OCCUPATIONAL THERAPY
FOR PSYCHIATRIC DISEASES

OCCUPATIONAL THERAPY FOR PSYCHIATRIC DISEASES

MEASUREMENT AND MANAGEMENT OF COGNITIVE DISABILITIES

Claudia Kay Allen
M.A., O.T.R., F.A.O.T.A.

Clinical Associate Professor of Occupational Therapy, University of Southern California, Los Angeles; Chief of Occupational Therapy, Department of Psychiatry, Los Angeles County–University of Southern California Medical Center, Los Angeles

with illustrations by
Catherine A. Earhart, O.T.R.

Occupational Therapist II, Department of Psychiatry, Los Angeles County–University of Southern California Medical Center, Los Angeles

Little, Brown and Company
Boston/Toronto

Copyright © 1985 by Claudia Kay Allen

Fourth Printing

Library of Congress Catalog Card No. 84-82544

ISBN 0-316-03263-8

Printed in the United States of America

HAL

Po 2228

TO ROBERT, MEGAN, AND BEVIN

CONTENTS

PART ONE   THEORY

CONTRIBUTING AUTHORS

Catherine A. Earhart, O.T.R.
Occupational Therapist II, Department of Psychiatry, Los Angeles County–University of Southern California Medical Center, Los Angeles

Lois M. Heying, M.A., O.T.R.
Occupational Therapist, Keystone Area Education Agency, Elkader, Iowa

Noomi Katz, Ph.D.
Vice Chairperson, School of Occupational Therapy, The Hebrew University of Jerusalem Faculty of Medicine, Jerusalem, Israel

Linda Riska Williams, M.A., O.T.R.
Formerly Occupational Therapist, Psychiatric Hospital, Los Angeles County–University of Southern California Medical Center, Los Angeles

PREFACE

The purpose of this book is to provide a description of the relative severity of mental disorders. The problem that the text seeks to correct is a tendency to think of people with mental disorders as being either well or sick. The either-or approach can be taken to extremes by stating that a person residing in an institution is sick while a person living in the community is well. Deinstitutionalization, with its provision of few services for people with chronic mental disorders, has taught us other dangers of this oversimplification. At the present time health care planning for people with mental disorders is in chaos and, in this author's view, order cannot be achieved without objective, realistic descriptions of what these people can and cannot do.

Occupational therapists are regarded as a professional group that can contribute to the clarification of cognitive disabilities because they spend a lot of time watching disabled people try to perform their activities of daily living. The therapist's observations provide detailed descriptions of the degrees of ability and disability associated with acute and chronic mental disorders. A systematic method of communicating the individual and social implications that can be drawn from these specific observations is required in order to coordinate the efforts of all caregivers, both professional and familial. The text will suggest a behavioral hierarchy for evaluating the patient's competence to perform activities, with criteria for analyzing the relative difficulty of any activity.

The evolution of the description of a cognitive disability has been slow; it was hampered by a need to reorient ourselves to a new way of describing behavior. For example, within the last decade the way to describe appearance, in a typical case, has changed from "bizarre and inappropriate" to "does not align buttons correctly." The earlier descriptions were general and often influenced by the value judgments of the rater. The descriptions contained in this text are more specific, often lengthy, and restricted as much as possible to a report of what the patient does or does not do. The kind of description sought is seldom found in the literature, and we have relied on clinical observations. The behaviors are not new; we have always seen patients who had trouble with their buttons. The change is that while we used to talk about these behaviors over coffee, we now need to describe them in our literature.

The development of a new approach to the description of cognitive disabilities has been accompanied by a persistent lesson: Theory, practice, and research are highly interdependent. The text is divided into these three parts with the understanding that a refinement in any part implies a corresponding change in the other two. Theory (Part One) is emphasized during the educational process, defining expectations of what will be found in practice. A therapist is not in practice long before encountering observations neglected by the theory or observations that run contrary to theoretical expectations (Part Two). Clinical confusion is objectively studied by doing research (Part Three); the research findings suggest theoretical refinements that can, in turn, be implemented in practice. The process has been dynamic and circular: from theory to practice to research to theory, etc. The absence of any one of these perspectives usually produces an unsatisfactory result, while the presence of all three is exhilarating.

The process of developing this text has spanned two decades and has been shared with more people than it is possible to acknowledge. A few people can be highlighted, with ongoing gratitude to those who are not mentioned by name. Gail S. Fidler introduced me to an expanded definition of cognition and the value of a good intellectual argument with a colleague. The discontinuities between theory and practice became evident to a number of us working at Eastern Pennsylvania Psychiatric Hospital in the late 1960s. We teeter-tottered between theory and practice, and the first descriptions of the cognitive levels were critiqued by Ellen Kolodner, Linda Levy, Nancy Lewis, and Elizabeth Tiffany. Application of the cognitive levels in a private hospital was supported by Mary Kay Bailey at Johns Hopkins Hospital. Therapists working at Los Angeles County–University of Southern California (USC) Medical Center have continuously examined their observations of behavior, participating in research studies and answering thousands of questions: Florence Barna, Patricia Butler, Nancy Dion, Ann Dunkle, Deborah Edmond, Joyce Elkin, Angela Espinoza, Francine Finklestein, Jeanne Langdon, Michelle Parolise, and Linda Riska Williams. Particular thanks are extended to Catherine A. Earhart; her writing of Chapter 10 and the illustrations in the text are examples of her astute observational abilities.

The research reported in Part Three was done by graduate students in occupational therapy at USC: Susan Herzig, Deborah Moore, Noomi Katz, Linda Riska Williams, Lois Heying, and Nanci Heimann. Their critical analysis and courage in pursuing an emerging theory added an invaluable dimension. The academic traditions established at USC by Mary Reilly and A. Jean Ayres have been an inspiration for academic excellence. Associates at USC have furthered these traditions by continuously underscoring (more than I wanted to hear at times) the need to avoid unwarranted theoretical bias; I am grateful to Susan Aoki, Florence Clark, Linda Davis, Doris Hill, Holly Holyk, Jerry Lindquist, Janice Matsutsuyu, Joan Rogers, Gerald Sharrott, Sarah Stocking, Alicia Trujillio, Ana Verran, Robert Wolfe, and Elizabeth Yerxa.

I have depended on Robert E. Allen, in the roles of psychiatrist, scientist, and husband, to dispatch with his keen sense of humor the development of any illusions of grandeur. Our daughters, Megan and Bevin, have contributed to an understanding of the differences between normal children and disabled adults.

I appreciated the good sense of humor of Ann Jones who typed the manuscript and helped me in my many confrontations with the idiosyncrasies of the English language. Barbara Ward, former Allied Health Editor for Little, Brown and Company, has shared with me a deep commitment to the importance of this project. In addition, she and her husband, Jim, were especially helpful with the most demanding and difficult task of placing the cognitive levels in a philosophic context. Cynthia J. Baron, Book Editor, skillfully balanced my perfectionist tendencies with the realistic demands of publishing. It has been a pleasure to work with Cynthia and with other discerning people assigned to this book.

C. K. A.

THEORY

The theoretical part of this book formulates the apparent relationships between mental diseases and functional disabilities. The text emphasizes the main points by including a set of theoretical propositions that have been verified to some degree; it is my hope that they will stimulate further investigation and refinement.

In an applied profession, the criteria for acceptable theory are influenced by social forces. Health professionals work within complex social, legal, and health care systems that influence both the definition of a health problem and what is to be done about it. The definition of mental diseases has changed during the last thirty years, and there is ample reason to suspect that more changes will occur. Chapter 1 examines these changes in order to establish a context for reputable occupational therapy theory. Theory is applied in practice where therapists observe functional behavior and try to explain the meaning of their observations to patients and other caregivers. Chapters 2, 3, and 4 refine the therapist's observations of a patient's functional assets and limitations. The functional disabilities are associated with disease processes, and Chapters 5 and 6 describe the relationships between diseases and disabilities.

This theoretical part of the book describes similarities that can be generalized. As much as possible, it has been my goal to enhance the therapist's ability to generalize from clinical observations: from one patient to the next, from one day or year to the next, from one cultural group to another, and from observations in the occupational therapy clinic to accurate predictions of community adjustment. In my opinion, the current theoretical need is for objective descriptions of the severity of functional disabilities. In addition, I think that similarities should be emphasized because similarities enhance generalization and prediction. The impetus for refining theory came from a desire to clarify the meaning of my observations of functional behavior.

If reading difficulty correlates with writing difficulty, the first two chapters will be tough reading.

The problem in the first chapter is that the advances in the neurosciences have produced varied responses in our social systems; the challenges to occupational therapy theory are numerous and complex. Chapter 1 is long, but the review of each issue is brief (where possible the references given are recent classics). The problem in the second chapter is to describe the function of the human brain, a description that has a tendency to become philosophical. To keep the discussion as clear as possible, standard dictionary definitions of terms and clinical examples are used. The reading is easier once this important framework is established.

CHAPTER 1

NEUROSCIENCE VIEWS OF ROUTINE TASK BEHAVIOR

Treating patients with cognitive disabilities has always been a prominent part of occupational therapy practice; the profession began by delivering services to psychiatric patients, and gradually expanded to include those with other disorders. Throughout our history the profession has been influenced by neuroscientific explanations of how the brain functions. Advances in the understanding of brain function have been occurring at an exponential rate during the last three decades. The biomedical application of this knowledge has shortened hospital stays, made diagnosis and treatment more specific, and sharpened the distinctions between acute and chronic mental disorders.

Currently many health professionals are reexamining their roles within the context of these changes. As a large portion of occupational therapy practice consists of providing services to people with mental disorders, we must also reexamine our role to make the indicated changes in our services. Change is not easy because it implies that some of our favorite ideas may have to be discarded and replaced by new ideas that may not have the same appealing qualities. The alternative seems to be to ignore the need to change, but since that approach would jeopardize our professional credibility it does not seem to be realistic. This book focuses on the identification of concepts that should be reexamined and suggests changes that seem to correspond with our current understanding of how the brain functions.

The depth of the changes brought about by new neuroscientific findings can be illustrated by the changing perception of the functional-organic split. Throughout this century people have thought of mental disorders as being functional (psychiatric) or organic (neurologic). That separation now appears to be artificial. The implication for this text is that even though the information presented is applied to the traditional psychiatric disorders, some of the information may also be helpful with neurologic disorders. An effort has been made to leave this possibility open to future exploration.

Another example of the depth of the changed perspective provided by neuroscientific research is the expanding of the definition of the unique feature of the human brain: the ability to speak. It appears that this definition neglects large elements of human performance, and now voluntary motor actions are receiving more attention within the neuroscientific community. Some attributes of voluntary motor actions, such as creating tools, seem to be unique to humans; others, such as walking, are shared with other species. One implication of this change is that therapists can be expected to find and produce neuroscience research that more directly addresses our areas of interest. The other implication is that occupational therapists should be more specific about our view of the human brain to differentiate ourselves from people working in other therapeutic disciplines. An occupational therapy view of brain functions (Fig. 1-1) can be suggested: Therapists make inferences about the functions of the human brain while watching a patient with an identified mental disorder perform activities. The behavior of interest is a voluntary motor action. The mental disorder may be an acute disease or a long-term disability. Priority in observation is placed on routine tasks because frequently performed tasks are usually most important to patients and their caregivers. The patient is evaluated to determine the current level of function, and the therapist asks the patient to identify desirable tasks. These tasks are analyzed by the therapist to identify steps in the typical procedure that the patient cannot do. As much as possible tasks are adapted to avoid procedures that patients cannot do, while making it possible for them to use their remaining abilities.

This view of brain functioning begins with the universe of voluntary motor actions and progressively refines the focus of study. Each layer in Fig. 1-1 is narrower. The factors that narrow the focus are external to the therapist: the concerns and desires of the patients and their caregivers, and the biologic state of the patient. The unique focus of the therapist is on adapting to these conditions.

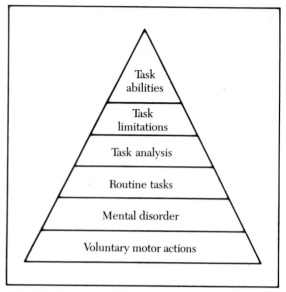

Fig. 1-1. Occupational therapy view of brain functions.

This chapter begins by defining the terms in Fig. 1-1 and by providing a perspective common to the rapidly changing fields of neurology and psychiatry. The remainder of the chapter attempts to identify the major implications of recent advances in the neurosciences and suggests theoretical approaches that may influence all of the areas of occupational therapy specialization. The range of topics is broad: theory of practice, the generalist approach, the medical model, treatment objectives for acute diseases, and service objectives for residual disabilities. One can infer from these topics that the advances in the neurosciences require an extensive reexamination of the way we conceptualize occupational therapy services.

TASK PERFORMANCE

Some historical perspective on the study of task performance may be helpful. Researchers at the turn of the twentieth century faced the problem of selecting the best approach to studying voluntary motor actions. The term *voluntary motor actions* replaced the nineteenth century concept of free will, a concept that could not be objectively studied. Two eminent neuroscience researchers made a similar decision that was not published until after their deaths. Sigmund Freud in 1895 wrote a book, often referred to as the "Project" (1966), containing theoretical speculations about the way the brain functions. Freud was a neurologist by training, and many of his speculations have been confirmed by more recent research in neuropsychology (Pribram and Gill, 1976). Vygotsky, an influential Russian neuropsychologist, wrote a similar book in the 1920s (cited in Luria, 1979). The two men took a parallel approach to the study of voluntary motor actions: They used human speech to study the notion of *voluntary*. Consequently, the literature contains a large number of paper-and-pencil tests and standardized verbal interviews, and we know a great deal about language and language disorders. What has been neglected is our understanding of how human beings use voluntary motor actions to manipulate and change physical objects. There is a growing recognition that the manipulation of objects deserves more study (Bronowski, 1973; Filskov and Boll, 1981).

Occupational therapists have been concerned about the lack of interdisciplinary information concerning the manipulation of physical objects, a deficiency that becomes readily apparent in practice. For example, therapists in psychiatric practice often sense that they are the only ones watching what the patient is doing (Fidler, 1978); everyone else seems to be talking to the patient. Verbally facile patients are particularly troublesome if their motor performance does not match their verbal abilities; a discussion with a colleague in another profession can leave one wondering if the colleague is talking about the same patient. Planning for the patient is problematic too, because members of an interdisciplinary treatment team may not agree on which is more important, verbal ability or motor performance. Moreover, the lack of evidence to support our view that the manipulation of physical objects is

a critical aspect of functioning may erode our confidence in our own observations. Many therapists have emulated the verbal methods employed by the other mental health professions, probably because of the strength of the supporting literature. Increasingly the neuroscience literature is addressing motor performance as an important element of human behavior. Therapists can draw on this literature to refine their observations of task performance.

Activity

In this discussion I will draw on occupational therapy's traditional use of activity in an effort to add greater specificity to our view of human functioning. It is assumed that purposeful activity is occupational therapy's treatment method. Further, it is assumed that activity is influenced by the disease process; that is, our patients' diseases cause restrictions in task performance. Observations of these restrictions in task behavior constitute our unique view of task performance.

Recent advances in the neurosciences are challenging some of our assumptions about the value of purposeful activity or human occupation. There has been a tendency to think that purposeful activity, or human occupation, is brought about by *learning* the activity:

Each individual is able to reach his or her potential only through purposeful interaction with the human and non-human environments. This philosophical assumption emphasizes the belief that *learning* [emphasis added] is facilitated through doing, through interaction in concrete, immediate situations (Mosey, 1981, p. 62).

Implicit in this philosophical view of activity, however, is the assumption that learning is unrestricted. Disorders of the brain can impede a person's ability to learn and to remember. The assumption must be modified to examine the task performance of people whose ability to learn and remember is impaired. A clearer distinction must be made between the process of doing the activity and the implied treatment objective. The process of doing the activity should be freed from an association with learning how to do an activity.

A therapist observes restrictions in task behavior and considers several plausible explanations for the restrictions. Cognitive deficits confound the explanations. One wonders if the patient is unable or unwilling to do the task, or if some other element in the task itself is causing the problem. Distinctions among the complexity of the task, the desirability of the task content, and the cognitive deficits of the person are difficult to make because each one contributes to our observations of behavior. To make these distinctions, a comprehensive description of voluntary motor actions is required.

Voluntary Motor Actions

Voluntary motor actions are a behavioral response to a sensory cue that is guided by the mind. Thus this discussion of voluntary motor actions is divided into three sections: matter, behavior, and mind. An orientation to the following discussion may be helpful. Brain functions are usually described by dichotomous terms: An action is voluntary or involuntary; one is conscious or unconscious. This discussion aims toward the identification of dichotomous descriptions that can be expanded into a continuum of six cognitive levels. The reason for the expansion is that the either-or descriptions provided by dichotomous variables fail to clarify the various degrees of function that therapists observe in practice. The six levels of function will be described in detail in Chapters 2 and 3. The present discussion will outline a comprehensive description of voluntary motor actions from a philosophical perspective.

Arthur F. Bentley (cited in Ward, 1984), an American philosopher, developed a list of 14 dichotomous descriptions that are used ambiguously in mathematics and in other sciences. I believe this list can be used to guide a comprehensive description of voluntary motor actions. I have added one addi-

tional dichotomy (for tool use), applied the dichotomies to important aspects of motor actions, and organized them into the framework presented here.*
The organization has imposed some delineations in common usage of these terms to restrict their reference to voluntary motor actions.

Matter

Matter is "that which is material and physical, occupies space, and is perceived by the senses" (*Funk and Wagnalls*, 1977). Sensory cues (Table 1-1) have been selected as the major feature of interest in describing matter in relation to motor actions because they seem to have the best potential for being exhaustive and mutually exclusive. The dichotomy that is used to describe sensory cues is inner and outer. A voluntary motor action is often a response to sensory cues provided by material objects, but that is not always the case; walking, for example, is an exception. What is required is a continuum that extends from the inner sensory cues of the body to sensory cues in the outer environment.

Matter is concrete or abstract according to the degree of perceptibility of a sensory cue. Perceptibility is an attribute of sensory cues. Concrete cues are embodied in physical existence, while abstract cues are considered apart from their real existence.

A setting is the spatial location in which a voluntary action is performed. Spatial proximity and extension are the modifying descriptions. Spatial proximity can be restricted to the confines of one's own body; a continuum can extend spatial awareness into infinity.

A sample is an example that is selected to represent a whole group of sensory cues. The scientific method uses samples as operational definitions. In this framework the sample represents sensory cues. The sample is described by *particular* and *general*. Particular samples are related to inner body movements. The continuum will extend to all of the attri-

---

*One of Bentley's dichotomies, mind versus matter, has been used to organize the description.

Table 1-1. Matter

Attribute	Dichotomy
Sensory cues	Inner vs. outer
Perceptibility	Concrete vs. abstract
Setting	Spatial proximity vs. extension
Sample	Particular vs. general

Table 1-2. Behavior

Attribute	Dichotomy
Motor action	Part vs. whole
Tool use	Accidental vs. instrumental
Number	Finite vs. infinite
People	Individual vs. collective
Directions (verbal or demonstrated)	Discrete vs. continuous

butes of matter. This continuum suggests sample selection criteria that can be used to generalize from one task to a related group of tasks.

Classification criteria for describing matter in relation to motor actions are needed for very practical reasons. Life is composed of a rich diversity of activities. This diversity causes problems when we try to explain performance. We need a classification system that organizes the diversity, and numerous attempts to devise such a system have been made. Most systems for classifying activities are organized by topics, for example, work, rest, and play. The problem is that topics are not mutually exclusive; tennis can be work or play. In addition the topics do not suggest criteria for generalizing from one task to a related group of tasks. A prediction is based on a generalization from one task to another, and at present social scientists are not very good at making predictions. What is being suggested is that classifying by sensory cues, along with criteria for selecting representative samples, may improve our ability to predict. Then therapists may have a better idea of how to select clinical activities that are representative of performance within the community.

Behavior

Behavior is the way a person acts under given material circumstances (*Funk and Wagnalls*, 1977). The material circumstances are described by the sensory cues that are related to observable motor actions. I have selected motor actions as the primary feature of behavior because of their observability during spontaneous and imitated performance (Table 1-2). Motor actions are described by the dichotomy of part and whole. The whole is the rich diversity of planned motor actions portrayed by the human species. A smaller part of our motor actions are shared with other living species.

Tool use can be a part of voluntary motor actions. Human beings use tools in ways that are unique to our species, as well as in ways that we share with other species. The dichotomy derived from the work of anthropologists is accidental versus instrumental (Cohen, 1968). Accidental tools are found by chance, while instruments are manufactured to carry out a part of a planned motor action.

Number is described by the dichotomy of finite versus infinite. The number of motor actions can stretch from the finite number of one (for example, peeling a potato with a peeler is one action, which may be repeated many times) to the seemingly infinite number that can characterize normal life.

Other people may, or may not, be included in a voluntary motor action. People are described by the dichotomy of individual versus collective. *Individual* is restricted to the self. *Collective* suggests a group of people with autonomous motor actions.

Motor actions may be observed as a response to directions from an external source. The directions may be verbal or demonstrated; both range from discrete to continuous. Discrete verbal directions begin with the one-word commands and extend to continuous, self-generated conjectures. Discrete demonstrated directions begin with physical contact and extend to a continued adherence to planned actions.

There have been numerous attempts to classify behavior according to motor actions; as a single criterion it does not work very well. The suggestion here is that the motor action be considered as an association with a sensory cue. The association is formulated in the cortex of the brain.

Mind

The associations made between sensory cues and motor actions form the basis for voluntary motor actions. Voluntary actions are guided by the mind. The mind is "the faculty, or function of the brain, by which an individual becomes aware of his surroundings and of their distribution in space and time, and by which he experiences feelings, emotions, and desires, and is able to attend, to remember, to reason, and to decide" (*Dorland's*, 1981). This definition implies that there are numerous ways of forming a sensorimotor association (Table 1-3). One's purpose in forming the association is probably the most important. Purpose is the intended objective of the voluntary motor action. Purpose is described by the dichotomy of existence versus transition. The most basic purpose is to maintain one's existence or to sustain life, for example, by eating and drinking. The other end of the dichotomy is transition or change: All of matter can be associated with a diversity of motor actions to create a new purpose.

Experience, within this framework, is a subclassification of purpose. An experience is what one actually lives through. A sensorimotor experience is most apt to produce sensations and reasoning. The emotions and desires that are produced are likely to be related to events in an individual's history, for example, stubbing your toe on the edge of the bed for the fourth time. Experience is described by the dichotomy of subjective versus objective. Subjective experiences are sensorimotor associations that produce a sensation. Objective experiences are sensorimotor associations that produce reasoning.

A process is a course of action followed to achieve a purpose. Sensorimotor associations establish a cause-and-effect relationship between a motor ac-

Table 1-3. Mind

Attribute	Dichotomy
Purpose	Existence vs. transition
Experience	Subjective vs. objective
Process	Inactive vs. active
Attention	Structural vs. functional
Time	Instantaneous vs. long-lasting

tion and its effects. A process is described by the dichotomy inactive versus active. Inactive processes are sluggish, dull, listless, motionless, or lethargic. Active processes are quick, animated, flexible, alert, or industrious.

Attention is selective responsiveness to sensory cues. The sensorimotor associations that can be formed are largely determined by the selections made. The available choices can be influenced by the material objects present and the biologic condition of the organism; one cannot assume that all choices are always available. Attention is described by the dichotomy structural versus functional. A function is the normal or proper action of an organ, in this case the brain. Functional attention occurs when sensorimotor associations are within normal limits for human adults. An organic disease is accompanied by alterations in the structure of an organ. Structural attention occurs when sensorimotor associations are inhibited, or overactivated, by the biologic condition of the brain. Potential explanations for structural attention include psychiatric diseases, organic brain syndromes, and a lack of maturation of the brain.

Time is a measure of duration, in this case the length of a purpose, from beginning to end. Memory, in terms of the length of time that sensorimotor associations are recalled, is a part of this dimension, as are projections into the future. Time is described by the dichotomy instantaneous versus long-lasting. Instantaneous time occurs within the moment, or within a few seconds. Long-lasting time draws on past sensorimotor associations and extends into the future, spanning years.

Voluntary motor actions are influenced by all of these attributes of matter, behavior, and mind. We know that mental disorders restrict a person's ability to use many of these attributes; such disorders may restrict the use of them all. The question is When is a restriction severe enough to require the services of a therapist? As a general guideline an occupational therapist may be consulted when the restrictions are severe enough to limit performance of routine tasks.

Routine Tasks

Routine tasks are the activities that a person does on a daily basis. Routine tasks usually involve food, clothing, shelter, transportation, general health precautions, and money management. Routine tasks are commonly referred to as the activities of daily living (ADL), which is the interdisciplinary term (Allen, 1982).

Occupational therapists approach routine tasks from a unique perspective. Therapists change the task so that a person with a disability can do it successfully. Therapists place a high priority on changing routine tasks for the following reasons: (1) A routine task is done frequently, on a daily or weekly basis, year in and year out. (2) The typical procedures of routine tasks are generally more standardized than are those of tasks done sporadically. (3) A schedule of routine tasks provides the basic structure or framework of a person's life-style (Cynkin, 1979).

Tasks that are causing difficulties for the patient or the caregiver can be identified, and the process can be changed through the application of task analysis (Allen, 1982).

Task Analysis

Task analysis is the specialized system of knowledge that guides the therapist in changing tasks. Task analysis, a part of the theory of practice developed by the Fidlers (1963), is also found in the use of activity suggested by Mosey (1970), is manifest in the interest checklist and play history of the occupational behavior frame of reference (Matsutsuyu, 1969; Reilly, 1974), and is further illustrated in the development of special equipment created for sensory integration disorders (Ayres, 1972, 1979). These theorists represent different approaches to task analysis. Some task analyses focus on task content; others, on task procedures. The approach taken here is to examine the procedures. The first requirement is the identification of each step in a typical procedure. Steps that cannot be done by the disabled person are identified, and alternative procedures are selected. A task analysis for a disabled population identifies problems in following a typical procedure that are common to that population (Allen, 1982).

The procedures for doing a task have a beginning, middle, and end. The therapist uses knowledge of the typical procedure for doing the task to evaluate the relative difficulty of performing each step of the task. The criteria that the therapist applies to the task analysis vary according to the problems that the patient may have in doing the task. For example, a different task analysis is required for someone who is blind than for a patient in a wheel chair. A task analysis for the cognitively disabled will be described in Chapter 3. The specialized criteria for analyzing tasks vary within the specialties of occupational therapy in accordance with the health problems that therapists encounter in practice; each area of specialization may require a specific task analysis. The unifying element of the specialized task analyses is that they all analyze the procedures involved in performing routine tasks (Allen, 1982).

Task Analysis Similarities: Process

The baseline of a task analysis is in the similar procedure that various people employ during the performance of the same task. The tasks that are easiest to analyze are those that are fairly well standardized in the method of performance. The processes involved in doing routine tasks contain similarities; some processes, such as cutting, chopping, mop-ping, wiping, and sweeping, are employed cross-culturally (Allen, 1982).

The frequency of task performance is an important consideration. Tasks that are done daily or weekly, such as brushing and shampooing one's hair, have a standardized routine containing cultural similarities. The similarities in the procedures are of interest to therapists because they establish a normative baseline for task analysis. The typical procedure for performing a task must be established first, because the therapist uses this information to establish the relative complexity of a task. The therapist's assessment of a problem in routine task performance requires the development of semistandardized task processes to distinguish between the complexity of the task and the capabilities of the patient. Semistandardized task procedures are developed by observing a number of people who have the same disability perform the same task. If they all have trouble doing one step in the typical procedure the therapist concludes that the problem is the complexity of the step. The task is then adapted by changing or eliminating the troublesome step. The adapted task is tried with more people with the same disability; if they can do each step, the task has been successfully modified for that disability. Then if a therapist observes a performance that does not follow the pattern for that disability, other explanations for a problem in performance can be considered.

Task Analysis Differences: Content and Past Experience

The typical procedure for doing a task can be influenced by differences in culture, age, sex, and personal experience. Cultural variations, such as eating with chopsticks instead of a knife and fork, include distinctions in both the tools used and the way they are used. Age and experience are also factors to consider in a typical procedure. The basic patterns for doing routine tasks are habits established early in life. Young children learn to put on their clothes, tie their shoes, go to the bathroom alone, peel carrots, wash the spinach, and wipe off the table. People continue to refine their patterns for doing routine tasks throughout their life span, so that a chef may master the variations of chopping an onion with a French knife and a Chinese cleaver. Age, past experiences, and cultural differences suggest the flexibility that the task analysis must contain; these factors can blur the distinction between an assessment of the complexity of the task and an evaluation of the capabilities of the patient.

Patients vary in the tasks they choose to include in the schedule of their daily lives. Therapists are in a better position to respond to these individual differences if the task analysis can be applied to any task content, that is, any activity the patient wants to do. The approach taken here is to suggest a task analysis that can be applied to any task content—crafts, play, work, or ADL. The task content is selected by the patient to minimize the confounding influence of the relative desirability of the task, that is, to ensure that the patient is willing to do the task. Choice in task content should be made by the patient as much as possible so as to minimize difficulties with making value judgments for other people. The distinction between the complexity of the task and the capabilities of the patient is easier to make when patients select their own task content.

Summary: Task Analysis Application

The therapist must be flexible in applying task analysis to respond to individual differences in task preferences and past experiences. Although general guidelines based on task analysis similarities can be suggested, the application of these guidelines must take individual differences into account. The unifying element of task analysis within the field of occupational therapy is our interest in the similarities observed during the process of doing a task. Diversification occurs according to the health problems, ages, cultural backgrounds, and personal preferences of the populations we serve.

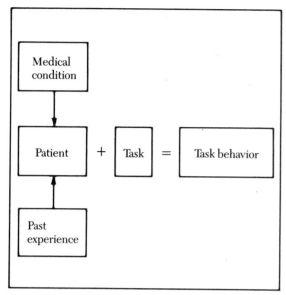

Fig. 1-2. Factors affecting routine task behavior.

Routine Task Behavior

Routine task behavior is what is observed during the process of completing a routine task. In an observation of task performance, therapists must take several factors into account: the capabilities of the patient, the medical diagnosis, the individual's past experience at doing the task, and the complexity of the task (Fig. 1-2) (Allen, 1982).

Limitations in Task Behavior

Limitations in routine task behavior are widely recognized. In fact the epidemiologic and economic scope of this issue may be one of the complications of the advances in modern medical knowledge. People can be kept alive, but after they leave the hospital someone else may have to prepare their meals, do their laundry, and perform other routine chores. The number of people who are permanently disabled is astonishing. Goldman, Gattozzi, and Taube (1981) estimate that there are between 1.7 million and 2.4 million chronically mentally ill

people in the United States. Colvez and Blanchet (1981), using the United States National Health Interview Survey, estimated that the number of persons whose activities are limited increased by 8 million in one decade—from 21.9 million people in 1966 to 30.2 million in 1976. The disorders that showed a significant change, in rank order, were as follows: arthritis and rheumatism, heart conditions, visual impairments, hypertension (without heart involvement), diabetes, mental and nervous conditions, asthma and hay fever, and hearing impairments. The only disorders to show a reduction were mental and nervous conditions: from 1.7 million in 1966 to 1.5 million in 1976, a 14 percent reduction. The number of women over the age of 65 with mental conditions showed a significant decrease of 46 percent; of men over 65, a decrease of 33 percent, which did not reach statistical significance (Colvez and Blanchet, 1981). (Women have a higher incidence of depression than men do.) These decreases may be partially explained by the development of antidepressant medications. This view of the health care system suggests a need to consider disability rates, in addition to mortality rates, in health care planning.

Occupational therapy planning may also be influenced by these disability figures; an estimated 19,000 occupational therapists and 8,500 occupational therapy assistants were employed in 1980 ("Job outlook," 1983). Thus there was less than one therapist per 1,000 disabled people. The presence of a disability, in and of itself, is not an adequate referral criterion. Referral criteria delineating the conditions that therapists serve the most effectively are required. Severely incapacitating mental and nervous conditions seem to be our top priority (see Table 1-4).

Policy makers have been concerned about the increasing cost of health care throughout the last decade, with mounting concern for the viability of the Social Security system. The number of beneficiaries and the cost of the benefits is increasing more rapidly for the disabled population than for the retired

Table 1-4. Primary health problem of patients served by OTRs

	Percent of clients served		
Primary health problem	1973	1977	1982[a]
Disorders with potential for cognitive impairment			
CVAs, hemiplegia	25.0	26.7	28.3
Developmental disabilities	5.8	8.0	13.0
Cerebral palsy	13.2	12.4	12.6
Mental retardation	7.5	10.2	10.3
Psychosis	14.3	12.4	8.7
Behavior disorder	5.5	3.6	2.7
Neurosis	6.2	4.3	2.2
Organic brain syndrome	—[b]	—	1.7
Personality disorder	—	—	1.5
Alcoholism, drug abuse	2.1	1.8	1.4
Head injury	—	0.5	1.4
Autism	—	3.6	0.5
Character disorder	0.8	0.8	—
Total	80.4	84.3	84.3
Disorders with less potential for cognitive impairment			
Hand injury	4.4	2.1	4.4
Spinal cord injury	2.7	2.2	2.1
Arthritis, collagen disorder	1.5	2.1	1.5
Heart disease	0.7	1.1	1.2
Fracture	0.8	0.6	0.8
Arteriosclerosis	4.1	2.8	0.7
Neuromuscular disorder	—	—	0.7
Multiple sclerosis	0.3	0.2	—
Muscular dystrophy	0.0	0.1	—
Burns	0.6	0.7	0.6
Cancer	0.3	0.4	0.4
Visual disability	0.6	0.5	0.3
Amputation	0.6	0.4	0.2
Respiratory disease	0.6	0.3	0.2
Kidney disorder	0.2	0.1	0.1
Spina bifida	—	—	0.1
Hearing disability	0.1	0.2	0.1
Peripheral nerve injury	0.2	0.0	—
Total	17.7	13.8	13.4
None			
High-risk population	0.5	0.7	—
Well population	1.0	0.8	0.3
Total	1.5	1.5	0.3
Other	3.0	3.8	2.2

CVA = cerebral vascular accident.
[a]Provisional data.
[b]Throughout this table a dash indicates that the category is not included in that year's survey.
Source: Membership data survey, Rockville, Md.: American Occupational Therapy Association, 1982.

population. Stone (1979) estimated the government expenditure for all disability programs at $23.3 billion in 1975. A prevalent problem in containing costs and planning health care systems is the lack of clear-cut guidelines for establishing a cognitive disability. Guidelines exist for physical disabilities, but defining and counting mental disorders is ambiguous. Part of the difficulty is that mental disabilities have been divided into psychiatric and neurologic disorders; this separation appears to be artificial. The aspects of chronic psychiatric and neurologic disorders that seem to be the most disruptive to the individual and to society are limitations in routine task behavior, limitations that span the split between psychiatric and neurologic disorders. Occupational therapists may be able to describe these limitations in task performance objectively.

Task Abilities

Task abilities are what the patient can do successfully. Of course, a mild disability leaves more abilities than a severe one. A therapist who is trying to change a routine task so that a severely disabled person can do it successfully may be able to identify few remaining abilities. The number of abilities can be very small when compared with the universe of voluntary motor actions. The description of task abilities is, in some ways, the opposite of the description of normal growth and development: A description of development looks at increasing abilities; a description of task abilities of a person with a disability looks at decreasing abilities.

The task abilities that a therapist describes correspond to a reduced level of function caused by a disease. The natural course of the disease produces expected changes in the level of function. Therapists work within these restraints, seeking to identify abilities that can be utilized to improve the quality of life for our patients and their caregivers. Thus descriptions of task abilities must be made within the context of current knowledge of psychiatric and neurologic conditions.

ORGANIC AND FUNCTIONAL DISORDERS

The first populations served by occupational therapists were those with mental disorders, and our membership surveys indicate that we continue to be principally involved with these conditions. Therapists responding to the American Occupational Therapy Association's (AOTA's) membership surveys indicated that approximately 80 percent of the primary health problems seen in practice continue to be neurologic (organic) or psychiatric (functional) conditions (see Table 1-4) (membership data survey, 1982). It seems that abnormalities of the brain characterize the majority of our patients.

Over the years the categorization of organic and functional disorders has been subject to change. The twentieth century has witnessed a number of advances in our understanding of how abnormalities in the brain (organic impairments) can produce deviant behavior (functional impairments); this understanding has made a brain-behavior association more credible. The first advance can be attributed to the discovery of the cause and medical management of pellagra and general paresis, or syphilis. Both diseases had been regarded as functional disorders. The identification of an organic impairment in these diseases led to a search for other linkages between disturbed behavior and organic pathology (Robbins and Ziegler, 1979). The electroencephalogram (EEG), described by a psychiatrist, Hans Berger, in 1924, led to an explanation of the association between seizure disorders and functional symptoms. The EEG recordings are influenced by the patient's behavior; the tracing looks different when a person is asleep, awake, or excited. EEGs are still used to detect abnormalities in the brain that are associated with behavioral problems (Shagass et al. 1982; Trimble, 1981).

Computerized tomography (CT or CAT scans) have led to the identification of focal brain lesions that have been associated with poor performance on a number of behavioral tests (Strub and Black, 1981). CT obviates postmortem studies to identify the brain lesion. The brain and behavior tests are administered at the same time in the patient's life, which lends greater credibility to the association between the brain lesion and the behavioral deficit. A further interest in the association between brain and behavior has been stimulated by the effectiveness of psychopharmacologic drugs and the recent discovery of the neurotransmitters. Psychopharmacologic drugs are thought to be neurotransmitter specific and effective in reducing or eliminating specific psychiatric symptoms (Swonger and Constantine, 1983; Trimble, 1981). All of these technical advances have facilitated our ability to detect brain abnormalities that cause deviant behavior and have strengthened the association between brain and behavior. A whole new approach to explaining physical and mental disorders is suggested by this association (Kandel, 1979).

The brain-behavior association has been accompanied by a growing recognition that the division of the study of the brain into components (i.e., neuroanatomy, neurochemistry, neurophysiology, neuropsychology) was artificial. These divisions, which were useful earlier in the century, are being replaced by interdisciplinary study. Current thought is that the brain consists of functional units; each discipline or specialty contributes to the study of these functional units. The hope is that studying the functional units of the brain will promote unity in the neurosciences (Satz and Fletcher, 1981).

Occupational therapists have always been concerned with functional behavior, and it now appears that the orientation of the neurosciences is recognizing these concerns. There is now a chance for occupational therapists to make a stronger contribution to the neuroscience literature through interdisciplinary collaboration. In addition the opportunity exists to identify more clearly the uniting elements of the occupational therapy profession (DiJoseph, 1982). These opportunities exist at a time when knowledge is expanding at a tremendous pace, and we must keep up with these advances if we are to realize these opportunities. A brief review of the present state of the art in neurology and psychiatry will now be presented to identify a perspective common to these two rapidly changing fields.

Neurology

Neurologists have introduced the term *neurobehavioral disorders* to connote the organic cause of such diseases while also stressing the behavioral manifestations. These disorders are commonly referred to as organic brain syndromes. Strub and Black (1981) have subdivided them as follows: (1) acute confusional states that are caused by temporary metabolic or toxic conditions and create generalized behavioral disturbances that disappear once the patient's physiology is normalized; (2) the dementias, which are usually caused by irreversible damage to, or atrophy of, the brain and result in a deterioration of intellectual and social behavior; and (3) focal lesions, identified anatomic abnormalities with correlated disturbances in behavior, for example, aphasia. What is evident in each of these neurologic disorders is that an organic impairment is associated with a functional disturbance in behavior. Neurologists have turned to neuropsychologists and speech pathologists for measures of the behavioral disturbances. Occupational therapy assessments are cited infrequently.

Neurologists use the functional assessments to assist in suggesting diagnosis as well as to describe the complications that can be produced by neurologic disease. Many of the consequences of these diseases are quite distressing to the patients and their families. It appears that an increased understanding of these behavioral deficits facilitates a neurologist's referral to other health-related disciplines (Strub and Black, 1981). In the future the problems in routine task behavior described by occupational therapists may be established as complications of neurologic diseases, and therapists may be able to refine their services in this area.

Neurologists address organic brain syndromes and so do psychiatrists. The nomenclature of the third edition of the American Psychiatric Association's *DSM III: Diagnostic and Statistical Manual of*

Mental Disorders (1980) includes organic mental disorders and organic brain syndromes. As more is learned about the brain-behavior association, the boundaries between neurology and psychiatry become less and less distinct (e.g., Fahn et al., 1983). Neurologists tend to emphasize neuroanatomy, while psychiatrists focus on neurochemistry. Both disciplines are expanding their awareness of the entire biopsychosocial organism.

Psychiatry

The terminology of psychiatry also reflects the brain-behavior association, as evidenced by the resurgence of the use of the terms *neuropsychiatry* (Trimble, 1981) and *biologic psychiatry* (van Praag et al., 1980). An organic explanation for some functional disorders, such as the schizophrenic and primary affective disorders, is an issue of intense consideration, because an organic explanation would be a clarification of how the psychotropic drugs reduce the behavioral symptoms of psychiatric disorders. Perhaps *DSM III*'s most dramatic departure from the previous edition (*DSM II*) is a change in the diagnostic criteria for schizophrenic and primary affective disorders. Epidemiologically, schizophrenic disorders were the largest population in *DSM II* (1968); now primary affective disorders are. This is not merely a change in label. The change in diagnostic classification reflects a change in the expectation for the outcome of medical intervention. Schizophrenic disorders may not be "cured" by current psychotropic drugs, but the neurochemical abnormalities associated with the primary affective disorders often can be normalized (Klawans et al., 1981; Swonger and Constantine, 1983).

The advances in our understanding of the brain-behavior association have been accompanied by a tremendous amount of change and rethinking about priorities in the care of psychiatric patients, and there is reason to suspect that the ripple effect of this rethinking may soon be felt in the care of neurologic patients. The last two decades have borne witness to considerable controversy over the correct definition of mental illness. Different theoretical points of view were offered by the proponents of psychoanalysis, behavior modification, and biologic psychiatry, while Szasz (1961) contended that mental illness is a myth. Advocates for each point of view were prolific. The problem extended into the social sciences, in which these theoretical biases could be detected in research designs (Fabrega, 1974). Caught up in this controversy were the patients who were "deinstitutionalized" and began to live in board-and-care homes, nursing homes, or on city streets, often carrying their belongings in shopping bags (Bassuk and Gerson, 1978). Patients' rights became a major issue, forming a new relationship between psychiatry and law that is extending into neurology and pediatrics (Stone, 1976). By the late 1970s the controversy over the definition of mental illness was creating so many problems that it was apparent that a major change was occurring.

DSM III

A major step in resolving these problems was the delineation of new classification criteria for the diagnosis of mental disorders (*DSM III*, 1980). The diagnostic criteria are purported to be "atheoretical," which is true in terms of the controversy that led to their inception. The criteria, however, do represent a point of view about mental illness. They are phenomenologic, based on motor actions or verbal statements. Priority was given to behavioral criteria that were supported by reliable and valid research studies. The "tough-mindedness" advocated by Goodwin and Guze (1984) appears to have been incorporated, in that the comprehensive factors that can influence a disease are being subjected to systematic and controlled studies with repeated demonstrations. This was required because it is easy for members of the various professions working in psychiatry to form conflicting opinions about psychological phenomena.

A classification system is the foundation of a discipline's literature. Medical treatment begins with diagnosis. Research studies begin with the selection of subjects. Interpreting research in psychiatry had become difficult because one could never be certain about the diagnosis of the subjects included in the study and because the unreliability of psychiatric diagnosis left questions about the existence of a medical disease—"the myth of mental illness." The situation had gotten so bad that some researchers stopped reporting diagnoses; nonphysicians were especially prone to this for the obvious reason that medicine has purview over diagnosis. The credibility of the *DSM III* criteria is being studied, and most researchers report an improvement in the reliability and validity of psychiatric diagnoses. Those of us who have struggled through years of ambiguity are thrilled to see some clarity emerging from these classification criteria. Refinements will, of course, be required, and a *DSM IV* is already under consideration. The excitement generated by the recent studies comes from the recognition that the phenomenologic approach to diagnosis is working. As we develop clearer diagnostic criteria we can expect to be clearer about treatment effectiveness and health care planning. One hopes that as the literature becomes clearer, research dependent on precise diagnostic criteria can be done, thereby adding to the treatment repertoire of all disciplines and contributing to the clarification of psychiatric enigmas that have existed since people first had the notion that patients' behavior could be altered in a positive direction.

Competence

Issues surrounding patients' rights are particularly challenging. The problem centers around defining *competence*, that is, determining whether a person is competent to recognize and exercise his or her legal rights. Questions about competence are beginning to emerge in psychiatry (Appelbaum et al., 1981; Geller, 1982). These questions are being generalized to other mental disorders such as mental retardation, dementia, and cerebral vascular accidents (CVAs) (Stone, 1976). Competence is particularly relevant to the content of this text.

Different levels of competence may be defined by the descriptions of voluntary motor actions. The descriptions can, conceivably, be used as an ordinal scale to measure functional abilities. In addition caregivers could use the scale to clarify the type of assistance required by those with disabilities. The present health care system is besieged by questions about how to identify fair and objective criteria that would assist with the measurement and management of functional abilities and disabilities. I hope this text will provide answers to some of these questions. Competence will be discussed further in Chapters 2 and 11.

The brain-behavior association is having a major impact on the practice of psychiatry, shifting the physician's attention from psychotherapy to correlations between behavioral symptoms and neurochemistry. Greater specificity in diagnosis and psychopharmacology appears to be associated with shorter stays in the hospital, shorter periods of acute illness, a greater return to normal levels of function, and fewer prolonged mental disabilities (Goodwin and Guze, 1979; Swonger and Constantine, 1983). All of these technical advances have facilitated the ability to detect brain abnormalities that cause deviant behavior and have strengthened the psychiatrist's ability to treat mental disorders.

IMPACT ON OCCUPATIONAL THERAPY

Psychiatrists and neurologists are not alone in experiencing the impact of the advances made in the neurosciences. Nearly every mental health profession is having to reexamine the value of its services and state new objectives that are consistent with these treatment advances. The brain-behavior association may be expected to have an important impact on occupational therapy as well.

There is evidence to suggest that therapists have been trying to adapt to the changes. Numerous attempts have been made in recent years to identify occupational therapy's domain of concern (Christiansen, 1981; Clark, 1979; Diasio, 1968, 1979; Ethridge, 1976; Fidler, 1978, 1981; Fine, 1983; Gillette, 1979; Kielhofner, 1983; Llorens, 1976; Mosey, 1981; Reilly, 1971; Williamson, 1982).

Shapere (1977) describes a domain of concern, in sophisticated areas of science, as the association between items of information that are the objects of investigation. Scientists generally consider it desirable to examine the domain of concern when there is an important problem in the domain. Occupational therapy is an applied profession. Our domain is defined by the patient populations we serve. Within Shapere's framework the advances in the neurosciences can be interpreted as troublesome background information that suggests a need for more precision and accuracy in defining our patient populations. The characteristics of a domain of concern (in this case, patient populations) have been identified as follows:

1. The association is based on some relationship between the items [patient populations].
2. There is something problematic about the body [of patients] so related.
3. The problem [the patient has] is an important one.
4. Science is "ready" to deal with the problem (Shapere, 1977, p. 525).

These characteristics will be used to suggest more precision and accuracy in defining our patient populations. The establishment of a relationship is not sufficient, in and of itself, to establish a population; almost any group of patients can be related in some way or another. The patients must have a problem that requires our services. Currently occupational therapy lacks clarity in selecting important problems. The various attempts to describe the domain of concern contain long lists of associated items, but they lack guidelines for the selection of important problems that respond to our services. The difficulty becomes most pronounced when one examines the AOTA's "Uniform Terminology for Reporting Occupational Therapy Services" (1979); this is an extraordinarily long list of evaluation areas, and therapists are instructed to report on every one of them. The list is simply too long to promote clarity and precision in the selection of service objectives. These long lists of associated items are often thought to reflect occupational therapy's generalist approach.

I have been frustrated by our generalist approach to identifying the parameters of practice. The difficulty is that the generalist approach fails to establish an important problem. As a result, our professional discussions contain the implicit assumption that a therapist needs to read every book in the library and offer services to every person in the community; the scope of the domain of concern becomes unmanageable in our literature and in our practice. Examining the scope of practice from a broad theoretical perspective seems to foster professional role ambiguity. We need a better method of identifying our patient population.

Some objective data on patient population can be supplied by the AOTA's membership data surveys (1982). OTR responses to the question regarding the health problems most often seen in practice were used. The data were examined to identify the disorders that might be associated with a brain impairment (Table 1-4). The results were surprising because the accepted divisions within the field disintegrated. Cognitive disabilities were known to be associated with psychosis, but, as Table 1-4 shows, they may also be associated with other health problems. The survey data suggested that basic theoretical concepts concerning cognitive disabilities should be stated in terms that allow for broader application—not just to psychosis, but to other disorders as well.

The member data survey was also examined to identify health problems that are less likely to be associated with a brain impairment. Hand injuries and spinal cord injuries lead the list (Table 1-4). These two physical disabilities were used as a conceptual model during the process of contrasting and comparing a cognitive disability with a physical disability. The data were then examined to identify the services offered to people with no health problem (Table 1-4). The survey suggests that few therapists are involved in this area of practice, and a well population is not the focus of this text.

Occupational therapy's patient population seems to consist of people who have a disability. The disability may be physical, or cognitive, or both. A disability is caused by a disease or accident. Occupational therapy is a health-related profession in the sense that the parameters of our practice are defined by the establishment of a medical diagnosis that is associated with a disability. Some of these disabilities are long-term or permanent, while others are temporary. The natural course of the most prevalent health problems (CVAs, hemiplegia, developmental disabilities, cerebral palsy, mental retardation, chronic schizophrenic disorders) dictates that residual disabilities are a common part of practice and that the health–illness–health continuum may be an erroneous part of our theoretical foundation. Three conclusions were drawn from this data: (1) We should maintain a constructive view of the medical model because the presence of a disease is an important part of practice. (2) More attention should be paid to residual disabilities and the kinds of services that can be offered to people with permanent limitations. (3) We must be far more selective in adopting theories that apply to physical and cognitive disabilities. For example, theories that assume normal learning and memory need to be reexamined for their clinical utility with the cognitively disabled. These conclusions have guided the selection of content for this text.

The second characteristic suggested by Shapere (1977) presents difficulties: Little is known about how a cognitive disability restricts routine task behavior. More is known about how a physical disability restricts routine task behavior, for example, the restrictions placed on the physically handicapped by architectual barriers are well understood. Less is known about the restrictions imposed by a cognitive disability, and there is evidence to suggest that we have been ignoring the problems that these patients encounter.

The membership data survey suggests that a large portion of our practice consists of delivering services to people who may have a cognitive disability. Recent medical advances seem to be successful in keeping people alive longer, but then they, and their families, may have to live with cognitive restrictions in the performance of their routine tasks. More information about the nature of these cognitive restrictions is required. The problem is important to occupational therapy, as well as the social community, the third characteristic suggested by Shapere (1977).

This text aims in the direction of fulfilling Shapere's fourth characteristic, getting us ready to deal with the cognitively disabled. A theory of practice to guide investigations is suggested; propositions that may be feasibly tested are identified; preliminary instrumentation is described. This text is not regarded as a final product, and further development of the instruments and the theory are invited.

The refinements in defining our patient populations necessitate some changes in the way therapists view the medical model, the generalist approach, and our service objectives. Some suggestions for the type of changes that seem to be indicated are offered in the following discussion.

Medical Model

Medical model has not been a popular term for many therapists in recent years. Various definitions of the medical model exist, and the profession of occupational therapy should select one that facilitates a cooperative response to a health problem. The sociologic perspective, as described, for example, by Parsons (1951), tends to lead to a discussion of a political process, as if professional effectiveness were some sort of social reform. Sociologic definitions may divert our attention from patient care and are not recommended.

A definition of the medical model is needed to help to establish cooperative lines of communication between therapists and physicians. Communication is difficult when there is ambiguity about the presence of a disease. The medical view is usually that a disease is a biologic abnormality (Rogers,

1982). A problem exists when the biologic abnormality is unknown; with these disorders social conventions have a major impact on the definition of the disease (Goodwin and Guze, 1979). Therapists often provide services to people with diagnoses that fall within the social definition of disease; alcoholism, the personality disorders, and developmental disabilities appear to be the most ambiguous. Physician involvement varies according to the effectiveness of known medical treatments—if there is no known effective treatment, there is usually little physician involvement. The level of physician involvement in turn influences the amount of collaboration between physician and therapist. Many points of consultation between a physician and a therapist do occur, however, and this also must be a recognized part of our theories of practice.

Confusion about the medical model probably stems from the treatment methods used by psychiatrists. Mental illnesses were regarded as functional disorders and treated by talking to the patient. If this approach is taken to an extreme, anyone who talks to a patient can say that he or she is "treating" a functional disease. The definitions of treatment of functional disease were extended to include the activities of many health professionals; these professionals began to think that their treatment methods were as effective as the methods used by physicians. It now appears that the various verbal treatment methods were equally ineffective with many mental disorders. Psychotropic drugs have been proved to be more effective for many of the mental disorders requiring inpatient care. These advances in treatment effectiveness require some changes in our treatment objectives.

Numerous attempts to redefine treatment objectives have been suggested during the last decade. Therapists in every area of specialization often review these efforts to describe occupational therapy with a note of skepticism. The skepticism is a response to laudable promises that can be kept only by ignoring elements of reality. Efforts to describe the value of occupational therapy services tend to share three problems:

1. They fail to account for learning and memory deficits.
2. They neglect the increasing effectiveness of psychotropic drugs.
3. They fail to address residual disabilities.

These neglected factors are becoming increasingly important in all of the disorders that may be associated with a brain abnormality (Table 1-4). An accurate description of the value of occupational therapy services must account for these factors. The neglected factors can be used as theoretical exclusion criteria, eliminating numerous theories from our basic education. Our curriculums are currently clogged with theories of questionable utility, and a theoretical housecleaning is required. The process will probably resemble the process of cleaning out the clinic storage closet: It will take a long time, it will generate a lot of discussion, and many people will resist approaching the task. The current confusion about the roles and functions of therapists suggests that a theoretical reorganization must be confronted. Time to address the neglected factors can only be made available after we eliminate the useless information.

Generalist Approach

Greater precision in defining our patient population generates some discussion about the value of the generalist approach. The generalist approach must be reexamined within the context of the way this approach is used in other professions and its utility in generating treatment objectives.

The last decade has lent increasing credibility to a generalist approach in every profession, and it would be naive to claim that this consideration is unique to occupational therapy. This approach is frequently implemented through interdisciplinary studies done by multiple authors, each providing an in-depth knowledge of one area of specialization (e.g., a psychologist, a neuropsychologist, a neuropharmacologist, a psychiatrist, and an anthropologist). Interdisciplinary study is the epitome of the generalist approach, and it is being done by researchers all over the world. The results are exciting. By comparison, however, occupational therapy's generalist approach tends to produce a rehash of information borrowed from other professions. The unique in-depth knowledge of the occupational therapist is all too frequently missing. Our generalist approach appears to have facilitated the borrowing of knowledge, but not the in-depth refinement of clinical practice.

There is a tendency to think that a field is either specific or general; the concern is that a specific focus of study will cause the specialist to lose sight of the patient as a total person. This concern may be misplaced. Specificity and generalization have been described, in general systems theory, as two complementary processes that must occur in tandem. General systems theory attempts to solve the problem of too much data. Specialization produces thousands of bits of information. General systems theory is helpful in identifying the relationships between units of information (Berrien, 1968).

Occupational therapy has the opposite problem—a very small amount of specific, self-generated data. The lack of specific, self-generated data makes it difficult for the practicing therapist to identify the unique value of occupational therapy services. A number of attempts have been made to apply general systems theory to occupational therapy practice (Diasio, 1979; Kielhofner, 1983). The models are usually very complex and abstract, and applying them to the clinical realities of practice seems to be problematic (Cubie and Kaplan, 1982). The intellectual gymnastics are dazzling but most remarkable for their lack of practical utility. The reason these models are so difficult to work with is that we lack the specifics that serve as the foundation for abstract models. Some specific questions that are left unanswered will illustrate this problem: How much television do disabled people watch? Do the physically and cognitively disabled spend different amounts of time watching television and performing self-care tasks? Does television watching, self-

care, or both become a substitute for the normal activities of work and play? If so, does the disabled person or the caregiver regard this as a problem that ought to be solved? Are there differences (in length of illness, degree of disability, age, cultural background) between those who regard prolonged television watching as a problem and those who do not? We lack answers to questions like these and have no way of knowing if major elements of current theories about such matters are valid or not. Without that information we are all just guessing. The intellectual gymnastics tend to obscure the fact that we may be imposing our values on patients, and that is the danger in the generalist approach. A continuation of the generalist approach is not recommended.

Service Objectives

A therapist identifies an area of specialization each time he or she writes a treatment objective in a patient's chart. Interdisciplinary credibility is affected by all of the treatment objectives we each write every day. Currently objectives are difficult to write; we require specific measurable objectives that can be achieved within a specified period of time and that convey our special contribution to patient care. The generalist approach provides a vast array of possible objectives of questionable relevance to the patient and the caregiver. Currently the clinician confronts a long list of possible evaluation areas and makes choices; guidelines for setting priorities among the possible problems are missing ("Uniform terminology," 1979). Naturally enough, many different objectives are selected, and there is a great deal of ambiguity, both in and out of the profession, about what occupational therapy is.

For the last 20 years therapists have tended to prefer views of mental disorders that permit stating treatment objectives in terms such as "to teach" a patient how to do a task or "to increase" or "to improve" a patient's ability to do a task. There are two problems with these objectives: (1) They treat all mental disorders as conceptually equivalent, and (2) they assume that the performance of a routine task produces a change in behavior while neglecting other explanations for such a change. A change in the quality of task behavior of patients with some psychiatric disorders, such as primary affective disorders, can be explained by psychotropic drugs. A change in the quality of task behavior of patients with some neurologic disorders, such as CVAs, can be explained, in part at least, by the natural healing process. A change in the quality of task behavior of a child might be explained by normal growth and development. These alternative explanations for change suggest that our treatment objectives need to be refined. The challenge resides in identifying the profession's area of specialization. Some suggestions are offered in the following section. They are based on the assumption that there is something important occurring in the profession's traditional use of routine tasks.

DISEASE AND DISABILITY OBJECTIVES

Identifying the kind of treatment we are actually providing has been, and will probably continue to be, a struggle. Objectives are an operational definition of what we think the value of our services is. Some clarity may be achieved by dividing health problems into stable and unstable medical conditions. The task of stating clearer service objectives can be facilitated by making sharper distinctions between treatment of a disease and compensation for a disability: Treatment of an acute disease may be palliative, expectant, or supportive; compensation for a disability may be biologic, psychological, or environmental (Allen, 1982). Each of these potential objectives will be generally described, with diagnostically specific objectives suggested in Chapters 5 and 6. The services of the therapist can be aimed at treating a disease or compensating for a disability. No distinction is made between functional and organic diseases, but a distinction be-

tween an acute mental disease and a long-term disability is made.

Acute Disease: Treatment

Strictly speaking, treatment is the prerogative of physicians, and their treatment of mental disorders will be discussed first.

Cause of a Disease

Ideally, active treatment aims at the cause of disease. When a cause is known, steps can be taken to cure or prevent the disease. The causes of many abnormalities of the brain, however, are unknown.

Palliative Treatment

When the cause is unknown, treatment can be aimed at reducing the symptoms. Such treatment is referred to as palliative. Psychotropic drugs are palliative in that they help to normalize the neurochemistry of the brain, but we do not know why the neurochemistry became abnormal in the first place (Strub and Black, 1981). The treatment of diabetes is a common analogy: The metabolic abnormality is known; the treatment is known; but the cause of the abnormality is unknown. Treatment with psychotropic drugs is increasingly diagnosis specific, and this is a major factor in the new classification system suggested in *DSM III* (1980).

Expectant Treatment

Expectant treatment relies on the natural healing process for improvement in a condition. The common cold is a good example. When we get a cold we have to wait for our bodies to heal the damage done by the virus. Expectant treatment can also be preventive, as when antibiotics are given to prevent the complication of pneumonia in the example of a cold. Physician treatment for many mental disorders is expectant; the physician watches for a spontaneous remission of symptoms. For example, some neuroanatomic conditions produce abnormalities that cannot be altered or improved by physical or chemical treatment. The physician can (1) diagnose and monitor the condition and (2) relieve untoward symptoms, but cannot (3) alter the biologic condition (Strub and Black, 1981). This has the potential for becoming an important issue in effectiveness studies conducted in physical rehabilitation settings (Allen, 1982).

Supportive Treatment

Supportive treatment aims at sustaining a patient's strength and is often supplemental to other forms of treatment. Nutritional supplements, cheerful colors in the hospital room, the presence of family members, and a television set are all examples. Supportive treatment recognizes the importance of biopsychosocial factors in sustaining the life and well-being of a patient (Engel, 1980). Some supportive treatments are initiated by physicians, and in the nineteenth century many supportive treatments now carried out by members of other health-related professions also were the responsibility of the physician. Physicians encouraged the development of occupational therapy to implement a form of supportive treatment for patients with mental disorders (Hopkins and Smith, 1978; MacDonald et al., 1970).

The medical condition can be regarded as unstable while the physician is changing, or monitoring a change, in the physical or chemical abnormalities of the patient. Unstable medical conditions are seen during an acute illness, an acute phase of a chronic illness, and the recovery period after an acute assault. Changes in the clinical picture are expected when the medical condition is unstable, but the degree and rate of change vary considerably. A favorable response to psychotropic drugs may be observed within 2 weeks, while favorable recovery from neurosurgery may taken 2 years or more (Allen, 1982).

Treatment	Method
Expectant	Report in patient's chart
Supportive	Change the task
Palliative	Change the task

Fig. 1-3. Potential treatment of a disease.

Occupational Therapy Treatment

The occupational therapy treatment provided when the medical condition is unstable can be expectant, supportive, and palliative (Fig. 1-3). Expectant treatment aims at documenting the alterations and improvements in functional abilities associated with biologic changes in the patient's condition. The therapist selects routine tasks that are sensitive to the expected changes, observes the patient's behavior, and reports these observations to the patient, family, and other involved professionals (Allen, 1981). The cognitive levels described in Chapter 2 indicate the severity of an acute mental illness and can be used to monitor changes produced by the medical interventions of the physician. For example, a primary affective disorder is an episodic illness that is associated with a temporary cognitive disability. The cognitive level is low at admission and improves as the psychotropic drugs take effect. The therapist can assess the cognitive level at admission and report changes in cognitive level as the patient's condition improves. The cognitive levels can be used to provide an objective record of changes in the severity of an acute illness. Used in this way, the cognitive levels are analogous to a person's temperature: One takes the temperature, gives some aspirin, and takes the temperature again to see if the fever has gone down. The therapist's report monitors the expected change in functional behavior.

Supportive treatment aims at sustaining the patient's strength and is especially important when the patient states that he or she feels hopeless and says, "I can't go on like this." The therapist selects routine tasks that the patient can do successfully and that provide a concrete measure of improvement in his or her condition. The therapist can assist the patient in accurately assessing the severity of the disease. This may be especially important with mental diseases that are severe enough to influence the way one thinks and feels. To be supportive, the therapist must be honest without being judgmental.

Palliative treatment reduces the pain and distress associated with symptoms. The therapist selects tasks that the patient can do successfully and that are designed to avoid symptom areas. For example, some people report that their auditory hallucinations go away while working on a project.

Criteria for selecting tasks for palliative and supportive treatment are needed. The task analysis described in Chapter 3 assists with the selection of tasks that can be done successfully. The steps in the typical procedure of the task are changed to match the task to the patient's level of ability (Fig. 1-3). Tasks that are above a person's level of ability are distressing and fail to fulfill palliative or supportive objectives (Allen, 1982).

One-to-one Correspondence

With an unstable medical condition, neuroscience professionals often assume a one-to-one correspondence between the state of the brain and behavior (Trimble, 1981). This assumption is helpful in monitoring the biologic changes in the patient—in answering such questions as these: Is this medication working? Should more or less medication be given? Is spontaneous remission occurring? What degree of recovery can be anticipated? Is the diagnosis correct? Therapists can help answer these questions by accurately reporting their observations of routine task behavior. To do this the therapist needs to know how biologic changes in the patient are expressed during routine task behavior, which will be described in Chapters 5 and 6.

Biologic influences are of paramount importance as long as the medical condition is unstable. Once the medical condition has stabilized, the assumption of a one-to-one correspondence between the state of brain and behavior is troublesome because other factors that can explain disturbances in routine task behavior become more pronounced (Jette, 1980; Lang and Jette, 1981). A distinction between a disease and a disability helps to clarify this problem (Allen, 1982).

A disease is characterized by symptoms that serve as indications that something is biologically wrong. Confusion occurs because the brain-behavior association suggests that behavioral symptoms are indicators of a disturbance in the central nervous system. Behavioral symptoms are neurogenic in the sense that they are caused by diseases that affect the brain. The one-to-one correspondence between the state of the brain and behavior is a view of disease that accounts for the biologic influences on behavior that respond to natural healing or medical intervention.

Disability: Compensation

A disability, on the other hand, is a residual restriction in behavior that persists after the medical condition has stabilized. A residual restriction does not respond to medical intervention or natural healing. One waits for a disease to end, but one must live with a disability. A context for the assessment of, and compensation for, residual restrictions in behavior is required. Such a context is also required in the practice of speech pathology and in occupational therapy practice with physical disabilities. These two areas of health care will be examined for their approach to the distinction between disease and disability.

Physical Disabilities

The association between biologic impairment and disturbance in behavior has face validity in physical disabilities. One can easily recognize, for example, that an impairment to the dominant hand will alter a person's routine task behavior. Selecting hand impairments as an example of frequent concern, we can ascertain that a variety of diseases, from peripheral hand injuries to CVAs, can cause hand impairments. The disability, then, cuts across diagnostic categories. The measure of the disability is a measure of deviance from normative ability, and the content of the measure considers factors not required to establish a diagnosis. Poor grasp, for example, is not diagnostic, but it is a factor in predicting future ability to perform routine tasks. Thus disabilities are problems in behavior that should be measured and classified independently from diagnostic causes. Separate typologies, with different evaluation instruments, should be employed to categorize disabilities and diseases.

Language Disabilities

Speech pathologists make this distinction. The behavior of interest is language that is impaired by neurogenic disorders. Some correspondence between the neurogenic disorder and the communication disorder is recognized, but speech pathologists have found it necessary to develop their own classification system—including aphasia, apraxia, dysarthria—for disabilities (Darley, 1979; Johns, 1978). Here again, similar problems in behavior can span diagnostic categories and suggest treatment methods that are disability specific.

Disability Divisions

Physical disabilities are frequently divided into three components: organic, functional, and social. The organic impairment is the biologic condition produced by the natural course of the disease. The functional disability is the limitation in function imposed by the biologic impairment and the individual's reaction to that impairment. The social disability, or handicap, is the restricting effect that the biologic impairment and functional disability have on the performance of social roles (Susser and Watson, 1971). These divisions are also helpful in describing cognitive disabilities.

Cognitive Disabilities

The experiences of speech pathologists, occupational therapists working with physical disabilities, neurologists, and psychiatrists suggest an approach for describing cognitive disabilities. A cognitive disability is caused by a biologic defect. The defect may be temporary, as in unstable medical conditions, or may produce long-term deficits. Deficits in routine task behavior can be observed in stable and unstable medical conditions. Some deficits in routine task behavior are characteristic of the diagnosis; others span diagnostic categories. Restrictions in routine task behavior that are shared by many diagnostic categories require a separate classification system. The cognitive levels described in chapter 2 provide such a classification system.

Recognizing that the biologic abnormality is unclear for some psychiatric disorders, therapists must be cautious in assessing a disability. For a disability to be established a disease must be present. The failure to establish the presence of a disease would expose us to the criticism aptly expressed by Szasz (1961), that is, falsely identifying an illness that is beyond the realm of a biologic defect and that actually represents a social value judgment about deviance (Fabrega, 1974). To avoid the problems of describing a myth of mental disability, therapists must understand the diagnostic criteria used to establish the presence of a disease. The assessment of a cognitive disability is safest with those diagnostic classifications that are supported by research studies documenting a biologic abnormality. Chapter 5 describes psychiatric disorders that stem from relatively clear biologic abnormalities. Chapter 6 contains a brief description of psychiatric disorders that may or may not be associated with a biologic abnormality. The phenomenologic approach to psychiatric diagnosis, coupled with the recent development of several objective laboratory tests, can be regarded as major advances in establishing psychiatric diagnoses as diseases. These advances make it much easier for therapists to assess a disability.

Stable medical conditions may leave residual restrictions in routine task behavior that are not corrected by the natural healing process or by current medical treatment. These restrictions represent residual disabilities. Biology may explain the cause of the disability, but the consequences can be expressed in psychological and sociologic terms. Occupational therapy incorporates information from the medical and social sciences to facilitate the process of compensating for a residual restriction in routine task behavior. Compensation may be biologic, psychologic, or environmental (Fig. 1-4).

Biologic Compensation

Biologic compensations have been the selected goal of some occupational therapists. Ayres (1972) aims sensory integrative treatment at developing alternative central nervous system pathways. The neurodevelopmental approaches also are directed at biologic compensation (Trombly and Scott, 1977). Biologic compensations seek to change the level of function. The advantage of biologic compensations is that they can be expected to generalize to a wide number of routine tasks (Moore, 1973). Biologic compensations for mental disorders are dependent on the neuroscientific study of brain plasticity. This dependency can be uncomfortable because it is very difficult to generalize from the study of the nervous system of animals to the treatment of hu-

Compensation	Method
Biologic	Change the biology
Psychological	Teach a skill
Environmental	Change the task

Fig. 1-4. Potential compensation for a disability.

mans. Bach-y-Rita (1980) has recently edited an excellent theoretical discussion of brain plasticity that can be applied to the rehabilitation process. There are those who argue that the brain has a considerable degree of plasticity that can be developed; however, the indications for professional versus nonprofessional assistance, as well as the criteria for selecting the various treatment methods, are largely unknown. This is a serious deficiency, and people in other professions are beginning to demand, rightly, that therapists correct the deficiency (Bach-y-Rita, 1980, pp. 257–259). Currently, biologic compensations enjoy popular appeal among therapists, but we can expect this type of treatment objective to decrease in popularity if it remains unsupported by effectiveness studies. Biologic compensations may be possible to achieve, but we must recognize that they are the most difficult objective to substantiate. Continuing to claim that we can produce this type of compensation without the support of well-controlled, replicated studies, places the credibility of the entire profession in jeopardy. A distinction that will certainly be problematic is between an expectant treatment (in which restoration of function is expected) and a biologic compensation (which depends on plasticity) (Satz and Fletcher, 1981). Instruments that measure the level of function are also required.

This text will not emphasize biologic compensations and will seek alternative treatment objectives for the cognitively disabled.

Psychological Compensation

An alternative to biologic compensation is psychological compensation. Psychological compensation is a "form of behavior whereby an individual attempts to make up for some personal lack or defect, as by development of substitute goals or abilities" (*Funk and Wagnalls*, 1977). Again, therapists have attempted to apply this form of compensation (Cynkin, 1979; Fidler and Fidler, 1963; Reilly, 1974; Rogers, 1982). Psychological compensation has proved to be unsatisfactory because it rests on the assumption that the patient has the ability to learn and remember substitute goals and abilities; the presence of abnormalities of the brain calls this assumption into question. Psychological compensations may be most appropriate in physical disabilities that do not involve the central nervous system. Brain abnormalities that impair learning and memory seem to jeopardize the fulfillment of this objective (Allen, 1982). Again, this objective will not be pursued within this text.

Environmental Compensation

The task environment contains the physical objects that human beings manipulate during the course of their daily lives. Environmental compensations offset defects in the structure or function of the disabled person through the modification of the task environment. This view of compensation can be seen in the use of adaptive equipment designed for people with physical disabilities; a piece of adaptive equipment is a modification of the task environment that enhances routine task behavior (Allen, 1982;

Trombly and Scott, 1977). The advantage of this view of compensation is that it provides an avenue of change in what might otherwise be regarded as a hopeless situation. The disadvantage is that the patients may be limited in their ability to generalize from one task to another. The treatment methods proposed in this text implement environmental compensations by structuring the task environment.

To structure is "to form into an organized structure" (*Funk and Wagnalls*, 1977). To structure a task is to use an element of the physical environment as a substitute for biologic deficiencies in the disabled person. This is especially subtle in mental disorders, because we are substituting for deficient patterns of thought. The structure of an activity consists of patterns, samples, prefabricated kits, or other items that the therapists use to compensate for the steps in a procedure that the patient may be unable to do. Some improvements in routine task behavior can be attributed to the ingenuity of the therapist in designing a structure that acts effectively as an environmental compensation.

Environmental compensations aim at changing the task (Fig. 1-4). Biologic and psychological compensations aim at changing the patient. All of these forms of compensation may produce an improvement in task behavior; they differ in the location of the change. A therapist may decide to aim treatment toward any one of these forms of compensation. The selection is not easy, because we know very little about our actual effectiveness in facilitating compensation. The choice will probably continue to be an emotional issue until we produce more objective evidence to substantiate, or refute, the varying points of view.

The therapist's ability to provide environmental compensations is particularly important in stable medical conditions that produce residual cognitive disabilities. Environmental compensations may be the only objective that we can realistically fulfill within the near future. If so, they may be our only defense against therapeutic nihilism for this patient population. Throughout our history we have been saying that we could fulfill biologic and psychological objectives. There are shocking deficiencies in our ability to substantiate those claims. Occupational therapy was founded during a period of history when no one questioned a profession's ability to fulfill its objectives, but the times have changed. Objectives must be fulfilled, and they must be cost-effective. We must be very careful about the statement of objectives for this patient population.

Our society, during the last 15 years, has found a number of ways to avoid assuming responsibility for people with permanent cognitive disabilities. It is economically convenient to avoid the problem. There is a growing concern that economic convenience may be producing serious consequences for the disabled and their caregivers (Borus, 1981). Society has not decided what to do about these problems, but the political climate suggests that any promised objectives will have to be substantiated by empirical studies. As of this writing our society is avoiding payment for services wherever possible. If any services are to be available for this population we must be candid about what can, and cannot, be achieved.

CHANGING

The advances in the neurosciences are wreaking havoc on occupational therapists' view of activity. We thought that doing an activity would prevent illness or restore health. That now appears to be a naive oversimplification. As a cherished idea it has been woven through the entire fabric of our thought, and the readjustments required are major. The most astonishing change, to me at least, is the switch from trying to change the patient to changing the activity. The change runs deep because everything seems to be set up backwards, and it takes time to turn things around. We still seem to be somewhere in the middle of this process.

Some of the changes outlined in this chapter are far easier to adapt to than others. Concepts that we are in control of—our treatment objectives, for example—are the easiest. Changes that are interdisciplinary in nature, such as those involving voluntary motor actions, ADL, and the brain-behavior association, will require mutual respect and collaboration. Designing programs that effectively deal with the social handicap associated with cognitive disability will take much time and energy. On the optimistic side there is a growing recognition that residual cognitive disabilities exist, and the pretense of a promised cure unsupported by effectiveness studies is diminishing. On the pessimistic side societies are concerned about health care costs and suspicious about promises of program effectiveness because many promises have not been kept. The remainder of this book seeks to clarify what we therapists have to offer to our patients, and to our colleagues in other professions, in an effort to help us adapt to some of these changes.

REFERENCES

Allen, C. K. Independence through activity: The practice of occupational therapy (psychiatry). *Am. J. Occup. Ther.* 36:731–739, 1982.

Appelbaum, P. S., Mirkin, S. A., and Bateman, A. L. Emergency assessment of competency to consent to psychiatric hospitalization. *Am. J. Psychiatry* 138:1170–1176, 1981.

Ayres, A. J. *Sensory Integration and Learning Disorders.* Los Angeles: Western Psychological Services, 1972.

Ayres, A. J. *Sensory Integration and the Child.* Los Angeles: Western Psychological Services, 1979.

Bach-y-Rita, P. (ed.). *Recovery of Function: Theoretical Considerations for Brain Injury Rehabilitation.* Baltimore: University Park Press, 1980.

Bassuk, E. L., and Gerson, S. Deinstitutionalization and mental health services. *Sci. Am.* 238:42–50, 1978.

Berrien, K. F. *General and Social Systems.* New Brunswick, N.J.: Rutgers University Press, 1968.

Borus, J. F. Deinstitutionalization of the chronically mentally ill. *N. Engl. J. Med.* 305:339–342, 1981.

Bronowski, J. *The Ascent of Man.* Boston: Little, Brown, 1973.

Christiansen, C. H. Toward resolution of crisis: Research requisites in occupational therapy (editorial). *Occup. Ther. J. Res.* 1:115–124, 1981.

Clark, P. N. Human development through occupation: A philosophy and conceptual model for practice, Part 1. *Am. J. Occup. Ther.* 33:577–585, 1979.

Cohen, A. (ed.). *Man in Adaptation: The Biosocial Background* (2nd ed.). Hawthorne, N.Y.: Aldine, 1974.

Colvez, A., and Blanchet, M. Disability trends in the United States population 1966–76: Analysis of reported causes. *Am. J. Public Health* 71:464–471, 1981.

Cubie, S. H., and Kaplan, K. A case analysis method for the model of human occupation. *Am. J. Occup. Ther.* 36:645–656, 1982.

Cynkin, S. *Occupational Therapy: Toward Health Through Activities.* Boston: Little, Brown, 1979.

Darley, F. L. (ed.). *Evaluation of Appraisal Techniques in Speech and Language Pathology.* Reading, Mass.: Addison-Wesley, 1979.

Diasio, K. Psychiatric occupational therapy: Search for a conceptual framework in light of psychoanalytic ego psychology and learning theory. *Am. J. Occup. Ther.* 22:400–414, 1968.

Diasio, K. Specialization: Perspectives from a systems approach. *Am. J. Occup. Ther.* 33:31–33, 1979.

DiJoseph, L. M. Independence through activity: Mind, body, and environment interaction in therapy. *Am. J. Occup. Ther.* 36:740–744, 1982.

Dorland's Illustrated Medical Dictionary (26th ed.). Philadelphia: Saunders, 1981.

DSM II: Diagnostic and Statistical Manual of Mental Disorders (2nd ed.). Washington, D.C.: American Psychiatric Association, 1968.

DSM III: Diagnostic and Statistical Manual of Mental Disorders (3rd ed.). Washington, D.C.: American Psychiatric Association, 1980.

Engel, G. L. The clinical application of the biopsychosocial model. *Am. J. Psychiatry* 137:535–544, 1980.

Ethridge, D. A. The management view of the future of occupational therapy in mental health. *Am. J. Occup. Ther.* 30:623–628, 1976.

Fabrega, H. *Diseases and Social Behavior: An Interdisciplinary Perspective.* Cambridge, Mass.: MIT Press, 1974.

Fahn, S., Calne, D. B., and Shoulson, I. (eds.). *Advances in Neurology: Experimental Therapeutics of Movement Disorders.* New York: Raven, 1983. Vol. 37.

Fidler, G. S. Doing and becoming: Purposeful action and self actualization. *Am. J. Occup. Ther.* 32:305–310, 1978.

Fidler, G. S. Overview of occupational therapy in mental health (white paper). Rockville, Md.: American Occupational Therapy Association, 1981.

Fidler, G. S., and Fidler, J. *Occupational Therapy: A Communication Process in Psychiatry.* New York: Macmillan, 1963.

Filskov, S. B., and Boll, T. J. (eds.). *Handbook of Clinical Neuropsychology.* New York: Wiley, 1981.

Fine, S. B. Occupational therapy: A role of rehabilitation and purposeful activity in mental health practice (white paper). Rockville, Md.: American Occupational Therapy Association, 1983.

Freud, S. Project for a Scientific Psychology (1895). In *The Standard Edition of the Complete Psychological Works of Sigmund Freud*, transl. and ed. by J. Strachey with others. London: Hogarth and of the Institute of Psycho-Analysis, 1966. Vol. 1.

Funk and Wagnalls Standard College Dictionary. New York: Harper and Row, 1977.

Geller, J. L. State hospital patients and their medications: Do they know what they take? *Am. J. Psychiatry* 139:611–615, 1982.

Gillette, N. Practice, Education and Research. In *Occupational Therapy: 2001.* Rockville, Md.: American Occupational Therapy Association, 1979.

Goldman, H. H., Gattozzi, A. A., and Taube, C. A. Defining and counting the chronically mentally ill. *Hosp. Community Psychiatry* 32:21–26, 1981.

Goodwin, D. W., and Guze, S. B. *Psychiatric Diagnosis* (3rd ed.). New York: Oxford University Press, 1984.

Hopkins, H. L., and Smith, H. P. (eds.). *Willard and Spackman's Occupational Therapy* (5th ed.). Philadelphia: Lippincott, 1978.

Jette, A. M. Health status indicators: Their utility in chronic-disease evaluation research. *J. Chronic Dis.* 33:567–479, 1980.

Job outlook is bright for new occupational therapists in next decade. *Occup. Ther. Newspaper*, 37:1–4, 1983.

Johns, D. F. *Clinical Management of Neurogenic Communication Disorders.* Boston: Little, Brown, 1978.

Kandel, E. P. Psychotherapy and the single synapse: The impact of psychiatric thought on neurobiological research. *N. Engl. J. Med.* 301:1028–1037, 1979.

Kielhofner, G. (Ed.). *Health Through Occupation: Theory and Practice in Occupational Therapy.* Philadelphia: Davis, 1983.

Klawans, H. L., et al. *Textbook of Clinical Neuropharmacology.* New York: Raven, 1981.

Lang, M. H., and Jette, A. M. Measuring functional ability in chronic arthritis: A critical review. *Arthritis Rheum.* 24:80–86, 1981.

Llorens, L. A. *Applications of Developmental Therapy for Health and Rehabilitation.* Rockville, Md.: American Occupational Therapy Association, 1976.

Luria, A. R. *The Making of Mind: A Personal Account of Soviet Psychology.* Cambridge, Mass.: Harvard University Press, 1979.

MacDonald, E. M., MacCaul, G., and Mirrey, L. (eds.). *Occupational Therapy in Rehabilitation* (3rd ed.). London: Bailliere, Tindall and Cassell, 1970.

Matsutsuyu, J. S. The interest checklist. *Am. J. Occup.*

Ther. 23:323–328, 1969.

Membership data survey (provisional data). Rockville, Md.: American Occupational Therapy Association, 1982.

Moore, J. C. *Concepts from the Neurobehavioral Sciences in Relation to Rehabilitation of the Mentally and/or Physically Handicapped.* Dubuque, Iowa: Kendall/Hunt, 1973.

Mosey, A. C. *Three Frames of Reference for Mental Health.* Thorofare, N.J.: Charles B. Slack, 1970.

Mosey, A. C. *Occupational Therapy: Configuration of a Profession.* New York: Raven, 1981.

Parsons, T. *The Social System.* New York: Free Press, 1951.

Pribram, K. H., and Gill, M. M. *"Freud's Project" Reassessed: Preface to Contemporary Cognitive Theory and Neuropsychology.* New York: Basic Books, 1976.

Reilly, M. Occupational therapy—a historical perspective: The modernization of occupational therapy. *Am. J. Occup. Ther.* 25:243–246, 1971.

Reilly, M. (Ed.). *Play as Exploratory Learning.* Beverly Hills, Calif.: Sage, 1974.

Robbins, E., and Ziegler, V. E. The History and Scope of Biological Psychiatry. In H. M. van Praag et al. (eds.), *Handbook of Biological Psychiatry.* New York: Marcel Dekker, 1979. Part 1.

Rogers, J. Order and disorder in medicine and in occupational therapy. *Am. J. Occup. Ther.* 36:29–35, 1982.

Satz, P., and Fletcher, J. M. Emergent trends in neuropsychology: An overview. *J. Consult. Clin. Psychol.* 49:851–865, 1981.

Shagass, C., Roemer, R. A., and Straumanis, J. J. Relationships between psychiatric diagnosis and some quantitative EEG variables. *Arch. Gen. Psychiatry* 39:1423–1435, 1982.

Shapere, D. Scientific Theories and Their Domains. In F. Suppe (Ed.), *The Structure of Scientific Theories* (rev. ed.). Chicago: University of Illinois Press, 1977.

Stone, A. A. *Mental Health and Law: A System in Transition.* New York: Jason Aaronson, 1976.

Stone, D. A. Diagnosis and the dole: The function of illness in American distributive politics. *J. Health Polit. Policy Law* 4:507–521, 1979.

Strub, R. L., and Black, W. F. *Organic Brain Syndromes: An Introduction to Neurobehavioral Disorders.* Philadelphia: Davis, 1981.

Susser, M. W., and Watson, W. *Sociology in Medicine* (2nd ed.). London: Oxford University Press, 1971.

Swonger, A. K., and Constantine, L. L. *Drugs and Therapy: A Handbook of Psychotropic Drugs* (2nd ed.). Boston: Little, Brown, 1983.

Szasz, T. S. *The Myth of Mental Illness: Foundations of a Theory of Personal Conduct.* New York: Hoeber Med. Div., Harper and Row, 1961.

Trimble, M. R. *Neuropsychiatry.* New York: Wiley, 1981.

Trombly, C. A., and Scott, A. D. *Occupational Therapy for Physical Dysfunction.* Baltimore: Williams and Wilkins, 1977.

Uniform terminology for reporting occupational therapy services. Rockville, Md.: American Occupational Therapy Association, 1979.

van Praag, H. M., Lader, M. H., Rafaelsen, O. J., and Sachar, E. J. (eds.). *Handbook of Biological Psychiatry: I. Disciplines Relevant to Biological Psychiatry.* New York: Marcel Dekker, 1979.

Ward, J. F. *Language, Form, and Inquiry: Arthur F. Bentley's Philosophy of Social Science.* Amherst: University of Massachusetts Press, 1984.

Williamson, G. G. A heritage of activity: Development of theory. *Am. J. Occup. Ther.* 36:716–722, 1982.

COGNITIVE LEVELS

A *cognitive disability* is a restriction in voluntary motor action originating in the physical or chemical structures of the brain and producing observable limitations in routine task behavior. A limitation can be detected during a patient's performance of a voluntary motor action; just as physical disabilities restrict the physical ability to do a voluntary motor action, a cognitive disability restricts the cognitive ability to do a voluntary motor action. The deficit is in the mental processes that usually guide motor actions. Just as a therapist measures range of motion to evaluate physical disability, he or she can assess cognitive level to evaluate impairments in thinking.

Cognition is "that operation of the mind by which we become aware of objects of thought or perception; it includes all aspects of perceiving, thinking, and remembering" (*Dorland's*, 1981). This global definition of thought has been selected in the hope that the numerous mental impairments presented by our patient populations can be organized into a single classification system. The system is divided into six levels, ranging from profound disability at level 1 to normal ability at level 6. The levels comprise an ordinal scale (see p. 40) arranged in hierarchical order.

Therapists might assume that a description of six levels will direct our services toward increasing the cognitive level. Implicit in the assumption is a question: Can occupational therapy services change the cognitive level? The answer is no, at least for the present. This is a shocking answer because we have hinged the value of our services to an ability to improve the patient's level of function. Some scary questions come to mind: What good are we doing, if any? Who will pay for our services? Is anything that we do important? Is occupational therapy going out of business? I have asked myself these questions, and in all honesty I suspect they are too radical. We do need to refine our treatment objectives, as suggested in Chapter 1, but we do not have to start looking for another job.

The idea that we can change the level of function has been with us for so long that the suggestion that we give it up requires some discussion. The initial description of the cognitive levels was derived from Piaget's description of the sensorimotor period (Ginsburg and Opper, 1969; Piaget, 1952). Piaget wrote extensively about the transition from one stage or period to another (Piaget, 1971, 1972, 1978, 1980). It seemed reasonable to assume that the principles that guide the acquisition of knowledge in children could be applied to disabled adults, that is, that adults could be encouraged to make a transition from one stage to another. The problem was that the principles did not work. For example, when we gave a level 4 patient a level 5 task, one of the following occurred: The patient listened to our instructions with a facial expression that suggested incomprehension; the patient ignored our directions; the patient refused to continue to work on the task; if we pressed the patient to continue to try, the patient refused to come to occupational therapy (OT); if we really pressed the patient, he or she had the fight-or-flight response that is sometimes referred to as a catastrophic reaction. The question remains: How can the cognitive level be changed?

Sometimes change in the cognitive level is observed: Acute conditions change. The changes in the cognitive level that we see do not seem to be explained by the patient's experiences in the occupational therapy clinic. The changes have alternative explanations with a great deal of credibility: the effectiveness of psychotropic drugs, the natural healing process, and the natural course of the disease. Although the cognitive level changes in many acute conditions, it is remarkably stable in most chronic conditions. Numerous professionals are trying to use attributes of the psychosocial environ-

ment to change the level of function of chronic mental patients. Over the years I have been struck by the stability of chronic disorders; no one seems to be able to increase the cognitive level.

The clinical observations are confusing because they do not correspond with the expectations derived from the developmental literature. There is a theoretical problem here, and some thoughts about what it might be can be shared. Piaget uses the concepts of equilibrium and disequilibrium as a way of explaining the acquisition of knowledge. However, the concepts of equilibrium, homeostasis, and adaptation do not provide us with a satisfactory explanation of how abilities improve. The problem extends beyond Piaget's work into other psychological theories that rely on these terms (Haroutunian, 1983). Most psychological theories assume that abilities improve through interaction with the external environment. An alternative has been suggested by Mounoud (1982). He suggests that the development of cognitive abilities is ". . . a maturational process that depends only very indirectly on the interactions of the child with the environment . . ." and that development is ". . . strongly determined by a genetic regulation. . . ." The development of cognitive abilities may be analogous to the development of other human abilities such as learning to walk. Mounoud's view is biologic in orientation. Biologic development may be associated with emerging cognitive abilities, and biologic impairment seems to be associated with cognitive disabilities. The influence of the external environment on both may be less than we had thought.

Accepting a reduced influence of the external environment requires a reorientation in the way we think about the value of our services. I suggest *measurement* and *management* as alternatives to *improvement* as goals of occupational therapy. A measurement can be important for a number of reasons. An objective measurement can clarify whether or not a positive change in an acute condition is actually occurring. To some people that does not sound very important, but imagine physicians without blood and urine tests. Physicians use these tests to guide their treatment decisions. Psychiatrists and neurologists have very few objective measures that can guide their decisions; the cognitive level can be used that way. In addition, a measure of the cognitive level can be used to identify realistic expectations for people who have chronic disabilities.

The cognitive levels can be also used to guide the management of people who are disabled. The condition can be acute or stable. An analogy with children is apt. Parents provide activities for children that are within the child's present range of ability. Therapists can do the same thing. The cognitive levels clarify what the range of ability is. In addition, the clarification can be shared with other caregivers who can incorporate it into their own management techniques. The specifics of measurement and management are related to the patient's diagnosis, as will be discussed in Chapters 5 and 6.

VOLUNTARY MOTOR ACTIONS

Chapter 1 provided lists of attributes of matter, behavior, and mind that contribute to voluntary motor actions (see Tables 1-1 to 1-3). The continuums for each attribute will be developed within this chapter and the next. An overview of the continuums to be developed in this chapter may be helpful. The discussions of matter will focus on sensory cues and their perceptibility. These attributes are closely related and are easily described together. The description of behavior will focus on motor actions. Most of the emphasis in this chapter will be on the mind. Continuums for purpose, experience, process, attention, and time will be described. These continuums describe the cognitive levels (Table 2-1). The attributes and related continuums will be discussed, and cognitive levels described.

Matter: Attention to Sensory Cues

Sensory cues are not perceived unless the person pays attention to them; one seldom pays attention to all of the sensory data found in the environment. Attention is selective responsiveness to sensory cues. The therapist must infer what the patient is perceiving by identifying the sensory cues that are capturing the patient's attention. Attention is the means by which the elements of matter enter into a sensorimotor assocation. Attention to matter will be discussed in relation to the inner versus outer dichotomy that describes sensory cues. In addition inner versus outer will be used to clarify the concrete versus abstract dichotomy that describes perceptibility. Perceptibility refers to the attributes of matter, not to perception. Perception is the act or process of perceiving a sensory cue and forming an internal representation of it. The perception of a sensory cue does not occur if the patient ignores the cue. Perception has not been used in describing matter because in the process of perception an input (cue) and a throughput (an internal representation or a distortion of the internal representation) are combined. This combination is difficult to observe during task performance. A failure to attend is easier to observe; attention to sensory cues was selected for that reason. The other attributes of matter, the setting, and the sample, will be described in Chapter 3.

Attention is highly selective; we make distinctions between various sensory cues and select the details that we choose to heighten and ignore. Children acquire this selective ability by adding sensory systems to their field of attention (Kinsbourne and Caplan, 1979). The sequence in which these systems are added suggests a natural hierarchy of sensory cues (Ginsburg and Opper, 1969; Piaget, 1952).

The sensory cues noted at level 1 are subliminal cues (Table 2-1). Most of this sensory information is inhibited from our conscious awareness. Some familiar examples are hunger, thirst, taste, smell, and a gross awareness of one's physical being.

Proprioceptive cues are the sensory cues added at level 2. Proprioceptive cues provide information concerning the position and movement of the parts of the body. Attention is still internal, but the parts of the body are discriminated.

Visual-motor stimuli are divided into four types at

Table 2-1. *Cognitive levels*

Attribute	Level 1: Automatic Actions	Level 2: Postural Actions	Level 3: Manual Actions	Level 4: Goal-directed Actions	Level 5: Exploratory Actions	Level 6: Planned Actions
Attention to sensory cues	Subliminal cues	Proprioceptive cues	Tactile cues	Visible cues	Related cues	Symbolic cues
Motor actions						
Spontaneous	Automatic	Postural	Manual	Goal-directed	Exploratory	Planned
Imitated	None	Approximations	Manipulations	Replications	Novelty	Unnecessary
Conscious awareness						
Purpose	Arousal	Comfort	Interest	Compliance	Self-control	Reflection
Experience	Indistinct	Moving	Touching	Seeing	Inductive reasoning	Deductive reasoning
Process	Habitual or reflexive	Effect on body	Effect on environment	Several actions	Overt trial and error	Covert trial and error
Time	Seconds	Minutes	Half hours	Hours	Weeks	Past and future

levels 3, 4, 5, and 6: touchable cues, visible cues, the relationships between two perceivable cues, and symbolic cues. Touchable cues are the attributes of a physical object that are perceived by touch, such as texture or shape. Many of these cues suggest a manual action. For example, a ball suggests bouncing and throwing, and sand paper and a wooden box suggest sanding the box. Visible cues are those sensory stimuli that are readily seen. Visible cues include color, size, and shape; these attributes of physical objects are attended to at level 4. At level 5 relationships between two visible cues—the space between objects, the overlapping of objects, or the blending together of objects—are attended to. Symbolic cues are intangible attributes of objects including evaporation, gravity, absorption, time, and temperature; these are noticed at level 6. Words, in the form of written directions or spoken instructions, provide the sensory information that is being processed. Visual images (pictures or diagrams) may be used also.

The course of normal growth and development as observed during the first 2 years of life suggests a natural evolution of the relative complexity of the sensory cues that capture attention. This evolution begins with a partial recognition of, and then heightened attention to, internal cues. The first external cues are tactile. First we feel an object, then we examine its most striking visual attributes, and then we consider the related qualities. Finally, we use words and symbols to consider the intangible qualities.

Behavior: Motor Actions

The behaviors exhibited by patients are motor actions. There are two types of motor actions, spontaneous and imitated. Spontaneous motor acting is by its own impulse, energy, or natural disposition, without external cause or influence. Imitated motor acting is to try to copy the movements of an external source. The source is usually another human being, but the self and other material objects are included as well.

Motor actions exist within the context of material circumstances. The continuum of sensory cues from inner to outer defines the material circumstances. The continuum for motor actions is guided by the part versus whole dichotomy. The inner parts of motor actions begin the continuum; the end contains the outer wholes or the universe of potential human actions on the external environment.

The other attributes of behavior—tool use, number, people, and directions, both verbal and demonstrated—will be described in Chapter 3.

The motor actions that a person spontaneously performs or imitates are suggested by a sensory cue. The word *voluntary* implies that the person has some degree of conscious control over the motor action. Physical disabilities are often characterized by involuntary motor actions, that is, reflexes and paralysis; conscious control is not involved. Cognitive disabilities are characterized by motor actions in which some degree of conscious control is available. The sensory cue, coupled with the associated action, helps to specify the degree of control.

Automatic motor actions are associated with subliminal sensory cues at level 1 (Table 2-1). Examples of automatic movements in infants include sniffing, licking, biting, swallowing, retching, and eye movements. Adults have additional automatic movements including sitting, standing, walking, eating, and drinking. Individual adults may have other automatic motor actions such as knitting, crocheting, driving, or biting their fingernails; we are not concerned with these actions here. The automatic movements of concern are related to life's basic necessities, the most important of which are eating and drinking. Imitation does not occur at level 1.

The voluntary motor actions associated with proprioceptive cues are postural actions. Gross body movements such as gesturing, turning, pacing, scratching, bending, and doing calisthenics are examples. The spontaneous action is a response to an internal cue. The response to a cue demonstrated by the therapist may be an approximation of the therapist's movement.

The action associated with tactile cues is usually

manual—people use their hands to feel physical objects. The manual action is applied to objects found in the external environment. The action, at level 3, is not goal directed. Actions that are not goal directed are often repetitive. The patient is able to imitate manipulative actions demonstrated by the therapist.

Visible motor cues are associated with goal-directed actions. Visible qualities are relevant to an identifiable purpose; for example, one sands until the wood is smooth, or strings green beans until there are enough for dinner. Voluntary motor actions in response to visible cues contain an implicit goal. Actions that can be imitated successfully are clearly visible actions demonstrated by the therapist.

Two or more perceivable cues are related at level 5. The most common cues are visible. Perceivable cues are associated with exploratory actions. Visible relationships foster experimentation, for example, getting equivalent spaces between mosaic tiles so that they fit evenly into a trivet. Novelty that the patient has not discovered is imitated.

Symbols are associated with planned actions. Words are used to select the intention of the motor action before it is executed. In addition words are used to distinguish among alternative motor actions and to select the best alternative. The intangible effects of material objects can be predicted, and the information can be used in selecting the best alternative. Visual images and words are implicit in selecting the best alternative for motor actions. Visual images form the background for a planned action because they are fleeting and hazy. Words and drawings may be generated from visual images, and even drawings seem to be associated with some explanatory words. Words are the predominant symbol used in planning motor actions.

Mind: Conscious Awareness

Attention to sensory cues and motor actions produces sensorimotor associations in the cortex of the brain. The brain is an interrelated network, and the anatomic location of the cognitive levels is still unclear. It seems reasonable, however, to suggest that associations involve the cortex, except perhaps at level 1 (Ayers, 1979; Noback and Demarest, 1975; Plum and Posner, 1980; Strub and Black, 1981).

Purpose

Purpose is the intended objective that guides the selective response to the sensory cue as well as the selection of the muscle movement. The continuum for purpose is indebted to the work of Kopp (1982), who postulated a sequence of self-regulation acquired during Piaget's sensorimotor period (birth to two years of age). Kopp's emphasis is on the psychosocial influences of learning. Her descriptions have been modified to describe an internally generated purpose for forming a sensorimotor association.

Purpose may have some biologic correlates of interest to therapists. Purpose may come into play when a patient enhances his or her awareness of some sensory cues or motor actions while inhibiting awareness of others. The reason for inhibition or enhancement may be self-regulated or biologically determined. My approach to cognitive disabilities is primarily concerned with biologic explanations, but we cannot afford to neglect self-regulated explanations.

Self-regulation of the reason for doing a task is a relatively recent idea. Reese and Overton (1970) suggest that the idea represents a change in world views. The mechanistic world view supports the notion that the patient is the passive recipient of the therapist's reason for doing a task. The organismic world view supports the notion that the patient actively selects a preferred sensory stimuli and a motor action. The organismic world view seems to be evident in the medicolegal system, which recognizes a patient's right to accept or refuse treatment. In turn, we must respect a patient's right to accept or refuse the tasks we offer. The therapist, of course, would like to suggest tasks that are acceptable to the patient. The therapist provides suggestions or opportunities. The patient decides whether to accept or reject these. This is a subtle, and profound, change in the way that many of us learned to think about patient care; new lines of responsibility must be drawn. Methods of adapting to the organismic world view are suggested throughout the text.

The dichotomy of existence versus transition will be expanded into a continuum for the description of purpose. The basic purpose of a living organism is to sustain life. To perform the actions of eating and drinking, a state of arousal must exist (Table 2-1). Arousal is a state of responsiveness to sensory stimuli; at level 1 the stimuli may be provided by the material object (food) or by a verbal command ("Chew").

The natural disposition for comfort is the purpose behind the combination of proprioceptive cues and postural actions. At level 2 the person may move because it feels good or to relieve distress.

Interest guides the manual manipulation of material objects at level 3. Interest in tactile cues introduces awareness of the external environment into the continuum. Interest is curiosity about the tactile properties of objects that can be manipulated in one's hands. The manual action is often repeated several times until curiosity is satisfied.

Compliance governs the association between visible cues and goal-directed actions at level 4. The individual yields to the procedure that must be followed to achieve the goal, but the goal must be desirable to the individual. Compliance is sustained when visible properties are present.

Self-control over one's own actions occurs during the explorations of the relationships between the properties of objects at level 5. The results of the explorations are perceivable, and motor actions are self-controlled so as to produce the desired effect. Novel actions may be discovered during explorations, and these may be self-controlled to repeat the effect. Novel actions that are demonstrated by others are also repeated. In this fashion self-control guides new learning from the visible properties of objects.

Reflection is the contemplation of a number of possible plans that could guide motor actions at level 6. New possibilities are imagined. Changes in the conditions of material objects are considered before manipulating the objects. Pauses to think, to reconsider the original plan, or to select a new purpose occur.

Experience

Experience is what one actually lives through; the term is used here as a subclassification of purpose. The characteristics of experience that seem to be most related to sensorimotor associations are sensations and reasoning. A sensation is an impression conveyed by an afferent nerve to the brain; the seat of sensation is the sensorium. A person who can receive sensations is conscious, with varying degrees of mental clarity that may be further clarified by the cognitive levels. Reasoning is the drawing of inferences or conclusions from known or assumed facts. The continuum for experience makes an abrupt shift from sensations, in levels 1 to 4, to reasoning, in levels 5 and 6 (Table 2-1).

The continuum for experience goes from subjective to objective. The experience at level 1 seems to be indistinct or indefinite most of the time. The patient is awake, has his or her eyes open, but is largely unresponsive to external cues. A change in the level of arousal requires vigorous and repeated stimuli, and the responsiveness lapses when one discontinues the stimulation.

The sensations for levels 2, 3, and 4 are readily understood. Moving is the sensation produced by proprioceptive cues and postural actions; touching, by tactile cues and manual actions; and seeing, by visible cues and goal-directed actions.

Inductive reasoning goes from the specific to the general. The specifics, as used here, are provided by the relationships between the properties of objects. Patients at level 5 generalize from one exploratory action to another motor action on the grounds of analogy. The induction is based on the notion that what is true for one motor action will extend to a class of actions.

Deductive reasoning goes from the general to the

specific. The general is provided by a class of motor actions coded by symbolic cues. The general classes of motor actions are used to generate hypothetical possibilities. One selects the best possibility for an unknown situation. The possibility selected is a planned or designed mode of action at level 6.

Process

Process is a course of action followed to achieve a purpose. A sensorimotor process establishes a cause-and-effect relationship between motor actions and their effects on sensory cues. Processes occur during the typical procedure for doing a task. The continuum for process goes from inactive to active. Inactive mental processes are characterized as sluggish, passive, dull, listless, motionless, or lethargic. Active mental processes are characterized as dynamic, operative, alert, busy, energetic, or flexible. The process is thus described by the degree of liveliness invested in forming sensorimotor associations.

The process is inactive at level 1. Few associations are made, and those that are formed are reflexive or habitual (Table 2-1). Although a reflex is an involuntary activity, it is included here because reflexes such as swallowing can be elicited to aid functional performance. Habitual actions are fixed by constant practice and established by frequent repetition. Habitual actions that can be elicited at the level of arousal, such as walking or bending one's knees, characterize level 1.

The level 2 process establishes a relationship between a chance movement and its effect on the body. The movement is frequently repeated several times to verify the effect. These postural movements are sluggish, like movements in a film projected in slow motion. This limited degree of activity occurs infrequently.

The level 3 process establishes a relationship between a chance movement and an effect on the external environment. Again, this movement may be repeated several times to verify the effect. These manual actions are slow and can be characterized as dawdling, distracted, lagging, unhurried, dilatory, delaying, or snail-paced. Patients at level 3 plod along, manipulating the objects in their hands without an awareness of other objects, people, or goals.

The level 4 process establishes a relationship between a goal-directed action and its visible effects on material objects. Goal attainment frequently requires several different motor actions, for example, sanding, staining, and gluing. The pace is still slow and can be characterized as deliberate, leisurely, decelerated, or interrupted and resumed. Several manual actions are done in compliance with the required procedure.

The level 5 process is characterized by overt trial-and-error problem solving. The relationship between an exploratory action and its effect on material objects is established after the action has been performed. Errors are not anticipated but are recognized. After an error has been made new actions that would avoid the error are explored. The active pace is injudicious and can be characterized as impulsive, abrupt, hasty, inefficient, careless, or imprudent. Supervisors must take precautions to prevent errors that are dangerous or costly.

The level 6 process is characterized by covert trial-and-error problem solving. The relationship between an anticipated action and its effect on material objects is established before the action is performed. Several possibilities can be considered, and many errors can be avoided. The active pace is judicious and can be characterized as dynamic, operative, alert, busy, energetic, flexible, or creative.

SOCIAL AND EMOTIONAL RESPONSES. The process of doing an activity is also characterized by emotional and social responses. Attempts to develop continuums for these responses have not produced descriptions that differentiate the levels. The best that can be offered is a general description to provide a snapshot for readers who are unfamiliar with the cognitively disabled.

The emotional responses at levels 1 through 4 are dulled. Level 1 might be characterized as numb, desensitized, impassive, or without spirit. Social relations are remote or essentially nonexistent. Emotional responses at level 2 are a little less dulled and could be described as apathetic, indifferent, or placid. The dullness may be lightened by engaging the patient in postural actions. Social withdrawal is apparent, and the patient's attempts to communicate are usually unintelligible. The dullness is still oppressive at level 3. Much of the patient's day may be spent in a dispirited, nebulous condition. Caregivers may organize the manual actions of patients at level 3 so that they attain a goal; when this happens they express surprise. A faint smile or a momentary gleam in their eyes may be observed. Their social relations are detached. Some intelligible communications do occur; they are usually terse, curt, vague, or difficult to decipher.

The emotional expression of those at level 4 remains generally dull. Patients at this level follow the typical task procedure and rarely talk or show an emotional response when performing successfully. Groups of level 4 patients are very quiet. Additional responses do, however, accompany goal directness. Preferences for task content, shape, and color may be expressed. Goal achievement may elicit a response of contentment or accomplishment. Errors that are recognized may produce impatient, irritable, distressed, confused, or depressed responses. Recognition that a procedure contains steps produces demands for demonstrated directions with a disregard for other concerns of the therapist. Level 4 patients may interrupt the social conversation of others to make their demands in a rude or abrupt fashion. Their reliance on visible cues extends into their efforts to make conversation: They may make comments on aspects of others' physical appearance, such as gray hair, weight gain, blemishes, race, or aging, that may be sensitive issues.

The dullness clears at level 5. Friendly conversation during task performance occurs in an outgoing, chatty fashion. Overt trial and error is accompanied by discovery and frustration. Reflection does not occur, and some social transactions may be tactless, intolerant, insensitive, or superficial. At level 6 covert trial and error can be accompanied by en-

joyment or disappointment. Self-congratulatory responses, or admonishments about preventing errors, may occur. Reflection seems to be accompanied by a responsiveness to others as autonomous people; sympathetic, tolerant, and grateful responses are observed.

The emotional and social responses occur, and they must be managed in practice; chapter 7 will elaborate on their management. However, these responses cannot be objectively measured. What, for example, is the difference between frustrated and disappointed? The adjectives that have been used in this description are ambiguous. Ambiguities in our language make it difficult if not impossible to develop description, or classification criteria, that are mutually exclusive. For that reason emotional and social responses will not be emphasized in the description of the cognitive levels.

Time

This discussion of time focuses on attention span, the length of time that sensorimotor associations are sustained. Time is a subclassification of purpose because intention governs duration. Memory—recall of past events plus the ability to acquire new recollections—is related to time. Time also includes projections into the future.

The continuum for time is from instantaneous to long-lasting. Instantaneous time occurs within the moment, while the years of the past and future are long-lasting. Attention at level 1 is instantaneous. Memories from the past are barely relevant, except perhaps for food preferences. The future is not considered. The actions that are observed are transitory and rarely sustained for more than a few seconds (Table 2-1).

Attention at level 2 lasts a few minutes, approximately 5 to 10. Memories about past postural actions can be evoked, but the reporting of these and other memories may be incoherent to those who do not share the memories. The future is not considered.

The level 3 attention span is a little longer, approximately 30 minutes. Patients at level 3 may be disoriented to time, place, or person. If active, they have a tendency to get lost. Memories about past manipulations of objects can be evoked, but the time when these events occurred may not be clear to those who do not share the memories. The future is not considered or is considered unrealistically. The person's concept of time is restricted to an interest in the here and now.

The attention span at level 4 is approximately one hour. Patients may be oriented to present time, place, or person. Memories about past goal-directed actions can be described coherently. Reports of life history may be disorganized. Immediate goals that can be achieved within their attention span are understood, but projections into the future may be rigid or unrealistic. Realistic goals do not extend beyond compliance with immediate events.

Attention to exploratory actions can be sustained for approximately one week at level 5. Orientation to the present is clear. Memories can be organized into a coherent life history, and new recollections from overt trial and error are acquired; memory is clear. Projections into the future fail to consider all the relevant possibilities, and plans may reflect poor judgment.

At level 6 the attention span is related to other priorities that the individual selects for himself or herself. The amount of time devoted to a task is contingent on external factors, for example, appointments, birthdays, length of hospitalization, or role responsibilities. Judgment is clear.

The continuums that describe the attributes of voluntary actions are difficult to separate because they are interrelated. The attributes of the mind form an association between the sensory cue that the patient pays attention to and the related motor action. The sensorimotor associations are also interrelated. These interrelationships suggest organized systems of abilities and disabilities that I call the cognitive levels.

The cognitive levels are probably arranged into an ordinal scale, that is, a scale that specifies the or-

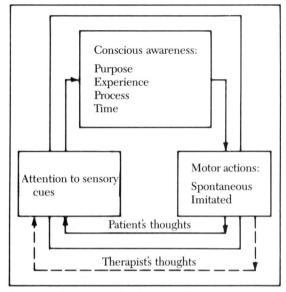

Fig. 2-1. The cognitive levels as an information processing system.

der of the items but not the distance between items. It seems less likely, given our current understanding of the levels, that they comprise an interval scale (one in which there is an equal distance, or interval, between the levels). A cognitive disability is a restriction in routine task behavior that has social consequences. At present we do not know what the intervals between social consequences might be and have no way of validating an interval scale.

The attributes of the cognitive levels can be organized into an information processing system (Fig. 2-1). The input is attention to sensory cues. The throughput is conscious awareness of purpose, experience, process, and time. The output is a motor action that can be spontaneous or imitated. The model indicates that there are two thought processes going on simultaneously, the patient's and the therapist's. This seemingly obvious fact must be kept in mind. We are always on the outside trying to make guesses about the patient's conscious awareness. Our guesses or inferences are based on the input and the output. Thus our descriptions of attention to sensory cues and motor actions need to

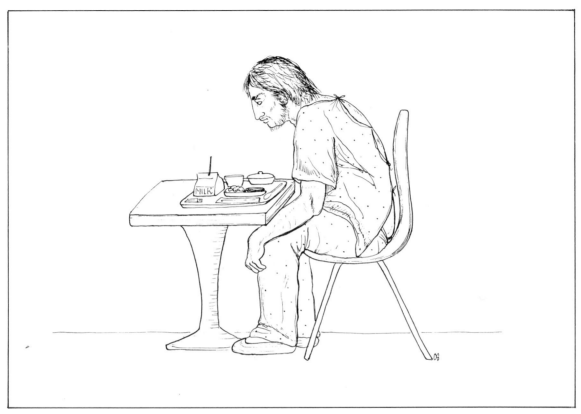

Fig. 2-2. Level 1. A glazed look on the face of a patient who seems to be unaware of the external environment. This patient is ignoring the food placed in front of him.

be as clear and objective as possible. In addition our descriptions of conscious awareness should be closely related to these cues and actions.

The following descriptions of the cognitive levels will be divided into two parts: the assets, or what the patient can do; and the limitations, or what the patient cannot do. Within each part, attention, motor actions, and conscious awareness are discussed.

LEVEL 1: AUTOMATIC ACTIONS
Assets

Attention

Level 1 is difficult to describe but fairly easy to observe. People functioning at this level are conscious and their reflexes are working, but their level of awareness is markedly impaired. Their attention may be captured by familiar objects, but their recognition of these objects seems to be subliminal (subliminal cues are at the threshold of consciousness). These people often have a glazed look (Fig. 2-2) and seem to be responding to internal cues. Calling their attention to the external environment requires vigorous stimulation; one may literally have to yell at them and shake them to get their attention.

Motor Actions

Automatic actions, or habits, are spontaneously performed at level 1. Examples include eating, drinking, and walking. An automatic action is done with very little thought, and the difficulty in defining the quality of thought can be illustrated by the example of drinking a glass of water. Some attention is required to grasp the glass and bring it to the mouth, but the degree of attention, when compared with that needed for other actions, is very small. The problem occurs in attempting to classify other actions that might also be regarded as automatic, such as reading, knitting, or driving. These actions appear to be in a different class in that they are not performed by profoundly disabled people. The automatic actions of concern at level 1 are those that are vital to one's health and well-being. We are concerned about whether or not a person can literally eat, drink, and walk to the bathroom.

An action that is demonstrated to a person functioning at level 1 is seldom imitated, largely because the therapist does not have the patient's attention. Attention may be gained by waving a hand in front of the patient's face. Sometimes actions may be generated by one-word commands such as "Chew"— verbs that identify the desired action.

Conscious Awareness

Arousal at level 1 has been reduced by inhibiting information coming from the environment, but such patients can produce some change in their level of arousal on command from a caregiver. The sensations experienced seem to be indistinct or faded. What is experienced seems to be based on an assumed similarity between a present object and past experience. That is, water tastes and smells like water one has had in the past. The automatic action is connected to the individual's past experiences. Cause-and-effect relationships are barely recognized; they are subjective. The patient responds to internal signals but not to elements of the external environment. Introspection does not occur.

The person is literally conscious but barely responding to the external environment (Fig. 2-3). The person may spend long hours sitting or lying motionless. The actions that are elicited may be dull

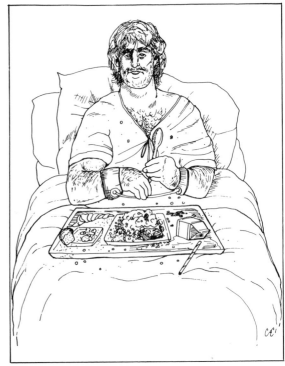

Fig. 2-3. Level 1. Automatic actions with a disregard for their effect on the external environment. This patient responds to his food by making a mess: the peas are strewn about the bed, the milk is spilled, and the meat and potatoes are mashed together. The face is expressionless and adequate nutrition is disregarded.

and lethargic. Caregivers may need to elicit reflexes to stimulate eating or drinking. The attention span is momentary; attention may last a few seconds.

Limitations

Attention

Most sensory cues are ignored at level 1. Awareness of the external environment is restricted to a subliminal recognition of familiar cues. Attention is transient, slipping away unless commands are constantly repeated.

Motor Actions

Automatic actions have a meaningless quality. Level 1 may also be characterized by no action at all, that is, sitting and staring into space. There is often reason for concern about the amount of food and fluid that is actually consumed, and sometimes people functioning at level 1 must be fed or given intravenous supplements. They may be brought into the hospital on a stretcher and may require bed rest until they reach a higher level of function.

The therapist's efforts to reach these people rarely meet with much success. They stare at a demonstrated action as if they do not see it. They do not clap their hands when the action is demonstrated, nor will they take an object when it is placed in their hands. If the patient is moving the therapist can imitate the patient's action, but at level 1 the patient does not recognize that his or her own action has been imitated.

Conscious Awareness

Changes in the level of arousal, required to do tasks that sustain life, must be initiated by an external stimuli to obtain a habitual action. One can infer that the sensations of those at level 1 must be restricted to subliminal recognition of familiar objects. They seem to be unaware of any cause-and-effect relationship beyond this subjective awareness.

The major cognitive limitation at level 1 appears to be that awareness of time is restricted to the few occasional moments when arousal is stimulated. The major asset is that the person is conscious and may be able to pursue the vital tasks of eating and drinking.

LEVEL 2: POSTURAL ACTIONS

Assets

Attention

The sensory cues that capture attention at level 2 are proprioceptive. People at this level attend to the

Fig. 2-4. Level 2. Attention is captured by proprioceptive cues. This movement if displayed with disregard for the social context may look peculiar.

movements of their own muscles and joints. They also watch the movements of objects and other people. Gross body movements sustain their attention; a part of the body is moved, and the movement is intentionally repeated (Fig. 2-4). Material objects such as clothing and furniture that come in contact with the body or restrict range of motion are noticed.

Motor Actions

The spontaneous actions observed at level 2 are postural actions such as bending, stretching, and

Fig. 2-5. Level 2. Imitation of a gross body movement. The imitation is an approximation of the demonstrated movement.

pacing. These gross body movements may be initiated by chance, seeming to occur for no particular reason, or they may be in response to some internal cue.

The simplest form of imitation is actually the reverse of the usual understanding of the term: Level 2 patients can recognize their own actions when imitated by others. Some patients, especially those with dementia, may have trouble initiating a movement; the therapist may guide them through the

first part of the movement to see if this facilitates imitation. Approximations of the postural action demonstrated by a therapist may be expected; what is important to note is that the patient is attending to a demonstration and attempting to replicate the action (Fig. 2-5). In selecting an action the therapist should consider the amount of coordination and balance required; obviously, jumping jacks that require coordination of all four extremities are much more difficult than bending as if to touch one's toes. Exercises that can be done in the upright position— movements of the arms, waist, and neck, for example—may be preferred. These exercises move one body part at a time. Floor exercises may be refused.

The therapist may accompany a demonstrated direction with words. Verbs and pronouns appear to be the most meaningful: "Look," "Watch me," "You try it." The words selected should be simple and the sentences short.

Conscious Awareness

The physical sensation is of moving the position of the body in space. The self-regulated process may be initiated by a chance connection made between a somatosensory cue and a postural action; the purpose of moving is that it feels good. The movement may be sustained until a feeling of discomfort is experienced, which is influenced by the physical stamina of the individual. Postural actions seem to orient people to the present. Attention can usually be sustained for 5 to 10 minutes.

Limitations

Attention

Awareness of the external environment does not extend beyond the limits of body movements. The postures, gestures, and pacing are done in response to internal cues of what feels good; their appearance to others in the external environment is not considered. Attention is easily distracted by the movements of others, by their own movements, and by music. Material objects and people are given only transient notice.

Motor Actions

The spontaneous postural actions characteristic of level 2 often appear to be purposeless or idiosyn-

cratic. Gestures, staring at parts of the body, finger movements, and self-mutilating actions may even seem to be bizarre. At level 2 a person's ability to imitate a demonstrated direction is restricted to gross body movements; other demonstrations and verbal instructions are ignored.

Conscious Awareness

Sensations seem to be limited to the subliminal recognitions of level 1 and the physical sensations of position in space and movement. There is a failure to account for external cues that can act as an intervening cause in a cause-and-effect relationship. There is an inability to comply with directions of other people or the qualities of material objects. Movements are usually slow with a sluggish quality; much of the day may be spent sitting idly staring at a television set or into space. Memories about past events are nearly unintelligible to people who do not share those memories. The future is not considered.

The major cognitive restriction is that at level 2 people are not aware of the effect that their actions have on objects or other people; instead, attention is directed to parts of their bodies. The major asset is that these people are able to organize their actions to imitate postural actions.

LEVEL 3: MANUAL ACTIONS

Assets

Attention

Attention shifts from the internal self to the external environment at level 3. The cues that capture attention at level 3 are tactile. Physical objects found in the external environment that suggest a motor action, for example, a ball, capture their attention. Attention is also directed to the exterior surfaces of objects; the patients may rub, pat, or visually inspect these surfaces in great detail even when manipulating common objects.

"One Our Father... Two Our Father..."

Fig. 2-6. Level 3. A repetitive action. The action may resemble a familiar movement—the rosary in this illustration. Other actions may relate to a personal sense of physical well-being.

Motor Actions

The spontaneous actions observed at level 3 are manual actions; people use their hands to manipulate material objects. The action may be initiated by a chance awareness of an object that suggests an action, for example, picking up a telephone receiver even though the phone has not rung (Fig. 2-6).

A manual action may be initiated by another person by demonstrating the motion. For apraxic patients imitation may be produced by placing an object (e.g., a bar of soap) in the patient's hands and beginning the associated motion (washing). Most people assessed at level 3 can imitate a demonstrated action. Examples of tasks with single repetitive actions are stringing beads, peeling carrots, folding linens, and washing tables. The accompanying words are limited to simple nouns and verbs in short sentences.

Manual actions are sustained at level 3 by repetitive actions. A pattern of action is performed and then repeated several times, for example, bouncing the ball from a wall to the floor and catching it several times. Obvious gross motor sequences—taking turns or passing a ball around in a circle—are noticed. (Sometimes patients functioning at level 2 will bounce a ball, but they do not follow such sequences.) The repetitive action may be continued until an obvious stopping place has been reached. For example, a craft project may be continued until supplies or space run out. Intense concentration on seemingly monotonous actions may be observed (Fig. 2-7).

Conscious Awareness

Material objects are manipulated because the properties are interesting to the patient. Sometimes people at level 3 will fondle objects in a way that looks peculiar to outside observers. They caress, stroke, pick at, twist, hit, drop, or tap an object for no apparent reason beyond an interest in connecting a manual action to a material object. Noisy or destructive actions can be annoying to caregivers.

Tactile cues and manual actions produce the sensation of touching. Related feelings may include weight, pressure, and temperature. The sense of touch can be evaluated with stereognostic tests. Stereognosis is the faculty of perceiving the form and nature of objects by the sense of touch. Stereognosis is usually assessed by giving a person a common object, such as a key or a coin, and asking him or her to identify it without looking at it. The person must feel the object and draw an inference about what it is, based on past experiences with the object. Stereognosis is a form of thought that is based

The attention span at level 3 is measured in half-hour units, with some variability according to the diagnosis and other individual differences. Some memories about past task experiences that are related to present manual actions can be elicited.

Limitations

Attention

Awareness of material objects is restricted to tactile cues; visual and auditory cues do not seem to have much meaning. Attention is restricted to what can be touched and manipulated.

Motor Actions

Spontaneous repetitive actions can appear to be monotonous, foolish, idiosyncratic, or purposeless. By ordinary standards the behavior of those at level 3 may be inappropriate and unpredictable: spooning soup into the fish tank, eating poisonous houseplants, rearranging the personal belongings of other people, picking up the telephone whenever they walk by it, or carrying away all of the ashtrays. The manual actions are not goal directed, and people functioning at level 3 are often quite surprised to see that they have completed a project. The only actions that they will imitate are concrete manipulations of material objects, one action at a time. The repertoire of actions that fulfill these criteria is quite restricted. In addition the quality of these actions is usually poor because the actions are not connected to a goal.

Conscious Awareness

At level 3 people fail to connect their manual actions to a purposeful goal. Their understanding of the external environment is restricted to their own actions on objects; other cause-and-effect relationships are frequently ignored or misinterpreted. The misinterpretation takes the form of magical thinking, the belief that their actions cause an effect that is really

Fig. 2-7. Level 3. A chance awareness of a familiar object may elicit a familiar action. The chance awareness of the flag stimulates the placement of the hand over the heart.

on a sensorimotor connection between a tactile cue (key) and a manual action (feeling the key). This connection should be made at level 3.

The person at level 3 is aware of cause-and-effect relationships as a connection between a tactile cue and a manual action. The tactile cue is produced by an object that is external to the organism; to understand the object as separate from oneself, one must think. The separation between the self and the object, made at level 3, is based on tactile cues and manual actions. The action may produce a chance effect on the external environment and may be repeated as long as the effect is interesting.

the result of other causes not taken into account (e.g., stomping one's foot turns on the television set). Socially these people appear quite egocentric; they are interested in their own motor actions and are unable to consider a large number of external perspectives.

The motor actions are slow at level 3. These people move at a snail's pace: They dawdle with material objects, lag behind others when moving from room to room, and appear to be unhurried even when encouraged to move faster. The exception is the person who is hyperactive but distractible; the motor actions of such patients are fast, but their functional achievement is slowed by their distractibility.

Disorientation of time, place, person, may be present at level 3. Disorientation to place is assessed by asking patients to identify their current location in an institutional setting, such as in a psychiatric hospital. Disorientation to space can be assessed by observing patients' movements within the institutional setting, such as finding their bedrooms, the bathroom, or the OT clinic. Empirical study of this potential correlation with the cognitive level would be of interest. Disorientation is thought to be diagnosis specific, but it may be more related to the degree of disability. Clinical experience suggests that a disorientation to space has important functional implications for the cognitively disabled. While walking is not physically restricted, it is cognitively restricted. Disoriented patients get lost. In the hospital they have trouble remembering where their bedroom, the bathroom, the ward, and the OT clinic are located. Active people at level 3 have a tendency to walk around and get lost. Others adapt by following the lead of other people, often to the wrong location. Locked doors may be required to protect them from getting lost. Recently I heard of a clever alternative to locked doors. The theft detector clamps that trigger an alarm at the doors of department stores can be attached to a garment worn by a wandering person at level 3. That way caregivers can be alerted if the patient leaves a protected area.

The attention span at level 3 seems to be defined by the length of time that a repetitive action can be performed. External factors such as physical fatigue, running out of space, or running out of supplies seem to influence the length of attention. The attention span is short, and attention is easily diverted by other tactile cues found in the environment.

Memories about when past events occurred are frequently unclear to others who do not share them. Reports of memories may be misinterpreted or uninterpretable. Some reports entail confabulation, that is, patients draw on past events to fill gaps in memory in an attempt to give an organized report. Memories of the past are unreliable. A life history may not be organized into a meaningful time frame. The future is not considered or is considered unrealistically. An awareness of time is restricted to an interest in the here and now.

The major restriction at level 3 is that the patient's actions are slow and meaningless unless directed by another person. The major asset is that the patients do notice the effect their manual actions have on tactile cues and they repeat the actions.

LEVEL 4: GOAL-DIRECTED ACTIONS

Assets

Attention

The visual-motor cues that capture attention at level 4 are clearly visible (Fig. 2-8). Color and shape seem to predominate, and two-dimensional objects seem to provide clearer cues than do three-dimensional objects. A sample of a project captures their attention; the sample is concrete in the sense that they often want to make an exact replication of it. Attention will also be paid to other strikingly visible distinctions such as up or down, right or left, front or back, vertical or horizontal, number, and amount. Attention is directed toward one cue at a time. Their questions—Is this smooth enough? Is

Fig. 2-8. Level 4. A clearly visible cue. This coffee pot is an invitation to have a cup of coffee, but all of the required supplies must be visible. As a rule, people at level 4 will not go to the refrigerator to find the cream, which is "hidden."

this enough stain?—indicate that they are aware of the purpose of their actions. Implicit in the questions is an awareness of an intended goal.

Motor Actions

Spontaneous actions are goal directed at level 4. Several familiar manual actions may be used to achieve the goal. People at level 4 may spontaneously perform a familiar task that does not involve new instructions, for example, crocheting granny squares without reference to a pattern. They notice visible errors in task performance and may seek assistance in correcting these errors.

People at level 4 imitate a demonstrated direction one step at a time. The directions must be clearly visible, and objects that cover things up, such as carbon paper, are confusing. An action involving a relationship between two objects can be imitated if it can be easily seen. Words that describe such actions, for example, "Move the picture up a little on the wood," may accompany the demonstration. The relationship between two objects can be used to guide one movement, as in moving the pic-

Fig. 2-9. Level 4. Visible demonstration is required. Here the therapist is showing how much batter to pour for each cupcake. A verbal direction such as half-full is usually confusing at level 4.

ture, but attention to it may not be sustained through several movements, as in correctly spacing mosaic tiles. Generally, people have to be shown what to do, and they can rarely follow a spoken direction without a demonstration (Fig. 2-9). Those who speak a foreign language can usually follow a demonstration without verbal direction.

Conscious Awareness

To imitate a goal-directed action one must comply with the demonstrated procedure. People at level 4 comply with a typical procedure to reach a goal. The sensory cues that are attended to, and therefore provide information, are things that the person can see and touch. Touchable and visible cues will be referred to as tangible cues. The motor actions are intentional and therefore meaningful. *Purposeful behavior* is a common occupational therapy term; it is introduced into the continuum of the cognitive levels at level 4.

Seeing is the sensation at level 4. That seems like a simple statement but is very important. If level 4 patients can see a property of an object they can deal with it. Their abilities can be used if the properties of the material objects that must be attended to are visible. At level 4 seeing really is believing.

The cause-and-effect relationship established at level 4 connects a striking visual cue to a manual goal. Visible cause-and-effect chains are understood. This applies to social behavior as well; the visible normative rules of behavior are understood (e.g., shirts can be buttoned correctly). Both the process of doing a task and the goal achieved are verified by a visual examination of a completed project. During the process a completed sample guides the behavior of those of level 4. After a project is completed these people can verify the results of their actions by comparing their project to the sample. The visual comparison verifies the thought that their motor actions have been directed toward achieving a desired goal.

A goal orients people to what they have done and what they need to do next; behaviors that would interfere with a visible purpose can be self-inhibited. Several familiar actions can be a part of the steps of task procedure, with an awareness of how several types of motor actions are combined to complete the desired task.

The pace is slowed at level 4. Many people seem to function in a leisurely or decelerated fashion. There is no hurry about reaching the goal. For others the process is deliberate and intense but the pace of reaching the goal is still slow. Distraction at level 4 is characterized by self-directed resumption of the required motor actions after an interruption. These differences between patients seem to be related to the diagnostic symptoms of psychiatric diseases.

Visual cues and goal-directed actions mark the passage of time at level 4. People notice regular patterns of events and base expectations on the notion that these patterns will be followed. The actions of other people in establishing routine sequences and schedules are noticed and used to anticipate future events.

An awareness of time extends to the completion of the task, but attention does not usually extend beyond one hour. Level 4 patients are usually oriented to the present time, place, and person, with the possible exception of the exact date. Dates that are important to the individual are remembered but he or she may not know the today's date at level 4. The date may not be a good measure of orientation: I, for one, frequently have to verify the date when I write a check. Day of the week may be a better measure of time orientation at level 4. Memories about past goal-directed actions can be described coherently.

Limitations

Attention

The awareness of material objects is restricted to tangible cues. Their visual dependence on understanding reality can be observed in the difficulty people at level 4 encounter with familiar items that cover things up—carbon paper, storage closets, grout—or that are themselves covered up—the bottom, inside, or back of a project. Sustained relationships between the perceivable properties of objects—overlapping the edges of two objects or leaving empty space between two objects—are also problematic. Color and form seem to be the most striking visual cues. Attention is further restricted to one cue at a time; two cues cannot be considered simultaneously. The differential between levels 3, 4, and 5 is influenced by these attention limitations. The making of a mosaic tile trivet illustrates the differences. At level 3, patients are interested in the manual action of placing tiles on the trivet form, usually placed in rows until they run out of space. No attention is paid to the color of the tiles. If a mixture of colors is given to them, a random pattern of colors is usually produced because no color selection criteria are used. The chance location of the tiles, at the top of a pile or closest to the patient, determine what is used. At level 4, patients do attend to the color of the tiles and usually prefer a checkerboard pattern. During the initial placement, no attention is paid to the space between tiles or the overall fit into the trivet form; later adjustments are usually required (Fig. 2-12). Too much or too little glue may be used. Spacing, gluing, and grouting require attention to the relationships between visual properties of objects. Related cues are attended to at level 5. Attention limitations have associated task performance errors that can be used to differentiate between the cognitive levels.

The use of a sample to identify a goal is concrete in the sense that people at this level prefer making an exact match of the sample that they see. The reason for this may be that they lack the higher-level abilities needed to imagine changes that a different color, size, or shape would make in a project.

The reliance on visual cues influences goal selection. The selection is restricted to what they see. Occupational therapy clinics often have sample cases containing projects that patients can make. Sample cases contain the real thing. Other visual presentations, such as pictures or drawings, seem to cause confusion at level 4. Verbal discussions about possible goals are even more troublesome. The goals patients select seem to be restricted to the activities that other people design for them. Other goals are seldom requested or undertaken.

If the physical materials require the understanding of a relationship between objects, the person will have to be told exactly what to do. For example, in decoupage the individual may not spread the glue all of the way to the edge of the picture, and when the picture is placed on a wood backing the edges will stick up from the wood. The problem with the glue is not readily apparent. At level 4 people do not draw inferences about the cause of a problem that they cannot see. They must be shown what the cause of the problem is. The relationship must be concrete and must be pointed out. Abstract

Fig. 2-10. Level 4. Failure to notice partially hidden cues. The shoes are under the bed and not visible unless he bends down, an action performed because he thinks they might be there. At level 4 he may not generate the hypothesis that is the prerequisite for searching behavior.

relationships are not understood when they are explained.

Motor Actions

At level 4 spontaneous actions are goal directed and restricted to tangible objects found in the environment. There is very little initiative taken to find objects that cannot be seen (Fig. 2-10) or to suggest a goal unless a visible sample is present. People at level 4 are restricted to the goals and objects placed in their environment by other people. Spontaneous actions of those at level 4 are restricted by another factor: They do not have the ability to invent new motor actions. They are restricted to familiar motor

Fig. 2-11. Level 4. Failure to notice partially hidden cues. The appearance of this man portrays his lack of attention to cues that are not clearly visible: He has not shaved under his chin, combed the back of his hair, tucked in the back of his shirt, or been concerned about wearing a dirty shirt.

actions. Tasks that require learning cannot be done independently.

Imitation is also restricted to actions that are tangible, and the preferred actions are replications of familiar actions. Unfortunately, many tasks involve numerous intangible and interrelated abstract properties. Failing to account for these cues causes numerous errors (Fig. 2-11). What is important to note here is that people at level 4 cannot correct many errors, even when the solution is demonstrated to them. One of two things usually happens: They stop working, or they repeat the motor action that was wrong the first time. Their success in following a demonstration of how to correct a mistake is influenced by the visibility of the correction. Obvious corrections can be imitated, but symbolic

ones cannot. As a result therapists spend a great deal of time correcting errors for these people because they are unable to see how to do it themselves.

Demonstrations are followed one step at a time. Two motor actions demonstrated at one time are not retained; the client will do the first one and then stop and ask, "What do I do next?" At level 4 people are aware of the fact that there must be another step because the goal has not been achieved; their project does not look like the sample. They will imitate the demonstration to achieve the goal, but they do not have the ability to explore the relationship between two steps.

Conscious Awareness

Thought is restricted to compliance with typical procedures. People at level 4 fail to explore new motor actions, and they do not direct their attention to relational properties of material objects. They may or may not recognize mistakes made in completing a task, and they may be unable to correct these errors (Fig. 2-12).

Errors cause difficult problems with interpretation, especially when a person says, "I want it that way," or "It doesn't matter." The person is denying the existence of an error. The therapist may be in the awkward position of confronting a personal value judgment about the quality of workmanship that results from inattention to the related properties of objects. Arguing with these patients is usually pointless; they disregard the abstract properties of material objects. A similar problem occurs when these people deny the existence of their disability. Numerous activities of daily living (ADL) require attention to the relationships between concrete and abstract cues. We must refine our understanding of the difficulties those with cognitive disabilities have with these cues.

The social behavior of people functioning at level 4 is also influenced by the connections made between their goal-directed actions and visible cues. The normative rules of behavior that are followed

Fig. 2-12. Level 4. Errors that must be corrected by the therapist. The problem in this example is clearly visible: The mosaic tiles do not fit the trivet. The correction of the problem depends on a concrete relationship, the space between the tiles. At level 4 there is variability in the correction of this problem: Some people can correct it, usually with difficulty; others cannot.

are restricted to the patient's intended goal and must be visibly apparent. Subtle rules and the goals of others are usually disregarded (Fig. 2-13). Purpose is tied to the here and now of their motoric goal and still contains an egocentric quality.

The attention span, which is measured by the hour, is restricted to the here and now of an immediate goal. People at level 4 prefer quick projects, usually tasks that can be completed within one session, scheduled for about one hour. Projects that require three or more sessions may be rejected. Purposeful actions that are restricted to visual cues are difficult to retain when the person is separated from the visual cue. Generally those at level 4 like to complete the goal before they have to leave the

clinic area and are therefore restricted to short-term tasks.

The clock has a recognized association with immediate goals that are important to the individual, for example, lunchtime, time for a cigarette, or the end of a work period. Other uses of clocks and calendars are disregarded; the clock does not provide meaningful information. Therapists compensate by saying, "It's time to clean up now," or "You have 10 minutes left." People at level 4 look at the clock, but the time registered does not influence the pace of their behavior.

Memories of their life histories may be disorganized, misinterpreted, uninterpretable, or delusional. Memory deficits are currently thought to be diagnostic, but here again the deficit may be more characteristic of the severity of the disability. Goals for the future often reflect the life-style of the past. When new goals for the future are required they are often unrealistic.

The major limitation at level 4 is that these people fail to explore new motor actions and they do not direct their attention to the related properties of material objects. Procedures for new actions and

Fig. 2-13. Level 4. Disregard for the goals of others. These patients are waiting to go through a locked door. The idea that they might be blocking the path of the therapist, who has the key, is not considered.

goals must be invented by others. The major asset is that actions are goal directed.

LEVEL 5: EXPLORATORY ACTIONS

Assets

Attention

Related cues capture attention at level 5. Related cues contain properties that can be perceived by one of the five senses; visible cues seem to be the most important. The relationship is between two or more material objects.

The relationship between cues can be further distinguished by its perceptibility, that is, whether it is concrete or abstract. Concrete relations are between two or more properties that are perceivable (visible). In abstract relations one of the related properties is perceivable and another property is intangible or requires the use of images. Examples of actions involving concrete relations are overlapping the edges of objects, leaving space between objects, fitting irregular shapes together, selecting the correct volume of a supply such as glue, matching shades of color such as makeup to skin tone, blending ingredients together as in cooking, and, to a lesser extent, mastering the over and under of weaving. Examples of actions involving abstract relations are getting the air bubbles out of clay, rotating objects in space, measuring and cutting supplies that fit together such as pieces of wood, closing the square knot in macrame that combines over and under with right and left, and working with patterns that contain a diagonal line. Concrete relations may

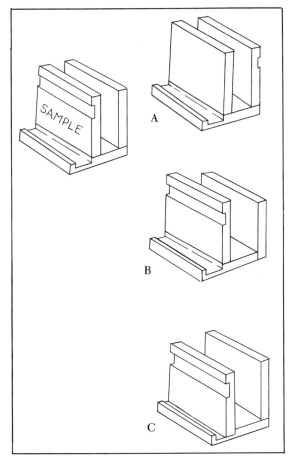

Fig. 2-14. Level 5. Exploratory actions. The assembly of the letter holder requires attention to the orientation of the pieces. Potential errors that are noticed and corrected at level 5 are incorrect placement of front and back pieces (A), failure to place both pieces on top of the bottom (B), and failure to place the front piece above the pencil trough (C).

be observed at level 5; abstract relations are used at level 6.

Attention at level 5 is sustained by variations in motor actions. Familiar actions are augmented by new information suggested by related concrete cues (Fig. 2-14). The motor actions are varied in response to the new information.

Motor Actions

Spontaneous motor actions at level 5 are exploratory, producing variations in physical objects and working methods. More or less pressure, strength, speed, or space will be used. The actions produce an observable effect on the material objects. The individuals will check to see how a variation in their actions influenced the physical objects. Initiative in discovering new ways of doing things is observed.

A series of directions can be imitated at level 5. The length of the series varies according to the degree of familiarity the individual has with the task; as a general rule, three familiar steps plus one new step seem to make up a comfortable series. These people are able to follow a demonstration of a new motor action that involves the presence of related concrete cues.

Written directions and diagrams can be followed to a limited extent. The directions must contain familiar motor actions. New actions that the individual must learn how to do must be demonstrated (Fig. 2-15).

Conscious Awareness

Actions exploring the related properties of material objects are self-controlled. The effects of exploratory actions are evaluated. Desirable effects are continued, and actions that produce undesirable effects are inhibited. Explorations may uncover new effects that are evaluated and, if desirable, repeated. This evaluation makes it possible for the individual to guide his or her own behavior; the purpose is self-controlled. The experience at level 5 is thought about the effect of one's motor actions on material objects. The form of thought is inductive reasoning. Inductive reasoning goes from the specific to the general. The induction is based on the notion that what is true for the effects of one motor action will extend to a class of motor actions. The formation of these inductions characterizes the experience of thought at level 5.

The process is overt trial-and-error problem solving. An overt action is tried and evaluated. Errors

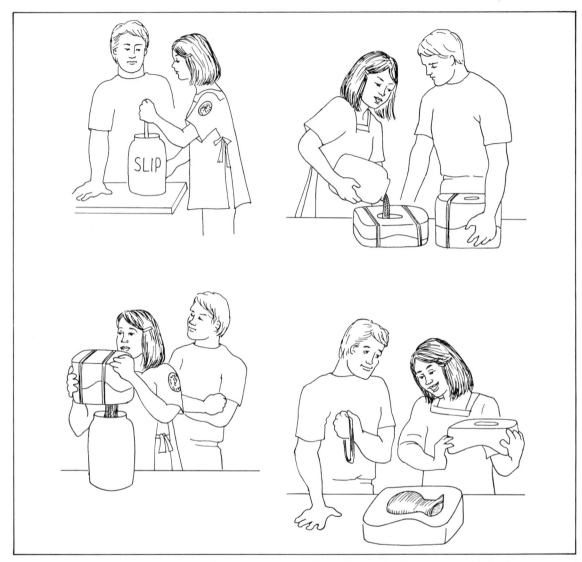

are understood after the action has been performed. The pace of the process is clear, that is, it is
moving at a normal speed, at level 5. Attention span
is still linked to the task but can be extended from
one session to the next. Generally, people prefer
tasks that can be completed within two to five sessions. Providing an estimate of the time it takes to
complete a task usually supplies enough information to permit an independent decision. Several

*Fig. 2-15. Level 5. New actions must be demonstrated.
Pouring a ceramic mold is an unfamiliar process for
many people. A new process can be learned at level 5,
but the procedure must be demonstrated by the
therapist. The length of time the slip is left in the mold is
influenced by absorption and evaporation, abstract
properties. Errors related to these symbolic cues must be
explained by the therapist.*

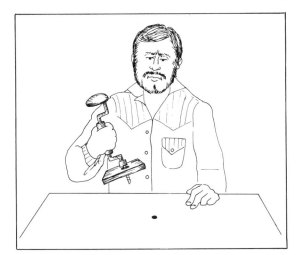

Fig. 2-16. Level 5. Failure to think before acting. Drilling a hole in the table is an unfortunate mistake. The seriousness of the consequences of a potential error is an important consideration for the therapist working with patients at level 5.

variations of one type of task—completing three or four patchwork pillows, for example—can sustain attention. Orientation to the present is clear. Memory is clear as well: Past events are organized into a coherent life history, and new recollections gained from overt trial and error are acquired.

Limitations

Attention

Awareness of material objects is restricted to the effect that a manual action has on material objects. The effect must be perceivable. People at level 5 do not anticipate the effect and therefore fail to anticipate errors. Numerous errors are made because they fail to think before they act (Fig. 2-16).

Motor Actions

Spontaneous exploratory actions are restricted to tasks and settings with a tolerance for error. Exploratory actions can be costly, inefficient, or danger-

ous, and this must be taken into consideration (Fig. 2-16). People at level 5 still rely on a demonstration for direction. The demonstration may show a potential error, explained by an abstract relation, and steps to avoid the error. These people must be shown how to do things; a verbal explanation without a demonstration is not meaningful.

Conscious Awareness

People at level 5 do not think before they act; they do not pause to reflect about possible courses of action and their potential consequences. This is often described as poor judgment or a neglect of the rules of scientific reasoning. The person fails to use symbols to plan motor actions. Thought is restricted to inductive reasoning; deductive reasoning does not occur. Self-control is restricted to a consideration of the relationships between the perceivable attributes of material objects. Abstract relations must be anticipated and explained by others. The social behavior may have a rigid or pedantic quality as well (Fig. 2-17). Those at level 5 do not pause to consider the possibility that other people have autonomous plans. The thought that there may be alternative actions, needs, or rights does not seem to occur to them.

The process of doing a task is injudicious at level 5. Supervision or restricted access is required to protect these people from errors that may be costly or dangerous. They can be "an accident waiting to happen." They may be hasty in reaching a decision about what to do, impulsive in trying it out, and abrupt in changing the course of action; the result can be a series of careless mistakes. The whole process can be inefficient or imprudent. Projections into the future are similar; patients fail to consider possibilities, and their plans reflect poor judgment (Fig. 2-17).

The attention span is set by the number of errors made, the individual's tolerance for error, the type of error made, and whether or not the error can be corrected. Errors in tasks vary according to the task content, for example, dropped knitting versus cro-

Fig. 2-17. Level 5. Social behavior considers one factor
at a time. Relevant factors that must be considered to
form a realistic plan of action are often neglected at level
5. Patients may have to "learn the hard way" because
they do not comprehend the need to plan ahead.

chet stitches. The attention span may be increased
by selecting task content so as to minimize the potential for error.

The major disability at level 5 is that costly, imprudent, or dangerous errors must be prevented by
someone else. The major ability of people at level 5
is that they can learn through inductive reasoning.

LEVEL 6: PLANNED ACTIONS

Assets

Attention

The sensory cues that capture attention at level 6
are symbolic cues. The symbolic cues take many
forms, including spoken instructions, written instructions, visual images, diagrams, and drawings.
Visual images seem to correspond naturally to vol-

untary motor actions in efforts to imagine what the
effects of one's actions are apt to be. Images are then
translated into words or diagrams or both. Symbols
are required to account for the intangible elements
of objects: gravity, evaporation, absorption, heat,
time, speed, and three-dimensional space. More
specific examples include anticipating the speed of
a machine, putting together three-dimensional objects, using word classification systems for such
things as glaze types (shiny versus matt), or anticipating lead poisoning from ceramic glazes. Sym-

Fig. 2-18. Level 6. A pause to think. The making of a patchwork pillow can include a number of symbolic decisions: the length of time required to complete the project, the probable rate of shrinkage and bleeding of dyes, and the coordination of fabrics and colors with each other and with the other furnishings.

the pupils of the eye (Fig. 2-18). Movement of the pupils reflects mental activity and can be differentiated from a blank stare, which indicates a lack of symbolic mental activity.

Motor Actions

Spontaneous actions are preceded by a pause to think or to ask questions. The person may inquire about potential errors that have not occurred. Spontaneous actions are autonomous in that new information required to do a new motor action can be

bolic cues are used to design a course of action before doing the action.

A designed mode of action sustains attention. A design attempts to minimize errors, but should one occur symbolic cues will be used to solve the problem. The use of symbolic cues is often accompanied by a pause in motor performance and movement of

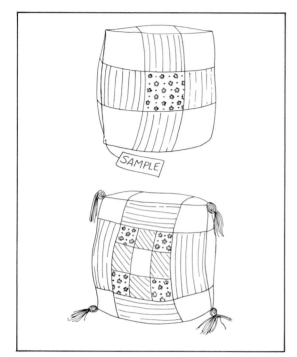

Fig. 2-19. Level 6. Departure from available samples. Individual expression and creativity are related to the characteristics of the patient, as opposed to the samples and supplies suggested by the therapist.

obtained from a book or diagram. Supervision, in the form of needing to be shown how to do a task, is not required. Demonstration may occur in conjunction with other symbolic forms of instruction, and verbal instructions can be followed without a demonstration.

The spontaneous actions observed at level 6 have an individual character. Independent thoughts and interests guide these actions, and the cues provided by the material objects are not a determinant of behavior (Fig. 2-19). Original approaches to task performance may be planned and may be accompanied by a question as to whether needed supplies are available or not.

Delayed imitation, the ability to follow a demonstration after a period of time has elapsed, occurs at level 6. The demonstration is retained by translat-

ing a new motor action into words; these words can be self-generated. Many new motor actions are easier to learn by watching a demonstration. Disabilities seem to impair a person's ability to generate the symbolic cues required to retain new information for later use; this difficulty is not present at level 6.

Conscious Awareness

Reflection about a number of possible planned actions generates the purpose at level 6. The purpose may be the original plan, a reconsideration of the original plan, or a whole new creation. The experience is thought in the form of deductive reasoning. Symbolic cues are required to go from the general to the specific. A specific mode of action is selected from a generalized data base. The experience is thinking about the best way to go.

The process is covert trial-and-error problem solving. The understanding of cause-and-effect relationships is based on assumptions concerning sensory cues and motor actions, assumptions that are premises stated in symbols. Several premises may be considered, along with their inferred consequences. The mode of action that is selected is thought to have the best consequences. Motor actions are fully self-regulated in that the person can think before acting. The thought contains the numerous contingency rules of behavior that are applied to a more specific plan (Fig. 2-20). The original plan can be redesigned or modified as other contingency rules become apparent (Fig. 2-21). The process is characterized by a flexible reflection about the quality of performance.

Symbols are used to project a person into the past and the future. The attention span depends on factors beyond the immediate task such as length of hospitalization, visiting hours, or birthdays. The amount of time that the person will commit to a task is decided within the context of his or her other priorities. Events from the past and future are considered and used to guide the individual's priorities. Judgment is clear.

Fig. 2-20. Level 6. Planning ahead. The contingency rule in this illustration is the need for exact change to use the public transportation system. A person who does not have the correct change cannot ride the bus.

Disability

Level 6 was designed, theoretically, to describe the absence of disability. The empirical investigation of a nondisabled population (Chap. 14) indicates that this is not always true. Level 6 is associated with a high educational and occupational background, while level 5 is associated with a lower educational and occupational background. This distinction is important when treatment is expectant; one must decide whether a patient is expected to return to functioning at level 5 or 6. The decision is based on

Fig. 2-21. Level 6. Departure from the usual route. People at level 6 are able to change plans when necessary.

the individual's educational and occupational history.

Attention at level 6 is directed toward anticipating errors and planning modes of action to prevent mistakes. The attention span is defined by the individual's desires and priorities. Spontaneous actions are planned autonomously, and directions need not be demonstrated. Deductive reasoning can confirm, or refute, the validity of a course of action and aid in the selection of an alternative course of action. Covert trial-and-error problem solving is applied to a reflective purpose. This description may not be complete, because some attributes of a disability have been observed in people who are assessed at level 6. Their problem may be related to classification abilities; this will be further explored in Chapters 13, 14, and 16.

LIMITATIONS IN ROUTINE TASK BEHAVIOR

This chapter began with a definition of *cognitive disability* that indicated that such disabilities produce "observable limitations in routine task behavior." Identifying the limitations has proved to be a greater challenge than originally anticipated. Numerous therapists have approached the problem from a variety of perspectives over an 8-year period; what follows is a summary of our experiences and frustrations.

The Person with a Disability

The first problem in identifying restrictions in routine task behavior is a personal one, and it seems to vary from one therapist to the next; the problem is fear. A cognitive disability is a nasty and insidious phenomenon that robs a person of some of his or her conscious awareness of the external environment. One can hope that the neurosciences will continue to identify treatment methods that reduce cognitive disability, because this type of disability instills dread and denial in the patient, the family, and the therapist. Our fear is that we will be robbed of our human dignity and our personal identity. People who have this disability struggle to maintain their integrity. Their struggle seems to be facilitated by our understanding of their level of awareness. Perhaps the greatest human need, in the disabled person's battle for a better quality of life, is to be understood.

To facilitate an appreciation for what people with cognitive disabilities have been robbed of, let us start at level 6 and work backward, or down the levels of ability. At level 6 no cognitive disability in the performance of voluntary motor actions is, theoretically, apparent. Performance at level 5 is characterized by a failure to generate words that would facilitate deductive reasoning. Performance is inefficient, judgment is impaired, and many errors are made. The normal range of individual variety or creativity is absent. Level 4 is characterized by an inability to account for the relationships between two material cues. People are limited to what they can see and touch; other elements of the universe seem to have no meaning to them. Some mistakes are recognized, but many of these cannot be self-corrected. Goal-directed behavior is lost at level 3. Actions at this level have a repetitive, meaningless quality but are still related to the external environment. The external environment is essentially lost at level 2; postural actions respond to internal cues, and external objects are generally ignored. At level 1 people can still perform automatic actions to a limited degree.

The second problem in identifying restrictions in task behavior is that cognitive disabilities are so overpowering that it is difficult to find the person behind the disability. Cognitive limitations obscure the personality. What is required is a description of the cognitive levels that facilitates locating the elements of the personality that are still available to the cognitively disabled, their assets and how they can be applied.

The approach I have taken to locating the healthy aspects of the personality has been to look at the individual's history in doing routine tasks. Routine tasks are done with great frequency, and the ability to do these tasks, or a few steps in the tasks, is retained even when a great deal of pathology is present. This is an individualized approach, and it rapidly produces bits of information that are difficult to organize.

Organization is confused further by two other important considerations: the natural course of the disease and the method of collecting data. Some patients, principally those with primary affective disorders, improve dramatically while they are in the hospital, and their routine task behavior improves as well. Other patients remain functionally the same from admission to discharge, and a few patients get worse. Therapists need an objective way of assessing these variations in functional performance. Therapists also need a way to avoid the problem of confusing patient assessment with the assessment of the value of the therapist's services. A routine task inventory that contains descriptions of observable routine task behavior will help to meet these needs.

Routine Task Inventory

Numerous ADL inventories are reported in the literature of mental disorders. The methods of collecting the data are to interview the patient, to interview a caregiver, or to observe performance. Each method has some pros and cons. Therapists working in psychiatric hospitals with large numbers of involuntarily committed patients cannot expect to get reliable information from a patient interview; such patients tend to deny the presence of any difficulties. Reports from caregivers may be confounded by their fears and concerns about the illness. Interviews with either patients or caregivers, however, are preferred to observations of performance because interviews are an efficient approach to gaining a large amount of information. Performance inventories take a long time to administer and require a standardized setting; the advantage, of course, is that they entail direct observations of behavior. The selection of tasks is an additional problem; food, clothes, and shelter are an agreed-on foundation, but many variations remain. The relevance of a task to a particular patient is an ongoing problem. The tasks selected for the present inventory are taken from Lawton's (1970, 1971) inventory developed for assessing the elderly. This instrument

was selected by Heying (1983) to study cognitive disability in people with dementia (see Chap. 15). Lawton's inventory is divided into two categories: physical self-maintenance and instrumental ADL. The divisions were based on community placement (Lawton and Brody, 1969) and use for that purpose may be somewhat misleading. The divisions have been retained, however, for statistical analysis of data currently being collected.

Identifying the relevant details of task behavior proved to be more troublesome. The details could not be located in the professional literature. Heimann (in preparation) and I attempted a revision of Lawton's inventory and showed a draft to experienced therapists; they identified numerous problems. It became apparent that the information we required is contained in anecdotes, that is, in the stories that staff tell about patients over coffee. What follows is a collection of this information, tracked down by Heimann, Heying, myself, and numerous other therapists. This process may have resulted in numerous errors of omission.

Before presenting the inventory, I must state an important precaution. The inventory, as of this writing, is in the process of being subjected to empirical study. Nothing is known yet about its association with the cognitive levels or its internal validity. The presentation of an inventory without empirical study could be regarded as problematic. This inventory (along with much of the content of this text) is presented to stimulate research. Philosophical support for this approach is given by Shapere (1969), who maintains that the current "revolution" in the philosophy of science is a reversal in the place of theory and observation. Observation used to guide theory; now it appears that theory guides observation.

The routine task inventory (RTI) is an observational guide, derived from the theory presented in this text (Fig. 2-22). The RTI includes 14 tasks, each of which may have a description for each of the 6 cognitive levels, for a possibility of 84 descriptions. Obviously 84 descriptions provide plenty of oppor-

---

Routine Task Inventory
Physical Scale

Scoring: Circle the number that best describes your observations of behavior.

A.   Grooming (Care of hair and nails; cosmetics)

    5.   Initiates and completes grooming without assistance.

    4.   Initiates grooming tasks but neglects features that are not clearly visible.
        May not match makeup to skin tones, or
        May not shave all parts of the face and neck for men or underarms and legs for women, or
        May neglect the back of the head or body.

    3.   Does daily grooming (brushing teeth; washing hands or face or both).
        May need to be reminded, or
        May not use sharp instruments required for nail trimming safely, or
        May not shave safely with a nonelectric razor.

    2.   Needs total grooming care.
        May cooperate with efforts of others by spontaneously moving hands, feet, or head, or
        May resist the caregiver's help.

    1.   Ignores personal appearance and does not spontaneously cooperate with, or resists, the caregiver's help.

Additional comments:

B.   Dressing

    5.   Selects own clothing and dresses without error.

    4.   Dresses self. May have minor errors in selection or method of dressing.
        Colors or patterns of garments may not be coordinated, or
        May disregard the appearance of the back of garments, or
        May require a limited choice of garments.

    3.   Dresses self. May have gross errors in selection or method of dressing.
        May ignore weather conditions, social conditions (e.g., dining out, guests), social customs (e.g., underwear on top, garments inside out or backwards, misuse of sex-specific garments), button alignment, or daytime versus nighttime garments.

    2.   Spontaneously alters the position of the body to facilitate dressing.
        May be unable to dress self, or
        May resist caregiver's help.

    1.   Must be dressed by caregivers and does not spontaneously alter position of the body to facilitate dressing.
        May hold still or move body position on command.

Additional comments:

Fig. 2-22. Routine task inventory.

C. Bathing

   5.   Bathes without assistance, using shampoo, deodorant, and other desirable toiletries.

   4.   Bathes the front of the body.
        May not bathe the back of the body, or
        May not rinse shampoo from the back of the hair, or
        May not remember to use deodorant, or
        May not obtain a safe water temperature.

   3.   Uses soap and washcloth in a repetitive action.
        May not bathe entire body unless given verbal or tactile direction, or
        May refuse to soap the entire body.

   2.   Stands in the shower or sits in the bathtub.
        May not try to wash self, or
        May move body parts to assist the caregiver, or
        May resist the caregiver's help, or
        May refuse to enter the shower or bathtub.

   1.   Does not try to wash self and is given a sponge bath by another person.
        May move body position on command.

Additional comments:

D. Walking

   5.   Goes about new grounds or city and finds way home.

   4.   Walks in familiar surroundings without getting lost.
        May require an escort in unfamiliar surroundings, or
        May refuse to go to unfamiliar places.

   3.   Initiates walking within a room to do a familiar activity.
        May get lost unless escorted from room to room, or
        May follow the lead of other people to the correct or incorrect location, or
        May pace or wander about and manipulate physical objects that happen to capture attention.

   2.   Follows the lead or pointed direction of others.
        May not initiate movement to do a familiar activity such as going to the dinner table, or
        May pace or wander about aimlessly without regard for objects unless they obstruct his or her path, or
        May resist the guidance of others.

   1.   Walks or transfers from bed to chair with physical guidance.
        May be bedridden, or
        May remain in a supportive chair, or
        May not notice objects that obstruct his or her path, or
        May require tactile assistance to bend knees.

Additional comments:

Fig. 2-22. *(continued)*

E. Feeding

    5. Considers the size of food portions and shares a limited quantity of food with others.
Usually self-monitors a balanced diet.

    4. Everyday table manners are consistent with social standards.
May not share a limited quantity of food with others, or
May not self-restrict portion size of desirable foods.

    3. Uses table utensils.
May not comply with a restricted diet, or
May not self-monitor a balanced diet, or
May not use table manners expected by social standards.

    2. Uses a spoon or adapted eating devices (e.g., nonslip or scoop-edge plate).
May not use utensils correctly, or
Eating may be untidy.

    1. Chews and swallows voluntarily.
May eat food with fingers, or
May need to be told to chew, or
May need to be fed.

Additional comments:

F. Toileting

    5. Cares for self at toilet completely and locates an unfamiliar bathroom with little or no assistance.

    4. Cares for self at toilet completely.
May need to have the location of an unfamiliar bathroom pointed out, or
May need to be escorted to an unfamiliar bathroom.

    3. Uses the toilet.
May need to be reminded to go to the bathroom, or
May not adjust garments correctly (e.g., zipping up zippers), or
May not wipe the body clean.

    2. Uses the toilet inconsistently.
May void in unacceptable locations, or
May need to be escorted to the toilet, or
May need to be positioned on the toilet.

    1. Fails to control bowel or bladder.

Additional comments:

Fig. 2-22. (continued)

Instrumental Scale

Scoring: Circle the number that best describes your observations of behavior.

A. Housekeeping

6. Organizes home environment, plans a schedule for completing chores, and plans for long-term maintenance.

5. Recognizes and completes less visible tasks (e.g., dusting under objects and cleaning corners).
May not plan for long-term maintenance, or
May not design a new organization of home environment (e.g., reorganize cupboards and drawers).

4. Completes familiar, simple household tasks at an acceptable level of cleanliness.
May not recognize the need to do tasks that are not clearly visible (e.g., dusting under furniture, cleaning corners, or washing windows), or
May not be able to find things that are out of place or in a new location.

3. Uses repetitive familiar actions (e.g., dusting) to be of assistance in housekeeping.
May not obtain an acceptable level of cleanliness, or
May not complete the usual procedure for doing a task, or
May unnecessarily do the same task over and over again.

2. Does not participate in any housekeeping tasks.

Additional comments:

B. Preparing Food

6. Plans menus for adequate nutrition and anticipates potential substitutions and problems.

5. Supplies ingredients and utensils and follows a new recipe for food preparation.
May not anticipate burning, or
May not coordinate the timing of several dishes, or
May not plan variations by substituting ingredients.

4. Prepares familiar, simple dishes if supplied with the ingredients.
May not avoid burning food, or
May not consistently remember to turn off the stove, or
May handle a knife or hot food and cooking equipment hazardously.

3. Uses repetitive familiar actions to be of assistance in meal preparation (peels potatoes, pours milk, sets the table).
May not prepare a meal, or
May not recognize mealtime.

2. Does not participate in food preparation.

Additional comments:

Fig. 2-22. (continued)

C. Spending Money

6. Anticipates infrequent expenses and plans for financial security.

5. Manages routine weekly and monthly purchases and income.
    May not anticipate infrequent major expenses, or
    May not plan for long-term financial security.

4. Manages day-to-day purchases but is slow at making change; may calculate correct change with paper and pencil, calculator, or by counting cash.
    May not calculate change in his or her head, or
    May not accurately anticipate weekly or monthly purchases, or
    May make errors in calculating cost or change.

3. Hands cash to another person.
    May realize that a caregiver is handling money for him or her, or
    May not consider amount of cash given or received, or
    May forget to pay bills, or
    May run out of money, or
    May not understand why he or she owes money.

2. Does not handle money.
    May not realize that money transactions are occurring.

Additional comments:

D. Taking Medication

6. Complies with new dosages and anticipates drug effects accurately.

5. Is responsible for taking routine medications in correct dosage at correct time. Explains why medication was prescribed and reports individual effects.
    Compliance with complicated dose schedules (such as every 6 hours) may be inaccurate, or
    May have trouble distinguishing concepts such as drug effect, drug side effect, drug synergies, drug tolerance.

4. Takes desirable medication in simple dosages at routine times, such as with meals.
    May use a pill dispenser to keep track of medications.
    May not understand why a psychopharmacologic drug was prescribed, or
    May refuse to take psychopharmacologic drugs, or
    May need to be reminded to take medications correctly.

3. Medications are given by a caretaker.
    May refuse to take medications, or
    May not distinguish among types of pills (e.g., vitamins versus psychopharmacologic drugs), or
    May not know what he or she is taking, or
    May not recognize that it is time to take medication.

Additional comments:

Fig. 2-22. *(continued)*

E. Doing Laundry

   6. Anticipates shrinkage and bleeding of dyes without error.
       Anticipates clothing needs (e.g., takes clothes to the cleaners or does laundry ahead of time).

   5. Sorts clothing.
       May not anticipate shrinkage or bleeding of dyes of new garments, or
       May not anticipate clothing needs.

   4. Does familiar hand laundry or uses a washing machine to do a load of clothing. Puts dirty clothes in a hamper.
       May not sort clothing, or
       May not consider care instructions for new garments, or
       May not distinguish between machine laundry, hand laundry, and dry cleaning.

   3. Does not participate in doing laundry.
       May not place dirty clothes in a hamper, or
       May not realize that clothing is dirty.

   Additional comments:

F. Traveling

   6. Uses a map to anticipate directions and determine present position.

   5. Drives a car or finds way in less frequently traveled or unfamiliar routes.
       May make a wrong turn, or
       May get on a wrong bus, or
       May forget where car is parked.

   4. Independently travels familiar routes in vehicles driven by others.
       May get lost on unfamiliar routes, or
       May avoid unfamiliar routes, or
       May not be able to drive a car safely.

   3. Gets in and out of a familiar vehicle without tactile assistance.
       May get lost without an escort, or
       May not know, or may be confused about, destination.

   2. May ride in a vehicle but is unaware of passing external environment.

   Additional comments:

Fig. 2-22. (continued)

G. Shopping

6. Anticipates and plans for shopping needs.

5. Does routine shopping
    May not anticipate long-range shopping needs, or
    May not follow a monthly budget.

4. Shops for small, familiar purchases.
    May not do comparison shopping, or
    May not have enough money for selected purchases, or
    May refuse to purchase items because of an exaggerated concern for lack of funds.

3. Goes to a store.
    May not recognize correct change, or
    May not remember what he or she went to the store to purchase, or
    May accompany another person without an awareness of, or with confusion about, desired purchases.

2. Does not go shopping.

Additional comments:

H. Telephoning

6. Uses a classification system to find a number in the Yellow Pages or in the listing of governmental agencies.

5. Looks up numbers in the White Pages or in a personal address book.
    May not use the Yellow Pages or consider subclassifications such as governmental agencies, or
    May become confused when calls must be transferred.

4. Dials familiar numbers and calls information for new numbers. Relays a message.
    May not look up new numbers in the telephone book, or
    May have trouble locating infrequently used numbers in an address book, or
    May be slow in writing down new numbers or messages.

3. Answers the phone when it rings and may answer even if it does not ring. May dial one or two well-known numbers.
    May not relay a message, or
    May not call a person to the phone, or
    May forget the telephone number he or she was trying to find, or
    May take the receiver off the hook.

2. Does not use the telephone.

Additional comments:

Fig. 2-22. (continued)

tunity for error. Refinements and revisions can be expected. The inventory should be used with this precaution in mind; application to individual cases will necessitate verifying performance on as many tasks as possible. The use of the inventory for health care planning is not warranted at this time.

This precaution applies to much of the content of this text, but it is stated here because the inventory is particularly vulnerable to abuse. People seek simple, easy answers to complex problems. Developing the inventory has not been simple or easy, and it may be wrong. We don't know yet.

The description of each task in the inventory has a beginning point and an end point. The beginning point describes normative ability; the end point describes a failure to do the task. Normative ability varies, according to task content, from level 6 to level 5; failure to do a task also varies, ranging from level 3 to level 1. The descriptions of behavior between these points refer both to what the person does and to what the person may not do. The behaviors identified are potential observations of performance.

The RTI is a description of the functional severity of a disability; it is a here-and-now assessment of the impact of a disease. Use of the inventory should identify only those changes in functional behavior that can be attributed to an illness. This should be kept in mind because some tasks, such as food preparation or housekeeping, may not be done because a person has never done them, because the person lacks access to the facilities required to do them, or because a person at level 6 places a low priority on the task. The descriptions are meant to be applied to behaviors associated with the diagnosed mental disorder. Other reasons for not doing a task are not applicable.

When a patient has a caregiver who can reliably describe what the patient does and does not do, the use of the RTI is relatively straightforward: The caregiver can be asked to identify current behaviors that are attributable to the illness. A person who denies the presence of a mental disorder, or any functional deficits, is troublesome; the difficulty can

be further confounded by an absence of caregivers. The problem in these cases is that it is easy to impose our own value judgments about tasks that ought to be performed. One solution to this problem is to ask the patient to identify tasks that he or she regards as relevant and to observe the performance of those tasks. If the patient does not communicate any relevant tasks one must assume that some form of physical self-maintenance must take place and observe that behavior.

Scoring the Routine Task Inventory

This discussion is directed to therapists who would like to use the RTI for research purposes. Heimann (in preparation) has developed scoring criteria that can be shared for use during an interview of a reliable informant. The 14 routine tasks of the RTI are divided into two scales, the physical scale and the instrumental scale. The six tasks on the physical scale are grooming, dressing, bathing, walking, feeding, and toileting. The eight tasks on the instrumental scale are housekeeping, preparing food, spending money, taking medication, doing laundry, traveling, shopping, and telephoning. Under each of the 14 tasks, behavioral descriptions are written in connection with each cognitive level listed. In some cases several behaviors are rated at the same cognitive level. The tasks within each scale can be randomized or asked in sequence by the researcher.

Administration of the interview requires the identification of an informant who is well acquainted with the individual's daily performance and willing to provide information. The inventory is reviewed by the informant and tester together. Under each task, the behaviors listed are read, beginning at cognitive level 6. The behavioral description that matches the individual's routine task performance is circled. Estimated time needed to administer the RTI is about 1 hour.

Scores on the physical scale of the RTI range from cognitive level 1 to 5. Scores on the instrumental scale range from cognitive level 2 to 6, except for task D, taking medication, and task E, doing laundry, which range from level 3 to level 6. The disparity in scoring between the physical and the instrumental scale is a reflection of the pattern of restriction in routine tasks that accompanies a cognitive disability. Lawton (1970) theorized that the complexity of instrumental ADL is greater than the complexity of physical self-maintenance. The greater complexity may be associated with the cognitive levels. Because of their complexity, the tasks on the instrumental scale of the RTI cannot be completed by persons at cognitive level 2. However, tasks that involve bodily needs (those on the physical scale) must be done, even at level 1. Heying's (1983; see Chap. 15) research on a group of adults with senile dementia supports the view of differential change in performance in physical versus instrumental tasks. Accordingly, a scoring system has been devised by Heimann (in preparation) to account for the differing scoring ranges. To prevent the deflation of scores in an individual functioning above cognitive level 5, the average score on the instrumental scale is calculated and the amount greater than 5 is added to each score of 5 on the physical scale. Likewise, inflation of scores is prevented by the following procedure. If the average on the physical scale is less than 3, the amount under 3 is subtracted from scores of 3 on the medication and laundry items. If the average on the physical scale is less than 2, the amount less than 2 is subtracted from all instrumental scale items that have been rated at level 2. These procedures prevent distortion of the score and statistical analyses by the presence of varied scoring boundaries associated with the nature of the task. The content of the RTI has been informally validated through consensus by the occupational therapy staff at Los Angeles County/University of Southern California Psychiatric Hospital. Statistical evaluations of the quality of the RTI as an interview are in progress (Heimann). Work is also being done to develop the inventory as an evaluation of performance (Kratz and Regan, 1984).

The information derived from the inventory can be used to make decisions about the community placement of an individual, but numerous other social factors must be considered as well. Increasingly, legal considerations are influencing these decisions. The central problem seems to revolve around establishing objective criteria for mental competence.

Competence

Competence, like consciousness, is usually regarded as a binary concept; one either is or is not competent to manage one's own affairs. The cognitive levels suggest a continuum of degrees of competence. Mental competence is a complex phenomenon, and establishing objective criteria that are fair to the disabled, their family members, and the community is not going to be easy. I will not be so bold as to offer final solutions to the problem, but some suggestions can be made.

Competence Measure: An Inference

A competence measure is a theoretical device used when theorists are trying to explain ambiguous and complex phenomena. Cognition is such a phenomenon. The problem with competence measures is that they are apt to produce false assessments, referred to as false negatives and false positives. A false negative is saying a person does not have an ability when, in fact, he or she has. A false positive is saying a person has an ability when, in fact, he or she does not (Brown and Desforges, 1979). Obviously, a therapist's credibility is jeopardized by the possibility of making false assessments. Factors that can distort the therapist's estimate of competence are the patient's past experiences, the complexity of the task, and behaviors that are symptoms of a disease. A large portion of this text is devoted to suggesting ways of controlling for these potentially confounding factors. Chapter 11 will expand on some of the problems to be encountered in using a competence measure. What is important to recognize here is that a competence measure is less than ideal and it should not be taken literally. There is a tendency to do that; the pressure comes from our-selves and from our colleagues in other professions. We would like our knowledge to be clearer than it is. A competence measure is an estimate, or infer-ence, and as such it is subject to error.

Making a distinction between performance and competence seems to be helpful in interpreting be-havior. Performance is the task behavior we see the patient do. Competence is an inference we make about the prerequisite ability required to do the task procedure. Competence is an estimate of the level of thought required to do a step in the task. The therapist sees the patient's performance and tries to estimate the prerequisite ability required, which explains the performance.

Application of a Competence Measure

Proposition 1. The observed routine task behavior of disabled patients will differ from the observed behavior of nondisabled populations.

Competence measures presume that there is a difference between the routine task behavior of people with a disability and that of people who do not have a disability. This concept must be empiri-cally tested. I have defined it operationally by a leather lacing task and a motor performance task. The motor performance task ("Clap your hands three times") contains familiar gestures that the per-son is asked to imitate to assess the lower cognitive levels (levels 1 and 2). The leather lacing task uses different lacing stitches to assess the higher end of the hierarchy (levels 2 to 6). A standardized assess-ment procedure is provided in Chapter 4, and the research studies completed as of this writing are presented in Part Three. The RTI is an important step in developing a description of a cognitive disa-bility that has face validity. The disability must be understood by the patients, their families, and health care planners. I am also working on the de-velopment of a work inventory. There is a reformist tradition in occupational therapy, and my inheri-

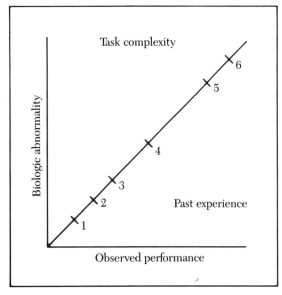

Fig. 2-23. Cognitive levels: a correlation between biologic pathology and observed task performance. The assessment of the cognitive level can be confounded by the complexity of the task and the individual's past experience in doing the task.

tance of this tradition can be detected in these in-ventories. My hope is that we can use them to re-form the health care delivery system for the cognitively disabled.

The cognitive levels are inferences about a per-son's capabilities that are used to predict restrictions in routine task behavior associated with biologic pa-thology in the brain. The cognitive levels are thought to represent a correlation between the bio-logic state of the organism and an observed perfor-mance (Fig. 2-23). Confounding factors are past ex-perience and task complexity. The levels are benchmarks arranged in an ordinal scale to describe the severity of a disability. The intervals between the levels vary in the degree of clinical importance attributed to restrictions in task behavior. Accept-able task behavior is socially defined because some restrictions in routine task behavior may be more easily tolerated in one family or cultural group than another.

Proposition 2. Limitations in task behavior can be hierarchically described by the cognitive levels.

The hierarchy of the cognitive levels is presumed to be correct as described. Testing the validity of the hierarchy is difficult. The approach taken has been to study different diagnostic groups. *DSM III* (1980) contains a hierarchy, also untested, but some correspondence between the two hierarchies is expected. One can also expect to see an improvement in the cognitive level during acute hospitalization from admission to discharge. The descriptive studies reported in Part Three examine, among other things, the validity of the hierarchy. The notion that the cognitive levels may also be used to describe a level of function within the traditional neurologic disorders finds some clinical support. The levels of cognitive functioning as used on the head trauma service at Rancho Los Amigos Hospital resemble the cognitive levels described above. Eight levels have been delineated at Rancho Los Amigos; these seem to expand the lower levels described in this chapter (Halzer et al., 1982).

Theoretical support for the validity of a hierarchical approach can be obtained from recent changes in the neurosciences. There is increasing agreement among people working in the neurosciences that the brain is organized into functional units. The practice of dividing the study of the brain into the components of neuroanatomy, neurochemistry, and neurophysiology is being replaced by the thought that these components are interrelated. Numerous biologic correlates with behavior have been identified, but behavior is expressed as a complex picture of memory, learning, motivation, and emotion. There have been repeated suggestions that a new classification system is required for the study of this phenomenon (Angevine and Smith, 1982; Brooks, 1981; Daube and Sandok, 1978; Ojemann, 1982; Pribram, foreword to Luria, 1973; Satz and Fletcher, 1981; Scheibel, 1981). The problem has been that the components of the new classification system lack names. One approach to suggesting the functional units of the brain is suggested by the cog-

nitive levels describing voluntary motor actions.

Eliciting task behavior is influenced by the sensory system involved as well as by the person's motor actions themselves. Neurobiologic correlates with these descriptions of behavior abound, and our observations of psychiatric patients may be instructive in sorting through the complex problems encountered in the neuroscience literature.

Change in Level of Competence

The greatest challenge presented by the recent advances in neuroscience knowledge is to our theoretical expectations for change. We have assumed that when we noted an improvement in a patient's task behavior, we could attribute the improvement to the value of our services. This cause-and-effect assumption now appears to be naive.

One of our areas of difficulty can be traced to our attempts to state general expectations for change that could be applied to many diagnostic categories. This approach ignores variations in the natural course of different diseases. Primary affective disorders have periods of acute illness followed by a return to normal functioning. Dementias, such as Alzheimer's disease, are characterized by functional decline ending in death within a few years (Goodwin and Guze, 1979). In the former we would expect the cognitive level to improve; in the latter we would predict decline. The natural course of the disease is a primary consideration in stating expectations for change. General expectations for change that span different diagnostic categories, characterized by different courses of disease, appear to be naive.

A cognitive disability is caused by a biologic defect. The physician's ability to correct the biologic abnormality is a relevant consideration. Expectations for change need to recognize the benefits, and limitations, of current medical knowledge. The rate at which knowledge is changing must also be considered, because the fast pace produces variability in application. Expectations for change must account for the medical interventions of the physicians, which influence the level of competence whenever the condition is unstable.

It may be possible to identify some stable medical conditions in which the cognitive level has remained the same for a number of years. A careful analysis of the routine task behavior and social support systems of patients with these conditions is required to clarify our understanding of what a cognitive disability means to the individual, family, and community.

Incompetent: What It Means

Many authors in the social and behavioral sciences tend to ignore the debilitating effects of psychiatric disorders. A rather romantic view of psychiatric illness exists (e.g., Foucault, 1965) that can be infuriating to the caretakers of psychiatric patients (Wing, 1978). This conflict has extended into the legal system in the United States, and a case-by-case analysis is underway. The states are struggling with the need to identify fair criteria for involuntary commitment to psychiatric hospitals and other institutional settings (Stone, 1976). A step toward resolving the conflict may be facilitated by identifying the behaviors that lead to institutional care.

A list of behaviors that provide evidence of a disability before hospital admission was sought (Table 2-2). The list was generated by reviewing the reason for admission as recorded by therapists on the interview and chart data cards described in Chapter 4. My colleagues and I reviewed all the available cards recorded at the LAC/USC Medical Center during 1982—about one thousand cards. It is our clinical impression that most patients were functioning at level 4 or below, and that many of them lack any contact with a social support system. In many cases the only informant available at the time of admission was a police officer.

The amount of support required from a group home or a social network is of particular interest to health care planners. Determining the amount of support needed is especially troublesome with people who deny the presence of a mental disorder and have good verbal abilities. Adult psychiatric patients can often draw on their learned verbal abilities to present a functional picture of themselves during a social conversation or when testifying in a legal proceeding. This may be in marked contrast to their task behavior, which indicates that they cannot respond to the ordinary demands of daily life. A great deal of professional effort needs to be directed toward clarifying these hidden disabilities.

I have been particularly interested in people who have been living alone or on the streets without any contact with a social support system. This population provides a clearer picture of the social handicap because it is not confounded by compensations made by other people.

People who have been living alone seem to have trouble paying their bills: Their utilities may be turned off, and they may be evicted from apartments or houses for failure to pay rent or taxes. The public health authorities report that they are living in squalor—trash is not removed, the house is not cleaned, dishes are not washed, clothes are not put away, and cupboards and counters are disorganized. Numerous potential fire and health hazards are identified: a can of spray bug killer placed beside a similar can of spray cooking oil, or an electrical cord draped across a stove. The neighbors complain about the vermin that this situation tends to breed.

The dangers from such patients that we have observed in the OT kitchen are a failure to turn off the stove or to take adequate precautions in handling boiling water. Heat is the invisible cue that is often neglected. Obviously, this can have some serious consequences.

People who live on the streets tend to neglect their personal hygiene. Lice and scabies are a common problem, fingernails and toenails are untrimmed, and hair is matted and dirty. Money management can also be a problem; when they run out of money they eat at the missions or out of trash cans. They carry their belongings with them and report frequent experiences of theft.

The presence of any mental disability is often

Table 2-2. Evidence of disability before admission

I. Gravely disabled
  A. Orientation
    1. Cannot state own name
    2. Cannot state address or residence.
    3. Cannot state present location in a psychiatric hospital
    4. Wandering, lost
  B. Eating
    1. Not eating
    2. Eating nonedible objects
    3. Eating out of trash cans
    4. Overeating
    5. Hiding food from others
    6. Throwing edible food away
    7. Unsafe in cooking food
  C. Sleeping
    1. Not going to bed
    2. Unable to fall asleep
    3. Early morning awakening
    4. Sleeping too much
  D. Dressing
    1. Nude in public
    2. Partially dressed in public
    3. Putting on clothes of others
    4. Wearing dirty clothes
    5. Informant reports failure to change clothes
  E. Personal hygiene
    1. Failure to use toilet
    2. Lice, scabies
    3. Dirty skin, feet
    4. Untrimmed fingernails, toenails
    5. Malodorous
    6. Informant reports failure to initiate self-care
  F. Shelter
    1. Living on streets
    2. Living where unwanted
    3. Living in unsanitary conditions
    4. Living in car
    5. Evicted
  G. Finances
    1. No money
    2. Less than $25
    3. Lost money or check
    4. Failure to pay bills
    5. Recent job loss
  H. Medical compliance
    1. Noncompliance with psychotropic medication
    2. Noncompliance with other medication, treatment
    3. Inaccurate administration of prescribed medication
    4. Does not seek care for health problem
  I. Communication, relating to others
    1. Mute
    2. Unintelligible speech
    3. Talking incessantly
    4. Disturbing others with yelling
    5. Disturbing others with banging
    6. Masturbating in public
  J. Belief system
    1. Controlled by external source
    2. Others are trying to harm
    3. Has serious medical illness, is dying

II. Danger to self
  A. Suicide
    1. Voices telling patient to harm self
    2. Suicidal thoughts
    3. Suicidal plans
    4. Self-mutilation
    5. Suicide attempt
    6. Suicide attempt requiring hospitalization in a general medical facility for less than 10 days
    7. Suicide attempt requiring hospitalization in a general medical facility for 10 days or more

Table 2-2. (continued)

   B. Transportation risks
     1. Jumping from moving vehicle
     2. Jumping in front of vehicle
     3. Directing traffic
     4. Obstructing traffic

III. Danger to others
   A. Assaultive toward others
     1. Voices telling patient to harm others
     2. Threatens to assault
     3. Assault without injury
     4. Assault with injury requiring
       a. Home care
       b. Outpatient medical care
       c. Hospitalization
     5. Sexually abusive
   B. Child care
     1. Does not feed child
     2. Leaves child unattended
     3. Exposes child to harmful drugs
     4. Threatens to hit child
     5. Hits child
     6. Sexually abuses child
   C. Destructive to property
     1. Threatens to set fire
     2. Sets fire to object, building
     3. Cigarette burn holes in clothing
     4. Threatens to damage property
     5. Damages property
     6. Rearranges property of others
     7. Trespasses on property
     8. Steals

denied. Some people recognize their restrictions while others cannot, and the factors that facilitate recognition are still unclear. The denial of a disability may necessitate legal actions for the management of the disability, for example, obtaining a legal guardian or involuntary placement in a locked facility.

It is my clinical impression that cognitive functioning at level 4 or below is a grave disability that necessitates some form of social support to protect the patient and the community. This clinical impression requires further investigation.

CONCLUSION

The assessment of the cognitive level is an inference about a person's competence. The assessment can be obscured by a number of factors, and therapists must control for these alternative explanations for limitations in routine task behavior. The task analysis described in Chapter 3 controls for the complexity of the task, the therapist's knowledge of the expression of symptoms during task behavior controls for the patient's medical condition, and the assessment of the individual's history in doing tasks controls for past experiences. The remainder of Part One is devoted to suggesting methods of controlling for confounding factors in the assessment of the cognitive levels.

REFERENCES

Angevine, J. B., and Smith, M. S. Recent Advances in Forebrain Anatomy and Their Clinical Correlates. In R. A. Thompson and J. R. Green (eds.), *New Perspectives in Cerebral Localization.* New York: Raven, 1982.

Ayres, A. J. *Sensory Integration and the Child.* Los Angeles: Western Psychological Services, 1979.

Brooks, U. B. Task-related Cell Assemblies. In O. Pompeiano and C. A. Marson (eds.), *Brain Mechanisms of Perceptual Awareness and Purposeful Behavior* (International Brain Research Organization [IBRO] Monograph Series, Vol. 8). New York: Raven, 1981.

Brown, G., and Desforges, C. *Piaget's Theory: A Psychological Critique.* Boston: Routledge & Kegan Paul, 1979.

Buscaglia, L. *The Disabled and Their Parents: A Counseling Challenge.* Thorofare, N.J.: Charles B. Slack, 1975.

Daube, J. R., and Sandok, B. A. *Medical Neurosciences: An Approach to Anatomy, Pathology and Physiology by Systems and Levels.* Boston: Little, Brown, 1978.

Dorland's Illustrated Medical Dictionary (26th ed.). Philadelphia: Saunders, 1981.

DSM III: Diagnostic and Statistical Manual of Mental Disorders (3rd ed.). Washington, D.C.: American Psychiatric Association, 1980.

Foucault, M. *Madness and Civilization: A History of Insanity in the Age of Reason.* New York: Random House, 1965.

Ginsburg, H., and Opper S. *Piaget's Theory of Intellectual Development: An Introduction.* Englewood Cliffs, N.J.: Prentice-Hall, 1969.

Goodwin, D. W., and Guze, S. B. *Psychiatric Diagnoses* (2nd ed.). New York: Oxford University Press, 1979.

Halzer, M. L., et al. Head Trauma. In M. K. Logigian (ed.), *Adult Rehabilitation: A Team Approach for Therapists.* Boston: Little, Brown, 1982.

Haroutunian, S. *Equilibrium in the Balance: A Study of Psychological Explanation.* New York: Springer, 1983.

Heimann, N. Investigation of the reliability and validity of the Routine Task Inventory with a sample of adults with chronic mental disorders. University of Southern California Master's Thesis, in preparation.

Heying, L. M. Cognitive disabilities and activities of daily living in persons with senile dementia. University of Southern California Master's Thesis, 1983.

Kinsbourne, M., and Caplan, P. J. *Children's Learning and Attention Problems.* Boston: Little, Brown, 1979.

Kopp, C. B. Antecedents of self-regulation: A developmental perspective. *Dev. Psychol.* 18:199–214, 1982.

Kratz, B., and Regan, T. Personal communication, May 8, 1984.

Lawton, M. P. Assessment, integration, and the environments of older people. *Gerontologist* 10:38–46, 1970.

Lawton, M. P. The functional assessment of elderly people. *J. Am. Geriatr. Soc.* 19:465–481, 1971.

Lawton, M. P., and Brody, E. M. Assessment of older people: Self-maintaining and instrumental activities of daily living. *Gerontologist* 9:179–186, 1969.

Luria, A. R. *The Working Brain: An Introduction to Neuropsychology,* transl. by B. Haigh. New York: Basic Books, 1973.

Mounoud, P. Revolutionary Periods in Early Development. In T. Bever (ed.), *Regressions in Mental Development: Basic Phenomena and Theories.* Hillsdale, N.J.: Lawrence Elbaum, 1982.

Noback, C. R., and Demarest, R. J. *The Human Nervous System: Basic Principles of Neurobiology* (2nd ed.). New York: McGraw-Hill, 1975.

Ojemann, G. A. Interrelationships in the Localization of Language, Memory and Motor Mechanisms in Human Cortex and Thalamus. In R. A. Thompson and J. R. Green (eds.), *New Perspectives in Cerebral Localization.* New York: Raven, 1982.

Piaget, J. *The Origins of Intelligence in Children,* transl. by M. Cook. New York: International University Press, 1952.

Piaget, J. *Biology and Knowledge: An Essay on the Relations Between Organic Regulations and Cognitive Processes,* transl. by B. Walsh. Chicago: University of Chicago Press, 1971.

Piaget, J. *The Principles of Genetic Epistemology,* transl. by W. Mays. New York: Basic Books, 1972.

Piaget, J. *Behavior and Evolution,* transl. by D. Nicholson-Smith. New York: Pantheon, 1978.

Piaget, J. *Adaptation and Intelligence: Organic Selection and Phenocopy,* transl. by S. Eames. Chicago: University of Chicago Press, 1980.

Plum, F., and Posner, J. B. *The Diagnosis of Stupor and Coma* (3rd ed.). Philadelphia: Davis, 1980.

Reese, H. W., and Overton, W. F. Models of Development and Theories of Development. In L. R. Goulet and P. B. Boltes (eds.), *Life-span Developmental Psychology: Research and Theory.* New York: Academic, 1970.

Satz, P., and Fletcher, J. M. Emergent trends in neuropsychology: An overview. *J. Consult. Clin. Psychol.* 49:851–865, 1981.

Scheibel, A. B. The Problems of Selective Attention: A Possible Structural Substrate. In O. Pompeiano and C. A. Marson (eds.), *Brain Mechanisms of Perceptual Awareness and Purposeful Behavior* (International Brain Research Organization [IBRO] Monograph Series, Vol. 8). New York: Raven, 1981.

Shapere, D. Notes Toward a Post-positivistic Interpretation of Science. In R. Achinstein and S. F. Barker (eds.), *The Legacy of Logical Positivism: Studies in the Philosophy of Science.* Baltimore: Johns Hopkins University Press, 1969.

Stone, A. A. *Mental Health and Law: A System in Transition.* New York: Jason Aaronson, 1976.

Strub, R. L., and Black, W. F. *Organic Brain Syndromes: An Introduction to Neurobehavioral Disorders.* Philadelphis: Davis, 1981.

Wing, J. K. *Reasoning About Madness.* New York; London: Oxford University Press, 1978.

CHAPTER 3

TASK ANALYSIS

COMPETENCE CAN ONLY BE MANIFEST THROUGH PAR-
TICULAR PERFORMANCES BUT ALL SORTS OF TRANSIENT
FACTORS RELATING TO THE PERSON, THE TASK, AND
THE ENVIRONMENT CAN SERVE TO IMPEDE PERFOR-
MANCE.
G. Brown and C. Desforges, 1979

The cognitive levels are a measure of competence as observed during task performance. There are a number of competing, and equally plausible, explanations for a problem in task performance. For example, a therapist's report of a problem in performance can be reasonably challenged by questions such as the following: Did the patient think the task was silly? Is the task relevant to the individual's life in the community? Was the task too easy or too complicated? Was the setting too distracting? Questions such as these challenge the therapist's judgment in selecting tasks and in predicting future task behavior. The selection of the task seems to be facilitated by dividing performance into two parts: the task and the person doing the task. This discrimination looks easy enough, but in practice it tends to be confusing.

An observation of task performance is confusing because it is difficult to separate the person doing the task from the task itself; occupational therapists have trouble with this distinction, and so do the Piagetians. Piagetians engaged in concurrent validity studies generally assume they are measuring mental processes. Brown and Desforges (1979) have challenged this assumption, suggesting that the studies address the structure of tasks. Piaget did not seem to recognize this problem and had very little to say about task selection; task analysis is more implicit than explicit in his work (Piaget, 1952, 1970a, b, 1971a, b). Our practice requirements are such that we cannot accept this ambiguity. We need a quick, flexible guideline that can be accurately applied to a variety of potential tasks. Therapists analyze a wide range of tasks daily, and explicit criteria for selecting and recommending tasks are required.

The idea that activities can be graded, from simple to complex, or from concrete to abstract, is a well-established tradition in occupational therapy. This grading tends, however, to be an either-or approach to task analysis; the task is either simple or complex. Tasks at either end of a continuum can be identified, but those that fall in the middle are ambiguous. A more refined gradation of task complexity is required.

One approach to grading tasks is evident in the behavioral hierarchies used in behavior modification. These hierarchies are done on a task-by-task, and often a case-by-case, basis. It is difficult to generalize from one task or one case to the next. The reason for this difficulty can, in part, be traced to an absence of theoretical criteria for analyzing tasks. The validity of a behavioral modification task analysis rests on the face validity of each behavioral hierarchy; criteria for selecting tasks are not identified.

TASK EQUIVALENCE

What is required is a method of establishing task equivalence. Establishing task equivalence is to say that tasks A, B, and C are of equal value according to a meaningful set of criteria. The need to determine task equivalence seems to be recognized relatively rarely; Holyk (1981) and Trujillo (1980) reviewed the literature and were disappointed by the neglect of task equivalence in the social and behavioral sciences. Goldman (1970) recognized the need to establish criteria for equivalence, but unfortunately the criteria he chose were the same person and the same time. Goldman's criteria severely restrict generalization.

The Piagetian literature has suggested an implicit means of arriving at a task analysis for the cognitively disabled (Kopp, 1974; Kopp and O'Connor, 1975). The Piagetians, however, have encountered a problem in conducting cross-cultural studies, and an important lesson about task equivalence can be gleaned from these studies. Familiarity or lack of familiarity with materials can confound task equivalence (Cole, 1975; Price-Williams et al., 1969). Obviously, there is a difference between someone who has never seen a screwdriver and someone who

uses one daily. The problem lies in controlling for individual differences in task experiences and for task preferences. Familiarity with materials is a relatively recent concern in Piagetian studies, but it is a ubiquitous problem in occupational therapy practice. Criteria for task equivalence must consider individual differences in experiences and preferences.

The occupational therapy literature suggests some criteria for establishing task equivalence, too. Tasks have been categorized according to the content of the task or the process of doing the task (Trujillo, 1980). For example, laundry is the content, doing the laundry is the process. The content is what is being done, and the process is how it is done. Task equivalence may be influenced by what is being done and how it is done.

The literature provides limited assistance in suggesting criteria for task equivalence. Indeed, the need to establish task equivalence is difficult to justify in theoretical terms. It is in practice that therapists encounter the need. A therapist may observe someone making a salad on Tuesday and applying nail polish on Thursday. The question is Is the patient's condition better, worse, or the same? The answer is influenced by task equivalence. Nail polishing and salad making may or may not be equivalent tasks for this individual. The criteria for establishing task equivalence must control for the numerous factors that can influence performance.

The scope of the factors that can influence task equivalence is large enough to warrant the use of comprehensive, journalistic guidelines; the criteria will be related to the following questions: who, what, where, when, why, and how? Fig. 3-1 provides a graphic display of the relationships among these factors.

What? Task demands and directions specify the mental operations required to do a task successfully. How? Successful performance occurs when the task demands and directions match the patient's cognitive level, that is, when a level 4 task is given to a level 4 patient. Who? The mental operations are performed by a patient, and the behavior is ob-

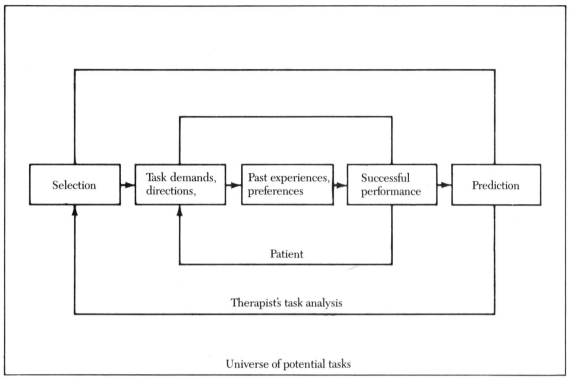

Fig. 3-1. Perspective on the therapist's task analysis. Task analysis requires criteria for establishing task equivalence so that a therapist can generalize from one task to the next.

served by the therapist. Where? The stimuli to initiate and sustain the mental operations are located in the external environment. When? The task analysis is used by the therapist to select items from the universe of possible tasks that can be done now or at some future date. Why? The purpose of the therapist's selection is to facilitate successful task performance in the present and to predict future task performance.

The therapist selects potential tasks, provides task demands and directions, observes behavior, and predicts future performance. These functions require criteria for generalizing from one task to another; task equivalence makes the generalization possible. The attributes of voluntary motor actions

that describe task equivalence are as follows: (1) matter, the sensory cue and its perceptibility, setting, and sample, and (2) behavior, the motor action and its use of tools, number, people, and directions (Table 3-1; see also Table 1-1). The same motor actions and sensory cues that specify the cognitive levels are used to specify task equivalence. This specification makes it possible to provide an activity that is within a patient's range of ability. The suggested criteria for task equivalence are (1) task demands—the requirements and structure of the task, including the material objects needed, the samples and choices provided (if any), the steps of the task, the tools used, potential errors, the length of task time, the procurement and preparation of supplies to be used and their storage, and the task setting; (2) task directions—the directions given by another person, including demonstrations, verbalizations, and number of steps explained at one time; and (3)

Table 3-1. *Task analysis*

Attributes	Level 1: automatic actions	Level 2: postural actions	Level 3: manual actions	Level 4: goal-directed actions	Level 5: exploratory actions	Level 6: planned actions
Matter						
Sensory cue	Threshold of consciousness	Proprioceptive cues	Tactile cues	Visible cues	Related cues	Symbolic cues
Perceptibility	Penetrates subliminal state	Own body Furniture and clothing	Exterior surfaces	Color and shape	Space and depth	Intangible
Setting	Internal	Range of motion	Arms reach	Visual field	Task environment	Potential task environment
Sample	Alerting stimuli	Demonstrated action	Material object	Exact match	Tangible possibilities	Hypothetical ideas
Behavior						
Motor actions	Automatic	Postural	Manual	Goal-directed	Exploratory	Planned
Number	One action	One action	One action	One step at a time	Several steps at a time	Infinite
Tool use	Stimulated use of body parts	Spontaneous use of body parts	Chance use of found objects	Hand tools used as a means to an end	Hand tools used to vary means and end	Tool making Power tools
Other people	Shouting Touching	Moving	Manipulating objects	Sharing goals	Sharing explorations	Sharing plans and recognizing autonomous plans
Direction						
Verbal	Verbs Introjections	Pronouns Names of body parts	Names of material objects	Adjectives Adverbs	Prepositions Explanations	Conjunctions Conjectures
Demonstrated	Physical contact	Gross motor and guided movements	Action on an object	Each step in a series	Each step and precautions for potential errors	Not required

individual differences—past experience in doing a task and stated preferences.

Task Demands

The task demands are introduced by the presence of *material objects*. Objects vary in the cognitive complexity required for successful use, and the task demands specify the degree of complexity introduced by different types of objects.

A *sample* is a standard of performance, providing an initial sensory cue of what can be done. *Choice* specifies the degree of autonomy or independence permitted in departing from the standard of performance.

The *steps* identify the sensory cues and motor actions that require attention during the process of doing a task. *Tools* can be used during the process of doing a step; because tools can increase the hazards of performance, precautions in tool availability merit special consideration. *Potential errors* are a departure from the standards of performance. Recognition of an error and a correction of the error can be considered separately. Recognition may be an anticipation of a potential error or an acknowledgment after the error has occurred. A correction may be a direct response or the avoidance of a repeated error. The *length of task time* is the duration of the task, how long it usually takes to complete the task. Length of time is given as a guideline for program planning, but it is influenced by diagnosis (e.g., manic episodes versus depressive episodes) and cultural factors (e.g., verbally facile people versus taciturn people).

Supplies specifies what the therapist or another caregiver must do to procure and prepare material objects for successful use by the disabled person. *Storage* is the procedure for maintaining supplies, including the degree of autonomy provided in organizing and using storage areas.

The *setting* is where the task is done, including the background characteristics of the room and the presence or absence of other people and irrelevant supplies. Restricted access to potentially hazardous objects that may be located in a setting is a consideration.

Task Directions

The *directions given by another person* identify the type and degree of assistance required to complete a task successfully. A *demonstration* is a motor action done by another person. The motor action is to be imitated; the demonstration provides a model of an action that is to be copied. The action may or may not have an effect on an external object. *Verbalizations* are words used to explain motor actions and are regarded as ancillary to the demonstration (Derevensky, 1976). The type of motor action required by the task dictates the parts of speech required. The *number of steps explained at one time* specifies the frequency with which a caregiver must be present to provide instruction.

Individual Differences

Task selection is influenced by individual differences in *task experience* in some ways that are fairly consistent. The task analysis identifies similarities in the way people utilize their past experiences. Past experiences also determine the individual's familiarity with the process of doing a task.

Preferences are the individual's likes and dislikes, expressed in selecting one task over another and in deciding whether to do a particular task. A cognitive disability may restrict the number of alternatives or the opportunity to choose. The task analysis identifies the opportunities that are available and seem to be preferred. Recognizing and honoring stated preferences is regarded as an essential component of task equivalence.

Each of the factors outlined above will now be described for each of the cognitive levels. The discussion will begin with level 6 and move down the hierarchy, because disease takes awareness of elements of the task environment away from the individual.

LEVEL 6: PLANNED ACTIONS

The task analysis at level 6 is influenced by the individual's ability to use symbolic cues to plan actions and anticipate events. Task opportunities that are enhanced by these abilities include freedom of choice, expression of individuality, creativity, and independence.

Task Demands

The task demands supplied by material objects include all elements of the physical environment. The sample of a desired task can be presented in the form of an illustration, diagram, or picture; these are symbolic samples (Fig. 3-2). An inexact sample of a material object can be used as well to stimulate an individual idea. Several choices in materials, tools, and tasks can be supplied. A unique pattern or mode of action can be designed successfully.

Steps that require reflection about the symbolic properties of material objects can be done. Power tools and unfamiliar hand tools can be used safely because potential errors are anticipated and plans are made to avoid these errors. The length of time that a task will be pursued is based on the individual's priorities in allocating time (e.g., someone's birthday or an anticipated discharge date).

There is a creative use of available supplies, and substitutions are used in a flexible manner. Supplies are obtained and returned to storage areas in an independent and logical fashion, while a disorderly storage area can be organized independently. Labels on drawers and cabinets may be helpful in new storage areas but are not required in familiar areas. The individual may have free access to all elements of the physical setting.

Task Directions

A demonstration may be given but is not required. Verbal directions may contain (1) a symbolic explanation of a cause-and-effect relationship, (2) the location of a requested supply, or (3) an explanation of the next step in a task. In addition multiple direc-

Fig. 3-2. Level 6. Symbolic sample.

tions and written directions can be followed with some variation that seems to be explained by the individual's past experiences with similar tasks.

Individual Differences

Prior task experiences are used to anticipate the effect that motor actions will have on present tasks. Preference is expressed in the form of selecting tasks that can be individualized with distinctive features or personal modes of action. Individualized tasks may combine prior preferences with present task demands.

LEVEL 5: EXPLORATORY ACTIONS

The task analysis at level 5 is influenced by the individual's ability to learn from direct experience with material objects. People at this level are able to invent new ideas to guide their actions. Errors and hazards, however, are not anticipated, but once they have occurred they are avoided.

Task Demands

Task demands can include properties of objects that are related to each other. The sample can be an inexact match of a task that can be done several different ways. Several choices in supplies and patterns can be offered.

Fig. 3-3. Level 5 errors. The design on this leather belt is not centered; a partial correction of the error is made by adding the flowers.

Steps requiring attention to one's direct experience with the relationships between objects (e.g., over and under) are preferred. Variation within the steps is desirable, for example, making three leather belts with different patterns or procedures. The variability permits exploration of how changes in motor actions have different effects on material objects. Planning a variation before beginning the task requires images and symbolic cues present at level 6 but not available at level 5.

Tools provided may include hand tools that act as linear extensions of the hand and arm (e.g., a hammer). Familiar power tools may be desirable at times, but the potential hazards are apt to be underestimated by the patient. The range of risk with power tools is great (compare a table saw with a toaster). Power tools should be used with supervision and under the assumption that the worst risk will occur (one can tolerate burnt toast but not an amputated hand). Potential errors are recognized after the mistake is made. Motor actions can be modified to avoid a second error when the error is due to a failure to consider a partially hidden cue. The length of time that it takes to complete a task can span two to five one-hour sessions. The number of errors made and their ease of correction seems to influence sustained effort; many mistakes that are hard to fix lead to a desire to quit (Fig. 3-3).

Patterns and procedures that have been designed or planned by other people are a part of the required supplies. Materials should display a perceivable difference when voluntary motor actions are varied (e.g., sanding across or with the grain of wood). Supplies can be located in an open storage area but their return to the proper location may be inconsistent; misplaced tools and supplies will be searched for in reachable locations. The organization of the storage area must be provided by others; labels and transparent storage containers are helpful. Access to all of the potential objects in a given setting must be supervised, and access to hazardous materials such as power tools, toxins, and flammable objects should be restricted. The task setting can include a number of different kinds of stimuli: other people working on projects and making noise, music, and even clutter.

Task Directions

The relationships between the properties of objects must be shown to the individual by a demonstration. Verbal directions augment the demonstration. Two or more steps can be demonstrated at one time; as a general rule, in a series of three steps one step may be unfamiliar. With practice new steps will be remembered.

Individual Differences

Past experiences in doing tasks are used to recognize new cause-and-effect relationships. Novel tasks that contain unfamiliar steps are preferred; people at level 5 like to try something new. Novel tasks combine prior task experiences with new relationships between perceivable cues.

LEVEL 4: GOAL-DIRECTED ACTIONS

The task analysis at level 4 is influenced by the individual's ability to use visible cues to achieve a goal. The features of material objects that are not clearly visible are not anticipated or understood.

Task Demands

Task demands must contain clearly visible cues. The sample must be such that an exact match can be produced from available supplies. The choices offered to the patient should include the opportunity to produce an exact match or to change one striking feature such as the color.

The steps should require attention to the clearly visible properties of objects. Unfamiliar hand tools may be used when they produce a clearly visible effect on an object, for example, winding yarn around a weaving hand shuttle. Hand tools that partially cover objects (e.g., a stapler or paper punch) may produce qualitative errors if the patient is unfamiliar with the tool. Errors that are visible cannot be anticipated but they can be recognized, and a correction of an error can be made when the required action is visible. If the correction requires attention to an intangible property of an object (as many corrections do), the correction must be made by someone else. For example, the misalignment of the diagonal line in the candle in Fig. 3-4 cannot be corrected by the level 4 patient. The patient can see the error but does not know how to correct it. An important part of task selection at level 4 is a consideration of the mistakes that are apt to occur and how quickly and easily they can be corrected. Expensive and dangerous errors must be avoided.

The length of time required to complete the task is usually one session lasting approximately one hour. People with verbal facility may talk while working and extend the task through two sessions. Goal-directed actions are self-sustained until the goal is achieved. As a general guideline, the sample should take about fifteen minutes for the therapist to make, and most disabled people will require approximately forty-five minutes to do the same steps.

Fig. 3-4. Level 4. Visible error. The beeswax candle on the left is made by cutting a rectangular piece of beeswax along a diagonal line, forming two triangular pieces. The wax is rolled by keeping the straight edge even and allowing the diagonal line to produce the spiral effect. A failure to attend to the straight edge and the diagonal side produces the misshapen candle on the right; this is an example of a visible error produced by inattention to the sides of the wax.

A real challenge exists in designing a simple, quick, error-proof task that does not look childish. A good measure of experience, creativity, and preparation on the part of the therapist is required.

The supplies required are two-dimensional objects with striking colors and clearly discernible shapes or forms. Primary colors and realistic representations seem to have more appeal than subtly muted colors and abstract shapes. Useful objects that avoid childish connotations are recommended for adults. Independent use of supplies is restricted to the visible properties of objects; all other steps must be done by someone else. Supplies provided often require much preparation before being given to an individual at level 4; a good deal of assistance is also needed during the task process.

Fig. 3-5. Levels 3 and 4. Room preparation. The project is decoupage, and a sample is placed in the center of the table. Each person has his or her own supplies.

Access to storage areas is problematic. Frequently used storage areas with clearly visible supplies can be used independently. Frequently used areas must be organized by others, and items must be stored there consistently; variability is disturbing. Infrequently used storage areas must be organized and maintained by others. For example, a person may be able to find things in the kitchen but not in the garage, assuming kitchen use is more frequent. Access to material objects in the external environment is restricted to visible tasks. The required supplies may be laid out by another person so that the task expectations are clearly visible. The setting may include other people who are working on the same, or similar, tasks.

Task Directions

A visible effect on an object should be demonstrated and augmented with verbal statements. Directions must be given one step at a time. After one step is demonstrated the therapist must wait until that step is completed before demonstrating the next step. One-step-at-a-time directions necessitate constant assistance during task performance, which places real demands on the therapist. In a group setting people at level 4 may have to sit and wait for the therapist to show them how to do the next step. The delay can be overcome by placing people who require one direction at a time (levels 3 and 4) in a group together and having them all do the same task. The therapist can give directions one at a time to the whole group, and the slower patients can imitate other patients. The necessary tools and supplies can be laid out in advance, and a sample can be placed in the middle of the table (Fig. 3-5). Patients seldom complain about not being allowed to select the project, and requests for the next day's project can be honored. Having a number of people doing the same task improves the therapist's efficiency in giving instructions and doing the necessary preparation. In addition the reliability of the therapist's observations and reports may be strengthened by this procedure.

Individual Differences

Past experience is used to modify familiar motor actions in accordance with their effect on the visible properties of objects. Familiar, short-term tasks are preferred. Familiar tasks combine prior task experiences with the visible properties of objects.

Fig. 3-6. Level 3. A repetitive action with a disregard for a goal.

LEVEL 3: MANUAL ACTIONS

The task analysis at level 3 is influenced by the person's ability to act on the external environment without connecting his or her actions to a goal. Manual actions have a beginning and a middle, but no end point or goal is recognized (Fig. 3-6).

Task Demands

The word *sample* usually refers to an example of a finished product or a goal. At level 3 attention is not focused on the sample but rather on the manual action used during the task process. The "sample" at level 3 is a repetitive action. The choice of materials or supplies may be a meaningless question at level 3, because these people are not attending to an end product and may not comprehend why a choice should be made. Even when a choice is limited to two items, a pattern for an apple or a pear, the level 3 patient may be immobilized. In that case the therapist may suggest that one of them is nicer and essentially make the decision for the patient. The repetitive manual actions must be familiar. Familiar actions can be identified by reviewing routine tasks that are done cross-culturally and selecting manual actions that most people learn to do as children. These actions, such as peeling a potato, have usually been done many times and seem to be retained better than other actions that are done less often. The manner in which the action is done may be fixed, such as using a peeler versus a paring knife or sitting down versus standing up to peel the potato.

The steps of the process should require attention to the tangible properties of objects. The step is an action that has an interesting effect on the external environment. The effect is repeated. A uniform effect is desirable and can be enhanced by selecting steps that are consistent and highly predictable.

Hand tools that are used habitually to do a task may be used. A distinction must be made between tools that are used habitually (a fork, pencil, or brush) and tools that are used automatically (a spoon or a glass). A habitually used tool is used repeatedly in a fixed manner to produce an effect on the external environment; conscious awareness of the external environment is ongoing throughout the process. With an automatically used tool a flicker of conscious awareness of the external environment is used to initiate the action (grasping the glass) but is not sustained. A few habitually used hand tools—for example, pens, pencils, brushes, or a needle and thread—may be used at level 3. The quality of use may be poor, and this may be distressing to the disabled person or his or her caregivers. Actions that can be done directly with the hands, without tools, may be done with better quality.

The definition of what constitutes an error takes a marked shift at level 3, because the actions are not goal directed. The usual standard of performance, the sample, is disregarded. People at level 3 fail to recognize that their actions have an outcome, an effect on objects and other people. Clearly visible errors are disregarded; this is often misinterpreted as having a malicious intent such as hiding or stealing. Intent involves a goal, which is not evident at level 3. The errors that are recognized at level 3 occur during the process of performing a repetitive manual action. Manual actions that fail to produce a consistent effect on the external environment, for example, dropping a bead while stringing beads, are recognized as errors.

A one-hour session can be scheduled for people at level 3, but attention to a task will probably be maintained for approximately thirty minutes. The longer period of time is scheduled because the attention of people at this level is distracted by extraneous elements of the environment. Moving from one location to another is slow and may be distracted by an urge to go to the bathroom, get a drink, or put on a sweater. Those at level 3 must be escorted to and from the clinic as they may be disoriented in space and apt to get lost. Talking to other people or to themselves or hearing voices may interrupt manual performance; some people cannot

talk and work at the same time. Other extraneous objects may suggest a familiar action, such as picking lint off of clothing or turning the pages of a magazine, and divert attention away from the caregiver's original intent.

The therapist selects supplies and places them in front of the disabled person. In selecting supplies the therapist must consider attention span, because the manual action may be repeated until an obvious end, suggested by the material object, is reached. For example, carrots may be peeled until they are "all done," or beads may be strung until the person runs out of thread. Some people continue the repetitive action until they come to an obvious end point, while others are highly distractible. This may be diagnosis specific. A level 3 person observed during a manic episode may place unique demands on a clinical setting, because these people are very distractible and the clutter that has a tendency to accumulate in occupational therapy clinics provides additional distractions. A regular effort is required to keep the clutter down to a minimum.

At level 3 the storage of supplies and maintenance of the environment is taken care of by others. Access to potentially hazardous materials including matches, cigarettes, knives, and other sharp objects, must be restricted. Any use of such objects must be supervised; if supervision is inconsistent these objects should be removed.

The storage of materials, supplies, and projects is taken care of by the therapist. Preparation for a level 3 task can be quite extensive because the steps that are unfamiliar and unrepetitive need to be completed by the therapist. Therapists generally find it easier to do as much preparation as possible before the patients' arrival. Some steps simply cannot be done ahead of time; these can be done for the patients during the session.

A task that has two or three different repetitive steps can be done by patients at level 3: A wooden box with a tile mosaic in the recessed top, for example, would require sanding the box, staining the box, and gluing the tiles. Therapists conducting groups have found it is easier to demonstrate directions if the supplies are laid out on the table before the patients' arrival. Level 3 patients, however, will be distracted by a large number of supplies placed in front of them, so the supplies for only the first step or two are placed on the table. In the example cited above, the sandpaper, water-base stain and brush, and wooden box could be placed in front of the patients, while the tiles can be kept on a nearby counter or cart until the patients are ready to use them. In this manner it is possible to provide tasks for level 3 and level 4 patients simultaneously.

Task Directions

A manual action is demonstrated and augmented with the nouns and verbs that name the object and the required action. One direction is given at a time; numerous repetitions may be needed. The repetition of the demonstration refocuses attention; other cues such as inquiring about how things are going can be used as well.

Individual Differences

Past experiences are used to recognize a familiar manual action that has a consistent effect on a tangible property of an object, for example, paint changes the color of an object and goes from wet to dry. Preference is expressed for objects that have a consistent effect, for example, paints that are pre-stirred so that each brush stroke is an even color. The effect should be observable in the here and now, for example, paints that dry rapidly. Individual differences are related to the physical properties of objects observed during the process of performing a manual action.

LEVEL 2: POSTURAL ACTIONS

Task analysis at level 2 is influenced by a decrease in attention to material objects in the external environment. The actions of other people are noticed, however, and can be used to capture and sustain attention.

Task Demands

The sample selected is a gross motor action. The action may be initiated by a caregiver or by the disabled person. A number of different postural actions can be demonstrated with the expectation that each will provide a comfortable sensation of movement. Simple, repetitive movements that most people learn in physical education classes can be used. The therapist's knowledge of sensory integration and neuromotor development can be applied here to select exercises that require the least amount of coordination and balance. A sequence of exercises that is routinely followed is helpful.

The steps should contain simple movements of one body part at a time that direct attention to the internal properties of movement such as bending, stretching, or rotating a body part. Hand tools are restricted to very few, familiar, objects that are used automatically (as defined above under level 3). A soft rubber ball may be caught and tossed automatically when familiar to the individual, and other objects that are associated with gross body movements, such as jump ropes or exercise bicycles, may be used. Music, however, may pose problems. Music frequently accompanies calisthenics in adult exercise classes, but it is an additional sensory stimulus for the cognitively disabled. Attention may be directed toward the music and away from the exercising, with the music becoming an undesirable distraction. Rhythm instruments can be distracting, too, and in addition they have childish connotations that may lead to their rejection. Therapists should be cautious because potential errors are introduced by the presence of all material objects; objects may be bumped into or tripped over or broken. An error caused by a gross motor action will be recognized, but it will not be anticipated.

The length of time that attention can be directed to gross motor actions is usually 5 to 15 minutes. This varies according to the physical exertion required to do the chosen action and the physical condition of the individual.

Supplies, in the traditional sense of changing material objects for use of oneself or others, are generally not used. Storage is taken care of by others and is beyond the disabled person's awareness. Postural movements must be done in a supervised setting where potentially hazardous furniture and objects have been moved out of reach. The setting in which gross body movements are done need not be difficult to obtain; I have found that it is possible to use a hallway, the seclusion room, or a conference room (after wheels were mounted on the table so it could be moved easily).

Task Directions

The demonstrated direction is a postural action that may be initiated by physically guiding the person through the first sequence of the movement, for example, bringing the arms up over the head and clapping the palms together. Another means of capturing attention is to imitate a movement that the disabled person is performing and follow it with another action.

Verbalizations should be restricted to a few simple verbs and pronouns and the names of parts of the body, for example, "Move your arms." Directions must be given one at a time, and frequent repetition may be needed. Counting the number of times that an action has been done seems to help sustain attention.

Individual Differences

Individuals at level 2 use their past experiences to recognize a familiar physical action that has a positive effect on their state of physical well-being—that feels good. They prefer actions that have a known positive effect. Actions with unknown effects may be regarded with suspicion or refused. Clinical examples include a refusal to do floor exercises, to move from one room to another, or to try novel exercise equipment. This tendency to refuse to try unknown gross motor actions further restricts the available voluntary motor actions.

LEVEL 1: AUTOMATIC ACTIONS

The task analysis at level 1 is influenced by a lack of responsiveness to other people. The only detectable response to the external environment is a change in the individual's level of arousal. Some cooperation with the essential tasks of living (eating, drinking, voiding, walking, sitting, and lying down) can be elicited.

Task Demands

A change in the level of arousal can be elicited by an object or a tactile direction that draws attention to the part of the body to be moved. No choice in the selection of the task to be done is offered; the task is selected by another person.

The steps of the task that can be done require transient attention to an automatic movement. Hand tools and other material objects are not used. Individuals may be able to use their hands to do some tasks such as picking up and eating finger foods. Potential errors include the misidentification of objects, such as eating nonedible objects and confusing bathing routines with toileting routines. Attention to an external demand may be sustained for approximately one minute. Awareness of the external environment seems to be restricted to things within arm's reach or immediately in front of the individual. Objects that are behind the person, such as a chair, bed, or toilet, may cause confusion. Placing the person's hand on the object may reassure him or her that the object is there. All other steps in tasks required to sustain life must be taken care of by another person.

Task Directions

Tactile commands may accompany demonstrated directions and seem to be helpful in initiating movements. For example, walking can be initiated by placing one arm around the disabled person's waist and pressing firmly while pointing in the desired direction with your other hand. Demonstration can include physically guiding a patient through the movement as in placing food in a person's hand and guiding the hand to the mouth. Guided actions may be followed by spontaneous repetitions of the guided action.

One-word verbal commands, such as "Sit!" or "Chew!" may be used to change the level of arousal, and shouting may be required. One direction must be repeated many times, as attention is lost numerous times during the process of doing a task.

Individual Differences

Individuals use their past experiences to alter their state of arousal and retain their fixed movements for doing an automatic action. Established eating and drinking preferences may continue to influence intake, and there may be an expressed desire to be, or not to be, fed. If the person is unable to attend to the survival tasks of eating and drinking, intravenous feeding may be required.

SELECTION OF TASK CONTENT

Proposition 3. The choice of task content is influenced by the diagnosis and the disability.

The presence of a cognitive disability may necessitate a distinction between the activities of daily living (ADL) and routine tasks. People with cognitive disabilities are often restricted in their ability to earn and spend money; work is not a routine task. As societies become more technical and specialized, there are fewer jobs for people with mental limitations, and unemployment produces long hours of nothing to do. Some people with associated physical disabilities can fill these hours with self-care and grooming tasks, but people who can do these tasks within a normal period of time require additional routine tasks. Given a choice, people who do not have physical disabilities may prefer crafts. A choice of task content has been offered to psychiatric inpatients for several years in a program large enough to permit a wide selection. Choices have included real

work tasks, grooming, cooking, sewing, educational materials reviewing basic community survival skills, games, and crafts. I am struck by a consistent clinical pattern: at levels 3, 4, and 5 the most popular tasks are crafts.

Crafts

Crafts are a professional problem; they lack professional mystique. We each have to prepare ourselves for the inevitable occasion when a disabled person proudly displays a project of poor quality to a professional colleague. The opportunity to crack jokes at our expense is tempting. This should not be regarded as a humiliating experience for the therapist. Differences in the quality of task behavior are expected between disabled and nondisabled populations. Differences in the quality of ADL tasks are easily apparent and may be humiliating to some patients. Differences in the quality of craft performance are not so readily apparent and may help in preserving the patient's sense of integrity. There is a tendency among therapists to avoid crafts, which may be for our own personal benefit and not the patient's.

Crafts may be our professional Achilles' heel, but they do have an asset that we can take advantage of. By using craft activities to assess the cognitive level, the assessment occurs in a naturalistic setting and is not confounded by the testing situation, which obscures many other psychological assessments (Maloney and Ward, 1976). The assumption that the individual wants to do the task and that observed problems in task performance can be attributed to lack of ability has greater credibility in a naturalistic setting. This is especially true when the individual selects the task according to his or her own preferences.

The preferences of the disabled may differ from the preferences of the nondisabled. The choice of the task should reflect the preferences of the individual doing the task, which we can accommodate. Therapists working with the cognitively disabled place a high value on crafts because they capture and sustain the attention of the people we serve. People who have physical disabilities are often willing to spend long hours attending to self-care and grooming, and, as should be expected, therapists working with these people place a high value on self-care tasks. Each therapist is recognizing the patient's right to a freedom of choice in selecting the task content. *ADL* is a term that is frequently used in physical rehabilitation settings, and it is biased in the direction of the preferences of those with physical disabilities. The preferences of the physically disabled have extended to the curtailment or elimination of crafts from curriculum and clinical programs. The content of a clinical program should reflect the interests and desires of the people participating in the program; freedom of choice in selecting task content must be protected for people with all kinds of disabilities. *ADL* is a term that has led to some infringement in this area, and the relative desirability of crafts should be reexamined with the patient's preferences in mind. Crafts, or any voluntary motor actions that a person wants to do (as long as they are legal), are within the scope of routine tasks.

Balance of Work, Rest, and Play

As of this writing, a troublesome problem with the selection of task content is posed by the assumption made in the occupational behavior frame of reference. The assumption is that people should have a balance of work, rest, and play (Reilly, 1974). Why patients should have a balance is unclear. Implicit in the application of the assumption is the notion that an imbalance has something to do with a disease or disability. A health problem assumes a biologic defect; the connection between the defect and a balance of work, rest, and play has been neglected. Lacking such a connection, therapists are in the awkward position of telling patients or clients how to "balance their lives" without any idea of how their advice is related to the person's disease or disability. The occupational behavior emphasis on the social aspects of a disability is a positive contribu-

tion, but it should not be made at the expense of neglecting the biologic restrictions on the choice of task content. The assumption needs to be restated to account for these restricted choices: People with cognitive or physical disabilities may express preferences in the selection of task content that are influenced by their disease or disability. The occupational behavior assumption sought one statement that would cover all diseases and disabilities. This may be an overgeneralization, and more progress may be achieved by multiple statements that are disease and disability specific. Some suggestions are offered in Chapters 5 and 6.

TASK ENVIRONMENT

Proposition 4. The task environment may have a positive or a negative effect on a patient's ability to regulate his or her own behavior.

Task environment refers to people, objects, and spaces that are external to the patient (Dunning, 1972). The positive effect of the task environment can be observed when patients successfully follow the task procedure delineated by the therapist. The negative effect can be observed when patients are unable to do a step in the procedure or refuse to participate, or when a procedure elicits symptomatic behavior. The task environment should be designed to have a positive effect on the patient's ability to regulate his or her behavior.

Negative Effect

The negative effect the task environment may have on behavior can be illustrated by projective techniques. Projective techniques are designed to elicit symptomatic behavior, and many of them are quite successful in producing hallucinations, delusions, and suicidal ideation (Hammer, 1967). Projective techniques are evaluation instruments that expose pathologic behavior by asking the person to do an open-ended task in which very little structure is provided: Draw a house. Paint the way the music makes you feel. Draw a picture of a person in the rain. The instructions are minimal. The task often deliberately introduces an emotional component, such as "the rain" or the color or music chosen. People who are finding it difficult to organize their behavior to follow specific, demonstrated instructions can be expected to be further disorganized by open-ended instructions and emotionally charged content. The creative or expressive arts are especially prone to elicit displays of pathology, because the typical procedure for completing these tasks is subject to endless variations and instructions for completing the task are self-generated; that is the creative process. It does not take any special training to design a number of tasks that will elicit pathology from people with an Axis I diagnosis (*DSM III,* 1980). The projective techniques illustrate the ease with which one can design tasks that will elicit symptoms, or a refusal to do the task, from people with psychosis. The negative effects of the task environment are evident in neurologic conditions as well. Catastrophic reactions are described in some cases of head trauma and dementia. Catastrophic reactions occur when a person encounters a task that was done easily in the past that he or she can no longer do. The reaction is a fight or flight response. This reaction may occur anytime a higher level task is given; the task is beyond the patient's range of ability. The question must be asked: Is there ever a justification for deliberately eliciting the negative effects of the task environment? As a general rule, psychiatric symptoms and catastrophic reactions do not need to be encouraged; they are rather like a headache in that they occur whether you want them to or not. The task environment may interfere with task behavior in spite of our best efforts to design an environment that minimizes negative effects.

Positive Effect

Treatment and compensation for a cognitive disability call for the suppression of symptoms and the support of successful task behavior. It is very diffi-

cult to do this, and therapists should recognize that this is not an either-or issue. Despite our best intentions, some symptoms and errors continue to occur. We try to restrict the degree of discomfort the person is experiencing. A task that is beyond the patient's capability will often elicit more severe symptomatic behavior or a desire to stop working on a project. When this occurs, the therapist can change the task by changing the step or providing a simpler project. Sometimes one step in the procedure is causing the difficulty, and the therapist can offer to do that step for the patient. The therapist's efforts are directed toward resolving difficulties encountered in doing the task so the patients can proceed to do those elements of the task that are within their capabilities.

Evaluation

The exception to the rule of suppressing symptoms and supporting successful task behavior is the evaluation process. The negative effect of the task environment may be used to assess a person's cognitive level, to elicit symptoms essential for a differential diagnosis, or to assess a person's ability to apply past experiences to essential routine tasks. Therapists may encounter an ethical consideration here because the task environment can be designed to provide an unpleasant experience. Tasks that rob people of their dignity and their integrity can be designed; however, displays of pathology should be avoided when possible.

The introduction of the negative effect of the task environment is justified during the assessment process. The task environment, for example, can be used to elicit suspected, but hidden, symptoms that would aid with differential diagnosis. To illustrate, a 60-year-old woman who had been living in squalor and neglecting self-care was admitted to the hospital. On the ward she was quiet and verbal performance showed no pathology, but she wore a knitted hat on her head all of the time. The correct diagnosis was in question. The therapist invited her to a grooming group and asked her if she would like to wash her hair. The therapist was seeking to uncover a delusional symptom that might be elicited by this task. The presence of a delusion might be confirmed by a refusal to wash her hair if accompanied by an illogical explanation. The negative effect of the task environment can be deliberately introduced to help solve an identified clinical problem. This, of course, should be done with caution.

Some guidelines as to when and how to conduct assessment can be suggested. First, the reason for the assessment should be clear in the therapist's own mind and clearly stated to the patient. The current occupational therapy literature is loaded with evaluations of questionable utility, and practice is burdened with duplications of effort. The questions to be asked are Do we really need the information? and Do we already have the information? Second, the patient should be told what the therapist plans to do with the assessment information. Reports to treatment teams and legal proceedings should be identified. Third, an unpleasant assessment should not be extended any longer than necessary. If, for example, an assessment can be made after two leather lacing stitches there is no reason to continue to struggle through the production of an entire wallet. These processes are uncomfortable for patients and therapists, and whenever we get into such a situation we should stop and consider the reason for continuing. Often there is no reason to continue the misery except "We have always done it that way" or "You should finish what you start." Neither of these reasons seems to be a valid justification for prolonging the negative effects of the task environment. The fourth guideline has to do with the degree of unpleasantness elicited by an assessment procedure. The diagnosis of depression will serve as an example. The diagnosis can be made by using a structured interview, a laboratory test, or finger paints. Each process will be unpleasant, but finger paints are more apt to elicit profound depressive feelings and suicidal ideation. The selected assessment procedure should be as objective and free of unpleasant emotions as possible. These guidelines

are provided to help therapists reassess some of our current evaluation methods.

Self-regulation

Inherent in the positive and negative effects of the task environment is a view of the patient as a person who regulates his or her own behavior. For some therapists this view represents a major change, at the level of a different world view. The mechanistic world view holds that the therapist changes the patient. This view is being replaced by the organismic world view, which assumes that people regulate their own behavior (Reese and Overton, 1970). Ayres (1979) and Reily (1974) have accepted an organismic world view, and I accept it here as well. Simply stated, the assumption is made that patients will do the best they can given the situation they encounter in the task environment. Therapists, as providers of task environment, can give them an opportunity to do what they can do. Therapists provide the task demand. Patients regulate their own response to that task demand by applying their available cognitive abilities, and the therapist and the patients see the outcome in the patients' task behavior.

This is a shift in the way we think about our observations of behavior from a mechanistic to an organismic world view. Those of us who have pursued this shift have not found it to be easy; our old thoughts guide our thinking in insidious ways. Reading helps, but applying the concept consistently takes time.

An intriguing observation will be used to illustrate the challenge. A young man with a diagnosis of a primary affective disorder in a manic episode was assessed at cognitive level 4. Given a level 4 project, his task behavior at first appeared to be as expected: rushing through the steps in the task and getting up out of his chair to walk around the room or get a cup of coffee. On one of his trips around the room he did an unusual thing—he picked up a can of cloves and dumped approximately three tablespoons into his coffee. His next cup of coffee consumed the remaining cloves. This behavior seemed to be peculiar, but it could be interpreted as an expression of personal taste. When, however, he dumped half of a can of oregano into his coffee and tried to sneak the rest of the can into his pocket, his behavior seemed too unusual. At this point it was time for me to reexamine my observations. I had been thinking that the project was holding this young man's attention. An alternative explanation could be that he was seeking spices to put into his coffee, behavior that is associated with polydrug abusers because they hope the spices will make them feel high. The alternative explanation led to laboratory tests to assess that possibility, which confirmed my suspicions. The important thing to note is that I, the therapist, offered an experience in the task environment—a project. What I had in mind was different from what the patient had in mind. The patient was self-regulating his task behavior according to his own purposes. The therapist can offer an opportunity for a positive experience in the task environment; the patient decides whether or not to accept that opportunity. The young man in this illustration left his projects in the clinic; he laughed when asked if he wanted to take his project with him. The service we have to offer may not be recognized or accepted by many patients, and adjusting to this notion is a major challenge of the organismic world view.

Semistandardized Tasks

Task analysis for the cognitively disabled provides a method of objectively analyzing the cognitive complexity of many activities. A therapist can analyze the task as a separate entity before the patient enters the clinic. The task analysis may be used as an integral part of the process of evaluating a person's level of function while the person is doing a desirable activity. An effort has been made to avoid restricting the content of the activity so that evaluation would not be invalidated by undesirable content. The evaluation process can, however, be invalidated by a therapist's error in task analysis.

These errors can be controlled for by developing semistandardized tasks. The tasks selected are expected to vary according to the interests and preferences of various patient populations, the size of the occupational therapy program, the age of the population, and the interests and ingenuity of the therapists.

The procedure for checking for task analysis errors begins with selecting the task content and the cognitive level, for example, sewing at level 4. The therapist designs a project (a pot holder) so that it can be done successfully at the selected level. The therapist verifies the analysis by watching the task behavior of a number of people presumed to be at the same cognitive level, level 4 in this example. When a number of people assessed at level 4 have difficulty in successfully performing the same step in a procedure, an error in the task analysis can be identified. A task analysis error is a step in the task procedure that impedes performance. The location of an error indicates that the therapist must reanalyze that step. The step in the task is modified because the problem in task behavior is produced by the complexity of the task. With the pot holder project the therapist observed that the patients had trouble attaching the loop; this problem was eliminated by doing the first few stitches for them as a part of the preparation (Fig. 3-7).

Errors in task analysis are a common occurrence when new tasks are introduced; we, too, learn by trial and error. Our attitude must be to recognize that despite our best efforts there is a good chance we will overlook something. I recommend that therapists observe a number of people at the same cognitive level following a task procedure before using the task as an assessment of competence. In this way therapists can develop semistandardized tasks that provide some measure of control for the complexity of the task as a confounding factor in the explanation for a problem in task behavior.

Semistandardized tasks are the projects used most frequently. An experienced therapist has had an opportunity to observe a number of people following the same procedure and has learned what to

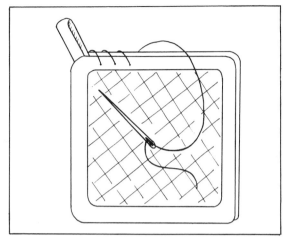

Fig. 3-7. *Modification of a task. The first few stitches can attach the loop of the pot holder and begin the stitching for the patient.*

expect. The tasks that are used vary according to the interests and preferences of the patient population, current fads, and the interests of the therapist. Generally these semistandardized tasks are done in a group setting, and some suggestions can be offered that seem to help in getting started.

Starting a Group

The treatment and compensation objectives are based on an assessment of the cognitive level. The selection of the cognitive level of the group participants is the first step; this selection is based on program needs. The second selection is the task content, for example, sewing, grooming, or games. The content is based on the preferences and past experiences of the patient population. Before beginning a group a therapist must obtain two things: a selection of tasks and a well-organized task environment. As a general guideline therapists seem to require about 10 projects, analyzed and prepared, before starting to see patients. The following period of about two months is required to develop an expanded selection of semistandardized tasks.

Task selection seems to go through an evolutionary process once the group has begun. The first step is to test the validity of our task analysis by watching a number of people at the same cognitive level doing the task. Task analysis errors are identified, and steps are modified. The second step is to identify the relative advantages and disadvantages of various tasks. For example, some tasks are easily confounded by visual impairments, while others are sensitive to a change in the cognitive level. The third step is to refine further the task procedures to maximize the desired advantages.

The other part of getting ready for a patient group is the organization of the task environment. During a group session a therapist needs to observe the patients' task behavior and so must control for factors that can divert his or her attention. The task environment must be organized to avoid unnecessary hassles. The following questions should be considered: If a patient needs a supply, can the therapist find it easily and quickly? Are the necessary supplies in the immediate clinic area, or does the therapist have to leave the room? Does the therapist have immediate access to well-organized cupboards and drawers? Are the patients apt to have trouble with a particular step? If so, can that step be done ahead of time or eliminated? What other steps need to be done ahead of time? For example, one can thread the sewing needles (for patients with blurred vision) and unplug the glue bottles in advance of the patients' arrival. Many tasks have a first step that the patients cannot do. This step can also be done ahead of time so that therapists do not spend the first part of a session running around getting everyone started. Therapists need to be meticulous in planning and maintaining the task environment if there is to be any hope of having the group run smoothly. Nothing breeds frustration and animosity faster than a sloppy clinic.

Semistandardized tasks are far from ideal, and we need to understand the risks involved as well as the potential benefits of using these tasks. The control for error is partial: We watch a number of people, at level 4, for example, performing the same task and draw some conclusions about the directions, tools, and materials that seem to work best. This is a gross, superficial procedure when compared with the standardization of psychological tests. Standardization is a lengthy process, usually involving numerous studies and large populations. The present approach leaves the standardization of psychological tests to the psychologists. In doing so we must be prepared to recognize that a refined, pinpointed, and accurate assessment of a cognitive problem is more apt to be produced by a thoroughly examined task than from a task that has only partial standardization. This is the disadvantage.

There are some advantages to this occupational therapy approach of using semistandardized tasks. The advantages are greater flexibility in the selection of task content and the naturalistic setting. These advantages seem to be consistent with our historical traditions. We have favored activity typologies that were exhaustive at the expense of mutual exclusivity. Our methods have emphasized a practical approach to living with medical problems. Numerous activities are preferred by our patients, and numerous medical problems can influence their performance. Routine task behavior involves many problems; we are observing a cumulative effect that needs to be divided into the component parts. To identify a routine task that a person with multiple limitations can do successfully can be a real challenge. We increase our potential for meeting that challenge by maintaining flexibility in our task selection. Furthermore, a testing situation can be regarded as an adversarial relationship by people with mental disorders. We have attempted to avoid this difficulty by providing a naturalistic and cooperative setting. These advantages are essential in the clinical setting, but it has been difficult to do research on them because they are responsive to individual differences. What we need is a clearer identification of what an individual difference is and what a similarity is. One similarity can be found in the complexity of the task. If a number of people have a problem in the same step in a task procedure, the problem is explained by the task's complexity, not by the individual's motivation, interest, or past experience. One can analyze the similarities in the step of the task apart from individual considerations. The identification of similarities in routine task behavior helps to distinguish between a disability and an individual difference.

Scope of the Environment

Proposition 5. Patients with cognitive disabilities attend to those elements of the task environment that are within their range of ability.

The task environment can offer the opportunity to engage in a large number of different projects, but only a selected portion of them will sustain the patient's attention. Useful tasks contain sensory stimuli that capture attention; other stimuli are ignored. A higher cognitive level increases the number of tasks that can be successfully done, thereby expanding the usable task environment (Fig. 3-8).

The task environment can be viewed from two perspectives, the therapist's and the patient's. An occupational therapy clinic illustrates the differences. The therapist is usually aware of a large number of supplies that can be employed to complete a variety of projects. The therapist is expected to acquire a comprehensive knowledge of the clinical area (the outer square of Fig. 3-9). The therapist knows, for example, where the ceramic molds and slips are stored and remembers to put the rubber bands on the mold before pouring the slip (even if some of us learned that lesson the hard way). The patient with a cognitive disability will not perceive the clinic from the therapist's perspective. Patients may learn the location of tools and supplies that are frequently used, but the formation of new patterns of thought to comprehend the workings of such things as ceramic molds and kilns is beyond their present ability. The patient's perspective is limited to a part of the environment, the part he or she can understand. The size of the part can vary with the cognitive level, and it can also be influenced by materials procured by the therapist. A clinic richly sup-

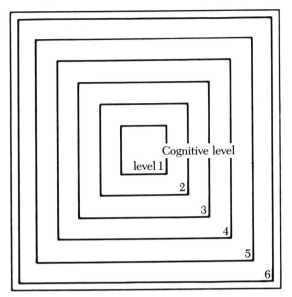

Fig. 3-8. The usable task environment. The higher the cognitive level, the broader the usable task environment.

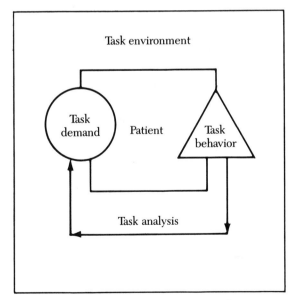

Fig. 3-9. The therapist's awareness of the task environment.

plied with expensive materials and equipment can be useless to a cognitively disabled patient if there is nothing there that he or she can successfully do. In this respect it is the therapist's responsibility to expand the patient's environment by providing the materials required for successful task behavior.

I use the term *task environment* to assist in generalizing from observations made in the clinic to other settings. The importance of suitable objects can also be stressed in the cognitively disabled person's home, work, and community. Listening to people with long-term disabilities describe recent typical days, one frequently hears very little about task behavior beyond eating meals. One could hypothesize that constricted task environments are contributing to this problem, and that change would occur if meaningful materials were made available to this disabled population. The necessity of having a therapist present to show the patient how to use the materials is of interest to us. Therapists will need to study the question of when it is possible to consult with a family member or some other interested persons in modifying task demands and directions versus when it is necessary for a therapist to have direct contact with the patient.

The usable environment for a person with a cognitive disability is quite different from the objective environment: (1) Specific aspects of the environment may capture attention, and other components may be ignored. (2) Past experiences may result in ascribing meanings to the environment that are not shared by others. (3) Deviant perceptions and hallucinations may lead to the belief that things exist in the environment that are not there. For people with a cognitive disability, the usable environment is most constricted because they only attend to a limited number of sensory stimuli (Fig. 3-10).

The Therapist in the Task Environment

The opportunity to interact successfully with the environment requires that people, objects, and space be within the patient's range of cognitive ability. The therapist is a part of the task environment

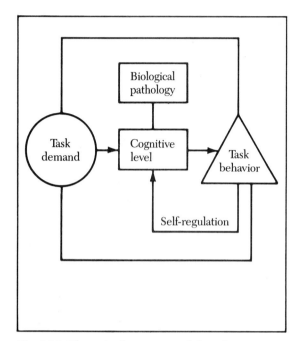

Fig. 3-10. *The patient's awareness of the task environment.*

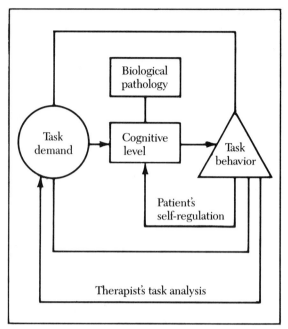

Fig. 3-11. *Transactions between the therapist and the patient.*

and expands the usable environment for the patient through the application of task analysis. The opportunity to interact successfully with the environment exists when the therapist creates a task that matches the patient's level of ability.

Proposition 6. Therapists can select and modify a task so that it is within the patient's range of ability through the application of task analysis.

The therapist is an intermediary between the task environment and the patient. The need for the assistance of a therapist is indicated when the patient's biological pathology interferes with routine task behavior. The patient may require a change in the task environment that will enhance the self-regulation of task behavior. The first form of intervention is to measure the cognitive level. The evaluation consists of an observation of standardized task behavior as well as an interview to establish history

and experience in doing tasks (Chap. 4). The second form of intervention is to analyze the available tasks to obtain a set of semistandardized tasks that are desirable to the patient population, for example, adults versus children. The therapist modifies the task, eliminating, altering, or completing those steps that are beyond the patient's capability. Modifications utilize attributes of the physical environment as a substitute for deficient patterns of thought; the therapist designs a structure for the process of doing a task. In this way the therapist brings a usable task environment to the patient by designing task demands that are within the patient's level of ability. The therapist's expertise in evaluating task behavior and in analyzing and modifying task demands becomes the cornerstone of practice.

Interactions between a therapist and a patient involve two feedback loops (Fig. 3-11). The patient is assessing his or her own task behavior. The therapist is also assessing the patient's task behavior and formulating plans regarding task demands. Two dynamic processes are occurring simultaneously. The distinction between these two processes is relatively simple to explain and teach. They are, after all, occurring in two different people. This rather simple idea is difficult to operationalize, however, because task behavior is influencing both the patient and the therapist. The intermediary between the patient and the therapist is the task behavior, and the therapist can change the task demand or continue with the task demand.

Beginning students often find it difficult to know when to step in and change a task demand. As a general rule environmental compensation objectives are fulfilled by initiating a change in the task demand as soon as a difficulty in behavior is detected. Expectant treatment objectives are fulfilled by standing back and watching for a change in the quality of task behavior. In practice standing back or assisting can produce chaos in the therapist's mind. For example, a therapist may be helping 10 people, all doing the same project but for whom the therapist has different objectives in mind. Suppose the project has two difficult steps in the typical procedure. The therapist must decide which patients need help immediately and which patients should be observed carefully to see if they can do the step independently. When 10 people begin to do a difficult step in a typical procedure, the therapist needs to be clear about the actions and observations required to fulfill the objectives. Therapists seem to have a tendency to err in one direction or another, either helping too much or too little. A number of things seem to help therapists in making this decision: familiarity with a set of semistandardized tasks, experience in keeping track of different objectives, and a well-organized task environment.

CONCLUSION

The task analysis is closely related to the patient's cognitive level; the pattern of thought used to guide behavior is evident in the patterns of performance (Fig. 3-12). The cognitive levels indicate qualitative differences in patients' ability to do a task. The task analysis indicates qualitative differences in the complexity of the task and suggests changes in a typical procedure that will alter the task's complexity. A distinction is made between the measurement of the cognitive level and the treatment process. Compensation is done by matching the complexity of the task to the patient's cognitive ability so that the patient has the opportunity to experience the successful manipulation of material objects. Evaluation of the cognitive level is done by providing tasks throughout the hierarchy of the cognitive levels until the complexity of the task is beyond the patient's cognitive level. The analysis of the task environment assists therapists in controlling for problems in behavior that can be explained by the complexity of the task environment. It would be nice to report that successful task behavior suppresses psychiatric symptoms. Unfortunately clinical experience does not support such a statement. *Successful* and *pleasant* are really relative terms indicating that we aim to make a person as comfortable as possible, but the basic fact of the matter is that the person has a disease that is making him or her uncomfortable. Mental disorders produce symptoms that are observed during task performance, and the type of experience people have in the task environment can be unpleasant if their symptoms are unpleasant. Therapists need to be realistic and objective about how these symptoms influence task experiences (Chaps. 4 and 5).

Problems with this view of task analysis are apparent. We need to know more about the influence of different diagnostic categories and cultural groups. A variety of methods are used to delineate the brain-behavior association; we will need to increase our sophistication in this area so that we can collaborate with psychopharmacologists, neuroanatomists, neuropsychologists, psychiatrists, and neurologists in refining our understanding of the brain-behavior association. The rapid explosion of knowledge about the brain makes this an exciting and promising area of study.

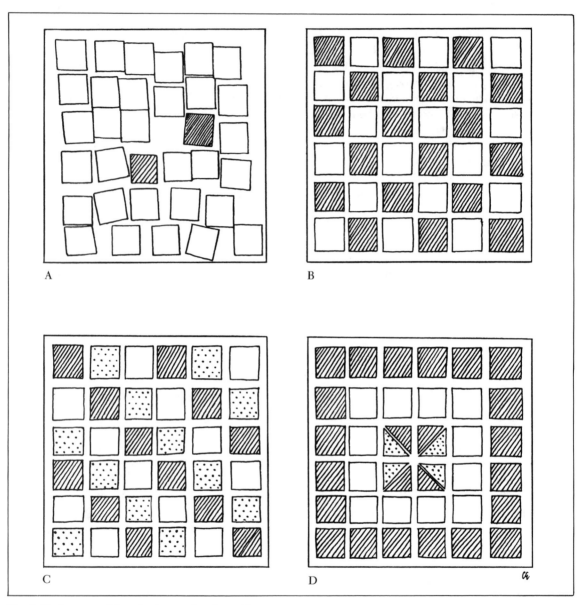

Fig. 3-12. Patterns of thought that can be observed in patterns of performance. A. Level 3. B. Level 4. C. Level 5. D. Level 6.

REFERENCES

Ayres, A. J. *Sensory Integration and the Child*. Los Angeles: Western Psychological Services, 1979.

Brown, G., and Desforges, C. *Piaget's Theory: A Psychological Critique*. Boston: Routledge & Kegan Paul, 1979.

Cole, M. An Ethnographic Psychology of Cognition. In R. W. Brislin et al. (eds.), *Cross-cultural Perspectives on Learning*. New York: Sage, 1975.

Derevensky, J. Developmental changes in the effect of verbal, non-verbal, and spatial-position cues for memory. *J. Exp. Educ.* 45:52–60, 1976.

DSM III: Diagnostic and Statistical Manual of Mental Disorders (3rd ed.). Washington, D.C.: American Psychiatric Association, 1980.

Dunning, H. Environmental occupational therapy. *Am. J. Occup. Ther.* 36:292–298. 1972.

Goldman, A. I. *A Theory of Human Action*. Princeton, N.J.: Princeton University Press, 1970.

Hammer, E. *A Clinical Application of Projective Drawings* (2nd ed.). Springfield, Ill.: Thomas, 1967.

Holyk, H. L. A model of cognitive planning of self-care in the brain injured. University of Southern California Master's Thesis, 1981.

Kopp, C. B. An application of Piagetian theory: Sensory-motor development. *Am. J. Occup. Ther.* 28:217–219, 1974.

Kopp, C. B., and O'Connor, M. J. Task characteristics and a stage 6 sensorimotor problem. *Child Dev.* 46:569–573, 1975.

Maloney, M. P., and Ward, M. P. *Psychological Assessment: A Conceptual Approach*. New York: Oxford University Press, 1976.

Piaget, J. *The Origins of Intelligence in Children*, transl. by M. Cook. New York: International University Press, 1952.

Piaget, J. *The Place of the Sciences of Man in the System of Sciences*. New York: Harper & Row, 1970a.

Piaget, J. *Structuralism*, transl. by C. Maschler. New York: Harper & Row, 1970b.

Piaget, J. *Biology and Knowledge: An Essay on Relations Between Organic Regulations and Cognitive Processes*, transl. by B. Walsh. Chicago: University of Chicago Press, 1971a.

Piaget, J. *Psychology and Epistemology*, transl. by A. Rosin. New York: Viking, 1971b.

Price-Williams, D. R., Gorden, W., and Ramirez, M. Skill and conservation: A study of pottery-making children. *Dev. Psychol.* 1:769, 1969.

Reilly, M. (ed.). *Play as Exploratory Learning*. Beverly Hills, Calif.: Sage, 1974.

Reese, H. W., and Overton, W. F. Models of Development and Theories of Development. In L. R. Goulet and P. B. Boltes (eds.), *Life-span Developmental Psychology: Research and Theory*. New York: Academic, 1970.

Trujillo, A. A study of the meaning of activity as conveyed to occupational therapists. University of Southern California Master's Thesis, 1980.

CHAPTER 4

ASSESSMENT PROCEDURES

The cognitive levels are a measure of a person's functional abilities. The assessment is done in the here and now, recognizing that a person's capabilities in the past and future may differ from present abilities. The evaluation is a competence measure, an inference about the person's capabilities from observation of performance. This chapter will present two methods for assessing the cognitive levels: the Allen Cognitive Level Test (ACL) and the Lower Cognitive Level Test (LCL). These assessments are done within the context of other information about the patient and the mandate of the institution in which occupational therapy services are delivered. The evaluations were designed for an acute psychiatric hospital, and other settings will necessitate modifications.

A request for occupational therapy services is initiated by a referral. Two types of referrals are used; both have their pros and cons. (1) A blanket referral indicates the need for an assessment of *every* patient admitted to a unit (ward, service, or hospital). The assessment is usually done within a specified period (e.g., 3 to 10 days). The therapist has free access to all patients and is responsible for determining who shall and shall not receive occupational therapy services. (2) Referral may also be made on a case-by-case basis in cases selected by the physician. The therapist's access to a patient is contingent on a referral from the physician.

The blanket referral in an acute hospital can generate the need to write many "trash notes." A trash note essentially says, "Yes, I know the patient is here, and no, I cannot assess him or her because _____." The blank is filled in with a description of a dysfunctional behavior. Seemingly the only person interested in the trash note is a chart auditor; experienced members of the treatment team learn to ignore them. Obviously, therapists are frustrated by having to write useless notes. A method of dealing with this difficulty will be suggested under Preliminary Occupational Therapy Evaluation.

A case referral requires the physician's signature, usually before the therapist can escort a patient to the clinic area. The therapist, under this system, must track down the physician to get the signature. Most of the time the physician agrees, and both the therapist and physician regard the signature as a nuisance. The purpose of the referral, for many years, simply read: "OT eval." Currently some regulatory agencies require more detail, and some referral guidelines will be suggested.

The last two decades have borne witness to tremendous changes in charting requirements and reviews. Changes in social mandates, such as the standards set by the Joint Commission on Accreditation of Hospitals (1983), state laws, the policies of third party payors, or the recommendations of the American Occupational Therapy Association ("Uniform terminology," 1981), seem to produce a typical response—therapists develop a new form to fill out. A number of different formats will be used in the chart examples found in this chapter and Chapter 8. Ultimately we come up against the same problems: The therapist's notes are no better and no worse than the therapist's understanding of all of the issues involved in a case. True, some outlines seem to work a little better than others, but the quality of the note ultimately reflects the individual therapist's expertise.

Evaluations, progress notes, and discharge summaries represent the application of a therapist's knowledge to patient care. Evaluation acts as a bridge between theory and practice. Evaluation instruments are operational definitions of theory and, as such, cut across patient populations and institutional settings. Theoretical similarities are expected. Dissimilarities are expected as well. The evaluation methods must be modified according to patient, population, and institutional demands. The balance of similarities and dissimilarities places the evaluation process in the position of acting as a bridge between a theoretical description of a cognitive disability and our actual observations in practice. Theoretical and operational definitions are not regarded as bifocal entities but are described as dynamic interactions between theory and practice (Shapere, 1969). The existence of a cognitive disability is expected. In addition the assessment must be open to important functional problems related to other bodies of information (such as the diagnostic symptoms). The therapist uses theory and observations to aid in the delineation of the patient's functional assets and limitations (Shapere, 1977).

CHART REVIEW

The first step in the assessment process is to review the medical chart to determine the reason the patient was admitted to a health care program and to identify the preliminary occupational therapy goals. In setting reasonable goals one must consider two factors: the context in which the therapist works and the medical treatment of the disease. The therapist works within a health care system that has an identified mandate for service: for example, inpatient or outpatient, day care or residential, long-term or short-term care. The mandate for service will partially delimit the goals that can be achieved. The medical knowledge available to intervene in the disease (or diseases) will also influence the service goals. Individualized patient care emerges from a determination of how each person fits into the available system of health care and responds to the available medical intervention.

The first review of the medical chart completed by students frequently results in a copious reproduction of everything there. Judgment and knowledge are required for a more efficient selection. Some headings that will fit onto a $6'' \times 9''$ index card are suggested in Fig. 4-1.

The review of the medical chart begins with the identification of a list of problems to be addressed during treatment; the problem list usually contains assorted difficulties present at admission and a probable diagnosis along with several other diagnoses that may be considered, for example, bipolar

Problem list _____ Working diagnosis _____

_____

_____

_____

_____

Risks _____ Medication _____

Reason admitted _____

_____

Past hospitalizations _____

_____

Medical complications _____

Physician _____

Mental status _____

_____

_____

_____

_____

Fig. 4-1. Format for collecting chart data.

affective disorder, rule out schizophrenic disorder, schizoaffective disorder. In addition, the evaluations and plans of people trained in other disciplines provide information about what else is known and being done for the patient. The therapist reviews the chart to begin to formulate the contribution occupational therapy might make. Reference to current medical textbooks and articles (*DSM III* 1980; Strub and Black, 1981; Goodwin and Guze, 1979, Swonger and Constantine, 1983) may assist the therapist in recognizing the expected symptoms, complications, medical treatment, and natural course of the disease. The interrelationships between a cognitive disability and a psychiatric disease will be discussed in Chapters 5 and 6. A medical formulation of the problem provides an indication of the short-term and long-term limitations that may influence task behavior.

The therapist working with a person who has a cognitive disability needs to address the following question: What information or services can I supply that will help solve the disease or disability problem? Answers that frequently occur in a short-term psychiatric hospital include (1) to assist with differential diagnosis, (2) to assist with the titration of medication, (3) to identify the time when stabilization of improvement is noted, (4) to provide symptom relief and (5) to assist with discharge planning.

The chart review helps in identifying counterindications for clinic attendance. Occupational therapy clinics are generally located away from the hospital ward to separate potentially dangerous supplies from potentially dangerous or self-injurious patients. Therapists are responsible for maintaining that separation. The reason for admission may be an important factor in determining whether or not a person is able to come to the occupational therapy clinic. Patients who may not be escorted to the clinic area include those who are elopement or suicide risks, those who require physical restraint, and those whose behavior is unpredictable and potentially violent. Other counterindications include muteness and refusal to come to the clinic area. Thus the chart review may act as a screening device, identifying who is eligible or ineligible for clinic attendance (see Fig. 4-2).

PERFORMANCE ASSESSMENTS OF THE COGNITIVE LEVEL

Another reason for delaying clinic attendance is that the person's current cognitive level is too low for him or her to interact successfully with the task environment. As a general guideline patients are usually seen on the ward at levels 1, 2, and sometimes 3. Patients seen in the clinic area are usually functioning at levels 4, 5, and 6, with a few people functioning at level 3. Two performance tests have been designed for the initial estimate of the patient's cognitive level: the Allen Cognitive Level Test and the Lower Cognitive Level Test. The ACL has the benefit of longer clinical use and is backed by more empirical study.

Allen Cognitive Level Test

The ACL is a leather lacing test that has been in clinical use for some time. Moore (1978; see Chap. 12) played a major role in refining the format so that this clinical tool can be used as a research instrument.

The ACL is based on an assessment of the complexity of the leather lacing stitch that the patient is able to imitate (Tables 4-1 and 4-2). Using the running stitch as a criterion for levels 2 and 3 is based on the assumption that the stitch is a familiar, repetitive manual action for most American adults (consider, for example, the sewing cards used in kindergarten). Therapists should be alert for a potential sex bias, which has not been detected in the research studies but is a logical possibility with the sewing stitch. The whip stitch is more difficult than the running stitch, requiring visual attention in going from the front to the back of the piece of leather. The single cordovan stitch contains a series of steps with the potential for a number of interrelated errors: twisted lacing, tightening out of sequence, and getting the lace tangled up in the loop.

Patient identification

Evaluation indicates that patient is

Eligible for OT groups

Ineligible because

Mute

Refusing

Elopement risk

Suicidal risk

In restraints

Unpredictable

Other

Cognitive level

Comments

Plan

Fig. 4-2. Preliminary occupational therapy evaluation.

Table 4-1. Allen cognitive level test: scoring criteria

Level	Criterion
2	Unable to imitate the running stitch
3	Able to imitate the running stitch, two stitches
4	Able to imitate the whip stitch, two stitches
5	Able to imitate the single cordovan stitch using overt trial-and-error methods (physically trying out various ways of completing the stitch), two stitches, two demonstrations
6	Able to imitate the single cordovan stitch using covert trial-and-error methods (mentally trying out various ways of completing the stitch before physically completing it), two stitches, one demonstration

Table 4-2. Allen cognitive level test: materials

1	natural cowhide carving weight Tom Thumb purse kit, #4109, Tandy Co.[a] (Do not use zippered piece included in kit.)
2	30-inch-long ³⁄₃₂-inch English calf lace, #5004, Tandy Co.[a]
2	Golka[b] needle tips
1	pair Golka[b] needle pliers
1	15-inch-long 5-cord linen thread, beeswaxed, dark brown
1	large-eyed, blunt-ended sewing needle

[a]Tandy Leather Co., P.O. Box 791, Fort Worth, TX 76101
[b]Robert J. Golka Co., P.O. Box 676, Brockton, MA 02403

Preparation

The preparation of the ACL, as refined by Moore (1978; see Chap. 12), follows the steps outlined below:

1. The therapist divides the leather into thirds and attaches the two pieces of leather lacing, completing at least two whip stitches with one piece of lacing and at least two single cordovan stitches with the other piece of lacing. The linen thread is attached, and two running stitches are completed.
2. The therapist selects a relatively distraction-free setting with adequate lighting and sits beside the patient at a slight angle. The therapist shows the patient the leather lacing stitches and asks if he or she knows how to do leather lacing. The response (yes or no) is recorded.

Running Stitch (Levels 2 and 3)

The therapist says,

"I am interested in seeing how you learn. This will help me place you in occupational therapy groups. I will show you how to do a stitch now, so watch what I do carefully."

(This explanation of purpose can, of course, be changed according to the treatment setting. I recommend keeping the explanation brief.)

The therapist then holds the leather project so that it is facing both the therapist and the patient and both sides of the leather's edge are visible. Therapists should practice holding their hands in a manner that affords the patient a clear view of the stitching process.

"Take the needle and push it through the hole, then pull the thread through the hole. Now push the needle back up through the next hole. Pull the thread through the hole and tighten it. Don't skip any holes. Now you do it."

These directions may be repeated once if the patient cannot complete the stitch on the first attempt.

The individual is scored at level 2 if unable to complete two running stitches and at least at level 3 if able to complete two running stitches.

Whip Stitch (Level 4)

If the patient is able to complete the running stitch, the therapist proceeds to the whip stitch. These directions may be repeated once if the subject cannot complete the stitch on the first attempt.

"See how this leather lace has one rough side and one smooth side. Always keep the smooth side up as you do each stitch, being careful not to twist the lace. Now I will show you another stitch. Watch me carefully."

"Take the lace and bring it around to the front, over the edge of the leather. Push the needle through the hole, and tighten it. Make sure the lace isn't twisted. Don't skip any holes. Now you do it."

The individual is scored at least at level 4 if he or she is able to complete two whip stitches, that is, twice bringing the lacing over the edge and pushing the needle from front to back. A score of level 3 is assigned to those who are able to do the stitch but cannot untwist the lacing. (Clinically we have noticed that people who score at level 4 usually stop after two stitches have been done, while the level 3 patients continue. While this difference has not been empirically tested it might prove to be an important differential between levels 3 and 4.)

Single Cordovan Stitch (Levels 5 and 6)

If the individual is able to complete the whip stitch, the therapist gives the following directions, which may be repeated once if the patient cannot complete the stitch on the first attempt.

"Now I will show you another stitch. Watch me carefully. Bring the needle around to the front of the leather. Push the needle through the next hole, toward the back of the leather. Don't pull the lace tight, but leave a small loop in it. Bring the lace around to the front of the leather again. This time put the needle through the loop you have made, and pull the lace through it toward the back of the leather. Keep the lace to the left side of the loop. Tighten the loop from the back, then tighten the long lace end. Make sure the lace isn't twisted. Now you do it."

A score of level 5 is given if inductive reasoning is used (physically trying out various ways of completing the stitch) or if the patient requests a second demonstration after noting an error. A score of level 6 is given if deductive reasoning is used (mentally trying out various ways of correcting an error or pausing to think and select the best course of action) and one demonstration is all that is required. Two stitches must be completed correctly at level 5 and 6; twists in the leather lacing are scored as errors that must be corrected. If the errors are not corrected, the score is level 4. The final score is the highest level achieved on the test. Any unusual circumstances, events, behaviors, or reactions occurring during testing are noted by the therapist.

The ACL has been used as the operational definition of the cognitive levels in four studies, which are reported in Chapters 12 through 15. A summary of the findings and a discussion of the relative strengths of the test are provided in Chapter 16. In general interrater reliability is strong enough to inspire confidence that different therapists will obtain the same score; $r = 0.99$, $n = 23$, degrees of freedom (df) $= 21$ for five independent rater pairs (see Table 12-6). The test has not yet been replicated in a different setting. Validity has been tested in a number of ways, but the most important test has not been completed: an examination of the internal consistency between the ACL score and routine task behavior. The development of the Routine Task Inventory (see Table 2-2) is regarded as an important step in that direction.

False Negatives and False Positives

Any single task that we use to assess the cognitive levels will produce some incorrect results, referred to as false negatives and false positives. A false negative indicates that a person does not have an ability that he or she actually has. Leather lacing is a visual-motor task, and deficits in this area can obscure the assessment. Visual problems seem to pose the largest clinical difficulty. People who are newly admitted to a psychiatric hospital may not have their glasses with them. In addition blurred vision is a common side effect of psychopharmacologic agents. An attempt to reduce visual problems was made by selecting leather with large, machine-punched holes and using contrasting colors. Therapists can also modify the setting in which the task is administered, being sure that the area has good light and providing a light-colored background to enhance color contrasts. Even with these precautions, however, visual deficits can still produce false negative results.

Hand impairment can also invalidate the test. Clinically therapists have held the leather for the patient or placed the leather in a vise or a lacing pony. The resulting scoring seems to be correct, but a controlled study would probably answer a number of lingering questions about hand impairments. The leather selected is heavy and thick so that it will stand up by itself and not fold over. This selection was based on concern about hand impairments.

A lack of cooperation can influence the test results and seems to be especially troublesome in those with paranoid ideations. Such patients will not attempt anything that resembles a test. A lack of cooperation is difficult to interpret; one does not know whether one is seeing a lack of ability or not. In such cases the assessment is deferred, and an effort is made to encourage attendance in the OT clinic so that task performance can be observed. Speaking a foreign language may also influence the patient's comprehension of the therapist's verbal instructions. Clinically therapists who routinely use this instrument have not encountered many problems with this factor; however, total reliance on demonstration has not been studied.

The research studies have excluded non-English-speaking subjects as well as subjects with visual, auditory, or hand impairments. Clinical exclusion of patients is more difficult. One may omit the ACL and substitute a different task that is not apt to be confounded.

The leather lacing test can also produce false positive results, indicating that a person has an ability

that in fact he or she does not have. Previous leather lacing experience seems to be the factor that could produce a false positive. The research studies indicate that this is not a factor when the mean score is around level 5 or 6, but it can be a factor at level 3 or 4. This is expected theoretically, based on the lack of new learning at levels 3 and 4. Thus therapists should ask about previous leather lacing experience and observe for false positives.

The leather lacing test does not achieve 100 percent accuracy; it is doubtful that any one test can achieve that kind of accuracy. Therapists should observe behavior on a variety of tasks to rule out other plausible explanations for a functional incapacity. That is the reason for developing the semistandardized tasks suggested in Chapter 3. I recommend that some of these tasks be designed to compensate for the impairments or past experiences that can confound the leather lacing test.

Clinical Considerations

Clinical use of the leather lacing introduces another problem; the lacing gets worn and floppy after it has been used a large number of times. Worn lacing twists easily, which may invalidate the test. Worn lacing should, obviously, be replaced.

Therapists frequently inquire about substituting a Life-eye needle for the Golka tip. Therapists have not had much luck with this substitution because the Life-eye needle has a tendency to come off the lacing. When that happens we seem to be measuring frustration tolerance rather than cognitive abilities.

Clinicians do not always follow a standardized format to the letter. The ACL seems to tolerate some modification; however, a modification that can invalidate the test has been discovered at levels 5 and 6. Telling a person to stop and think may prompt the use of images that would not spontaneously occur. A false level 6 result may be produced by this added instruction.

The instrument for measuring the cognitive levels was designed with clinical utility in mind. The

ACL can be administered quickly in many locations. The materials are small and flat so that they fit into the pocket of a 6″ × 9″ three-ring notebook, which therapists can use to keep track of current patient information. Therapists can carry these notebooks to the ward so that they have all of their evaluation materials with them. The test is designed to be administered on a one-to-one basis; this gives the therapist an opportunity to meet an individual patient, establish rapport, and offer some choice in the selection of the clinic program. Therapists usually conduct a brief interview before administering the ACL, because the initial rapport seems to enhance cooperation.

Lower Cognitive Level Test

Heying (1983; see Chap. 15), in a study of senile dementia, anticipated that her sample would include subjects at levels 1, 2, and 3. Differentiation of these levels with the ACL was questionable so an alternative, the LCL, was designed. The LCL asks the patient to imitate a motor action. The motor action selected is clapping hands because it is familiar and cross-cultural, and the ability seems to be retained by most of the disabled population. Clapping is an action learned by small children that is not confounded by a need to cross the midline. Clapping also lends itself to interrater reliability. Scoring criteria appear in Table 4-3.

Verbal Directions

"I'd like to see how well you can follow directions. Please clap your hands loudly three times. Watch me."

Demonstration

At the midline, the therapist claps three evenly spaced beats that are distinguishable and clearly audible. The directions may be repeated one time. The therapist may say, *"I did not hear you,"* when there is some doubt about the claps' being audible.

Table 4-3. Lower cognitive level test: scoring criteria

Behavior	Score
Three audible, consecutive, evenly spaced claps; contact at the palmar surface (May be more than three)	Level 3
One or two claps, claps not audible	Level 2
Other movements between claps	
Clapping initiated by therapist	
Attempts to clap, but contact with other than palmar surface (e.g., fist into palm, pads of digits)	
No response	Level 1
Refusal	No score

The therapist may also help to initiate the action by placing the palmar surfaces of the hands together.

Setting

The test should be given in a setting where the patient and therapist can hear the clapping.

The interrater reliability was examined by Heying with four staff therapists at Los Angeles County–University of Southern California Medical Center. Interrater reliability was 100 percent for 22 subjects selected because it was thought they might be functioning at levels 1, 2, and 3. The validity of the test needs further investigation. With the ACL as the independent variable, the LCL gave a false positive (i.e., a score of level 3) to 70 percent of the subjects who scored at level 2 on the ACL. It may not be possible to differentiate between levels 2 and 3 with the LCL; for the present we have discarded the level 3 score on the LCL.

Object Classification Test

A third test for measuring cognitive abilities has been developed and will be discussed in Chapters 13, 14, and 16. The test is designed to measure classification abilities and is divided into two parts, structured and unstructured. Our current understanding of the test (Riska Object Classification Test or ROC) is largely theoretical; it has been useful in developing the descriptions of the cognitive levels in Chapter 2. The clinical utility of the test is unclear, and a study of the correlations between the ROC score and the items on the Routine Task Inventory (see Table 2-2) might add some clarity to this instrument. Because of uncertainty about how to interpret the ROC in practice, it has not been included in this chapter.

PRELIMINARY OCCUPATIONAL THERAPY EVALUATION

The preliminary assessment (Fig. 4-2) can be made within the first few days of admission. The therapist's data base may be confined to the chart review and performance on one or both of the cognitive levels tests. Additional functional history may be unavailable or of questionable reliability. Three frequent examples illustrate a preliminary assessment.

Case Example I: Preliminary Occupational Therapy Evaluation

Patient Identification

A 36-year-old man who was dishevelled, cachectic, and disoriented to date was brought in by police after masturbating in a public park. Differential diagnosis includes mental retardation, organic mental disorder. He is unable to provide any history of past function to this therapist.

Brief interview indicates that patient is

    Eligible for OT groups
X Ineligible because
      Mute
      Refusing
   X Elopement risk
      Suicidal risk
      In restraints
      Unpredictable
      Other

Cognitive Level

ACL score = Level 3, severely impaired on motor evaluation. Patient engaged in repetitive actions and failed to detect errors in shifting from the running stitch to the whip stitch. No evidence of goal-directed actions or recognition of errors was observed.

Comments

Patient states he wants "to go to work in a factory" and wants glasses. He was suggestible during interview (wanting whatever was suggested to him) and repeated his desires endlessly in a childlike voice.

Plan

Patient will be seen in basic crafts at 2:00 in OT clinic area when allowed off ward.

Case Example II: Preliminary Occupational Therapy Evaluation

Patient Identification

This 19-year-old single man was brought in by family after several months of bizarre behavior including secluding self, believing Mafia and FBI were after him, hearing voices. No previous psychiatric hospitalizations. Working diagnosis is atypical psychosis, rule out schizophrenic disorder.

Brief interview indicates that patient is

X Eligible for OT groups
    Ineligible because
      Mute
      Refusing
      Elopement risk
      Suicidal risk
      In restraints
      Unpredictable
      Other

Cognitive Level

Level 5. Patient appears able to learn with difficulty and only with repeated encouragement. He used direct experience and inductive reasoning to correct errors in task performance.

Comments

Patient displayed normal range of affect. His thought process was intact. No abnormal thought content was elicited during interview. He is vague about events before admission, however, denying problems. He is unsure about what he wants to do after discharge other than "get a job doing something."

Plan

Patient agrees to participate in daily woodworking so therapist can monitor his function in tasks as medication is titrated.

A preliminary evaluation may be indicated when a patient refuses to come to the clinic area or refuses to attempt a performance measure (ACL or LCL).

Case Example III: Preliminary Occupational Therapy Evaluation

Patient Identification

A 51-year-old divorced (?) woman was brought in by self for "euthanasia." She has multiple delusions and refuses to provide much history because of guardedness. Working diagnosis unclear; rule out schizophrenic disorder, paranoid disorder, and bipolar affective disorder.

Brief interview indicates that patient is

   Eligible for OT groups
X Ineligible because
     Mute
  X Refusing
     Elopement risk
     Suicidal risk

     In restraints
     Unpredictable
     Other

Cognitive Level

Testing deferred owing to patient's refusal. It is estimated (from ward activity this date) that patient is goal directed when completing short-term tasks. She may be capable of exploratory actions: level 4, possibly higher.

Comments

Patient states that "security has determined that I must stay in this area" (i.e., on the ward); therefore she refuses to participate in any off-ward activities.

Plan

When patient agrees to participate in OT evaluation she will be assigned to groups. Ward tasks will be offered.

ROUTINE TASK HISTORY: INTERVIEW

An interview to obtain the routine task history is usually conducted for one of two reasons: to gain information that may help in differential diagnosis or to predict future task behavior. The chart review helps in selecting the purpose of the interview. Because many people interview patients, the unique focus of the therapist must be identified. The therapist asks questions about task behavior, and the interview is directed towards establishing the patient's functional history of experience in the task environment. The interview may be deferred until the patient can cooperate in providing a reliable self-report—usually at level 3 or 4.

An objective description of a person's functional abilities throughout the life span can be difficult to organize. Some organization may be imposed by dividing the description into past, recent, present, and future behavior.

Name _____ Age _____ Ward _____ Date _____

Living situation _____

Social support _____

Self-care responsibilities _____

Educational history _____

Work history _____

_____

_____

Interests, friends _____

_____

Reason for admission _____

Past hospitalizations _____

_____

Usual day PTA _____

_____

ADL _____

_____

Assets and limitations _____

_____

Goals for the future _____

Groups _____ Cognitive level _____

_____

Fig. 4-3. Routine task history: interview guidelines. (PTA
= prior to admission; ADL = activities of daily living.)

Past experience is addressed by asking the patient to identify the period of life when he or she was functioning the best. The context of that period may be elicited by inquiring about social situations such as living arrangements and main social role (e.g., worker, student, or homemaker). Asking the patient to identify the specific year or years may elicit helpful information regarding the onset of an illness. The patient's description of his or her best adaptive function may help predict future task behavior.

The patient's medical chart usually contains a description of maladaptive behavior that occurred during the days, weeks, or months before admission. The therapist can ask the patient to describe the reason for admission. This description may disclose the patient's ability to assess his or her own behavior. An inaccurate self-assessment of maladaptive behavior may predict medical noncompliance after discharge.

The questions the therapist asks are inquiries about the patient's past and recent experiences. The interview is semistructured in that the major topics to be considered are provided. The phrasing of the questions and the depth of coverage of selected topics are determined by the purpose of the interview. The interview can be conducted in a quiet corner of a room or in an office as long as an effort is made to minimize distractions and assure privacy. Some patients seem to be reassured by seeing the headings for the interview typed or printed on a piece of paper. The therapist should take notes during the interview and should show the notes to the patient if requested. The headings as they can be arranged on a 6″ × 9″ file card are shown in Fig. 4-3. The reverse side of the card can be used to take notes from the medical chart (Fig. 4-1); this is handy in that therapists can easily carry the file cards about and file them alphabetically in the OT office for rapid retrieval for readmitted patients.

Each of the topics of the verbal interview will be described, with some suggestions for questions that can be asked. A review of the questions in conjunction with a review of a patient's chart will indicate that many of them are irrelevant to a particular case. Some of the information may already be on the chart, and duplication can be avoided unless there is some reason for asking the question again. (An outline of the written evaluation is provided in Fig. 4-4 in the following section.)

Living Situation

Where the patient has been living recently and whether he or she can or wants to continue that living arrangement is explored. The use of the living environment can include the use of the neighborhood, a telephone, a television set, a collection of personal belongings, and a living space shared with others. Some living situations for the cognitively disabled have budgeting arrangements for the allocation of money, cigarettes, meals, snacks, and television programming, which may explain a patient's response to the living situation.

Social Support

The availability of family, friends, or other people in the community who take an interest in the patient is explored, along with the frequency of contact. Many cognitively disabled patients experience isolation from family and friends, and the degree to which this has occurred needs to be identified. This area is frequently explored by psychiatric social workers and may represent unnecessary duplication of effort in some cases or settings.

Self-Care Responsibilities

The patient's recent responsibility for purchasing supplies and initiating self-care tasks and the frequency with which these tasks are done is investigated. Specific questions can be addressed to laundry, general housekeeping, personal hygiene, and meal preparation. Patients at level 4 and below usually have difficulty fulfilling these responsibilities,

Data base
Axis V functional history prior to admission

Functional observations during this admission
    Symptoms of illness

    Awareness of illness

    Cognitive level

    Patient's goals

Occupational therapy plan
    Ineligible for OT at this time because

    Eligible for the following OT groups:

Functional observations for
    Verification of cognitive level
    Titration of medication
    Clarification of symptoms
    Assessment of potential grave disability

Occupational therapist

Name

P.F. #

Ward

4

Fig. 4-4. Routine task history: written report.

and a response that these survival skills are attended to independently can be regarded with suspicion. The extent of a person's past experiences with self-care tasks will influence his or her repertoire of familiar tasks.

Work History

The onset of the illness and the natural course of the disease can be expected to have an impact on the patient's work history. Patient's work experience will influence both their willingness to participate in work tasks and the familiar motor actions that are available to them. If the person has worked, how long ago, for how long, the type of job, the reason for leaving the job, and his or her desire to work in the future can help predict future work potential.

Educational History

The onset and natural course of a disease can also influence the patient's educational history. Successful motor actions and desirable task content can be explored by inquiring about educational level, favorite subjects, grades, friends, and participation in social activities while in school. During the discussion of educational and work history the patient can be asked to identify the time when he or she was functioning best. Patients who have had pleasant educational experiences may prefer tasks that have an intellectual connotation (the basic skills group described in Chap. 10, for example) rather than craft or work tasks.

Interests

The patient's preferences for hobbies, crafts, sports, and community organizations can be explored to identify motor actions that are apt to be familiar. The interviewer may need to inquire about participation in these tasks in the distant past for patients with long-term cognitive disabilities because many have not pursued their interests recently.

Recent Typical Day

The patient is asked to describe a recent day, beginning with getting up in the morning. The patient's ability to organize the description of everyday tasks provides an internal assessment of the credibility of previous answers. For example, a patient who reports responsibility for self-care but fails to include self-care in a typical day raises some questions about whether or not self-care is actually being done. The patient's ability to organize time independently is assessed; the therapist should avoid guiding responses by suggesting times or tasks. After the assessment of independent organization is complete the therapist can inquire about medical symptoms related to a typical day such as sleep disturbance, disorientation, nutrition, cycles in energy level, or substance abuse.

The skill of the interviewer in pursuing cues provided by the patient is particularly evident during this part of the interview. Frequently patients hint at problems that have not been revealed until they begin to describe the tasks that compose their daily life. A therapist who is knowledgeable about how symptoms are apt to influence daily life functioning can often elicit data that are valuable in differential diagnosis. In addition to the medical symptoms cited above, delusions, hallucinations, suicidal ideation, child neglect, and hyperactivity can be suggested by the description of a recent typical day.

Assets, Limitations, and Goals

The degree of accuracy of self-assessment is evaluated by asking the patient to identify his or her assets, limitations, and goals. Diseases that influence the way one feels or thinks make accurate self-assessment difficult. The degree of distortion, as well as the content of the distortion, may influence the patient's willingness to cooperate with a treatment program. For example, the patient may be delusional about the cause of the problems, and reference to objectives that would solve the problems may elicit the delusional symptoms. The patient's view of him- or herself is evaluated to determine the type of program that is apt to be meaningful to the individual patient.

Self-assessment questions are difficult for anyone to answer, and a cognitive disability makes them particularly hard. Many people with a mental disease refuse to recognize the presence of an illness. Phrasing the questions as follows seems to help: What do you like best about yourself? What would you like to change about yourself? What do you plan to do when you leave the hospital? The therapist may need to rephrase the question in several different ways before a meaningful response is elicited. Sometimes a self-assessment can be facilitated by asking the patient what other people say: What do other people like about you? What do other people think you should do differently? Do you agree? Distorted self-assessment frequently results in a symptomatic response to these questions; the stability, duration, and content of these symptoms is useful information for differential diagnosis and predictions of future behavior.

Past Hospitalizations

Patients with long-term illnesses have frequently experienced many hospitalizations and treatment programs. Information about past hospitalizations provides a measure of the age at onset, duration, and course of the illness, when examined in conjunction with the educational and work histories. Examination of past hospitalizations also affords an opportunity to explore the patient's past experiences with occupational therapy programs. The patients' expectations will be based on their past experiences, which may or may not conform to your present approach. Clarification of the patient's expectations may be required to foster a desire to participate in the occupational therapy program. When this problem occurs, therapists frequently suggest that the patients come and watch the first day, assuring them they will not have to do anything.

The questions asked during the interview concern the individual's functional history before admission (Fig. 4-3). The information that can be obtained from an interview varies and is influenced by the patient's diagnosis. People who are depressed give one-word answers to questions and volunteer very little information. The therapist may have to reexamine important areas when the depression has lifted somewhat. The other extreme is observed in the pressured speech that is symptomatic of mania. The therapist may need to interrupt the patient to return to the topic. The questions asked of people with schizophrenia should be concrete and specific, and the responses are specific, generally reflecting isolation and exclusion from the task environment. The recent memory loss observed in organic brain syndromes may produce an interview in which people enjoy talking about the past, but they may not recall recent events. Sometimes people with recent memory loss try to avoid the problem by making things up that could be quite plausible; the credibility of their responses must be verified.

The medical chart and the interview data are obtained by talking to patients and are subject to the problems of patients' credibility and cooperation. The data obtained can be constricted by the symptoms of the disease and by the skill of the interviewer. Performance measures (such as the ACL and LCL) are freer from these problems. The therapist may observe symptoms of the disease while interviewing the patient or watching task performance. Behavior that the therapist actually sees or hears is described under the heading of Functional Observations During This Admission (see Fig. 4-4).

Interview and chart data cards are filed in the occupational therapy office of my clinic for rapid retrieval during a subsequent admission. The consistency of the data obtained during subsequent admissions is striking even though the interviews are often conducted by different therapists and years apart. Patients with a chronic disability do not seem to develop new interests or aspirations, but they do seem to develop a set of stable answers to common questions asked in a psychiatric interview.

ROUTINE TASK HISTORY: WRITTEN

At this point the therapist may have a great deal of information about the patient. Organizing this information into a meaningful interdisciplinary communication (Fig. 4-4) is a challenge. Because most people do not have the time to read lengthy records, the length of the note should be limited to one handwritten page. Experience shows that there seems to be a negative correlation between the length of a note and its readership; long notes are rarely read by anyone. The self-imposed restriction on length, however, probably makes the note harder to write because the therapist usually has enough information to fill several pages. The therapist must be selective. The criteria for selection will vary with the purpose of the interview. New therapists and students report that they save time in the end by completing a working outline before writing.

Two forms of reporting a routine task history will be described. The first format is fairly straightforward, reporting what the patient and/or the chart says about the patient's past, along with observations made during this admission. The first format is all that is required in many cases. The second format is indicated when a change in the patient's lifestyle is being considered. The recommended change is based on a prediction of the future capabilities of the patient. Predictions are difficult to make, and a different format will be suggested.

Data Base

The source of the information is identified, including the date of the interview. Therapists may be using a combination of chart information, interview data, and task observations to write the note. The data base gives the reader some idea of the reliability and validity of the information that follows.

The history can be divided into two parts: the highest level of function ever and the level of function during the last year. The year of the highest

level of function should be noted and compared to functioning during the last year. The information usually makes more sense when it is presented in chronological order.

Axis V Functional History Before Admission

DSM III (1980) describes adaptive functioning as best performance during the past year (Axis V). Axis V is not required to make a diagnosis, and the criteria are ambiguous enough to generate concern about their reliability and validity. Some refinements are suggested in Table 4-4, but little is known about the predictive validity of best functioning during the past year. Therapists should note that there may be a difference between the best ever and the best during the past year. This distinction should be inquired about during the interview and dated in the written evaluation.

Functional Observations During This Admission

Information related to the current level of function is divided into four categories: symptoms of the illness observed by the therapist, the patient's awareness of his or her illness, the patient's cognitive level, and the patient's stated goals.

The symptoms of the illness observed by the therapist are reported as they relate to *DMS III* (1980) criteria. The awareness of the illness is taken from the patient's description of his or her assets and limitations. Additional information can be obtained from the patient's understanding of why he or she is in the hospital or needs help. Diseases that affect the brain often obscure a person's awareness of a problem. The cognitive level is stated by number, followed by a description of what the patient can and cannot do. Behavioral responses to the task evaluation can be noted. The patient's stated goals are also identified, usually in quotation marks, from comments made during the interview.

Occupational Therapy Plan

If the patient is eligible for clinic attendance the recorded plan should include the specific groups and times the patient will attend. Ineligibility follows the same rationale described above in relation to the preliminary assessment. The need for further assessment is identified under the heading of Functional Observations for. Four common objectives in acute psychiatric hospitals are listed: verification of cognitive level, titration of medication, clarification of symptoms, and assessment of potential grave disability. One or more of these objectives may be checked by the therapist. Other objectives, of course, can be added as necessary. A verification of the cognitive level may be required because of a recognized potential for error in the ACL or LCL. Assistance with the titration of medication is indicated when neuropharmacologic medications are being adjusted by the physician. Clarification of symptoms is indicated in cases in which differential diagnosis is uncertain. Assessment of a potential grave disability is indicated when there are questions about a person's competence to manage his or her personal affairs.

PREDICTED FUNCTION

Most functional observations reflect behavior that is related to one or more of the objectives checked on the history form (Fig. 4-4). These observations are of behavior seen or heard during the course of hospitalization. The observations acquire a more important meaning when applied to a predicted level of function.

A prediction about a person's future level of function is a synthesis of the following pieces of information: the highest level of function, the recent level of function, the current level of function, the natural course of the disease, and the expected effects of medical intervention (Fig. 4-5).

Highest Level of Function

The time in the patient's life when the patient was functioning at his or her best should be established;

the patient's age, the calendar year, and the patient's role at that time may have predictive value. The patient's own words are preferred. A lack of response or an unrealistic response may necessitate an estimate from the therapist based on a review of the patient's education, work, and social histories.

Recent Level of Function

Entrance into the health care system may be precipitated by an inability to do daily tasks successfully. This is represented on Axiv V in *DSM III* (1980), in which recent is defined as the best adaptive functioning during the last year (see Table 4-4). Therapists may expand the definition of "recent" functioning to include maladaptive behavior during the past year. It should be noted that people will assume the *DSM III* definition is being followed unless an exception is explicit.

Predicted Future Function

Predictions in medicine, and especially in psychiatry, are difficult to make with any degree of accuracy, and a prediction is difficult to write. A prediction of what the patient will do on discharge from a facility is a working estimate. Members of the treatment team use the estimate to identify expectations for change and make discharge plans. Examples of occupational therapy predictions, with related progress notes, are provided.

Case Example IV: Routine Task Predictions

Data Base

Information gained from interview, 6/12/82; patient chart.

Highest Function

Probably before 1979, when he was employed for 5 years as machinist helper and living alone. Pt had to quit work because of neck spasms and has not

Data base

Highest function

Recent function

Current function

Symptoms of illness

Cognitive level

Awareness of illness

Patient's goals

Predicted future function

OT plan

Occupational therapist

Name

P.F. #

Ward

4

Fig. 4-5. *Routine task predictions.*

Table 4-4. Suggested refinements in Axis V, highest level of adaptive functioning during past year

Level	Criteria	Level	Criteria
1. Superior	Performance consistent with Hollingshead's (1958) social class 1, 2, or 3; no subjective complaints or history of problems in work, social relations, or leisure pursuits	5. Poor	Clear-cut deficit: unable to sustain employment for more than a few weeks; evidence of strain on social support system; leisure pursuits are initiated by others or are solitary (television or reading)
2. Very good	Performance consistent with Hollingshead's (1958) social class 4 to 5; no subjective complaints or history of problems in work, social relations, or leisure pursuits	6. Very poor	No attempt to work or pursue leisure tasks other than watching television and eating meals can be identified; may be living in a group home or on the streets; no contact with social support system or withdrawal from social interactions
3. Good	Subjective complaints of impaired functioning but no objective deficits in employment, social situations, or leisure pursuits	7. Grossly impaired	Largely unable to identify recent events and experiences; personal hygiene and a balanced diet neglected unless others assist
4. Fair	Performance decreased when compared with usual social class expectations; objective deficits in employment, social settings, or leisure pursuits		

Source: Adapted from *DSM III: Diagnostic and Statistical Manual of Mental Disorders* (3rd ed.). Washington, D.C.: American Psychiatric Association, 1980.

worked since, though he has made attempts. He has had several short psychiatric hospitalizations after stressful events ('70 divorce; '73, '80 unemployed).

Recent Function

Pt has lived in downtown hotel since 11/80, supported first by brother, then recently by VA benefits. He has lost 20 pounds in last year, sleeps all day, watches TV all night in the hotel lobby. Became upset before admission because his check was lost in the mail; attacked hotel owner.

Current Function

SYMPTOMS OF ILLNESS. Pt has slowed speech, slow response time to questions; is hypoactive. Affect blunted, sad. Thought content reflects realistic concerns about his medical and social problems.

AWARENESS OF ILLNESS. Pt describes self as unhappy about his disabling neck problem; does not understand what caused his behavior before admission.

COGNITIVE LEVEL. Level 4 on ACL evaluation: Pt able to be goal directed but gives up rather than attempting to solve problems.

PATIENT'S GOALS. Vague and apparently resigned: "Continue on."

Predicted Future Function

Present symptoms and recent lab tests (positive results on dexamethasone suppression test, + DST) are consistent with depression, which seems to be recurrent. When acute symptoms remit pt should be able to return to some form of independent living. His medical problems may prevent employment and limit other leisure pursuits; evaluation of extent of this disability is warranted when acute depression lifts.

OT Plan

Pt agrees to participate in daily 1:00 woodworking group in which response to medication and remission of acute symptoms will be monitored.

Case Example V: Routine Task Predictions Deferred

Data Base

Information taken from interview 6/13/81, patient's chart, and ACL.

Highest Function

Possibly 4 years ago when employed as busboy at a restaurant, though pt cannot remember how long he worked. Chart reports periodic hospitalizations ($\times 9$?) since age 26.

Recent Function

Pt has received Social Security Insurance and has lived in a board-and-care home, a hospital, or on the street for the last 4 years. He moved in with sister 4 days before admission. Daily activities include "walks," eating once or twice a day; pt takes "vitamins" but cannot recall other medications. Recently (3/81) left board-and-care home to live on streets for 6 months.

Current Function

SYMPTOMS OF ILLNESS. Pt displays flat affect, poverty of speech, delusions ("My family are supermen; I'm half a superman"). Differential diagnosis was unclear to this therapist. Symptoms suggest schizophrenic disorder, rule out chronic depression.

AWARENESS OF ILLNESS. Apparently poor. Pt does not know why he is here, nor does he identify what helps him.

COGNITIVE LEVEL. ACL score = level 3. Pt failed to recognize an error and was unconcerned when the error was pointed out.

PATIENT'S GOALS. Quite limited: "Move in with my sister" (feasible?); "get crutches."

Predicted Future Function

Deferred until diagnosis is clarified.

OT Plan

Pt agrees to participate in daily basic crafts group at 2:00.

Functional Observations for

X   Verification of cognitive level
    Titration of medication
X   Clarification of symptoms
    Assessment of potential grave disability

Progress Note on Deferred Predictions

OBSERVATION. Pt has attended basic crafts group $6\times$ for the last 2 weeks. He sits quietly working on his project with intense concentration and seems to be unaware of other people and objects around him. No complaints about a loss of energy have been heard or observed. Within the last 2 days he has noticed the sample of a finished project and begun to ask questions such as "Is this enough?" which indicate an awareness of a goal.

ASSESSMENT. Behavior shows some improvement; level 4. Present symptoms are consistent with the working diagnosis of schizophrenic disorder: poverty of speech, working while sitting in the "eggshell" posture (see Chap. 5, Fig. 5-5 for a description of this common posture associated with a schizophrenic disorder).

RECOMMENDATION. Cognitive level has improved to the point that pt could return to a sheltered community living arrangement with continued financial aid and medical supervision.

PLAN. Will continue to monitor response to medication and remission of symptoms.

Case Example VI: Routine Task Prediction

Data Base

Verbal interview and task evaluation, 11/29/83.

Highest Function

Pt reports that this was probably in 1966 when he was living at home with his mother and not working. He has never had a job that lasted for more than one month and reports that he did poorly in school. Functioning may have always been poor.

Recent Function

Recent history is obscured by an unclear report of his encounters with the legal system and his mother. Says he has been in jail nine times and has had numerous psychiatric hospitalizations; I am unable to determine if any of these events occurred during the last year.

Current Function

SYMPTOMS OF ILLNESS. Pressured speech, rushing through task in a hyperactive fashion. Impression: mania.

AWARENESS OF ILLNESS. Seems to be aware of difficulties in functioning; response is angry and blaming.

COGNITIVE LEVEL. Level 4; performance impaired by lack of attention. Saw some potential for level 6 behavior.

PATIENT'S GOALS. He has a "floating date" when he thinks he will be able to "get the judges," his "mother's Social Security." The relationship between these statements was unclear to this observer.

Predicted Future Function

Long history of poor functioning would seem to indicate that this man has not had a positive response to available medical treatment. The fact that current functioning is not good is a poor prognostic indicator.

OT Plan

Pt has not liked many of his experiences in OT, reports "poor finger dexterity." Refused to attend, and no immediate plans for clinic attendance have been made.

Progress Note

DATA BASE. I have talked to pt on several occasions and offered an opportunity to attend OT; he has refused, saying he prefers recreation therapy (see note dated 12/15 above). Verbal performance on ward seems to be less pressurized and rushed. I asked pt to attend OT so that I could observe for an improvement in motor behavior; he did, making it clear that it was a personal favor to me.

OBSERVATION. Some pressured speech while waiting on elevator to go to the clinic. Speech subsided within a minute or two after he began working. He said that he enjoyed basic crafts but did not want to come again. Performance responded to striking visible cues; less obvious errors were ignored. An error pointed out by the therapist was disregarded.

ASSESSMENT. Pressured speech is diminished, but the cognitive level is unchanged, still level 4. Long history of poor functioning indicates that this man has not had a favorable response to lithium. That the cognitive level has not changed is a poor prognostic indicator (therapeutic blood levels were reached 14 days ago).

PLAN. No immediate plans for clinic attendance. If further improvement is noted I will encourage clinic attendance again.

PROGRESS NOTES

A progress note is a record of ongoing evaluation of a patient's response to treatment. Many formats are followed to write such notes, but the problem-oriented record is a common selection. A central problem list is established, and people in the multidisciplinary team direct their notes to the problems. A distinction is made between an observation and assessment. An observation is what the patient says or does. An assessment is what the therapist thinks the behavior means. The distinction between observation and assessment is frequently blurred with mental disorders because meaning is derived from observations. Some examples are provided.

Progress notes should be related to the reason for admission and the overall institutional objectives. The relationship between a therapist's observations of routine task behavior and medical interventions

should be clearly stated. Implications for discharge planning and long-term treatment objectives should be made as explicit as possible. The information included should be relevant to other members of the treatment team. The multidisciplinary team requires an explicit explanation of why the therapist thinks the information is important.

Case Example VII:

Progress Note

PROBLEM. 2. Bipolar Affective Disorder

OBSERVATION. Patient has been seen in OT five times this week. He continues to show improved concentration on tasks and is able to sit one hour doing written exercises without extraneous verbalizing. He recognizes an error after a mistake is made and can vary his actions in response to the partially hidden properties of objects. He continues to disbelieve that his present medication has produced changes in himself. He perceives the changes but ascribes them to the "changed environment." He therefore is reluctant to continue with medication after discharge. Goals are more realistic (see above nursing note).

ASSESSMENT. Improved in manic symptoms. Level 5. Judgment about need for medication appears poor. While patient can probably perform familiar work, his stability long-term is highly questionable without medication compliance.

PLAN. Continues daily groups. OT continues to encourage medication compliance by pointing out patient's improved performance and explaining the association between medication and behavior.

Case Example VIII:

Progress Note

PROBLEM. 5. Bizarre Behavior

OBSERVATION. Patient attended the OT clinic groups four times this week for familiar sewing and grooming tasks. She was noted to be markedly stiff, with "wooden" expression 6/3. The attending physician was notified, resulting in additional medications ordered. Yesterday she was noted to be less stiff, and her affect was improved; she smiled on approach. In tasks she shows good concentration and some limited exploratory actions with great effort. No actions are taken to avoid problems.

ASSESSMENT. Less stiff. Level 4 with some indication of potential level 5 behavior. Improved from last week. Moderate cognitive impairment persists, but there is evidence of higher ability.

PLAN. Continue to monitor patient in clinic groups.

Case Example IX:

Progress Note

PROBLEM. 2. Bizarre Behavior

OBSERVATION. Patient has attended work evaluation twice and woodworking group once this week. He easily follows verbal, multiple-step directions; there is evidence of planned actions and deductive reasoning. He initiates appropriate social interactions. He is no longer sleepy during the groups but continues to have stiffness in his extremities.

ASSESSMENT. No bizarre behavior during OT groups. Level 6.

PLAN. Continue with woodworking and work groups. Add advanced crafts five times weekly.

Case Example X:

Progress Note

PROBLEM. 3. Depression

OBSERVATION. Patient has been seen three times this week for familiar sewing tasks. Patient no longer initiates these tasks on the ward, though she has the materials to do this. In groups her concentration continues to be episodically poor; she stops working in midstream while she stares and mumbles to herself. She states she is praying. On 6/3, stereotypic, repetitive hand movements were noted for first time; patient also displayed inappropriate smiling.

ASSESSMENT. Continues to show poor concentration, low energy of depression, with some inappropriate affect and gesturing that resemble symptoms of PCP [phencyclidine hydrochloride] toxicity.

PLAN. Continue daily sewing and grooming groups. Observe for changes in symptoms as ECT [electroconvulsive treatment] is started.

CONCLUSION

The relationships between the symptoms of illness and the level of function become more explicit in the reported observations of behavior. The assessments show how the information can be used by therapists and other members of the treatment team.

The written notes make it clear that the therapist expects other members of the treatment team to know something about the cognitive levels. Many of the tables and figures in this text have been used to orient people in other professions: Table 2-1 provides a brief orientation to the cognitive levels, Table 2-2 describes the practical consequences of a cognitive disability, and the illustrations in Chapter 2 show patient appearances that are familiar to many health professionals. Their use in enhancing communication with other members of the multidisciplinary team is recommended.

The written notes also imply that the therapist needs to know how other members of the multidisciplinary team can use our observations and assessments. The next two chapters describe the interrelationships between the cognitive levels and the most frequently seen psychiatric diseases.

REFERENCES

Consolidated Standards for Child, Adolescent and Adult Psychiatric, Alcoholism and Drug Abuse Programs. Chicago: Joint Commission on Accreditation of Hospitals, 1979.

DSM III: *Diagnostic and Statistical Manual of Mental Disorders* (3rd ed.). Washington, D.C.: American Psychiatric Association, 1980.

Goodwin, D. W., and Guze, S. B. *Psychiatric Diagnosis* (2nd ed.). New York: Oxford University Press, 1979.

Heying, L. M. Cognitive disability and the activities of daily living in persons with senile dementia. University of Southern California Master's Thesis, 1983.

Hollingshead, A. B., and Redlich, F. C. *Social Class and Mental Illness.* New York: Wiley, 1958.

Moore, D. S. An occupational therapy evaluation of sensori-motor cognition: Initial reliability, validity and descriptive data for hospitalized schizophrenic adults. University of Southern California Master's Thesis, 1978.

Shapere, D. Notes Toward a Post-positivistic Interpretation of Science. In P. Achinstein and S. F. Barker (eds.), *The Legacy of Logical Positivism: Studies in the Philosophy of Science.* Baltimore: Johns Hopkins University Press, 1969.

Shapere, D. Scientific Theories and Their Domains. In F. Suppe (ed.), *The Structure of Scientific Theories* (rev. ed.). Chicago: University of Illinois Press, 1977.

Strub, R. L., and Black, F. W. *Organic Brain Syndromes: An Introduction to Neurobehavioral Disorders.* Philadelphia: Davis, 1981.

Swonger, A. K., and Constantine, L. L. *Drugs and Therapy: A Handbook of Psychotropic Drugs.* Boston: Little, Brown, 1983.

Uniform terminology for reporting occupational therapy services. Rockville, Md.: American Occupational Therapy Association, 1981.

CHAPTER 5

MAJOR PSYCHIATRIC DISEASES THAT PRODUCE COGNITIVE DISABILITIES

Some of the behavior that therapists observe represents symptoms of various diseases. This chapter and the next will focus on those symptoms that may be observed during the performance of a task. In this chapter relationships between the cognitive levels and symptomatic behavior will be discussed for the primary affective disorders (mania and depression), dementia, and schizophrenic disorders. Other mental disorders may also cause cognitive disabilities; the selection presented in this chapter is related to frequent clinical exposure and the relative degree of clarity or ambiguity in the supporting literature.

A disease produces specific problems in behavior that are helpful in making a differential diagnosis, for example, distinguishing between schizophrenia and depression. The behavior discussed here in association with a particular disease has been selected because it is specific to one diagnostic category and sensitive to a probable behavioral disturbance (Baldessarini et al., 1983; Galen and Gambino, 1975). The identification of a disability rests on the assumption that a biologic abnormality is present. Mental disorders that are supported by sensitive and specific tests, indicating the existence of a biologic defect, make this assumption easier to sustain.

The assessment of a disability also rests on the assumption that the disabled person functions differently from a nondisabled person. The identification of problems in functional behavior goes beyond the selected diagnostic criteria. Descriptions of function reflect the overwhelming number of behavior similarities that are disability specific but not necessarily disease specific. The identification of a disability can be sustained easily at levels 1, 2, and 3, becomes more difficult at level 4, and is questionable at level 5.

Changes in the cognitive levels are observed during the course of acute psychiatric hospitalization. The degree of change is, in many cases, diagnosis specific. This chapter describes the relationships between the diagnosis and the disability with respect to the reason for admission, the observed task behavior, the cognitive level, management precautions, treatment objectives, and rehabilitation.

The impact of the rapid advances in neuroscience knowledge become more explicit within this chapter. Medication effectiveness has done more than shorten the length of hospitalization; it has called our treatment objectives into question. We had thought we produced changes in the patient's task behavior, and now we learn that some changes can be produced by pills in a couple of weeks. The question that creeps into our minds is "What am I doing here?" A famous hypothesis stated by Mary Reilly (1961) presents our former view succinctly: "That man, through the use of his hands as they are energized by mind and will, can influence the state of his own health." During the last 20 years, the meaning of *mind* and *will* has changed. It is now understood that neurobiologic abnormalities influence the mind and will, and there has been an explosion in the physician's knowledge about how to treat these abnormalities. We had sometimes thought we were treating the cause of the disease. That now appears to be erroneous. The neurosciences are wreaking havoc with our definitions of treatment and therefore with our explanations of the value of our services. What is required from our clinical impressions is greater specificity in our clinical descriptions of patient behavior. At present our clinical impressions and hunches are not strong enough to predict future task behavior or prescribe effective rehabilitation programs. We must have clearer descriptions of what we see, and we must show how these descriptions are related to other, well-known descriptions of mental disorders. This chapter aims in that direction, recognizing there is a great deal of work yet to be done.

The following description of psychiatric information assumes the reader has access to introductory texts consistent with the diagnostic criteria contained in *DSM III* (1980). Some readers may need to do some prerequisite reading. It is common to talk to students and therapists who have taken courses in abnormal psychology and psychiatry that

reflected the state of the art as it was in 1960 or 1970. This is hopelessly out of date. Recognizing this difficulty, I have made an effort to identify and use consistent introductory references. An introduction to psychiatry can be found in Goodwin and Guze (1984). An introduction to neuropharmacology can be found in Swonger and Constantine (1983). The *Textbook of Clinical Neuropharmacology* by Klawans and Weiner (1981), written for medical residents, is organized by diagnosis and covers neurologic, psychiatric, and developmental disabilities. Other introductory texts may, of course, be used.

PRIMARY AFFECTIVE DISORDERS

The change in classification criteria (*DSM III*, 1980) has made primary affective disorder an increasingly common diagnosis, perhaps the most common in inpatient psychiatry. The disorder is a disturbance in mood, producing either a major depressive episode or a manic episode. The two types of episode will be discussed separately, with psychiatric information most relevant to therapists being presented.

The classification criteria of *DSM III* essentially accept Kraeplin's (1919) view that functional psychosis can be divided into two disorders: schizophrenia (dementia praecox) and affective illness (manic-depressive insanity). The validity of this division is still being explored, but recent studies are supportive of the division (Boyd and Weissman, 1981; Helzer et al., 1981; Kendler et al., 1981a, b, c). The validity of the division supports the notion that a careful diagnosis is required, and since the criteria changed in 1980 many people all over the world have been reevaluated to see if an alternative diagnosis is indicated. Many physicians prefer to diagnose and treat for affective disorder first because the prognosis is so much better. The prognosis for a schizophrenic disorder is generally poor. Differential diagnosis continues to be a clinical challenge. Some task observations that may aid in diagnosis can be suggested.

Manic Episode

Reason for Admission

Therapists usually see people who are experiencing an acute manic episode when they are admitted to a psychiatric hospital. Their behavior before admission has been disruptive—they may talk incessantly, be in perpetual motion, neglect sleeping and eating, have unrealistic ideas of what they can do while accomplishing virtually nothing, engage in behavior that for them is "oversexed," or spend money in a reckless fashion. A manic episode may be accompanied by a major depression, or it may be isolated to mania; in either case, the diagnosis is bipolar affective disorder. Sometimes the patients recognize their disturbances and seek help. In other cases patients deny the disturbance, and complicated social and legal arrangements precede admission.

The disturbance in mood and motor activity is usually normalized through the administration of lithium salts. The dosage is gradually increased until a therapeutic serum lithium level is reached, usually between 0.9 and 1.4 mEq/L (Goldsmith, 1977; Klawans and Weiner, 1981; Swonger and Constantine, 1983). The development of a tolerance to lithium can be accompanied by a number of annoying side effects. A decrease in energy such as weakness, fatigue, or drowsiness may be experienced. Gastrointestinal side effects may include diarrhea, nausea, vomiting, and abdominal pain. Renal symptoms may include polyuria, dry mouth, and thirst. These side effects are transient and usually go away within a few weeks. Some people, however, complain bitterly about these side effects, and their presence may be a major factor in leaving the hospital against medical advice or in noncompliance with prophylactic treatment (the prevention of recurrent manic episodes). Weight gain, postural or intention hand tremors, and edema are side effects that may occur after drug tolerance has developed (Goldsmith, 1977; Klawans and Weiner, 1981; Swonger and Constantine, 1983).

A few people, even at low serum lithium levels, have a toxic reaction to lithium. Therapists should be alert for behavior that resembles symptoms of an organic brain syndrome: ataxia, memory loss, disorientation, dizziness, increased confusion, or increased lability. One indication of lithium toxicity that is especially noticeable during task behavior is hand tremors. Two kinds of hand tremors are associated with lithium. At therapeutic levels of lithium the therapist may notice a fine postural or intention hand tremor, which is a lithium side effect that does not interfere with task performance. Fine hand tremors in someone who has already developed a tolerance for lithium are not a cause of concern. Gross, bilateral hand tremors, however, may indicate lithium toxicity. As toxicity begins to develop, gross hand tremors appear and become pronounced; they are usually bilateral, and they do interfere with task performance. Ataxia is also apparent and may be observed in the trips to and from the clinic or as the patient gets up out of his or her chair. These symptoms should be reported to the physician immediately as the consequences of lithium toxicity can be severe (Goldsmith, 1977; Klawans and Weiner, 1981; Swonger and Constantine, 1983).

Task Behavior

Task behavior during a manic episode may reflect an inability to inhibit thoughts and behavior. The therapist may observe an elevated or expansive mood when a person makes an inflated assessment of his or her ability to do tasks. Projects done by those in a manic episode may be flamboyant collections of colors, designs, and materials. The elevated mood may result in calling these projects creative works of art. Some such projects are imaginative, while others are of questionable aesthetic value.

An irritable mood may be expressed by a resistance to directions or suggestions about the typical procedure used to complete a task. There may also

Fig. 5-1. Manic episode: distractibility.

be a reluctance to recognize and correct errors. Hyperactivity produces a restlessness that interferes with sitting in a chair while working on a task; manic patients may choose to stand or pace while working. Patients may rush through the steps of the task, producing a speedy but sloppy project. They may express the desire to start a new task while being unable to attend to their current project (Fig. 5-1).

Pressured speech can become a distraction to the patient and to others around him or her. People in a manic episode talk instead of working on a task, and once talking begins they may be unable to stop themselves and must be interrupted. Racing thoughts may accompany hyperactivity and pressured speech, and some of the patients seem to rush to keep up with their thoughts. As the disturbance subsides, the rushing is under better control and may only be elicited by specific topics or tasks.

Cognitive Level

A person in a manic episode seems to be hyperresponsive to the external environment. At admission such a patient may be a hyperactive level 3 and a real management problem, buzzing around the hospital ward or occupational therapy clinic, getting into everything not nailed down or locked up. Highly distractible, they pursue one chance movement after another, and it is very difficult for them to slow down or to sit down. Repetitive actions can be sustained, and gross motor activities such as folding linens may be preferred. If fine motor tasks are used they should be easily portable because people in a manic episode at level 3 have a tendency to carry projects around the room while working on them. If, for example, a person is stringing beads, be sure you have a secure knot at the end so the beads do not drop all over the floor.

The level 4 patient in a manic episode is less distractible and shows an awareness that a project is being produced and that there is a typical procedure to be followed. Voluntary motor actions are usually rushed and may be accompanied by talking, singing, or joking, which results in careless actions of poor quality. Projects of such patients are frequently embellished with some additional decoration not contained in the sample (Fig. 5-2). The therapist's suggestion that these embellishments are undesirable is usually disregarded.

At level 5 patients are able to work on a project for a longer period, but it is difficult for them to pause to think before they act. The action occurs suddenly or impulsively, popping out before the consequences are considered. As a result their projects often contain errors that could have been avoided if they had paused to think. At level 5 people in a manic episode act as if they are in a hurry to finish, and slowing down to do a task carefully is difficult and often impossible. Many people reach level 6 soon after their lithium serum levels reach a

Fig. 5-2. Embellished projects are a common feature of a manic episode.

therapeutic level; their task behavior then reflects their educational and social background. The improvement in the cognitive level often lags behind the lithium serum level. There may be a 2-week gap between a therapeutic blood level and a return to a premorbid level of functioning. If the cognitive level does not improve as the lithium increases, the treating physician should be notified.

Management Precautions and Treatment Objectives

The clinical features of manic episodes suggest that an important consideration for the task environment is a neat and tidy clinic. Extraneous items should be put away, preferably behind locked doors. Assuming that materials and supplies are inaccessible seems to help people in a manic episode control their hyperactivity and distractibility. They will request additional supplies, usually bright and shiny things such as glitter, paint, and makeup, which the therapist can provide. (One begins to wonder if a request for glitter might achieve statistical significance in a correlation with the diagnosis of mania.)

There is a tendency for a tug-of-war to develop between a therapist and a patient experiencing a manic episode. The therapist has one idea about how a project should be done, and the patient has another. Obviously some patient ideas, such as building a yacht or a water bed, are beyond the realm of possibility. These ideas can be managed by showing the patient samples of projects that are possible. The embellishments patients add to their projects can be unduly distressing to the therapist; understanding the reason for our distress helps us to eliminate the potential tug-of-war.

Nothing elicits a therapist's need to be in control of a situation as well as mania. A person buzzing around the clinic, cracking jokes (often obscene), getting into things, and making silly-looking projects can be unduly upsetting to us. Some of our discomfort is valid—manic behavior can be distracting to other patients, and some people assessed at level 3 are impossible to manage in groups. Another part of our discomfort can be traced to our former explanations of psychiatric illness.

Recent medical advances have had an impact on our view of psychiatric disease and, in turn, our own role as therapists. We used to think that patients were unwilling to control their own behavior and that the therapist's role was to encourage internal control by teaching, counseling, or confronting people. In this view the therapist was in some sense responsible for symptomatic behavior, in that pathologic behavior was a reflection on the therapist's methods of producing a change in behavior. We were in a bind because a continuation of pathologic behavior was regarded as evidence of the ineffectiveness of our treatment methods. Silly projects were a reflection on us. The realization that pathologic behavior is caused by chemical imbalances in the brain eliminates this problem. Pathologic behavior is a reflection of brain abnormalities and the physician's ability to normalize brain function. This realization has changed the role of the therapist from controlling to reporting and managing. The therapist observes behavior and objectively reports how the brain pathology is expressed in task behavior; treatment is expectant. Silly projects are a reflection of the illness. The therapist also manages the task environment to minimize the distress of pathologic symptoms. The task environment offers supportive treatment, providing symptom relief until brain pathology can be normalized. The patient's experience while engaged in doing a task should be as pleasant as possible. There is no reason to confront patients or to attempt to force them to conform to the typical procedures for doing a project. Most people will be able to follow a typical procedure soon after their serum lithium level reaches a therapeutic level.

Projects like the one in Fig. 5-2 reflect the symptoms of the illness. Patients may make excuses for their projects, but the therapist recognizes that patients in manic episodes lack the internal control needed to follow the typical procedure. They seem to be overly responsive to novelty (Pribram, 1981). Attempts to force patients to follow the typical procedure often elicit anger or rage. Forcing patients to conform is a confrontation that makes them realize that internal control is deficient. Therapists can avoid causing this distress by allowing these patients to move around the clinic area and to use the supplies they have requested. The therapist does not need to attempt to control the pathologic symptoms unless they are harmful to the patient or other people. Once the lithium takes effect, the production of silly projects ceases.

Hypersexuality, when it occurs, can pose some management concerns for therapists. Steps should be taken to prevent potential problems by being aware of the patient's whereabouts. Placing patients in treatment groups is especially problematic when a person in a manic episode has exaggerated homosexual mannerisms that may be offensive to other people. Obscene jokes can also be offensive to many people. While we do not have to be responsible for silly-looking projects, we do have to be responsible for preventing unwanted pregnancies, fights, and other distressful situations that can be provoked by manic behavior. Therapists frequently treat people in groups of 6 to 10. Limiting the number of people present who are experiencing a manic episode is a common practice. The number varies according to the management problems posed by the individual patients and the experience of the therapist, but two or three people in a manic episode seems to be pushing the limit for groups at cognitive levels 3 and 4.

The euphoria experienced during some manic episodes makes some patients feel terrific. Their behavior may be disorganized and unproductive, but they may be totally unaware that any problems exist. In these cases families and friends may have gone to considerable lengths to get these people into the hospital, and there is real concern about the social consequences of a lack of recognition that a problem exists. Confrontation and forcing recognition, as already discussed, are seldom effective. What seems to help is providing objective data that help the patient make a distinction between an expression of his or her personality and an expression of the manic episode. The manic symptoms generally decrease as the lithium is adjusted. The therapist can point out improvements in behavior that accompany a change in the lithium level. These patients need to see a connection between the medication and their behavior; voluntary motor actions provide a tangible means for making that connection. For example, the therapist might say to a patient, "You are sitting down longer today; the lithium must be effective for you." The discussion should be short, objective, and straightforward, avoiding any connotation of blame, self-righteousness, or guilt. Regular feedback at frequent intervals seems to be effective.

Euphoria accompanied by lithium side effects presents a special management consideration. A poor response to lithium carbonate has been linked to a premature termination of treatment, usually because the patient decides to leave the hospital. Taylor and Abrams's (1981) study of treatment response found no significant predictor of treatment response among family history, personal history, electroencephalogram, an aphasia screening test, or 40 signs and symptoms of depression, mania, and schizophrenia. The factor that was significant in predicting a poor response was premature termina-

tion of treatment. My clinical experience suggests that people in a manic episode start talking about leaving the hospital in conjunction with their complaints about lithium side effects. Therapists should be alert to this problem and reassure patients that the side effects are temporary. Sometimes numerous reassurances from many sources are needed, and even then the information may be disregarded. Mania can be very difficult to treat when people do not believe they have any task deficits, fail to recognize improvements, and are only aware of the medication side effects. Numerous straightforward, honest comments about how their behavior is related to their medication are required if there is to be any hope of preventing premature termination of treatment.

A prevalent complication of affective disorders is self-medication with alcohol or drugs. The therapist may observe symptoms of an organic brain syndrome that are not attributable to lithium toxicity but may be attributable to substance abuse. If a patient does not improve beyond cognitive level 4 or 5, the therapist should begin to watch for a disturbance in memory, which is discussed in relation to dementia. Substance abuse tends to present an ethical dilemma for many health professionals, raising prejudicial attitudes and lowering expectations for treatment effectiveness. Care must be taken to be as fair and objective as possible when a history of self-medication is present.

Major Depressive Episode

Reason for Admission

A discussion of depression is often confusing because one word is used to describe two different types of experience. First there is the experience that everyone has—feeling "down in the dumps" when we get a virus or when life does not seem to be going quite right. That kind of depression is not a reason for admission to a hospital. A major depressive episode, on the other hand, produces experiences that do not make sense, given the person's life situation. The person may lose weight because food is unappealing. He or she may have trouble sleeping, usually with early morning awakening, or the reverse—sleeping most of the day—may occur. Voluntary motor actions may be very slow, so that it takes hours to do what could formerly be done in a few minutes. Sometimes psychomotor agitation makes people so restless and tense that they find it difficult to do anything productive. All of this is accompanied by a profound sadness that the person feels unable to change, which leaves him or her feeling hopeless and often suicidal. A major depressive episode is sometimes referred to as endogenous depression, or nonbipolar affective disorder, or a unipolar affective disorder.

A number of antidepressants have been explored since the 1950s, with more being developed each year (Goldsmith, 1977; Klawans and Weiner, 1981; Swonger and Constantine, 1983). They can be divided into two categories: monoamine oxidase (MAO) inhibitors and the tricyclics. The tricyclics are usually preferred because they seem to be more effective and produce fewer side effects, but knowledge in this area is expanding rapidly; current knowledge can be found in this month's journal articles. Generally a favorable response is first noted in about one week; a lack of response usually produces the decision to try a different medication. At present there is a great deal of trial and error in prescribing antidepressant medications, and the length of hospitalization varies accordingly. Patients and families find it difficult not to know how long a person will be in the hospital and can be reassured by the therapist's recognition of this difficulty. Patients also need to know that many medical researchers think the study of the neurochemistry of the brain is the most exciting and promising area of study in medicine, producing greater treatment specificity and shortening hospital stays. Reassurance is especially important when these people feel hopeless about their condition.

The psychiatric literature reflects the refinements in the physician's ability to treat depression. The dexamethasone suppression test (DST) is being studied carefully to determine its clinical utility in diagnosing depression (Baldessarini et al., 1983; Dewan et al., 1982; Greden et al., 1983; Raskind et al., 1982; Targum et al., 1983). A number of other studies are aimed at refining the subtypes of major depression (Keller et al., 1983; Keller and Shapiro, 1982; Lewis et al., 1983; Nelson et al., 1982; Pattison and Kahan, 1983; Puig-Antich et al., 1983; Schuckit, 1982; Winokur, 1979). These studies are clarifying ambiguous clinical impressions and altering the course of treatment for individual adults and adolescents (Carroll et al., 1981; Crumley et al., 1982; Targum et al., 1982). The current psychiatric literature is loaded with studies that are improving treatment effectiveness. Some physicians think that the treatment of depression is one of the most promising areas of medical practice.

The tricyclic antidepressants, however, have some side effects that patients complain about: constipation, edema, and dry mouth. Postural hypotension is also a problem. Therapists should be careful about this when getting someone out of bed to bring him or her to the clinic—a person with postural hypotension who gets up too fast may get dizzy and fall. This seems to be especially true in the elderly. It is a good idea to stand beside the person so that you can put your arm around his or her waist if the patient feels dizzy. You should also suggest that the person get up slowly.

The MAO inhibitors are accompanied by drug and dietary restrictions (Goldsmith, 1977). A therapist who plans to cook with patients who are taking MAOs must be aware of these restrictions, as well as the physician's recommendations about following them. These lists vary, and some food items seem to be more problematic than others; aged cheeses and liquors seem to produce headaches.

Electroconvulsive treatment (ECT) is actually the treatment of choice for severe depression, but the general public has heard so many wild stories about "shock" treatment that a trial on medication is often initiated before using ECT. Occupational therapy students have also heard the myths and seen the movies; I suggest that students observe

ECT and talk to the treating physician. Of all the medical interventions a therapist can observe in a hospital, ECT is remarkable because it is so undramatic. A person usually receives 6 to 12 treatments over a span of 2 to 4 weeks. During that time the person may have trouble remembering new instructions or may forget the project he or she was working on. The memory problem will probably disappear when the treatments are finished. Short-term, familiar projects are recommended.

Task Behavior

A loss of energy is the most noticeable symptom when people in a depressive episode do a task (Akiskal et al., 1983; Cohen et al., 1982). They take frequent breaks during the process, putting their heads down on the table, yawning, or sighing while working (Fig. 5-3). When asked what the trouble is they usually say they feel tired. The difficulty is not expressed as an inability to do the task but is seen as an inability to sustain their efforts. Psychomotor retardation produces movements that are slow and laborious; they will be the last ones to get their projects done. Transporting these people from their bedrooms to the OT clinic can also be a problem; it seems to take forever because their pace is so slow.

The loss of interest or pleasure can be expressed by no interest in coming to OT and no satisfaction in completing projects that are really quite nice. Sometimes they leave their projects behind because they do not like them. Feelings of worthlessness, self-reproach, or excessive and inappropriate guilt are also observed during task performance (Fawcett et al., 1983; Matussek and Feil, 1983). The therapist may hear statements such as "I'm sorry, I've wasted your supplies" or "Don't waste your time on me, dear. Spend your time on someone who can benefit from your help."

A diminished ability to think or concentrate is also observed. Depressed patients may be unable to organize and sustain their attention. This deficit is usually accompanied by an increase in other depressive symptoms. Indecisiveness is also apparent;

Fig. 5-3. Depressive episode: loss of energy.

if a therapist offers a choice in projects or supplies, some depressed people seem to become immobilized.

A study by Smouse and associates (1981) found high correlations between the following factors that seem to measure the severity of a depression: depressed mood, guilt feelings, suicidal ideation, decreased work and interests, retardation, agitation, psychic anxiety, gastrointestinal symptoms, and somatic symptoms. Many of these symptoms appear during task performance, and their presence should be communicated. Many physicians will heed this communication and make medication adjustments that clear the impairment (Glass et al., 1981).

A distinction between psychomotor agitation and hyperactivity can pose a difficult problem in differential diagnosis. Hyperactivity, as expressed during a manic episode, tends to put people into a consistent and constant pattern of motion; they move about all of the time. The accompanying mood may be euphoric or irritable. Psychomotor agitation, as expressed during a major depressive episode, tends to produce inconsistent restlessness. The person may sit working on a project in a posture that looks tense and then suddenly stand up and start walking. He or she may go get a cup of coffee or go to the bathroom and come back and resume working. This inconsistent restlessness is accompanied by discomfort: "I can't do this any more!" In some cases these behavioral observations are helpful in deciding whether to administer lithium or antidepressant medication.

Cognitive Levels

A few people with severe depression are admitted at level 1; usually they have not eaten for several days. ECT may be initiated as soon as possible to sustain the person's life. At level 2 depression may be accompanied by psychomotor retardation or psychomotor agitation. As noted agitation can be confused with hyperactivity, and the therapist should look for postural tension and sporadic restlessness. At level 3 there is usually a profound loss of energy. People cannot sustain their attention to complete a task they could normally do in 5 to 15 minutes. The patients are often aware that they are not getting the task done and complain about their lack of energy. Motor actions are slow and laborious and usually of poor quality. They may be unable to complete the task or may skip steps in the typical procedure.

At level 4 people can complete a task they would usually do in 5 to 15 minutes but it will take 45 minutes to an hour. They are usually very quiet while working on a project, focusing all of their efforts on the task. Depression is often accompanied by circular ruminations—worrying about the same thing over and over again. Some patients tell me that focusing on a task provides some relief from these ruminations. Any mistake or error, however, throws them right back into their depressive symptoms. At level 5 it still takes too much energy to think about

designing a project or planning one's task behavior. Their task behavior indicates that depressed people at this level select the avenue that takes the least amount of effort. For example, when they encounter an error, they do not give up, as they did at level 4. They try to correct the problem by physically trying solutions. They poke, pull, and fuss with the material objects, but they do not stop and think or try to analyze the situation (Selberman et al., 1983). This picture is disconcerting to someone with a high educational and occupational background because they are accustomed to analyzing tasks and they realize their behavior is not quite right. Pleasure in task performance occurs at level 6, when they are able to plan their projects and create their own designs.

The cognitive level can be deceptive with patients who hide their motor limitations behind good verbal skills; this seems to be especially true of depressed patients with a high educational and/or occupational background. Therapists working in plush, private psychiatric hospitals are especially prone to encountering this problem. To assess the cognitive level, most therapists report that they maintain a pleasant social conversation but focus their observations on motor performance. People who sound like they should be functioning at level 6 are often functioning at levels 4 or 5. Motor performance is slow; they do not get much done during the course of an hour. In addition, they may not invest much energy in their projects. Sometimes there is a prima donna quality, as if motor performance is beneath their vanity, and they may blame OT for their reluctance to perform. Avoiding a defensive posture can be tricky; I recommend an objective appraisal of the cognitive level while ignoring any unpleasant social connotations. Communicating the cognitive level to other members of the multidisciplinary team can also be tricky when the therapist is observing a performance limitation that the other members of the team are not seeing. It takes time, study, and experience to develop enough credibility to convince the team that these limitations are real and important. The greatest credibility seems to be achieved by accurately predicting how the cognitive limitations will affect performance outside of the OT clinic.

Management Precautions and Treatment Objectives

The threat of suicide is the major concern during major depressive episodes, and therapists must be vigilant in controlling sharp objects and toxic substances. Currently available tools are not adequate to predict suicidal behavior in individual cases (Murphy, 1983; Pokorny, 1983). Vigilance begins when ordering supplies by making an effort to select nontoxic materials and eliminating any potential weapon. Every hazard admitted to the clinic area must be counted and kept under lock and key; the fewer the better.

People who are suicide risks are usually treated on the ward to eliminate the risk of transporting them to a clinic area. Treating them on the ward is not easy. First, many of these people complain that they want something to do, and they hate being confined to a hospital ward. Experience has taught us, however, that almost any physical object can be transformed into a dangerous weapon: Ping-Pong balls can be swallowed; pencils and plastic crochet hooks can be broken into sharp points. Institutional policies vary and so do the decisions regarding which projects an individual patient can do on the ward. The therapist should collaborate with other members of the treatment team in deciding which supplies to take on the ward, and no supply should be left with the patient unless other people are aware of its presence. Ward projects require a collaborative relationship with the nursing staff.

Depression interferes with a person's ability to mobilize the energy required to do a routine task. Participation in an occupational therapy program is difficult for these people. Some people at levels 2 and 3 refuse to make the effort, and we can accept their refusal as an indication of the severity of their illness. Others at level 3 attend reluctantly, and the

experience is far from pleasant. We usually encourage them to attend because the change in environment seems to reduce the depressive complaints and early attendance establishes a baseline for the patient so he or she can see improvement. Once some improvement is noted it is possible for the patient to be more optimistic about the future. Therapists can accept the fact that these people really do feel miserable without succumbing to their sense of hopelessness. Conversations that include the phrase "when you get better" seem to reassure those people who are finding it difficult to believe getting better is possible. Supportive treatment can be provided, but it must be realistic.

It is very easy to insult the dignity of a person experiencing a major depressive episode. These people are often aware of the deficiencies in their behavior and are frustrated by their difficulties. Being spoken to as if they were children or being given projects with childish connotations can be upsetting to anyone and is especially upsetting to people who are depressed. Furthermore people who are depressed are suffering, and some of them complain a great deal about that suffering. One can get very tired of listening to the same complaints over and over and over again. There is a tendency to get mad at the patients or to ignore them. One way of coping with the complaining is to reassure them that the complaint is going to get better and then direct their attention to a task. The task helps to pass the time until the mental anguish is reduced by diverting their attention away from the source of pain. The palliative powers of the task are temporary and discomfort will resume again, but the task does seem to help for a short period of time.

Rehabilitation

The majority of the people who experience an acute episode of a primary affective disorder will respond to medication and will resume their lives as they were before the episode. Rehabilitation is unnecessary. The outcome, however, is not so benign for everyone. This discussion will focus on intractable conditions.

Sixty-five to 85 percent of those with mania will respond to preventive lithium treatment (Davis, 1976) if you can convince them to take their medication. Many people prefer not to take medications, and some avoid doing so until they experience recurrent episodes in close proximity. Not taking medication between episodes can be a logical way of managing an episodic disorder for those who are able to recognize their illness and seek help when needed. Those people who feel terrific but exercise poor judgment in their personal affairs are far less fortunate (Connelly et al., 1982). They may ruin their personal finances, strain their marriages to the breaking point, alienate their family and friends, get into trouble with law enforcement agencies, abuse drugs and alcohol, or jeopardize their jobs (Flaherty et al., 1983; Merikangas et al., 1983). Recent changes in American civil commitment proceedings often mean that concerned family, friends, and health care providers can do nothing to alter the self-destructive course of a person who refuses treatment. A history of following an uncharacteristically self-destructive course before seeking, or being forced to obtain, treatment is an indication for preventive treatment to avoid these social complications. Many social complications can be avoided, but a disease that affects the way one feels and thinks is difficult to self-assess. A major factor in predicting rehabilitation requirements is the manic patient's ability to recognize problems and take steps to obtain help. Once the social consequences have developed the patient may need some help in sorting through the current situation, and a prevocational assessment may be indicated.

Recent epidemiologic and outcome studies are confirming the separation of bipolar and nonbipolar affective disorders. A person with a bipolar disorder may have only manic episodes or manic and depressed episodes. A bipolar disorder has a lifetime risk of less than 1 percent with no significant differences found between men and women (Boyd and Weissman, 1981; Winokur and Crowe, 1983). The age of onset may be 10 years younger in bipolar disorders than in nonbipolar disorders, and fewer neurotic personality characteristics have been identified in those with bipolar disorders (Hirschfeld and Cross, 1982). Depression occurs almost twice as often in women (42%) than men (23%) (Winokur and Crowe, 1983). A more favorable outcome occurs when there is a supportive social network, which may include husbands and wives as well as other patients with the same diagnosis who can support compliance with the medication regimen. The value of self-help groups is an area of practice that merits further attention from therapists. Helping people identify behaviors that may be early signs of an episode, suggesting tasks that can be done at home during a minor episode, or suggesting environmental compensation that might prevent social complications may also be valuable to these patients.

Bipolar disorders seem to be homogeneous, but depressive disorders seem to have several subclassifications. People who have nonpsychotic depression tend to respond to antidepressant medications and avoid social complications; later episodes, if they occur, are nonpsychotic (Brockington et al., 1982). Rehabilitation will probably not be required for nonpsychotic depression. Two types of psychotic depression are identified in *DSM III* (1980): mood-congruent and mood-incongruent psychotic depression. People with mood-incongruent psychotic depression tend to have schizophrenic symptoms in subsequent episodes (the diagnosis may be changed to schizophrenic disorder). Mood-incongruent psychotic depression may have a benign course that does not resemble schizophrenic or bipolar disorders in severity (Brockington et al., 1982). Mood-congruent, or delusional, depression may not respond well to the currently favored medications, the tricyclics, but there is a better response to ECT (Brockington et al., 1982; Glassman and Roose, 1981). Some people seem to have chronic depression that may be associated with a residual cognitive disability. How this fits in with these subclassifications is unclear (Keller and Shapiro, 1982).

Chronic depression with residual disabilities may necessitate some sort of long-term support. The type of support required is unclear, but some coping behaviors have been suggested by Barraclough and Brown (1982). Clinically I have been struck by the observation that a number of people with chronic depression also have a *DSM III* (1980) Axis II diagnosis (a histrionic, narcissistic, borderline, dependent, compulsive, or passive-aggressive personality disorder). The dual diagnosis may be further compounded by a history of severe suicide attempts. If these clinical observations are correct, the prevention of suicide through the establishment of realistic psychological or environmental compensations could be very difficult. Outpatient, psychosocial rehabilitation might be possible, but I certainly agree with the minimum standards for its staff members suggested by the American Association of Partial Hospitalization: Therapists should have a minimum of 2 years' experience working in an acute, inpatient hospital before attempting to work in psychosocial rehabilitation (Casarino et al., 1982). Some psychosocial rehabilitation agencies have had a tendency to hire inexperienced staff members with their hearts set on grandiose objectives. Very few therapists in the United States are working in the community mental health system, and care for the chronically mentally ill is badly neglected (Sharfstein, 1982). We lack experienced therapists who know what they are doing in this area. The British have also attempted to care for the chronically mentally ill in the community, with seemingly less neglect than in the American system. The British system, however, also seems to have a tendency to underestimate the difficulties of providing a realistic and positive outcome in psychosocial rehabilitation (Shepherd, 1982). These problems are not limited to chronic depression, but history of suicide attempts complicated by personality disorders makes them more critical. The best way to approach this difficult area of practice may be to establish short-term objectives with readily apparent measures of success. Diagnosis specificity is badly neglected in the community-based programs, which makes it very difficult to evaluate program effectiveness.

Depression has always been a concern in patients with physical disabilities. Two studies that have taken advantage of the new classification criteria are of interest. Thirty spinal cord injury patients were evaluated for a possible psychiatric diagnosis before the injury and after the injury. Before the injury four had a history of alcohol abuse, two had hypomania, and one had endogenous depression. After the injury there were eight new psychiatric diagnoses: three endogenous depressions, four minor depressions, and one case of delirium. The new diagnoses appeared in about 3 weeks, and seven of the eight cases cleared without medication. Medication was tried with all three endogenous depressions but was discontinued for two people because of medication side effects (Fullerton et al., 1981). The prior psychiatric diagnosis is interesting because it may have an effect on the individual's rehabilitation potential. This is an idea often talked about in physical rehabilitation centers that might profit from further study. The finding that the depression cleared without medication is also interesting. It can be hoped the distinction between endogenous depression and minor depression will be helpful in distinguishing a reaction to injury from a neurochemical abnormality. Therapists should note that 7 new cases of depression were reported in a sample of 30. It seems not everyone reacts to a spinal cord injury by becoming diagnosably depressed. One important aspect of this study is that it seems to indicate we are making progress in writing classification criteria that are helpful in distinguishing despondency, or situational depression, from a mood disorder that reflects a biochemical abnormality.

An accurate diagnosis of major depressive episode in people who have brain damage is difficult because the symptoms can be easily confused with situational adjustment reactions, agitation, or a symptom of the neuroanatomic lesion. Five cases whose course of rehabilitation was improved by administering antidepressant medications are reported by Ross and Rush (1981). They suggest some patterns of behavior that may be helpful to therapists in recognizing a biologic depression in people with brain damage: a lack of cooperation in a rehabilitation program; poor, erratic, or unusual recovery from injury; a worsening of neurologic deficits after some recovery; and vegetative signs. In addition lesions to the right inferior frontal lobe with depression produced pathologic laughing and crying. Ross and Rush (1981) describe these behavioral patterns as "clues" because it will require an experienced therapist to interpret them accurately. Since three of these cases had a positive response to the DST and all showed a clinical improvement when treated, these clues merit further consideration.

DEMENTIA

Reason for Admission

Dementia is a chronic organic brain syndrome (OBS) that impairs memory, orientation, and intellectual functioning (Goodwin and Guze, 1979). People may be brought to the hospital because their routine task behavior has deteriorated so much that they are a hazard to themselves or others. They may get lost, start a fire, or neglect personal or household cleanliness to the point of jeopardizing their health. Admission to a psychiatric hospital usually indicates there is some suspicion of dementia with depression. This combination poses some of our most puzzling problems in differential diagnosis. Dementia is more frequent in the elderly, as are many other medical diagnoses. Several physical health problems can, and frequently do, explain some of the difficulties elderly people have in routine task behavior. This discussion focuses on the mental problems that can obscure the management of dementia.

A great deal of effort has gone into attempts to equate organic disease with cognitive impairments. The other simple equation is between affect and functional disease. Neither equation works very well (Wells, 1982). The functional-organic split led to the thought that there were separate forms of dementia: organic dementia and pseudodementia. Organic dementia was diagnosed in the presence of cognitive loss, often measured by neuropsychological tests. Clinicians began to notice that the cognitive impairment was reduced by treating a demented patient for biologic depression, and the separation between dementia and pseudodementia became less and less distinct. More recently it has been suggested that dementia and depression coexist in approximately 25 percent of outpatients with dementia (Reifler et al., 1982; Maletta et al., 1982). The clinical importance of this coexistence is that although organic dementia may not be treatable, depression is. The present concern is that we lack clinical signs and symptoms that would mark the presence of a treatable condition. Ambiguous diagnostic criteria are especially worrisome in severe cases in which the cognitive impairment can obscure the depression and lead to a misdiagnosis of "far-advanced Alzheimer's disease" (McAllister and Price, 1982). The clinical result of this distinction is that someone who is treated may return home at cognitive level 4, as opposed to being untreated and sent to a skilled nursing facility at cognitive level 1 or 2. It seems reasonable to advocate a clinical trial of treatment for depression before accepting a diagnosis of a purely organic condition (McAllister and Price, 1982). Identification of coexisting biologic deficits is unclear (dementia may be neuroanatomical; depression may be neurochemical). For example, one computed tomography (CT) study found a decrease in the density of brain tissue in the frontal and temporal lobes of people with senile dementia that could be related to a change in tissue structure or chemical composition (Bondareff et al., 1981). The coexistence of dementia and depression would predict both abnormalities—changes in the neuroanatomy and the neurochemistry. The neurochemical deficit can be treated; ECT may be the treatment of choice because the tricyclic antidepressants may produce delirium in the elderly (McAllister and Price, 1982).

The most common form of dementia is primary degenerative dementia. Other forms include multi-infarct and dementia with alcoholism or other neurologic disorders. A number of assessment tools are available; these generally reflect the difficulties encountered in making a diagnosis when the impairment is mild (Drachman et al., 1982; Gurland, 1980; Katzman et al., 1983). The deficits that most commonly lead to institutionalization have been given an acronym by Drachman and colleagues (1982): SWID—sleep disorder, wandering, incontinence, and danger to self or others. A correctable cause of these problems may be found during acute hospitalization. Selecting the best disposition plan is a common consideration. The patient's ability to perform his or her activities of daily living is a major concern (Weintraub et al., 1982; Wilson et al., 1973).

Task Behavior

Some task behavior of patients with dementia resembles that seen in depression, but some difficulties specific to dementia can be identified. Disorientation to time, place, or person is often described as characteristic of OBS, but it may not discriminate between dementia and depression. Some people cannot recall the month or the year, while others retain this information but do not know the day of the week. Disorientation may be observed when patients are unable to learn their OT schedule. They may not realize they are in a hospital or may develop delusions about why they are there and try to escape. Precautions need to be taken with people who are trying to escape if transportation to the OT clinic area is required. Many people get lost in the hospital; they don't know which way to turn to get to their bedrooms, the bathroom, or the OT clinic. All of the new faces confuse them, and they may not learn your name but may come to associate your face with OT.

Memory problems are often regarded as diagnostic of organic disorders. Patients may not recall the project they worked on the day before or the one completed an hour ago. Instructions they followed successfully on one day may be forgotten the next day. Memory of their past experiences is often intact, but they may forget recent task behavior that the therapist has observed.

Cognitive Level

Patients with dementia may be admitted at cognitive level 1, reluctant to eat and having bowel or bladder accidents. At level 2 they may pace around the ward, posing a real elopement risk, but they seldom get very far because they get lost. Their speech may be incoherent, and they may refuse to cooperate with any suggestion. At level 3 they may be more responsive to the therapist's approach and willing to engage in familiar tasks. They are generally most successful at routine tasks they have been doing all of their lives, and therapists can draw on the intact memory of their past experiences to identify these activities. People functioning at level 3 may forget they are working to complete a task and stop in the middle. At level 4 they finish the task as long as the steps are familiar to them, but new learning and adjusting to novel situations is impaired. It has been my clinical experience that if a person begins to function at cognitive level 5 the final diagnosis is depression and the diagnosis of dementia is dropped (see Reisberg et al., 1982; Rosen and Mohs, 1982; Weingartner et al., 1982).

Management Precautions

Most people with a diagnosis of dementia are elderly and are hyperresponsive to medication. Therapists should be alert for medication side effects that the patient may notice during task performance but forget to report to the nurse or physician. Patients may also forget they have other somatic problems

Fig. 5-4. Dementia: confabulation. A patient may not remember a step and seek direction by watching another patient. Errors in following directions, such as pasting the picture upside down, may be observed.

they experience during task performance; again the therapist should report these difficulties. The therapist can also collaborate with nursing in stimulating attention to grooming and personal hygiene. Some self-care tasks can be attended to by nursing personnel on the ward, while other supplies are easier to manage in the OT clinic.

Memory is an elusive term. The operational definition of memory in psychological tests (Maloney and Ward, 1976) is different from the definition in *DSM III*, which is also different from our observations of task behavior. Memory seems to mean something different to everybody and is an area that obviously needs more study. Recently a neuropsychologist has suggested that memory problems are secondary to an attentional dysfunction involving arousal, mental processing speed, spontaneous elaboration, and analysis of detail (Albert, 1981). This becomes very confusing when we consider the

notion that the cognitive levels probably measure an attentional dysfunction. The distinction between dementia and other diagnostic categories seems to be that people with dementia seem to have trouble remembering common, simple bits of information—for example, a retired business executive assessed at level 4 who could not place sponges in groups of five. He repeatedly asked, "Now how many was that?" He could not remember *groups of five*, which is a small amount of new information that most people have frequently encountered. The task behavior of those with dementia is characterized by difficulty in remembering common, simple directions.

Memory is very difficult to assess in a natural environment when it is confounded by confabulation. *Confabulation*, as used here, is not limited to verbal behavior but is extended to voluntary motor actions. People with organic deficits use imitation to compensate for their deficits (Fig. 5-4). If they are disoriented to space they follow the lead of other people and may or may not find themselves in the right place. If they cannot remember what to do next they imitate the person next to them. Imitation can be an effective compensation, and successful task behavior is not necessarily an indication that no deficit is present. Therapists should be alert for a puzzled look on their faces and take note of the environmental cues that may be guiding their behavior.

Violence is a surprising consideration with OBS. Craig (1982) reports in a study of violence among psychiatric patients that 10 percent of people who were admitted to a psychiatric hospital had been assaultive before admission. Assaultiveness was associated with anger and agitation and linked to the diagnoses of OBS and schizophrenic disorders. Assaultiveness was not prevalent during manic or depressive episodes. Craig's results correspond with the clinical impression that elderly people who appear fragile can be amazingly forceful in attempts to leave a locked psychiatric unit.

Treatment Objectives

The treatment objectives pursued during hospitalization for dementia may be the same as the objectives for depression because depression is the illness being treated. Expectant treatment with dementia will differ, of course, because the cognitive level is not expected to go beyond level 4.

Many dementia patients prefer to work in groups with other elderly patients who also have dementia or depression or both. People in a manic episode may frighten them, and they are at the mercy of people with a personality disorder. Many elderly people enjoy reminiscing together, and this seems to help them preserve their dignity.

Reality orientation is a treatment method that is often associated with this population, but one critical appraisal of the literature indicates there is reason to doubt its effectiveness (Powell-Proctor and Miller, 1982). Reality orientation has a mechanical quality in that one continuously repeats orienting statements such as names, dates, and day of the week. Some improvement in these specific behaviors has been noted in patients treated this way, but it is doubtful that the improvement generalizes to other forms of behavior. In fact more improvement in a wider range of behavior was produced by a British occupational therapy program than by reality orientation (Powell-Proctor and Miller, 1982).

Zarit (1980), a gerontologist, has noted that "the aged typically perform better on simpler or familiar types of tasks than on tests involving novel responses, unfamiliar activities, or increasing levels of complexity." Thus the elderly seem to prefer environmental compensations over psychological compensations. For people who have deficits, Albert (1981) suggests the use of real objects and the provision of structure by limiting choices and redirecting attention. Albert essentially recognizes limitations and suggests environmental compensations for the deficits.

Adult day care may provide a welcome relief for families of people with dementia. A few hours of freedom from the burden of caring for these people may facilitate a continued placement in the home (Sands and Suzuki, 1983).

The literature seems to support the provision of environmental compensations. Whether or not the long-term provision of environmental compensations will produce any biologic compensations is unknown. One study seems to cast some doubt on biologic compensations for dementia. The question is related to brain plasticity and the physical mechanisms that produce plasticity. Neuroanatomically this might be observed through the growth of long dendrite trees (Bach-y-Rita, 1980, 1981). Large dendrite trees have been found in normal adults and the aged, but they have not been found in those with senile dementia (Buell and Coleman, 1981). Rehabilitation of central nervous system deficits has had a tendency to equate restoration of function with reorganization of function in the form of dendrite growth and environmental compensation. There are three separate explanations for a recovery of function—biologic, psychological, and environmental (Satz and Fletcher, 1981). Refined program planning would benefit from clearer distinctions among these alternative explanations. The objective that can be achieved with the greatest degree of certainty is environmental compensation.

Potential Rehabilitation Issues

The course of many of the dementias is variable, and the factors that influence it are unknown (Schneck et al., 1982). Psychiatric hospitalization may occur when a person can no longer live safely in the community, and alternative living arrangements are frequently considered. This may mean placement in a nursing home, which is justifiable at cognitive levels 1, 2, and 3. A number of legal issues may arise because very few people want to go to a nursing home. Increasingly therapists are faced with the unpleasant task of documenting that persons cannot safely perform their routine tasks. Better assessments of cognitive level 4 are badly needed; especially important is a consideration of the required social network (Greenblatt et al., 1982). Dementia poses all the legal problems surrounding residual cognitive disabilities. It is my clinical impression that people assessed at cognitive level 4 are gravely disabled and a potential danger to themselves or others. These dangers can be avoided if a nondisabled person is present to supervise routine tasks. Perhaps the biggest concern is that these people frequently forget to turn off gas or electric stoves and fail to take precautions when pouring boiling water. People living alone seem to have some common problems: forgetting to pay bills and so being evicted from their apartments or having telephone, gas, and electric services discontinued; neglecting housecleaning and living in squalor; neglecting bathing and acquiring lice; neglecting nutrition. We are often required to predict whether these problems are apt to occur in individual cases; the accuracy of our predictions is unknown.

Social services have the ominous task of placing these people in the community. Therapists can collaborate in identifying the least restrictive environment available. At present there are not many good activity programs for people with dementia. We must be highly selective in utilizing the limited community resources (Mace and Rabins, 1981; Sands and Suzuki, 1983).

SCHIZOPHRENIC DISORDERS

The classification criteria for the schizophrenic disorders have posed problems throughout this century. *DSM II* (1968) subdivided schizophrenia into different types of reactions: simple, hebephrenic, catatonic, paranoid, acute, latent, residual, schizoaffective, childhood, chronic undifferentiated, and others. These subdivisions did not work very well, and people in the neurosciences were frustrated. The subclassifications could vary from one hospitalization to the next, and research populations could easily be contaminated by the inclusion of subjects who would be more properly diagnosed with a primary affective disorder. Recently, attention has turned to attempting to use the CT scan to help clarify this baffling disorder.

A number of controlled and replicated studies have shown abnormally large ventricular sizes in a subset of people with schizophrenic disorders (Andreasen et al., 1982b; Golden et al., 1979; Johnstone et al., 1976; Weinberger et al., 1979). Enlarged ventricular size has been reported in a number of mental disorders and is not diagnostic of schizophrenia (Rieder et al., 1983). Of interest to us is that enlarged ventricular size has been associated with cognitive impairments in schizophrenic disorders (Andreasen et al., 1982a; Johnstone et al., 1978; Weinberger et al., 1980a, b). These findings led Crow (1978) to suggest that schizophrenia can be divided into at least two types, a division that has received some empirical support from the Andreasen group (1982a). These types will be used in the following discussion of schizophrenia.

The two types of schizophrenia suggested by the literature are a type that seems to have a neuroanatomic defect and a type that seems to have a neurochemical defect. The neuroanatomic group has ventricular enlargements associated with impaired cognitive functioning on neuropsychological tests, poor premorbid social adjustment, and a poor response to neuroleptic (antipsychotic) medications (Golden et al., 1979; Johnstone et al., 1976; Rieder et al., 1979; Weinberger et al., 1980a, b). A marked poverty of speech, loss of drive (involuntary), and a loss of the ability to experience pleasure (anhedonia) are the symptoms characteristic of this type of schizophrenia. The prognosis may be poor because these people have an intellectual impairment and they do not respond to neuroleptic medications (Andreasen et al., 1982a).

The neurochemical group is thought to have a dopaminergic disturbance that responds to neuroleptic medication (Crow, 1978; Sternberg, et al., 1983; Weinberger et al., 1980b). The disturbance is not associated with intellectual impairment but is associated with delusions, hallucinations, and bizarre behavior (Andreasen et al., 1982a; Crow, 1978). The absence of intellectual impairment, plus the positive response to neuroleptics, predicts a more favorable outcome. The finding that people with the neuroanatomic deficit are usually older than those with the neurochemical defect has led to speculation about the influence of aging in this disorder, and slow-acting viruses, such as herpes, are being explored as a potential cause of the disorder (Crow, 1978; Harrow et al., 1983; Kety, 1981). Neuroscience research is being directed toward identifying defective neurochemical pathways with the hope that medications can be further developed to normalize these pathways and alter the schizophrenic state.

This description of schizophrenia is somewhat misleading in that it is a simple explanation of a befuddling subject (Ariel et al., 1983; Fogelson et al., 1982; Morihisa et al., 1983; Morstyn et al., 1983; Rieder et al., 1983; Travin and Protter, 1982; Tune et al., 1982). People in the neurosciences are always coming up with new explanations for the cause and cure of this disorder; there must be hundreds of them in the literature of this century. Everything imaginable seems to have been done to these peo-

ple. The various treatment methods studied have had little success in that there are many people who remain gravely disabled by the disorder (May et al., 1981).

Reason for Admission

Delusions, hallucinations, bizarre behavior, and social withdrawal are the symptoms that lead to seeking help. The symptoms may be disturbing to the patient, but sometimes it is other people in the patient's environment who are disturbed by the symptoms. Patients may actively respond to delusions and hallucinations and pose a danger to themselves or others. Neuroleptic medications are usually prescribed. Therapists should note that these medications reduce the seizure threshold.

Hospitalization may begin by casting a shadow of doubt over a former diagnosis of schizophrenia. The *DSM III* (1980) criteria are restrictive in that they require 6 months of illness before the diagnosis can be made. Furthermore the criteria seem to contain a high degree of predictive specificity in that the schizophrenic symptoms and disabilities are apt to persist (Helzer et al., 1981). Conservative treatment may consist of avoiding this diagnosis until after the treatment of disorders with a more favorable outcome has been explored. Frequently people are treated for a primary affective disorder first, and if that fails the diagnosis of a schizophrenic disorder is considered.

Identifying the biologic deficit or deficits associated with schizophrenia fascinates many researchers, and one cannot help but think clinical practice would be much easier if the deficit were clearer. No attempt to review these ambiguities in the literature will be made here, but recent studies may be found in the Additional Readings. Some discussion of the reasons for the difficulties in this area may be helpful.

The diagnostic criteria for schizophrenic disorders are heavily dependent on verbal behavior. Delusions and hallucinations must be verbally reported, but many patients refuse to talk about these symptoms. The diagnostic difficulty is to distinguish between primary affective disorders and a schizophrenic disorder. What, for example, is the difference between a marked poverty of speech (schizophrenia) and a loss of energy (depression); it can be argued that the person is too depressed to talk. Another distinction that often seems to be impossible to make is between a loosening of associations (schizophrenia) and a flight of ideas (mania). Discriminating between the thought disorder of schizophrenia and the psychosis of primary affective disorder is ambiguous as well. In clinical practice these problems can be observed during team meetings when an individual patient's diagnosis is debated. In research sample selection criteria and interrater reliability of the diagnosis are problematic. The recent development of laboratory tests is helpful, but it must be remembered that these tests are not the final answer; accuracy is not 100 percent. There is, in fact, an ongoing debate about the relative accuracy of all of these tests. Therefore a laboratory report does not exclude or verify the diagnosis and clinical judgment in establishing the diagnosis is required (Carroll et al., 1981). The same thing is true of CT scans, which can produce false negatives. Recently a laboratory test, the protirelin test, that may help distinguish mania from schizophrenia has been suggested (Extein et al., 1982). Currently it is difficult to diagnose a schizophrenic disorder. Therapists can use their observations of voluntary motor actions to help with this problem.

Task Behavior

Motor Performance

The attention deficit observed in schizophrenic disorders seems to differ from the difficulties observed in other mental disorders. In schizophrenia attention is riveted to voluntary motor actions. Motor actions may be slow, but a great deal of effort seems to be expended in guiding the actions. External stimuli seem to be blocked from awareness, and the patients' posture seems to reflect this limited aware-

Fig. 5-5. *Schizophrenic disorder: the eggshell posture.*

ness of the task environment (Fig. 5-5). The typical posture is called the eggshell posture, because the patients seem to build a shell around themselves, intensely attending to their actions on the physical objects within this space while blocking out other stimuli.

There is some support for an attention deficit in schizophrenia that extends beyond motor slowness (Zahn et al., 1981). This may be related to difficulties in monitoring motor behavior through the use of self-generated cues (Malenka et al., 1982). Slow information processing has been found in schizophrenic subjects but not in manic control subjects (Saccuzzo and Braff, 1981). The deficit may be related to low metabolic activity in the superior frontal-premotor cortex (Buchsbaum et al., 1982). These deficits in attention as observed during the performance of voluntary motor actions are gaining credibility in the literature, but they are not yet a part of the diagnostic criteria. Other symptoms that interfere with task behavior must also be considered.

Verbal Performance

Delusions may produce a response to the task environment that is highly emotional and subjective. Therapists should be alert to observations of idiosyncratic responses. The reasons for the response can be elicited by asking an open-ended question such as, "Why did you do that?" Hallucinations are often auditory, and some people say the voices go away when they focus their attention on a task. Other people say the voices interrupt them, drawing attention away from the task. Some patients deny the presence of hallucinations; professionals can only infer their presence from observations of behavior. Giggling, talking, or gesturing in a manner out of context with the task environment may be an indication that hallucinations are occurring. During task behavior a cessation in task behavior accompanied by eye movements or rapid blinking may be an indication that hallucinations are occurring.

A marked poverty of speech is seen. People with schizophrenic disorders are unusually quiet while working in a group situation. Efforts made by others to begin a social conversation are barely acknowledged, often with a one-word answer to a question. The patient usually complies with the therapist's directions but does not request supplies, projects, or assistance when needed. A poverty of speech is often accompanied by a poverty of response to the task environment.

Movement Disorders

Therapists may observe a number of abnormal movements during task performance, and putting a label on these movements is tricky. A common explanation for these movements in psychiatric patients is tardive dyskinesia: spontaneous abnormal movements about the face and neck that may be accentuated by high dosages of high-potency neuroleptics (Mukherjee et al., 1982). These movements can be confused with symptoms of other disorders, however. An excellent differential and definition of terms is provided by Granacher (1981). A review by Kane and Smith (1982) found relatively few studies to support the common assumption that neuroleptics increase the risk of tardive dyskinesia. One study, by Owens and associates (1982), seriously challenges this assumption. The study compared 47 chronic schizophrenics who had never received neuroleptics with 411 who had, and no differences were found. Both groups had a number of movement disorders; most occurred around the face but all regions of the body were affected. This study suggests that tardive dyskinesia may be partly explained by age and perhaps the length of illness. The best way to learn to recognize movement disorders is through clinical experience combined with frequent reference to a definition of terms (Granacher, 1981).

Cognitive Levels

All of the cognitive levels have been observed in people with a diagnosis of schizophrenic disorder. Level 1 may be assessed when people are in a catatonic stupor, a symptom that is rarely seen. At level 2 a person may be engaged in odd postures, often repeated and accompanied by no emotional expression. I have also seen people consciously guide their movements by talking to themselves: "Move," "Turn," "Sit down." Their movements may have a wooden, robotlike quality to them that is often considered to be, but is not always, a side effect of medication. Akathisia, expressed as discomfort relieved by moving, is a neuroleptic side effect; the person may pace, wiggle the feet and legs, or suddenly get out of his or her chair (Klawans and Weiner, 1981).

The eggshell posture is observed at levels 3 and 4. At level 3 patients' awareness is limited to the immediate action they are performing, and they do not seem to be aware of the fact that there is an end product. I have heard patients express surprise that they have made something: "Oh, it's a pot holder!" At level 4 they are aware of the end product and realize their actions are directed toward making something that looks like the sample. Hallucinations may interrupt task performance. The therapist can redirect attention by pointing to the action at level 3 and the end product at level 4. Social conversation is virtually nonexistent at level 3 but does occur at level 4 in a stereotyped, artificial fashion. Their conversation lacks emotional tone. The words may be right, but their meaning is unclear: The sentence "I like that project" can have a variety of meanings, depending on voice inflections. When it is said without inflection, the therapist may wonder what the patient means.

It is my clinical impression that I know some people with a schizophrenic disorder who have been functioning at a level 4 for a number of years. On admission they test at level 4, and no change in cognitive level is observed during hospitalization. Their symptoms resemble those associated with ventricular enlargement. I have not noticed further deteriorization to level 3. Level 4 may reflect the disabling effect of this type of schizophrenia. Community placement poses problems similar to those described above for dementia.

Levels 5 and 6 with a schizophrenic disorder are somewhat unclear. First of all, these levels may be confounded by education and occupation; beginning efforts to sort through these confounding factors are discussed in Chapters 14, 15, and 16. The second problem is posed by differential diagnosis; we must decide whether we are looking at an affective disorder, rather than a schizophrenic disorder. It may be that these levels are achieved by people who have a neurochemical defect that responds to neuroleptics. Clinically I have observed a favorable response when neuroleptics are combined with treatment methods designed for primary affective disorders. This area seems to be in a state of flux right now, with more questions than answers.

The symptoms of schizophrenia may be reduced at levels 5 and 6, and the person may appear eccentric but not bizarre. Task behavior adheres to the typical procedure in a constricted fashion. At level 5 patients can learn new schemes and seem to enjoy new procedures, but they do not fool around with the materials in a spontaneous effort to create or invent new schemes. They may be eager to do a good job, and the process has a serious emotional tone. A compliment from the therapist produces satisfaction, but they seem to have a limited sense of self-satisfaction. At level 6 there does not seem to be any intellectual impairment, but task behavior may still lack spontaneity and pleasure. These qualities are difficult to describe and even harder to measure. We have a sense that something is not working quite right but are not sure what it is. It does not seem to be a problem in learning new directions or in remembering them. Rather, it seems to be a problem in using the information in a flexible fashion. These people rely on the therapist to set priorities in information for them; this clinical observation is one of the reasons Williams decided to study classification (see Chaps. 13 and 14).

Management Precautions

A therapist who is treating the mental disorders that have been described to this point may require a large number of tasks for the lower cognitive levels. Some tasks work better than others, and it is difficult to keep coming up with new ideas. If we don't come up with any new ideas, we get bored and so do the patients. We need to be careful, however, about some of our brainstorms. It is very easy to design a task that will humiliate a person at the lower cognitive levels. No one wants to do this, but sooner or later we all do. The patient's dignity can be spared if we are open and honest about this: "I'm sorry, that's not a good project." Special precautions need to be taken with people with schizophrenic disorders because these people are compliant and will attempt to struggle through a task that is really a frustrating failure. The therapist should ask patients if they would like to stop working on such projects.

The usual problem with our worst projects is that they do not match the patient's cognitive level. A step in the procedure that is too hard for them will increase the expression of their symptoms. Symptoms are an unpleasant experience and, as a general rule, are to be avoided as much as possible. Delusions and hallucinations are stimulated, at times, by emotionally laden symbols. The meaning varies from individual to individual, but a therapist should be aware of patriotic and religious symbols that frequently take on bizarre meanings. Their use may be warranted in cases in which delusions or hallucinations are suspected but are denied by the patient, or when these symbols are reassuring to an individual patient. No general rule for the use of symbols is advocated; it varies with the individual case.

Potential Rehabilitation Issues

Those people who have stabilized at cognitive level 4 pose real problems when it comes to placement in the community. Generally they require a sheltered living situation, such as a personal care home, and professionally planned programs, very few of which exist. Gradually studies are beginning to describe the seriousness of this disability. Young adult men with schizophrenia have a mortality rate significantly higher than the norm (Haughland et al., 1983). Patients who refuse neuroleptic treatment are usually more disorganized than those who comply, and the refusers do not think that they are disabled (Marder et al., 1983). Institutionalized chronic psychiatric patients scored lower than mentally retarded patients on an adaptive behavior scale developed for use with the retarded (Sylph et al., 1977).

Chronic mental patients, in one study, did *not* report an improvement in their life satisfaction when provided with more autonomy in menu planning and cooking and structured activities during the day. They reported dissatisfaction with their social isolation (25% had not seen a single family member during the last year) and their lack of employment (Lehman et al., 1982). Currently, very few psycho-

social rehabilitation programs are designed to respond to the findings of this study.

Those people who stabilize at cognitive level 5 and 6 require an environment that can tolerate their eccentricities. Many families provide a supportive environment for these people, often without much appreciation from those of us in the medical community. We spent many years thinking the cause of the disorder was poor child rearing, for which we blamed the family; now we need to think about how to help the family.

Treatment Objectives

Program objectives for people with a schizophrenic disorder have undergone considerable change during the last two decades. Some controversy still exists, but this is abating as it becomes clearer that there are biologic defects associated with the disorder. Acute hospitalization is aimed at reducing symptoms. Therapists can observe and report a reduction in the degree to which symptoms interfere with task behavior. Those whose cognitive level remains at level 4 throughout the course of hospitalization seem to enjoy tasks that match their cognitive level; treatment is palliative. Those who are experiencing a change in their cognitive level should be observed for these changes. A step in a typical procedure that is slightly higher than their assessed level of ability can be demonstrated to see if a positive change is occurring; treatment is expectant. Many people with a schizophrenic disorder think their OT experience is supportive: It gives them something to do, gets them off of the ward, gives them a chance to work with their hands, or refreshes their memory of things they learned in school.

Long-term program objectives that would reduce the residual disabilities of a poor-prognosis schizophrenic disorder are largely unknown. Recently therapists have been interested in applying the sensory integrative techniques developed by Ayres (1972) to this disorder. A number of sophisticated and subtle confounding factors are being encountered. Biologic compensations for defects in the brain are hard enough to deal with when the location of the deficit is known. Schizophrenia may involve several neuroanatomic locations with additional neurochemical abnormalities. The search for the biologic defect has been so extensive and refined that reading the literature requires an educational background few occupational therapists possess, and the studies employ instrumentation far more sophisticated and exact than the tools clinically available to therapists (see for example Lathan et al., 1981). Additional confounding factors, such as medication and institutionalization, make it even harder to identify a deficit or explain a change in behavior. Ottenbacher (1982) cautions against making therapeutic claims that lack empirical support, and this seems to be sound advice.

Similar difficulties in determining the effectiveness of psychosocial rehabilitation can be encountered. Selection criteria are often vague, and one may have serious questions about the adequacy of the medical workup, diagnosis, and treatment. Attempts to guess the average cognitive level are often futile because adequate detail is lacking. People in a number of mental health professions use activities of daily living as a treatment method, and it is difficult to tell whether these tasks are being presented as psychological or environmental compensations. It is also difficult to determine whether programs for poor-prognosis schizophrenia should be time limited or offer support for the remainder of the person's life. The American rehabilitation system tends to be time limited; the British system, lifelong. Obviously rehabilitation of schizophrenic patients is a very difficult area to work in, and acute hospital experience, as in chronic depression, is essential. The best chance of substantiating program effectiveness may be achieved by aiming program objectives toward environmental compensations for a lifelong deficit. That way, program failure is less apt to occur.

During the last decade program objectives in the American community mental health system have had a tendency to neglect chronic schizophrenia. Occupational therapy objectives have had a tendency to be overly optimistic (Harvey and Jellinek, 1981). There is, however, some evidence to suggest that occupational therapy service objectives are cost-effective (Feigenson et al., 1981; Robin, 1957). Descriptive studies like the ones reported above under Potential Rehabilitation Issues seem to provide the clearest guidelines for selecting treatment objectives.

CONCLUSION

Primary affective disorders, dementia, and schizophrenia can all produce a cognitive disability. The impairment may be temporary, as in primary affective disorders, or permanent, as in dementia. Schizophrenia seems to produce some permanent impairments, but this may not always be the case. Therapists are apt to see temporary disabilities during acute hospitalization. A change in the cognitive level can be anticipated in primary affective disorder, dementia with depression, and good-prognosis schizophrenic disorders. Residual disabilities can be expected with poor-prognosis schizophrenia and dementia. The selection of program objectives for people with residual disabilities is uncertain. These psychiatric disorders present different patterns of improvement, and greater specificity in diagnosis seems to be helpful in presenting clearer descriptions of task behavior, in identifying management precautions, and in selecting treatment objectives (Fig. 5-6).

The cognitive levels are designed to provide a relatively objective measure of the severity of a mental illness. A patient's cognitive level may indicate a temporary disability and provide an objective appraisal of the physician's treatment methods that improve functional performance. The cognitive level may also reflect a residual disability and may prove to be helpful in predicting restrictions in social role performance. Therapists can use the assessment of the cognitive level to change a task so that

Fig. 5-6. A heterogeneous group of patients with different diagnoses.

patients do not encounter their restrictions in routine task behavior. Therapists can also consult with others in suggesting changes in a task that will enhance successful performance, in the hospital and in the community.

REFERENCES

Akiskal, H. S., Hirschfeld, M. A., and Yerevian, B. The relationship of personality to affective disorders. *Arch. Gen. Psychiatry* 40:801–810, 1983.

Albert, M. S. Geriatric neuropsychology. *J. Consult. Clin. Psychol.* 49:835–850, 1981.

Andreasen, N. C., et al. Ventricular enlargement in schizophrenia: Relationship to positive and negative symptoms. *Am. J. Psychiatry* 139:297–301, 1982a.

Andreasen, N. C., et al. Ventricular enlargement in schizophrenia: Definition and prevalence. *Am. J. Psychiatry* 139:292–296, 1982b.

Ariel, R. N., et al. Regional cerebral blood flow in schizophrenia. *Arch. Gen. Psychiatry* 40:258–263, 1983.

Ayres, A. J. *Sensory Integration and Learning Disorders.* Los Angeles: Western Psychological Services, 1972.

Bach-y-Rita, P. (ed.). *Recovery of Function: Theoretical Considerations for Brain Injury Rehabilitation.* Baltimore: University Park Press, 1980.

Bach-y-Rita, P. Central nervous system lesions: Sprouting and unmasking in rehabilitation. *Arch. Phys. Med. Rehab.* 62:413–417, 1981.

Baldessarini, R. J., Finklestein, S., and Arana, G. W. The predictive power of diagnostic tests and the effect of prevalence of illness. *Arch. Gen. Psychiatry* 40:569–573, 1983.

Barraclough, G. P., and Brown, L. B. Coping behaviors that mediate between life events and depression. *Arch. Gen. Psychiatry* 39:1386–1391, 1982.

Bondareff, W., Baldy, R., and Levy, R. Quantitative computed tomography in senile dementia. *Arch. Gen. Psychiatry* 38:1365–1368, 1981.

Boyd, J. H., and Weissman, M. M. Epidemiology of affective disorders: A reexamination and future directions. *Arch. Gen. Psychiatry* 38:1039–1046, 1981.

Brockington, I. F., et al. Definitions of depression: Concordance and prediction of outcome. *Am. J. Psychiatry* 139:1022–1027, 1982.

Buchsbaum, M. S., et al. Cerebral glucography with positron tomography. *Arch. Gen. Psychiatry* 39:251–259, 1982.

Buell, S. J., and Coleman, P. D. Quantitative evidence for selective dendrite growth in normal human aging but not in senile dementia. *Brain Res.* 214:23–41, 1981.

Carroll, B. J., et al. A specific laboratory test for the diagnosis of melancholia. *Arch. Gen. Psychiatry* 38:15–22, 1981.

Casorino, J. P., Wilner, M., and Maxey, J. T. American Association of Partial Hospitalization (AAPH) standards and guidelines for partial hospitalization. *Int. J. Partial Hosp.* 1:5–21, 1982.

Cohen, R. M., et al. Effort and cognition in depression. *Arch. Gen. Psychiatry* 39:593–597, 1982.

Connelly, C. E., Davenport, Y. B., and Nurnberger, J. I. Adherence to treatment regimen in a lithium carbonate clinic. *Arch. Gen. Psychiatry* 39:585–588, 1982.

Craig, T. J. An epidemiologic study of problems associated with violence among psychiatric patients. *Am. J. Psychiatry* 139:1262–1266, 1982.

Crow, T. J. Disorientation in chronic schizophrenia: The nature of the cognitive deficit. *Br. J. Psychiatry* 133:137–142, 1978.

Crumley, F. E., et al. Preliminary report on the dexamethasone suppression test for psychiatrically disturbed adolescents. *Am. J. Psychiatry* 139:1062–1064, 1982.

Davis, J. M. Overview: Maintenance therapy in psychiatry: II. Affective disorders. *Am. J. Psychiatry* 133:1–13, 1976.

Dewan, M. J., et al. Abnormal dexamethasone suppression test results in chronic schizophrenic patients. *Am. J. Psychiatry* 139:1501–1503, 1982.

Drachman, D. A., Fleming, P., and Glosser, G. The Multidimensional Assessment for Dementia Scales. In S. Corkin et al. (eds.), *Alzheimer's Disease: A Report of Progress in Research* (Aging, Vol. 19). New York: Raven, 1982.

DSM II: Diagnostic and Statistical Manual of Mental Disorders (2nd ed.). Washington, D.C.: American Psychiatric Association, 1968.

DSM III: Diagnostic and Statistical Manual of Mental Disorders (3rd ed.). Washington, D.C.: American Psychiatric Association, 1980.

Extein, I., et al. Using the protirelin test to distinguish mania from schizophrenia. *Arch. Gen. Psychiatry* 39:78–81, 1982.

Fawcett, J., et al. Assessing anhedonia in psychiatric patients: The pleasure scale. *Arch. Gen. Psychiatry* 40:79–84, 1983.

Feigenson, J. S., et al. The cost-effectiveness of multiple sclerosis rehabilitation: A model. *Neurology (N.Y.)* 31:1316–1322, 1981.

Flaherty, J. A., et al. The role of social support in the functioning of patients with unipolar depression. *Am. J. Psychiatry* 140:473–476, 1983.

Fogelson, O. L., Cohen, B. M., and Pope, H. G. A study of *DSM III* schizophreniform disorder. *Am. J. Psychiatry* 139:1281–1285, 1982.

Fullerton, D. T., et al. Psychiatric disorders in patients with spinal cord injuries. *Arch. Gen. Psychiatry* 38:1369–1371, 1981.

Galen, R., and Gambino, S. *Beyond Normality: The Predictive Value and Efficiency of Medical Diagnosis.* New York: Wiley, 1975.

Glass, R. M., et al. Cognitive dysfunction and imipramine in outpatient depressives. *Arch. Gen. Psychiatry* 38:1048–1051, 1981.

Glassman, A. H., and Roose, S. P. Delusional depression: A distinct clinical entity? *Arch. Gen. Psychiatry* 38:424–427, 1981.

Golden, C. J., et al. Cerebral ventricular size and neuropsychological impairment in young chronic schizophrenics. *Arch. Gen. Psychiatry* 37:725–739, 1979.

Goldsmith, W. *Psychiatric Drugs for the Non-medical Mental Health Worker.* Springfield, Ill.: Thomas, 1977.

Goodwin, D. W., and Guze, S. B. *Psychiatric Diagnosis* (2nd ed.). New York: Oxford University Press, 1979.

Granacher, R. R. Differential diagnosis of tardive dyskinesia: An overview. *Am. J. Psychiatry* 138:1288–1297, 1981.

Greden, J. F., et al. Dexamethasone suppression tests in antidepressant treatment of melancholia. *Arch. Gen. Psychiatry* 40:493–500, 1983.

Greenblatt, M., Becerra, R. M., and Serafetinides, E. A. Social networks and mental health: An overview. *Am. J. Psychiatry* 139:977–984, 1982.

Gurland, B. J. The Assessment of Mental Status of Older Adults. In J. E. Birren and R. B. Sloane (eds.), *Handbook of Mental Health and Aging.* Englewood Cliffs, N.J.: Prentice-Hall, 1980.

Harrow, M., Silverstein, M. L., and Marengo, J. Disordered thinking: Does it identify nuclear schizophrenia? *Arch. Gen. Psychiatry* 40:765–771, 1983.

Harvey, R. F., and Jellinek, H. M. Functional performance assessment: A program approach. *Arch. Phys. Med. Rehab.* 62:456–461, 1981.

Haugland, O., et al. Mortality in the era of deinstitutionalization. *Am. J. Psychiatry* 140:848–852, 1983.

Helzer, J. E., Brockington, I. F., and Kendell, R. E. Predictive validity of *DSM-III* and Feighner definitions of schizophrenia: A comparison with research diagnostic criteria and CATEGO. *Arch. Gen. Psychiatry* 38:791–797, 1981.

Hirschfeld, R. M. A., and Cross, C. K. Epidemiology of affective disorders. *Arch. Gen. Psychiatry* 39:35–46, 1982.

Johnstone, E. C., et al. Cerebral ventricular size and cognitive impairment in chronic schizophrenia. *Lancet* 7992:924–926, 1976.

Johnstone, E. C., et al. The dementia of dementia praecox. *Acta Psychiatr. Scand.* 57:305–324, 1978.

Kane, J. M., and Smith, J. M. Tardive dyskinesia: Prevalence and risk factors. *Arch. Gen. Psychiatry* 39:473–481, 1982.

Katzman, R., et al. Validation of a short orientation-memory-concentration test of cognitive impairment. *Am. J. Psychiatry* 140:734–739, 1983.

Keller, M. B., et al. "Double depression": Two-year follow-up. *Am. J. Psychiatry* 140:689–694, 1983.

Keller, M. B., and Shapiro, R. W. Double depression: Superimposition of acute depressive episodes on chronic depressive disorders. *Am. J. Psychiatry* 139:438–442, 1982.

Kendler, K. S., Gruenberg, A. M., and Strauss, J. S. An independent analysis of the Copenhagen sample of the Danish adoption study of schizophrenia: I. The relationship between anxiety disorder and schizophrenia. *Arch. Gen. Psychiatry* 38:973–977, 1981a.

Kendler, K. S., Gruenberg, A. M., and Strauss, J. S. An independent analysis of the Copenhagen sample of the Danish adoption study of schizophrenia: II. The relationship between schizotypal personality disorder and schizophrenia. *Arch. Gen. Psychiatry* 38:982–984, 1981b.

Kendler, K. S., Gruenberg, A. M., and Strauss, J. S. An independent analysis of the Copenhagen sample of the Danish adoption study of schizophrenia: III. The relationship between paranoid psychosis (delusional disorder) and the schizophrenia spectrum disorders. *Arch. Gen. Psychiatry* 38:985–987, 1981.

Kety, S. S. Current Problems and Opportunities for Research in the Major Mental Illnesses. In J. J. Schwak (eds.), *Psychiatry, Psychopharmacology, and Alternative Therapies.* New York: Marcel Dekker, 1981.

Klawans, H. H., and Weiner, W. J. *Textbook of Clinical Neuropharmacology.* New York: Raven, 1981.

Kraeplin, E. *Dementia Praecox and Paraphrenia* (1919), transl. by R. M. Barclay and G. M. Robertson. New York: R. E. Krieger, 1971.

Lathan, C., et al. Optokinetic nystagmus and pursuit eye movements in schizophrenia. *Arch. Gen. Psychiatry* 38:997–1003, 1981.

Lehman, A. F., Ward, N. C., and Linn, L. S. Chronic mental patients: The quality of life issue. *Am. J. Psychiatry* 139:1271–1276, 1982.

Lewis, D. A., et al. Differentiation of depressive subtypes of insulin sensitivity in the recovered phase. *Arch. Gen. Psychiatry* 40:167–170, 1983.

McAllister, T. W., and Price, T. R. P. Severe depression pseudodementia with and without dementia. *Am. J. Psychiatry* 139:626–629, 1982.

Mace, N. L., and Rabins, P. J. *The 36-Hour Day: A Family Guide for Persons with Alzheimer's Disease, Related Dementing Illness, and Memory Loss in Later Life.* Baltimore: Johns Hopkins University Press, 1981.

Malenka, R. C., et al. Impaired central error-correcting behavior in schizophrenia. *Arch. Gen. Psychiatry* 39:101–107, 1982.

Maletta, G. J., et al. Organic mental disorders in a geriatric outpatient population. *Am. J. Psychiatry* 139:521–523, 1982.

Maloney, M. P. and Ward M. P. *Psychological Assessment: A Conceptual Approach.* New York: Oxford University Press, 1976.

Marder, S. R., et al. A comparison of patients who refuse and consent to neuroleptic treatment. *Am. J. Psychiatry* 140:470–472, 1983.

Matussek, P., and Feil, W. B. Personality attributes of depressed patients: Results of group comparisons. *Arch. Gen. Psychiatry* 40:783–790, 1983.

May, P. R. A., et al. Schizophrenia: A follow-up study of the results of five forms of treatment. *Arch. Gen. Psychiatry* 38:776–784, 1981.

Merikangas, K. R., Bromet, E. J., and Spiker, D. G. Associative mating, social adjustment and course of illness in primary affective disorder. *Arch. Gen. Psychiatry* 40:795–800, 1983.

Morihisa, J. M., Duffy, F. N., and Wyatt, R. J. Brain electrical activity mapping (BEAM) in schizophrenic patients. *Arch. Gen. Psychiatry* 40:719–728, 1983.

Morstyn, R., Duffy, F. N., and McCarley, R. W. Altered P300 topography in schizophrenia. *Arch. Gen. Psychiatry* 40:729–734, 1983.

Mukherjee, S., et al. Tardive dyskinesia in psychiatric outpatients. *Arch. Gen. Psychiatry* 39:466–469, 1982.

Murphy, G. E. On suicide prediction and prevention. *Arch. Gen. Psychiatry* 40:343–344, 1983.

Nelson, J. C., et al. Desipramine plasma concentration and antidepressant response. *Arch. Gen. Psychiatry* 39:1419–1422, 1982.

Ottenbacher, K. Sensory integration therapy: Affect or effect? *Am. J. Occup. Ther.* 36:571:578, 1982.

Owens, D. G. C., Johnstone, E. C., and Firth, C. D. Spontaneous voluntary disorders of movement. *Arch.*

Gen. Psychiatry 39:452–461, 1982.

Pattison, E. M., and Kahan, J. The deliberate self-harm syndrome. *Am. J. Psychiatry* 140:867–872, 1983.

Pokorny, A. D. Prediction of suicide in psychiatric patients. *Arch. Gen. Psychiatry* 40:249–257, 1983.

Powell-Proctor, L., and Miller, E. Reality orientation: A critical appraisal. *Br. J. Psychiatry* 140:457–463, 1982.

Prikram, K. H. Emotions. In S. B. Filskov and T. J. Boll (eds.). *Handbook of Clinical Neuropsychology*. New York: Wiley, 1981.

Puig-Antich, J., et al. Sleep architecture and RE sleep measures in prepubertal major depressives. *Arch. Gen. Psychiatry* 40:187–192, 1983.

Raskind, M., et al. Dexamethasone suppression test and cortical circadian rhythm in primary degenerative dementia. *Am. J. Psychiatry* 139:1468–1471, 1982.

Reifler, B. V., Larsen, E., and Hanley, R. Coexistence of cognitive impairment and depression in geriatric outpatients. *Am. J. Psychiatry* 139:623–625, 1982.

Reilly, M. Occupational therapy can be one of the great ideas of the twentieth century. *Am. J. Occup. Ther.* 16:1–9, 1961.

Reisberg, B., Ferris, S. H., and Cook, T. Signs, Symptoms and Course of Age-associated Cognitive Decline. In S. Corkin et al. (eds.), *Alzheimer's Disease: A Report of Progress in Research* (Aging, Vol. 19). New York: Raven, 1982.

Rieder, R. O., et al. Sulcal prominence in young chronic schizophrenic patients: CT scan findings associated with impairment on neuropsychological tests. *Psychiatry Res.* 1:1–9, 1979.

Rieder, R. O., et al. Computed tomographic scans in patients with schizophrenia, schizoaffective and bipolar affective disorder. *Arch. Gen. Psychiatry* 40:735–739, 1983.

Robin, A. A. The stabilizing effect of occupational therapy in chronic psychotics with a tendency to aggressive forms of behavior. *J. Ment. Sci.* 103:597–600, 1957.

Rosen, W. G., and Mohs, R. C. Evolution of Cognitive Decline in Dementia. In S. Corkin et al. (eds.), *Alzheimer's Disease: A Report of Progress in Research* (Aging, Vol. 19). New York: Raven, 1982.

Ross, E. D., and Rush, A. J. Diagnosis and neuroanatomical correlates of depression in brain damaged patients: Implications for a neurology of depression. *Arch. Gen. Psychiatry* 38:1344–1354, 1981.

Saccuzzo, D. P., and Braff, D. L. Early information processing deficit in schizophrenia: New findings using schizophrenic subgroups and manic control subjects. *Arch. Gen. Psychiatry* 38:175–179, 1981.

Sands, P., and Suzuki, T. Adult day care for Alzheimer's patients and their families. *Gerontologist* 23:21–23, 1983.

Satz, P., and Fletcher, J. M. Emergent trends in neuropsychology: An overview. *J. Consult. Clin. Psychol.* 49:851–865, 1981.

Schneck, M. K., Reisberg, B., and Ferris, S. H. An overview of current concepts of Alzheimer's disease. *Am. J. Psychiatry* 139:165–173, 1982.

Schuckit, M. A. Prevalence of affective disorder in a sample of young men. *Am. J. Psychiatry* 139:1431–1436, 1982.

Selberman, E. K., Weingartner, H., and Post, M. Thinking disorder in depression: Logic and strategy in an abstract reasoning task. *Arch. Gen. Psychiatry* 40:775–780, 1983.

Sharfstein, S. S. Medicaid cutbacks and block grants: Crisis or opportunity for community mental health? *Am. J. Psychiatry* 139:466–470, 1982.

Shepherd, G. Day care and the chronic patient: What we have here is the same old problems in different places. *Int. J. Partial Hosp.* 1:23–31, 1982.

Smouse, P. E., et al. The Carroll Rating Scale for Depression: II. Factor analysis of the feature profiles. *Br. J. Psychiatry* 138:201–204, 1981.

Sternberg, D. E., et al. CSF dopamine B-hydroxylase in schizophrenia: Low activity associated with good prognosis and good response to neuroleptic treatment. *Arch. Gen. Psychiatry* 40:743–747, 1983.

Swonger, A. K., and Constantine, L. L. *Drugs and Therapy: A Handbook of Psychotropic Drugs*. Boston: Little, Brown, 1983.

Sylph, J. A., Ross, H. E., and Kedward, H. B. Social disability in chronic psychiatric patients. *Am. J. Psychiatry* 134:1391–1934, 1977.

Targum, S. D., Rosen, L., and Capodano, A. E. The dexamethasone suppression test in suicidal patients with unipolar depression. *Am. J. Psychiatry* 140:877–879, 1983.

Targum, S. D., Sullivan, A. C., and Byrnes, S. M. Neuroendocrine interrelationships in major depressive disorder. *Am. J. Psychiatry* 139:282–286, 1982.

Taylor, M. A., and Abrams, R. Prediction of treatment response in mania. *Arch. Gen. Psychiatry* 38:800–803, 1981.

Travin, S., and Protter, B. Mad or bad? Some clinical considerations in the misdiagnosis of schizophrenia as antisocial personality disorder. *Am. J. Psychiatry* 139:1335–1338, 1982.

Tune, L. E., et al. Serum levels of anticholinergic drugs and impaired recent memory in chronic schizophrenic patients. *Am. J. Psychiatry* 139:1460–1462, 1982.

Weinberger, D. R., et al. Cerebral ventricular enlargement in chronic schizophrenia: Its association with poor response to treatment. *Arch. Gen. Psychiatry* 37:11–13, 1980a.

Weinberger, D. R., et al. Poor premorbid adjustment and CT scan abnormalities in chronic schizophrenia. *Am. J. Psychiatry* 137:1410–1413, 1980b.

Weinberger, D. R., et al. Lateral cerebral ventricular enlargement in chronic schizophrenia. *Arch. Gen. Psychiatry* 36:735–739, 1979.

Weingartner, H., et al. Determinants of Memory Failures in Dementia. In S. Crokin, et al. (eds.), *Alzheimer's Disease: A Report of Progress in Research* (Aging, Vol. 19). New York: Raven, 1982.

Weintraub, S., Baratz, R., and Mesulam, M. Daily Living Activities in the Assessment of Dementia. In S. Corkin et al. (eds.), *Alzheimer's Disease: A Report of Progress in Research* (Aging, Vol. 19). New York: Raven, 1982.

Wells, C. E. Refinements in the diagnosis of dementia. *Am. J. Psychiatry* 139:621–622, 1982.

Wilson, L. A., et al. Mental status of elderly hospital patients related to occupational therapist's assessment of activities of daily living. *Gerontol. Clin.* 15:197–202, 1973.

Winokur, G. Unipolar depressions: Is it divisible into autonomous subtypes? *Arch. Gen. Psychiatry* 36:47–52, 1979.

Winokur, G., and Crowe, R. R. Bipolar illness: The sex-polarity effect in affectively ill family members. *Arch. Gen. Psychiatry* 40:57–58, 1983.

Zahn, T. P., Carpenter, W. T., and McGlashan, T. H. Autonomic nervous system activity in acute schizophrenia: Method and comparison with normal controls. *Arch. Gen. Psychiatry* 38:251–258, 1981.

Zarit, S. H. *Aging and Mental Disorders: Psychological Approaches to Assessment and Treatment.* New York: Free Press, 1980.

Ross-Stanton, J., and Meltzer, H. Y. Motor neuron branching patterns in psychotic patients. *Arch. Gen. Psychiatry* 38:1097–1103, 1981.

Saccuzzo, D. P., and Braff, D. L. Early information processing deficit in schizophrenia: New findings using schizophrenic subgroups and manic control subjects. *Arch. Gen. Psychiatry* 38:175–179, 1981.

Smith, R. C., et al. RBS and plasma levels of haloperidol and clinical response in schizophrenia. *Am. J. Psychiatry* 139:1054–1056, 1982.

Wahba, M., Donlon, P. T., and Meadow, A. Cognitive changes in acute schizophrenia with brief neuroleptic treatment. *Am. J. Psychiatry* 183:1307–1310, 1981.

Wilkinson, C. B., and O'Connor, W. A. Human ecology and mental illness. *Am. J. Psychiatry* 139:985–990, 1982.

Yarden, P. E., and Raps, C. S. Identity alterations and prognosis in schizophrenia. *Br. J. Psychiatry* 138:495–497, 1981.

ADDITIONAL READINGS ON SCHIZOPHRENIC DISORDERS

Crow, T. J. Disorientation in chronic schizophrenia: The nature of the cognitive deficit. *Br. J. Psychiatry* 133:137–142, 1978.

Iacono, W. G., Tuason, V. B., and Johnsen, R. A. Dissociation of smooth-pursuit and saccadic eye tracking in remitting schizophrenics. *Arch. Gen. Psychiatry* 38:991–996, 1981.

Karson, C. N., et al. Haloperidol-induced changes in blink rates correlate with changes in BPRS score. *Br. J. Psychiatry* 140:503–507, 1982.

Luchins, D., et al. HLA antigens in schizophrenia: Differences between patients with and without evidence of brain atrophy. *Br. J. Psychiatry* 136:243–248, 1980.

CHAPTER 6

OTHER PSYCHIATRIC DISORDERS

All of the mental disorders presented in this chapter are confounded by complex social, legal, medical, and ethical ambiguities. Effective treatment methods are essentially unknown, and the prognosis is often poor. The disorders discussed are the anxiety disorders, anorexia nervosa, the borderline and antisocial personality disorders, the somatoform disorders, and some types of substance abuse. Patients with all of these disorders, with the exception of substance abuse, tend to be functioning at level 5 or 6. Patients who are functioning at levels 5 or 6 are rarely admitted to a psychiatric hospital; a suicide attempt is the typical reason for admission. Difficulties with differential diagnosis are common, usually accompanied by numerous staff disagreements about social values. The staff disagreements develop because objective criteria for establishing the presence of a disease are missing. In one instance the very existence of a disorder is challenged—borderline personality disorder. In addition a large number of the patients admitted to the hospital with agoraphobia, multiple phobias, anorexia nervosa, somatization disorders, alcoholism, and drug abuse may have a treatable primary affective disorder. Of genuine concern to me is the thought that treatable, mild affective disorders are being overlooked because alternative diagnoses, which entail a priori excuses for treatment failure, are available. The approach taken in this chapter is to review the ambiguities discussed in the recent psychiatric literature and to suggest precautions in the way a therapist interprets observations of task behavior.

PERSONALITY DISORDERS

The personality disorders are located on Axis II of *DSM III* (1980) and represent a fundamental difficulty in defining mental disorders. Axis I contains disorders that are linked to a biologic abnormality. The existence of a medical disease is less clear with the Axis II disorders. Axis II contains enduring personality patterns. The fundamental problem resides in trying to describe pathologic personality patterns while avoiding descriptions of behavior that can be used as a subtle form of character assassination. The descriptions of the personality disorders in *DSM III* (1980) can be misleading and are of particular concern when used to restrict continued access to medical treatment. The most dramatic determinations involve an involuntary placement in a hospital or a jail. The social stigma associated with the personality disorders can be severe, and for that reason these diagnoses should be avoided whenever possible.

The challenge of trying to describe pathologic personality patterns has been pursued by Millon (1981), who proposes a three-level hierarchy defined by the *social severity* of the disorder. The first level contains disorders in which the patients seek out and maintain social relationships: dependent, histrionic, narcissistic, and antisocial personality disorders. The second level includes socially distant behaviors and contains compulsive, passive-aggressive, schizoid, and avoidant disorders. The most severe social level contains borderline, paranoid, and schizotypal personality disorders (Millon, 1981). Millon's theoretical discussion of pathologic personality reminds me of the puzzles encountered in attempting to make a distinction between a disease and a disability. The Axis II personality disorders may represent the *social disability* produced by neurogenic disorders. If so, this would represent a major conceptual change.

Theories of personality have shared an assumption that is familiar to occupational therapists: "That early experience plays a decisive part in determining personality is assumed by psychiatrists and psychologists of all theoretical persuasions" (Millon, 1981, p. 103). Early development is examined to identify experiences that would explain the later manifestations of pathology. This assumption has never been supported by well-designed, replicated research studies. Discarding the assumption would have major treatment implications: Treatment methods that focus on past experiences would be considered less relevant than treatment methods

that focus on present and future behaviors. The remedial interventions recommended by Millon (1981) seem to be making such a change. Principally recommended are teaching psychological compensations, locating environmental compensations, providing supportive treatment, and recommending psychotropic drugs. An intensive examination of early, developmental experiences is rarely recommended because this treatment approach has not worked very well. A shift in theoretical orientation is occurring, and more change may be required (Gunderson et al., 1983).

Matuzas and Glass (1983) have cited the dangers of linking treatment response, or treatment methods, with the cause of a disorder. The personality disorders may or may not be caused by early childhood experiences. A treatment response (to a pill or psychotherapy) may be achieved without affecting (or knowing) the causes. The familiar diabetes example, cited in Chapter 1, illustrates this. The point is made again because when a cause is unknown there is a tendency to think in simple cause-and-effect relationships. Effective treatment response is not wedded to an explanation of cause. The explanation of the cause could continue to be unknown for several centuries.

Occupational therapy theories have been influenced by the early-experience assumption (for example, Fidler and Fidler, 1963; Llorens, 1976; Mosey, 1970; Reilly, 1974). Studying normal growth and development may be helpful in determining the severity of a disorder; that may be all that can be learned from early childhood experiences. The evaluation and treatment of a disability does not have to depend on an explanation of the cause of the disorder. The therapist can assess the severity of the disability, along with the patient's interests and desires, and suggest tasks and social environments that enhance functional performance.

The following sequence displays the theoretical utility of early childhood descriptions when applied to adults with a disability. To change an early childhood description into a description of an adult disability, one would follow these steps:

1. Select descriptions of early childhood experiences.
2. Observe for similarities in disabled adults.
3. Refine childhood descriptions for better correspondence with adult descriptions.
4. Identify frequent observations omitted from childhood descriptions.
5. Refine adult descriptions.
6. Identify observations of adults that continue to cause confusion.
7. Refine adult descriptions.

The similarities between early childhood and adult disability are examined in steps 1 and 2. Steps 3 through 7 are required to complete the description of the adult's disability. Early childhood experiences are still of some value but may be far more restricted in their usefulness than we had thought. Many of our descriptions of adult disabilities contain unanswered questions about the nature of the problem. The descriptions of most of the personality disorders are ambiguous enough to raise reasoned questions about the existence of the disorders as a medical diagnosis.

Currently these disorders are associated with a persistent personality pattern, and the prognosis is poor. The social disability can be severe. Physicians are uncertain about treatment specificity. These diagnoses can be regarded as a justification for discontinuing medical interventions or as a justification for psychotherapy with a rationale for treatment failure. The difficulty one encounters in distinguishing between a primary affective disorder and a personality disorder is alarming, because a primary affective disorder is usually treatable. The question of concern is Do we treat the people we like and not the people that we do not like? People who would benefit from medical treatment may be erroneously denied available care. The question is disturbing enough that I recommend that these diagnoses be used with considerable restraint.

The personality disorders may reflect the social disability associated with an Axis I or an Axis III (physical) disease. If this speculation is correct, suc-cessful treatment of the alternative disease should reduce or eliminate the social disability. A disorder that cannot be treated could produce a residual social disability. The personality disorders may need to be reconceptualized as a social disability with treatment objectives that compensate for the disability.

Borderline Personality Disorders

Perhaps the most puzzling personality disorder is borderline personality disorder. A number of studies have questioned the construct validity of the disorder (that is, whether this disorder really exists) (Koenigsberg et al., 1983; Kroll et al., 1981; Mellsop et al., 1982; Pope et al., 1983; Soloff and Millward, 1983). There was a debate about whether the diagnosis should be included in *DSM III*, and the debate will probably continue into the fourth edition. The problem is that the criteria for making the diagnosis are not reliable. The overlap with other diagnoses—primary affective disorder, schizophrenia, other functional psychoses, organic mental disorder, anxiety disorder, factitious disorder, anorexia nervosa, and other personality disorders—is extensive. The scope of this overlap generates a concern that once again a "wastepaper basket" diagnosis has been created.

Weak interrater reliability coupled with extensive overlap with other diagnoses produces major clinical problems. For example, using *DSM III* criteria the Kroll (1981) group diagnosed 8 of 117 consecutive admissions as borderline personality disorder. Discussions with therapists from different institutions suggest that there is a marked variation in the prevalence of diagnosing borderline personality disorder. Some therapists report that they rarely see the diagnosis. Others report a rate as high as 50 percent of consecutive admissions. This diagnosis seems to be used by people with a psychodynamic orientation.

The attempt to keep *DSM III* atheoretical may not have been successful here. The debate will probably continue to pose clinical problems because the diagnostic criteria do not appear to be reliable. We should not expect to develop specific treatments for this disorder until we achieve greater clarity about who has the disorder. Lacking clear diagnostic criteria, one wonders if the disorder even exists. This problem is shared to some extent by the other personality disorders. The lack of clear diagnostic criteria may have some alarming ramifications because borderline personality disorder is associated with a poor prognosis and a failure to comply with medical instruction (Millon, 1981). The diagnosis can be used as an explanation for a treatment failure. The alternative diagnosis of a primary affective disorder may be considered, and the differential may be confused by affective instability. I recommend that top reporting priority be given to any symptoms of depression that might respond to psychopharmacologic medications. A further recommendation is that therapists guard against the all too human temptation to make informal, prejudicial comments about any patient; the temptation seems to be escalated by the disorders described in this chapter.

Antisocial Personality Disorder

Antisocial personality disorder seems to be associated with alcoholism in men, hysteria in women, and nonmajor affective disorders. Admission to a hospital may follow a suicide gesture and may be accompanied by a history of drug and alcohol abuse. Psychiatric hospitalization may be associated with social stress such as legal difficulties, and there may be some suspicion that the hospital is being used to avoid legal procedures.

People with an antisocial personality disorder infringe on the rights of others, and many of them show no interest in changing that pattern of behavior. Many of them refuse to comply with prescribed treatments, and repeated medical and legal complications are common (*DSM III*). Therapists who specialize in working with physical disabilities may

see people with this disorder when their reckless behavior results in physical injuries.

The detection of this disorder is apt to raise ethical questions for therapists (Purtilo and Cassel, 1981). The dilemma is expressed by the purpose of hospitalization and imprisonment. The American prison system has always had rehabilitative goals, but it now appears these goals were overly idealistic. People who engage in repeated crimes raise questions about whether any changes in behavior can be realistically expected from incarceration. American society may decide that the purpose of imprisonment is punishment (Andersen, 1982). The problem is compounded by studies of prison populations that disclose numerous psychiatric and neurologic problems (Lamb and Grant, 1982; Shanok and Lewis, 1981). Primary affective disorders, schizophrenic disorders, temporal lobe epilepsy, and multiple medical problems contribute to antisocial behavior, and, of course, some of these disorders are more readily treated than others. *DSM III* implies that a jail history is limited to antisocial personality disorders, but this seems to be a gross oversimplification.

Antisocial personality disorders exemplify some of the chaos in our current medical legal system. Some people with medical disorders that can be treated are in jail, and criminal offenders with disorders that may not be treatable are in hospitals. Institutional care of any kind is expensive, and people are searching for admission criteria that would result in a better use of our resources. Therapists are often in a position of making recommendations for long-term treatment or rehabilitation; these recommendations merit careful consideration when an antisocial personality disorder is present. The presence of the disorder may raise doubts about the individual's ability to cooperate with the program.

Acute psychiatric hospitalization lasts about 2 or 3 weeks, and it is doubtful that a persistent maladaptive pattern of behavior can be changed in that time. A specific biologic treatment for antisocial personality disorder is unknown, and the available verbal therapies require a longer time. A coexisting diagnosis (Axis I or Axis III) may be treated during acute hospitalization.

Long-term treatment programs for those with an antisocial personality disorder do exist. It is generally thought that they are most effective for adolescents and young adults. Long-term care seems to require a minimum of 3 months; some programs require 2 years (Simpson, 1981).

Child and Adolescent Conduct Disorders

Diagnosis specificity for adolescents has been greatly increased by *DSM III*, and it now appears that the diagnostic pattern follows the pattern seen with adults. This suggests that a diagnostic division according to age may be artificial (Strober et al., 1981). The change in diagnostic patterns may have a major impact on some long-term care facilities. Adolescent programs may need to make clearer distinctions between disorders that respond to acute care and those that necessitate long-term care. Personality disorders may require long-term care, but the primary affective disorders respond to acute care. Greater treatment specificity is required, and the financial considerations are substantial. The selection of the most effective long-term treatment method remains obscure. Graded behavioral objectives are frequently used (Moss and Rick, 1981).

Diagnostic specificity for children is still a problem. The reason for admission is often confused by the following questions: Is this a bad kid? Are these rotten parents? Is the referral from a stupid teacher? Earls (1982) applied the *DSM III* criteria in an epidemiologic study of 100 3-year-olds unselected for psychopathology. Fourteen were diagnosed, and 9 of the 14 had a social stress, with marital separation of the parents being the most common. Rogeness and colleagues (1982) are looking for biochemical differences in conduct disorders, and one hopes that studies like this will produce the clarity that is noticeably lacking at the present time.

Task Behavior

Most of my clinical observations of task behavior in personality disorders have been of people who have an antisocial personality disorder, and that will be the focus of the following description. People with an antisocial personality disorder would usually rather talk than work (Fig. 6-1). Their task behavior takes the avenue of least effort, with a lack of interest in learning new procedures and lack of persistence in correcting errors. They tend to do the minimum required of them and are not distressed by deficiencies in their performance. An apparent deficiency may be blamed on external factors: lousy supplies, poor equipment, bad instructions. The therapist may find it difficult to get these people to do anything at all, and what they do do may not be up to their "level of ability." People with an antisocial personality disorder may sell their projects for money, and steps may need to be taken to protect the supply inventory. Rules become important to the therapist during task performance because of their tendency to be inconsiderate of other people. The therapist must set the limits on infringement.

The problem occurs in making a distinction between depression and antisocial personality disorder; patients with both disorders take a course that requires the least amount of effort. People with depression tend to comply with the social rules that govern polite behavior, while the antisocial people do not. The concern is, Are we missing a treatable depression? The question should be considered before suggesting an Axis II diagnosis.

Cognitive Level

Most people with an Axis II diagnosis are assessed at cognitive level 5 or 6, which seems to be consistent with their educational level and social backgrounds. At level 5 they have a low tolerance for error and resist suggestions about how an error can be corrected. They usually take an easy way out and produce a project of poor quality. They are uncon-

Fig. 6-1. Personality disorder: "I'd rather talk than work."

cerned about the quality of their workmanship and tend to indicate that the therapist's standards are unnecessarily high. No interest in improved performance is evident. At level 6 they usually select task content that is familiar to them and refuse opportunities to learn something new. They prefer short-term projects that produce a quick and easy end product. Spontaneous performance is below the assessed level of ability.

Antisocial personality disorder has been associated with attention deficit disorders (Wender et al., 1981). My clinical observations tend to support the notion that a subtle and persistent attention deficit is present. There is an unusual lack of response to novelty. At levels 5 and 6 novelty usually sparks interest, creativity, and learning. People with an antisocial personality disorder tend to disregard novelty. Coercion can be used to focus their attention on novelty, and they are capable of learning new procedures. Their natural inclination, however, seems to be to avoid novelty. This deficit has also been observed in the associated disorders: drug abuse, alcohol abuse, and hysteria. One continues to hope that physicians will discover a way to treat this deficit; a recent report that minimal attention deficits may be improved by pemaline (Cylert) is encouraging (Wender et al., 1981).

The lack of response to novelty may or may not aid in differential diagnosis. The distinction between depression and a personality disorder poses the largest problem. People who are depressed fail to respond to novelty in the sense that they lack the energy to do more. Depressed people are disturbed by poor workmanship and seek to improve their task behavior and comply with the therapist's standards of performance. People who have a personality disorder disregard suggestions that the quality of task performance could be improved and say that the therapist's standards of performance are unwarranted. The therapist's standard of performance must be consistent. We should remember that we are using compliance with our value judgments to make an important differential diagnosis.

Management Precautions and Treatment Objectives

People with a personality disorder can be vexing to therapists, and it is difficult to know when and if one's annoyance is legitimate. Clear standards for the use of supplies, the quantity of time spent working, and the quality of performance expected seem to help. Standards are especially important in acute psychiatric settings where programs are designed to make allowances for deficits. People with a personality disorder may stretch those allowances to the limit. Ultimately therapists must be clear about what attendance in occupational therapy is accomplishing. Acute hospitalization is generally aimed at treating a coexisting disorder, not the personality disorder. The therapist's objectives should be directed toward the acute disorder. The therapist must protect the institution and other patients by the long-term maladaptive behavior.

Long-term treatment objectives generally aim toward psychological compensation, which is realistic at cognitive levels 5 and 6. The problem is that people with a personality disorder are usually not interested in learning new skills and abilities. The selection of the skills and abilities to be learned is also problematic. A selection made by the therapist tends to take on an element of coercion—the patient is forced to learn a skill the therapist thinks is important but the patient does not want to learn. A selection made by the patient may be restricted to familiar skills and abilities; thus no learning would occur. A suggestion for avoiding this difficulty can be offered. A contract between the therapist and the patient might stipulate a graded amount of time spent in learning a skill or an ability. The selection of the content, cooking versus grooming, for example, would be the choice of the patient. I have had limited clinical experience with this approach and

think it resolves some immedia the long-term effectiveness is unk.

Rehabilitation Issues

Personality disorders can follow recurrent of behavior for years, and a marginal social a ment can be expected. Therapists working w these people must recognize that their rehabilita tion potential is linked to the theoretical confusion surrounding these disorders. There is an obvious need to change the behavioral pattern, with many unknowns about what explains the disorders. Greater clarity about the biologic defect may help focus treatment methods in this confusing area of practice.

SOMATOFORM DISORDERS

The most common somatoform disorder producing admission to a psychiatric hospital is a somatization disorder referred to as hysteria or Briquet's syndrome. Hospitalization may follow a suicide attempt. There may be a need to distinguish between the somatic complaints of a major depressive episode and a somatization disorder. Somatization disorders are associated with depression, anxiety, histrionic personality disorders, and antisocial personality disorders. History and present medical complaints are apt to be complicated and confusing. There has been a tendency to conceptualize somatization disorder in psychological terms such as "secondary gain" and to regard the complaints as manipulative. These psychological explanations now appear to be in error and analogous to blaming the patient for having a disease we do not understand. The familial pattern and consistency of the organ systems involved suggest a biologic deficit.

The other somatoform disorders are seldom seen by therapists. Conversion disorders are relatively rare. Psychogenic pain and hypochondriasis should be used as diagnoses with considerable restraint; the correct diagnosis may be "pain of unknown origin."

Fig. 6-2. Histrionic personality disorders: dramatic, self-indulgent projects.

Task Behavior

The lack of response to novelty observed with the personality disorders may also be seen with the somatization disorders. People who are hospitalized with this diagnosis often have a concurrent diagnosis of endogenous depression, and much of their task behavior can be explained by the depression. A histrionic personality disorder may be expressed by the selection of a dramatic, self-indulgent project (Fig. 6-2). Some patients may resist motor performance, spending their time in the clinic talking rather than working. The assessed cognitive level may be level 5 or 6, but spontaneous performance may be below the assessed level.

ANXIETY DISORDERS

The anxiety disorders include phobic neurosis, anxiety neurosis, obsessive-compulsive neurosis, and posttraumatic stress disorders. Anxiety may be a general, predominant symptom, or it may be aroused by a particular situation. A similar pattern

in task behavior is noted. These disorders will be discussed as a general category.

Reason for Admission

People with these disorders who are admitted to a psychiatric hospital are usually severely incapacitated. They may have a recent history of being unable to leave their homes or complete ordinary household activities. They may be given antianxiety medication, and a question of a concurrent diagnosis of primary affective disorder is common. There seems to be some overlap between phobic attacks and primary affective disorders (Leckman et al., 1983; Munjack and Moss, 1981; Pecknold et al., 1982). Overlap has also been found among anxiety disorders, panic attacks, and primary affective disorders (Holhn-Saric et al., 1981). This overlap may be present in people who are admitted to hospitals; a diagnosis of a primary affective disorder, a dual diagnosis, or a differential diagnosis may be considered. Laboratory tests that aid in the diagnosis of primary affective disorder are helpful with these problems, even though false negatives may make individual cases baffling.

Drugs may benefit patients with spontaneous panic (agoraphobia or mixed phobia), but there is some question of their effectiveness with isolated phobias (e.g., toward snakes) (Zitrin et al., 1983). Unexpected good results occurred during supportive therapy, as compared with behavior therapy, when both groups were given a placebo; even so, both placebo groups expressed concern about their level of function (Klein et al., 1983).

Task Behavior

The functional incapacity that leads to psychiatric hospitalization is evident in the task behavior of those with anxiety disorders. The first problem in working with these people is getting them into the OT clinic; they can often think of a hundred good reasons for staying on the ward. Once in the clinic they may think of numerous ways to avoid working:

washing their hands, washing a paintbrush, going to the bathroom, getting a cup of coffee, discussing a current event (Fig. 6-3). It seems to be difficult for them to start working, but once they begin their performance is consistent with their assessed cognitive level. The therapist may notice that during a one-hour session they have actually been engaged in working for approximately five minutes. Time spent working seems to be a good measure of improvement. Most of these people are assessed at cognitive level 5 or 6, which seems to be consistent with their educational and social background.

People who have primary affective disorder also find it difficult to get anything done, but the process looks different. People who are depressed lack energy; they sit quietly or take a nap. People with an anxiety disorder move around the clinic area and initiate conversations. Even though they are not working on their task they are usually busy doing something. The amount of activity can suggest the hyperactivity associated with a manic episode, and differentiating these disorders can be difficult. Mania is characterized by hyperresponsiveness to the task environment; the behavior is rushed, and attention is easily distracted. People with an anxiety disorder usually move at a steady pace, and they are not distracted by extraneous objects. Even so, the behavior could be interpreted as a mild form of mania.

Management Precautions

Task performance may represent a terrifying confrontation with their symptoms, and understandably those with anxiety disorders are reluctant to come to the clinic. It is even more difficult if the person has trouble with doorways or elevators that may be encountered in route. The therapist can appreciate the discomfort the person is experiencing but may need to observe his or her task performance. Simple direct commands similar to those issued by a drill sergeant—"Go," "Now"—can be effective in getting these people going. The therapist need not be harsh but must be firm.

Fig. 6-3. Anxiety disorders: numerous ways to avoid working.

Realistic improvements in task performance should be pointed out to these people. The anxiety may be overwhelming to them, and they may find it difficult to assess their own behavior objectively. A rating sheet filled out by the patient may also be helpful when self-assessment is a problem.

Potential Rehabilitation Issues

Life-style complications similar to those seen in primary affective disorders may be seen with anxiety disorders. Medications are often effective in reducing the symptoms, and the person may then need to develop a plan for reentry into the social community. Interdisciplinary collaboration and treatment objectives are similar to those described under primary affective disorders.

ANOREXIA NERVOSA

Reason for Admission

Anorexia nervosa used to be a relatively uncommon disorder that occurs more frequently in girls than boys. The incidence may be increasing: why is unclear. The fact that eating disturbances are associated with primary affective disorders is of particular concern, and some questions about whether anorexia is a separate disorder still need to be answered. People are admitted to a hospital when their weight loss is dangerous to their health. Often the self-imposed starvation places their lives in jeopardy. The goal is weight gain.

Task Behavior and Cognitive Level

These girls have usually been through endless discussions about food and weight and prefer to avoid the topic. They invest energy in a variety of tasks, and their performance is usually diligent and persistent. Their cognitive level is consistent with their educational and social backgrounds, usually level 5 or 6.

Management Precautions

Some people with anorexia self-induce vomiting, and the therapist may have to monitor trips to the bathroom. Solid food may have been avoided for a long period of time. Using a blender to puree food was effective in one case; the pureed food resembled baby food and seemed to be easier to digest. Physical exercise may have to be controlled, too, because these people often pursue strenuous exercise to avoid weight gain. Exercise may resemble the hyperactivity of a manic episode and suggest a need for a differential diagnosis. People experiencing a manic episode may engage in physical exercise, but it is usually not sustained for very long because their attention is distracted. This kind of an attention deficit is not associated with anorexia nervosa.

Fig. 6-4. *Anorexia nervosa: bloated stomach.*

Therapists are often tempted to make a dress or skirt with these patients, which seems to result in an argument about the cause of their bloated stomachs. Starvation produces a bloated stomach (Fig. 6-4). A girl who thinks the bloated stomach is fat seldom changes her mind while making a dress, and the discussion resembles an attempt to talk someone out of a delusional system. This kind of confrontation does not seem to be effective in facilitating weight gain. The therapist may be more effective by making the task experience as pleasant as possible and by gently reminding the patient that the way to get out of the hospital is to gain weight.

Verbal discussions about body size have led to some speculations about a possible thought disorder in some cases of anorexia nervosa. The way these patients think about their bodies certainly seems to be unrealistic. I have not, however, been able to detect a cognitive disability unless there was another diagnosis that could explain it. Impairments in task behavior may be attributed to the second diagnosis, and therapists should be alert for this possibility. The principal consideration is a primary affective disorder.

Behavior modification techniques are sometimes used with anorexia, and the place of occupational therapy can be problematic. Attendance in occupational therapy may be used as a reward for weight gain. Many therapists have trouble with this because there is an element of coercion in it. The therapist may not be in a position to alter the reward list and may have to wait until permission to attend OT is granted.

SUBSTANCE ABUSE

Substance abuse is difficult to treat because of the uncertainty surrounding its definition: Is it a bad habit, a complication of another mental disorder, or a unique biologic defect? Each of these definitions of substance abuse suggests a different treatment approach. The bad habit definition is prevalent in psychosocial rehabilitation programs and self-help groups in which people are taught new forms of behavior. Defining substance abuse as a complication of another mental disorder is prevalent in hospitals, where the reason for admission may be a primary affective disorder. A biologic defect is sought in the basic science research with the hope that greater treatment specificity can be achieved. The last three decades have been characterized by controversy over these definitions. It now appears that genetics and the environment both play a major role in producing the problem, but there is continued uncertainty about the best treatment approach.

Occupational therapists have had limited participation in rehabilitation programs for substance abusers, predominantly alcoholics (see Table 1-1).

Therapists working in other settings may encounter substance abuse that is a complication of another diagnosis. The most commonly abused substance is alcohol, and this will be discussed. A street drug that is currently causing concern in psychiatric hospitals, phencyclidine hydrochloride (PCP), will also be discussed.

Alcoholism

Alcoholism, like depression, is difficult to define because it is hard to distinguish between behavior that many people engage in (drinking) and abnormal behavior. Ninety percent of the adults in some societies may consume alcohol, but only one percent may develop alcoholism (Turner, 1980). The question has been Where does one draw the line between use and abuse? *DSM III* departs from a bifocal definition by expanding use and abuse into a number of subclassifications. The organic mental disorders include alcohol intoxication, alcohol idiosyncratic intoxication, alcohol withdrawal, alcohol withdrawal with delirium, alcohol hallucinosis, alcohol amnestic disorder, and dementia associated with alcoholism. The substance use disorders include alcohol abuse and alcohol dependence. A history of drinking, social and occupational impairment, and a response to abstinence are used to make the diagnosis; the criteria for subclassifying are behavioral.

Another method of subclassifying alcoholism is suggested by the genetic studies. The medical and legal history of the biologic and adoptive parents of adopted children has been examined. Several patterns of biologic predisposition to alcohol abuse seem to be emerging (Table 6-1). A link is found between biologic fathers who abuse alcohol and alcohol abuse in their children, even though the children are reared by adoptive parents (Table 6-1). Alcoholic biologic mothers also increase the risk of abuse in both their sons and daughters; in utero and postnatal exposure may produce the increased risk of later abuse. No increased risk is associated with

Table 6-1. Biologic predisposition to alcohol abuse

Alcohol use in parents	Alcohol use in son	Alcohol use in daughter
Biologic father with adolescent onset of alcohol abuse, criminal history, extensive treatment	Abuse is recurrent or moderate; may be severe	No significant findings
Biologic father with mild abuse		Increased risk of abuse
Biologic mother alcoholic	Increased risk of abuse	Increased risk of abuse
Adoptive parents alcoholic	No increased risk; nonsignificant reduction in abuse	No increased risk

Source: Data from Bohman, M., Sigvardsson, S., and Cloninger, C. R. Maternal inheritance of alcohol abuse: Cross-factoring analysis of adopted women. *Arch. Gen. Psychiatry* 38:965–969, 1981; Cloninger, C. R., Bohman, M., and Sigvardsson, S. Inheritance of alcohol abuse: Cross-factoring analysis of adopted men. *Arch. Gen. Psychiatry* 38:861–868, 1981.

placement with alcoholic adoptive parents (Bohman et al., 1981; Cloninger et al., 1981).

Therapists working in acute psychiatric hospitals are apt to encounter a problem with alcohol abuse associated with other *DSM III* disorders. Nace and associates (1983) report that of a group of alcoholic patients 13 percent had a borderline personality disorder. The rate of affective disorder was 5 percent in men and 20 to 25 percent in women. A higher incidence of posttreatment, alcoholic relapse associated with depression has been recorded as well (Hatsukami and Pickens, 1982). Short-term care may focus on the affective disorder, and a decision regarding a referral to a long-term rehabilitation agency for alcoholism may be required. In some cases the alcohol problem is corrected by treating the affective disorder (Goodwin and Erickson, 1979). Some patients may be interested in a rehabilitation program; however, some substance abuse rehabilitation agencies will not allow their clients any type of medication, including antidepressants and lithium. This rule may be a contraindication for a referral for those with a primary affective disorder.

The natural history of alcoholism received some clarification from a prospective longitudinal study of a normative sample of 110 men from ages 14 to 47. Stable abstinence for a period of one year was associated with severe alcohol abuse but *not* with clinical treatment or a good premorbid adjustment (that

is, recovery was not associated with professional help or strength of character). An ability to return to social drinking without abuse was associated with few symptoms of abuse (Vaillant and Milofsky, 1982). A return to social drinking is sometimes said to be impossible. The current programs for treating alcoholism may be based on concepts that are incorrect.

The recovery process in chronic illnesses such as alcoholism is difficult to evaluate because individuals may have experienced numerous treatment interventions and differences in premorbid status may account for treatment success (Edwards and Grant, 1981). A suggestion has been made that recovery may aim at maximizing the natural healing process (Vaillant and Milofsky, 1982). A natural healing process may be self-regulated and correspond to the theoretical view of drinking supplied by Gaines (1981), who describes drinking as a planned act that is self-monitored and influenced by the situational context. The Vaillant and Milofsky (1982) study suggests a number of activities that have been spontaneously employed as a substitute for drinking: compulsive eating, candy binges, chain-smoking, marijuana, compulsive work or hobbies, compulsive gambling, increased religious involvement, meditation, a new love relationship, and regular involvement in Alcoholics Anonymous (AA). The "willpower" to stop drinking may be fostered by identifying activities to replace the time spent drinking. The selection of the activity should be made by the individual, as it appears the choice is influenced by individual values. Therapists can suggest options (Matsutsuyu, 1969) and facilitate the identification of priorities (Lakein, 1974). The effectiveness of this approach is unknown, and it is based on the assumption that no cognitive impairment is present.

The organic mental disorders do impair cognition; some of the impairments, such as intoxication, withdrawal, and hallucinosis, are temporary. The recovery process begins after the acute condition has cleared. Long-term cognitive impairments are associated with alcohol amnestic disorders and dementia associated with alcoholism. The treatment objectives in these cases may be similar to those suggested for dementia in Chapter 5.

Phencyclidine-Hydrochloride Abuse

There is some evidence to suggest that an urban epidemic of phencyclidine hydrochloride (PCP) abuse is occurring (Allen et al., 1981). Studies conducted at Los Angeles County–University of Southern California Medical Center indicate that a large number of patients have positive results on blood tests for PCP: 78.5 percent of 135 consecutive psychiatric patients (Aniline et al., 1980). The dangers of this drug have been well known to law enforcement officials and are a growing concern in psychiatric hospitals.

The popular way to ingest the drug is to dip a cigarette into a PCP solution and smoke it, which induces a calm state of "nothingness." Easily manufactured from readily available chemicals, the drug can be purchased at low cost in most urban areas. PCP is nonbiodegradable and poorly metabolized; it may accumulate in the lipid tissue of the body. Some users have a psychotic reaction to the drug and appear in psychiatric hospital admitting areas with symptoms that mimic those of schizophrenic disorders, affective disorders (especially mania), and other nonspecific dementias. The identification of PCP abuse as the primary problem, or a complicat-

ing problem, is hampered by the inability of prevalent laboratory tests to detect abuse in known abusers. The test must be done within 24 hours after ingestion and is indicated by the presence of nystagmus (an involuntary rapid movement of the eyeball) observed at the end of the horizontal plane (moving the eyes from side to side without turning the head) or the vertical plane. A misdiagnosis will probably produce a negative response to treatment (Allen et al., 1981).

Reason for Admission

People with toxic PCP psychosis are often brought to the psychiatric emergency room by the police, or others, and require physical restraint. Recent history may include unpredictable violence, extraordinarily senseless actions, and highly changeable mood and behavior. Behavior within the hospital is often unpredictable, and preserving the safety of other patients and staff is a genuine concern. Treatment involves turning the body acidic. The theory is that the acid washes the drug out of the patient's system.

Close observation of patient task behavior on hospital wards and in the occupational therapy clinic has revealed several distinguishing features of PCP intoxication. This description has been facilitated by the laboratory evidence of the USC group (Aniline et al., 1980). The clinical description aims at facilitating the identification of PCP toxicity.

Task Behavior and Cognitive Levels

PCP toxicity seems to produce an attention deficit that differs from the other attention deficits observed by therapists. Therapists may observe lapses in attention and rapid change in the cognitive level in PCP abusers. The attention lapses that are associated with the cognitive levels will be described and followed by a discussion of differential diagnosis.

At cognitive level 1 the PCP abuser's attention is focused inward most of the time. Patients may sit

Fig. 6-5. Phencyclidine hydrochloride abuse: "Fading Out."

immobile for long periods, staring into space, not responding to touch or verbal commands. Such patients do not initiate automatic actions. At cognitive level 2 patients appear aware of the environment, but their behavior is unpredictable and unusual, for example, climbing up on tables. In these patients violent behavior may suddenly erupt without any external provocation. Diminishing external stimulation may have a calming effect; placing these patients in the seclusion room has a calming effect not observed in mania, depression, or organic syndromes. Differential diagnosis is very difficult to make at cognitive level 1 or 2 if there is no known history of PCP abuse.

Cognitive levels 3 and 4 are marked by recurrent lapses of attention lasting a few seconds to several minutes. Patients stop what they are doing suddenly and unpredictably, and stare fixedly into space. Their gaze appears to lack focus, giving it a glazed appearance, and body positions at the time

of "fading out" may be maintained in statuelike immobility. A person who had been functioning at level 4 suddenly appears to be functioning at level 1 (Fig. 6-5). Attention appears to be focused inward, though the immobility of facial expression and the lack of pupil movement provides no indication that the person is "listening" to internal stimuli or even thinking particular thoughts. A spontaneous return of attention to the level 4 task is usually seen, though the patient often forgets what he or she was doing and needs to reorient himself or herself: ". . . Now what was I doing?" PCP abusers at cognitive levels 3 and 4 require frequent reorientation to their environment. Their periodic inattentiveness results in incomplete learning. Patients may forget instructions they had evidently mastered a few minutes before.

Perhaps because of their faulty attention, PCP patients are typically indecisive. Given several choices these patients ponder endlessly, often remarking, "I just can't decide" or "I can't remember the choices." Concretizing alternatives by writing down options or presenting samples of tasks facilitates decision making. Attention to a task may be diverted by excessive tactile and visual exploration of objects in their environment. Episodic repeated fingering, tapping objects on tables, and careful visual scrutinizing of common objects seems to engross patients for long periods. Typically these patients' motor movements are slow and deliberate, with some variations in their actions suggesting true exploration. Misuse of common objects, such as trying to sand a box with a pencil, is sometimes seen. Patients appear inattentive at these times and do not spontaneously recognize their errors. Patients' perception of any aberrant behavior varies: Most report only that they feel "slowed down" in their thinking and actions, and only a few have noted difficulty in maintaining attention.

Systematic trial-and-error problem solving at level 5 is confounded by the patient's inability to remember previously attempted unsuccessful solutions. Some patients are aware of their imperfect recall and inattentiveness and spontaneously seek to reorient themselves; others are quite unaware of their deficits.

Variability in cognitive level frequently occurs. Formal assessment may indicate they are capable of a certain level of ability, but their behavior may change by the minute or hour. Therapists find this very unnerving because we cannot predict their task behavior. As a rule people who test at levels 5 and 6 cannot function in groups designed for those levels and must be placed in groups for levels 3 and 4. Even in a group for levels 3 and 4 the patient may exhibit behavior characteristic of levels 1 and 2 for several minutes at a time and then resume behavior characteristic of levels 3 and 4. These sudden changes in the level of behavior are not observed in other psychiatric conditions.

Differential Diagnosis

PCP toxicity is frequently confused with the schizophrenic and primary affective disorders and the dementias. The most common problem is a failure to identify the toxicity and wash the drug out of the

person's system. The description of the task behavior must rule out other plausible explanations for our performance observations. The transient and unpredictable attention lapses are the most salient feature of PCP toxicity.

Attentional difficulties in schizophrenic disorders are more stable and predictable than those observed in PCP psychosis. For instance, patients with schizophrenic disorders will experience the same level of concentration difficulty day to day or display an increase in hallucinatory preoccupation at predictable times, such as during times of inactivity or stress. Persons with schizophrenic disorders often indicate they are listening or watching unseen stimuli by inclining their heads to the side or holding the pupils at the right or left upper corner of the eyelids, and they may talk or laugh in response to their hallucinations. Toxic PCP patients, on the other hand, typically display a glassy-eyed straightforward gaze when their attention is disrupted, and they are very quiet and still.

Distractibility is common in patients with bipolar affective disorder. At level 3 their inability to sustain attention could be described as hyperreactivity to the external environment. Objects, people, colors, and movements are all apt to capture the attention of the manic patient in rapid succession. By contrast the intoxicated patient's attention is inward. Though physically active they are hyporesponsive to the external environment in that they respond to objects in front of them but do not readily shift their attention. It has been observed that unmanageable manic patients when placed in a nonstimulating seclusion room will continue to rage, talk, or sing. The unmanageable PCP patient will usually become quite still and withdrawn.

Persons with depression also display attentional difficulties in task behavior, but typically this arises from an inability to sustain effort in a task. Their attention is focused on a task but they fatigue after a predictable period. If depressed persons display distractibility, they usually confirm that ruminations or a loss of energy are diverting their attention from the task at hand. PCP patients distinguish themselves by the variability of their task performance hour to hour. This variability is doubtless due in part to their frequent fade-outs. In addition their task performance seems to be affected to an unusual degree by the presence or absence of environmental cues. Given an unstructured task environment, such as a level 5 or 6 group for a person assessed at level 5 or 6, the PCP patient becomes suddenly perplexed and indecisive. The unstructured group places excessive demands on the patient. The PCP patient's response differs from the response of other patients. The manic patient's response to an unstructured task environment is to proceed to do many things, all at the same time; the depressed patient will either decline or select and execute the task requiring the least energy; the patient with a schizophrenic disorder may become anxious and withdrawn. Given a level 4 task, the PCP patient will usually proceed readily. With environmental cues these patients spontaneously display level 5 abilities. In this way they differ from the typical patient with a cognitive disability, who requires continued environmental alterations to compensate for the apparent absence of these same level 5 patterns of thought. PCP psychosis produces an inconsistent cognitive impairment, and the inconsistency seems to correspond with the severity of the attentional lapses.

The misuse of common objects is rarely seen in syndromes other than organic mental disorders. PCP patients who misuse objects do so only sporadically and when in a preoccupied, inattentive state. Other signs of dementia, such as disorientation and consistent memory problems, are not generally seen. Perceptual exploration (e.g., fondling common objects) may suggest autism, but in PCP patients perceptual exploration too is transient and episodic.

Implications for Management

Once the presence of PCP is confirmed and treatment begun, the objectives for management include monitoring for signs of diminishing toxicity and providing a safe environment for the patient and those around him or her. The rapid changes in behavior, coupled with unpredictable violence, indicate that therapists should be cautious with these people. Transporting PCP abusers to the OT clinic should be avoided during the first few days of hospitalization and should only be done after violent outbursts have subsided. Sometimes it is difficult to know when these outbursts are really under control; therapists should be in frequent contact with nursing personnel to be informed of the patient's current behavior.

Patients may continue to slip into behavior characteristic of level 1 or 2 for several days after violent behavior is controlled and cognitive levels 3 through 6 have been assessed. When they slip back to level 1, they are usually unresponsive to therapist's directions and the therapist must wait for the episode to pass, usually in a minute or two; the longest fade-out observed to date lasted 20 minutes. Level 2 behavior can be interrupted by bringing their attention back to the task at hand. Therapists are advised to avoid forcing these people to do anything and to avoid confrontations with people with a history of violence. Emergency procedures for calling for assistance should be clearly established but with an exercise of cautious judgment will probably not be needed. I suspect that the structure provided by the task is a great asset in managing this difficult condition.

Adequate nutrition and hydration can be problematic in severely toxic patients, though helping to focus attention through loud verbal commands or guiding the patient's movements have met with limited success. Secluding violent patients, far from being cruel, often has a calming effect. Such patients should be watched very closely, however, for possible self-injurious behavior. Sedating neuroleptic drugs are used to treat both agitation and psychotic symptoms.

Compliance with hospital routines, schedules, and rules can be facilitated by providing reminders such as lists of staff names or schedules of activities. As soon as patients are predictable, daily activities in which patients are closely observed will allow documentation of remitting attentional difficulties and other toxic signs. Structured task environments with concrete, demonstrated instructions result in success for the inattentive patient. Patients should be counseled to postpone resumption of hazardous occupations or household tasks if they leave hospital before attention problems are resolved.

CONCLUSION

A cognitive disability is not associated with all of the psychiatric diagnoses. The presence of maladaptive behavior is an indication that some kind of an impairment is present, and we are uncertain about the best way to describe the problem. A therapist's observations of routine task behavior may be helpful in refining some of these descriptions. Clear descriptions contain specific aspects of behavior associated with specific biologic defects. Greater descriptive specificity is producing greater treatment specificity and a reduction in maladaptive behavior. The diagnoses cited in this chapter are still ambiguous, and the references cited are regarded as an indication that greater clarity is being achieved.

REFERENCES

Allen, R. E., Aniline, O., and Pitts, F. N., Jr. The urban epidemic of phencyclidine (PCP). *Urban Health*, pp. 45–47, Nov. 1981.

Andersen, E. What are prisons for? No longer rehabilitation, but to punish and lock the worst away. *Time*, pp. 38–41, Sept. 13, 1982.

Aniline, O., et al. The urban epidemic of PCP use: Laboratory evidence from a public psychiatric hospital inpatient service. *Biol. Psychiatry* 15:813–817, 1980.

Bohman, M., Sigvardsson, S., and Cloninger, C. R. Maternal inheritance of alcohol abuse: Cross-factoring analysis of adopted women. *Arch. Gen. Psychiatry* 38:965–969, 1981.

Cloninger, C. R., Bohman, M., and Sigvardsson, S. Inheritance of alcohol abuse: Cross-factoring analysis of adopted men. *Arch. Gen. Psychiatry* 38:861–868, 1981.

DSM III: Diagnostic and Statistical Manual of Mental Disorders (3rd ed.). Washington, D.C.: American Psychiatric Association, 1980.

Earls, F. Application of *DSM III* in an epidemiological study of preschool children. *Am. J. Psychiatry* 139:242–243, 1982.

Edwards, G., and Grant, M. (eds.). *Alcoholism Treatment in Transition*. London: Croom Helm, 1981.

Fidler, G. S., and Fidler, J. *Occupational Therapy: A Communication Process*. New York: Macmillan, 1963.

Gaines, L. S. Cognition and the Environment: Implications for a Self-awareness Theory of Drinking. In T. C. Harford and L. S. Gaines (eds.), *Social Drinking Contexts*. Washington, D.C.: Government Printing Office, 1981.

Goodwin, D. W., and Erickson, C. K. *Alcoholism and Affective Disorders*. New York: Spectrum, 1979.

Gunderson, J. G., Siever, L. J., and Spaulding, E. The search for a schizotype: Crossing the border again. *Arch. Gen. Psychiatry* 49:15–22, 1983.

Hatsukami, D., and Pickens, R. W. Posttreatment depression in an alcohol and drug abuse population. *Am. J. Psychiatry* 139:1563–1566, 1982.

Holhn-Saric, R., et al. Effects of clonidine on anxiety disorders. *Arch. Gen. Psychiatry* 38:1278–1282, 1981.

Klein, D. F., et al. Treatment of phobias: II. Behavior therapy and supportive psychotherapy: Are there any specific ingredients? *Arch. Gen. Psychiatry* 40:139–145, 1983.

Koenigsberg, H. W., Kernberg, O. F., and Schomer, J. Diagnosing borderline conditions in an outpatient setting. *Arch. Gen. Psychiatry* 40:49–53, 1983.

Kroll, J., et al. Borderline personality disorder: Construct validity of the concept. *Arch. Gen. Psychiatry* 38:1021–1026, 1981.

Lakein, A. *How to Get Control of Your Time and Your Life*. New York: Signet, 1974.

Lamb, H. R., and Grant, M. S. The mentally ill in an urban county jail. *Arch. Gen. Psychiatry* 39:17–22, 1982.

Leckman, J. F., et al. Anxiety disorders and depression: Contradictions between family study data and *DSM III* conventions. *Am. J. Psychiatry* 140:880–882, 1983.

Llorens, L. A. *Application of Developmental Theory of Health and Rehabilitation*. Rockville, Md.: American Occupational Therapy Association, 1976.

Matsutsuyu, J. S. The interest checklist. *Am. J. Occup. Ther.* 23:323–328, 1969.

Matuzas, W., and Glass, R. M. Treatment of agoraphobia and panic attacks (comment). *Arch. Gen. Psychiatry* 40:220–222, 1983.

Mellsop, G., et al. The reliability of Axis II of *DSM III*. *Am. J. Psychiatry* 139:1360–1361, 1982.

Millon, T. *Disorders of Personality: DMS-III Axis II*. New York: Wiley, 1981.

Mosey, A. C. *Three Frames of Reference for Mental Health*. Thorofare, N.J.: Charles B. Slack, 1970.

Moss, G. R., and Rick, G. R. Overview: Applications of operant technology to behavioral disorders of adolescents. *Am. J. Psychiatry* 138:1161–1169, 1981.

Munjack, D. J., and Moss, H. B. Affective disorder and alcoholism in families of agoraphobics. *Arch. Gen. Psychiatry* 38:869–871, 1981.

Nace, E. P., Saxon, J. J., and Shore, N. A comparison of borderline and nonborderline alcoholic patients. *Arch. Gen. Psychiatry* 40:54–56, 1983.

Pecknold, J. C., et al. Does tryptophan potentiate clomipramine in the treatment of agoraphobic and social phobic patients? *Br. J. Psychiatry* 140:484–490, 1982.

Pope, H. G., et al. The validity of *DSM III* borderline personality disorder: A phenomenologic, family history, treatment response, and long-term follow-up study. *Arch. Gen. Psychiatry* 40:23–30, 1983.

Purtilo, R. B., and Cassel, C. K. *Ethical Dimensions in the Health Professions*. Philadelphia: Saunders, 1981.

Reilly, M. (ed.). *Play as Exploratory Learning*. Beverly Hills, Calif.: Sage, 1974.

Rogeness, G. A., et al. Biochemical differences in children with conduct disorder: socialized and undersocialized. *Am. J. Psychiatry* 139:307–311, 1982.

Shanok, S. S., and Lewis, D. O. Medical histories of female delinquents: Clinical and epidemiologic findings. *Arch. Gen. Psychiatry* 38:211–213, 1981.

Simpson, D. D. Treatment for drug abuse: Follow-up outcomes and length of time spent. *Arch. Gen. Psychiatry* 38:875–880, 1981.

Soloff, P. H., and Millward, J. W. Psychiatric disorders in families of borderline patients. *Arch. Gen. Psychiatry* 40:37–44, 1983.

Strober, M., Green, J., and Carlson, G. Reliability of psychiatric diagnoses in hospitalized adolescents: Interrater agreement using *DSM III*. *Arch. Gen. Psychiatry* 38:141–145, 1981.

Turner, T. B. Clinical Aspects of Ethanol Tolerance and Dependence. In H. Rigter and J. C. Crabbe (eds.), *Alcohol Tolerance and Dependence*. New York: Elsevier, 1980.

Vaillant, G. E., and Milofsky, E. S. Natural history of male alcoholism. *Arch. Gen. Psychiatry* 39:127–133, 1982.

Wender, P. H., Reimherr, F. W., and Wood, D. R. Attention deficit disorder ("minimal brain dysfunction") in adults: A replication study of diagnoses and drug treatment. *Arch. Gen. Psychiatry* 38:449–456, 1981.

Zitrin, C. M., et al. Treatment of phobias: I. Comparison of imipramine hydrochloride and placebo. *Arch. Gen. Psychiatry* 40:125–138, 1983.

PART TWO

PRACTICE

Theories tell us what should occur most of the time, and Part One described common observations. Practice introduces additional variables that are specific to individuals being treated in various institutional settings. Perhaps the most startling variation to beginning therapists is the wide range of emotional responses that can be elicited by identical task demands; Chapter 7 will provide some explanations for these variations and suggest methods for managing emotional responses. The teaching case examples in Chapter 8 may help the reader fit an appreciation for individual differences into the framework of theoretical similarities.

The variations introduced by institutional settings will be discussed in Chapters 9 and 10. A health institution responds to social mandates for service. The issues of frequent concern to the administration of a treatment program will be discussed. Some examples of activity groups that have a good clinical track record will be presented.

Practice examples invariably raise concerns about a "cookbook approach," that is, following the examples without making the adjustments indicated for an individual patient or treatment setting. Part Two assumes that therapists are "creative cooks"—that they can read a recipe and modify it according to the available ingredients. The examples selected present common clinical problems, and the solutions suggested may be imitated in similar instances. The examples are not ideal in that they are not intended to represent the only way that a therapist could manage a treatment program. The examples are designed to facilitate the application of theory in clinical practice.

CHAPTER 7

EMOTIONAL RESPONSES TO TASK DEMANDS

SURVIVAL IS KEEPING ONE'S DIGNITY INTACT.
D. Nyad, 1978

The emotional responses to a task demand can be volatile, vitriolic, apathetic, glacial, sensitive, or just about any other reaction that one can imagine. The clinical application of a theory is confusing when variations in emotional responses are elicited by identical tasks demands. The therapist may not be concerned when a pleasant emotional response occurs, but an unpleasant, vitriolic, or catastrophic reaction can lead to undesirable consequences. By and large this chapter aims at suggesting methods for enhancing pleasant task experiences and preventing unpleasant task experiences. It is assumed that people with a disability are at risk for encountering more than their fair share of unpleasant task experiences. Furthermore, it is assumed that pleasant task experiences are essential to the preservation of human dignity and that pleasant, successful experiences are especially important to disabled people. As used here, an *emotional response* is what the therapist observes and a *task experience* is what the patient feels.

Human beings find it difficult to understand and explain human experience. The last two centuries have witnessed considerable advancement in detailing the neural apparatus that forms the biology of experience (Crockett et al., 1981; Freud, 1895; James, 1890; Luria, 1979; Pribram and Gill, 1976). The advantage of a biologic explanation lies in the relative objectivity that it brings to a subject that tends to be fraught with metaphysical speculation. The view of experience contained in this chapter relies on a biologic explanation with emphasis on the tremendous advances made during the last three decades. It is hoped that these biologic advances will be helpful in objectively explaining a subjective experience.

Neuroscience research into the relationship between an emotional response to a task and a mental disorder usually proceeds along two courses: associations with focal lesions or general impairments. Patients with small, discrete focal lesions are studied in order to develop anatomic models of the brain that show how these lesions are correlated with disturbances in behavior. Patients with such lesions are clinical rarities. Most patients have a general impairment. Therapists require a functional model that speaks to the total organization of the brain (Crockett et al., 1981). A functional model of an emotional response to a task demand, based on a general description of total brain organization, is required. This chapter is indebted to the description of total brain organization suggested by Pribram (1981).

The theoretical discussion may be easier to follow if I first cite some examples of the kinds of emotional responses to a task demand that I am seeking to clarify. The clinical observations that puzzle us are best seen in an OT program that we have called the basic crafts group (Chap. 10). Every day for the last 10 years therapists have been conducting a basic crafts group for patients assessed at cognitive level 4. Thousands of wooden boxes and felt eyeglass cases have been made by people diagnosed as having schizophrenic or primary affective disorders. Each therapist has an opportunity to observe 8 to 12 people doing the same project with some degree of control for the following variables: the cognitive level, the task complexity, the method of giving instructions, and the diagnosis. Patients respond to basic craft projects in different ways, especially when they make a mistake. Some people calmly ignore or disregard a mistake. Other people get angry; they may blame the therapist and tell him or her that the materials are shoddy. Some say that they want to stop working on the project or leave the project to get a cup of coffee. Other people work with intense concentration; I have seen people perspire profusely while doing something as physically undemanding as staining a small wooden box. Clearly people vary in their emotional response to a task demand.

A number of questions are posed by these variations. The most immediate is How should we, as therapists, respond to these variations? The second question is How should we report these variations?

The therapist's response and the report are influenced by the therapist's theoretical interpretation of these emotional reactions.

This chapter addresses the following topics: (1) a description, based on current neurobiologic knowledge, of normative responses to task demands, (2) emotional responses to task experiences that appear to be diagnosis specific, (3) management techniques that can promote a pleasant or an unpleasant task experience, (4) a possible neurobiologic basis for the positive and negative effects of the task environment, and (5) implications for occupational therapy's treatment objectives.

NORMATIVE TASK EXPERIENCES

A description of a "normal" emotional response is required before one can describe a "disabled" response. Piaget has written extensively about the self-regulation of normative task experiences, and therapists have utilized his work (Ayres, 1979; Reilly, 1974). Usually self-regulation refers to development, to the transformation that occurs during the process of moving from a lower to a higher cognitive level (Furth, 1969; Piaget, 1971, 1978; Reiss and Overton, 1970). What can be gleaned from Piaget's description is that self-regulation is invariant, that it is always occurring in a dynamic fashion throughout the process of doing a task. The individual patient is in control of his or her own exchanges with the task environment.

Self-regulation is linked to adaptive functioning (Fig. 7-1). Piaget divides adaptive functioning into two complementary processes: assimilation and accommodation. *Assimilation* refers to taking matter into the organism, as in the nutritional process; *accommodation*, to the organism's adjusting according to external demands, as in chewing soft or tough foods. The terms are derived from biology and are more readily applied to solid matter such as food than to abstracts such as information processed by the brain. Assimilation and accommodation have escaped attempts to define and test operationally Piaget's concepts (Brown and Desforges, 1979). I

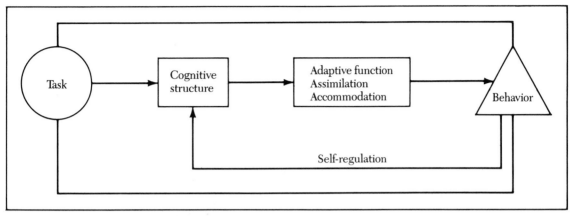

Fig. 7-1. *Piagetian view of self-regulation.*

have shared this confusion. Piaget (1971) makes a clear distinction between a cognitive structure and an adaptive function. Attempts to measure adaptive functions have resulted in measures of the cognitive level, not the adaptive function. The Piagetian concepts are interesting, but they seem to require further clarification.

Subjective and Participatory Experiences

A method for studying assimilation and accommodation has been suggested by Pribram (1981). Pribram's conceptualization of the way the brain works has been instructive because it suggests the neurologic pathways that produce different kinds of experiences (Pribram, 1981). This association between brain and emotional response is promising in that it may lead to theoretical clarity that has been lacking heretofore.

It is obvious that a therapist cannot experience what the patient experiences. The source of information about an emotional response to a task experience is the same as the source for information about task performance: the analysis of task demands and our observations of task behavior (Fig. 7-2). Task demands can elicit an emotional response that may be observed during the process of doing a task. The emotion observed by a therapist or re-

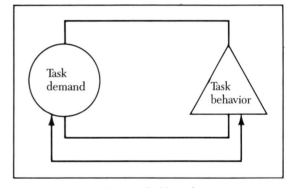

Fig. 7-2. *Therapist's view of self-regulation.*

ported by a patient can be pleasant or unpleasant (Arieti, 1967).

Two internal processes, identified as subjective experiences and participatory experiences, may be operating while a person is doing a task. Briefly described, subjective experiences operate to inhibit awareness of disturbing information, while participatory experiences operate to enhance awareness of novel information. Inhibition and enhancement interact to balance each other. Thus subjective and participatory experiences are two reciprocal processes that can be visualized as two feedback loops firing with equal density (Fig. 7-3). Assimilation

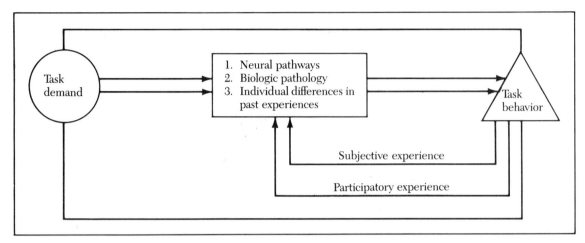

Fig. 7-3. Biologic view of self-regulation.

may be subjective, while participation may require accommodation.

Subjective Experience: Inhibition

Information that is not relevant to the present task is normally inhibited by the brain. Examples are blocking out the feel of the chair you are sitting on or being unable to remember confusing directions. Information that is irrelevant to the present task is eliminated because the information would disturb continuity in task performance. Subjective experiences are conservative in that they aim to preserve the status quo that existed before the introduction of irrelevant input. Internal control and stability are maintained by self-inhibiting, de-emphasizing, or eliminating irrelevant information. Successful inhibition produces the emotional experiences of relief, calm, or tranquility (Table 7-1).

Participatory Experience: Enhancement

Information that is novel to the person is usually enhanced by the brain. A task demand that contains novelty, contrasts, or new information may produce a temporary instability. A novel task demand increases the probability that a change in mental or-

ganization is required. Participatory experiences introduce new information, and some mechanisms of the brain highlight the uniqueness of the information, accommodating to the uniqueness of the task demand. Participatory experiences require some mental flexibility. When mental reorganization occurs, the emotional experience is satisfaction, delight, joy, exhilaration, or aesthetic appreciation (Table 7-1).

Balance

The brain is balanced, or equilibrated, by either eliminating irrelevant information or restructuring the mental organization to accommodate to novel information. Brain pathology jeopardizes this balance. An inability to inhibit irrelevant information produces distress. An inability to accommodate to new information increases confusion (Pribram, 1981). The type of imbalance that occurs may be diagnosis specific.

DIAGNOSIS-SPECIFIC EXPERIENCES

Clinical experience suggests that differential diagnosis may be facilitated by therapists' observations

Table 7-1. Emotional experiences related to the biologic processes of the brain

Subjective experience	Participatory experience
NORMATIVE EXPERIENCES	
Successful inhibition	Successful reorganization
Relief	Satisfaction
Calm	Delight
Tranquility	Joy
	Exhilaration
	Aesthetic appreciation
DISORDERED EXPERIENCES	
	Unsuccessful
Unsuccessful inhibition	reorganization
Racing thoughts	Loss of energy
Pressured speech	Confabulation
Hyperactivity	Inflexibility
Ruminations	Poverty of speech
Hallucinations	Avoidance of novelty
Information	Confusion
bombardment	Apathy

Source: Data from K. H. Pribram, Emotions. In S. B. Filskov and T. J. Boll (eds.), *Handbook of Clinical Neuropsychology.* New York: Wiley, 1981.

of the type of imbalance in self-regulation that may be occurring (Table 7-2).

People in a manic episode are hyperresponsive to novelty, as seen in their distractible task behavior. There is a diminished ability to inhibit information as expressed by racing thoughts, pressured speech, and hyperactivity. Conversely, people in a depressive episode have a diminished response to novelty expressed by a loss of energy, which may be accompanied by a diminished ability to inhibit ruminations and somatic complaints. Novelty is bewildering to people with dementia. Their bewilderment produces confabulation, guessing, and an inflexible adherence to their familiar patterns of motor action.

People with a schizophrenic disorder have an intense response to novelty expressed by a flat affect, social withdrawal, marked poverty of speech content, and working in the egg shell posture. Atten-

tion is stimulus bound; patients block out other stimuli and lack initiative in seeking novelty. In addition, schizophrenic disorders are characterized by a diminished ability to inhibit unusual stimuli such as delusions, hallucinations, and bizarre behavior.

Anxiety disorders may be accompanied by excessive inhibition of novelty expressed by avoidance procedures, rituals, and trouble getting started on a task. People with personality disorders may have a selective response to novelty, preferring easily mastered novelty for immediate personal benefit. PCP psychosis may be accompanied by a trancelike response to common physical objects and rapid, cycling variability in the ability to inhibit and reorganize information.

MANAGEMENT TECHNIQUES

A therapist who sees the symptoms of a disease must decide whether to stand back and observe them or intervene to suppress them. It is appropriate to stand back and observe the symptoms when one has questions concerning differential diagnosis or medication effectiveness. Observation is recommended for the purpose of evaluation. The purpose of intervention to suppress the symptoms is treatment, which should be initiated as soon as the therapist has obtained the required assessment. The therapist's purpose may change within a matter of seconds. Making the shift seems to be easier when we have a clear reason for eliciting observations of potential pathology.

A therapist should intervene to suppress symptoms as quickly as possible. Task performance is a participatory experience that can easily require capabilities beyond the patient's level of ability. Task demands that are too complex can elicit a catastrophic reaction. A catastrophic reaction occurs when patients recognize, to some degree, that they are unable to do a simple task and the personal disaster of a mental disorder becomes apparent. The experience is unpleasant and the emotional response may be fear or anger. Other common participatory experiences include distress, confusion,

Table 7-2. A biologic disruption in self-regulation

Disorder	Subjective experience	Participatory experience
Manic episode	Diminished inhibition of information Hyperactivity Pressured speech Racing thoughts	Hyperresponsiveness to novelty Distractibility
Depressive episode	Diminished inhibition of information Ruminations Somatic complaints	Diminished response to novelty Lack of energy
Dementia	Hyperstable inhibition of information Inflexible	Bewildered response to novelty Confabulation Poor recent memory
Schizophrenia, acute	Diminished inhibition of information Hallucinations Delusions Bizarre behavior	Diminished response to novelty Social withdrawal Flat affect Poverty of speech content Functional decline
Schizophrenia, chronic	Hyperstable inhibition of information Lack of initiative Stimulus-bound attention	Diminished response to novelty Continued functional decline Poverty of speech content Eggshell posture
Anxiety disorders	Hyperstable inhibition of information Rituals Phobias	Hyperresponsiveness to novelty Avoidance of tasks Novelty increases anxiety
Personality disorders	Excessive neglect of abstract information Rights of others Social consequences	Selective response to novelty Immediate benefit Egocentrism
PCP toxic psychosis	Variable inhibition of information Unpredictable behavior Fade-outs Disregard for common properties of objects	Variable response to novelty Novelty in common objects Indecisiveness

perplexity, uncertainty, and apathy. The therapist's management techniques are aimed at minimizing these unpleasant experiences. Therapists can prevent unpleasant experiences, but doing so requires considerable therapeutic skill because the therapist must overcome the natural tendency for unpleasant experiences to occur. The description of the subjective and participatory experiences that follows presents the pleasant and unpleasant experiences that can occur. Therapeutic management techniques that aim at fostering pleasant experiences are suggested.

Proposition 7. An effective outcome of occupational therapy service occurs when successful task performance is accompanied by a pleasant task experience.

An opportunity to engage in a pleasant task experience is present when the therapist reduces the novelty required to do a task. The task analysis described in Chapter 3 provides some guidelines for grading novelty. Individual differences in past experience in doing tasks can guide the degree of novelty as well.

Past Experiences

Experience is usually regarded as participatory, occurring within the present tense. The baseline for present experience, however, is provided by past experience. Past experience is the history people bring with them when first seen by a therapist. Many disciplines are involved in collecting historical information with different emphases: medical, social, vocational, and educational histories. Often there is some overlap in these histories, and institutions vary with respect to which discipline collects what information. The emphasis in occupational therapy is on routine task history.

Therapists collect information about the specifics of past experience that is apt to influence present and future task behavior. For example, one of our favorite questions is to ask a person to describe a recent typical day, from getting up in the morning to going to bed at night. A person's response provides a picture of the content of his or her day as well as an indication of the person's ability to establish a routine. As might be expected, many people at lower cognitive levels are unable to organize their time and establish their own routines. If the patient is unable to identify recent task experiences, other parts of the history can be used to identify meaningful tasks.

Therapists rely heavily on the use of familiar voluntary motor actions when designing tasks for people assessed at levels 2, 3, and 4. The search for familiar actions can be facilitated by inquiring about a person's education, work, and social history. The therapist uses this information to select task content that is apt to be interesting and meaningful to the individual. The routine task history establishes a baseline for what the person already knows how to do. The routine task history also aims at establishing the individual's feelings about various tasks: likes and dislikes, successes and failures. Past experience continues to influence routine task behavior throughout the delivery of services, and therapists should be alert to this influence. Therapists should inquire continually about a person's experience with similar tasks.

A patient's past experiences in occupational therapy may be influential. For example, I have heard psychiatric patients say, "I don't want to finger-paint." We can infer that their past experience involved a therapeutic transaction with projective techniques. The patient's response to participation in all kinds of tasks can be influential; a person brings a baseline of experience to the first encounter with a therapist. People with cognitive disabilities seem to respond favorably to familiar processes that their past experience suggests they can do successfully. The task provides them with an opportunity to act positively on the external environment in a manner that can be produced by their defective neurochemical and neuroanatomic mechanisms. The therapist's management techniques can be directed toward providing experiences of satisfaction and sometimes delight.

Present Experiences

The performance of a task requires that the individual attend to and respond to the demands of the external environment. Task behavior produces a participatory experience for the patient. Doing a task is apt to introduce novel demands and produce instability; the task analysis can be regarded as a vehicle for controlling the degree of instability introduced by a task demand. It is assumed that a person at a lower cognitive level is at risk for experiencing overwhelming task demands; achievable demands can be provided by matching the task demand to the individual's assessed cognitive ability and past experiences. Participatory experiences can be designed to minimize the mental adjustment required by external task demands. The experience produced can be one of symptom relief.

Accommodation to novel information discovered in the task environment begins at cognitive level 3 and is established at level 6. A degree of emotional satisfaction may be expressed when mental reorganization occurs. An absence of mental reorganization may be accompanied by a bland emotional response, that is, no personal investment in the task or the outcome.

Emotional response during task performance is based on an internal awareness of one's success or failure in meeting the task demands. A positive self-assessment produces a positive task experience, and the converse also appears to be true. Feelings of competency and mastery are influenced by this self-appraisal (Pribram, 1981; White, 1959). Simple task demands that appear to be beneath a person's usual expectations for himself or herself can produce a feeling of shame. This is a major reason for avoiding childish connotations in task content. The individual's self-assessment is accepted as a valid indication of a task experience. If a negative task experience occurs, the therapist asks the individual for an explanation and attempts to remove the problem in a new task. Negative emotional responses are frequent during depressive episodes; these patients can be encouraged to observe their performance for signs of improvement.

Unpleasant experiences can produce some emotional responses that are difficult to manage: blame, anger, rage, fear, or flight. The neurologic literature refers to these responses as catastrophic reactions. Generally these emotions are observed when there is a mismatch between the task complexity and the individual's cognitive ability. The therapist can do a difficult step in the task procedure for the individual or supply a different and easier task. A discussion with the individual is counterproductive, tending to

escalate the negative emotional response and producing even greater management problems.

Some people make mistakes in a task procedure that they simply ignore. When mistakes are pointed out by a therapist, one may hear a rationalization such as "I wanted it that way." Asking the person to correct a mistake in such cases may result in a firm refusal or a great deal of self-defensive anger. These observations may be interpreted as a breakdown in internal control produced by novelty in the task demands. Therapists seem to have a natural urge to have mistakes corrected, and we can become a bit zealous in our insistence. Our insistence can escalate the negative emotional response. If the mistake bothers us, we can offer to correct the error for the patient, respecting, of course, the patient's right to refuse the offer. Sometimes we have to learn to tolerate mistakes that bother us but are of no concern to the patient.

Internal control is usually stabilized by inhibiting input into the brain. Information is deemphasized, eliminated, or discarded so that people are not bombarded by redundant information. Internal control prepares a person for participation in a specific task; the person discards useless information and attends to the information required to do the task (Pribram, 1981). Inhibition seems to be a problem in those with cognitive disabilities; distractibility, hyperactivity, hallucinations, and depressive ruminations are all acute examples of an inability to block input. Acute problems in inhibition of information can be ameliorated by the therapist. The therapist refocuses attention on the task; this can be done by demonstrating the next step in the task or by asking a question about how the current step is progressing. A gentle nudge is frequently all that is required to bring the person back to the task at hand. Many patients tell us they value task experiences because doing projects helps to block these disturbing symptoms.

Stable Experiences

Long-term cognitive disabilities seem to produce a hyperstable and inflexible method of maintaining internal control that is often divorced from reality (Pribram, 1981). Some people maintain delusions and bizarre thoughts in a manner that is divorced from reality. Participatory experiences may frighten them; their fear is expressed as a total refusal to come to OT or engage in activity. Tasks that are new or different to them may be rejected or regarded with suspicion. Arousing their interest in making a first attempt at a task can be a therapeutic challenge. Mendel (1975) uses a metaphor that seems to apply here: The therapeutic transaction is rather like attempting to feed a bird out of one's hand. Any unexpected movement or comment is apt to frighten the person away. Therapists can ignore delusions and accept bizarre thinking as "real"; the delusions and irrational thoughts are real to the patient. Participation begins within the context of the patient's present reality; the first efforts may be tenuous and brief. The first task selected by the therapist should be familiar to the patient and as unlikely to elicit errors as possible. The therapist's demeanor should be calm, accepting, and gentle. Any indication that you are going to "make" them do something or confront their irrational thoughts can frighten them. An accepting management technique can stimulate satisfaction in having successfully met the task demands.

Some people with long-term cognitive disabilities keep their internal realities a secret. For example, people with a delusional system may decide simply to stop talking about it. The delusional system may still guide their thinking, but they can avoid arguments and detection if they refuse to discuss their thoughts. A therapist can easily say or do something contrary to a secret delusional system that threatens the patient's internal control. The therapist can apologize by saying, "I'm sorry, I didn't mean to do that." Saying "I'm sorry, I didn't mean to scare you" can make the situation worse—the person may not recognize his or her own fear or may be alarmed that someone else recognized a vulnerability. The emotional response to suppressing these secret thoughts successfully may be an expression of calmness and tranquility.

NEUROBIOLOGIC RESEARCH ON EFFECTS OF THE TASK ENVIRONMENT

Research studies in cognitive psychology and psychopharmacology are beginning to clarify the positive and negative effects of task demands. The terminology used in the neurosciences is inconsistent, which makes the reading difficult. What seem to be emerging are some consistent findings about how the brain functions during a task experience. Two examples will provide an illustration of the type of studies being conducted. Shallice (1981), in a study of frontal lobe lesions associated with reading impairments, divided reading control processes into primitive selection methods and supervisory attentional mechanisms. Primitive selection methods utilize "routine experience" and "well-learned 'triggers'." Supervisory attentional mechanisms are utilized during the "correction of unexpected errors . . . where the desired response is novel or ill-learned, where habitual responses have to be overcome, and where the response is judged to be dangerous or technically difficult" (Shallice, 1981, p. 191). Shallice's division seems to follow the distinction between subjective and participatory experiences, with a hierarchical distinction made between familiar tasks and new learning. New task demands evoke the supervisory attentional mechanisms.

A psychopharmacologic study based on Gray's (1981) paradigm for the effectiveness of the antianxiety drugs (benzodiazepines, barbiturates, and alcohol) is interesting. In animal studies the usual response to the stimuli of punishment, omission of an expected reward, and novelty are counteracted by the antianxiety drugs. (Therapists should note that novelty here is associated with punishment and nonreward.) The usual response to novelty, punishment, or nonreward is an increase in attention to novelty, an increase in arousal, and a pause in or discontinuation of ongoing behavior. "Anxiety . . . consists of a central state elicited by threats of punishment, frustration, or failure, and by novelty or uncertainty" (Gray, 1981, p. 194). Gray hypothesizes that the septo-hippocampal system with its se-rotonergic and noradrenergic effects is the locus of anxiety and further suggests that the system functions in two modes. The first mode is to check incoming stimuli for a "match" between expected stimuli and actual stimuli. The second mode, which is called into operation when a "mismatch" occurs, increases arousal and attention (Gray, 1981). Novelty in a task demand may be associated with a pause in task behavior and an increase in anxiety. A mismatch between the cognitive level and the task demand may trigger this psychopharmacologic system, which may be the biologic basis of the negative effects of a task demand.

Research in neuropsychology, cognitive psychology, and psychopharmacology such as that just described supports the notion that there are two processes operating in the brain. One process is a match or correspondence with past experience. The other process goes into operation when there is a mismatch, an actual error, or a potential threat. The experience produced by a mismatch has a high potential for being aversive. People with a cognitive disability are at risk during task performance of encountering a mismatch between the past experiences that they can apply to a task and the actual task demands. The risk is an aversive task experience.

Task Demands

Task demands are external stimuli. The type of sensory stimuli seems to be an important consideration. Matching the task demand to the person's current cognitive level seems to produce an experience that is within a person's comfortable range of tolerance. A task demand that is above the person's current cognitive level elicits reluctance, resistance, and sometimes a stubborn refusal to participate in tasks. Arousal, activation, and effort seem to be impeded by sensory stimuli that stimulate the neurobiologic mechanisms beyond a comfortable range of tolerance.

Proposition 8. Steps in task procedures that require abilities above a person's level of ability will be refused or ignored.

The complexity of the task demand is analyzed as an autonomous unit, separated from the person doing the task, according to the guidelines of the task analysis. The task analysis provides an objective measure of the task demand. A person's response to the task demand is influenced by his or her past experiences. Past experience is important in arousal, activation, and sustaining effort. Within a patient population, some cultural similarities can be identified by therapists. Detailed information concerning an individual's past experience in doing something like threading a needle is often lacking, and therapists are forced to draw on cultural similarities to supply this information. Of course, dissimilarities between patients also occur, which can make the selection of a task demand quite difficult.

The selection of a task demand utilizes the task analysis and cultural similarities as much as possible. We must recognize, however, that this is not a fail-safe system. Individual differences in past experience can affect arousal, activation, and effort. The best way to account for individual differences seems to come from a clear recognition that individuals regulate their own task behavior. Self-regulation is based on the assumption that most patients will do their best to comply with task demands, given the cognitive limitations imposed by the disease process. This assumption is a major theoretical change.

Novelty, increased arousal, attention, learning, adaptation, and anxiety produce some theoretical knots for us. Our theories have been focusing on novelty by deliberately introducing novelty to stimulate the learning of new behaviors. This sounds great when you read it or teach it. In practice, however, it has not always worked out so well. In the extreme, some terrible scenes between therapist and patient have occurred, with the patient screaming at the therapist and actively resisting the therapist's best efforts to help. Some patients hate to come to OT, and we must look at the possible validity of their complaints. The question is: Is it really beneficial to put ourselves and our patients through catastrophic or adverse reactions? We do not know. The first problem, in some cases, is a pretense that unpleasant experiences do not occur. Clearly, this problem should be solved by objective observation. The second problem is that we have pretended that improvements in behavior resulted from these task experiences, lulling ourselves along by ignoring spontaneous remission and the effectiveness of psychotropic drugs. If improvement is going to happen anyway, we certainly do not need to insist that patients continue unpleasant task experiences. The third problem is that we have not separated those patients who are able to learn new behavior from those who cannot; the separation seems to be between level 4 and level 5. Task demands, which introduce novel relationships and abstract properties, do seem to be pleasant at levels 5 and 6. Levels 1 through 4 are characterized by inattention to, or an inability to retain, subtle or intangible properties of objects. At the lower levels an unpleasant experience is easy to generate and difficult to prevent.

PLEASANT EXPERIENCES

I recommend that therapists take on the challenge of preventing unpleasant emotional responses and become proficient at doing so before experimenting with potentially noxious stimuli. That way a therapist can quickly change the task if a task demand becomes painful to an individual patient. Changes in task demands can be used to prevent unpleasant participatory experiences by matching the task demands to the person's assessed cognitive level. Therapists can modify the task so that people who have mental limitations can experience their remaining human dignity. The therapist's response to individual differences must be done on a case-by-case basis. Therapists cannot be expected to anticipate every problem introduced by individual differ-

ences, and some modifications are usually required during treatment. The indication for a modification in the task demand is an unpleasant experience.

The medical interventions that can change the natural course of mental diseases are undergoing major changes. As a general rule neurologists cannot change the course of a disease, but increasingly psychiatrists can. At present we are all struggling to select the best course of action for the confusing clinical pictures we encounter in practice (Allen and Mendel, 1982). The change in our theoretical orientation is profound.

Consider, for example, the recent history of American psychiatry. Thirty years ago the American psychiatrist was taught to consider dreams, symbols, ego defense mechanisms, and oral and anal needs (English and Finch, 1954). Psychotropic drugs were introduced in the 1950s, but it took a number of years to discover the reason for their effectiveness. Now psychiatrists are taught to consider chemical formulas, neurotransmitters, drug synergies, and dosage levels (Goodman and Gilman, 1975). Obviously there is a big difference between the study of dreams and symbols and the study of neurochemistry. Kuhn (1970), in his historical review of scientific revolutions, identified some of the psychosocial responses to radical changes in knowledge: Some people refuse to recognize the new knowledge, and the discipline awaits their retirement; some people try to combine the old and new knowledge in complicated models that are incongruent because the knowledge is contradictory; and the younger people in the discipline tend to embrace the new knowledge and make most of the advances. Psychiatry can be regarded as an applied profession in transition; physicians trained in the 1960s may still be in practice at the turn of the century. We can safely assume that we will continue to see variances in physicians' use of the new knowledge for some time. Age, inclination to study neurochemistry, the effectiveness of medication on the psychiatrist's patient population, and geographical location seem to be relevant factors in influencing adaptation to the new knowledge. We should not assume, as some wish, that psychotropic drugs are going to be discontinued because the side effects are so awful. Medications do have side effects. Diseases also have complications, such as suicide, divorce, and unemployment. Many people choose to tolerate the side effects of medications because the pathologic experiences and the associated social complications are so severe.

Physicians are not alone in needing to adapt to the new knowledge. Adaptation to the neuroscience knowledge is the focus of this book. A particularly difficult problem is posed by occupational therapy's interpretation of an emotional response to a task demand. A person's emotional response may be influenced by individual and cultural differences in past experience, by the complexity of the task, by a neurochemical imbalance, and by neuroanatomic damage. Each of these factors must be considered in observing and managing the routine task behavior of those with a cognitive disability. The advances in the neurosciences are making it possible for us to be more objective, specific, and realistic about the effectiveness of our services. This is bound to have a positive effect on the quality of our services. These gains are not without their losses; some long-cherished ideas require a reexamination, because we have been deliberately introducing potentially noxious stimuli to fulfill learning objectives.

Reexamination of Learning Objectives

The cognitive levels provide a measure of the severity of an illness at a specific time. Concepts of change identify how the cognitive levels can be expected to change over a span of time, from weeks to years. The presence of long-term limitations in those with cognitive disabilities creates a challenge for us if we hope to show that change has occurred as a result of our services. Long-term limitations are characteristic of all chronic diseases, which, by definition, show little change or a slow progression and long continuance (*Taber's*, 1977; *Dorland's*, 1981). *Progression*, in the medical use of the term, means

that the condition is getting worse. Improvement is implicitly excluded from the meaning of chronic disease. The challenge is to define an expectation for change in conditions that are known to stay the same or get worse. The therapist's view of change must consider the natural course of the disease, as well as the other forms of medical and social intervention that influence the kind of change that can be expected. Ultimately, the effectiveness of our services will be measured by the criteria established by our expectations for change.

Recognition of permanent limitations that medical science cannot now, or in the foreseeable future, alter is a confrontation with grim reality. Many new clinicians in every health discipline are shocked to discover the large number of patients with residual impairments that cannot be corrected. Perhaps it is a part of the human condition to avoid unpleasant realities. At any rate many of the views of change that underlie our theories of practice require reexamination in light of these limitations. Perspective on our difficulty in confronting long-term limitations can be gained by a review of three prevalent models of change. Each model represents the most striking features of a system of thought about change (Lippitt, 1973); each model's explanation of change in chronic disease will be critiqued.

Change can be observed in the structure of the biologic organism, in the external environment, and in the process that the human organism uses to interact with the environment (Fig. 7-4). The change models that will be described differ in (1) the location of the problem requiring a change, (2) the location of their target of intervention, and (3) the location of the point at which the results of intervention can be observed (Allen and Mendel, 1982).

The magical cure model attempts to locate a physical or chemical problem and change the anatomic or physiologic structure so that a normative laboratory report or x-ray results (Fig. 7-5). In some diseases (e.g., primary affective disorders) this expectation can be fulfilled. It is assumed that the structural change will permit the individual to re-

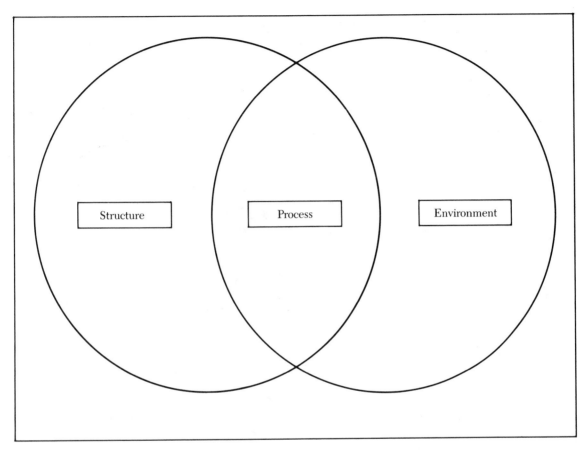

Fig. 7-4. Potential locations of change. (From C. Allen and W. Mendel, Chronic illness and staff burnout: Revised expectations for change in the supportive-care model. Int. J. Partial Hosp. *1:191–201, 1982.)*

sume a healthy life. This assumption is apparent when morbidity rates, without disability rates, are used to illustrate medical effectiveness. Obviously the problems of residual limitations are not addressed by this model, and no experienced clinician in any health discipline would claim it as an accurate reflection of reality. The point being argued is that the model is recognizable and that it probably represents the hope we all bring with us when we seek medical attention. Health care practitioners face the unpleasant duty of recognizing and informing many patients that these hopes cannot be fulfilled.

The hope for a magical cure may have also influenced our career choice. The realities of clinical practice may then become an unpleasant encounter with the realization that we cannot solve many of our patients' problems. Forced to confront residual limitations, the clinician can experience discouragement, burnout, anger toward the patient, and a desire to pursue a different career. Those who follow a discipline such as ours that serves people with long-term limitations may be well advised to guard against expectations of change that are influenced by the magical cure model.

The environmental model places the cause of a mental disorder in the external environment. Intervention is directed toward having the patient learn a new process for coping with the environment, the

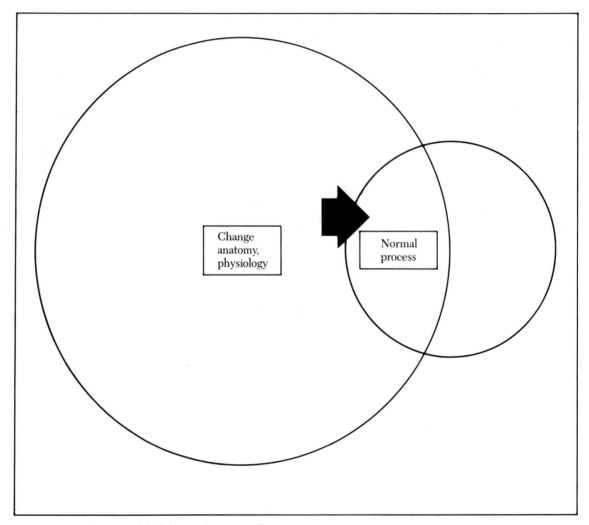

Fig. 7-5. Magical cure model of change. (From C. Allen and W. Mendel, Chronic illness and staff burnout: Revised expectations for change in the supportive-care model. Int. J. Partial Hosp. 1:191–201, 1982.)

expectation being that the patient will return to the mainstream of society (Fig. 7-6). The patient is expected to learn new patterns of behavior that have typically been described by hierarchies of normal growth and development. Application of these hierarchies to long-term illness is based on the assumption that such illness does not alter the sequence, content, or terminus of normal growth and development. The validity of this assumption has not been substantiated by research. The environmental model, described by Freud and carried into other psychosocial formulations, has not proved to be an effective explanation of change for patients with long-term mental disorders.

The vocational rehabilitation model locates the source of the problem as a structural deficit that may be compensated for through adaptive equip-

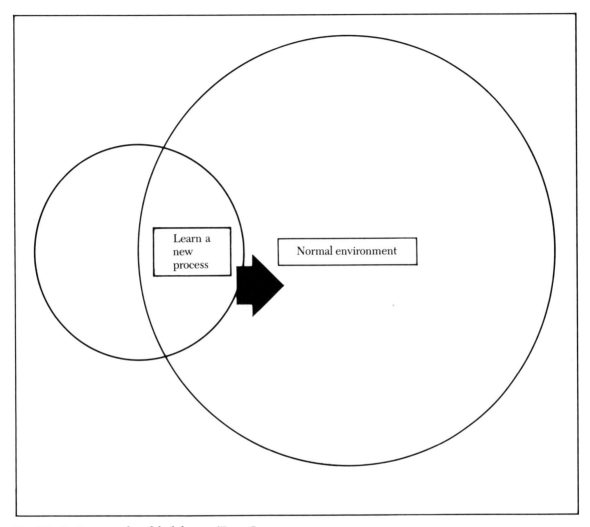

Fig. 7-6. Environmental model of change. (From C. Allen and W. Mendel, Chronic illness and staff burnout: Revised expectations for change in the supportive-care model. Int. J. Partial Hosp. *1:191–201, 1982.)*

ment or adaptive behavior. Competitive employment used to be the only criterion for successful rehabilitation and remains an important consideration (Fig. 7-7). Alternative criteria are still being considered in the literature (Anthony, 1979; Talbott, 1978) because many people with long-term illness cannot work; clearly, a new rehabilitation objective is

needed. Realistic, long-term objectives are largely unknown.

The simplified presentation of these views of change tends to hide their prevalent influence on our thoughts. The clearest encounter with them occurs when we try to write long-term objectives or to describe the positive outcome of our services. Textbook examples frequently cite a return to work, functional independence, functional restoration, or a balanced life-style (Hopkins and Smith, 1978).

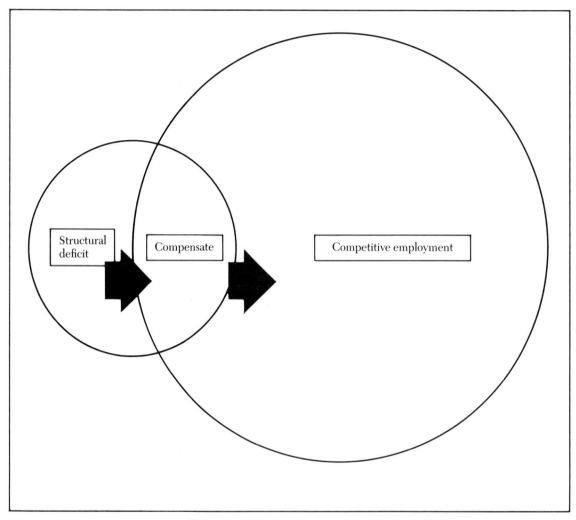

*Fig. 7-7. Vocational rehabilitation model of change.
(From C. Allen and W. Mendel, Chronic illness and staff
burnout: Revised expectations for change in the
supportive-care model. Int. J. Partial Hosp. 1:191–201,
1982.)*

These phrases sound encouraging but, with the exception of returning to work, they cannot be measured. From these models of change we gain some perspective on the difficulty we have in establishing expectations for change that realistically account for the long-term limitations associated with many mental disorders (Diller and Gordon, 1981).

Unfortunately payment for occupational therapy services is often tied to documenting improvement, and therapists who provide services to people with chronic conditions are trapped. Maintenance and decline are not recognized by third-party payers. Frequently, the therapist's progress notes must show some kind of improvement or the services will be discontinued. The question is: What kind of improvements are we really seeing? The difficulty lies in trying to show improvement in conditions characterized by progressive decline.

CONCLUSION

A therapist offers an opportunity to feel the effects of a task experience. A therapist can modify the task demands so that the task experience is successful and pleasant, and steps can be taken to prevent unpleasant mistakes and failures. A pleasant emotional experience is a realistically achievable objective. A here-and-now benefit can be provided. That may be the value we are describing when we discuss improving the quality of life of people with a chronic cognitive disability. If this view is accepted, the concept will require further clarification. I do not think occupational therapists should be in the business of providing pleasant experiences for everyone who has a chronic cognitive disability; the numbers are too great, and the cost is too high. I suspect that clearer distinctions need to be made between the need for direct services and the need for consultation. Direct services may be required to fulfill treatment objectives, while evaluation and consultation may be adequate to fulfill compensation objectives. Empirical investigation of this possibility certainly would be helpful.

REFERENCES

Allen, C., and Mendel, W. M. Chronic illness and staff burnout: Revised expectations for change in the supportive-care model. *Int. J. Partial Hosp.* 1:191–201, 1982.

Anthony, W. A. *The Principles of Psychiatric Rehabilitation.* Amherst, Mass.: Human Resources Development, 1979.

Arieti, S. *The Interpsychic Self: Feelings, Cognition and Creativity in Health and Mental Illness.* New York: Basic Books, 1967.

Ayres, A. J. *Sensory Integration and the Child.* Los Angeles: Western Psychological Services, 1979.

Brown, G., and Desforges, C. *Piaget's Theory: A Psychological Critique.* Boston: Routledge and Kegan Paul, 1979.

Crockett, D., Clark, C., and Klonoff, H. Introduction: An Overview of Neuropsychology. In S. Filskov and T. Boll (eds.), *Handbook of Clinical Neuropsychology.* New York: Wiley, 1981.

Diller, L., and Gordon, W. A. Rehabilitation and Clinical Neuropsychology. In S. Filskov and T. Boll (eds.), *Handbook of Clinical Neuropsychology.* New York: Wiley, 1981.

Dorland's Illustrated Medical Dictionary (26th ed.). Philadelphia: Saunders, 1965.

English, S. O., and Finch, S. M. *Introduction to Psychiatry.* New York: Norton, 1954.

Freud, S. Project for a Scientific Psychology (1895). In *The Standard Edition of the Complete Psychological Works of Sigmund Freud*, transl. and ed. by J. Strachey with others. London: Hogarth and Institute of Psycho-Analysis, 1966. Vol. 1.

Furth, H. G. *Piaget and Knowledge: Theoretical Foundations.* Englewood Cliffs, N.J.: Prentice-Hall, 1969.

Goodman, L. S., and Gilman, A. *The Pharmacological Basis of Therapeutics.* New York: Macmillan, 1975.

Gray, J. A. Anxiety as a Paradigm Case of Emotion. In D. M. Warburton and A. Summerfield (eds.), *Psychobiology: Introduction.* New York: Churchill Livingstone, 1981.

Hopkins, H. L., and Smith, H. P. (eds.). *Willard and Spackman's Occupational Therapy* (5th ed.). Philadelphia: Lippincott, 1978.

James, W. *Principles of Psychology.* New York: Dover, 1890. Vols. 1 and 2.

Kuhn, T. S. *The Structure of Scientific Revolutions* (2nd ed.) (International Encyclopedia of Unified Science). Chicago: University of Chicago Press, 1970.

Lippitt, G. L. *Visualizing Change: Model Building and the Change Process.* La Jolla, Calif.: University Associates, 1973.

Luria, A. R. *The Making of Mind: A Personal Account of Social Psychology*, M. Cole and S. Cole (eds.). Cambridge, Mass.: Harvard University Press, 1979.

Mendel, W. M. *Supportive Care: Theory and Technique.* Los Angeles: Mara Books, 1975.

Nyad, D. *Other Shores.* New York: Random House, 1978.

Piaget, J. *Biology and Knowledge: An Essay on the Relations Between Organic Regulations and Cognitive Processes.* Chicago: University of Chicago Press, 1971.

Piaget, J. *Behavior and Evolution*, transl. by D. Nicholson-Smith. New York: Pantheon Books, 1978.

Pribram, K. H. Emotions. In S. B. Filskov and T. J. Boll (eds.), *Handbook of Clinical Neuropsychology.* New York: Wiley, 1981.

Pribram, K. H., and Gill, M. M. *Freud's "Project" Re-Assessed: Preface to Contemporary Cognitive Theory and Neuropsychology.* New York: Basic Books, 1976.

Reilly, M. (ed.). *Play as Exploratory Learning.* Beverly Hills, Calif.: Sage, 1974.

Reiss, H. W., and Overton, W. F. Models of Development and Theories of Development. In L. R. Goulet and P. B. Baltes (eds.), *Life Span Developmental Psy-*

chology: Research and Theory. New York: Academic, 1970.

Shallice, T. Neurological Impairment of Cognitive Processes. In D. M. Warburton and A. Summerfield (eds.), *Psychobiology: Introduction.* New York: Churchill Livingstone, 1981.

Taber's Cyclopedic Medical Dictionary (13th ed.). Philadelphia: Davis, 1977.

Talbott, J. A. *The Chronic Mental Patient: Problems, Solutions and Recommendations for a Public Policy.* Washington, D.C.: American Psychiatric Association, 1978.

White, R. W. Motivation reconsidered: The concept of competence. *Psychol. Rev.* 66:297–333, 1959.

CHAPTER 8

TEACHING CASE EXAMPLES

The teaching case examples presented in this chapter provide the reader with an opportunity to apply concepts to case material. The case examples presented here are meant to be used for educational purposes; the case method is a research technique. A distinction must be made between a case example and the case method. The case method discusses real cases, while a teaching case, though based in reality, is fictional. The process of developing a teaching case resembles the process described by some authors in the preface of their novels (see Michener, 1982, for an example). The first step is to select a topic and identify the type of patient that would best illustrate the topic. Then one can look around for a real patient who is representative of common observations. Certain salient features are selected; other, irrelevant factors are discarded. Finally, the individual's confidentiality is protected by changing the name and other identifying clues. The teaching cases should not be confused with the case method of investigating the validity of research hypotheses.

The topics for the teaching case examples will emphasize the assessment of the cognitive level and differential diagnoses. Case examples I through X provide a brief description of the history and task observations, with questions that can be used to assess the cognitive level. Case examples XI through XIV provide a brief description of common psychiatric diagnoses. The brief case examples (I through XIV) make practice look a lot easier than it is; case examples XV through XVII are longer, illustrating the scope of available data that a therapist must analyze to establish a professional opinion. Frequent answers to the questions for case examples I through XVII are found at the end of the chapter; it should be noted that these answers do not always hold true; exceptions will probably be encountered in practice.

ASSESSMENT OF COGNITIVE LEVEL

An understanding of the cognitive levels seems to be facilitated by starting at level 6 and working down the hierarchy. The cases will begin at the normative level 6 and examine the loss of abilities.

Case Example I: Level 6

History

Marcia is a 26-year-old black woman who was admitted to the hospital after one month of outpatient treatment. She did not respond to outpatient treatment, and information on her history and symptoms is still incomplete. The admitting diagnosis is primary affective disorder, unipolar.

Marcia has a bachelor's degree in education and worked as an elementary school teacher until 6 months ago, when she quit working. Her husband is concerned about her and reports that there is a gradual decline in her performance of housekeeping chores. At present he does most of the housework.

The therapist gained little information during the initial interview. Marcia gave one-word answers to questions and picked at her nail polish while talking. When the therapist asked Marcia to do the leather lacing evaluation she sat up, looked at the therapist, and said, "Honey, don't waste your time on me. I know you mean well, but I can't do anything any more. I never will. You'd better try someone else." The therapist decided to try a different approach and suggested that she come and watch a cooking group. Marcia agreed to come if she didn't have to cook.

Observations of Task Performance

In the cooking group Marcia looked uncomfortable sitting at a table by herself. The therapist suggested she make macaroni and cheese from a mix. She agreed. Marcia read the directions on the box and then got out a pan, lid, and measuring cup from two cupboards with opened doors. When the water boiled she added the macaroni, placed a colander in the sink, and then checked the clock to time the cooking. During the cooking she talked a little with

the other patients and watched them work. At the correct time she removed the pan from the burner, turned the burner off, and poured the macaroni and water into the colander. Without being told she looked around the kitchen and then went to the correct cupboard and drawer to obtain a serving dish and spoon.

Questions

1. Select observations that indicate
   a. Attention was captured by a symbolic cue.
   b. Attention was sustained by a designed mode of action.
   c. Motor actions were planned.
   d. Imitation was not necessary.
2. After telling Marcia that she could observe in cooking, was it good therapeutic practice to suggest that she make macaroni and cheese? Why?
3. Was it good therapeutic practice to suggest a cooking group to this patient?

Case Example II: Level 6

History

Eileen is 21 years old, white, and married. Her first hospitalization occurred when she was 17 and lasted 9 months; the diagnosis was an adolescent adjustment reaction. This hospitalization was preceded by a suicide attempt—jumping out a window five flights up—that resulted in a broken pelvis and left arm that required surgery and a pin, as well as other injuries. She has been in the hospital 5 months. The diagnosis being considered is schizo-affective disorder. Her highest level of function probably occurred before this admission when she was married and was completing a course as an x-ray technician one week before her suicide attempt.

Observations of Task Performance

The cast was removed from her arm 2 weeks ago, and Eileen has been able to pursue her interest in weaving. Initially the therapist taught Eileen how to weave by demonstrating and verbally explaining how the loom works. Within a few minutes Eileen could do a tabby weave. Looking in a weaving book, she selected a herringbone pattern with three weft colors for a striped effect. (The warp was already on the loom.) Eileen wrote down and taped the weaving pattern's sequence to the loom and began to weave. At the beginning of the second weaving session the therapist complimented her earlier work and encouraged her to get started again. Periodically Eileen checked her progress to see if variations in her original pattern or her weaving technique needed to be made. She considered several possibilities for use of the fabric but finally stayed with the original idea of making a pillow.

Questions

1. Give an interpretation for the following observations:
   a. Selecting a weaving pattern from a book.
   b. Checking her progress periodically.
   c. Taping the pattern sequence to the loom.
   d. Comprehending the therapist's directions on how the loom operates.
2. Was it necessary to praise and encourage Eileen when she started weaving in the second session? Why?
3. Should Eileen be allowed to do another weaving project when she finishes the pillow? Why?

Case Example III: Level 5

History

Lauren is a 31-year-old Japanese-American woman who is single. After graduating from high school, she began a professional dancing career, and one year before this admission she danced a supporting role in a major musical on Broadway. She has been unemployed for approximately one year, during which time she moved to Los Angeles and began living with her boyfriend. Recently she was seen by a psychologist for anxiety and depression. He encouraged her to admit herself to the hospital after noticing an increase in withdrawn behavior, intermittent muteness, and extremely depressed mood. This is her first psychiatric hospitalization.

Observations of Task Performance

Lauren has been making ruffled patchwork pillows. She has sewn with patterns in the past. When choosing her project, Lauren initially could not decide which of the many sewing projects available she wanted to do. When the therapist showed her three patchwork pillow patterns, she chose one of them. By placing various fabrics next to each other, she was able to determine which fabric she wanted for each patch of the pillow top. As she sewed the pieces together, she made mistakes occasionally (which she recognized) and had to rip the patches apart. In sewing the back to the front of the pillow, Lauren had difficulty figuring out how to position the front, back, interlining, and ruffle so that the pieces would be in the proper positions when the pillow was turned. Lauren liked the end product so much that she decided to make another patchwork pillow using different fabric. She expressed surprise that the second pillow was much easier to make, which she ascribed to "having a finished one to look at."

Questions

1. Select an observation of task performance that can be interpreted as
   a. Attention captured by relationships between material objects and not by symbolic cues.
   b. Attention sustained by variations in actions.
   c. Spontaneous motor actions that are exploratory.
   d. Imitation of novel motor actions.
2. Could the mistakes in sewing the fabric pieces together have been avoided?
3. Do you think that Lauren's explanation of why she had less difficulty with the second pillow is correct? Why?

Case Example IV: Level 5

History

Ernest is 25 years old, black, and married with three children. After dropping out of high school in his senior year he was in the army for 9 months. Ernest received a total medical discharge from the army and has been supporting his family with the army disability checks; the family also receives public assistance. This is his fifth hospitalization, the first occurring when he was 19 years old. His diagnosis is schizo-affective disorder, with a question of manic-depressive psychosis and a possible passive-dependent personality. His highest level of function probably occurred in high school.

Observations of Task Performance

Ernest has been making a series of leather belts in OT. When he made the first belt the therapist was able to show him two directions at a time, for example, creasing and beeswaxing the edge or tracing and cutting the leather belt keeper. On his second belt Ernest remembered all of the steps until he got to the buckle, at which point he requested help from the therapist. Now he has made a series of belts with stamped patterns and words on them. He tests out several patterns on scrap leather and chooses one. (Spacing may not work out quite right at the end of the belt.) While working on a belt Ernest is able to get his own tools from the cabinet, search in several likely locations for a missing tool, alter the force applied hitting the stamping tool, determine how much leather dye to apply, follow directions to avoid getting dye on other things, and wait 24 hours for the dye to dry. Ernest takes pride in each one of his belts.

Questions

1. Give an interpretation of the following:
   a. Creasing and beeswaxing the edge.
   b. Requesting help in attaching the second belt buckle.
   c. Searching for a missing tool.
   d. Determining how much leather dye to use.
   e. Determining how hard to hit the stamping tool.
2. Why does Ernest want to make so many belts? Should the therapist permit this? Why?

Case Example V: Level 4

History

John is a 33-year-old man who was recently admitted for his eighth psychiatric hospitalization. There has been a consistent diagnosis of schizophrenia. John graduated from high school, where he got C's and D's and had few friends. His work history consists of two janitorial jobs of short duration; he has not worked for the last 5 years. John has been living in a board-and-care home and was admitted to the hospital when he became unruly and difficult to manage.

Observations of Task Performance

John scored at level 4 on the Allen Cognitive Level Test (ACL), as he had during past hospitalizations. He agreed to attend a basic crafts group but refused basic skills group (educational content described in Chap. 10). John told the therapist that he still had two projects that he made during a past hospitalization and asked if he could make a duplicate of one that had been broken. The project requested was a decoupage that entailed the following steps:

1. Sanding the wood
2. Staining the wood
3. Wiping the stain
4. Selecting a print
5. Trimming the print
6. Gluing the print

7. Attaching a hook to the back
8. Applying polymer

John looked at the sample and self-initiated sanding the wood. He refused to wipe off some of the stain, which was so dark that the grain of the wood could not be seen. The glue on the print did not cover the edges. The therapist, at John's request, showed him how to add more glue so that the corners of the print would stay down. John successfully imitated the other steps one step at a time.

Questions
1. Select observations that indicate the following:
    a. Attention was captured by a clearly visible cue.
    b. Attention was sustained by purposeful actions.
    c. Voluntary motor actions were goal directed.
    d. The motor actions that were imitated were similar to other, familiar actions.
2. Suppose the therapist suspects that John's level of function is worse, possibly level 3. Without changing the decoupage project, predict the steps in the task that will require extra assistance from the therapist.
3. Both basic crafts and basic skills utilize level 4 capabilities. Why did John agree to basic crafts and not basic skills?
4. Identify the verbal statements that seem to indicate that John is functioning at level 4.

Case Example VI: Level 4

History

This is the second hospitalization for Bev, a 19-year-old white woman. Her first admission was one year ago; the diagnosis was schizo-affective disorder. ACL score at admission was level 3. The therapist suspects that her functional abilities may be improving because she has begun to style her hair and

is wearing her own clothing: tight-fitting, pressed designer blue jeans.

Observations of Task Performance

Bev has been attending a level 3 and 4 sewing group and has been too distractible to complete a project. A pot holder in the shape of a strawberry (precut and with the first stitches done) is given to her. She is able to sit in her chair until the project is completed and looks to see if her pot holder matches the sample. There is time to make a second pot holder; this is offered. Bev rejects the offer, saying, "I can't do two of those in one day." The last half of the session is spent chatting with the therapist and another patient.

Questions
1. Identify the interpretations that may be made from the following observations:
    a. Looking at the sample after her project is completed.
    b. Sitting in her chair long enough to complete one pot holder.
    c. A refusal to make a second pot holder.
    d. Wearing her own clothes and styling her hair.
2. Write an interdisciplinary progress note.

Case Example VII: Level 3

History

Mary is a 29-year-old married Mexican-American woman. Her first psychiatric hospitalization occurred at age 15, when she was in the tenth grade. Since that time, Mary has been unable to return to school and has had numerous hospitalizations. Work history is limited to brief periods in sheltered workshop evaluation programs. The diagnosis is schizophrenic disorder, rule out primary affective disorder. The patient lives in an apartment with her husband, who is an alcoholic. Her husband does the cooking and cleaning. Mary states she has no friends and spends her day caring for her cats. In the past Mary has been hospitalized for regressive behavior and agitation. This admission was precipitated by a separation from her husband. On admission the patient stated, "I will kill myself if my husband divorces me."

Observations of Task Performance

A mosaic tile trivet project using one color of tile and without spacing and grouting was selected by the therapist. A choice of color was offered; Mary indicated that she would use the color that happened to be in front of her. The therapist showed Mary how to squeeze a line of glue across the first row and place the tiles on top of the glue. Mary followed the direction with intense concentration until the first row was completed and then stopped to smoke a cigarette. The therapist redirected her attention to the mosaic tiles. Mary continued to place the tiles, but her actions contained striking errors: Great globs of glue covered adjacent tiles, the rows were crooked, and the tiles were skewed. Mary was unconcerned about the errors in the trivet. She stopped at midpoint and asked to wash her hands. She washed her hands and indicated that she was finished for the day.

Questions

1. Identify the observations that would support the following interpretation:
   a. Attention was captured by a tactile cue.
   b. Attention was sustained by a repetitive action.
   c. Spontaneous actions were manual.
   d. Familiar actions were imitated.
2. Select observations that help differentiate between level 3 and level 4.
3. Select observations that may help with a differential diagnosis.

Case Example VIII: Level 3 or 4

History

Bob is a 27-year-old white man; this is his third hospitalization. Previous diagnosis was schizophrenic disorder; he is presently being treated for primary affective disorder, unipolar. He has been in the hospital for 2 weeks. He has been tearful, with suicidal ideation. Recently his behavior has changed: pressured speech, hyperactivity, and teasing, suggesting an affective disorder. He will not take an ACL.

Observations of Task Performance

Bob refused to have anything to do with arts and crafts but did agree to attend a work group. The task suggested by the therapist was preparing new medical charts for use in the psychiatric hospital, which entails removing unused forms, collating new psychiatric forms, punching holes in the psychiatric forms, and inserting new forms into the chart. The complexity of the charting task can range from a high level 3 to level 6. The part that Bob said he could do was typical of a high level 3: punching holes in new forms. He was able to insert a group of forms into a two-hole punch, check placement, and operate the lever. Bob did not press the lever; he hammered at it with a broad, loud, and heavy punch. He continued to punch until all of the forms were done, working longer than the 35 minutes he had contracted for at the beginning of the session. He talked frequently and tended to forget about hole punching. Attention to the task was redirected with ease.

Questions

This is an example of observations of behavior that are difficult to interpret.

1. Explain the following observations of behavior:
   a. A broad and heavy punch.
   b. Punching beyond 35 minutes.

c. Correct placement of the hole punch.

d. Easy redirection of attention by the therapist.

2. Select behaviors that could differentiate between level 3 and 4.

3. The cognitive level could essentially be assessed when the patient selected the part of the chart that he would do. Describe how the therapist should present this task. What should the therapist do after Bob has begun to punch holes in the charts?

4. Write a progress note on these observations.

Case Example IX: Level 2

History

Ruby is a 67-year-old white woman brought to the hospital by police officers after she was found in her nightgown in a shopping center. At the time of admission she could not state her name or address. A daughter that she lives with has been located; the daughter works during the day. This is Ruby's first psychiatric hospitalization. The ACL score was level 2; she could not go from front to back with the sewing stitch.

Observations of Task Performance

Another patient directed Ruby to the food cart at lunchtime. She took a food tray and sat down at a nearby table. She was unable to get the plastic utensils out of a cellophane package, open a milk carton, or remove the cellophane from around a slice of bread; the therapist offered assistance. Ruby ate with her fingers and a spoon. Another patient guided her in returning her tray to the food cart.

Questions

1. Select examples of the following behavior:

   a. Attention to somatosensory cues.

   b. Gross body movement.

c. Postural action.

d. Approximate imitation.

2. Give a rationale for observing eating behavior.

Case Example X: Level 2

History

This is the first hospitalization for Richard, a 28-year-old white businessman who came to California to have fun in the "frontier to the new evolutionary universe." He was brought to the hospital by the police after he was found nude on Sunset Strip. The diagnosis is primary affective disorder, acute mania.

The therapist ended the initial interview quickly because Richard's loose associations rendered his answers to questions meaningless: "What is your name?" "Name, lame, same, life is a meaningless game. . . ."

Richard's hyperactivity and pressured speech were a constant disruption on the ward so the therapist decided to do some calisthenics with Richard.

Observations of Task Performance

The therapist took Richard to a large room and asked him to put some shoes on his bare feet. Richard began to talk about shoes. Ignoring the words the therapist took him by the arm and pointed to a chair. After Richard sat down he continued to talk. The therapist handed him a shoe and pointed to his foot, saying, "Put your shoe on, please." Finally, the therapist put the shoe on Richard's foot, and he worked his foot into the shoe.

Richard was able to imitate the therapist in touching his toes, did an approximation of a jumping jack, and then got distracted by a magazine with a picture of a Christian cross on the cover. First he folded his hands in a praying posture, then he shifted to a gesture of saluting the flag (an American flag could be seen through the window, flying from an adjacent building). The therapist took him by the arm and showed him the next exercise.

Questions

1. Interpret the behavior:
   a. Calisthenics.
   b. The way Richard put his shoes on.
   c. Richard's folding his hands in a praying position.
   d. The therapist's taking him by the arm.
2. Give a rationale for ignoring the patient's words.

DIFFERENTIAL DIAGNOSIS

The first few days that a patient spends in an acute psychiatric unit may be directed toward establishing a diagnosis. The therapist can assist with a differential diagnosis from the perspective of a limited data base: a review of the medical chart, an interview, and an ACL. The objective of the following case studies is to show how this data base can be related to the *DSM III* (1980) criteria and to the interdisciplinary treatment plan.

Case Example XI: Depressive Episode

History

Mabel is a 66-year-old woman who was admitted because of severe depression, which has been worsening for the last 2 years since the death of her husband. One year ago she retired, having worked successfully as a special education teacher for 30 years; 9 months ago she was forced to admit her mother to a nursing home, about which she feels guilty. During the last 2 years she has lost 40 pounds, has had intermittent difficulty sleeping at night, and has been progressively unable to manage at home. She has been seeing a psychiatrist as an outpatient; the psychiatrist has been treating her with antidepressants and chlorpromazine, but there is some question of her reliability in taking medication.

OT Interview

When seen, Mabel sat huddled in a chair in a wrinkled dress, hair half-combed, with slight perspiration, probably caused by her constant leg and hand movements. Her response to questions was minimal, with no identification of interests or goals. Mabel stated that she wanted out of "jail" but knew the name of the hospital. She made a vague effort to do the ACL but then stopped, listing a number of reasons: "I can't do anything anymore. I never will. You'd better try someone else. My eyes are too bad to see this. They'll never let me out of this place."

Questions

1. List the diagnostic symptoms of depression that are identified in the history and OT interview (*DSM III* criteria).
2. Cite examples of task behavior that you can anticipate.
3. After 2 weeks, the therapist notices that Mabel is showing some improvement; she has been smiling, and her personal appearance is better. Mabel completes the steps in level 4 tasks but shows no initiative in varying her actions or in exploring the relationship between objects. Her task behavior is limited to 30 minutes. The physician must evaluate the effect of medication at this point.
   a. Write your observations of Mabel's performance; include observations and terminology useful to the physician.
   b. Write an interpretation of the observations.
   c. Write your plan.

Case Example XII: Manic Episode

History

Fawn is a 38-year-old mother of five children. This is her third psychiatric hospitalization; the first occurred after the birth of her fifth child. Three weeks before this admission Fawn quit her job as a teacher's assistant. She reports periods of not being sure of where her body is and feels that the Mafia may have taken control of her because they want her to be a call girl. She sought admission because she was too "keyed up" for the last 2 or 3 months and has not been sleeping well at night.

OT Interview

The therapist's impression of Fawn was that of a pleasant person who talked fast, teased, and joked. During the 15-minute interview Fawn left and returned twice; once to get coffee and once to talk to another patient who passed by.

Fawn's hospital goal is "to get in balance." Her future goals include vocational rehabilitation. She has had a good work history as a waitress and hostess. Her interests include radio, concerts, her children's activities, sewing, embroidery, and making friends. ACL score was level 5, with one interruption during the performance of the evaluative task.

Questions

1. The diagnosis is primary affective disorder, bipolar; rule out unipolar affective disorder, schizophrenia. List factors that would support each diagnosis. From the above information, what is your diagnostic impression?
2. Describe the observations you would expect to make in the OT clinic.
3. Identify your initial treatment plan.

Case Example XIII: Schizophrenic Disorder

History

Basil is a 33-year-old man brought to the hospital for his fourth admission by his family. The first admission occurred in his early twenties; there is a consistent diagnosis of schizophrenia. The family reports that he has gradually become more and more difficult to manage at home and has displayed unruly behavior for which they can determine no cause. The patient lives at home with his mother and two brothers (ages 36 and 38). He has stayed at home and has not worked for the last 2 years.

OT Interview

During the interview, the therapist noted that Basil's response to questions was a brief one- or two-word answer without elaboration. There was no eye contact, and no emotion was shown. Basil reported that he completed the twelfth grade but had few friends and received C's and D's in school. His work history until 2 years ago consisted of 9 years of employment in three unskilled jobs.

Basil has no goals for the hospital, no goals for the future, and no interests. His usual day before admission was to get up, eat, and "help out a bit." ACL score was level 4.

Questions

1. Identify another psychiatric diagnosis that closely parallels this picture of schizophrenia. Identify the symptoms and task behaviors that would help you distinguish between the disorders.
2. The natural course of chronic schizophrenia may include acute symptoms interspersed with a progressive decline in functional ability. Review Basil's present assets and limitations and predict his abilities at the time of discharge from the hospital.

Case Example XIV: Organic Brain Syndrome

History

Hazel is a 77-year-old woman who has had no previous psychiatric hospitalizations and was admitted because of difficulty in caring for herself and her home. In the last year and a half she has experienced the death of her mother and her husband. Her 55-year-old daughter and 18-year-old nephew have been living with her; however, the daughter has spent the last 2 months in a general hospital. Diagnostic impression is organic brain syndrome (OBS).

OT Interview

The general impression was of a sweet, friendly lady who was shabbily dressed and depressed: "What's an old lady like me still doing around?" She did not know why she was admitted to the hospital, and her goal is to go back home and keep house. On the ACL she could do the sewing and whip stitch but could not put the needle through the loop of the simple cordovan stitch, stating she could not see well enough to do it.

Questions
1. Identify the symptoms of OBS that the therapist might observe:

SYMPTOMS	OBSERVATIONS
a.	a.
b.	b.
c.	c.

2. On learning that the nephew is seldom home, you realize that Hazel is alone most of the time. In making recommendations for discharge plans, what information do you need? Describe a method of selecting additional observations of performance.

LONGER CASE EXAMPLES

The case examples presented thus far have been highly selective in the information presented. Three longer case examples will be presented to provide exercises with clinical complexities. Here again identifying features have been changed, and numerous extraneous considerations have been eliminated.

Case Example XV: Differential Diagnosis

Present Illness

David, age 28, was brought to the psychiatric admitting area by his mother, who states that he has been refusing to eat for one month and has lost over 20 pounds. David's mother has noted a deterioration in her son since he stopped taking prescribed haloperidol (Haldol) 6 months ago. The patient talks to himself constantly; he has stopped washing his clothes; he throws away valuable possessions (claiming, "This radio is old"); he stands and postures for hours in doorways; he roams the streets, leaving the house key in the door. His mother can no longer manage him.

Social History

David is single, unemployed, and an only child. He is 6 feet 2 inches tall and weighs 151 pounds. There is no psychiatric history on the mother's side of the family, but his father, who left when David was 5, had mental illness of an unknown type. David completed high school and one quarter term at a local college. He transferred to a college in Alabama but attended no classes there. He reportedly stayed in his dorm room for 3 months, not eating, until he weighed 118 pounds. He was returned to Los Angeles and was hospitalized for the first time at age 18.

Psychiatric History

David has been hospitalized eight times in the last 10 years, for periods of up to 3 months. He has been diagnosed as having chronic schizophrenia and has been treated with fluphenazine hydrochloride (Prolixin) (good response with side effects of drooling and skin changes), thiothixene (Navane), and haloperidol. He has taken haloperidol for the last 7 to 8 years with side effects of postural rigidity. He has never been treated with electroconvulsive therapy.

Activities of Daily Living

In the last 10 years David has lived in several board-and-care homes, but never longer than 6 months. His mother describes him as decompensating at board-and-care facilities and then being rehospitalized. He has lived with his mother for the last 3 years. When he takes his medicine David can launder his clothes and make a sandwich for himself. He cannot budget his Social Security Insurance (SSI) check and is known to spend it in one day if allowed. His usual day consists of walking around for 4 to 5 hours or lying in bed. He cannot drive, although he can take the bus to familiar locations. There is no evidence of drug or alcohol abuse.

Work History

David has worked odd jobs but never longer than 2 months. He last worked 7 years ago and has received SSI for 10 years.

Results of Psychological Testing

The Bender-Gestalt, administered during this hospitalization, revealed no organic signs. Verbal measures on Wechsler Adult Intelligence Scale (WAIS) suggest an IQ around 90 (normal range); David refused WAIS performance measures.

OT Clinic Presentation

When the therapist first saw David, he was standing motionless in the hallway of the ward. His right arm and hand were stiffly extended at his side, and his other arm was rigidly flexed away from his body. His eyes darted back and forth continually, and he mumbled softly to himself. When the therapist approached him, he backed up, always maintaining a distance of about 2 feet from her. He established no eye contact, and he responded only with yes or no to a few questions asked of him. When asked to attend a crafts group that afternoon, he replied, "Crafts?" and after a long pause, "Okay."

David walked to the clinic very slowly with halting steps, following the other patients in the group at some distance. He held his arms rigidly extended at his sides. He stopped before going through each doorway, apparently unable to proceed, and the therapist heard him mumble repeatedly to himself, "Go through, go through." He entered the crafts room with great hesitancy, glancing from side to side continually. He sat down very slowly while saying to himself, "Bend your knees."

The project for the session was a small wooden jewelry box, selected and set up for each patient by the therapist. David did not pick up his sandpaper when the therapist demonstrated this instruction, but took it when it was placed in his hand. He began sanding the box only after the therapist guided his hands to begin the motion. He was noted to stop his actions frequently and glance around in a frightened manner. When the therapist said, "Keep sanding, David," he resumed his actions. David ignored the grain of the wood as he sanded. He was equally unaware of other patients working nearby. When one asked him for a cigarette, he gave no indication that he had heard, nor did he respond. When it was time to stain the box, the therapist again placed the brush in David's hand, starting the motion for him. He stiffly dabbed at the box in one place, rather than using a fluid, brushing motion. The therapist had to point to areas where David had not stained for him to cover the entire box. He often stopped painting and sat motionless with his eyes darting back and forth, mumbling to himself.

During the group activity David surprised the therapist by suddenly asking her, "What do you think of integration of knowledge?" When the therapist asked him what he meant, he repeated, "Integration of knowledge, you know. Some people say it is good." His affect was blunted, and he spoke in a rapid monotone. He again avoided all eye contact. Later he remarked quickly to the therapist, "Was that a real ball we used?" (referring to a ward activity of ball tossing done earlier in the day). When told it was he added, "Balls are nice. I thought I would learn all I could about balls." He suddenly grinned broadly as if quite amused.

When the box was sanded and stained, David asked, "What is this?" When told it was a box that he could keep, he slowly picked it up by one corner with his thumb and index finger. On the way back to the ward David walked very slowly, stopping again at all doorways. He edged through only when told to keep walking. When back on the ward he remarked without expression, "Well, I wasn't hurt." When asked what he meant he stated, "I have heard that surgeons cut up patients in the hospital," and added, "If my turning neck is not treated, I might die."

Questions

1. Identify evidence in the patient's history of schizophrenic disorder and major depressive episode.
2. Select the diagnosis you think is most likely.
3. From the section headed OT Clinic Presentation select three observations that reflect symptoms of the diagnosis.
4. Identify the diagnostic criterion that each observation supports.
5. From answers to questions 3 and 4, what could a physician learn from your progress note?
6. Write a progress note based on your answers to questions 3, 4, and 5. Use the headings Observation, Assessment, and Plan.

Case Example XVI: Rehabilitation Potential

History of Present Illness

Patient left an alcohol rehabilitation residential center about one month ago. For the past 3 weeks he has been hearing voices telling him "bad things," has been unable to communicate with others, and has become increasingly depressed. He felt he could not handle any situation any longer. He thought people were trying to put thoughts into his head, and he decided to kill himself by ingesting approximately one cup of toilet bowl cleaner. After emergency room treatment at a nearby hospital, he was medically cleared and transferred to this facility for continuing suicidal ideation: "If I had a gun now, I'd use it."

Mental Status on Admission

Forty-six-year-old black, widowed, unemployed man.

APPEARANCE. Medium height, thin, neat, and clean.

BEHAVIOR. Alert; posture: slumped; facial expression: sad; eye contact: avoided; attention span: poor; motor level: hypoactive; no unusual movements or features.

MANNER OF RELATING TO INTERVIEWER. Submissive.

SPEECH. English-speaking; quantity: answers questions only; amplitude: soft; speed: slow; associations: logical; style: unremarkable.

THOUGHT CONTENT (PREDOMINANT IDEA). "I can't communicate with people and no one can help me."

INSIGHT INTO PROBLEM. None.

DELUSIONS. None.

SUICIDAL THOUGHTS. Present ("If I had a gun now, I'd use it").

INTENT TO HARM OTHERS. None.

MOTIVATION FOR TREATMENT. Present.

PERCEPTIONS. Hallucinations: present (voices telling him bad things, 3 weeks' duration); ideas of reference: present ("Sometimes people put thoughts in my head").

MOOD. Depressed.

AFFECT. Blunted.

SENSORIUM. Oriented ×3: to person, place, and time. Memory somewhat impaired on recent events and recall of past events.

JUDGMENT. Impaired.

ESTIMATED IQ. Average.

Initial Diagnostic Impression

Axis I	Major depression with psychotic features (296.34)
	Alcohol dependence, episodic (303.92)
Axis II	Deferred
Axis III	Erosive gastritis secondary to ingestion of toilet bowl cleaner
Axis IV	4, moderate
Axis V	5, poor

Psychiatric History

First psychiatric hospitalization occurred in 1973, after wife's death and his subsequent suicide attempt (gunshot wound to lower abdomen). Two more short-term hospitalizations occurred in 1978 and 1979 for depression. The patient was placed each time in alcohol rehabilitation centers, where psychiatric medications were discontinued. Hallucinations and ideas of reference were not apparent at those times.

Family History of Mental Illness, Alcohol Abuse, or Suicide

Unknown. Wife died of cirrhosis of the liver in 1973.

Brief Social History

Patient was born in Louisiana where the rest of his family still resides. He moved to Los Angeles at the age of 14 and graduated from high school at age 18. He describes himself during adolescence as "having few friends, getting average grades, and not getting into trouble." Directly after graduation, he was employed by a tire manufacturer as a machine operator, a job he held 18 years until 1973. He was married in 1962, had first child in 1964 and second in 1972. His wife died in 1973, whereupon he attempted suicide for the first time and subsequently lost his job for absenteeism. He obtained another job, but his alcohol use increased at this time, and care for his children was given to relatives. He held his job for 4 years but was eventually fired for absenteeism; he lost his driver's license at this time. Unskilled short-term jobs followed, as did two more psychiatric hospitalizations for depression. For the last 3 years, the patient has been on general relief, living in a downtown hotel. He states he cannot work because of his arthritis and prostate pain (neither of these complaints has been verified). Patient is reluctant to reveal specifics concerning his recent life-style.

Results of Psychological Testing

Quick Test: average to high average IQ. Rorschach results: conventional, yet underproductive with no evidence of thought disorder. Minnesota Multiphasic Personality Inventory: results consistent with diagnosis of either psychotic depression or schizo-affective disorder. The psychologist's report concludes: "The patient would appear to be lacking in internal emotional resources for coping with his environment in an adaptive and positive manner. This profile is probably the worst suicide risk pattern of all, in terms of actual risk of success."

Medication

Low-dose perphenazine for psychotic symptoms, imipramine hydrochloride for depressive symptoms.

Problems on Medical Chart
1. Depression
2. Incomplete data base

3. Suicidal ideation
4. Sore throat and erosive gastritis secondary to suicide attempt
5. No place to stay

Occupational Therapy Interview

The following notes were taken by the therapist during the first interview:

GENERAL IMPRESSION. During interview, pt was uncomfortable and restless, complained of not feeling well, and had poor eye contact, but was willing to answer questions for about 20 minutes. Was oriented ×3; affect was flat, sad.

LIVING SITUATION. Last private residence in 1978.

FAMILY HISTORY. No family contact in several years; no date of last contact. Wife died in 1973.

EDUCATIONAL HISTORY. High school graduate, on-the-job training.

WORK HISTORY. Machine operator until 1973, left owing to absenteeism. Smelter operator until 1977, left owing to absenteeism. Temporary jobs until 1978.

INTERESTS, FRIENDS. None.

REASON FOR ADMISSION. Still a suicide risk.

PAST HOSPITALIZATIONS. × 3. Does not think that medications affect his functional performance.

USUAL DAY BEFORE ADMISSION. Unable to describe a typical day after he left the rehabilitation program.

ADL. Hands and feet show evidence of neglect: long, broken, dirty nails, scabs, and calluses.

ASSETS AND LIMITATIONS. "I can't communicate with people; can't cope with my life any longer."

GOALS FOR THE FUTURE. None.

GROUPS. Work group?

COGNITIVE LEVEL. Level 4, quit after first error.

Questions

Write an initial occupational therapy evaluation:

Data base
Axis V functional history before admission
Functional observations during this admission
   Symptoms of illness
   Awareness of illness
   Cognitive level
   Patient's goals
Occupational therapy plan
   Ineligible for OT because
   Eligible for the following OT groups
Functional observations for
   Verification of cognitive level
   Titration of medication
   Clarification of symptoms
   Assessment of potential grave disability

Case Example XVII: Interpretations of Task Behavior

Chart Data

This is the second psychiatric hospital admission within one month for a 45-year-old white man. The diagnosis during the first admission was an adjustment disorder, apparently in response to a separation from his wife. He threatened to harm her. It now appears that his wife lives out of state, that they have been separated for 5 years, and that the legal status of two children is a concern of the patient's. The social worker has been unable to contact the wife or any local friends who could clarify the patient's history. The patient is the sole informant, and the information he supplies is often contradictory. Objective historical information is unavailable.

The patient is a tall, obese man whose appearance reflects an ongoing neglect of personal hygiene. He says that he came to California 2 years ago to start a new life for himself but has been unable to work because of medical problems. The presence of a number of Axis III problems has been verified. The patient says that he has worked for 20 years as a business consultant, a job that resulted in his learning eight foreign languages. His ability to speak some of these languages has been verified. The patient had planned, after the first admission, to work in a law firm where he claimed that he had a job. He apparently lost this job prospect and was readmitted with a diagnosis of major depression with suicidal ideation. His behavior on the ward has not shown much evidence of a dysphoric mood or a loss of energy, and there is some question about the need for continued hospitalization. The therapist has been asked to evaluate the patient's cognitive level.

Preliminary OT Evaluation

ACL score was level 3. The verbal interview indicated that the patient is unaware of current deficits in functional performance. This has been reported in an initial note. The patient is eligible to attend OT groups.

Clinical Observations

1. Cut apart strips of mailing address labels, a level 3 task. Patient could do this task. He held the scissors upside down, putting his fingers through the thumb hole.
2. Cut rags into 7-inch squares, given a sample—a level 4 task. The patient cut the rags into uneven squares ranging from 10 to 18 inches. Error was pointed out by therapist. Patient's response: "I'm sorry, I've ruined your rags," with genuine concern in voice inflection. Attempted to correct er-

ror by trimming around and around the edges but still unable to produce 7-inch squares.
3. Teapot memo pad,* a level 3 to 4 task. Patient applied far too much glue to the fabric and rickrack. Held rickrack up so that glue dripped over the memo pad and front of the fabric. Expressed concern and attempted to correct the mistake. Smeared glue around more. Attaching a pencil to message board was also difficult. He could not tie a string onto a pencil or attach the string to the handle of the teapot. The attempt was brief. He gave up quickly, saying, "I can't figure this out."
4. Decoupage, a level 3 to 4 task. Task behavior was as expected, with one exception. The picture hanger was placed on the front of the board with the points facing up. The patient was about to hit the hanger with the rounded end of a ball peen hammer.

Questions

Write a report of these observations for the patient's chart. The report should be addressed to the current issues of the patient's treatment—in this case, the need for continued hospitalization. The report should be meaningful to the readers, that is, people trained in other professions who are busy and apt to ignore lengthy reports. Use the following questions in preparing the report:

1. Did the ACL provide an accurate assessment of the cognitive level? What is the cognitive level? Select three observations that substantiate your answer. In selecting observations, take into account whether they will be clear and meaningful to the readers of the report.
2. Do any of the observations support the diagnosis of a major depression?
3. Do any of the observations suggest a diagnosis other than depression?
4. Write your observations and interpretations, along with recommendations regarding the need

*S & S Arts and Crafts, Coulchester, Conn.

for continued hospitalization and the current occupational therapy treatment plan.

FREQUENT ANSWERS TO QUESTIONS FOR CASE EXAMPLES I THROUGH XVII

Case Example I
1. a. Attention was captured by the written directions on the box.
   b. Attention was sustained by the written directions in correspondence with supplies and space available in this particular kitchen.
   c. The motor actions of locating the colander and placing it in the sink showed a plan for its use.
   d. Directions from the therapist were not required.
2. Yes. The task is familiar to most people and can be easily modified for levels 4, 5, and 6.
3. The history mentions a decline in the performance of housekeeping tasks. An assessment of the severity of this decline in function may be helpful to other members of the treatment team. Some patients, however, want a rest from their usual activities. In such cases a more desirable activity can be used.

Case Example II
1. a. Attention was captured by a symbolic cue, the pictures and diagrams found in the weaving book.
   b. Attention was sustained by a designed mode of action.
   c. Spontaneous motor actions were planned.
   d. A loom is a machine that operates in the horizontal and vertical planes through a set of relationships between treadles, heddles, warp, shuttles, and weft. The relationships on a floor loom can be seen but the number of relationships seem to be comprehended through the use of symbols.
2. Praise may not be necessary while assessing the cognitive level. The clinic is a naturalistic social setting, however, and praise can be a part of a supportive environment. Support can be offered when an assessment of the current cognitive level is not required.
3. Yes. A second project of the same content is a frequent request. The request can be honored unless some other factor, such as discharge date or further functional assessment, interferes.

Case Example III
1. a. Attention is captured by the relationships between the fabrics selected to make the patchwork pillows. The criteria for selecting from an array of sample projects may be symbolic and difficult at level 5 to generate.
   b. Attention was sustained by varying the placement of the fabric pieces using visual cues rather than conceptual criteria.
   c. Various fabrics were tried, and errors in the placement of the fabric were recognized and spontaneously corrected.
   d. Sewing the pillow pieces together was difficult. The therapist had to show Lauren how to do it. Verbal explanations were meaningless, but a demonstration could be followed.
2. Mistakes are not anticipated at level 5. Someone else, such as a therapist, must see a potential error and intervene to prevent it. This is not always possible.
3. The concept of self-regulation implies that a therapist should accept the patient's explanation of performance as much as possible. In this case the finished pillow may have reminded her of potential errors to be avoided.

Case Example IV
1. a. The therapist demonstrated the direction; imitation occurred. Creasing and beeswaxing the edge are finishing touches that are not strikingly apparent at level 4; the relationship between a finishing touch and the look of an entire project is understood at level 5.
   b. Attaching a belt buckle is novel for most peo-

ple. Repetitive actions, such as creasing and beeswaxing, are usually learned more easily than are new steps done only once (attaching a buckle).

c. Searching for a missing tool is usually a spontaneous exploratory action.

d. The amount of leather dye to be used must be coordinated with the amount of water recently absorbed in the leather. Determining the amount of dye may require attention to the partially visible effect of dye absorption.

e. Determining how hard to hit a stamping tool is influenced by water absorption and evaporation, factors that must be considered throughout the process. At level 6 these problems may be anticipated, but at level 5 a problem is noted after it occurs.

2. The variations explored at level 5 frequently are accompanied by a desire to complete several projects on the same theme. This may be permitted when possible. Leather belts are an example of an expensive project whose quantity must be regulated in some settings. Regulations for supply use seem to be especially important for patients with an Axis II diagnosis (*DSM III*, 1980).

Case Example V

1. a. Looking at the sample.
   b. Completing all of the steps.
   c. Spontaneously beginning to sand and asking for assistance when needed.
   d. The steps in the task contain actions that are familiar to most people.

2. Most of the steps in the project rely on one motor action, moving an object in the hand in a back and forth motion. The exceptions are selecting a print, trimming the print, and attaching the hook. The exceptions may require extra assistance.

3. Past experience of getting poor grades in school may lead to an avoidance of educational tasks.

4. The verbal request to duplicate a project that

had been broken suggests that motor performance is goal directed.

Case Example VI

1. a. The spontaneous action of looking at the sample may verify that a goal has been achieved. Her project looks like the sample.
   b. Sitting in a chair long enough to complete a project indicates that purposeful actions can be sustained.
   c. A refusal to do a second project may indicate that compliance cannot be sustained again.
   d. Attention to personal appearance is usually spontaneous, goal directed, and visible, all characteristics of level 4 behavior. A therapist may need to verify this interpretation with the nursing staff because the nurses may have initiated this activity.

2. OT Progress Note. An improvement in her personal appearance (hair styled and dressed in her own clothes) has been accompanied by an improvement in observed task performance. Previous note assessed performance at level 3; today some behavior was typical of level 4 (sat still to complete a project and verified her goal-directed actions by comparing her project with the sample).

Some evidence of disability is still present; she could not sustain her attention for the entire session, and her actions were still rushed. Will continue to observe to see if performance can be sustained, at a slower rate, for one hour.

Case Example VII

1. a. The best evidence for attention to a tactile cue may be the desire to wash her hands—tactile cues were of greater concern to her than the completion of the project.
   b. The repetitive action was the placement of the mosaic tiles.
   c. The spontaneous actions were smoking a cigarette and washing her hands; the actions were manual and probably familiar.

d. The familiar actions demonstrated by the therapist were squeezing glue from a plastic bottle and placing tiles.

2. The observation that differentiates level 3 from level 4 fairly clearly is Mary's response to errors; her interest was directed to a tactile cue, and she ignored goal-directed actions.

3. The observation that may help in differential diagnosis is the intense concentration in completing the first row. This observation supports the diagnosis of a schizophrenic disorder. An alternative in this case may be a depressive episode; however, depression is observed as a loss of energy and diminished concentration.

Case Example VIII

1. a. The broad and heavy motion applied to the hole punch is usually an example of attention that is captured by a tactile cue. The interpretation can be explored by asking the patient why he or she is doing it that way; level 3 patients often say that it feels good.

   b. Punching beyond the original agreement of 35 minutes suggests that an interest in the action superseded the original goal.

   c. The correct placement of the hole punch requires attention to a partially hidden cue, which is associated with level 5. Past experience seems to influence performance on this task, however; people who already know how to do it retain the ability. You can ask a level 3 patient if he or she knows how to use a hole punch, and if the patient looks puzzled you had better try something else.

   d. Easy redirection to the task at hand is common at level 3, especially during a manic episode. Numerous goals may be suggested, but the redirection of the therapist is required to complete one.

2. Level 4 involves purposeful, goal-directed behavior. The differential is based on the therapist's redirection to a single task. If a patient requires

redirection to get anything done, the level is 3. In this case the patient is probably functioning at level 3, but further observation may be required to confirm the assessment.

3. The therapist can say, "We would appreciate some help in fixing these charts for new patients. I'll show you what needs to be done, and you can decide what you would like to do." The choice is up to the patient. In most instances patients have a pretty good idea of what they can, and cannot, do. The challenge is to design tasks that they can do.

   After Bob has begun to punch holes in the charts, the therapist should watch Bob's spontaneous performance. The correct use of the hole punch is subject to individual variations and may fluctuate during sustained performance. If errors are made the task can be changed.

4. Progress Note. The cognitive level is uncertain after one clinic session in the work group; at least a level 3 and possibly a level 4. He was able to punch holes correctly in medical chart forms but needed redirection from the therapist to complete the task. Would like to continue observations.

Case Example IX

1. a. Walking to the food cart to pick up and return a tray is an example of attention to somatosensory cues.

   b. The most obvious gross body movement is walking; to some extent eating with fingers or a spoon seems to fit into this category.

   c. Postural actions that are voluntarily performed are walking and sitting.

   d. Following the lead of another person to get to and from the food cart is evident. Speed and route may vary. Eating manners are also approximations.

2. A failure to eat can be life threatening, and one can assume that eating is a desirable task that provides a reasonably accurate indication of a pa-

tient's abilities. Observations of eating behavior are helpful when patients refuse to try other performance measures.

Case Example X

1. a. Calisthenics are somatosensory actions that have an adult connotation. Physical education exercises are the most apt to capture attention.
   b. A shoe is an external object that may be ignored at level 2. In cases like this one the therapist may be relying on familiar tactile cues to elicit cooperation.
   c. A cross and a flag suggest a postural action. Religious and political symbols are elements of the external environment that frequently capture attention and elicit an associated motor action.
   d. Taking a person by the arm and demonstrating a gross motor action may recapture attention. Firm pressure seems to work better than light touch (Ayres, 1972).
2. Words that are confusing to the therapist can be confusing to the patient, too. Gross body movements seem to have an organizing and calming effect.

Case Example XI

1. *DSM III* criteria for depression in this case: weight loss, sleep disturbance, diminished ability, loss of interest or pleasure.
2. Anticipated OT observations: loss of energy with slow movements; indecisiveness in making choices; resistance to, or reluctance to attend, OT activities.
3. a. Mable's functional performance corresponds with the improvement in her personal appearance. She is able to sustain performance for about thirty minutes and shows interest in completing tasks selected by the therapist.
   b. Current level of function is typical of level 4.

Level 5 behaviors were not observed. Her functional history indicates that her quality of performance should improve to at least a level 5 and probably a level 6.
   c. Plan. Continue to observe for higher-level performance as her medication is titrated.

Case Example XII

1. Bipolar: increased activity, decreased sleep, talkativeness, distractibility, delusions. Unipolar: postpartum depression. Schizophrenia: delusions, depersonalization, decline in function. Diagnostic impression: Bipolar.
2. Hyperresponsiveness to the clinic area expressed in a number of ways: requests to do many different projects, talking while working, extensive movement around the clinic area, rushing through the steps of a task, short attention span.
3. Even though the patient tested at level 5, the initial plan may be to schedule a person in an acute manic episode for a level 4 group for a few days because such persons are so distractible and grandiose. The selection of the task can be made by the therapist, and the same standard of performance can be applied to all patients in the group.

Case Example XIII

1. A depressive episode is characterized by symptoms that are similar to those in this case of a schizophrenic disorder. People with a schizophrenic disorder usually work in the eggshell posture with an intense, sustained degree of effort. People with a depressive disorder have trouble getting started and quit easily.
2. This case example attempts to describe chronic schizophrenia at a fairly young age. Basil's functional decline seems to have been more pronounced during the last two years; there is no

evidence to suggest that he has been functioning above a level 4 during that time.

The question of progressive decline is interesting in cases like this. It is my clinical impression that people with a chronic schizophrenic disorder have a progressive decline to level 4 and then stabilize at level 4 for many years.

Case Example XIV

1. SYMPTOMS   OBSERVATIONS
   a. Disorientation to space   a. May not find the clinic room, bedroom, bathroom
   b. Recent memory loss   b. May not remember the project worked on or talking to the therapist
   c. Intellectual function is impaired   c. Level 4 or below
2. The reason for admission is that she was unable to care for herself and her home. The nephew should provide an account of problems with routine tasks that led to admission. Fire hazards such as not turning off the stove or iron should be explored. Alternative community resources such as assistance from a neighbor, Meals on Wheels, and a nursing home should be explored. In many settings the nephew will be talking to a social worker; the therapist and the social worker can collaborate in selecting observations of performance needed in this case.

Case Example XV

1. Evidence in patient's history
   a. Schizophrenic disorder
      (1) Markedly illogical thinking with catatonic or disorganized behavior
      (2) Deterioration from previous level of function (work, social relations, self-care)
      (3) Duration of more than 6 months with active phases and residual symptoms: social isolation, impaired role function, peculiar behavior
      (4) Onset before age 45
      (5) Not caused by mental retardation or organic mental disorder
   b. Major depressive episode
      (1) Major weight loss
      (2) Loss of interest
      (3) Psychomotor retardation
      (4) Loss of energy
2. Schizophrenic disorder
3. Observations of symptoms
   a. Speaks rarely, content difficult to understand
   b. Flat expression, silly laughter
   c. Stops at doorways, moves only with commands, postures
   d. States concern that surgeons might have cut him up when he went to the clinic
4. Interpretation of observations
   a. Incoherence, poverty of speech
   b. Inappropriate affect
   c. Catatonic or markedly disorganized behavior
   d. Potentially absurd thoughts (delusions)
5. Task performance suggests a schizophrenic disorder with a severe deterioration in functional abilities.
6. Progress note. Axis I: Schizophrenic disorder, rule out major depressive disorder

   Observation. The patient was seen once in OT clinic. He walked to the clinic slowly, requiring a verbal command from himself or the therapist to go through all doorways. No motor actions were initiated during the task unless the therapist started the action for the patient. He often stopped in midaction to mumble and glance fearfully around. He did not talk except to make nonsensical remarks to the therapist, accompanied by blunted and inappropriate affect. On returning to the ward he said, "Well, I wasn't hurt. . . . I have heard that surgeons cut up patients in the hospital."

Assessment. Symptoms observed during task performance include bizarre, markedly reduced motor behavior; social withdrawal; inappropriate affect; poverty of speech content and bizarre delusions. Symptoms suggest schizophrenic disorder in acute phase. Adaptive functioning is grossly impaired: level 2.

Plan. Monitor task behavior daily in 2:00 group as medication is titrated and report change in function as it occurs.

Case Example XVI

Initial Occupational Therapy Evaluation

10/4/1981 Data Base. Interview and ACL this date.

Axis V Functional History Before Admission. In 1973 patient was married with two children and a job of 18 years' duration as a machine operator. Wife died in 1973. By 1978 he had stopped working, given custody of his children to relatives, and no longer had a private residence. During the last year he has been in an alcohol rehabilitation program and on the streets.

Functional Observations During This Admission.

SYMPTOMS OF ILLNESS. "I can't communicate with people; can't cope with my life any longer."

AWARENESS OF ILLNESS. Does not think that medications affect his functional performance.

COGNITIVE LEVEL. ACL score was level 4. Gave up at the first sign of an error and refused to try any more. Score was explained to patient.

PATIENT'S GOALS. Suicide.

Occupational Therapy Plan

Ineligible for OT because
X   Suicide risk

When eligible for OT groups: work group. When risk is removed, will explain functional level and implications for potential rehabilitation objectives if medications are effective.

Functional Observations for

X   Verification of cognitive level
X   Titration of medication
X   Clarification of symptoms
Assessment of potential grave disability

Case Example XVII

1. Yes, the cognitive level is level 3. Patient was
   a. Unable to cut rags into 7-inch squares.
   b. Unable to secure string on a pencil or through a hole in wood.
   c. Unable to anticipate the dripping of clearly visible globs of glue.
2. The diagnosis of depression is supported by the patient's genuine concern when errors in cutting rags were pointed out and his inability to sustain energy to figure out how to attach the string to the pencil.
3. The misuse of tools (scissors) and supplies (picture hanger) is rarely seen with depression but may be observed with OBS.
4. Progress note. The patient has been seen ×4 in the OT clinic. Observations tend to confirm the ACL assessment, level 3:
   a. Can cut mailing address labels.
   b. Cannot cut rags into 7-inch squares.
   c. Cannot tie a string onto a pencil or attach the string through a hole in wood.
   d. Unable to anticipate dripping globs of glue.
   This behavior is consistent with level 3. Affective response to errors is consistent with a major depressive episode:
   a. "I'm sorry, I've ruined your rags," said in genuine tone of voice.
   b. After a brief attempt to attach string, stopping and saying, "I can't figure this out."
   A desire to stop problem solving and an apology for damaging supplies are typical responses to task errors during depressive episodes.

Two observations are puzzling:
a. The scissors were used upside down, with fingers through the thumb hole.
b. A picture hanger was placed on the front of a decoupage with the attachment prongs away from the wood.

The misuse of common tools and supplies is seldom observed at level 3 with depression and would be more consistent with OBS.

Recommendation. Task performance is severely impaired and independent living in the community is not advised. This patient's verbal abilities seem to exceed observed performance. The possibility of OBS merits further consideration.

Plan. Further observation in OT clinic area 10:30 A.M. and 2:00 P.M., Monday through Friday, for change in the cognitive level and any other signs of OBS.

CONCLUSION

The case examples illustrate the therapist's selected focus of attention. Practicing therapists know much more about their patients than is reported in these cases. In fact the longer case examples are really condensed summaries. In addition the longer we see the patient, the more we know about him or her. In the final analysis we are human beings, possessing a human brain that is capable of processing very few factors (3 to 6) while solving an abstract problem. We adapt to our human limitations by selecting a focus of study; some information is highlighted while other information is less important. The therapist chooses observations of task behavior that can be explained, and the kind of explanations required are usually related to the concerns of the patient and his or her caregivers. The case examples show how observations of task behavior can be related to those concerns.

REFERENCES

Ayres, J. *Sensory Integration and Learning Disorders.* Los Angeles: Western Psychological Services, 1972.
DSM III: Diagnostic and Statistical Manual of Mental Disorders (3rd ed.). Washington, D.C.: American Psychiatric Association, 1980.
Michener, J. A. *Space.* New York: Random House, 1982.

SUGGESTED READINGS

Goodwin, D. W., and Guze, S. B. *Psychiatric Diagnosis* (2nd ed.). New York; London: Oxford University Press, 1979.
Klawans, H. L., and Weiner, W. J. *Textbook of Clinical Neuropharmacology.* New York: Raven, 1981.
Maloney, M. B., and Ward, M. P. *Psychological Assessment: A Conceptual Approach.* New York: Oxford University Press, 1976.
Stone, A. A. *Mental Health and Law: A System in Transition.* New York: Jason Aaronson, 1976.
Strub, R. L., and Black, W. F. *Organic Brain Syndromes: An Introduction to Neurobehavioral Disorders.* Philadelphia: Davis, 1981.
Swonger, A. K., and Constantine, L. L. *Drugs and Therapy: A Handbook of Psychotropic Drugs* (2nd ed.). Boston: Little, Brown, 1983.

ADMINISTRATION

The administration of an occupational therapy program for people with cognitive disabilities has been influenced by the advances in the neurosciences. Perhaps the most obvious change is in the length of stay. Psychiatric hospitalizations used to be measured in years, then months, and now days. Part of this reduction can be explained by improvements in treatment methods; another part is derived from efforts to contain the mounting costs of hospital care. At present a distinction is made between an acute inpatient service and a long-time program for chronic disabilities; the suggested readings include references for both settings. This chapter will focus on programs designed for acute inpatient stays.

The mental health system is in a state of flux, as reflected in the numerous laws, policies, accreditation standards, and regulations that are subject to constant revisions and that often contain contradictory statements. The social mandates bestowed on institutions providing services to the cognitively disabled are changing. The American Occupational Therapy Association and state associations provide assistance in responding to these mandates. Ten years ago these social mandates were rather unimaginative, focusing on concrete realities such as unleaded ceramic glazes and the proper grounding of electrical plugs. Some discussion of administrative concerns is warranted. The issues to be considered include program objectives, staffing patterns, activity schedules, and the task environment. Once the pragmatic procedures are in place they are fairly easy to maintain. Keeping up with the advances in the neurosciences poses a different type of administrative problem, which will be discussed under the heading of In-service Education.

PROGRAM OBJECTIVES

The general program objectives that can be met during the course of an acute psychiatric hospitalization include the following:

1. To assist with differential diagnosis

Table 9-1. Cognitive levels: abilities and disabilities

Cognitive level	Ability	Disability
1	Automatic actions only, or patient does not move	Unable to initiate self-care tasks (feeding, toileting, dressing, bathing, grooming)
2	Gross body movements only; can approximate actions	Needs assistance to initiate and complete all self-care tasks consistently
3	Repetitive actions only; can act on external environment	Needs assistance to complete self-care tasks and other familiar activities
4	Goal-directed actions to accomplish visible goals only	Needs assistance to see the relationships between material objects; requires striking visual and tactile cues
5	Exploratory actions; can learn from direct experience	Needs assistance to anticipate the consequences of actions
6	Planned actions using deductive reasoning to anticipate effects of actions	None

Table 9-2. Occupational therapy goals for patients with cognitive disabilities

Cognitive level	Goal
1	Assess self-care tasks on ward
2	Assess self-care tasks on ward
3	Assess self-care tasks on ward or in OT groups; assist with completion of problem-free tasks
4	Provide short-term tasks and assist with problem solving to monitor functional abilities and the disease process
5	Provide novel tasks and assist with problem solving to monitor functional abilities and the disease process
6	Provide desirable tasks and assist with observations of symptom reduction to monitor the disease process

2. To assist with the titration of medication
3. To assist with discharge planning
4. To observe and treat the expressions of acute symptoms and disabilities in the task environment

The first three objectives are met by reporting information to members of the treatment team, principally the physician. The implication of these objectives is that therapists should devote time and energy to written and verbal reports. The fourth objective is fulfilled during task performance.

An accurate description of what a therapist does about a functional disability is required. Tables 9-1 to 9-3 constitute such a description. These tables were developed for distribution to the multidisciplinary team. The team is concerned with fulfilling the institutional objectives. The problems that must be addressed are frequently found in the reasons for admission (see Table 2-3). A reason for admission may be an expression of a disease, a disability, or both; both are considered by the therapist.

An occupational therapy program provides the opportunity to engage in various kinds of activities. The selection of program content is based on the pa-

Table 9-3. Occupational therapy
goals for acute psychiatric diseases

Disease	Goal
Major depression	Monitor cognitive level via task performance as antidepressant medication is titrated Assist with task performance as required by disability (see Tables 9-1, 9-2)
Bipolar affective disorder	Monitor cognitive level via task performance as lithium is titrated Assist with task performance as required by disability (see Tables 9-1, 9-2)
Schizophrenic disorder	Monitor cognitive level via task performance as neuroleptic medication is titrated Assist with task performance as required by disability (see Tables 9-1, 9-2) Make discharge recommendations based on residual disability
Substance abuse	Monitor cognitive level via task performance as substance is removed from system Assist with task performance as required by disability (see Tables 9-1, 9-2)

tient's abilities and personal preferences. Table 9-4 is an example of a brief orientation to program content; a brief orientation is helpful to new staff members, students, and visitors. Tables 9-1 to 9-4 are examples, presented with the expectation that institutional variations will occur.

People in other disciplines usually appreciate brief descriptions, but therapists and students require more detail. Chapter 10 gives examples of programs and attempts to answer questions of unique concern to therapists.

The occupational therapy program objectives must reflect the social demands placed on an institution. Funding procedures, admission and discharge criteria, length of stay, and service objectives become political questions as politicians and private payers attempt to reduce health care costs and ensure patients' rights. Some examples of social mandates that can influence program planning follow.

During the last decade we have witnessed an overall decrease in the cognitive level of inpatients (resulting in more groups designed for lower-level patients), a more rapid turnover of patients (resulting in more occupational therapy evaluations), an increase in medical complications accompanying psychiatric illness (resulting in a need to increase our knowledge about their effects on task behavior), an increase in phencyclidine hydrochloride (PCP) abuse (resulting in a need to increase our ability to assess and manage PCP abusers), an increase in requests for data that can be used in court (resulting in legal and ethical considerations), and the closing of inpatient wards (resulting in a loss of budgeted occupational therapy positions). Clearly, social and political factors have had an influence on the demands placed on the hospital, which have, in turn, altered the demands placed on therapists. These examples illustrate how institutional objectives influence occupational therapy objectives.

STAFFING PATTERNS

The organization of the personnel of the occupational therapy department is designed to fulfill two different roles. Therapists are accountable for (1) conducting a patient program and (2) for reporting observations to a multidisciplinary team. The division of these two roles has produced some interest-

Table 9-4. Activities available in occupational therapy

Level 3 and 4 groups

An opportunity to complete a task successfully within an hour is provided. Demonstrated directions contain obvious tactile and visual cues and use familiar tools and supplies. Patients assessed at level 3 or 4 can select from the following groups, according to their personal preferences:

1. *Basic crafts*. Monday through Friday, 2:00–3:00 P.M. Simple craft projects such as wooden jewelry boxes, decoupage, tile trivets and coasters, mosaics, and wooden letter holders are made.

2. *Basic skills*. Tuesday through Friday, 10:30–11:30 A.M. Pencil and paper tasks including alphabetizing, simple mathematical calculations, use of the telephone directory, map reading, and filling out of forms are reviewed.

3. *Basic woodworking*. Monday through Friday, 1:00–2:00 P.M. The projects, which may last two or more sessions, include decoupage, plant holders, recipe and jewelry boxes, cutting boards, and spice racks.

4. *Basic sewing*, Monday through Friday, 10:30–11:30 A.M. Familiarity with hand sewing is required to complete simple projects such as felt eyeglass cases, pincushions, and pot holders.

5. *Grooming*. Monday through Friday, 9:30–10:30 A.M. and 1:00–2:00 P.M. Nail, hair, and skin care are discussed and encouraged. Patients select grooming and cosmetic aids and are shown how to use them.

Special interests groups for levels 4, 5, and 6

1. *Work group*. Monday through Thursday, 10:30–11:30 A.M. Real work tasks ranging from simple collation to complex chart assembly and preparation for other craft groups are demonstrated. A limited number of vocational skills (typing, filing, and simple bookkeeping) may be refreshed. This group is frequently selected by depressed men.

2. *Senior group*. Tuesday through Friday, 1:00–2:00 P.M. People over the age of 55 can do craft projects, reminisce while listening to music, read senior newspapers, and discuss community resources.

3. *Medication group*. 2:00–3:00 P.M. Lithium and antidepressants on Monday; neuroleptics on Tuesday. Information and answers to questions about drug benefits, side effects, and compliance are presented. This group is coordinated with the pharmacist and pharmacology residents.

Level 5 and 6 groups

An opportunity to select and learn how to complete a new task is provided. Demonstrated, written, and verbal directions about the intangible properties of objects are provided. Project selection and length of time to complete project are based on personal preferences.

1. *Advanced crafts*. Tuesday through Friday, 3:00–4:00 P.M. Available projects include woodworking, ceramics, leather, macrame, candles, needlework, basketry, jewelry, drawing or painting, and educational activities.

2. *Advanced sewing*. Monday through Friday, 1:00–2:00 P.M. Projects that are sewn by hand and completed in one to four sessions include patchwork pillows, bargello, purses, embroidery, and stuffed animals or dolls. This group is frequently selected by depressed women.

ing side effects that I think are beneficial to our working conditions. Traditionally therapists have not made these divisions, and the therapist who observed the task behavior reported the observations. The following staffing pattern illustrates how the therapist who observes the task behavior is not necessarily the same therapist who reports the observation.

The need for the division of responsibilities evolved from activities preferred by patients at levels 3 and 4; therapists wanted to place all of these people in the same group, working on the same project. This was achieved by dividing the therapists' role responsibilities. Each therapist is assigned to one treatment ward and completes the evaluations and progress notes for all of the patients admitted to that unit (20 to 25 patients per ward, 6 to 9 therapists and treatment units). The patients admitted to a unit vary in their cognitive levels, personal preferences, and diagnoses. Flexibility in task content and level of function was the administrative goal.

The therapist assigned to the ward completes the initial assessment of a new patient and then presents the case to the rest of the OT staff. The presentation includes the treatment objectives and the selected activity groups. The selection of the activity group is based upon the patient's cognitive level and the task content preferred by the patient. The group may be conducted by any of the therapists; each therapist conducts two groups. A report on the patient's behavior is given to the ward therapist during feedback sessions and contains the content necessary for written and verbal reports to the multidisciplinary team.

The time required for occupational therapy departmental communication is formally defined by three lunch-hour meetings per week for new patient presentations and three feedback sessions per week, scheduled at the end of the day. In addition a great deal of informal communication occurs during the day because therapists are curious about the patients' performance.

The interdependency of the OT staff has sharpened our focus on patient care by increasing our mutual curiosity about why patients behave the way they do. Communication with other therapists has helped us refine descriptions of patient behavior and has pointed out questions and interpretations that require further study. In addition there has been a decrease in the tendency for therapists to assume too much personal responsibility for a patient's behavior (e.g., the fact that a patient is malodorous is not necessarily a reflection on the therapist). An atmosphere of collaboration and cooperation has developed. This is especially evident in bartering over who will do less desirable jobs, such as cleaning out the refrigerator or having a repelling patient in one's group.

An additional benefit of this mode of operation is that we hear a presentation on nearly every patient in the hospital and can rapidly compile data describing the patient population. Long-term changes in the hospital admission criteria can be assessed and responded to, while changes in ward admissions, which are temporary and occur more frequently, can be accommodated without major program changes. Furthermore, each therapist has some knowledge of how each ward's interdisciplinary team operates and can use that information to depersonalize communication problems. Overall, the division of role responsibilities seems to be conducive to focusing our attention on a careful interpretation of task performance and helps us avoid some of the temporary or personnel issues that can divert energy and attention.

A central issue with staffing patterns is the identification of a reasonable work load. The number of beds and the average length of stay are frequent considerations. The length of stay is a figure that is easily distorted by a few patients who stay a very long or a very short time. The average number of new patients evaluated each week may be a better figure. Five new acute patients per week, or one a day, seems to be manageable; ten a week seems to be far too many. This figure, of course, can be distorted, too: by readmissions, severe illness, and absence of social support systems.

Fulfilling the objectives that are met by communicating information to other members of the treatment team can be difficult. The therapist's report may be excellent, but is anybody listening? In general people who are interested in a psychodynamic formation of mental disorders have trouble understanding the severity of illness as reflected in a person's voluntary motor actions. People who are interested in a biologic formulation of the problem tend to take the cognitive levels as literally true and may disregard the factors that can produce an error. In both instances the therapist must provide information that is as accurate and objective as possible. Doing so seems to be facilitated by having two or more therapists make observations involving different task content, for example, grooming and crafts.

The staff of an occupational therapy department may be augmented by assistants, aides, and volunteers. There is a tendency to overestimate the amount of help provided by volunteers. The therapist's first thought may be to find some assistance with the formidable amount of preparation required for level 3 and 4 groups. Volunteers want to work with patients but do not understand the distinction between an evaluative observation and a treatment intervention. A volunteer who will help with preparation and stay out of the way during the activity is a rare individual. Aides often have experience and training as nursing aides; that background can be helpful in conducting grooming groups. Assistants have a basic education in disease and disability and often have a good crafts background. Aides and assistants can conduct groups as long as a therapist can provide some assistance with the standardization of the tasks.

Presently many long-term facilities for people with stable cognitive disabilities are poorly funded and cannot offer a salary that would attract a full-time therapist. A consultant's fee may be offered, but the rehabilitation objectives that can be realistically achieved by a consultant are unclear. Some guidance in setting practical objectives may be found by using the Routine Task Inventory (Table 2-2). Behavioral change may be possible, but it should be attempted with caution. Romantic promises should be avoided; a self-directed opportunity for change should be offered. Descriptive studies of long-term cognitive disabilities are scarce, and therapists are well advised to have experience working in acute facilities before attempting this confusing and often demoralizing area of practice.

ACTIVITY SCHEDULES

The scheduling of a patient program in a short-term hospital is always a problem. Other demands on the staff's and the patient's time, such as meals, meetings, laboratory tests, medication time, and change of shift, are often beyond the therapist's control. Therapists should probably avoid trying to change these realities unless there is a very compelling reason to do so.

Certain elements are within the therapist's con-

trol, and some suggestions about these can be offered. Groups for the cognitively disabled are more successful if they are offered at the same time of day 5 days a week. Groups that are offered once or twice a week at different times of day usually have a short life span or require extra time, and gaining a reasonable attendance is difficult. Ideally a patient should be assigned to one group in the morning and one in the afternoon. Groups generally are scheduled for one hour. The level 3 and 4 patients do not pay attention to their projects that long but transporting them between the ward and the clinic takes up the additional time. Transporting patients is an important consideration because they can get lost, become distracted, move slowly, refuse to come to the clinic area, or try to escape from an involuntary commitment to the hospital.

The transfer of a patient between the ward and the clinic is governed by policies and procedures, and some frequent issues can be identified. People who have a cognitive disability can act in unpredictable or harmful ways. A newly admitted patient may be observed on the ward and gradually allowed access to other areas of the facility and the community. A written policy describing the restrictions and privileges that govern the patient's whereabouts is usually available. The decision about an individual's plan is often discussed in a community meeting, attended by other patients and staff members; the final decision may be made by the physician. Therapists work closely with other members of the ward staff in deciding when a patient is ready to come to the clinic area. General criteria for clinic attendance can be suggested: Patients must be at level 3 or higher and predictable, nonviolent, and cooperative. The level can be measured objectively, but the other criteria are subjective; to err on the cautious side of delaying attendance is usually the best policy. Risks vary from one institution to another, and, of course, these variations should influence the criteria.

A schedule of activities (title of group, day of the week, and time of day) can be posted on the ward where the patients can see it. In addition, because the nursing staff is usually responsible for knowing the patients' whereabouts, they appreciate an up-to-date list (time of day, day of the week, names of patients).

Supplies taken from the clinic to the ward also necessitate collaboration with the nursing staff. Some items may be used independently, while others must be used only when supervised by ward staff. The following items are frequent concerns:

Sewing	Plastic or metal knitting, sewing, and embroidery needles and crochet hooks
Art	Felt-tip pens, pencils, chalk, watercolors, paper, acrylic paints, paint-by-number kits
Crafts	White glue, mosaic tiles, blunt-end scissors, leather lacing with or without a needle
Grooming	Glass bottles, toxic fumes, poisons, nail clippers, nail files, tweezers, items that may cause allergic or other potentially harmful reactions

Institutions vary in the permitted use of these objects. A written checklist helps prevent unnecessary ambiguity and conflict.

Another potential scheduling problem can develop between occupational therapists and the other activity therapists. Activity therapy is a term used to include recreation, art, music, movement, dance, horticulture, and many other types of activities. Scheduling patients can create conflicts unless a system is developed to minimize the problem. For example, the recreation therapists can schedule most of the level 3 and 4 patients for 1:00 P.M., and the occupational therapists can schedule them for 2:00 P.M.

Some psychiatric institutions have a history of a close working relationship between occupational therapy and one or more of the other activity therapies. Our theories have shared a psychodynamic formulation of disease, and in the business of conducting a program we have shared space, supplies, schedules, policies, and procedures. Role confusion and self-defensive statements about the relative value of one's own discipline have occurred. Lines of authority that entail supervision by a person from another discipline tend to heighten the conflict. Separate departments with autonomous space, programs, policies, procedures, and lines of authority can reduce friction. Autonomy may be essential as the activity therapists select their responses to the advances in the neurosciences. We are all struggling to adapt to these advances, and we are each responsible for placing these adaptations in our own treatment programs, documentations, literature, and curricula.

Scheduling an activity group often raises questions about the professional qualifications required to conduct a group. People in other professions have been telling us for years that one of the values of our services is that we can "keep the patients busy." The statement has a slightly annoying quality, because it implies that we are glorified babysitters. In a sense the statement is true, in that the purpose of acute hospitalization is to provide a safe place to "wait it out" until the medication takes effect. Professional qualifications become necessary when the patient and the multidisciplinary team require an objective assessment of how well the medications are, or are not, working. Attendance records provide an account of the number of opportunities that the therapist has had to appraise the patient's current level of function. The quality of the observations is not reflected by the numerical count.

Developing a program that aims at monitoring changes in the level of cognitive functioning is deceptively difficult. The projects look easy enough, but interpreting the degree of conscious awareness required to do a step can be confusing. Discussing an analysis of a task demand as well as observations of performance with another therapist helps. The process of developing semistandardized tasks for a given patient population usually uncovers numerous questions about the correct interpretation. A dialogue about the correct interpretation is easily achieved in settings with several therapists. Therapists who work alone in small units report that the absence of dialogue with other therapists is a major problem in working in these settings. A cognitive disability is an ambiguous phenomenon, and in the final analysis it is always possible to make a mistake. The preferred program design is one that provides some checks and balances for potential errors, such as observations by two or more therapists using desirable task contents and different types of tasks and done at different times of day. Activity schedules and personnel assignments should be designed to enhance a system of checks and balances. Therapists working alone can create this system by forming special interest groups designed to clarify puzzling observations.

TASK ENVIRONMENT

The management of cognitive disabilities emphasizes the task environment and places an administrative emphasis on supplies. Without supplies there simply is no program. Procurement, storage, preparation, and clutter are the natural hassles that accompany management of the task environment.

The supplies needed for a patient group are ordered by the therapist who conducts the group because that therapist has the greatest knowledge of the quantity and quality of the materials required. Supplies for several groups may be ordered from a single vendor; these orders can be combined once each therapist has determined his or her needs.

Cost containment objectives in the current health care delivery system can easily lead to a bureaucratic decision that occupational therapy supplies are not essential medical supplies. A considerable amount of institutional education can be required to obtain supplies successfully. The procurement of the materials necessary to conduct a program must be regarded as the top administrative priority. The institutional policies and procedures required to obtain supplies warrant careful scrutiny,

because an OT clinic without supplies is analogous to a hospital without beds or a doctor without medication.

Locating vendors who can supply projects that can be done successfully by adults with cognitive disabilities is difficult. Potential vendors are suggested at the end of this chapter (Appendix 9-1).

While the critical need for supplies is apparent, the therapist is also responsible for cost containment. One partial measure of the cost-effectiveness of the various task media is the supply cost per patient session. The cost of the supplies for a patient group can be divided by the number of patients attending the group to obtain a relative cost of the content. For example, inflation has had a serious effect on the cost of leather. It is possible that another medium can be substituted to meet the objectives met by a leather group, at reduced cost. The media that are most resistive to substitution are the routine tasks; a patient's safety in the kitchen is best assessed by placing the patient in a kitchen. The assessment of routine tasks raises questions about the disposition of the patient, and our ability to predict community adjustment is limited. At this time our predictive capabilities are not strong enough to permit substitution of less expensive supplies and capital equipment.

The storage of supplies involves another set of aggravations for the therapist. Supplies must be immediately adjacent to the patients during a group session, but the volume of materials needed to conduct a program usually makes additional, remote storage areas necessary. Therapists are constantly moving things from the supply room to the clinic areas. Recognizing the storage and organization of supplies as a perpetual reality, we should include time for this maintenance operation in our weekly schedules.

The preparation needed for successful task behavior for level 3 and 4 groups can be extensive if the therapist is not careful. Kits should be purchased from manufacturers whenever possible. The cost-effectiveness of a kit can be measured by adding the cost of the therapist's preparation time to the cost of the materials. Another solution to the problem of preparation, in institutions where a work evaluation group is indicated, is to have the work group help to meet the real need to prepare for other patient groups. Many patients express real satisfaction with having helped prepare for the finished product that other patients produce.

Clutter seems to be a natural accompaniment to the variety of tasks, tools, and materials we make available to patients. Unfinished projects and supplies that are not put away seem to accumulate with amazing speed. Constant vigilance is required to keep the clinic area neat and orderly—and this applies to the sample of an intricate project that the therapist likes but no cognitively disabled patient would ever be able to make. The war against clutter requires cooperation with the housekeeping department, and therapists must remember that a counter cannot be cleaned if it is covered with junk. Therapists have a tendency to place a low priority on clinic maintenance; cleaning the paintbrushes, unplugging the glue bottles, and cleaning cupboards are not our favorite examples of professional behavior. If these maintenance procedures are not attended to, however, patient care will suffer, because the therapist will miss observations of patient behavior while sorting through the clutter.

One of the surprising realities of clinical practice is that the therapist does the "unfun" steps of task completion. The therapist procures the supplies, stores them, prepares the material, corrects the patients' mistakes, and cleans up afterwards. The patient gets the pleasure of doing the project and showing it off after it is done. We must try to cooperate in finding methods of fulfilling these unpleasant requirements as efficiently as possible. One lesson occurs repeatedly: If specific assignments and regular schedules for doing these duties are not made, they simply do not get done. Suddenly we look around, and we are low on supplies and the clinic is a mess. The management of the physical and capital resources of the task environment deserve as much attention as the other issues involved in practice.

WHO OWNS CRAFTS?

There has been a tendency to confuse our professional identity with our media. Therapists working in psychiatric hospitals are often identified with crafts; in other settings they are identified with activities of daily living. This identification may be derived from the simple fact that we have easy access to supply catalogues. A problem in professional roles may develop when someone else wants similar supplies. The question is When does the use of these supplies require the presence of a therapist? An example of a limited use of a therapist's knowledge can be cited.

In maternity wards in general hospitals there are often a few women who must be in the hospital for a long time because of medical complications of their pregnancies. Staff on the ward are concerned about the detrimental effects of the patients' having nothing to do but sit and worry about their health problems. Needlework is a natural suggestion. A therapist can consult with a person assigned to the ward, perhaps a social worker, in selecting supplies and working through the institutional procedures for obtaining the supplies. A therapist is not needed to hand out the supplies or teach the typical procedure. No cognitive disability is present in these patients, and the special management skills of the therapist are not required. The therapist's knowledge is pragmatic: how to get the supplies to the ward. The availability of supplies, without a therapist, may produce a nice side effect—the patients may teach each other how to do the projects and thus reduce their social isolation.

SAFETY AND HEALTH REQUIREMENTS

The task environment must also comply with numerous federal, state, and local requirements for safety, fire prevention, health, and sanitation. Of particular note in the occupational therapy clinic are the following:

1. The ceramic glazes used must not contain lead.

2. The refrigerator temperature must be routinely taken and recorded on the door of the refrigerator.
3. Food purchased from the local grocery store, or obtained through the central kitchen, must be dated when brought into the clinic.
4. The kitchen area is particularly vulnerable to violations of health and sanitation requirements. These should be reviewed by the person conducting the cooking group. Coffee cups, glasses, and measuring and stirring utensils should be checked.
5. Fire extinguishers must be routinely checked to make sure that they conform with use requirements.
6. Staff must be trained in proper fire procedures—both the evacuation of patients and the extinguishing of various types of fires.
7. Security procedures for sharp objects and toxic materials must limit access; usually they are kept under lock and key and used only under staff supervision.
8. Flammables must be stored in the flammable cabinet, and an effort should be made to keep the quantity of these materials at a minimum. Recently a distinction has been made between flammables and combustibles: Combustibles blow up, flammables burn. Combustibles are not stored in the flammable cabinet. It is a good idea to check current wastepaper basket policies: metal cans, and special cans for sharp objects and flammables, may be required. Keep ashtrays in smoking areas only.
9. Toxins, if required, can be stored under lock and key in the clinic area, but they should not fill up the flammable cabinet unless, of course, they are flammable.
10. Hallways and doors must be kept free for easy access.
11. The space between the top of the storage cabinets and the ceiling must be checked; 18 inches for fire access may be required.
12. Sanitation of hand soap should be checked. Some hospital regulations prohibit the sharing

of bar soap, and individualized liquid soap dispensers may be required.
13. Connections and grounding of electrical appliances should be checked.

SECURITY

Careful security in the occupational therapy department is of real concern for the following reasons:

1. The patients seen in clinic may until recently have been suicide or elopement risks; some risk may still be present.
2. Materials and equipment in the department must be protected from misuse or theft.
3. The personal property of the staff must be protected from misuse or theft.

Some procedures to consider are as follows:

1. *Main door.* The main door to the clinic must be locked when patients are in the clinic unless the clinic policy clearly states that an open door is permitted.
2. *Tool cabinets—activity groups.* The group leader must be responsible for checking the tool cabinet to see that all tools are present when the cabinets are opened, observing the proper use of tools, replacing all tools in the cabinet, and locking it before leaving the area.
3. *Tool cabinets—individual use.* The individual therapist who opens the cabinet must be responsible for checking to see that all tools are present when the cabinet is opened, returning tools used, checking for any tools obtained by others while the cabinet was open, and locking the cabinet. If a therapist removes a tool for use outside the room, a note with the therapist's name and the date and time the tool was removed can be taped to the shadow board. If there are patients in any room in the clinic and you intend to leave the room, lock the cabinet before leaving the room.
4. *Supply cabinets.* Cabinets containing toxic materials or sharp items are to be locked when not in

immediate use and patients are in the area. As patients arrive in the clinic area, the individual who opens the cabinets is responsible for closing them.

5. *End of the day.* Before leaving the OT clinic or office at the end of the day, determine which cabinets and rooms are in use and lock all of those not in use. Check to see that lights, coffee pot, and kiln are turned off and that record players, tool cabinets, and storage closets are locked.

6. *Keys.* Keep track of your keys. Children and adolescents are especially prone to taking them if you put them down.

7. *Institutional identification badges.* Identification badges should be worn every day. This is especially important when you are new to a facility.

8. *Patients leaving the OT clinic.* Some patients may leave the OT clinic alone. If you do not know the patient, ask a staff member. If there is any doubt, escort the patient to the ward.

IN-SERVICE EDUCATION

The day-to-day operations of an occupational therapy program can easily consume all of a therapist's working hours. When we allow this to happen for an extended period, we have a tendency to get bored and restless. Necessary clinic maintenance has a tendency to isolate us from the dramatic changes in the neurosciences. In-service education can provide an essential link to interdisciplinary knowledge.

Various regulatory agencies require some evidence of continuing education, but the selection of the content is usually left to individual discretion. The generalist approach made it possible to develop a rationale for just about any topic. This discussion will aim at providing assistance in selecting a focus of study.

The first problem encountered in designing a continuing education program is the various levels of sophistication represented by the occupational therapy audience. A professional baseline is required, and the suggested readings found at the end of Chapter 8 can be suggested. There is a great deal

of variation in therapists' familiarity with that content, but deficiencies can be corrected through independent study.

Another independent approach to continuing education is reading professional journals. Therapists should not restrict themselves to occupational therapy journals but should select other, related journals. The journals cited in this text can be used as a start. If your aim is to keep up with the advances in the neurosciences you can examine the references cited in a given article to see if they are current. (Many "new" articles are restricted to "old" ideas.) Many journals publish overviews that are a wonderfully efficient way of gathering information, and the more reputable journals try to protect the reader from author bias, a well-recognized problem with overviews. Restricted access, because of time or geography, can be overcome by subscribing to interdisciplinary journals. For example, you do not have to be a psychiatrist to subscribe to the *Archives of General Psychiatry.* Interdisciplinary information is accessible; obtaining it requires an investment in time and money.

An easier access to information is provided by workshops, journal clubs, study groups, and guest lecturers. The information is selected for you, and your attendance is based on the anticipated relevance of the information. A stimulating new area of study can be suggested by these approaches to continuing education. Having designed and presented numerous continuing education programs I find that they have a common problem: An independent, critical analysis of the content is rarely possible in a group setting. Continuing education programs bear a resemblance to college courses in which one is tested on the lecture notes, not the assigned readings. One has the sense that one's knowledge of the subject is restricted. To be truly informed one must do some independent reading. The current design of continuing education units (CEUs) emphasizes attendance of the participants and neglects the need for further critical analysis. The enforced addition of critical analysis is probably not possible with CEUs, but critical analysis is an expectation that we can place on ourselves. Continuing education programs can be an effective stimulation, mobilizing us out of our complacency, but they should not be regarded as a substitute for independent study.

Independent study implies that each therapist must establish criteria for his or her own course of study. Criteria become especially important when one goes to the library; the available information can be overwhelming. It is very easy to waste a great deal of time in the library; thinking of the process as an applied literature review seems to help avoid interesting, but basically irrelevant, tangents. Some clinical questions that can suggest topics follow.

1. What is the most common medical diagnosis seen in your patient population? What is your current knowledge about any recent changes in diagnostic criteria, the effectiveness of medical interventions, and the natural course of the disease?
2. Are you seeing an increase in a medical diagnosis about which your knowledge could benefit from an updating, for example, a new street drug, an increasing interaction between alcoholism and an affective disorder, or a potential genetic link between Down's syndrome and Alzheimer's disease?
3. Is there something new being tried on your service unit, for example, a new psychotropic drug or a new diagnostic test? The person who initiated the idea is often willing to share a copy of the references.
4. Have there been any new studies describing residual physical and cognitive disabilities? Are there any new ideas for measuring treatment effectiveness in chronic disabilities?
5. Are there any new studies measuring attention deficits, voluntary and involuntary motor actions, sensory perceptions differentiated from attention to sensory cues, or self-directed behavior in those with cognitive disabilities?
6. In the social sphere, what progress has the legal system made in defining incompetency, and

what is the current thought in program planning for the cognitively disabled?

Searching for answers to any one of these questions can usually keep you busy for several hours. One precaution should be noted: When you begin to sense that you are beating your head against a revolving wheel, it is time to go home. The knowledge explosion is producing information from every conceivable direction; information overload is a common occurrence. When it happens it usually helps to leave the literature and go back to observing patients to develop a more specific formulation of the question. The identification of one or two common patient observations usually makes it possible to find some semblance of order in the literature. At the very least one can develop some criteria for deciding which studies can be safely ignored, and that, all by itself, can be a relief.

CONCLUSION

Designing and maintaining a program for the cognitively disabled is relatively straightforward. Reformulating a program is difficult because the changes must be consistent with current knowledge. Knowing when and how to change a program, or a progress note, requires a commitment, from each of us to continuing education.

APPENDIX 9-1. VENDORS

All Felt Products, Inc.
559 West Covina Boulevard
San Dimas, California 91773

Bucilla (Stitchery)
7026 East Slauson Avenue
P.O. Box 22198
Los Angeles, California 90040

Chaselle Arts and Crafts
9645 Gerwig Lane
Columbia, Maryland 21046

Craft House (paint by number)
Besco Associates
11222 La Cienega Boulevard
Inglewood, California 90304

Curriculum Resources, Inc.
2 Post Road, Box 923
Fairfield, Connecticut 06430

La Femme (cosmetics)
4570 Santa Monica Boulevard
Los Angeles, California 90040

Lakeshore Curriculum Materials
2695 East Dominguez Street
P.O. Box 6261
Carson, California 90749

Leisure Crafts
3061 Maria Street
P.O. Box 5528
Rancho Dominguez, California 90224

Nasco Arts and Crafts
1524 Princeton Avenue
Modesto, California 95352

S & S Arts and Crafts
Colchester, Connecticut 06415

Stewarts of California, Inc.
Division of American Art Clay Company, Inc.
16055 Heron Avenue
La Mirada, California 90638

Triarco Arts and Crafts, Inc.
14650–28th Avenue North
Plymouth, Minnesota 55441

Tandy Leather Company
P.O. Box 791
Fort Worth, Texas 76101

SUGGESTED READINGS

Drucker, P. E. *The Age of Discontinuity: Guidelines to a Changing Society.* New York: Harper & Row, 1968.

Drucker, P. E. *People and Performance: The Best of Peter Drucker on Management.* New York: Harper & Row, 1977.

Durham, T. M. Preparing the mentally handicapped for community living. *Br. J. Occup. Ther.* 41:25–27, 1978.

Hausman, K. APA task force issues report on long-term care facilities. *Psychiatr. News.*, pp. 6 and 12, Sept. 3, 1982.

Hillard, J. R., Holand, J. M., and Ramm, D. Christmas and psychopathology. *Arch. Gen. Psychiatry* 38:1377–1381, 1981.

Lefkovitz, P. M. The assessment of suitability for partial hospitalization: The day therapy appropriations scale. *Int. J. Partial Hosp.* 1:45–57, 1982.

Myler, A. A. Involving boarding home owners in the clinical process: A case study. *Int. J. Partial Hosp.* 1:99–104, 1982.

Nathan, J. Community occupational therapy in the mental health field. *Br. J. Occup. Ther.* 45:3–5, 1982.

Toeffler, A. *The Third Wave.* New York: Telecom, 1980.

CHAPTER 10

OCCUPATIONAL THERAPY GROUPS

Catherine A. Earhart

The occupational therapy groups described in this chapter have been selected to provide detailed examples of the behaviors that a therapist may observe in practice. Behaviors that seem to generalize from one patient population to another have been selected as much as possible. An attribute of our target population that facilitates generalization is our geographical location in Los Angeles. Los Angeles is home to a number of recent immigrants, and attendance in our occupational therapy program often resembles a United Nation's gathering, with patients from any number of racial, ethnic, and cultural groups. Therapists working in this setting must identify universal voluntary motor actions. Therapists also increase their reliance on demonstrated directions because many patients speak a foreign language and cannot understand verbal directions.

Our patient population contains some attributes that constrain generalization as well, and these constraints must be identified. The groups are conducted in a public institution that provides services to many people who lack private means of payment. Many of these people lack social support systems and have very few personal belongings. Practical projects that fulfill a utilitarian need are preferred by these patients. In addition the local inpatient hospitals have a limited number of beds, and people are treated as outpatients as much as possible; potential inpatients who can recognize a problem in their behavior and see a connection between functional performance and medication compliance are often treated as outpatients. Our inpatient population may be skewed in the direction of people who deny the presence of an illness, refuse to take medications, and seek a legal release from an involuntary stay in the hospital. These inpatients may refuse to take tests and avoid activities that would expose a disability. Tasks that have face validity (i.e., tasks that are vital to the patient's health and safety) may be refused. Therapists working in this setting have to be ingenious in designing tasks that will elicit cooperation; the therapist must obtain the patient's agreement to do a task in order to observe cognitive abilities.

WHAT'S IN A NAME?

The groups that will be described include movement, grooming, basic crafts, basic skills, basic sewing, clay and mosaics, cooking, work evaluation, and advanced crafts. The name of the group reflects the level of function and the task content. The patients are concerned about the content; they want to know what they are going to be doing. In a large facility with several therapists the group title can reflect the available choices. Smaller facilities can convey the available choices in other ways, such as a display case of sample projects. Craft projects are fairly easy to display, but some of the other tasks require more ingenuity, given that people at level 4 require a visible example.

The level of function, implicit in the group name, is a concern of the therapist's. A *basic* group in these examples is designed for people functioning at levels 3 and 4, while *advanced* is for levels 5 and 6. Dividing patients according to the level of function is a common practice of varying popularity. *Primary* and *secondary* are alternative names derived from Freud's description of primary and secondary processes (Hall and Lindzey, 1957). In recent years some therapists have avoided an expression of the level of function in the title of a group because of an implicit stigma conveyed by the lower-level groups. The stigma seems to be an extension of the notion that a label causes a disability. In fact the title of the group seems to have little effect on the quality of observed performance. The presence, or absence, of a term that signifies the level of function is for staff convenience. The inclusion of these titles is relatively unimportant.

Scheduling patients in groups according to their level of function is important. Therapists must have a program plan that organizes their observations of behavior. What must be remembered while planning a schedule is that we, too, have limitations; the human brain can only process so much information.

An example of a clinical practice that can hopelessly confuse a therapist is an "open clinic." In an open clinic, as described here, patients elect to meander in and out of the clinic according to the whim of the moment. The therapist often knows little or nothing about the patient and thereby lacks hypotheses that can suggest key observations of behavior. Therapist errors in deciding when to observe or intervene are likely. The therapist's report is apt to be redundant, stating obvious observations that are already known about the patient and contributing no new information. A scheduled program helps the therapist identify the kind of observations and interventions that can be provided by different task contents. Information about the individual patient helps the therapist predict the observations of performance to be expected and report the accuracy of the predictions. A planned program can give equal weight to the desires of the patients and the demands on the therapist's assessment and management skills. The groups described in this chapter show various approaches to balancing desirable content with therapeutic observations. The groups were selected to illustrate a wide range of program content and potential observations.

TREATMENT DELIVERY

Treating patients in groups makes it possible to manage a large number of patients efficiently in an acute hospital. The groups described here provide some examples of how a program can be organized in a relatively large (over 100 beds) hospital. These examples are a way of illustrating one type of schedule; of course, other program designs are expected.

Those groups that are consistently successful in meeting identified treatment objectives will be described. In designing a program, it is important to provide a variety of groups from cognitive level 2 through 6, and within each level a variety of tasks. As some patients can be expected to "move up" the cognitive scale as their acute symptoms remit, more complex tasks and environments are necessary to allow for an observation of reemerging abilities. For patients who stabilize at a lower cognitive level, a variety of tasks allows for the selection of a desirable task. The description of each group includes the referral criteria, the number of patients scheduled, the length of time required to complete the task, and environmental considerations. Methods, including specific tasks, and preparations are described, with samples of patient performances and possible assessments. In addition, the advantages and disadvantages of each group are discussed.

MOVEMENT

Movement group is designed to meet the needs of the level 2 patient. Referral to the group is indicated by the patient's behavior on the ward, consisting of gross body movements and an ability to follow the directions of the Lower Cognitive Level Test (see Chap. 4). In addition level 3 patients can be incorporated into this group if their interest is sustained by gross body movements. The maximum number of patients in this group with one leader is four; six can be accommodated if another staff person is present to provide an additional source of imitation. The length of the group activity is between 5 and 15 minutes. The group formerly met off the hospital ward, but because of the enormous difficulty of transporting level 2 patients a short distance more success has been achieved by holding the group on the ward in a large, barren room. Music, the obligatory accompaniment to many exercise programs, distracts the level 2 patient and is not advised.

The therapist should stand so as to be in full view of all of the patients. The activity consists of the therapist's demonstrating postural movements and asking patients to copy them. Very simple pronoun and verb phrases are used, such as, "Look at me. Bend your arms." The therapist can capture the patient's attention by imitating the patient's movements. Most actions may be repeated about five times before patients become distracted. Examples of movements that seem to engage attention and stimulate at least approximations are raising both

hands and clapping them overhead, raising hands overhead and stretching up, raising right and left arms alternately, twisting to right and left with hands on hips, bending over to touch toes, circling both arms at shoulder height, and raising shoulders up toward ears. These movements resemble physical education exercises and are familiar to most patients. Approximations of these movements by a patient are recognized by the therapist as attempts to conform to the task demand.

Tossing a large soft rubber ball often elicits well-established motor reactions in level 2 patients. With everyone in a circle facing inward, the ball can be handed around from person to person in one direction, or, in an expanded circle, the ball can be tossed from person to person. The level 2 patient is not particularly mindful of direction (i.e., clockwise versus counterclockwise); rather, it is the action of receiving and handing the ball that sustains attention. Patients at level 3, on the other hand, are aware of directionality as part of a repeated movement, and they may chastise the level 2 patient for disregarding direction.

During the process of attempting to repeat actions, level 2 patients are apt to produce a chance movement that surprises the therapist. Movements may elicit associated actions, as in the case of a young man who, after catching the rubber ball, began a series of basketball-like feints and pivots, or the ex-Marine who raised his arms over his head and then dropped on the floor and started doing military-style push-ups. Patients select spontaneous movements that feel good to them.

The group is ended when it becomes apparent that the patients are fatigued or are less successful at maintaining attention and approximating movements. A patient's withdrawal from the activity can be a signal that compliance with demonstrated directions cannot be sustained any longer. Thanking patients for their efforts can validate successful performance, and the recognition seems to be appreciated by some patients.

Movement group has the advantage of requiring little preparation (except to secure a room), and no equipment (except a ball, if desired). The group has provided level 2 and 3 patients with an alternative to the ward "community meetings," which are a traditional verbal group in some psychiatric settings. The discussion conducted during community meetings is interrupted by the restless level 2 and the distractible level 3 patient. Management of level 2 and 3 patients is difficult for staff members, and the staff and students who have assisted in conducting the movement group observe compliance with demonstrated directions, as an alternative to "bizarre," "manipulative," or "dependent" behavior. In addition, movement can be used to assess daily emerging ability to manipulate objects, like the directionality of the ball, which suggests that the therapist should begin to offer level 3 tasks.

The disadvantages of movement group include its necessarily small size (a therapist may have to schedule several groups to accommodate an unusually large number of level 2 patients). Medically ill patients may be unable to perform gross body movements, and patients taking certain psychotropic medications should avoid rapid postural changes and consequent blood pressure fluctuations that can induce faintness.

GROOMING

Most patients are familiar with basic grooming procedures such as washing one's face or hair or brushing one's teeth. Grooming tasks provide the immediate visible outcomes that are preferred at level 4. Level 3 patients retain the ability to do many of these everyday manual actions.

Grooming group is designed to accommodate level 3 patients whose ward behavior reflects an interest in performing manual actions. Many of their actions are characteristically unpredictable and troublesome: repeatedly removing the telephone receiver from the hook, making "arrangements" of assorted trash, or pacing the hall and systematically knocking on each office and bedroom door. Grooming group provides an opportunity to engage in constructive manual actions. The results of their actions

may be of no interest to the patient, but the group activity can keep them out of trouble for a little while. Level 4 patients will work towards completing grooming tasks with perceivable results.

The group can be held in the occupational therapy clinic twice a day, once in the morning and once in early afternoon, five days a week. All basic groups are easier to implement when they are scheduled for the same time of day, five days a week. Ten patients are accommodated per group, fewer if there are more level 3 than level 4 patients. The group has been successfully run by an occupational therapy assistant, a former nursing attendant whose nursing background facilitates assistance with the hair, skin, feet, and nail problems that result from prolonged neglect. The group lasts 50 minutes, though it is not uncommon for level 3 patients to return to the ward after 30 minutes, indicating that they are tired.

The grooming room contains one sink for washing hair, several counters at which patients may sit on tall stools, and two tables on which are placed several large, portable mirrors. Patients may wash their face and hair, soak their feet, set and dry their hair, apply makeup, do manicures and pedicures, apply facials, and shave their face or legs. Cutting hair and pressing hair are generally done for patients by the therapist.

When patients enter the room they are asked to take a seat at one of the tables or at the counter. Clearly visible in baskets on the tables are basic grooming supplies such as combs, brushes, clips, curlers (sterilized), and nail care supplies including nail polish remover, cotton swabs, nail polish, and emery boards. Shampoo and rinse, towels, and foot soak supplies are next to the sink (Fig. 10-1). The patients are individually asked what they would like to do. The visible objects suggest tasks to the level 4 patient; if making a selection is difficult, a goal can be suggested by the therapist. Level 3 patients are easily distracted by the equipment, materials, and choices, and may respond to a suggested activity. Distractibility can be reduced by seating the level 3 patient apart from the rest of the group. The thera-

Fig. 10-1. Room preparation for grooming. As the patients enter the room they see supplies that are organized according to the grooming tasks that they can choose to do.

pist gets additional supplies (e.g., a bottle of nail polish) from the closed storage cabinet in the grooming room and prepares them for use (e.g., shakes the nail polish for an even color). Level 3 and 4 patients cannot be expected to find the supplies or recognize the need for preparation; this observation holds true even when patients have a goal in mind and request supplies.

Manual actions that sustain attention at level 3 include filing nails, washing hair, and combing and brushing hair. These tasks provide a connection between a manual action and a tactile cue. In a task such as filing nails, the level 3 patient will perform the repetitive action of filing but will neglect the outcome of the action (i.e., shape, length, or smoothness). The patient at level 4 will be aware of

the goal of filing and will work toward achieving this with a visible sample of the desired outcome. The sample may be a picture of uniformly filed nails, or a nail filed by the therapist.

Level 4 patients are more successful than level 3 patients on all grooming tasks because the attention of level 4 patients is focused on the outcome of their actions. Tasks that have clearly visible cues are preferred. Washing and drying hair, removing nail polish and applying new polish, applying makeup, and lathering and shaving are examples. Slight modifications in familiar grooming procedures may be imitated. The therapist must remember, however, that level 4 patients do not engage in spontaneous exploratory actions, and experimentation, with different kinds of makeup, for example, does not occur. The therapist should provide makeup of the proper color for the patient rather than expect her, through experimentation, to find the best skin tones and lipstick shades.

Since level 3 and 4 patients' understanding of the environment is based on touching and seeing, it is not surprising that when shampooing their hair these patients may "forget" to shampoo and rinse the backs of their heads adequately. The back of the body is "hidden" and therefore not taken into account. Processes that are invisible, such as the action of a facial or hair remover, are not understood. The therapist may be unable to convince a patient that such a product should be left on for a prescribed amount of time in order to work. Use of heavy makeup that is in sharp contrast to the natural color of their skin is preferred by many patients because they can see the results of their actions.

Cutting hair and straightening naturally curly hair are often desired by patients but are problematic because of the presence of related properties and intangible cues. Intangibles such as the heat of a straightening wand and the passage of time (how long to keep the heat on hair before it burns) perplex the level 3 and 4 patient. Most haircuts require an even cut on both sides, and the relationship between the sides may be neglected at level 4. Cutting the hair at the back of the head may not even be considered at level 4. For the patient's own safety, these tasks are best done by the therapist or not at all.

Level 4 patients are given their own makeup, combs, and hairpins, if they desire these supplies, and are encouraged to bring these supplies to the clinic daily. Level 3 patients are apt to forget these "means" to the "end" of hair care.

The advantages of the grooming group are many. The familiar and tangible qualities of grooming tasks suit patients at lower cognitive levels. Grooming is generally desirable and valued by patients cross-culturally, and they often report feeling better when well groomed. Grooming also promotes the objective health and safety of the patient. In terms of clarifying diagnosis, it has been noted that men who request grooming are usually either experiencing a manic episode or have a homosexual orientation. Poor judgment in the manic patient is seen in the sloppy or garish application of makeup. Depressed persons, on the other hand, frequently avoid "beautification" tasks and choose low-energy tasks such as foot soaks.

Disadvantages of this group include the need for supplies such as sinks and water and the presence of potentially dangerous equipment (nail polish remover, dryers). The therapist must be knowledgeable about the medical precautions concerning foot, skin, and hair care and must be able to confront the severe and dismaying neglect of self-care by some chronic patients without repulsion or avoidance.

BASIC CRAFTS

Basic crafts group has been consistently successful in providing a desirable opportunity for task performance. Crafts are favored by many psychiatric patients. This is, without doubt, the most important group that has evolved from the description of cognitive levels. It is recommended that this group be implemented first when setting up a program for the cognitively disabled.

Basic crafts is designed for up to twelve level 3 and 4 patients, meeting daily. It is conducted by one therapist, and I recommend it to students for at least half of their field work experience.

The basic crafts environment is designed to minimize distraction. Patients sit at tables to work side by side for a one-hour period. Projects are designed to be completed in one session. Basic crafts projects are the result of many years of catalogue searching and therapist adaptation, producing end products that are predictable (when attending to shape and color), useful, adult in appearance, and aesthetically pleasing. Examples of projects include stained wooden boxes, beeswax candles, decoupage plaques, leather key cases and change purses done with whip stitch, tile trivets without grout, cork message boards, ribbon covered flower pots, greeting cards, hand-sewn bath mitts, and copper tooling.

The preparation for each craft is critical and time-consuming. Some of this work can be done by other patients (see Work Evaluation), but most is done by therapists. Each task is analyzed to identify familiar, visible actions; partially visible procedures, tools, or processes are eliminated. Since level 3 patients are also included in the group, manual actions are a desirable component of the task. Successful task performance can be achieved when the therapist pays careful attention to organizing the details of the task environment. The following example will illustrate the therapist's attention to such details.

Tile trivets can be completed successfully in basic crafts under the following conditions. The motor action of picking up and placing is a familiar action for most people. Since this action will be repeated many times, the task is suitable for level 3 patients. The squeezing action required to use the glue bottle is similar to that used with shampoo, mustard, catsup, or toothpaste dispensers, and so may be familiar. A tile cutter, a less familiar tool the use of which requires estimation of where and how to cut each tile, is judged to be potentially problematic and is avoided. A square trivet form that provides an exact fit for uniform square tiles is preferred. Round or irregularly shaped tile trivets and spaces introduce relationships between visible cues and are avoided. In addition a flat trivet eliminates the effect of gravity, observed when the tiles slide down a curved surface. If tiles fit exactly, the step of grouting can be eliminated. The procedure of grouting is problematic for level 3 and 4 patients for several reasons: First, mixing the correct proportions calls for reading a recipe or using good exploratory actions. Level 3 and 4 patients can do neither of these. Second, the grout must be applied quickly and tiles cleaned before the grout hardens. Level 3 and 4 patients cannot alter the speed of their actions to adjust to a time constraint. Finally, the grout temporarily covers up the tiles, making them disappear, a process that is most dismaying to the patients.

The crafts project is set up completely by the therapist before the patients arrive (Fig. 10-2). All materials needed for the project are clearly visible at each patient's place. A completed, exact sample is plainly visible for level 4 patients to examine. Glue bottles are unstopped, brushes cleaned, and stains prestirred. Sandpaper is right side up, as level 3 patients are known to sand with the wrong side if that is all they see. Plain newsprint can be used to cover the tables. Printed newspapers can also be used: Place the print upside down so the patients are not distracted by it, and remove advertisements with sexual connotations when hypersexuality is to be avoided. Too much clutter must be avoided; if necessary, some materials can be kept to the side until needed.

The therapist displays the project and demonstrates each step to the entire group. Verbal instructions are limited to simple nouns and verbs, since adjectives and adverbs, which specify variations in how an action is performed, are usually ignored or found confusing by the level 3 and level 4 patient. When all patients are performing the same actions, they become an additional source of imitation for each other, and also less of a distraction for the level 3 patient.

In giving instructions, the therapist will notice that the level 3 patients can repeat a single manual action, but have trouble putting two actions together. Some common problems and suggested modifications for solving them are as follows: In lacing a leather coin purse, level 3 patients attend to the action but cannot straighten out the twist in the leather lace. In this case the therapist can substitute waxed thread, eliminating the twist for the level 3 patient. In covering a box with torn pieces of masking tape, level 3 patients are known to perform the single action of placing quite well but cannot tear and place the pieces at the same time. By pretearing the pieces, the therapist reduces this short sequence to one manual action. To eliminate the step of picking up and squeezing a glue bottle, the therapist can place a puddle of glue on the newspaper and demonstrate how to dip a tile into the glue before placing it on a trivet. Ideally the therapist plans

Fig. 10-2. Room preparation for basic crafts. Materials needed to complete a wood box with tiled top are clearly visible at each patient's place. Premature use of materials is avoided by placing tiles to one side.

such adaptations beforehand, but unexpected difficulties may require a fast simplification of instructions.

When patients are distracted, the therapist can intervene to refocus their attention on the original motor action or to introduce a new action. For example, if not interrupted, some level 3 patients who enjoy the action of sanding wood may sand indefinitely, long after their project is smooth. Others lose interest quickly, before their project is smooth, and must be directed to the next action with more interesting results (e.g., painting on the stain). Knowing when and how to intervene requires close observation to distinguish among patients who are stopping an action because they are fatigued, because they have lost interest in the action, or simply because another stimulus has distracted them temporarily.

When problems arise for the patient in doing a task (e.g., the glue bottle becomes stopped, the patient uses too much glue, the tiles do not fit), the therapist must usually assist the patient. For the level 3 patient intervention may take the form of suggesting causes other than egocentric explanations ("No, you did not break the glue bottle. The glue stopped it up inside") and correcting the problem for the patient. Level 4 patients typically remark, "Something is wrong here," thus indicating an awareness of the problem. The therapist may give the patient the opportunity to attempt a solution through exploration in cases in which movement to level 5 is expected. If no experimentation is forthcoming, the therapist should quickly step in with a demonstrated action that the patient can see and imitate to correct the problem. The therapist's role in the group is to be a meticulous designer of the environment, a purposeful facilitator whose interventions are designed to promote successful performance of the task, and a careful observer of the patient's performance.

The therapist's assessment of the patient's cognitive level and any changes in it are based on careful observation of the patient as he or she works on tasks. Where the patients focus their attention is clearly observed in their use of the sample. Level 3 patients are unaware of the relationship between the sample and the material objects in front of them. Sometimes this manifests itself in "going to work" before the therapist has a chance to demonstrate instructions; their actions may or may not be what is required by the task. When level 3 patients lose interest in an action or are distracted by some environmental stimulus, they are apt to wander away or become engaged in a different action, such as talking, getting a cup of coffee, or going to the bathroom. In addition level 3 patients may not care about taking their completed projects with them.

In contrast, level 4 patients are very aware of the sample project. They will examine it carefully, refer to it repeatedly, ask questions about it, and often directly copy it. When they have completed a step, level 4 patients often ask, "What do I do now?" indicating their awareness of and interest in a sequence of actions leading to the end product. The level 4 patients' awareness of the end product sustains attention for up to an hour, and they usually wish to take the completed project with them.

The reliance on the tactile and visible properties of objects is evident during the process of doing many of the projects done in the basic crafts group. The level 3 patient's egocentric understanding of the properties of objects can be humorous: "We are making beads today because I am an Indian." A misinterpretation of the properties of objects can also be disruptive, as in the case of a patient who accused another of sabotaging his project when the patient himself failed to use enough glue to affix his tiles to a box. Level 3 and 4 patients habitually apply far too much glue to projects in the belief that

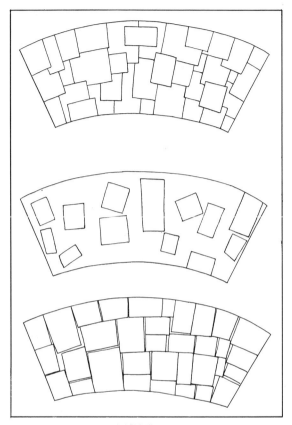

Fig. 10-3. *Overlapping objects. The objects that are to be overlapped here are pieces of ribbon cut by the therapist.* Top, *Sample prepared by the therapist.* Middle, *Typical placement at level 3.* Bottom, *Typical placement at level 4.*

the glue must be seen or felt to work properly. Gluing craft materials such as beans and dried peas onto a box for decoration simply does not make sense to a concrete thinker who knows those items to be *food*. The therapist should probably reserve such craft ideas for higher-level patients. Typically, level 3 and 4 patients forget to stain the bottom and the inside of boxes, parts they cannot see. In projects that require overlapping, patients often refuse to overlap objects, placing objects side by side instead (Fig. 10-3). Tracing around a pattern is done

Fig. 10-4. Verifying hidden cues. This patient is lifting the cardboard pattern that she has been tracing around to see the line drawn on the felt.

very tentatively. Patterns cover part of the surface and are often removed during tracing (Fig. 10-4). The patients seem to verify the continuing presence of the material being traced on and the results of their actions by looking at their progress. Copper tooling, a perennial favorite in occupational therapy crafts programs, is a relationship that baffles level 3 and level 4 patients unfamiliar with it; these patients express great surprise when the template is removed and the picture in the copper matches the template. Level 3 patients have been known to mount the plastic template, instead of the finished copper picture, onto their board. Copper tooling is a project that can be used when assessing potential improvement to level 5; patients vary the pressure applied to tools to get a clearer picture and turn the template over to see how the copper picture compares with the template. At level 4, part of the picture of fine details may be missed, and the relationship between copper and template is confusing.

In addition to identifying cognitive level and alterations in this level, the therapist can make the usual observations for medical symptoms reflecting diagnosis. Having patients work on the same task makes individual differences and symptoms clearly observable. The level 3 manic patient may display distractibility, pressured speech, increased motor activity, and elevated mood or irritability. The level 3 depressed patient may be distracted by ruminations and hampered by negativism and low energy. Both types of affective disturbance should resolve, and evidence of higher levels (5 or 6) is expected. On the other hand, patients with schizophrenic disorders who are initially seen at level 3 may, with suppression of their hallucinatory and delusional preoccupations, resolve into level 4 without further improvement.

In patients with a diagnosis of dementia, memory problems and confusion are often observable. Patients may forget how to perform a moderately novel process such as staining. Actions indicative of confusion associated with organic problems are usually grossly incorrect, such as gluing a decoupage picture upside down or backwards. Care must be taken to distinguish organic confusion from the non-goal-directed actions of the level 3 patient. Demented patients are usually working hard at replicating an end product but simply are too confused to succeed, while level 3 patients show no interest in end products.

Patients with toxic psychosis caused by phencyclidine hydrochloride (PCP) display a unique picture during basic crafts. Often indistinguishable from those with affective or thought disorders in symptoms, the patient with PCP psychosis displays a waxing and waning inattentiveness. While cognitive levels may vary from 2 to 6, episodic blank staring during task performance is observed in most patients. The behavior differs from that of the hallucinatory schizophrenic whose eyes may be fixed up and to the side or who may track or blink. When PCP patients "phase in" after a 1- to 5-second period of staring, they appear momentarily confused. They may or may not be able to reorient themselves to what they are doing. (Seizure disorders must be ruled out to verify that this is due to PCP.) Many PCP patients may rely on tactile input when learning tasks; they may use their hands tentatively and repeatedly feel materials and tools while closely scrutinizing them, as if tactile perceptions were dulled or somehow not quite "right." This tactile exploration can distract them sufficiently to necessitate redirection by the therapist. PCP patients do not tolerate the self-directed action expected in the advanced crafts group; they find it difficult to make decisions and carry out level 5 or 6 actions consistently. For this reason, they are often best treated in the basic crafts environment, regardless of their score on the Allen Cognitive Level Test (ACL) (see Chap. 4).

The advantages of basic crafts are many. Most occupational therapy departments are equipped with the basic supplies to run the group, and most therapists are familiar with the necessary procedures. Most patients enjoy the group, especially if care is taken to select projects that are adult, aesthetically pleasing, and useful. The method of supervision (step-by-step, nonverbal) and the nature of the tasks make the group suitable for non-English-speaking and nonverbal patients. Student therapists learning about cognitive disabilities can observe the limitations of level 3 and 4 most clearly in this group.

Disadvantages of basic crafts include difficulty in designing successful projects that are adult, aesthetically pleasing, and useful. Almost all catalogue projects require some type of modification. Therapists must spend time analyzing the actions and thought processes required by a task. Preparation, setup, and making samples all take time. The therapist will work hard supervising level 3 and level 4 patients, especially when the group exceeds eight patients.

BASIC SKILLS

Basic skills group capitalizes on the fact that since education is mandatory in the United States, most Americans have acquired basic academic skills in reading, writing, and simple math. The group is designed for level 4 patients who dislike crafts and for those who have had a cognitive disability for a number of years. The group consists of a one-hour writ-

ten lesson with exercises based on a topic related to community living. The group can be scheduled each day. Mornings may be preferred because patients are more alert at that time. It accommodates 10 patients, and it can be led by one therapist.

Educational materials designed to teach community survival skills to the mentally retarded have provided some resource material for basic skills, but it has generally been found that the materials must be rewritten to allow for the concreteness of thought and lack of new learning characteristic of a stable level 4 patient. The purpose of the group, unlike adult education classes, is not to teach basic living skills but to review what patients already know. Because of wide variations in educational achievement and exposure, some materal is inevitably new to some patients; new material is generally ignored.

Subject matter includes self-care topics (doing laundry, reading a prescription, using a thermometer, recognizing a balanced meal, making change), using community resources (riding the bus, ordering from a restaurant menu, using a telephone directory, using public agencies), and exercises that renew intellectual skills (reviewing vocabulary, following directions, doing picture crossword puzzles).

Each exercise is approximately thirty minutes in length and consists of some written material on the topic, followed by written questions or a task that allows the patient to apply the information in a specific situation. As much as possible, the application portion of the lesson is as concrete and real as possible. For example, patients take their own temperatures with conventional thermometers, use the local telephone directory to look up emergency numbers, and look at real servings of food when reviewing portion sizes.

The therapist selects the topic for the session, taking into account the interests and backgrounds of the patient. As in basic crafts, all materials needed for the session are laid out for the patient, including written materials, pencils, and other aids. Many patients with blurred vision (a side effect of many medications) appreciate the use of nonprescription magnifying eyeglasses that enlarge the printed page. A typewriter with a large typeface is effective in producing readable copy. Printed material is kept brief and to the point, with careful spatial placement of the copy to assist the focus of attention. Bright colors and pictures help to capture attention. The group uses as much as two hundred duplicated sheets of paper per week, which is facilitated by the purchase of a copy machine. The copier was selected for its ability to reproduce gray tones so that photographs, pictures of coins, and other graphics appear as realistic as possible.

Comprehension of written material is further facilitated when both visual and auditory cues are used to capture attention. Hence the therapist or a patient usually reads the material aloud while the rest of the group follow along on their papers. Written questions are generally considered one by one, as a group, and correct answers are given immediately. This method seems to appeal to the level 4 patients' interest in immediate outcomes. Completed papers are often taken back to the ward by patients as tangible evidence of their intangible learning experience.

Assessments in basic skills include identification of retained areas of knowledge and academic skills, as well as cognitive deficits. Retained skills often dictate interest and influence ability at level 4. For example, a depressed man with a high school education had trouble concentrating when doing a map-reading exercise. He was unable to answer simple written questions related to the map he was reading, despite the ability to identify verbally the main features of the map when asked. A short time later he was able to concentrate for 20 minutes without assistance while reading a mileage chart showing distances between United States cities. On this task he answered all questions accurately, though slowly. When asked about his varied performance, the man said that he had been a bookkeeper and was used to working with numbers, tables, and matrices. Presumably finding information on the mileage chart was more familiar than map reading for this particular man.

Basic academic skills (reading, writing, basic math) are easily observed as patients work on exercises. Rote learning is to be distinguished from problem solving, however. The ability to perform various mathematical computations, for example, does not necessarily guarantee that a patient can solve a mathematical problem that arises in daily living. Patients at level 4 typically are unable to set up a math word problem, especially if the problem contains more than two elements. The problem of figuring out how many days a prescription of 36 pills will last if taken one pill at meal time three times daily is rarely solved correctly by level 4 patients. While able to do discrete calculations correctly, they seem to be unable to generate a concept of how the elements of the problem are related. The math problem can be visualized for level 4 patients by physically dividing 36 pills into groups of 3 and seeing that this results in 12 piles, for 12 days. To assist patients in monitoring their own supply of prescription medication, transparent containers such as plastic bags or the boxes available in pharmacies may be helpful. The value of transparent containers generalizes to many level 4 tasks.

Stable level 4 thinking is characterized by other errors derived from these patients' reliance on visible cues. For example, in a lesson on the four basic food groups, patients have great difficulty accepting the idea that beans are in the meat group and not the vegetable and fruit group. Protein content is an intangible property of an object and is not convincing to them as a classification criterion. In discussing food groups a remark such as "Rice is starch, so it cannot be a grain" is not unusual.

A matrix, such as in the game of categories, provides a successful use of visual cues (Fig. 10-5). In this game the answers are provided and patients simply place them in the correct box according to class and first letter. (This letter "class" may really be a matter of matching only.) The dependence on the visible cue is seen as more patients make errors in boxes that are spatially farthest away from the class title (i.e., bottom righthand corner). An item that can fit into two boxes (e.g., chess is a pie and a

	Cleaning supplies	Celebrities	Pies	Magazines	Games
P					
B		James Brown			
C					
M					
S					
W					
R					
T					

Find the word(s) that go in each box from the list below. Match the category and the letter. The first has been done as an example.

James Brown
strawberry
People
cleanser
Scrabble
Better Homes and Gardens
Diana Ross
Pledge
Tinkertoys

mincemeat
whist
Suzanne Somers
Cosmopolitan
Monopoly
wax
rhubarb
Richard Thomas
bingo
banana cream
Time

Mademoiselle
Sports Illustrated
towel
Richard Pryor
cherry
Lawrence Welk
Reader's Digest
sponge
poker
Johnny Carson

broom
pecan
chess
Women's Day
rummy
Steve Martin
tamale
mop
rake
walnut

Fig. 10-5. Use of visual cues: categories game.

game), if placed incorrectly, is corrected by the patient with great difficulty or not at all. This may also reflect a difficulty with forming simultaneous classes.

Concrete associations and idiosyncrasies also characterize the stable level 4 patient's class formation. Patients are apt to place Diana Ross under the class *magazine* "because I saw her in a magazine," or *Sports Illustrated* under *games*. The patient who reasoned that "I have eggs for breakfast, but I never

have meat; therefore, eggs cannot be in the meat group" represents the peculiarly idiosyncratic logic of many level 4 patients.

Stable level 4 thinking appears to progress in a linear, rather than hierarchical, fashion. This may explain why the Yellow Pages, a monolith of hierarchical classification, is virtually never used by level 4 patients, who seem to find it much easier to telephone the information operator. The matrix and the Yellow Pages illustrate the difficulties encountered in generating and using classification criteria that seem to be characteristic of a cognitive disability; further elaboration on this difficulty can be found in Chapters 13 and 14.

As in basic crafts, having all the patients work on the same task simultaneously allows for the observation of individual symptoms. Memory lapses in the patient with dementia are more apparent in skills than in crafts, probably because in skills there are fewer tangible objects available for reorientation. This is also true for the PCP patient whose attention to the task waxes and wanes. Depressed persons experiencing concentration difficulties often do better in crafts, in which the physical activity of object manipulation assists concentration. On the other hand, some depressed persons who ascribe pejorative connotations to crafts will request basic skills. Manic patients with pressured speech can pose management problems for the therapist in basic skills as opportunities for discussion of answers are provided; these patients may not be able to stop talking. Schizophrenic patients often enjoy the basic skills group because they are able to use skills retained from high school, for many the last functional period in their lives. Patients with poor reading and writing ability, or a record of poor performance in school, will often refuse skills group.

The advantage of basic skills is its wide appeal to chronic patients. Patients are genuinely enthusiastic about the group and indicate by their comments that the information reviewed is valuable to them because it "makes me think" and is "useful." Since the main supplies are paper and pencils, the group is relatively inexpensive to run. Some sort of duplicating capability is necessary, preferably a machine that allows accurate reproduction of photographs.

Disadvantages of the group include its inappropriateness for non-English-speaking patients and patients with poor eyesight. Time is needed to formulate successful lessons that are concrete, short-term, familiar, and able to maintain attention yet provide opportunities for the therapist to assess cognitive changes as these occur.

BASIC SEWING

Basic sewing is designed for level 3 and level 4 patients who are familiar with hand sewing. The group is led by a therapist who can supervise up to 10 persons. Like basic crafts, the group activity lasts one hour to accommodate the limited attention span of lower-level patients. Unlike basic crafts, patients in sewing can work on different projects that may take more than one session to complete. The typical patient in the group is a depressed woman, though men, and women with other diagnoses, are seen.

All sewing is done by hand, and though machines are available, these are used only by the therapist. The action of a machine is incomprehensible to the level 3 and 4 patient unfamiliar with it; for those familiar with sewing machines, predictable problems arise from patients' inability to vary their accustomed actions to accommodate the peculiarities of a machine make or model different from their own. Examples of projects include hand-sewn makeup bags; patchwork pillows (using precut squares); felt eyeglass cases; tissue holders; pot holders; bargello of various sizes and complexity for pot holders, eyeglass cases, and pillows; burlap handbags made from 4-inch burlap strips sewn together; and simple embroidery. Knitting and crocheting are done only if the patient is extremely familiar with these tasks and can work without a pattern (unfamiliar projects are essentially level 5 or 6 tasks).

As in basic crafts, preparation and setup for the group is critical and time-consuming for the therapist. Samples of all projects that can be completed should be plainly visible for patients to examine. Yarn in skeins should be made into balls beforehand to eliminate this lengthy step for patients at level 4, who desire immediate results. Similarly, yarn for bargello is precut and fashioned into loosely braided "packets" so that patients do not have to measure and cut each piece.

When patients arrive they find regularly used items such as needles, thread of different colors, and scissors laid out on the table. Other supplies are located in a nearby cupboard, from which the therapist can secure additional materials. The therapist does not expect level 3 and 4 patients to get their own supplies but may direct an occasional level 5 group member to the cupboard. The therapist may suggest a simple project that can be completed during the first session. Level 4 patients may be given a choice between two or three selected alternatives. Instruction is always in the form of demonstration, one step at a time, usually on an individual basis.

Level 3 patients generally prefer the repeated action of the running stitch, and this on a fairly short-term project such as the ladybug pincushion (Fig. 10-6). The felt pieces for this project can be manufactured in the work evaluation group. The pieces are assembled by the therapist. The patient sews three-fourths of the way around the front and back pieces. At this point, the therapist shows the patient how to insert the stuffing. The rest of the bug is sewn, and the eyes and dots are glued on. Felt eyeglass cases that are precut and assembled are a slightly longer-term but essentially level 3 project when accomplished with a running stitch. The therapist should have threaded needles available so that this often frustrating step is eliminated for level 3 patients.

Sewing patchwork squares together with a running stitch to form a pillow requires awareness of the correct positioning of pieces before sewing. For the patient at level 3 whose actions are the focus of attention, the placement of the pieces right sides together may be ignored. The level 4 patient typically will not plan color coordination, seemingly unaware of these possibilities. Level 5 patients, on the other hand, will engage in exploratory actions to select and discard patches. Level 6 patients will do this with less experimentation because they can imagine possible combinations before acting. (Verification of their ideas by trying out possibilities may still occur at level 6). Stitching the front and back of a pillow together, right sides together, and then turning the pillow right side out, can be a confusing process for level 4 patients. The patients may turn the pillow after it is pinned to verify the outcome of this unseen process.

The whip stitch, or overcast stitch, requires an awareness of the direction of the needle when inserted, and is accomplished by patients at level 4 more readily than at level 3. Past experience seems to affect patients' preferences for using the whip (level 4) versus the running stitch (level 3). These stitches are used to assess the cognitive level on the ACL (see Chap. 4), but the spontaneously selected stitch does not always correspond with the cognitive level. Patients tend to use the most familiar stitch, and at level 3 an inconsistent use of both stitches is observed. Additional observations of behavior are required to discriminate accurately between the levels, and the patient's awareness of goal is an important consideration. Pincushions, eyeglass cases, small tissue cases, and fabric toys are goals that can be recognized and completed in one session by level 4 patients (Fig. 10-7).

While conventional needlepoint is typically quite difficult for patients, bargello is a needlework process that can be mastered at levels 3 through 6. It provides a good illustration of the patterns and task modification required for each level (Fig. 10-8). Bargello has been most successful with bright rug yarn on large scrim with plastic needles. Level 3 patients can accomplish a stripe pattern on a small project (such as a 6-inch-wide potholder) when masking tape is placed the width of the strip above the row of holes in which the needle will be placed. Instructions consist of demonstrating how to put the needle down through the scrim next to the tape, then in a separate action up through the next hole, until the row is completed. Successive rows can be made of different colors. Ends can be left loose or worked back in by the therapist for a level 3 patient.

Level 4 patients can figure out where to place the needle by counting up the correct number of holes without benefit of tape. They can begin with a stripe project but can be expected to expand on the counting and stitching sequence to modify the stripe pattern: Four stitches are made and one stitch skipped; the skipped stitch is filled in with contrasting yarn after the row is completed. A checkerboard design can be achieved by alternating

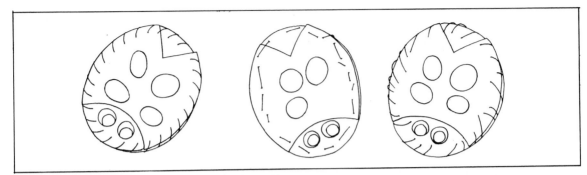

Fig. 10-6. *The running stitch and the whip stitch. (Left) Sample. (Middle) Quality of stitching frequently seen at level 3. (Right) Quality of stitching seen at level 4.*

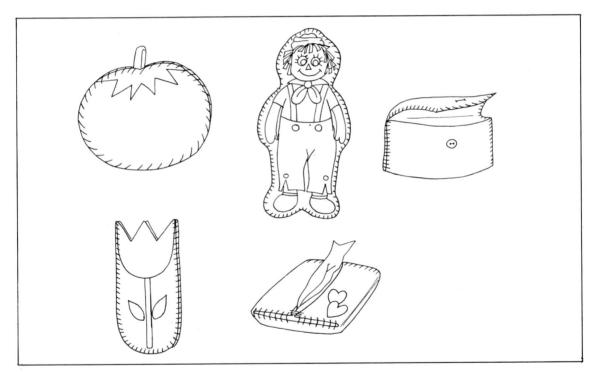

Fig. 10-7. *Successful sewing projects for level 4 patients. The tomato pot holder, purse, tulip eyeglass case, and tissue holder are made of felt. The doll is made from a printed fabric.*

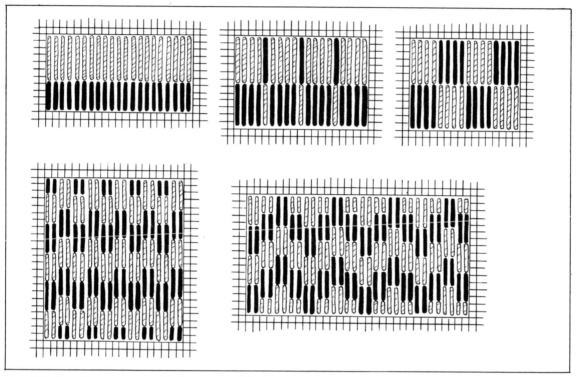

Fig. 10-8. Bargello patterns usually done successfully by patients at various levels. (Top left) Level 3. (Top middle and top right) Level 4. (Bottom left) Level 5. (Bottom right) Level 6.

colors every four or five stitches. Level 4 patients can imitate weaving yarn behind other yarn to secure ends. In a checkerboard pattern they can imitate running the unused thread under the stitching thread.

The diamond pattern typically associated with bargello is occasionally mastered by a compulsive level 4 patient but is far more successful with level 5 patients. The diamond patterns require not only awareness of front and back and counting, but also of the vertical displacement of each stitch. Level 5 patients understand the changing spatial relationship between stitches and can correct any errors by varying their actions.

If the patient masters a pattern (generally accomplished at level 4), he or she can take bargello to the ward along with precut yarn. On most of our wards, plastic needles are considered safe, while knitting needles and crochet hooks are not.

Some patients, particularly those with affective disorders, may display rapid improvements in cognition and require more complex tasks while in basic sewing. Weaving tasks contain good differentiation criteria for assessing changes in level of ability. Weaving on a table or floor loom can be done at level 3 if the therapist sits beside the patient and assists with changing the headles and untangling the shuttle when it gets stuck in the warp threads.

At level 3 the patient focuses on the repetitive manual action of putting the shuttle through the warp.

The over-and-under of tabby weaving can be followed at level 4. However, a tabby weave requires an alteration of the over-and-under pattern in successive rows. When doing off-the-loom weaving, the level 4 patient may recognize an error in a successive row but will require assistance to correct the error; the relationship between the rows is confusing. A tabby weave may be done on a table or floor loom. The treadling sequence can be taped to the loom (1-3, 2-4), or one can use two treadles when possible. The patient focuses on the amount of fabric woven, and thick yarn produces faster results. Assistance to move the warp, to correct treadling errors, and to keep the edges even will be required. Weaving at level 4 requires exceptional persistence from the patient and the therapist; continuous errors that must be corrected by the therapist occur. Weaving is usually avoided at level 4 with the exception of individual patients who think that the task is highly desirable.

Successive rows of weaving are understood at level 5; the relationship between one row and the next is understood. Short treadling sequences, like a twill (1-2, 2-3, 3-4, 1-4), can be taped to the loom, and some patients prefer a grid where they can mark their place in the sequence. Treadling errors may be confusing at level 5; some errors can be corrected by using overt trial and error to go through the correct treadling sequence while other errors require assistance. Attention is usually directed toward the space in front of the reed, successive rows and edges. The loom mechanisms that effect the warp are ignored. Off-the-loom weaving done in a two-dimensional plane is successful at level 5. A slightly more difficult project that contains a third dimension can also be suggested. Basket frames made out of plastic are commercially available; the frames provide a rigid warp. At level 5 patients can manage the over-and-under successive rows required to weave thick yarn around the baskets. The rigid frame essentially eliminates the need to consider depth; the project has a third dimension but the patient does not have to account for depth during the process of making the basket.

The third dimension becomes evident in weaving in two ways: understanding the loom's mechanisms and weaving baskets. A loom is a three dimensional object: The warp is altered by the vertical relationships between treadles, harnesses, and needles; the fabric is woven in the horizontal frame. At level 5 patients focus on the horizontal plane and do not comprehend the function of the heddles or harnesses; a broken warp thread must be fixed by the therapist. In addition, warping the loom is problematic at level 5. Weaving pattern books contain graphic symbols, similar to reading music; warping patterns are confusing at level 5. At level 6 the patient will understand that there is a relationship between the way the warp is run through the heddles and the pattern that is produced; errors in the warping and treadling sequences can be recognized and corrected by the patient.

Weaving baskets requires the creation of a three-dimensional shape; an image of a projected shape guides motor actions. The relationships between motor actions and ideal shape is not sustained at level 5; attempts to make baskets are usually lopsided, distorted, unsatisfactory, or tedious. Basket-weaving can be done successfully at level 6. Basket-weaving, contrary to folk mythology, cannot be done by the cognitively disabled.

Many level 4 patients who sew state that they do not use patterns, probably because patterns often look different from the finished piece. Patterns used successfully at level 4 should be two-dimensional and resemble the end product (see Fig. 10-7). Pieces that change shape or are hidden (facings, for instance) should be avoided.

The advantage of the basic sewing group lies in the gradability of its tasks from very simple to fairly complex, which accommodates patients whose remission is relatively rapid. Projects are generally handsome and adult in appearance. Projects can be sent to the ward with patients who want something to do. Diagnostically, it has been observed that many depressed women, and a few depressed men, select sewing. Typical symptoms, described more fully under Basic Crafts and Basic Skills, can be seen in the sewing group as well. Patients whose condition can be expected to fluctuate daily (e.g., the depressed woman who is receiving electroconvulsive therapy) can work on two projects simultaneously—using a running stitch (level 3) on treatment days if confused and doing a higher-level project on other days. The fact that many projects take two sessions to complete can be a disadvantage for the patient who wants an immediate end result.

CLAY AND MOSAICS

The clay and mosaics group is designed for patients at level 5 or level 6. Level 4 patients whose disorders are expected to remit quickly can also be assigned to this group. The group can meet daily, for one hour, and can accommodate 12 patients per therapist.

The media used in this group are selected for their potential for variation, since patients at level 5 are interested in exploring variation. Patients at level 6 can demonstrate planning abilities given the many options available to them in mosaic and clay materials. Examples of suitable tasks include ceramic tile trivets, ashtrays, bowls, and mosaic pictures; seed and bean mosaic pictures; glazed slip-molded projects; and hand-built and potter's wheel clay projects. It is important to have a wide variety of materials so that variation can be accomplished indefinitely. Ceramic tiles should be stocked in many colors, shapes, and sizes, along with flat and dished forms of varying sizes and shapes. A wide variety of seeds and beans and other dried foodstuffs suitable for mosaics is desirable. Glazes that require only one firing speed up completion time of ceramic projects, and these should be ordered in a variety of lead-free colors. Molds for slip casting are chosen for their aesthetic and utilitarian features but also with an eye for variety of shape and use. A potter's wheel is not mandatory but can be used by patients at level 6. It is important to have a kiln in the clinic area so that patients can verify for themselves the

effects of the unseen firing process on their projects. A padlock must be attached to it so that patients cannot open the kiln during firing. Stacking and firing are done by the therapist.

Mosaic tiles, beans, and seeds can be stored in covered cans, since level 5 and level 6 patients will explore their environment to find materials. Tools can be stored in closed cupboards. Unfamiliar tools, such as tile cutters, ceramic tools, and glazes, are mastered through experimentation by patients at levels 5 and 6. The therapist can verbally direct the level 6 patients.

The therapist in groups with higher-level patients will find that the careful one-step demonstrated instruction needed at level 4 is not required, yet demonstration is still very important at level 5. Demonstrations, however, can be done in a series, and therapists do not need to simplify their language. The number of steps that the level 5 patient can follow is related to the degree of novelty of the actions. Clinical experience tends to suggest that not more than one of a short series of actions should be novel.

Patients can be expected to be able to select projects from a variety of alternatives. Samples are still required at levels 5 and 6 but need not be exact. Since most projects, except for very small ashtrays and trivets, take two or more sessions to complete, and ceramic pieces even longer, patients often make selections based on time to completion. Level 5 and 6 patients are free from the need for immediate results but vary in the amount of time they are willing to invest in a project. Having some slip molds precast, ready for sanding and glazing, shortens ceramic projects. (These can be prepared by patients in the work evaluation group.)

The level 4 patients who are expected to advance to level 5 include those with remitting affective disorders, transient psychotic episodes, and toxic psychoses. Level 4 patients can begin a mosaic project, for example, a flat base with square tiles that fit exactly without grout. Tiles of two colors may be provided if an exact sample is available for the patient to copy. When patients begin to show interest in variations, the task lends itself to exploration. The patients may ask for more colors or different shapes. They may begin to experiment with forming patterns or alter how they apply glue or where they place the tiles. Once a patient shows interest in variation, he or she may want to do the same type of project over and over, with modifications each time.

The emergence of successful variations in motor actions allows the level 5 patient to sand prepoured slip molds without breaking them (a typical complication at level 4), to mix grout with water until the correct consistency for spreading is achieved, to wedge clay properly, and to roll out clay for slab or coil pots. As the patients work, they use feedback from their explorations to continue to alter their actions. The therapist will see the patient slice a lump of clay repeatedly to check for bubbles while wedging or place and replace coils to achieve a desired curve on a coiled pot. The overall process appears inefficient, yet the patient at level 5 does not become frustrated or bored with these explorations. Inductive reasoning, as observed at level 5, is accompanied by overt trial and error.

Invisible processes that are novel confuse the patient at level 5 because of continued dependence on tangible cues. Pouring a mold, for example, is enjoyed but not understood, as the process is hidden and unverifiable until the mold is opened. The patient's confusion is registered in the question, "Why pour out the clay when we just poured it in?" Similarly, patients at level 5 will have difficulty imagining what a glaze sample will look like on their project. Level 5 patients emphasize the perceptual cue (color) and disregard the chemical properties of the glazes. As a result they may select glazes based on their color before firing or combine glazes that are chemically incompatible. In grouting mosaic projects patients at level 5 usually mix far too much grout because they base their estimation of volume on the size of the trivet rather than the spaces between the tiles.

The inpatient at level 6 appears to be much more inventive and independent: thinking about possibilities, planning patterns, and requesting supplies. Access to all possible materials, representative samples, and idea notebooks can be used profitably.

Patients often ask to learn to throw a pot on the potter's wheel. While mastery of this process can be gained through exploratory actions, some planning ability shortens this process considerably. For instance, level 6 patients may deduce that increasing the speed of the wheel may affect how hard one needs to press down on the clay, and their actions will be far more purposeful and efficient than those of level 5 patients. Any wheel-thrown project can fail at many points during its creation. These pitfalls are better understood, and tolerated, at level 6 than at level 5.

Patients in the clay and mosaics group tend to have affective and personality disorders. The level 5 manic may show poor judgment and euphoria by initiating several overly complex and lengthy projects; the procedures will be rushed through, and end products are often sloppy. As medication takes effect, the therapist can expect projects to become less grandiose, neater, and perhaps more functional and the work rate to be less hasty. Depressed patients, on the other hand, are apt to select simple projects with relatively quick outcomes, because of their low energy and interest. Many patients with PCP psychosis who have been initially assessed to be at level 5 or level 6 become confused in the clay and mosaic group because of a seeming inability to sustain attention and make decisions about the many available choices.

Advantages of the clay and mosaics group are its potential for infinite variation and its ability to adjust to rapid changes in a person's cognitive level. Disadvantages include the storage challenges presented by many types of supplies. In addition, the length of time required to complete a project and to fire the kiln may be a problem in acute care settings where the length of the hospital stay is short.

Other media, such as woodworking and leather, also possess the potential for variation required at levels 5 and 6. Woodworking has been found to be a successful activity that appeals to many male patients. Leather, on the other hand, has been found to have the dual disadvantages of being prohibitively expensive and of attracting those with personality disorders almost exclusively. The therapist in a leather group may spend time setting limits on material use and watching for theft.

COOKING

Cooking group is designed for patients at levels 5 and 6 who have retained skills or are interested in acquiring skills in cooking. The group may accommodate seven patients and has been successfully planned to meet four times weekly: two 1-hour sessions are for planning meals, and two 1½-hour sessions are for cooking and eating. Patients can plan menus and discuss issues related to cooking, such as planning balanced meals, eating well on limited budgets, identifying meat cuts, storing food properly, using weights and measures, and meeting special dietary needs. Needed for this group is a kitchen equipped with refrigerator, stove, counters for working, basic cooking equipment, and foodstuffs. A dishwasher is optional. The group can be run by one therapist.

On days when meals are planned, the therapist provides each patient with a cookbook; the patients are encouraged to look through to select recipes that they like. A group discussion makes more sense when everyone has a copy of the same cookbook. Usually a main dish, salad, vegetable, bread (e.g., muffins), and dessert are selected. Level 6 patients are able to infer flavor from reading the recipe and are better able to select compatible combinations than are patients at level 5. Level 5 patients typically ask many questions since samples (or pictures) of most finished dishes are not available. The therapist provides information regarding available supplies and foodstuffs that may limit choices. Food preparation jobs are divided up according to each patient's interest. The therapist will find it necessary to identify various jobs for level 5 patients, while level 6 patients can use the recipes to plan their actions. A further distinction between level 5 and level 6 patients is that patients at level 5 find it

difficult to predict which tasks must be started first so that the entire meal is completed at the same time.

Discussions on planning days of information related to cooking resemble basic skills exercises in format. A topic of interest to patients is presented in written form. Unlike basic skills, in cooking the information may be new to the patients, since learning does occur at levels 5 and 6. The patients read and answer questions on the material, and the therapist encourages discussion.

Assessments can be made of patients' retained knowledge in cooking and of their safety in the kitchen. Safety is often related to cognitive level. The level 6 patient is apt to stop and consider before he or she acts. Level 5 patients find it difficult to account for the intangible variables of time and temperature. It is problematic for them to make gravies, sauces, or gelatin dishes that change consistency according to temperature. The time required to cook, versus burn, food can be miscalculated too; level 5 patients may check the progress in the refrigerator or on the stove, using perceptual cues in place of symbolic cues.

Level 6 patients, on the other hand, can be counted on to think about the actions before they start to work. This may include reading the entire recipe, gathering needed equipment, or preheating an oven. When patients at level 6 are unclear about an anticipated result, they will usually check out their hunches with the therapist or read the cookbook before proceeding. Cooking tasks allow level 6 patients to plan and carry out a new mode of action.

As in the clay and mosaics group, the therapist is apt to observe a predominance of patients with affective disorders in cooking. A few patients with schizophrenic disorders who are at level 5 or 6 may select this group. If so, their poor interpersonal skills are often clearly observed in the cooperative planning and conversational phase of the group. A depressed patient, on the other hand, may initially be withdrawn but may begin more conversations as the depression lifts. As in clay and mosaics, the therapist can monitor the initiative and energy level of the depressed patient. A decrease in hyperactivity and irritability with an increase in cooperation may be expected with a manic episode.

While the therapist can expect level 5 or level 6 patients to manage their cooking needs, the ability of the level 4 patient to cook safely and effectively is often questioned. The cooking group is not the best setting in which to answer such questions. The cooperative structure of the cooking group, the many distractions represented by many different tasks being performed simultaneously, and the written, serial instructions of recipes do not provide the opportunity for an accurate assessment of the level 4 patient's cooking ability. Such patients are best assessed on an individual basis, usually with a simple one- or two-step mix requiring use of selected visible appliances, such as the stove top. Making macaroni and cheese from a mix is a favorite suggestion. The therapist looks for the familiar knowledge possessed by the patient and must decide whether this knowledge base is essentially safe and healthful. The difficulty for a level 4 patient is the inability to predict problems or solve them by overt experimentation when they occur. A patient at level 4 who is not habitually careful could start a grease fire and not know how to put it out. Patients assessed at level 4 have a tendency to forget to turn off the stove, and again the potential fire hazard is a concern. Many level 4 patients who cook for themselves report that their cooking is limited to canned goods and convenience foods, which may represent a successful adaptation to their lack of ability. Individual assessments of cooking ability in older patients with dementia who anticipate cooking after discharge are also advised. The lack of empirical study in this area makes it a particularly difficult assessment.

The advantages of cooking are its wide appeal and almost universal necessity; many patients have familiar knowledge in this area. Cooking involves combinations and alterations in ingredients that uniquely suit it to level 5 and level 6 patients. Assessments of performance are thought to have extra validity because the environment and media closely resemble patients' home situations. Patients repeatedly state that they enjoy eating what they cook.

Disadvantages of the cooking group include the necessarily small group size and the need for a well-equipped kitchen area. Developing a system for acquiring both perishable and nonperishable food items on a regular basis is a necessity that frequently requires negotiating several layers of red tape to conform to regulations designed for a hospital's main kitchen. The therapist must be committed to the advantages of the cooking group to tolerate such predictable hassles.

WORK EVALUATION

The work evaluation group can accommodate up to 10 patients who may be referred for a prevocational assessment or for a stated preference for work tasks. Cognitive levels in the group can range from 4 to 6; the range is possible because the therapist individually assigns work tasks suited to the patient's level, and the work room is large enough to provide a minimally stimulating area for level 4 patients. This group is not generally suitable for level 3 patients as they are not concerned with end products and a correct end product is the desired outcome in any work setting.

Work tasks range from simple (one- to three-step) repetitious tasks suited to level 4 patients to tasks with several steps requiring inductive and deductive reasoning. Work tasks are selected to include a broad range of types of work, so that familiar work skills can be used. In addition all work is "real" work that needs to be done. This keeps patients from feeling patronized. Finding tasks that meet all of these criteria is a challenge for the therapist.

Examples of tasks that have been found to be successful with level 4 patients are punching holes in forms, cutting rags into 6-inch squares, putting strings in hospital identification tags, collating three-page forms with carbons and stapling them together, counting and bundling gauze surgical sponges into groups, bundling and counting forms, stamping and stuffing envelopes, tracing and cutting felt kit parts, cutting quilt blocks with a pattern, and cleaning sinks. Level 5 patients usually enjoy cutting and fitting copper onto copper tooling templates, counting and rolling plastic trash bags, sorting tiles and beads, and cleaning brushes, slip molds, and other hard-to-clean items. Level 6 patients are able to do tasks requiring planning and involving symbolic cues. They are successful at mixing and pouring plaster into molds, preparing slip and pouring it into molds, measuring and cutting wood on the band saw, putting away supplies in cupboards, and altering hospital charts by adding and removing forms. Retained skills that have been used at many levels include janitorial, clerical, typing, limited mechanical, woodworking, assembly, cooking, lettering, sewing, and painting skills.

The therapist selects tasks for patients based on their interests, retained skills, and cognitive level. A typist who is at level 4 can be given a typing task, for example, as long as the task does not demand planning or problem solving. Level 4 patients can type the interview card suggested in Chapter 4, for instance, when the margins on the machine are preset and the patients can copy an exact sample. Many typing jobs require attention to symbolic cues and planning a mode of action (margins, spacing); these standards of quality can be achieved at level 6.

The therapist sets up all materials for level 4 patients. For example, a stapler should be loaded with staples, hole punches preset, and an exact sample of a finished product provided. All materials should be visible, and only familiar tools used. Level 5 and 6 patients may be asked to secure their own supplies from nearby cupboards. The therapist provides demonstrated step-by-step instruction for level 4 patients and demonstrates novel steps for level 5 patients. The therapist's objective is to give patients an achievable task at their cognitive level that will give them the opportunity to use their current abilities. Evidence of returning abilities (e.g., the level

4 patient who spontaneously explores a new procedure) is noted, and a task that could provide confirmation of an improvement can be tried.

The work rating form (Fig. 10-9) can be completed by patients at the end of each work session. Originally, this form was filled out by the therapist for patients to determine payment in an experimental work rehabilitation project. It was found that patients seem more willing to perceive and accept corrective suggestions from the therapist when they themselves are rating their performance. The form is written in behavioral terms as these are most objectively identified and measured. The categories represented on the form reflect concerns gleaned from a survey of vocational rehabilitation and workshop evaluation forms. All work tasks are standardized in terms of outputs by having therapists, students, and staff perform the tasks. These figures are given to the patient so that he or she can calculate a rating for the quantity box. The therapist should take into account that cognitive limitations at level 4 are apt to affect performance, especially in the initiative and quality measures. Level 4 patients cannot be expected to replace their own supplies unless shown where they are and so instructed. Errors affecting the quality measure may simply represent poor planning on the part of the therapist who gives the level 4 patient a job that requires higher levels of ability. The work rating form is seen as a tool to allow patients to assess their performance, and changes in their performance, on a day-to-day basis. It can also be used to set goals for desirable behaviors.

The Work Performance Inventory (Fig. 10-10) was developed to convey assessments with minimal jargon to sheltered workshop supervisors, vocational counselors, and other non–occupational therapists. Sections I, II, and IV (work habits, work relationships, and motor skills) were identified as consistent areas of concern in most workshop evaluation forms. Section III was included to identify perceptions or emotions that particularly affect the work performance of psychiatric patients. Section

Name _____ Ward _____ Date _____

Rate yourself 1, 2, or 3 in each work habit area; look below for the meaning of 1, 2, or 3 for each area.

	Monday	Tuesday	Wednesday	Thursday	Friday
Punctuality					
Appearance					
Quantity of work					
Quality of work					
Attention					
Initiative					
Work with others					
Cooperation with supervisors					
Total					

Punctuality
1   More than 15 minutes late
2   0–15 minutes late
3   On time

Appearance
1   Hospital clothes
2   Needs grooming
3   Neatly groomed and dressed

Quantity of work
1   0–50% average output
2   50–75% average output
3   75–100% average output

Quality of work
1   more than 20% errors
2   10–20% errors
3   no errors

Attention
1   Three or more breaks
2   Two breaks
3   One or no breaks

Initiative (replaces, requests supplies)
1   Less than half the time
2   Half the time
3   All the time

Work with others
1   Unable to work next to others
2   Works next to others
3   Can converse and get work done

Cooperation with supervisors (accepts suggestions,
   reports to supervisors)
1   Unable to accept suggestions or reports
2   Accepts supervision, reports half the time
3   Accepts supervision, reports all the time

Fig. 10-9. Work rating scale: self-report.

Name of client _____ Date _____

Age _____ Sex _____ Years of education _____

Medicine (yes or no) _____ Precautions _____

I. Work habits

    Appearance   _____ Dirty, sloppy, bizarre, unsuitable
                             _____ Clean

    Attendance   _____ Irregular
                             _____ Consistent

    Punctuality   _____ On time
                             _____ Late

    Work rate   _____ 0–10% of normal output
                             _____ 10–25% of normal output
                             _____ 25–100% of normal output

    Accuracy   _____ 20% or more errors
                             _____ 10–20% errors
                             _____ 0–10% errors

    Behavior   _____ Under control, predictable
                             _____ Occasional or frequent outbursts precipitated by _____

Comments

II. Work relationships

    A.   Coworkers

        _____ Works best when in a room alone
        _____ Works in the presence of others with minimal sharing or interaction
        _____ Forms casual relationships with coworkers
        _____ Can work on a job requiring cooperation and competition

    B.   Supervisors

        _____ Passively compliant; unable to ask for directions
        _____ Asks for directions even when procedure is known
        _____ Critical to supervisors of their directions
        _____ Asks for directions when learning is required

Comments

III. Perceptions and emotions affecting work performance

    _____ Does not like to be touched   _____ Anxiety
    _____ Sensitive to smells   _____ Irritability
    _____ Sensitive to sounds   _____ Depression
    _____ Hallucinations

Comments

IV. Motor skills

    _____ Clumsy gross body movements
    _____ Plans own gross body movements
    _____ Accurate in using arms and hands
    _____ Accurate with tools
    _____ Changes position of body, objects for better task performance

Fig. 10-10. Work performance inventory.

Physical limitations in strength or endurance

| _____ Sitting | _____ Standing | _____ Bending |
| _____ Walking | _____ Lifting | |

Medical problems

_____ Hearing	_____ Arthritis	_____ Heart disease
_____ Seeing	_____ Allergies	_____ Back
_____ Obesity		
_____ Hand or wrist limitations		
_____ Memory impairment		
_____ Mental retardation		

Comments

V.   Task selection

_____ Level 2: postural actions

Client is highly distractible and requires constant guidance. Familiar postural actions can be performed. Demonstrated directions should be limited to one step repeated several times.

_____ Level 3: manual actions

Client's capacity to learn work tasks is limited to simple, one-step, repetitive tasks. Client generally works better with hands than tools. Interest is focused on the demonstrated directions and does not include other factors such as the end product or cleanup. Productivity may be sustained for an average of 15 to 30 minutes, but client is easily distracted and may need frequent refocusing of attention to the task.

_____ Level 4: goal-directed actions

Client is interested in achieving a visible end product. Tasks that include several standardized steps can be performed when directions are demonstrated one step at a time. Materials and simple familiar tools must be supplied and put away by the supervisor. Attention is focused until the identified job is completed. When the job becomes boring, the client is apt to quit.

_____ Level 5: exploratory actions

Several directions may be demonstrated to client at one time. Interest will be sustained in work tasks that require several sessions to complete. Client will discover methods of modifying work tasks and will resolve minor difficulties without assistance. Perseverance and improvement in task performance will be noticed, but client's problem solving is limited to inductive reasoning, seeing the effect of an action after it occurs. Plans and verbal directions are not understood. The client may be expected to search for needed equipment, tools, and supplies.

_____ Level 6: planned actions

While directions for unfamiliar tasks may still require demonstration, client is able to initiate familiar tasks from simple verbal, written, or diagrammed instructions. Little assistance is required in solving problems because client is able to think about solutions and retain directions. Quality control is maintained by client. Use of unfamiliar tools, with potential hazards, can be learned.

VI.   Self-regulation

| _____ Mechanically does tasks |
| _____ Resists change and unfamiliar activities |
| _____ Works to release tension or "keep busy" |
| _____ Works for cigarettes, snacks, or _____ |
| _____ Enjoys a "job well done" |

Fig. 10-10. (continued)

Comments

VII. Special skills and preferred tasks

VIII. Client most suited for
    _____ Closed setting
    _____ Activity program
    _____ Sheltered work setting
    _____ Job training
    _____ Competitive employment
    _____ Other (specify) _____

Disposition at discharge _____

Number of sessions observed _____

Inventory rater _____
    (Title) _____

Fig. 10-10. (continued)

V, task selection, describes, in five paragraphs, performance characterizing the various cognitive levels. The intent of these descriptions was to give supervisors an idea of how a client might be expected to perform and at the same time to give suggestions as to how to make their supervision more meaningful to the client. Section VI recognizes the importance of self-regulation and identifies what the patient states or what the therapist observes to be of prime importance to the patient. Section VII, special skills and preferred tasks, offers further suggestions of possible successful tasks for the patient.

Clinical experience suggests that Section VIII, the recommendation, often, but not always, parallels the degree of cognitive disability. Level 2 patients generally require continued care in a closed setting. Level 3 patients, who are distractible and lacking in goal direction, function best in either closed settings or activity centers. Level 4 patients without strong interest in work would be suited for activity programs as well. The 8-hour day and consistent attendance required in the sheltered workshop is within the capability of some level 4 patients if the supervision and tasks provided take into account their limitations in learning and problem solving. Experience in the work rehabilitation program with chronic schizophrenic patients strongly suggested that level 4 patients have great difficulty maintaining consistent attendance for 3 months. Patients were typically given jobs that were too difficult (i.e., those requiring exploratory or planned actions), or they became bored with repetitive jobs. The great dilemma for the level 4 patient appears to be that interest in achieving immediate end products wanes as the process becomes extremely familiar. Yet level 4 patients cannot create interest for themselves, as patients at level 5 can, by varying their actions. The only solution is to quit the job, which level 4 patients frequently do. Some level 4 patients with work experience are known to return to highly familiar jobs; in these cases the environment is supportive and the job is unskilled.

Level 5 patients successfully negotiate sheltered work settings and some training programs. They are able to generate interest in what can be monotonous routine in workshop jobs by varying their approach or exploring the environment, perhaps even asking for another job. If a training program includes participatory learning, the level 5 patient can learn effectively by engaging in exploratory actions. Some jobs are more suited than others to the level 5 patient's experimentation. Level 5 patients may be able to perform jobs that require the manipulation of material objects (janitorial, food service, assembly work), if the inevitable errors are not too dangerous or prohibitively expensive. Computer programming, typing, and dental technician programs, for instance, are inherently exacting and will not tolerate the "wasteful" exploration of the level 5 patient. Level 6 patients can be expected to learn effectively in conventional training programs in which information is often communicated by the written or spoken word. Competitive employment is indicated if the patient's retained skills and cognitive level are compatible with the job in question and work habits are at an acceptable level.

Patients with all diagnoses are seen in the work evaluation group. The quantified outputs and regular daily assessment allows the therapist to monitor accurately changes in work output (because of increased energy in a depressed patient or increased concentration in a schizophrenic patient) as a measure of response to medication. Quality measures often reflect increased care taken by a remitting manic or improvements in concentration of a toxic PCP user. Work histories are often gathered by the therapist to identify retained skills and patterns of employment that may have diagnostic importance. The work history of the manic patient may reveal "creative binges" as an actor, musician, or dancer between more mundane clerk or factory jobs. The paranoid schizophrenic's job history may reveal increasingly erratic adjustment to an unusually solitary vocation such as being a security guard. The inability of the employed alcoholic to remember instructions or placement of tools and supplies on a day-to-day basis can assist in substantiating the presence of dementia.

The advantages of the work group are many. It can be implemented with a limited budget in any institution in which there are many routine tasks and much collated paperwork to be done. Since it can accommodate a variety of cognitive levels, it could be considered a versatile group in a setting where staffing is too limited to run a variety of groups. Patients who view crafts as childish often enjoy work tasks, and work is often the group of choice of depressed patients who have no interest in doing a "gratifying" task but are willing to "help others." The procedures in most work tasks are prescribed and lend themselves to a step-by-step analysis. This makes identification of areas of patient difficulty easier. Work group can be regularly used to do preparation that would otherwise consume staff time for other activity groups such as basic crafts and basic sewing.

The work group excludes most non-goal-directed level 3 patients, though an energetic therapist can provide tasks such as ripping rags and folding linen. Some patients refuse to work without payment. The chief disadvantage of this group, however, is locating a variety of work tasks that range from level 4 to 6. If tasks are secured from outside agencies or departments, then deadlines and quality control are also considerations. Therapists may find supervising work evaluation a demanding experience, as they must be able to change their supervisory styles and interventions frequently for the variety of levels, as well as keep track of patients' progress on many different tasks to make accurate reports.

ADVANCED CRAFTS

Advanced crafts resembles the traditional occupational therapy group most closely. It is designed for level 5 and level 6 patients and can accommodate up to 20 patients with two therapists supervising, or one therapist and one aide or student. The group can last up to 2 hours. Patients are given the opportunity to select projects from a wide variety of craft media by referring to a display case of samples and a file cabinet of instruction books.

The environment should include working space for predicted attendance, with tools and equipment stored in easily accessible cupboards, and a sink.

Examples of projects that are successful include wood kits and boxes, decoupage with resin finish, macrame, hand weaving, basketry, jewelry, large copper tooling projects, machine sewing, stained glass painting on acrylic plastic,* leather work, and fine arts such as painting and drawing.

The therapist's role resembles that of a consultant, giving an orientation as to location of supplies and tools and demonstration of unfamiliar procedures. The therapist's interventions may not be immediately evident to the outside observer as patients appear independent. As in the clay and mosaics and cooking groups, however, the therapist is conscious of the level 5 patient's potential for disaster in using exploratory, unplanned actions and the level 6 patient's need for validation of a tentative plan of action. Demonstration is still preferable to diagrams and instruction books for the level 5 patient; diagrams can be used at level 6.

In guiding the patients' selection of tasks, the therapist should be aware of procedures that are best learned at level 6. For example, it has been observed that macrame is difficult for many level 5 patients, even with demonstration and a diagram for learning knots. The over-and-under scheme, while very familiar and usually successful in hand weaving, is complicated in the square knot by shifting the cords from right to left. Over versus under, plus left versus right, may be interpreted as two sets of classification criteria that must be considered simultaneously (see Chaps. 13 and 14). When a mistake is made, the level 5 patient may not be able to identify the cause of the error and subsequently vary his or her action, especially if the cords are the same color. Teaching the square knot with four different colors of cords has been found to be successful, presumably because the patient is cued by color as to which cord is on the right and which is on the left.

---

*See manufacturer's instructions for usage precautions.

The patient is able to locate a mistake easily by comparing his or her colors with colored diagrams of the knotting sequence; the diagrams are an environmental compensation for the classification criteria.

Following wood kit assembly instructions is usually far easier for patients at level 6 than those at level 5 because the former think about placement of the parts before they go to work. Level 5 patients can be encouraged to use a little glue during assembly instead of nails as glued pieces are much easier to disassemble if an error is made.

In this author's (CAE) facility a group of patients with minimal cognitive impairments typically includes a preponderance of patients with mild affective disorders or personality disorders. These patients may refuse to participate in the work evaluation group but enjoy advanced crafts. Besides assessing their cognitive level, the therapist can identify any social behavior patterns that interfere with compliance with standards of performance. Unlike work evaluation, where tasks are prescribed and quantity and quality are objectively measured, therapists' standards for effective performance in advanced crafts are less clear and usually need refinement. At this writing, patients who are functioning at levels 5 and 6 are expected to come to group punctually without reminders (patients are not escorted to advanced crafts), to work while in group on a task rather than socialize exclusively, and to work independently rather than asking others to get supplies or solve problems for them. Standards for quality are important for this population, but measurements of what constitutes adequate quality are difficult to define. If major problems can be identified in the patient's ability to complete a task, these can be brought to the attention of the patient. Presumably, patients who do not view their social behaviors as problems will do little to change them. When this occurs, adjustment to environments with imposed social standards could be predicted to be poor.

The advantages of advanced crafts include its potential for providing higher-level patients with unfamiliar processes and tools, which maximizes the opportunity for observing distinctions between level 5 and level 6. Patients can be observed for differences in response to a fairly unstructured task environment, in contrast to a structured one such as the work evaluation group. Patients enjoy the opportunity to explore new interests and to develop more complicated, longer-term tasks. The clutter and potentially chaotic cumulative effect of countless tools, machines, and supplies is a disadvantage and necessitates an organized clinic and regular attention to housekeeping. Another disadvantage occurs occasionally when a wave of patients with personality disorders begins to turn out projects in large numbers to sell them to staff and other patients. The lack of quality control measures makes it difficult for the therapists in this situation to preserve their inventory of supplies. Limitations on the number of projects, such as five per week, may be required.

REFERENCE

Hall, C. S., and Lindzey, G. *Theories of Personality.* New York: Wiley, 1957.

PART THREE

RESEARCH

The research studies presented in this part of the text are concerned with a central question: What can empirical science do to help objectify a theory of practice? It is not possible to investigate every idea suggested by the theory, so selections must be made. The choices made have been attempts to strike a balance between ideas that are often regarded as polar opposites:

1. Abstract ideals versus concrete realities
2. Reduced parts versus whole systems
3. Doubts versus convictions
4. Known facts versus intuitions
5. Individual analysis versus group synthesis

An effort has been made to avoid a dualistic, either-or position and to follow a synergistic approach. A synergistic approach considers each pole to be equally important, combining them to create a balanced ideal (Hampden-Turner, 1981).

1. Abstract ideals + concrete realities = realistic ideals
2. Reduced parts + whole systems = practical theory
3. Doubts + convictions = questioned commitments
4. Known facts + intuitions = inspirations
5. Individual analysis + group synthesis = professional cohesion

When synergies are formed the results can be delightful, but it is not always possible to do so.

The research studies presented are the first efforts to examine the theoretical description of cognitive disabilities. Necessity dictated a focus on instrument development—the identification of ideas that can be measured. The first thing that one has to do is establish the reliability of an instrument. Priority was placed on interrater reliability so that different therapists can be confident that they are all talking about the same thing when assessing the cognitive level. Validity has been examined by com-

paring the instruments with other instruments in the current neuroscience mainstream, so that therapists can identify similarities and differences in interdisciplinary assessments (Anastasi, 1982). Clinical significance is regarded as more important than statistical significance, and this value has been self-enforced by relating findings to routine tasks.

At the time of these studies, very little research in psychiatric occupational therapy had been done, and models for good research designs were lacking. These studies were conducted by master's degree candidates in occupational therapy at the University of Southern California (USC). Support was obtained from the USC-OT faculty, experienced therapists at Los Angeles County-USC Medical Center, and members of the USC faculty in the Department of Psychiatry. The studies contain some obvious limitations in sample size and geographic location. They are presented as examples of what research in psychiatric occupational therapy can look like. I hope that these studies will stimulate more research.

I would like to extend my thanks to the authors of the master's degree theses, some completed and some still in process: Susan Herzig, Deborah Moore, Linda Riska Williams, Noomi Katz, Lois Heying, Nanci Heimann, and (from San Jose State University) Debra Wilson. I admire their courage in working with an emerging theory and value their critical analysis.

REFERENCES

Anastasi, A. *Psychological Testing* (5th ed.). New York: Macmillan, 1982.

Hampden-Turner, C. *Maps of the Mind: Charts and Concepts of the Mind and Its Labyrinths.* New York: Collier, 1981.

CHAPTER 11

MEASURING COMPETENCE

There is growing recognition of a need for a competence measure for the cognitively disabled, stimulated by concern about the health care of the chronically ill and the legal decisions made about mental disorders. Competence has legal implications in matters such as responsibility for standing trial, civil commitment, and conservatorships (Stone, 1976). The cognitive levels may assist in untangling some of the problems in this area, but precautions must be taken to avoid oversimplification. If the cognitive levels are to be of practical assistance to our patients in their communities, we must have an indepth knowledge of what the levels do, and do not, describe. Research is needed to refine our understanding of the cognitive levels as descriptions of disabilities with inherent social consequences. Some of the theoretical and practical concerns that have been taken into account in measuring competence will be outlined in this chapter.

The cognitive levels are a measure of the severity of a disability as observed during the performance of a task. There are a number of potential approaches to the empirical study of the cognitive levels. This chapter will discuss some of the related issues, including a definition of cognition as a competence measure, the legal determinations of competency that may effect the cognitively disabled, instruments developed to measure cognitive disabilities, and the predictive validity of these measures.

Piaget (1971) describes increasing cognitive abilities as the self-regulation of the process of applying patterns of thought that organize and extend the usable environment (Furth, 1969). Cognition is the mechanism we all use to find order in our environment, and it is this mechanism for establishing order that guides behavior in the performance of routine tasks. Doing a task requires the prerequisite cognitive abilities for each step in the task's procedure. Doing a task also involves a choice to do the task (Piaget, 1978). The choice and the abilities are two features of the cognitive system. An illness that impairs the cognitive system can be expected to restrict the patients' abilities and limit the number of choices. A cognitive disability takes activities away from the patient, and competence measures seek to describe the loss.

A measurement of the loss of ability requires considerations not evident in the study of the development of abilities. A disability is caused by known or unknown biologic impairments, and the natural course of the disease, when treated or untreated, is an important part of the description of a disability. Expression of the cognitive disability is observed during routine task behavior because difficulties in this area are important to the patient, the family, and the community; a disability creates a social handicap. Individuals respond to biologic impairments and social handicaps in a manner that reflects individual differences and personal choice. Therefore the description of a cognitive loss must be comprehensive, encompassing the biologic, psychological, and social factors involved.

COMPETENCE: AN INFERENCE

A competence measure is an inference derived from observations of performance. Performance is what one sees or hears; competence is what one thinks it means. An error in ascribing meaning is easy to make, and the potential for error seems to increase when one attempts to explain changes in the cognitive level. How are we to explain change in a person's cognitive level? Piaget (1971, 1978) states that psychological experience with motor tasks produces psychological development. Occupational therapists provide experience with motor tasks, and at first glance it might appear that the occupational therapy experience would change the cognitive level. Spontaneous remissions and the somatic interventions of physicians, however, loom before us as alternative biologic explanations for change with a great deal of credibility. Disregarding alternative explanations for change makes measurement easier, but unfortunately it is a kind of naiveté that we cannot afford.

Acute Conditions

Developmental psychologists have encountered some difficulties in explaining changes in behavior, especially during the periods of transition from one developmental stage to another. The difficulty is in explaining periods of transition without rendering the stages meaningless (Flavell, 1971). I have shared this difficulty. It is especially apparent in acute conditions characterized by rapid changes in the cognitive level. For example, patients with a high fever or a primary affective disorder may go from level 1 to level 6 in a few days. Therapists may describe behavior as a "high 3" or a "low 4" or "a little bit of 5 but not solid." The fluidity in the therapist's report reflects the fluctuations in the acute condition. In these instances the assessment acts as a benchmark, giving a general impression, and in practice the meaning is interpreted with caution. A number of biologic factors, such as the time of day or a pill that was taken, can explain a fluctuation in the cognitive level. Inferences about the cognitive level in acute conditions are relatively imprecise, compared with assessments of the cognitive level in stable conditions. Empirical study of acute conditions will, predictably, be influenced by these fluctuations. Some of the studies that follow have dealt with this problem by testing the cognitive level at admission and discharge and examining the degree of change during the course of hospitalization. No effort to date has been made to describe the rate of change, and this may be desirable in the future. Examining the rate of change will probably require a fairly large sample to even out potential distortions explained by fluctuations.

Psychological and Social Factors

Psychological explanations for changes in the cognitive level seem to err in the direction of making pejorative judgments of patients. A comment like the following may be heard: "Joe is going to be discharged tomorrow. You watch, he is going to come into the clinic and show us how sick he is." Joe had been functioning at level 6 but that day his performance was typical of level 3. He used one color of mosaic tile in a disorderly fashion to make a tile trivet; glue oozed between irregularly spaced tiles, dripped on to the table and his trousers, and covered his fingers. We must ask this question: Did Joe know that this is typical of disabled performance? If he had no way of knowing, then it is probably unfair to say that he was *trying* to look disabled. Volitional explanations for poor performance are difficult to substantiate objectively. Inferences such as malingering or trying to qualify for disability insurance are tempting in some cases and for that reason should be used with restraint in practice.

Research designs that correlate the cognitive level with psychological and social factors may also be subjected to a prejudicial interpretation. Age, sex, and social class are examples of factors that need to be considered, and interpreted, with restraint. The empirical study of psychological and social factors is helpful in practice because the therapist has relatively objective criteria for knowing which factors are apt to influence the cognitive level.

Intelligence

Cognition, which guides behavior, is often referred to as intelligence, and the association between the cognitive levels and intelligence may be examined. The intellectual ability measured by psychologists in assessing intelligence is academic achievement. Emphasis is placed on the verbal demands that characterize normal school performance (Maloney and Ward, 1976). Psychological tests of intelligence measure abilities that develop after the sensorimotor period, and we would expect psychological tests to measure more complex abilities than those assessed by measures of cognitive level. The greatest correspondence between the cognitive levels and results of psychological tests of intelligence could be expected with motor performance tests such as the Block Design of the Wechsler Adult Intelligence Scale. The Block Design is a nonverbal perfor-

mance test that examines visual-motor coordination and sustained effort (Maloney and Ward, 1976). The greatest difference from the cognitive levels could be expected with tests that measure information recall and abstract problem-solving ability. Information recall is a good example of how a predictor of academic achievement draws on a person's past experiences to predict future performance. The stability of the test results is enhanced by drawing on prior learning. These tests are not designed to be sensitive to fluctuations in performance abilities seen in disease and disability. Some fluctuations may be detected, and these fluctuations may be the most promising associations with the cognitive levels.

Language intelligence is measured by people in linguistics and speech pathology. Here again we would expect the cognitive levels to be a simpler form of intelligence, and the highest correlations with them may occur with the simpler tests such as naming familiar objects and visual-motor performance. Some similarity may also be found with impaired listening tasks when a person has trouble attending to auditory cues (Keenan, 1975). The greatest differences are expected with measures for the use of abstract language. The correlation between cognitive level and a person's ability to profit from the retraining provided by speech pathologists may be a promising area for study. An example of potential associations between cognitive levels 1 through 4 and language abilities is suggested by the Porch Index of Communicative Abilities (Porch, 1967). The index is designed to be a sensitive measure of small changes in the communicative performance of aphasic patients. Eighteen subtests measure performance in gestural, graphic, and verbal abilities. The design and scope of performance are interesting because of the shared focus on describing a disability. Porch's index might be helpful in providing a more comprehensive description of the communication abilities associated with the cognitive levels.

At this point in the study of the cognitive levels, it is easier to state what is not being measured than what is. Some speculations can be offered. The cognitive levels identify the sensory cues that can capture attention. A measurement of the cognitive level can be made by observing spontaneous motor actions or imitated motor actions. Observations provide a data base for drawing inferences about the qualitative purposes, experiences, processes, and time frames that enter conscious awareness. The description of a cognitive disability focuses on the quality of intelligence used during the sensorimotor process of doing routine tasks.

Perception and Attention

The first step in using a sensory cue is to pay attention to it. The cognitive levels describe a hierarchy of cues that capture attention; slowly I have come to realize that what a person ignores is as important as what a person attends to. Large elements of the external environment are ignored by people with cognitive disabilities, which renders these elements useless. The therapist selects a sensory cue that captures attention. There is a tendency to confuse ignoring a sensory cue with a problem in perception. When a person ignores a cue, that does not mean he or she misperceived the cue; rather, the cue was not attended to at all. Ignoring a cue indicates the person is experiencing a problem in attention, not perception. The deficit seems to be an attentional deficit. In practice distinguishing between perceptual and attentional deficits requires careful observation. In research this could pose problems as well: The reliability of a test of the cognitive level may be influenced by the administrator's ability to capture the subject's attention. In the Allen Cognitive Level Test (ACL), this problem has been dealt with, in part, by specifying the number of directions that can be repeated. The process consists of refocusing the person's attention to the selected sensorimotor cue; attention is thought to be sustained when sustained motor action is observed. Even so, there will probably be instances when the therapist must use his or her own judgment in determining whether the subject was paying attention. If the subject was not attending, the direction does not count and should be repeated.

Therapists frequently ask: What about perception? The answer, to me, is unclear. The literature on perception is vast, containing numerous definitions of different types of perception. A readable introduction to this topic can be found in Matlin (1983). More is known about visual perception than about the other sensory cues. A sensorimotor association has not been a prominent part of the study of perception. Lacking that association, I find it difficult to generalize from the perception tests to the motor performance of routine tasks. The practical importance of the test score is unclear. Some psychologists recognize this problem and are working on broader theoretical models (for example, Wilding, 1982). As the models develop they may contain clearer guidelines for application in practice.

Test Materials

The cognitive levels describe a hierarchy of movements that correspond with sensory cues. Whether a movement will be successfully imitated is influenced by the individual's familiarity with the movement. I think familiar movements are especially important at levels 1 through 4: The person can draw on memories, or past experiences, to follow the demonstrated direction, but novel movements that involve learning a new motor action are often ignored or refused. Thus the assessment of the cognitive level is easily confounded by individual differences in the relative familiarity, novelty, or desirability of the test materials. These factors must be considered in research designs. In the studies that follow patients were asked if they had ever done leather lacing before, and refusals to try to do the lacing stitches of the ACL were recorded. One of the reasons for selecting leather lacing to measure cognitive level was that it does not look like a test—tests are apt to produce a refusal from patients who deny having a mental disorder.

COMPETENCE: LEGAL CONSIDERATIONS

Proposition 9. The assessment of the cognitive level can contribute to the legal determination of competency.

Forensic psychiatry seems to be in the vanguard in contending with the social impact of the advances in the neurosciences. As one might expect, forensic psychiatry is a rapidly changing field, fraught with complex controversies. As therapists we have been tempted to ignore these problems, but as legal constraints increasingly impinge on patient care we have been forced to examine our position within these controversies. This is difficult because the legal demands placed on a conceptual definition are often quite different from the treatment requirements we are accustomed to considering. The following discussion aims at placing the cognitive levels in a legal context.

Psychiatry and the law used to be regarded as two separate systems; this is changing, and the interaction between these fields is affecting practice in both professions, as well as our own. *Competence, dangerousness, insanity, civil commitment, right to treatment, right to refuse treatment,* and *gravely disabled* are legal terms therapists encounter. An overview of the moral, ethical, medical, and legal considerations connected with these terms can be found in Stone (1976). Competence is a basic issue in civil commitment proceedings, having an effect on determining who is hospitalized and for how long. Furthermore, decisions about competence are becoming important in other legal determinations.

Competence first referred to a person's ability to stand trial. This meaning of competence involves the person's understanding of his or her current situation and ability to cooperate in his or her defense. It is a here-and-now determination that may be reconsidered at many points during the judicial process. These assessments are verbal, usually based on a screening test (Bukatmen et al., 1981; Lipsitt et al., 1971). Here a verbal assessment

makes sense because a trial is a verbal process. The burden of responsibility during a trial falls on the trial lawyer, not the client. The trial lawyer acts in the defendant's behalf, and the question is, Can the defendant cooperate? The ability to cooperate with a trial lawyer is a narrow definition of competence. A trial is a specialized task not familiar, or routine, to most people.

Stone (1976) has identified four requirements of the legal system in determining competence: accuracy, fairness, efficacy of punishment, and the dignity of the judicial process. He did not include the requirements of the medical system, and the omission is noteworthy. The medical requirements in determining competence may be the efficacy of treatment and the dignity of the health and welfare system. There is a growing recognition of, and concern for, the arbitrary criteria used to admit people to a hospital and to enable them to receive disability insurance. The cognitive levels could be used as an objective measure, but this should be done with caution. We all like to find easy answers to complex questions. Unfortunately, easy answers often lead to a misuse of information. Safeguards are required.

The first safeguard is to recognize the distinction between results of an assessment of a disability and competence to stand trial. The assessment of cognitive level is not an assessment of a specialized verbal process used in a court of law. Patients at levels 1 and 2 would probably be assessed as incompetent and those of level 6 as competent. Ambiguity will probably surround those at levels 3, 4, and 5; other factors would have to be assessed to make a determination (Weinstein, 1980). The therapist's assessment of the cognitive level must be made in conjunction with other factors that can influence a person's ability to stand trial.

Competence is often confused with insanity, but the two terms are not synonymous. Historically, the insanity defense stems from English law, admitted as a plea in a murder trial to avoid capital punishment. The insanity defense is based on the nineteenth century concept of "free will" to choose between good and evil, and it acts as a vehicle for excusing a person from responsibility for committing a crime (Stone, 1976). The current outcome of a successful insanity defense is commitment to a hospital for treatment, instead of jail. The problem is that the law, in Britain and the United States, fails to distinguish between those conditions that respond to treatment and those that do not. Furthermore, while most psychiatrists would agree that personality disorders cannot be treated successfully, there are, no doubt, some who would testify that they can. It seems that a "prospect of benefit from treatment" (Hamilton, 1981) ought to be a requirement for being in a hospital, and that prospect should be backed up by effectiveness studies. The cognitive levels may be of assistance in measuring the functional benefits of treatment. The functional benefits of treatment must be considered in conjunction with other factors that could mitigate for, or against, sustained benefits, for example, patients' willingness to continue to take their medication after discharge from a treatment facility.

A broader view of competence seems to be working its way into American law at the state level under a variety of terms. This view comes into play when "the diagnosable illness impaired the person's ability to accept treatment; e.g., the person was either too disturbed to communicate, or because of incapacity arising from the illness such as delusions and hallucinations, the person was unable to comprehend the possibility of treatment" (Stone, 1976, p. 67). This quotation from Stone recognizes a need for acute treatment of mental diseases, and the states have adopted a variety of civil commitment proceedings to provide treatment while protecting the individual's rights. Arbitrary legal decisions about the length of hospitalization have been especially troublesome, producing a ripple effect that has extended beyond the hospitals to the courts and jails (Appelbaum et al., 1981; Daniel et al., 1981; Lamb and Grant, 1982; Munetz et al., 1981; Stone, 1981). The permitted length of hospitalization before a hearing has a nationwide range from 3 to 30 days, and the criteria applied to extended hospitalization are sometimes as arbitrary as the number of

days. Police officers, who are often called to remove a disordered person, may direct a person to the criminal system or a hospital, and there is a growing recognition of the arbitrary nature of the assignment (Daniel et al., 1981; Lamb and Grant, 1982; Shanok and Lewis, 1981). Justifying the need for acute treatment can be very difficult, and the situation is even more difficult in cases involving long-term disabilities. Some resolution of these problems has been suggested by a Utah law that provides a model for overcoming the presumption of competence before commitment to a hospital (Lebegue and Clark, 1981; Stone, 1981). Commitment hearings are held at the time of admission, and once committed the person no longer has the right to refuse treatment.

People at either end of the hierarchy of cognitive levels usually avoid the ambiguities in legal extensions of competence. The illness of those at levels 1 and 2 is easily detected, and people assessed at levels 5 and 6 can usually survive in the community. It is the people assessed at levels 3 and 4 who get into trouble, especially if they have good verbal skills. A man who cannot tie his own shoelaces but has good verbal abilities may pull himself together and present an adequate picture of himself during an interview or hearing. The distinction between verbal behavior and voluntary motor action is highlighted by the judicial process. Judicial processes are verbal, and what a person says he or she can do is not always evident in his or her motor actions. The twentieth century emphasis on verbal behavior has left the mental health professions largely unprepared to explain the discrepancies between verbal and motor competencies. The discrepancies are recognized by people working in the mental health professions, but providing evidence that is acceptable to the judicial process is difficult. The great challenge before us is to develop our assessments of routine task behavior so they have face validity in a court of law. The need is especially great at cognitive levels 3 and 4.

This point of view is based on the notion that a determination of competence is the basic assessment made in decisions concerning civil commitment, right to treatment, right to refuse treatment, and grave disability. There is some support for this notion (see, for example, Applebaum and Hamm, 1982, Appelbaum et al., 1981), but it is not always recognized (as in Munetz et al., 1981). American legal traditions contend that a person is competent until proven otherwise, and in some cases it may be difficult to enter the question of incompetence. By and large, forensic psychiatry focuses on the narrower definition of competence to stand trial, and the need for a broader determination is a recent development. The lack of recognition that a question of competence exists makes it even more difficult to raise the question and places even more stringent demands on the evidence. The best evidence is a specific observation of behavior that is relevant to the instrumental role performance of the individual (see Chap. 15).

The assessment of cognitive levels during routine task behavior may be helpful in resolving some of the complex problems encountered by psychiatry and the law—but we should not delude ourselves into thinking this contribution is easily achievable. A profession that requires only a bachelor's degree may be unable to meet this challenge, because our assessments lack the requisite empirical support or we fail to comprehend the other factors that are related to the assessment of competence. Our dreams and our realities may be crystallized at the interface between mental disorders and the law, where the social implications of a cognitive disability are coming into focus. Forensic psychiatry seems to be helpful in the selection of research priorities, supplying important problems that may alter the course of patient care. Inferences about mental abilities may be made credible through the association with routine task behavior. The absence of a credible assessment is certainly creating problems, and the validation of a determination of competence may be the challenge of the next decade.

This section might be read as implying that the only social use of the assessment of cognitive level is to make a legal determination of competence.

That is not the intent. The expectation is that in actual practice a small proportion of the cognitively disabled will require a legal determination. In most cases the patients and their caregivers can use information about cognitive levels without the intervention of the legal system. What the legal system provides is a social standard for the quality of information accepted in the formulation used to determine competence. Therapists can use these social standards as assistive devices in designing assessments that are as fair and objective as possible.

COMPETENCE: THEORETICAL CONSIDERATIONS

A clear distinction must be made between performance and competence. Performance is the behavior that the therapist observes during the process of doing a task. Observations can have a number of plausible explanations (Brown and Desforges, 1979). Competence is one possible explanation. Before the assignment of the competence measure (the cognitive level) the therapist attempts to rule out the other plausible explanations for a problem in task performance.

A competence measure is difficult to work with because the therapist must draw an inference about an ambiguous phenomenon. Inferences increase the probability of making a mistake. To guard against this possibility, an effort must be made to identify the factors that can confound the inference. The research studies in this part of the text dealt with this problem as follows: Some confounding factors, such as hand and visual impairments, were used as exclusion criteria—subjects who might obscure the interpretation of the data were excluded from the study. Other confounding factors, such as past experience, were tested. Eventually we will need to test the exclusion criteria to see if they really are confounding factors.

Translating an observation of performance into a number also entails some problems. The hierarchy of cognitive levels does seem to follow the sequence one would anticipate. This supports the notion that the scale is ordinal. There are some questions about the space, or intervals, between the numbers (some measurements, such as age, have equivalent intervals between the numbers). The cognitive levels are a functional intermediary between a biologic abnormality and a social handicap. Criteria for measuring the intervals between the levels are difficult to establish. I am not certain that the intervals are equivalent and suspect that a social dichotomy may exist between levels 4 and 5. This presents a problem when selecting statistical tools; parametric statistics assume equivalent intervals, while nonparametrics do not (Fox, 1969). Some parametric statistics have been used in the following studies. It could be that nonparametrics would produce different results. The selection of the best statistical procedure continues to be a problem, and more studies are needed to achieve greater clarity.

Sound research requires accurate data-gathering techniques. Much of the research presented in this part of the book has been concerned with instrument development. A decision was made to avoid borrowing instruments developed by people in other professions, with the hope that greater clarity about the uniqueness of occupational therapy would emerge. The question was, What can research do for us? The answer seems to fall somewhere between everything and nothing.

While it may seem obvious that an instrument cannot measure everything, occupational therapy's generalist tradition leads to a consideration of a great number of factors. Selecting a focus of study requires a setting of priorities and an elimination of much potentially important information. The discard pile always seems to be much larger than the retained pile. One fears that, indeed, one will come up with nothing. Finding a balance between everything and nothing is the challenge of the scientific method. Three or four major factors seem to be a manageable number to consider in each study. Clinical utility is helpful in establishing priorities. The research process stimulates an awareness of the relative importance of various theoretical concepts;

one discovers that many concepts are nice, but not essential.

INSTRUMENT DEVELOPMENT

Most of the tests of cognitive abilities have been designed by psychologists to fulfill their conceptual needs (Maloney and Ward, 1976). Measurements of the impact of a disease on the activities of daily living are relatively rare; the information is often obtained by interviewing a significant other (Albert, 1981; Jette, 1980; Liang and Jette, 1981). Measurements of the quality of observed functional performance usually contain numerous deficiencies. It is hoped that the description of the cognitive levels will facilitate the development of measures of functional performance.

The leather lacing test or ACL (see Chap. 4) was designed with clinical requirements in mind. Research requirements have been helpful in clarifying clinical ambiguities. The first requirement of a research instrument is the establishment of reliability (Fox, 1969). The cognitive levels are designed to be sensitive to rapid change in functional abilities; test–retest reliability is not expected in acute conditions but would be expected in stable conditions. Interrater reliability between therapists who administer the test is essential. Difficulties with using the leather lacing task can lead to a selection of a different task; both tasks should produce equivalent scores. The medical conditions of the patient and the content of the task influence the expected reliability of an instrument.

An assessment instrument is an operational definition of a larger body of information. A single task or test always contains limitations in the kinds of inferences that can be drawn from the data. Leather lacing, for example, can be influenced by visual impairments, hand impairments, familiarity with leather lacing, and lack of cooperation. Cooperation is an important factor with performance measures of cognitive disability; patients often refuse to attempt to do tasks that might expose a deficiency. Leather lacing, like many other crafts, lacks face validity; it does not look like a test of functional abilities. Patients who refuse to cooperate with psychological testing will often try to do the ACL or another task suggested by the therapist.

Face validity is the weakest kind of validity, but a lack of face validity can cause problems for therapists. Patients and staff members may think it is ridiculous for us to claim that we provide an objective measure of level of function from an observation of something like leather lacing. They are raising important questions, and generalizing from any observation of task performance should be done with caution. Another estimate of validity can be gained by comparing two or more instruments. The research studies described in this part of the text compare the ACL with other, frequently used, instruments. The similarities and differences between the instruments are helpful in defining the functional performance being measured (Fox, 1969). The instruments selected measure the symptoms of a disease and other definitions of cognitive functioning. Demographic characteristics that might supply alternative explanations for task performance are also considered. Task performance as restricted by a mental disorder can encompass just about anything. The performance of routine tasks has served as a conceptual target because they are apt to be the most important to the patient and their caregivers.

PREDICTING ROUTINE TASK PERFORMANCE

The cognitive level is assessed during the performance of a routine task. The quality of the process is measured. It is thought that one can generalize about the quality of the process from one task to another, that is, from leather lacing to the provision of food, clothing, and shelter. The predictive validity of this generalization requires empirical study. Some steps have been taken toward this goal.

Craft activities often seem to be removed from the provision of food, clothing, and shelter but were investigated first for clinical reasons: Most patients are willing to do them, and therapists have a great deal of experience in observing craft performance. The first generalizations made were from one craft project to the next, that is, from leather lacing to copper tooling. Gradually, criteria for generalizing to other tasks were postulated and refined.

Selecting specific tasks that operationally define the ability to provide oneself with food, clothing, and shelter can skew an assessment in several ways. Cultural bias, individual differences, and the personal values of the author or authors of the assessment tool can be detected. The tasks that are freest from bias are related to biologic functions; everyone must eat, drink, eliminate, and get dressed. Tasks that must be done by all human beings to sustain life and maintain physical health can be universally agreed on as important (see Chap. 2, Routine Task Inventory). The acceptable level of performance of the universal tasks is subject to individual differences.

"Street people" provide a startling example of individual choices. They sleep on the street, eat at missions or out of trash bins, and carry all of their personal belongings in shopping bags. The right to freedom of choice may include the right to live on the streets. The question must be asked: When is a person unable to make the choice? Probably somewhere around level 4, but performance of specific routine tasks may have to be assessed to make a decision in individual cases.

A prediction of routine task performance can be confounded by the selection of the task. If the patient has no intention of doing the task, a prediction is meaningless. The identification of universal tasks helps the therapist suggest tasks that are apt to be selected by many individuals. The quality of performance can be objectively observed by the therapist. Decisions involving the acceptable quality of performance extend beyond the patient and the therapist and may engage the patient's family or legal advocates.

Predictions of routine task performance are made to provide guidelines for establishing the patient's place in the community. A cognitive disability may necessitate restricting the patient's access to locations that would endanger the health and well-being of self or others. The goal is to provide as much access as possible. The assessment of the cognitive level can be used as a general indicator of the severity of the disability. In addition, the selection of a community placement that would restrict access must consider the individual differences presented by each case and the available community resources. It is hoped that the assessment of the cognitive level, coupled with observations of relevant routine tasks, will be useful in setting creditable standards of community support needed by people with cognitive disabilities.

Health Status Measures

There is a growing awareness of a need for health status indicators beyond the usual life expectancy measures. A number of ways of measuring health status are discussed in the recent literature (Anastasi, 1982; Bergner et al., 1981; Bergner and Gilson, 1981; Jette, 1980; Kaplan et al., 1976; Liang and Jette, 1981). Some of the measures identify physical disabilities or communication problems, but many contain routine tasks. The relationship between the cognitive levels and these health status indicators is just beginning to be explored, and they are mentioned here as a conceptual target. The process of setting priorities on information is easier when one has some idea about the potential use of the information; that may sound easy, but health status seems to be an easy target to lose.

REFERENCES

Albert, M. S. Geriatric neuropsychology. *J. Consult. Clin. Psychol.* 49:835–850, 1981.

Anastasia, A. *Psychological Testing* (5th ed.). New York: Macmillan, 1982.

Appelbaum, P. S., and Hamm, R. M. Decision to seek commitment: Psychiatric decision making in a legal context. *Arch. Gen. Psychiatry* 39:447–451, 1982.

Appelbaum, P. S., Mirkin, S. A., and Bateman, A. L. Empirical assessment of competency to consent to psychiatric hospitalization. *Am. J. Psychiatry* 183:1170–1176, 1981.

Bergner, M., Bobbitt, R. A., Carter, W. B., and Gilson, B. S. The sickness impact profile: Development and final revision of a health status measure. *Med. Care* 19:787–805, 1981.

Bergner, M., and Gilson, B. S. The Sickness Impact Profile: The Relevance of Social Science for Medicine. In L. Eisenberg and A. Kleinman (eds.), *The Relevance of Social Science to Medicine.* Dordrecht, Netherlands: Reidel, 1981.

Brown, G., and Desforges, C. *Piaget's Theory: A Psychological Critique.* Boston: Routledge & Kegal Paul, 1979.

Bukatmen, B. A., Foy, J. L., and Degrazia, E. What is competency to stand trial? *Am. J. Psychiatry* 127:1225–1229, 1981.

Daniel, A. E., Harris, P. W., and Husain, S. A. Differences between female offenders and those younger than 40. *Am. J. Psychiatry* 138:1225–1228, 1981.

Flavell, J. H. Stage-related properties of cognitive development. *Cognitive Psychol.* 2:421–453, 1971.

Fox, D. J. *The Research Process in Education.* New York: Holt, Reinhart & Winston, 1969.

Furth, H. G. *Piaget and Knowledge: Theoretical Foundations.* Englewood Cliffs, N.J.: Prentice-Hall, 1969.

Hamilton, J. R. Diminished responsibility. *Br. J. Psychiatry* 138:434–436, 1981.

Jette, A. M. Health status indicators: Their utility in chronic-disease evaluation research. *J. Chronic Dis.* 33:567–579, 1980.

Kaplan, R. M., Bush, J. W., and Berry, C. C. Health status: Types of validity and the index of well-being. *Health Serv. Res.* 11:478–507, 1976.

Keenan, J. S. *A Procedure Manual in Speech Pathology with Brain-Damaged Adults.* Danville, Ill.: Institute, 1975.

Lamb, H. R., and Grant, M. S. The mentally ill in an urban county jail. *Arch. Gen. Psychiatry* 39:17–22, 1982.

Lebegue, B., and Clark, L. D. Incompetence to refuse treatment: A necessary condition for treatment. *Am. J. Psychiatry* 138:1075–1077, 1981.

Liang, M. H., and Jette, A. M. Measuring functional ability in chronic arthritis: A critical review. *Arthritis Rheum.* 24:80–86, 1981.

Lipsitt, P. D., Lelos, D., and McGarry, L. Competency for trial: A screening instrument. *Am. J. Psychiatry* 128:105–109, 1971.

Maloney, M. P., and Ward, M. P. *Psychological Assessment: A Conceptual Approach.* New York: Oxford University Press, 1976.

Matlin, M. W. *Perception.* Boston: Allyn and Bacon, 1983.

Munetz, M. R., Kaufman, K. R., and Rich, C. L. Modernization of a mental health act: II. Outcome effects. *J. Clin. Psychiatry* 42:333–337, 1981.

Piaget, J. *Biology and Knowledge: An Essay on the Relations Between Organic Regulation and Cognitive Processes,* transl. by B. Walsh. Chicago: University of Chicago Press, 1971.

Piaget, J. *Behavior and Evolution,* transl. by D. Nicholson-Smith. New York: Pantheon, 1978.

Porch, B. E. *Porch Index of Communicative Ability.* Palo Alto, Calif.: Consulting Psychological Press, 1967. Vols. I and II.

Shanok, S. S., and Lewis, D. D. Medical histories of female delinquents: Clinical and epidemiologic findings. *Arch. Gen. Psychiatry* 38:211–213, 1981.

Stone, A. A. *Mental Health and Law: A System in Transition.* New York: Jason Aronson, 1976.

Stone, A. A. The right to refuse treatment: Why psychiatrists should and can make it work. *Arch. Gen. Psychiatry* 38:211–213, 1981.

Weinstein, H. C. Psychiatry on trial: Clinical and ethical problems in the psychiatric assessment of competency to stand trial. *Ann. N.Y. Acad. Sci.* 347:12–19, 1980.

Wilding, J. M. *Perception: From Sense to Object.* London: Hutchinson, 1982.

CHAPTER 12

RESEARCH WITH SCHIZOPHRENIC SUBJECTS

Schizophrenic disorders were selected for the first empirical studies for a number of pragmatic and theoretical reasons. At the time these studies were done it was thought that people with schizophrenia occupied one-third to one-half of all psychiatric hospital beds. In addition a disturbance in thinking has been accepted as a diagnostic symptom since the early distinction was made between schizophrenic and primary affective disorders. Finally Herzig (1978) had access to some collected data that might provide some answers to questions about the relationship between the cognitive levels and other predictors of community adjustment.

LITERATURE REVIEW

Studies of schizophrenia had been troubled by ambiguities in sample selection criteria, poor research design, and inconsistent descriptions of the thought disorder. Herzig (1978) and Moore (1978) decided to use the sample selection criteria referred to as the Feighner criteria (Feighner et al., 1972; Goodwin and Guze, 1979; Woodruff et al., 1974). The Feighner criteria (Table 12-1) were influential in establishing the *DSM III* (1980) criteria. Both require a 6-month duration of poor social adjustment that cannot be explained by an affective disorder. A later study lends additional support for requiring a 6-month duration (Helzer et al., 1981).

The numerous definitions of a schizophrenic thought disorder that have been used in the interdisciplinary literature can make a literature review seem analogous to reading written "production[s] making communication difficult due to lack of logical or understandable organization" (Feighner et al., 1972). At the time this literature review was done, most studies emphasized the verbal content of speech with few attempts to study motor performance. Herzig (1978) and Moore (1978) examined the literature to locate studies that explained the thought disorder in ways that might parallel the discription of a cognitive disability. They found that many of the studies used instruments that could be

Table 12-1. Feighner criteria for diagnosing a schizophrenic disorder

Schizophrenia (For a diagnosis of schizophrenia, A through C are required.)

A. Both of the following are necessary:
   1. A chronic illness with at least six months of symptoms prior to the index evaluation without return to the premorbid level of psychosocial adjustment
   2. Absence of a period of depressive or manic symptoms sufficient to qualify for affective disorder or probable affective disorder
B. The patient must have at least one of the following:*
   1. Delusions or hallucinations without significant perplexity or disorientation associated with them
   2. Verbal production that makes communication difficult because of a lack of logical or understandable organization (in presence of muteness, diagnostic decision deferred)
C. At least three of the following manifestations must be present for a diagnosis of "definite" schizophrenia, and two for a diagnosis of "probable" schizophrenia:
   1. Single
   2. Poor premorbid social adjustment or work history
   3. Family history of schizophrenia
   4. Absence of alcoholism or drug abuse within one year of onset of psychosis
   5. Onset of illness prior to age 40

*We recognize that many patients with schizophrenia have a characteristic blunted or inappropriate affect; however, when it occurs in mild form, interrater agreement is difficult to achieve. We believe that, on the basis of presently available information, blunted affect occurs rarely or not at all in the absence of B.1. or B.2.
Source: J. P. Feighner, et al. Diagnostic criteria for use in psychiatric research. *Arch. Gen. Psychiatry* 26:57–63, 1972. Copyright 1972, American Medical Association.

interpreted as classification tasks. Some of the earliest work was done by Goldstein and Scheerer (1941); Goldstein, (1946), used numerous object-sorting tasks, and he reported that schizophrenic subjects, as well as brain-damaged individuals, generally failed to sort objects according to conventional categories. Two modes of thinking, concrete and abstract, were proposed to explain this phenomenon. An alternative explanation for difficulties in object-sorting tasks was proposed by McGaughran and Moran (1956), who suggested that schizophrenic subjects group objects according to idiosyncratic or "private" concepts, as opposed to the "public" criteria used by normal subjects. Interference theory was used to explain problems in sorting tasks by Cameron (1939), who suggested that the patients were unable to screen out extraneous stimuli; other researchers thought the problem was caused by a deficit in attention and the arousal mechanisms (McGhie and Chapman, 1961; McGhie et al., 1965). While the explanations of the deficit varied, these studies consistently demonstrated that schizophrenic subjects had problems in doing object-sorting tasks.

The object-sorting tasks seem to be similar to the classification tasks described by Piaget. Classification schemes emerge during the preoperational and concrete operational periods of development (Furth, 1969; Inhelder and Piaget, 1964). However, the proposed cognitive levels were suggested by Piaget's earlier sensorimotor period. Herzig and Moore reasoned that object-sorting tasks might be above the schizophrenic patient's range of ability; this would explain the reported difficulties with such tasks.

Other studies that examined the schizophrenic thought disorder from a Piagetian perspective were examined. Studies conducted by Trunnell (1964, 1965) suggested some similarities and differences among normal adults, schizophrenic adults, and normal children (6 to 12 years old). Subjects performed four tasks requiring object sorting, puzzle solving, combining colors, and identifying a common property of a group of objects. On all four tasks there were significant differences ($p < .05$) between the following groups:

1. Among adults there were differences between normal and schizophrenic subjects.
2. Among normal subjects there were differences between adults and children.

The schizophrenic adults performed better than the children on two tasks requiring verbal ability ($p < .01$, $p < .048$), but the difference was not significant on the other two tasks. Trunnell's studies suggested that one can expect to find similarities and differences in thought processes between normal children and adults with a schizophrenic disorder. These studies suggested that the developmental perspective may have a limited application.

Preoperational and concrete operational thinking was studied by Hamilton (1966). Again, children (mean age 12.2 years) and schizophrenic adults were compared. Significant differences were found on conservation tasks ($p < .05$) and perspective tasks ($p < .001$) but not on seriation tasks. The children performed better than the schizophrenic adults, which suggested that those with the disorder may be at a lower developmental level.

Another interpretation of the Piagetian hierarchy as applied to schizophrenic adults has been suggested (Kay and Singh, 1975; Kay et al., 1975). Tests designed to tap the sensorimotor period examined color and form preferences. The proposed hierarchy, which included perseveration, random responsiveness, color dominance, and form dominance, was thought to span the second stage of the sensorimotor period to the preoperational period. A second version of the test examined symbolic representation. Subjects were asked to match a standard card with three comparison cards. The matching criterion was recorded. Kay and colleagues were able to differentiate schizophrenic subjects from normal controls and from nonpsychotic patients. An additional differentiation was made between acute schizophrenics with a favorable response to medication and chronic schizophrenics who did not respond. These studies used operational definitions of sensorimotor performance that are different from the description of the cognitive levels in this text. It does appear, however, that there is some kind of sensorimotor disturbance in schizophrenia that impairs performance and that a measure of this deficit can be used to describe treatment effectiveness.

The literature reviewed suggests that the thought disorder associated with schizophrenia contains some elements associated with early stages of development. Although these studies describe certain properties of normal cognition that differentiate schizophrenic thought from normal thought, their application is restricted. They tell us what the patient cannot do and neglect what the patient can do, and they do not account for past experiences. The description of the cognitive levels contains abilities and disabilities with some control for past experiences. The cognitive levels may be helpful in refining the similarities, and differences, between disabled adults, normal adults, and children.

The occupational therapy literature contains some interesting departures from the literature of other mental health disciplines. Early occupational therapists established a tradition of recognizing a hierarchical relationship between cognition and the performance of activities (AOTA, 1924; Bowman, 1922; Gustafson, 1925; Marsh, 1932; Meyer, 1922; Saunders, 1925; Slagle, 1934). Therapists have continued to suggest that early ontogeny can be used to describe a disability that must be considered during the presentation of therapeutic tasks (Gilfoyle and Grady, 1971; Gillette, 1971; MacDonald et al., 1972). The occupational therapy literature has suggested that the stages of the Piagetian sensorimotor period can be applied to disabled populations (Kopp, 1974; Levy, 1974; Wursten, 1974). It seems that early development is particularly helpful in identifying tasks that the patients can do. Occupational therapists are particularly interested in early development because our treatment methods require a description of what the patient can and cannot do. The emphasis on early development, however, is largely speculative; empirical investigation is required.

COMMUNITY ADJUSTMENT

A study of the relationship between cognitive level and community adjustment (Herzig, 1978) was influenced by a rare opportunity to take advantage of some data that had already been collected. Morguelan (1977) generously offered to enter the cognitive level at discharge into a series of factors that he had identified as predictors of community adjustment. The range of factors considered promised to provide some insight into the relative importance of the cognitive levels through a stepwise multiple regression analysis. Morguelan had identified 15 predictive factors; one was related to occupational therapy. The average earnings paid by an occupational therapist (Catherine Earhart) as a part of a token economy had some predictive validity. We were curious about the relative predictive validity of the cognitive level at the time of discharge from the hospital.

The problem that Herzig (1978) defined for study was the relationship between the cognitive levels and community adjustment in chronic schizophrenic subjects after discharge from a work rehabilitation unit of an inpatient psychiatric hospital. The questions investigated included the following (Herzig, 1978):

1. Is there a correlation between the schizophrenic individual's cognitive level and community adjustment? Will higher cognitive levels be associated with better community adjustment? Will lower cognitive levels be associated with poorer community adjustment?
2. Do the cognitive levels have a stronger relationship to certain dimensions of community adjustment than to others?

The specific objectives of the investigation (Herzig, 1978) were

1. To determine by retrospective study whether cognitive levels at time of hospital discharge predicted community adjustment three months post discharge, as measured by the Personal Adjustment and Role Skills Scale, fifth version (Ellsworth, 1975);
2. To determine by retrospective study whether cognitive levels had a stronger relationship to some dimensions of community adjustment than to oth-

ers, three months post discharge;
3. To establish interrater reliability in the assessment of cognitive levels utilizing a Work Performance Inventory;
4. To determine the extent to which two versions of the Work Performance Inventory correlated, in order to employ both versions for the assessment of cognitive levels.

Samples

The study used two samples. The first sample was composed of 20 inpatients on one ward of Los Angeles County–University of Southern California (LAC–USC) Medical Center who met the Feighner criteria (1972) for a schizophrenic disorder. Informed consent and review for the protection of human subjects were obtained. This sample was used to fulfill objectives 3 and 4.

The second sample consisted of those who had participated in Morguelan's (1977) study. Subjects had been inpatients on the same ward and also met the Feighner (1972) criteria.

Instruments

The validity and reliability of an assessment of the cognitive levels had never been investigated, so an effort was made to provide some control for these obvious deficiencies. Herzig's (1978) study included a retrospective analysis of the cognitive level that had been recorded on the Work Performance Inventory (see Chap. 10) by one therapist (Earhart). Morguelan's study was prospective, but the Work Performance Inventory had been revised during the course of his study. The problem of two versions of the form was corrected by having two independent raters (Earhart and Herzig) score the second version from data on the first version ($N = 20$); the scores were identical ($r = 1.0$).

The unestablished reliability of a retrospective assessment was a serious limitation of the study. Some credibility for the assessment was sought by selecting a common work task (scratch pad assembly), standardizing the procedure, and identifying evaluation criteria (see the appendix to this chapter). Interrater reliability (between Earhart and Herzig) was established in a new group of patients with a probable diagnosis of schizophrenia ($r = 1.0$; $N = 20$; range, levels 3 to 6); these patients were not included in Morguelan's study.

Records for the discharge cognitive level were located for 74 of the patients in Morguelan's study. The distribution of the cognitive level scores at discharge was as follows (Herzig, 1978):

LEVEL	NUMBER OF PATIENTS
2	2
3	4
4	26
5	12
6	30

The mean level was 4.82 (standard deviation, 1.07).

The cognitive level was added to the factors selected by Morguelan (1977) as predictors of community adjustment (Table 12-2). Items 1 through 7 were taken from the Ullman-Giovannoni scale (1964), a patient self-report measure; items 8 through 10, were taken from Langfeldt's prognostic features (1956); items 11 through 14 are demographic variables, and item 15 is the average earnings paid per day in the hospital by the occupational therapist. The factors are interesting in that most of them describe the patient's past experience, with emphasis on marital status and work history. These factors were used to predict community adjustment 3 months after discharge from the hospital.

The instrument used to measure community adjustment was the Personal Adjustment and Role Skills Scale, fifth version (PARS V) (Ellsworth, 1975). Originally designed with separate scales for males and females, Morguelan (1977) selected the items that pertain to both sexes (Table 12-3). Ratings were based on information obtained during a telephone interview of a significant other (e.g., family member, friend, group home operator). Item 29, on Factor Scale 2, was dichotomous (zero = no, one

Table 12-2. Biographic, demographic, and symptoms variables comprising a predictor scale of community adjustment

1. UGS item 1: When I leave the hospital I will live with my wife/husband.
2. UGS item 4: I have been married.
3. UGS item 7: As a civilian I have worked steadily at one job or for one employer for over two years.
4. UGS item 9: Adding up all the money I have earned in the last three years, it comes to less than $700 before deductions.
5. UGS item 16: Shortly before I came into the hospital there was some major change in my life (e.g., marriage, birth of a baby, death, injury, loss of job).
6. UGS item 19: My top wage in the last five years was less than $1.65 per hour.
7. UGS item 21: I have had to stay in a mental hospital for more than one year at a time.
8. LPF 1: Good premorbid adjustment.
9. LPF 2: Precipitating factors.
10. LPF 6: Dreamlike or altered state of consciousness.
11. Marital status.
12. Chronological age.
13. Sex.
14. Age at onset.
15. Average earnings per day in hospital.

UGS = Ullman-Giovannoni (1964) scale; LPF = Langfeldt (1956) prognostic feature.
Source: F. N. Morguelan, The development and validation of a measure including demographic, biographical and symptom-related items for the prediction of community adjustment of schizophrenic patients. University of Southern California Ph.D. Dissertation, 1978.

= yes). All other items were scored as follows. A score of 0 was entered if performance was unknown and 1 to 4 points were given for other responses: 1, rarely; 2, sometimes; 3, usually; 4, always; or 1, never; 2, rarely; 3, sometimes; 4, often. These scores are based on the *frequency* of performance. Reliability and validity data are available for this instrument (Ellsworth et al., 1968; Fontana and

Table 12-3. Community adjustment

Factor scale 1. household activities
  Item 1. During the last month, has he shown
         consideration for you?
  Item 4. During the last month, has he been able to
         talk it through when angry?
  Item 25. During the last month, has he helped with
         chores around the house?
  Item 26. During the last month, has he done
         household cleaning?
  Item 27. During the last month, has he prepared
         meals for the family?
  Item 28. During the last month, has he done laundry,
         ironing, or mending?
Factor scale 2. relationship with children
  Item 29. Are there usually children in the home?
  Item 31. During the last month, has he shown
         affection toward the children?
  Item 32. During the last month, has he kept his
         promises to the children?
Factor scale 3. excessive use of alcohol and/or drugs
  Item 20. During the last month, has he been drinking
         alcohol to excess?
  Item 21. During the last month, has he been using
         drugs excessively?
  Item 22. During the last month, has he become drunk
         on alcohol or high on drugs?
  Item 23. During the last month, has he had a drinking
         problem that upset his relationship with
         family?
Factor scale 4. anxiety
  Item 12. During the last month, has he been
         nervous?
  Item 13. During the last month, has he acted restless
         and tense?
  Item 14. During the last month, has he had difficulty
         sleeping?
  Item 17. During the last month, has he forgotten to
         do important things?
  Item 18. During the last month, has he been in a daze
         or confused?
  Item 19. During the last month, has he needed
         supervision or guidance?
Factor scale 5. outside and/or social activities
  Item 34. During the last month, has he been involved
         in activities outside the home?

  Item 35. During the last month, has he attended
         meetings of civic, church, or other
         organizations?
  Item 36. During the last month, has he participated in
         recreational activities outside the home
         (sports, movies, dances, etc.)?
  Item 37. During the last month, has he looked for or
         obtained employment?
  Item 39. From working, did he earn an adequate
         amount of money last month?

Source: F. N. Morguelan, The development and validation of a measure including demographic, biographical and symptom-related items for the prediction of community adjustment of schizophrenic patients. University of Southern California Ph.D. Dissertation, 1977; adapted from R. B. Ellsworth, Measuring community adjustment of clinic clients and hospital patients: A manual for the PARS V Adjustment Scale. Salem, Virginia: V.A. Hospital, 1975.

Dowds, 1975; Morguelan, 1977; Morguelan et al., 1978).

Results

The cognitive level at discharge showed a low correlation with social adjustment (PARS V scores) 3 months after discharge. The Pearson product-moment correlation coefficients between the cognitive level and PARS V scores (total score, the score for each of the five factor scales, and the score for each individual item), as well as the other predictive factors, were low, ranging from $r = -0.2$ to $r = +0.3$. The strongest correlation was between the cognitive level at discharge and the average earnings per day in the hospital ($r = 0.33$, $p < .05$, as a continuous variable). Low correlation coefficients indicate a weak contribution to a stepwise multiple regression analysis.

The cognitive level was a moderately promising predictor of one dimension of community adjustment, anxiety, factor scale 4. (The scale may be misnamed; the items may reflect some of the disabling effects of psychosis.) The cognitive level entered in at step 1 in the stepwise multiple regression analysis ($r = 0.216$; $r^2 = 0.047$; $r_c^2 = 0.033$; $F = 3.52$; $p <$

Table 12-4. Step entry of cognitive level as predictor of community adjustment of 74 schizophrenic subjects

Cognitive level	Step entry					
	Factor scale 1: household activities	Factor scale 2: relationship with children	Factor scale 3: drug or alcohol abuse	Factor scale 4: anxiety	Factor scale 5: outside or social activities	Total factor scale
As continuous variable	14	11	14	4	14	15
As dichotomous variable	9	13	14	1	14	9

Source: S. I. Herzig, Occupational therapy assessment of cognitive levels as predictors of community adjustment of chronic schizophrenic patients. University of Southern California Master's Thesis, 1978.

.10).* This contribution was made when the cognitive level was used as a dichotomous variable, separating the levels into two groups—one comprising levels 2 through 4; the other levels 5 and 6. The division was based on the clinical impression that there is a big difference between levels 4 and 5. The regression analysis indicated that the cognitive level, as a dichotomous variable, accounted for approximately 4.7 percent of the variance of the anxiety scale. The cognitive level, when entered as a continuous or a dichotomous variable, accounted for less than 1 percent of the variance of all of the other factors and the total scale score.

Discussion

The use of the cognitive level as a continuous and dichotomous variable has some statistical and practical implications. Cognitive level attained a higher predictive rank as a dichotomous variable than as a continuous variable on three scales: household activities, anxiety, and the total factor scale (Table 12-4). As a dichotomous variable, cognitive level had a lower rank on one factor, relationship with children. If we assume that the cognitive level is a stronger predictor as a dichotomous variable, the assumption may imply that the cognitive levels are an ordinal

*r = coefficient of multiple correlation; r^2 = coefficient of multiple determination; r^2_c = coefficient of multiple determination corrected for shrinkage; F = variance ratio.

but not an interval scale. This suggests that the rank order of the levels—the sequence from profound disability to normative ability—is correct. But on an ordinal scale the distance between items is not necessarily the same; in this case the differences in community adjustment may be greater between level 4 and level 5 than between 3 and 4 or between 5 and 6. Statisticians frequently recommend nonparametric statistics for ordinal scales. In practice therapists may need to recommend very different community placements for patients assessed at level 4 than for those at level 5; the recommendations for those at 3 and 4 may be similar, as may recommendations for those at 5 and 6. This difficulty—that what you assumed was an interval scale turns out, on closer inspection, to be an ordinal scale—is a common complication in the study of human behavior. While these data are far from conclusive, they did suggest a potential problem that merited further consideration.

The regression analysis suggested that the therapist's report of the patient's cognitive level is a poorer predictor of community adjustment than the patient's age at onset of the disease, sex, work history, altered state of consciousness, past record of hospitalizations, and marital history (Table 12-5). When all of the predictors are combined, about 42 percent of the variance is accounted for (Table 12-5, entry 16, $r^2 = 0.418$). Fifty-eight percent of the variance is unexplained by the predictor variables

Table 12-5. Stepwise multiple regression analysis of predictors of community adjustment

Order of entry	Predictor variable	r	r^2	r_c^2	F
1	Age at onset	0.339	0.115	0.103	9.36[b]
2	Sex	0.484	0.234	0.213	11.02[b]
3	UGS item 19: My top wage in the last five years was less than $1.65 per hour	0.560	0.313	0.284	8.07[b]
4	LPF 6: Dreamlike or altered state of consciousness	0.583	0.340	0.301	2.76[a]
5	UGS item 9: Adding up all the money I have earned in the last three years, it comes to less than $700 before deductions	0.604	0.365	0.318	2.69[a]
6	UGS item 21: I have had to stay in a mental hospital for more than one year at a time	0.620	0.385	0.330	2.18
7	UGS item 4: I have been married	0.629	0.396	0.332	1.25
8	Marital status	0.640	0.410	0.338	1.54
9	Cognitive level	0.643	0.413	0.331	0.35
10	LPF 1: Good premorbid adjustment	0.644	0.415	0.322	0.20
11	UGS item 7: As a civilian I have worked steadily at one job or for one employer for over two years	0.645	0.416	0.312	0.06
12	Average earnings per day in hospital	0.645	0.417	0.302	0.08
13	UGS item 1: When I leave the hospital I will live with my wife/husband	0.646	0.417	0.291	0.04
14	LPF 2: Precipitating factors	0.646	0.417	0.279	0.04
15	Chronological age	0.646	0.418	0.267	0.03
16	UGS item 16: Shortly before I came into the hospital there was some major change in my life, e.g., marriage, birth of a baby, death, injury, loss of job	0.646	0.418	0.254	0.04

r = coefficient of multiple correlation; r^2 = coefficient of multiple determination; r_c^2 = coefficient of multiple determination corrected for shrinkage; F = contribution of predictor variable to proportion of variance of the outcome measure; UGS = Ullman-Giovannoni (1964) scale; LPF = Langsfeldt (1956) prognostic feature.
[a]$p < .05$.
[b]$p < .01$.
Source: S. I. Herzig, Occupational therapy assessment of cognitive levels as predictors of community adjustment of chronic schizophrenic patients. University of Southern California Master's Thesis, 1978.

studied. One perspective gained from this study is that the cognitive level is one variable among many that can predict future task performance.

Another perspective began to emerge during the data analysis—a hunch that we were using apples to predict oranges. The discontinuity can be seen in the instruments. The scratch pad assembly (Appendix 12-1) involves a highly specific description of the quality of performance with controls for the available physical objects and interpersonal transactions.

The occupational therapy instrument is designed to provide sufficient detail so that another therapist could read the description and replicate the task. Elements of the task environment are controlled to obtain an objective appraisal of the patient's quality of task performance. The content and frequency of performance are a secondary consideration in the assessment of the *quality* of task performance. Content and frequency are separated from observations made during task performance; usually therapists discuss content and frequency with the patient before the task begins.

The PARS V scale provides a general description of task content (e.g., household cleaning, preparing meals) and asks how often the person has done it (never, sometimes, often, almost always). False results may be obtained with these measures. For example, a false negative result may be obtained with a person who has never done any meal preparation or has no access to cooking facilities. A false positive may be obtained with a person who dusts a corner of the dining room table several times a day but leaves the rest of the table dirty. Frequent efforts may or may not be adequate and respondents may vary in their interpretation of the question. Assessing adults with cognitive disabilities would seem to be more apt to produce false positives because adults retain some familiar responses to the environment but may not meet an *acceptable* standard of performance.

Two words that set off warning signals in the minds of many behavioral scientists are *acceptable* and *appropriate*. The danger is that these interpretations rely on a personal opinion that may be influenced by an awareness of a disability or reduced social expectations. It is hoped that detailed descriptions like the one given for scratch pad assembly can circumvent some of these problems with interpretation. Specific details are obtained at a cost; it takes a long time to observe the performance and record the observations. One cannot observe everything, selections must be made, but we lack selection criteria. Time constraints and the absence of selection criteria may explain the absence of detail in the professional literature. Most research instruments, like the PARS V, aim for a general estimate of performance over a wide scope of activities. This study led to a reexamination of general estimates.

The PARS V contains a scope of content frequently found in the occupational therapy literature. The frustration that resulted from attempting to analyze the correlations seemed to parallel common clinical frustrations: We kept wondering, What

is *really* happening here? Or, how can I convince someone that this person is *really* disabled? The generalist approach touches lightly on many daily living activities but fails to provide an adequate description of the quality of performance. The person can get an *A* for effort, but the outcome of this effort is not measured. Here the frustration is produced by a report that fails to examine the quality of the process, indeed, that actually seems to gloss over problems with a person's functional performance. One could look at a person and see evidence of a disability in his or her personal appearance, but it would not show up on the research instrument. The general estimate of a wide scope of activities may be achieved at the cost of obscuring the severity of a disability. A decision was made to attempt to find an alternative to the general estimates. The studies that follow trace those attempts.

INSTRUMENT DEVELOPMENT

A second study (Moore, 1978) also focused on problems in assessing the cognitive level. The largest methodologic problem encountered in Herzig's (1978) study was with a retrospective assessment of the cognitive level. The scratch pad assembly task indicated that one could develop a reliable instrument that measured performance on one task. Scratch pad assembly, however, has some practical constraints: The task takes at least 10 minutes to complete and may take appreciably longer (30 to 60 minutes) with depressed patients; it may also require the use of scissors. The first assessment of the cognitive level may be done on an acute inpatient ward with people admitted because they are a danger to themselves or others. Hence we wanted to avoid scissors, we wanted a test that could be scored quickly, and we wanted to continue doing an in-depth analysis of one task. Even with these decisions made, a confusing array of related issues remained to be considered.

Moore's (1978) study was divided into two sections: experimental and descriptive. The experimental section was devoted to the development of the Allen Cognitive Level Test (ACL; see Chap. 4). The reliability and validity of the test, as it was being used in practice (to place patients in occupational therapy groups), was examined. This section of the study also examined the reliability of a Group Performance Rating (GPR). The cognitive levels were also being used to report changes in functional abilities: The study examined the ACL score at admission and discharge and looked at potentially associated changes in physician ratings (the Brief Psychiatric Rating Scale or BPRS). The following questions were addressed:

1. What is the interrater reliability for the ACL?
2. What is the interrater reliability for the GPR?
3. What is the predictive validity of the ACL?
4. What improvement occurs in ACL scores between admission and discharge?
5. What improvement occurs on the BPRS?
6. Is there an association between ACL scores and BPRS scores?

The descriptive section of the study began the process of examining the demographic variables that might be associated with cognitive level, community placement, or this particular sample of hospitalized schizophrenic adults. The following questions were addressed:

1. What were the characteristics of this sample on selected demographic variables?
2. What was the relationship between discharge ACL score and type of community placement, that is, place of residence and type of employment?
3. Did the ACL scores, as measured at admission or discharge, or the degree of change in ACL score during hospitalization, correlate with any of the following variables: age, intelligence, education, length of time since first hospitalization, previous leather lacing experience?

The experimental section aimed at refining an operational definition of the cognitive levels by be-

ginning to examine the reliability and validity of the ACL. The descriptive section began to examine independent variables that might, or might not, be associated with the ACL score.

Subjects

Moore (1978) decided to continue the investigations with schizophrenic subjects. Subjects were excluded from Moore's study who were less than 18 or more than 65 years old or had evidence of (1) mental retardation (IQ below 75), (2) an organic mental disorder, (3) a seizure disorder, (4) a vision disorder, or (5) a hearing disorder. Subjects were inpatients on any ward of the psychiatric hospital at LAC–USC Medical Center; informed consent and review for the protection of human subjects were obtained.

Allen Cognitive Level Test

Reliability

The task that Moore (1978) decided to refine was the leather lacing task (see Chap. 4), which had been used in practice at the medical center for several years. The first step in instrument development is to establish the reliability of the instrument. Moore selected interrater reliability: five rater pairs, consisting of Moore and five experienced therapists, were established. The therapists had participated in developing the testing procedure, based on their clinical experiences in administering the test in a variety of ways. Independent ratings established interrater reliability as $r = 0.99$, by using the Pearson product-moment correlation (range, levels 2 to 6; $N = 32$; degrees of freedom, or $df, = 30$). Disagreement between independent raters occurred with one subject.

Prediction of Group Placement

Moore (1978) selected a modest approach to predictive validity: examining the ACL's value in placing patients in the correct occupational therapy groups.

Table 12-6. ACL scores at admission and discharge with reported change in score*

ACL	Cognitive levels				
	2	3	4	5	6
Admission ACL	4	2	14	2	3
Discharge ACL	0	2	7	9	7
Change in ACL	−1	−1; +1	0	+1; +2; +3	0; +1; +2
			0	+1 +3	0 +2
			0; +1; +2	+1	0 +2
			0	+1	
			0	+1	

ACL = Allen Cognitive Level Test.

*N = 25.

Source: Adapted from D. S. Moore, An occupational therapy evaluation of sensorimotor cognition: Initial reliability, validity and descriptive data for hospitalized schizophrenic adults. University of Southern California Master's Thesis, 1978.

Six pairs of therapists who had no knowledge of the ACL score or the past experiences of the patient rated the patient's performance for appropriateness of group placement (GPR): levels 3 and 4 versus 5 and 6. (The GPR was given within 48 hours after the ACL was administered.) The interrater reliability for the GPR was established ($r = 0.69$); there was one disagreement between two raters in a sample of 23 patients ($df = 21$). The validity of using the ACL score to place patients in groups was established ($r = 0.76$; $N = 23$; $df = 21$). Both independent raters agreed that one patient received an inappropriate group placement; another subject produced disagreement between the raters.

Associations with Descriptive Data

Moore (1978) also collected data on the relationship between the ACL score and other frequent variables considered with a schizophrenic population. The initial ACL was administered within 72 hours of admission to the hospital; a second test was administered at discharge. Of 25 patients tested twice, 16 had a change in ACL score from admission to discharge (Table 12-6). The change in ACL score ranged from −1 cognitive level (one patient) to +3 cognitive levels (two patients).

Practicing therapists have often expressed an interest in the raw data displayed in Table 12-6. The scores suggest that there is a wide variation in the severity of schizophrenic disorders and in the effectiveness of neuroleptic drugs. Less than half of the sample were discharged at levels 3 and 4, and only one-fifth were a stable level 4. Our clinical impressions may cause us to overestimate the number of people who have a chronic disability. In a replication of this study with a larger sample, it would be interesting to see if the cognitive levels can be helpful in differentiating between acute and chronic schizophrenic disorders.

Similarities and differences between the ACL score and the BPRS (Fig. 12-1) score were examined. The BPRS is a commonly used assessment of changes in psychopathology. Scores range from 18 to 126; 18 indicates an absence of psychopathology. The scoring system is the reverse of that for the ACL; lower numbers on the BPRS show improvement. Thus a negative correlation between ACL and BPRS scores would be expected. The interrater reliability on the BPRS has been established for each of the 18 items; it ranges from $r = 0.57$ to $r = 0.87$ (Overall and Gorham, 1962). The BPRS was completed by the treating physician on the days that the ACL was administered, at admission and

Date ____

Rater ____

No. ____

Patient ____

Directions: Draw a circle around the term under each symptom that best describes the patient's present condition.

1. Somatic concern — Degree of concern over present bodily health. Rate the degree to which physical health is perceived as a problem by the patient, whether complaints have realistic basis or not.
Not present   Very mild   Mild   Moderate   Mod. severe   Severe   Extremely severe

2. Anxiety — Worry, fear, or over-concern for present or future. Rate solely on the basis of verbal report of patient's own subjective experiences. Do not infer anxiety from physical signs or from neurotic defense mechanisms.
Not present   Very mild   Mild   Moderate   Mod. severe   Severe   Extremely severe

3. Emotional withdrawal — Deficiency in relating to the interviewer and the interview situation. Rate only degree to which the patient gives the impression of failing to be in emotional contact with other people in the interview situation.
Not present   Very mild   Mild   Moderate   Mod. severe   Severe   Extremely severe

4. Conceptual disorganization — Degree to which the thought processes are confused, disconnected or disorganized. Rate on the basis of integration of the verbal products of the patient; do not rate on the basis of the patient's subjective impression of his own level of functioning.
Not present   Very mild   Mild   Moderate   Mod. severe   Severe   Extremely severe

5. Guilt feelings — Over-concern or remorse for past behavior. Rate on the basis of the patient's subjective experiences of guilt as evidenced by verbal report with appropriate affect; do not infer guilt feelings from depression, anxiety, or neurotic defenses.
Not present   Very mild   Mild   Moderate   Mod. severe   Severe   Extremely severe

6. Tension — Physical and motor manifestations of tension, "nervousness," and heightened activation level. Tension should be rated solely on the basis of physical signs and motor behavior and not on the basis of subjective experiences of tension reported by the patient.
Not present   Very mild   Mild   Moderate   Mod. severe   Severe   Extremely severe

7. Mannerisms and posturing — Unusual and unnatural motor behavior, the type of motor behavior which causes certain mental patients to stand out in a crowd of normal people. Rate only abnormality of movements; do not rate simple heightened motor activity here.
Not present   Very mild   Mild   Moderate   Mod. severe   Severe   Extremely severe

8. Grandiosity — Exaggerated self-opinion, conviction of unusual ability or powers. Rate only on the basis of patient's statements about himself or self-in-relation-to-others, not on the basis of his demeanor in the interview situation.
Not present   Very mild   Mild   Moderate   Mod. severe   Severe   Extremely severe

9. Depressive mood — Despondency in mood, sadness. Rate only degree of despondency; do not rate on the basis of inferences concerning depression based upon general retardation and somatic complaints.
Not present   Very mild   Mild   Moderate   Mod. severe   Severe   Extremely severe

10. Hostility — Animosity, contempt, belligerence, disdain for other people outside the interview situation. Rate solely on the basis of the verbal report of feelings and actions of the patient toward others; do not infer hostility from neurotic defenses, anxiety nor somatic complaints. (Rate attitude toward interviewer under "uncooperativeness.")
Not present   Very mild   Mild   Moderate   Mod. severe   Severe   Extremely severe

11. Suspiciousness — Belief (delusional or otherwise) that others have now, or have had in the past, malicious or discriminatory intent toward the patient. On the basis of verbal report, rate only those suspicions which are currently held whether they concern past or present circumstances.
Not present   Very mild   Mild   Moderate   Mod. severe   Severe   Extremely severe

12. Hallucinatory behavior — Perceptions without normal external stimulus correspondence. Rate only those experiences which are reported to have occurred within the last week and which are described as distinctly different from the thought and imagery processes of normal people.
Not present   Very mild   Mild   Moderate   Mod. severe   Severe   Extremely severe

13. Motor retardation — Reduction in energy level evidenced in slowed movements and speech, reduced body tone, decreased number of movements. Rate on the basis of observed behavior of the patient only; do not rate on basis of patient's subjective impression of own energy level.
Not present   Very mild   Mild   Moderate   Mod. severe   Severe   Extremely severe

14. Uncooperativeness — Evidences of resistance, unfriendliness, resentment, and lack of readiness to cooperate with the interviewer. Rate only on the basis of the patient's attitude and responses to the interviewer and the interview situation; do not rate on basis of reported resentment or uncooperativeness outside the interview situation.
Not present   Very mild   Mild   Moderate   Mod. severe   Severe   Extremely severe

15. Unusual thought content — Unusual, odd, strange, or bizarre thought content. Rate here the degree of unusualness, not the degree of disorganization of thought processes.
Not present   Very mild   Mild   Moderate   Mod. severe   Severe   Extremely severe

16. Blunted affect — Reduced emotional tone, apparent lack of normal feeling or involvement.
Not present   Very mild   Mild   Moderate   Mod. severe   Severe   Extremely severe

Fig. 12-1. Brief Psychiatric Rating Scale. (From J. E. Overall and D. R. Gorham, The brief psychiatric rating scale. Psychol. Reports 10:799–812, 1962. Reprinted with permission.)

Table 12-7. Relation between ACL score and BPRS score

BPRS score	N	df	ACL at admission	ACL at discharge
Initial	29	27	−0.53*	−0.23
Discharge	22	20	−0.36	−0.43*

*$p < .05$.
ACL = Allen Cognitive Level Test; BPRS = Brief
Psychiatric Rating Scale; df = degrees of freedom.
Source: D. S. Moore, An occupational therapy evaluation of
sensorimotor cognition: Initial reliability, validity and
description data for hospitalized schizophrenic adults.
University of Southern California Master's Thesis, 1978.

discharge. Significant correlations were found as expected (Table 12-7). Both tests showed a significant change between the admission and discharge scores (Table 12-8). The correlations provide some concurrent validity for the ACL. The *t* values provide some support for an expectation of change during the acute hospitalization of schizophrenic subjects.

Selected demographic variables were examined (Tables 12-9 and 12-10). Previous leather lacing experience was recorded as a yes or no response at the time the ACL was administered. Leather lacing was discontinued as a treatment activity from the occupational therapy groups during the course of the study to minimize any practice effect. The intelligence quotient was obtained from psychologists' reports of the results of the Quick Test (Ammons and Ammons, 1962). The interrater reliability and concurrent validity for the Quick Test established at Los Angeles County-University of Southern California Medical Center is above $r = .80$ (Maloney and Steger, 1972). All correlations between demographic variables and ACL scores were low (Table 12-11). Four *r* values reached statistical significance. Previous leather lacing experience may explain part of the variance when the cognitive level is low; at admission the mean ACL score for those with lacing experience was 3.91, and the correlation was significant; at discharge it was not. A higher educational background was associated with a greater

change in the ACL score. A longer period of hospitalization was associated with a lower ACL score at admission and discharge.

Recognizing that many factors influencing the availability of social support systems can affect discharge plans, Moore (1978) decided to examine the clinical impression that the place of residence and place of employment to which a person is discharged are influenced by the person's cognitive level (Table 12-12). These discharge plans give an indication of the social support system required by schizophrenic patients. The data obtained on the relationship between cognitive level and discharge plans suggest that this may be a promising area for further descriptive study.

Discussion

The Moore (1978) study is descriptive, delineating changing functional abilities without reference to the cause of the change. No attempt was made to describe group attendance, group methods, or the physician's treatment methods. Moore's study marked the beginning of a series of descriptive studies designed to provide a clearer picture of what a cognitive disability is, before describing programs that might produce a change.

IMPLICATIONS

One cannot draw conclusions from two small studies carried out in one institution. The studies were helpful, however, in pointing out questions requiring further investigation. The issue of whether the cognitive levels are an interval or an ordinal scale is still a concern. Herzig's (1978) data on the differences in predictive strength of cognitive level as a dichotomous variable and as a continuous variable (see Table 12-4) are not clear enough to form a conclusion. Add Moore's (1978) data concerning discharge plans (see Table 12-12), and one wonders again about a continuous variable.

Establishing correlations with an operational def-

Table 12-8. Change in ACL and BPRS scores during hospitalization of schizophrenic patients

Score	N	Admission		Discharge		t	p
		Mean	SD	Mean	SD		
ACL	25	3.91	± 1.06	4.84	± 0.94	4.43	.001
BPRS	22	53.31	± 13.34	41.82	± 15.69	3.82	.002

ACL = Allen Cognitive Level Test; BPRS = Brief Psychiatric Rating Scale.
Source: D. S. Moore, An occupational therapy evaluation of sensorimotor cognition: Initial reliability, validity and descriptive data for hospitalized schizophrenic adults. University of Southern California Master's Thesis, 1978.

Table 12-9. Characteristics of a sample of schizophrenic subjects

Characteristic	N	Mean (range)	Standard deviation
Age (years)	32	33 (19–61)	± 11
Intelligence (IQ)	11	97 (82–121)	± 12
Education (years of schooling)	31	11	± 3
Length of illness (years since first hospitalization)	30	9	± 5
Length of current hospitalization (days)	32	21	± 10

Source: D. S. Moore, An occupational therapy evaluation of sensorimotor cognition. Initial reliability, validity and descriptive data for hospitalized schizophrenic adults. University of Southern California Master's Thesis, 1978.

Table 12-10. Demographic features of a sample of schizophrenic subjects

Variable	No.	Percent	Variable	No.	Percent
Sex			Ethnicity		
Male	17	53	White	13	41
Female	15	47	Black	13	41
Marital status*			Mexican American	5	16
Single	15	48	Oriental	1	3
Divorced	7	23	Previous leather lacing experience		
Separated	5	16	No	20	62
Married	4	13	Yes	12	37

*Marital status for one subject was not available.
Source: D. S. Moore, An occupational therapy evaluation of sensorimotor cognition: Initial reliability, validity and descriptive data for hospitalized schizophrenic adults. University of Southern California Master's Thesis, 1978.

Table 12-11. Relation of demographic variables to ACL score in schizophrenic subjects

Variable	N	df	Correlation with ACL score (r)		
			Admission	Discharge	Change
Previous leather lacing	32	30	+0.38*	+0.22	−0.10
Age	32	30	−0.15	+0.06[a]	−0.01
Education	31	29	+0.04	−0.27	+0.35[b]
Length of illness	30	28	+0.09	+0.14	−0.10
Length of current hospitalization	31	29	−0.38*	−0.43*	+0.26
Intelligence	11	60	−0.44	+0.03	+0.28

[a]Moore's (1978) thesis reads +0.59, which is a typographical error.
[b]$p < .05$.
ACL = Allen Cognitive Level Test; df = degrees of freedom.
Source: D. S. Moore, An occupational therapy evaluation of sensorimotor cognition: Initial reliability, validity and descriptive data for hospitalized schizophrenic adults. University of Southern California Master's Thesis, 1978.

Table 12-12. Discharge ACL scores and discharge plans of 31 schizophrenic subjects

Discharge plans	Mean score	Percent
Residence		
Acute care facility	3.0	3
Locked board-and-care home	3.5	7
Open board-and-care home	4.8	39
Private residence	5.1	42
Other or not known		10
Employment		
Training program for disabled population	4.0	7
None anticipated	4.6	65
Former job, competitive, part-time	5.0	3
New job, competitive, part-time	5.3	10
New job, competitive, full-time	5.5	10
Training program for general population	6.0	3
Former job, competitive, full-time	6.0	3

ACL = Allen Cognitive Level Test.
Source: D. S. Moore, An occupational therapy evaluation of sensorimotor cognition: Initial reliability, validity and descriptive data for hospitalized schizophrenic adults. University of Southern California Master's Thesis, 1978.

inition of community adjustment is a major problem. If one is to define a cognitive disability as a restriction in routine task behavior, then an operational definition of what the limitations are is required. Frequency of performance, as measured by the PARS V scale, seems to be misleading. Other measures that require a verbal self-report, or a report from a significant other, of the amount of assistance or supervision required also contain serious flaws. Reliability and validity seem to be enhanced by greater specificity in observations of performance. The instruments developed for these two studies (scratch pad assembly and ACL) contain promise for gathering credible data. The scoring methods, materials, and length of administration should facilitate daily clinical use. The question suggested by the studies is, Can we generalize from our observations of test performance to the performance of other routine tasks? We will return to this question in Chapters 15 and 16. The major implication, in retrospect, seems to be that therapists require criteria for establishing task equivalence if there is to be any hope of generalizing from our observations of performance in the OT clinic to predictions of performance in other settings.

ACKNOWLEDGMENTS

Thanks are extended to theses committee members: Susan Herzig's study was supported by Elizabeth J. Yerxa, Ed.D., O.T.R., and Robert E. Allen, M.D.; Deborah Moore's study was supported by Dr. Yerxa and Jytte Busk, Ph.D.

APPENDIX 12-1. SCRATCH PAD ASSEMBLY

Materials provided for each patient

1. Thirty sheets 8½″ × 11″ recycled paper, printed on one side, divided into two stacks of 15 sheets each.
2. One 2″ × 5½″ cardboard top.
3. Two rounded brads, 1-inch shank.
4. One pair of scissors.
5. One hole punch, preset.
6. One completed scratch pad.

Steps in assembly of scratch pad (Fig. 12-2)

1. Fold 8½″ × 11″ sheet in half.
2. Cut 8½″ × 11″ sheet in half along fold.
3. Punch holes in the center of the cut sheets and in cardboard top.
4. Assemble scratch pads:
   a. Place brads through cardboard top.
   b. Place paper, printed side up, over brads to form pad.
   c. Flatten brads over paper.

Scratch pad assembly score sheet

Familiar task   Yes _____   No _____

Level 2.   Folds fewer than 15 sheets of paper.   _____

Level 3.   Folds 15 sheets of paper with no more than one redirection.   _____

Level 4.   With demonstration but without redirection, folds, cuts, and punches 30 sheets of paper.   _____

Level 5.   Without demonstration and after one or more errors, correctly assembles the scratch pad.   _____

Level 6.   Without demonstration correctly assembles the scratch pad on the first attempt.   _____

Note that some of the scores require therapeutic interventions (redirecting attention and demonstrating directions), while others are dependent on the absence of these interventions. The administration of the instrument requires a decision about when and under what circumstances an intervention is to be made.

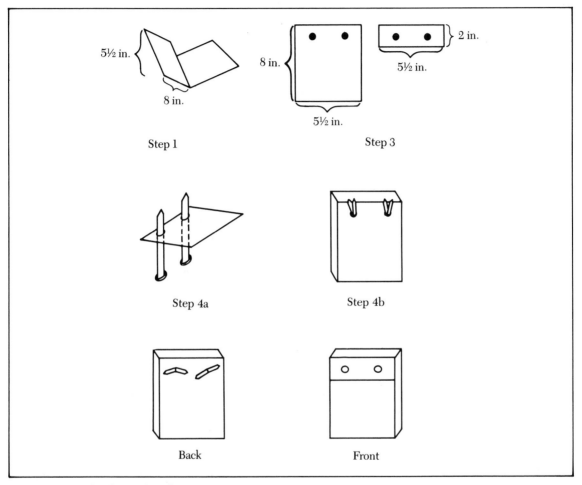

Fig. 12-2. Completed scratch pad.

Directions

1. All materials and tools are laid out for the evaluation.

2. The investigator will show the patient a scratch pad that is completed, saying, *"This is what we call a scratch pad. We make them from scrap paper for use in the hospital. Notice how the underneath side of each paper may have printing on it, while the top side is blank for jotting down notes. Have you ever made one of these pads before?"* The investigator

will record the patient's response (yes/no) to the question.

3. The investigator will demonstrate folding the paper in half, two times, saying, *"This is the first step in putting together a scratch pad. You fold each sheet of paper in half like this. Please go ahead and fold this stack of paper in half and then I'll show you how to do the rest of the job."* If the patient is able to fold 15 sheets of paper in half without requiring more than one redirection to the task or repetition of the demonstration, the therapist will pro-

ceed to step 4. If the patient is *not* able to fold 15 sheets of paper in half unless two or more directions to the task or repetitions of the demonstration are provided, the therapist will proceed to step 5, providing the patient with a stack of 8½″ × 5½″ prepunched paper and a prepunched cardboard top, and saying, *"I'd like you to try and assemble the pad now."*

4. The therapist will demonstrate folding and cutting the paper in half and punching holes in the paper one time, saying, *"Now you'll need to cut the paper in half along the fold and then put the paper into the hole puncher like this. Line up the edge of the paper with the paper guide, push the paper all the way back, and press here. Go back and cut and punch the paper you've already folded."* If the patient *is or is not* able to complete folding, cutting, and punching the entire stack of 30 sheets of paper without redirection to the task or repetition of the demonstration, the therapist will proceed to step 5.

5. The investigator will pick up the sample scratch pad and turn it over and back, saying, *"Now please assemble a pad just like this sample. Look at the pad carefully and think about what you are going to do before you begin."* If the patient is able to assemble the pad correctly on the first attempt, the investigator will thank the patient for his cooperation, and the evaluation will be completed. If the patient is *not* able to assemble the pad correctly on the first attempt, the investigator will say, *"You've made some mistakes here. Can you get your pad to look exactly like the sample?"* If the patient *is or is not* able to assemble the pad correctly by the third attempt, the therapist will thank the patient for his cooperation, and the evaluation will be completed.

6. The therapist will assign a cognitive level to the patient according to the behavioral criteria outlined on the score sheet.

Evaluation criteria

Observation during the construction of the scratch pad may consider three scoring criteria for each cognitive level: the generalizable, theoretical crite-ria from which specific task observations are derived; the specific task observations; and the criteria that would exclude the patient from the next higher level.

Level 2

Theoretical criterion: Patient can approximate gross body movements if they are familiar schemes.

Task criterion: Patient is able to fold sheets of paper in half after this scheme has been demonstrated to him.

Exclusion criterion: Patient will not be able to complete folding a stack of 15 sheets of paper in half unless the therapist provides at least two redirections to task or two repetitions of the demonstration after the initial demonstration.

Level 3

Theoretical criterion: Patient is able to focus attention on tasks that have repetitive actions.

Task criterion: Patient will be able to complete folding 15 sheets of paper in half. He will require no more than one redirection to task or one repetition of demonstration, after the initial demonstration, to complete the task.

Exclusion criterion: The patient will *not* be able to complete folding, cutting, and punching the entire stack of 30 sheets of paper, unless redirection to the task or repetition of the demonstration is provided.

Level 4

Theoretical criterion: Patient will utilize several familiar or moderately novel schemes to achieve a goal.

Task criterion: The patient will be able to complete folding, cutting, and punching the entire stack of 30 sheets of paper without redirection to task or repetition of demonstration. It is not necessary for the patient to be able to recognize or correct errors in any of these procedures.

Exclusion criterion: The patient will *not* be able to assemble a scratch pad correctly, that is, exactly like the sample, including printed sides of paper facing downward, when only a sample but no demonstration of the assembly process is provided.

Level 5

Theoretical criterion: Patient uses overt trial and error to discover the means of achieving a goal.

Task criterion: The patient will be able to discover how to assemble a scratch pad correctly when this procedure has not been demonstrated to him and only a sample is provided.

Exclusion criterion: The patient will *not* be able to assemble the pad correctly on the first attempt, but must assemble it correctly by the third attempt. He will recognize when he has assembled the pad incorrectly and will be able to correct his errors.

Level 6

Theoretical criterion: Patient is able to use covert trial-and-error problem solving, using images to test solutions to problems.

Task criterion: Patient will be able to assemble a scratch pad correctly on the first attempt when a sample is provided.

Source: S. I. Herzig, Occupational therapy assessment of cognitive levels as predictors of community adjustment of chronic schizophrenic patients. University of Southern California Master's Thesis, 1978.

REFERENCES

American Occupational Therapy Association. Report of committee on installations and advice, III. *Arch. Occup. Ther.* 3:459–472, 1924.

Ammons, R. B., and Ammons, C. H. *The Quick Test (QT).* Missoula, Mont.: Psychological Test Specialists, 1962.

Bowman, E. The psychology of occupational therapy. *Arch. Occup. Ther.* 1:171–178, 1922.

Cameron, N. S. Schizophrenic thinking in a problem-solving situation. *Br. J. Psychiatry* 85:1012–1036, 1939.

DSM III: Diagnostic and Statistical Manual of Mental Disorders (3rd ed.). Washington, D.C.: American Psychiatric Association, 1980.

Ellsworth, R. B. Measuring community adjustment of clinic clients and hospital patients: A manual for the PARS V Adjustment Scale. Salem Virginia: V.A. Hospital, 1975.

Ellsworth, R. B., et al. Hospital and community adjustment as perceived by psychiatric patients, their families and staff. *J. Consult. Clin. Psychol.* 32:1–41, 1968.

Feighner, J. P., et al. Diagnostic criteria for use in psychiatric research. *Arch. Gen. Psychiatry* 26:57–63, 1972.

Fontana, A. F., and Dowds, B. N. Assessing treatment outcome: I. Adjustment in the community. *J. Nerv. Ment. Dis.* 161:221–230, 1975.

Furth, H. G. *Piaget and Knowledge: Theoretical Foundations.* Englewood Cliffs, N.J.: Prentice-Hall, 1969.

Gilfoyle, E. M., and Grady, A. P. Cognitive-Perceptual-Motor Behavior. In H. S. Willard and C. S. Spackman (eds.), *Occupational Therapy* (4th ed.). Philadelphia: Lippincott, 1971.

Gillette, N. Occupational therapy and mental health. In H. S. Willard and C. S. Spackman (eds.), *Occupational Therapy* (4th ed.). Philadelphia: Lippincott, 1971.

Goldstein, K. Methodological Approach to the Study of Schizophrenic Thought Disorder. In J. S. Kasanin (ed.), *Language and Thought in Schizophrenia*. Berkeley: University of California Press, 1946.

Goldstein, K., and Scheere, R. M. Abstract and concrete behavior: An experimental study with special test. *Psychol. Monogr.* Vol. 53, No. 239, 1941.

Goodwin, D. W., and Guze, S. B. *Psychiatric Diagnosis* (2nd ed.). New York: Oxford University Press, 1979.

Gustafson, M. E. The kindergarten class in the mental hospital. *Occup. Ther. Rehabil.* 4:185–186, 1925.

Hamilton, V. Deficits in primitive perceptual and thinking skills in schizophrenia. *Nature* 211:389–392, 1966.

Helzer, J. E., Brockington, I. F., and Kendell, R. E. Predictive validity of *DSM III* and Feighner definitions of schizophrenia: A comparison with research diagnostic criteria and CATEGO. *Arch. Gen. Psychiatry* 38:791–799, 1981.

Herzig, S. I. Occupational therapy assessment of cognitive levels as predictors of community adjustment of chronic schizophrenic patients. University of Southern California Master's Thesis, 1978.

Inhelder, B., and Piaget, J. *The Early Growth of Logic in the Child.* New York: Norton, 1964.

Kay, S. R., and Singh, M. M. A developmental approach

to delineate components of cognitive dysfunction in schizophrenia. *Br. J. Soc. Clin. Psychol.* 14:387–399, 1975.

Kay, S. R., Singh, M. M., and Smith, M. M. Colour form representation test: A developmental method for the study of cognition in schizophrenia. *Br. J. Soc. Clin. Psychol.* 14:401–411, 1975.

Kopp, C. B. An application of Piagetian theory: Sensory-motor development. *Am. J. Occup. Ther.* 28:217–219, 1974.

Langfeldt, G. The prognosis of schizophrenia. *Acta Psychiatr. Neurol. Scand. [Suppl.]* 110:1–66, 1956.

Levy, L. L. Movement therapy for psychiatric patients. *Am. J. Occup. Ther.* 28:354–357, 1974.

MacDonald, E. M., MacCaul, G., and Mirrey, L. (eds.). *Occupational Therapy in Rehabilitation* (3rd ed.). London: Baillière, Tindall & Cassell, 1972.

Maloney, M. P., and Steger, H. G. Intellectual characteristics of patients in an urban community mental health facility. *J. Consult. Clin. Psychol.* 38:299, 1972.

Marsh, L. C. Borzoi: Suggestions for a new rallying of occupational therapy. *Occup. Ther. Rehabil.* 11:169–183, 1932.

McGaughran, L. S., and Moran, L. J. "Conceptual level" versus "conceptual area" analysis of object sorting behavior of schizophrenic and non-psychiatric groups. *J. Abnorm. Soc. Psychol.* 52:43–50, 1956.

McGhie, A., and Chapman, J. Disorders of attention and perception in early schizophrenia. *Br. J. Med. Psychol.* 34:103–116, 1961.

McGhie, A., Chapman, J., and Lawson, J. S. The effect of distraction on schizophrenic performance: I. Perception and immediate memory. *Br. J. Psychiatry* III:383–390, 1965.

Meyer, A. Occupational therapy. *Arch. Occup. Ther.* 1:1–10, 1922.

Moore, D. S. An occupational therapy evaluation of sensorimotor cognition: Initial reliability, validity and descriptive data for hospitalized schizophrenic adults. University of Southern California Master's Thesis, 1978.

Morguelan, F. N. The development and validation of a measure including demographic, biographical and symptom-related items for the prediction of community adjustment of schizophrenic patients. University of Southern California Ph.D. Dissertation, 1977.

Morguelan, F. N., Michael, W. B., and Allen, R. E. The design and development of a measure consisting of demographic, biographical and symptom-related items for prediction of community adjustment of schizophrenic patients. *Educ. Psychol. Measurement* 38:491–499, 1978.

Overall, J. E., and Gorham, D. R. The brief psychiatric rating scale. *Psychol. Rep.* 10:799–812, 1962.

Saunders, M. J. The relation of education to mental disorders. *Occup. Ther. Rehabil.* 4:311–364, 1925.

Slagle, E. C. Occupational therapy: Recent methods and advances. *Occup. Ther. Rehabil.* 13:289–299, 1934.

Trunnell, T. L. Thought disturbance in schizophrenia: Pilot study utilizing Piaget's theories. *Arch. Gen. Psychiatry* 11:126–136, 1964.

Trunnell, T. L. Thought disturbance in schizophrenia: Replication study utilizing Piaget's theories. *Arch. Gen. Psychiatry* 13:9–18, 1965.

Ullman, P. P., and Giovannoni, J. M. The development of a self-report measure in the process–reactive continuum. *J. Nerv. Ment. Dis.* 138:38–42, 1964.

Woodruff, R. A., Goodwin, D. W., and Guze, S. B. *Psychiatric Diagnosis.* New York: Oxford University Press, 1974.

Wursten, H. On the relevancy of Piaget's theory to occupational therapy. *Am. J. Occup. Ther.* 28:213–217, 1974.

CHAPTER 13

RESEARCH ON MAJOR DEPRESSION

Noomi Katz

The studies described in this chapter and the next were conducted in tandem and followed, in part, the recommendations made by Herzig (1978) and Moore (1978). The present study (Katz, 1979) employed a different population, depressed patients, and used different measures of cognition. Williams (1981; see Chap. 14) selected a nondisabled population and developed a classification instrument that could be used to examine further the Piagetian hierarchy when applied to an adult population. Williams's classification instrument was included in the study of depression (Katz, 1979).

A battery of five instruments was employed in the study of depression:

1. Allen Cognitive Level Test (ACL) (see Chaps. 4 and 12)
2. Riska Object Classification Test (ROC) (Williams, 1981; see Chap. 14)
3. Block Design (BD), a performance subtest of the Wechsler Adult Intelligence Scale (WAIS; Wechsler, 1955)
4. Zung Self-rating Depression Scale (SDS) (Zung and Durham, 1965, 1973; see Tables 13-1 and 13-2)
5. Physician Global Rating (PGR) for depression (Bech et al., 1975; Appendix)

The first three provide the operational definitions of cognition; the last two, of depression.

DEPRESSION AND COGNITIVE DISABILITY

Depression is one of the most extensively studied syndromes in psychiatry, probably because of its complexity and prevalence (Freedman et al., 1976; Goodwin and Guze, 1979). Depression as a syndrome usually presents a clinical picture in which the main symptoms are feelings of worthlessness, despair, ideas of self-harm, dysphoric mood (sadness), hopelessness, helplessness, irritability, fearfulness, worry, crying spells, anorexia with weight loss, insomnia, early morning awakening, loss of energy, psychomotor retardation or agitation, loss of interest, slowed thinking, inability to concentrate, decrease in activity, and suicidal thoughts.

The illness is episodic, and the length of an episode is extremely variable. Between episodes a patient usually functions well, so no permanent deterioration is expected. The episodes may consist of depression only (unipolar) or alternate with mania (bipolar) (Goodwin and Guze, 1979).

During the last fifty years many attempts have been made to classify depression, but there is as yet no agreement among the competing schools of thought (Kendell, 1976). The importance of diagnostic classification has increased with the development of more precise methods of treatment, especially chemotherapy (Zung and Durham, 1973). Recent advances in biologic research, especially genetic and pharmacologic studies, have led to new and probably more accurate classifications of depression (Cole et al., 1978).

The variety of subclassifications previously used for affective disorders were based on dichotomous distinctions. Newer criteria, represented by *DSM III* (1980), are based on symptoms and not precipitating factors, thus avoiding the unuseful distinction made between endogenous and reactive depression. The *DSM III* also includes "criteria for levels of severity of depression," which differentiate between psychotic and nonpsychotic depression, although both are included. These criteria by Feighner and colleagues (1972) for "primary affective disorder, depression" emphasize symptoms of mood as well as physiologic symptoms, with a decline in ability to act and think.

Depression is of special interest from the point of view of cognitive disability because one of the main symptoms of depression is a decrease in performance of daily life tasks. This decrease varies with the severity of the episode (Freedman et al., 1976). The cognitive impairment in depression is thought to be of a lesser magnitude than that of schizophrenics (Braff and Beck, 1974; Harrow and Quinlan, 1977; O'Leary et al., 1976). The main areas found to

be impaired suggest a cognitive disturbance in the higher cognitive levels, namely, in the concrete operational or formal operational period.

Some theorists have assumed that a cognitive distortion underlies the affective manifestation of depression (Arieti, 1967; Arieti and Bemporad, 1978; Beck, 1967, 1976; Beck et al., 1979; Ellis and Grieger, 1977). Devaluation and negative appraisal of oneself are seen as a basic component of depression, which suggests a negative correlation between a patient's self-rating of depression and his or her actual performance in structured tests (Andreasen, 1976; Colbert and Harrow, 1968; Friedman, 1964). An alternative assumption is to regard biologic factors, such as sleep disturbance, weight loss, and loss of energy, as the basic components of depression, which lead to the cognitive distortions (Kendell, 1976; Pincus and Tucker, 1978). Recent studies suggest that the cognitive distortions are symptoms of the disease; these distortions clear when the depression is treated effectively (Murphy et al., 1984; Nelson et al., 1984; Silverman et al., 1984; Simmons et al., 1984). These findings and clinical experience indicate the importance of using both self-rating scales and observer's rating scales in measuring the severity of depression (Biggs et al., 1978; Zung and Durham, 1973). The cognitive impairment has been found to be more obvious in a severe depression than in a mild one (Braff and Beck, 1974; Lanzito et al., 1974), and this finding provides an additional reason for using several measures for the severity of depression.

The course of depression indicates full recovery between episodes (Goodwin and Guze, 1979). This means that both the cognitive impairment and the decrease in performance of daily life tasks are temporary, and functioning should return to normal after the episode is over. The natural course of acute episodes provides a unique opportunity to study the changes in cognitive ability from the normal to the pathologic phase, as well as the relationship between cognition and routine tasks.

The occupational therapy profession is, at present, at an important phase of research and instrument development. The need for scientific research and accurate evaluation tools with demonstrated reliability and validity is steadily growing. The ACL was shown to be a reliable and valid test in Moore's (1978) study (see Chap. 12) of a sample of chronic schizophrenic adult inpatients. Her results, however, cannot be generalized to other psychiatric categories. Therefore the present study investigated further the validity of the ACL and its ability to evaluate cognitive levels in depressed adult inpatients. Furthermore, it utilized the ROC, which was a newly devised test for measuring cognition beyond the sensorimotor period, and thus added to the investigation of cognition in psychiatric illness by examining the preoperational and concrete operational periods of development (Piaget, 1971, 1978).

PURPOSE OF THE STUDY

The study aimed at answering the following questions: What is the relationship between cognitive disability and the syndrome of depression as manifested by adult inpatients? Furthermore, how accurate are occupational therapy evaluation tools—the ACL and the ROC—in measuring cognitive impairment in adult inpatients with depression?

Thus, the purpose of this study was twofold:

1. Investigation of cognitive impairment in depression and its relation to the depressed patient's ability to function
2. Further investigation of the ACL's validity and ability to measure cognitive levels in depression, as well as investigation of the ROC as a measure of cognition beyond the sensorimotor period

RELATED RESEARCH FINDINGS

Studies usually confirm the basic clinical observation that the cognitive disturbance in depression is less than that in schizophrenia, but more prominent in severe psychotic depression than in mild depres-

sion (Braff and Beck, 1974; Harrow and Quinlan, 1977; O'Leary et al., 1976). The literature review revealed a few studies examining the relationship between cognition and performance in depressed subjects. In these studies the main areas of cognitive impairment were speed, short-term memory, abstraction, mental flexibility to shift from one line of thought to another, visual-motor coordination, and sustained concentration (Friedman, 1964; Sternberg and Jarvik, 1976; Weckowicz et al., 1978). Depression was associated with impairments on the Block Design (BD) which suggested difficulties in visual and spatial perception and visual-motor coordination (Rapaport et al., 1968). In addition, a patient's self-rating of depression was found to be negatively correlated with performance measures, that is, the patient's depression was pronounced, but actual performance was still high (Lanzito et al., 1974). Success seems to have a positive influence on a depressed patient's performance, while failure lowers performance (Hammen and Krantz, 1976). Some researchers extend the performance observations into an assumption that it is possible to induce an elated or depressed mood by cognitive means; this assumption was not investigated in this study. This study assumes that an improvement in the biologic condition, attributed to interventions of the physician, will be associated with some improvements in performance.

INSTRUMENTS

Allen Cognitive Level Test

The Allen Cognitive Level Test measures subjects' cognitive ability on a 1- to 6-point scale with an occupational therapy activity. Extensive discussion of the test is provided in Chapter 4, while the first reliability and validity data are described in Chapter 12.

Riska Object Classification

The Riska Object Classification test is an occupational therapy instrument that was being developed during the course of this study. Interrater reliability was investigated before this study began. The ROC is divided into two parts: an open-ended part in which people are asked to place cardboard pieces in "groups that are alike" (ROCUN), and a structured part in which the cardboard pieces are to be placed in "groups that are like mine" (ROCST). The interrater reliability for the ROCUN was $r = 0.835$ ($p < .01$, $N = 20$; degrees of freedom, or df, = 18). The interrater reliability for the ROCST was $r = 0.826$; $p < .01$ ($N = 20$; $df = 18$). The test operationally defines sensorimotor, preoperational, and concrete operational classification (see Chap. 14).

Block Design

The WAIS is a standardized measure of intelligence devised by David Wechsler and published in 1955. The BD subtest is a cognitive performance test that measures especially nonverbal organization, visual-motor coordination, spatial and visual perception, flexibility to change patterns, ability to reproduce a given pattern, concentration and attention, and ability to solve a problem by overt versus covert trial and error (Cohen, 1957a, b; Matarazo, 1972; Rapaport et al., 1968). For instruction and statistical data, see Wechsler (1955). Raw scores on the BD subtest, which can range from 0 to 48, are transformed into scaled scores from 0 to 19 according to age groups. Higher numbers indicate higher performance. Each design is time limited (60 seconds for the first six designs, 120 seconds for the last four), with a time bonus for faster performance. In this study, following findings indicating psychomotor retardation in depression (Colbert and Harrow, 1968; Friedman, 1964; Weckowicz et al., 1978), additional time over the regular time limits was given to accomplish each design. Two scores were computed: one within the regular time limit (BDT); the other, assuming no time limitation (BDU).

Zung Self-rating Depression Scale

The Zung Self-rating Depression Scale was devised by Zung (1974) to measure severity of depression as rated by the patient himself or herself (Tables 13-1 and 13-2). The items included in the scale fit the *DSM III* criteria chosen for this study. There are 20 items, each of which is rated on a scale of 1 to 4. The raw score may range from 20 to 80 points, 20 indicating no or negligible depression and 80 representing the most severe state of depression.

The split-half procedure was used to estimate which was found to be $r = 0.73$ ($p < .01$) (Zung and Durham, 1973). Correlation between the Hamilton Rating Scale and the SDS is $r = 0.80$; between the SDS and the PGR, $r = 0.69$ (Biggs et al., 1978). These findings indicate the congruent validity of the SDS. The test was also used with normal and depressed subjects aged 20 to 64 years. In this study the SDS index of 0.50 was chosen as the cutoff point for morbidity. In the same age group 88 percent of depressed patients had scores higher than 0.50, while 12 percent of the normal population scored above 0.50 (Zung and Durham, 1973). These findings also provide construct validity for the SDS, which clearly differentiated between the two different populations.

Physician Global Rating

The Physician Global Rating for depression was employed by Bech and colleagues (1975) as an objective clinical assessment of the severity of depression. The scale consists of 11 intervals: 0 and 1, no depression; 2 to 4, mild depression; 5 to 7, moderate depression; 8 to 10, severe depression. A lower score indicates fewer symptoms of depression; a higher score, more severe symptoms. Interrater reliability was determined for the PGR scale and found to be $r = 0.88$, ($p < .001$) (Bech et al., 1975). Congruent validity was determined by correlating the depression scales developed by Beck et al. (1961) and Hamilton (1960): $r = 0.77$, ($p < .001$); $r = 0.84$, ($p < .001$), respectively (Bech et al., 1975).

OBJECTIVES

The objectives of this study were the following:

Table 13-1. Key for scoring the self-rating depression scale

Item	Score			
	A little of the time	Some of the time	Good part of the time	Most of the time
1. I feel down-hearted and sad	1	2	3	4
2. Morning is when I feel the best	4	3	2	1
3. I have crying spells or feel like it	1	2	3	4
4. I often don't sleep through the night	1	2	3	4
5. I eat as much as I used to	4	3	2	1
6. I enjoy looking at, talking to, and being with attractive women/men	4	3	2	1
7. I notice that I am losing weight	1	2	3	4
8. I have trouble with constipation	1	2	3	4
9. My heart beats faster than usual	1	2	3	4
10. I get tired for no reason	1	2	3	4
11. My mind is as clear as it used to be	4	3	2	1
12. It is easy to do things I used to do	4	3	2	1
13. I am restless and can't keep still	1	2	3	4
14. I feel hopeful about the future	4	3	2	1
15. I am more irritable than usual	1	2	3	4
16. I find it easy to make decisions	4	3	2	1
17. I feel that I am useful and needed	4	3	2	1
18. My life is pretty full	4	3	2	1
19. I feel that others would be better off if I were dead	1	2	3	4
20. I still enjoy the things I used to do	4	3	2	1

Source: Modified slightly from W. W. K. Zung, Privately printed. Copyright 1974.

1. Measuring and examining the trend of scores for each depressed subject from admission through discharge and follow-up on the ACL and ROC.
2. Determining congruent validity of the ACL and ROC by correlating scores with each other and with scores on the BD subtest of WAIS.
3. Examining the relationship between the results of the cognitive tests (ACL, ROC, BD) and scores on the scales of depression (SDS, PGR).
4. Comparing the ACL scores of the depressed sample with those of Moore's (1978) schizophrenic sample.
5. Comparing BD scores of the depressed sample in regular time with scores in unlimited time.
6. Describing the characteristics of the sample on selected demographic variables.

METHOD

The general approach of the study was descriptive correlational. The design was a short-term longitudinal one, with the same subjects being tested at three points (at admission, discharge, and follow-up).

Table 13-2. Converison of raw score to self-rating depression scale (SDS) index

Raw score	SDS index	Raw score	SDS index	Raw score	SDS index
20	0.25	40	0.50	60	0.75
21	0.26	41	0.51	61	0.76
22	0.28	42	0.53	62	0.78
23	0.29	43	0.54	63	0.79
24	0.30	44	0.55	64	0.80
25	0.31	45	0.56	65	0.81
26	0.33	46	0.58	66	0.83
27	0.34	47	0.59	67	0.84
28	0.35	48	0.60	68	0.85
29	0.36	49	0.61	69	0.86
30	0.38	50	0.63	70	0.88
31	0.39	51	0.64	71	0.89
32	0.40	52	0.65	72	0.90
33	0.41	53	0.66	73	0.91
34	0.43	54	0.68	74	0.92
35	0.44	55	0.69	75	0.94
36	0.45	56	0.70	76	0.95
37	0.46	57	0.71	77	0.96
38	0.48	58	0.73	78	0.98
39	0.49	59	0.74	79	0.99
				80	1.00

Source: W. W. K. Zung and N. C. Durham, A self-rating depression scale. *Arch. Gen. Psychiatry* 12:65–70, 1965. Copyright 1965, American Medical Association.

Subjects

The subjects were 32 adult inpatients tested at Los Angeles County University of Southern California Medical Center. All of the subjects had a clinical diagnosis of depression and met the *DSM III* criteria for major depressive disorder or bipolar affective disorder, depressed type.

The average subject seemed to be a white woman, 40 years old, single or divorced, with 11 or 12 years of education, belonging to social position class IV (second lowest class, Hollingshead and Redlich, 1958), with one or two previous hospitalizations for depressive episodes, and receiving psychotropic drugs during the tested hospitalization (Tables 13-3 and 13-4). Some of these characteristics are congruent with the literature on depression, for example, the prevalence of middle-aged women who are single, divorced, or separated. Contrary to the expectations for a sample in this particular setting, 62.5 percent of the group was white. The mean education, 11.6 years, was higher than expected. Despite the relatively high level of education, the social position class, as expected, was low (IV). The patient's occupations were of low status, which produced a low score in social position on the Hollingshead and Redlich (1958; see Chap. 14) scale.

Procedures for Data Collection

Subjects were selected according to a physician's diagnosis based on the *DSM III* criteria for major affective disorder, depressed type, and by my chart review. The study was explained to the selected patients, who then signed informed consent forms.

Each subject was tested within the first 5 days after admission to the hospital and a second time within 3 days before discharge. In each testing period, four instruments were administered in the following order: ROC, BD, ACL, and SDS. The battery as a whole took 30 to 45 minutes to complete.

The PGR scale was scored by the patient's physician on the same days the other tests were administered. Two months after discharge eight subjects were tested a third time for follow-up. (The number of dropouts was much higher than expected. Despite many attempts to bring subjects in for a third testing, only eight were obtainable.)

Demographic data on each subject were collected from chart review and subjects' interviews.

Data Analysis

The following statistical procedures were employed in analyzing the data: Pearson product-moment cor-

*Table 13-3. Characteristics of a sample
of depressed subjects* (N = 32)

Variable	Mean	Standard deviation
Age (years)[a]	39	± 10.4
Education (years of schooling)	12	± 2.7
Social position	53[b]	± 14.1
No. of previous hospitalizations for depression	2	+ 2.5

[a]Range, 21–61.
[b]Class IV, second lowest (Hollingshead and Redlich, 1958).

*Table 13-4. Demographic features of a
sample of depressed subjects* (N = 32)

Variable	No.	Percent
Sex		
Male	8	25
Female	24	75
Ethnicity		
White	20	63
Black	7	22
Mexican American	5	16
Marital status		
Single	11	34
Married	5	16
Divorced	11	34
Separated	4	13
Widowed	1	3
Previous leather lacing experience		
Yes	17	53
No	15	47
Electroconvulsive therapy		
Yes	4	12.5
No	28	87.5

relation, paired *t*-test, two sample *t*-test, two-by-two contingency table with chi-square statistics, and one-way analysis of variance for repeated measures, as well as descriptive statistics including means, standard deviations, and frequencies. The minimum level of significance accepted in this study was $p < .05$.

RESULTS

Descriptive Statistics

Table 13-5 presents descriptive statistics of all tests scores at admission and discharge. For two instruments (ROC and BD), two scores were obtained (ROCUN and ROCST; BDT and BDU). Seventy-five percent of the subjects (24 of 32) scored 4 to 6 on the ACL at admission; at discharge 91 percent (29 of 32) scored 5 or 6. All subjects (except two on ROCUN at admission) scored between 7 and 16 on the ROC test. In a two-by-two contingency table for ACL and ROC, a trend was noticed: Twenty subjects (62.5%) scored high on ACL (5 and 6) and ROC (11 to 16), but the only statistically significant relationship found was between ACL and ROCST at discharge ($\chi^2 = 4.99$, $p < .05$).

On the depression scales, only three subjects scored less than 40 on the SDS at admission and no one scored less than 5 on the PGR (40 and 5, respectively, were the cutoff points to differentiate between mild to moderate and severe depression). At discharge the SDS and PGR scores decreased. The upper scores were 56 for the SDS and 7 for the PGR, indicating moderate or mild depression.

Admission to Discharge

Table 13-6 presents correlations and paired *t*-test results between admission and discharge for each test. Improvement (higher cognitive functioning and decrease in depression) between admission and discharge was indicated by highly statistically significant *t* values for ACL, BDT, SDS, and PGR. No significant change was found on either part of the ROC or on the BDU.

Table 13-5. *Test scores at admission (1)*
and discharge (2) (N = 32)

Variable	Mean	Standard deviation	Range raw scores
ACL 1	5.0	0.7	4–6
ACL 2	5.5	0.7	4–6
ROCUN 1	11.9	2.9	3–16
ROCUN 2	12.6	2.0	10–16
ROCST 1	12.5	2.0	7–14
ROCST 2	13.1	1.4	10–14
BDT 1	9.2	3.3	3–16
BDT 2	10.5	3.0	6–17
BDU 1[a]	11.1	2.1	4–15
BDU 2[b]	11.9	2.2	8–15
SDS 1	52.8	9.8	32–74
SDS 2	41.0	10.4	20–56
PGR 1	7.3	1.1	5–9
PGR 2	2.7	1.9	0–7

ACL = Allen Cognitive Level Test; ROCUN = Riska Object
Classification Test, unstructured; ROCST = Riska Object
Classification Test, structured; BDT = Block Design, timed;
BDU = Block Design, untimed; SDS = Self-rating
Depression Scale; PGR = Physician Global Rating.
[a]N = 17.
[b]N = 18.

In a separate one-way analysis of variance for a
subgroup of eight subjects who were tested three
times (admission, discharge, and follow-up), significant improvement was found only on BDT, $F =$
8.95 ($p < .005$) and SDS, $F = 3.76$ ($p < .05$). The
ACL and both parts of the ROC showed no significant change. These findings should be viewed with
caution since the sample size was very small ($N =$
8); with such a small sample the statistical tool loses
much of its power. Still the tests that showed
change seem to be sensitive even with such a small
number.

Timed Performance

The difference between the mean score on the BD
in regular time (BDT) and in unlimited time (BDU)
is shown in Table 13-7. The scores were highly cor-

Table 13-6. *Pearson r correlations and*
paired t-test results for each instrument between
admission and discharge (N = 32)

Variable	r	t
ACL	0.61[a]	4.6[a]
ROCUN	0.08	1.2
ROCST	0.47[b]	1.9
BDT	0.88[a]	4.7[a]
BDU[c]	0.7[b]	1.6
SDS	0.3	5.6[a]
PGR	−0.03	11.9[a]

ACL = Allen Cognitive Level Test; ROCUN = Riska Object
Classification Test, unstructured; ROCST = Riska Object
Classification Test, structured; BDT = Block Design, timed;
BDU = Block Design, untimed; SDS = Self-rating
Depression Scale; PGR = Physician Global Rating.
[a]$p < .0001$.
[b]$p < .001$.
[c]N = 15.

related ($r = 0.908$, $r = 0.928$, $p < .0001$), and a
statistically significant improvement between admission and discharge was seen when the test was
scored with no time limitation (BDU) (Table 13-7).
The analysis included only 17 subjects at admission
and 18 at discharge since the other subjects did not
use additional time beyond the specified limits;
thus their BDT and BDU scores were identical.
(The test was given in a similar way for all subjects;
only the scoring for BDU was added.)

Cognition and Depression

From the data (Tables 13-8 and 13-9) it is evident
that the cognitive test scores correlated positively
and significantly with each other. Both occupational
therapy instruments (ACL and ROC) showed significant positive correlations with the BD, which was
chosen as a measure of concurrent validity.

The two depression scales (SDS and PGR) were
correlated significantly only at discharge, while the
only significant correlation with a cognitive test was
found between SDS and ROCST at discharge. The
statistically significant correlations expected be-

Table 13-7. Results of paired t-*test of BDT and BDU at admission (1) and discharge (2)*

Variable	Mean	Standard deviation	t	r
BDT 1[a]	8.2	2.7		
			8.15[b]	0.91[b]
BDU 1[a]	10.5	2.7		
BDT 2[c]	10.0	2.2		
			8.04[b]	0.93[b]
BDU 2[c]	11.6	2.2		

BDT = Block Design, timed; BDT = Block Design, untimed.
[a]$N = 17$.
[b]$p < .0001$.
[c]$N = 18$.

tween the depression scales and the cognitive measurements did not occur. The expected direction (negative), however, is seen in all of them.

In addition the instrument scores were correlated with some of the demographic variables. The only consistent positive correlations were found as expected between BDT and education, social position, and age.

Depression and Schizophrenia

The ACL scores of this sample of depressed adult inpatients were compared with scores of a sample of schizophrenic patients (Moore, 1978; see Chap. 12). A two-sample *t*-test was employed. Statistically significant differences between the two samples were found at all measurement times (Table 13-10); the difference was especially high at admission.

DISCUSSION

Allen Cognitive Level Test

As hypothesized, depressed patients did score at the highest levels of the ACL. It also seemed that subjects at the highest cognitive levels on the ACL also scored high on the ROC, namely, classifying at a concrete operational stage, even though only one

statistically significant result was found to support this conclusion (ACL with ROCST at discharge: $\chi^2 = 4.99$, $p < .05$).

Significant improvement of mean ACL scores from admission to discharge (see Table 13-6) indicates that the test is able to measure changes in cognitive ability. Although many of the subjects scored well from the beginning (mean, 5.0), they still had improved by discharge (mean, 5.5). Analysis of the follow-up subgroup shows that this sample started out higher (mean, 5.4) and improved only a small amount (mean, 5.6); therefore, no significant *t* value was found. The data supported the hypothesis that ACL scores would improve from admission to discharge and follow-up.

Congruent validity was determined by the results showing significant positive correlations between the ACL and BD (see Tables 13-8 and 13-9). These findings validate the content of the ACL test as a measure of cognition and support the hypothesis that the two instruments test similar areas of cognition.

ACL scores also correlated significantly with ROC scores at admission, providing additional validity for both tests. They had no correlation at discharge, probably because the ACL scores increased significantly while the ROC test scores remained almost the same.

No significant correlations between the demographic variables and ACL scores were found. No significant result was seen in analyzing the ACL scores with either previous leather lacing experience or with sex. These results indicate that ACL results, at the higher cognitive levels observed in this study, are relatively independent of previous experience, sex, socioeconomic status, and social factors. This supports its use as a measure of cognitive disability.

In comparing the schizophrenic sample with the depressed sample, significant differences were found, which indicated that the ACL was able to differentiate between schizophrenics and depressed populations. This difference was in the hypothesized direction: Schizophrenic patients are re-

Table 13-8. Pearson r correlations between all test scores at admission (N = 32)

Variable	ROCUN	ROCST	BDT	BDU	SDS	PGR
ACL	0.42[a]	0.38[b]	0.46[a]	0.29	−0.18	−0.01
ROCUN	—	0.58[c]	0.60[c]	0.38	−0.14	−0.19
ROCST	—	—	0.57[c]	0.45[b]	−0.19	−0.12
BDT	—	—	—	0.91[c]	−0.25	−0.07
BDU[d]	—	—	—	—	−0.09	−0.03
SDS	—	—	—	—	—	0.05

ACL = Allen Cognitive Levels Test; ROCUN = Riska Object Classification Test, unstructured; ROCST = Riska Object Classification Test, structured; BDT = Block Design, timed; BDU = Block Design, untimed; SDS = Self-rating Depression Scale; PGR = Physician Global Rating.
[a]$p < .005$.
[b]$p < .01$.
[c]$p < .0001$.
[d]$N = 17$.

Table 13-9. Pearson r correlations between all test scores at discharge (N = 32)

	ROCUN	ROCST	BDT	BDU	SDS	PGR
ACL	0.24	0.24	0.40[a]	0.17	−0.13	−0.08
ROCUN	—	0.62[b]	0.38[a]	0.18	−0.19	−0.03
ROCST	—	—	0.43[c]	0.34	−0.44[c]	−0.15
BDT	—	—	—	0.93[b]	−0.05	−0.06
BDU[d]	—	—	—	—	−0.11	−0.37
SDS	—	—	—	—	—	0.34[a]

ACL = Allen Cognitive Level Test; ROCUN = Riska Object Classification Test, unstructured; ROCST = Riska Object Classification Test, structured; BDT = Block Design, timed; BDU = Block Design, untimed; SDS = Self-rating Depression Scale; PGR = Physical Global Rating.
[a]$p < .01$.
[b]$p < .0001$.
[c]$p < .005$.
[d]$N = 18$.

garded as more severely impaired in cognitive ability than depressed patients.

The one hypothesis concerning the ACL test which was not confirmed in this study concerns the relation to severity of depression. It was hypothesized that significant negative correlation would be found between the cognitive measurements and the depression scales, but no significant correlation was found for any of the cognitive tests (ACL, ROC, or BD). Analysis and possible interpretation of this

finding will be presented later, as it occurred as a general pattern, raising some important questions.

Riska Object Classification Test

As was hypothesized, the scores on the ROC ranged from 7 to 17 (except for two subjects scoring 3 and 6 on ROCUN at admission). The results indicate that depressed patients were able to classify within the range of the preoperational or concrete

Table 13-10. ACL scores of depressed
(N = 32) and schizophrenic (N = 24)
patients at admission (1) and discharge (2)

Variable	Mean	Standard deviation	t
ACL 1			
Schizophrenic	3.9	1.2	
			4.34[a]
Depressed	5.0	0.7	
ACL 2			
Schizophrenic	4.9	0.9	
			3.04[b]
Depressed	5.5	0.7	
Change between ACL 1 and ACL 2			
Schizophrenic	1.0	1.0	
			2.57[c]
Depressed	0.5	0.6	

ACL = Allen Cognitive Level Test.
[a] $p < .0001$.
[b] $p < .005$.
[c] $p < .01$.

operational states of Piaget's cognitive development theory.

Significant correlations were found between the two parts of the ROC test as expected. Approximately 50 percent of subjects obtained the highest possible score of 14 on the structured part (ROCST) test but received a lower score on the unstructured part (ROCUN). It seems that the depressed patient has difficulty in producing a spontaneous pattern of thought or shifting to another pattern of thought. These patients' spontaneous thinking may be more restricted than their ability to comply with the standard of performance provided by the structured portion of the ROC. The ROCUN was the only instrument in this study in which the patient had to rely on spontaneous thought to obtain a high score. In addition after producing one pattern of thought the patients had difficulty shifting set (moving to another classification criterion). From observations

made during the administration of the test it became evident that most subjects classified first by shape. Some of them continued to use only combinations of shapes and could not change to another criterion (color). An additional problem was the lack of correlation between ROCUN at admission and discharge ($r = 0.08$). This finding indicates that the test is not measuring consistently, and better data on how an acute psychiatric disease may be affecting these processes is needed.

Contrary to the study's hypothesis, no significant improvement was found between admission and discharge on either part of the ROC test. On the ROCST 65 percent of the subjects scored 14 (upper limit) at admission, leaving no room for further improvement. Consequently, the ROC was not an appropriate measure of improvement.

On the other hand, a highly significant positive correlation was found between both parts of the ROC test and the BDT (see Tables 13-8 and 13-9). These findings are in the hypothesized direction and provide data for concurrent validity of the ROC test as a measure of cognition.

Like the ACL, the ROC showed no significant correlation with the depression scales.

The ROCST results showed no significant correlation with the demographic variables, and like the ACL this part of the ROC is probably culture free. ROCUN scores correlated significantly with education and social position (similar to BD scores), indicating their influence on a subject's unstructured, or spontaneous, classification score.

In summary, the ROC test was found to be a valid measure of cognition but was not appropriate as an indication of the change in cognition in depression between admission and discharge. The test's importance is in providing a measure of preoperational and concrete operational stage of cognition, as well as pointing out the difficulty the depressed patient has in abstraction and in initiating new patterns, which may not change as rapidly as other cognitive functions. It is important to investigate further the ROC's reliability and validity, especially that of the unstructured part. See Chapter 14 for data on a normal population that was collected after this study was finished.

Block Design

The BD was found to be a very sensitive test for measuring, and detecting change in the cognitive ability of the depressed patient even with a sample of eight. The BD test provided congruent validity for the ACL and ROC tests by showing highly significant correlations with them.

The procedure of providing more time to complete each design and obtaining two scores (BDT and BDU) gave important information. The results show a significant difference (see Table 13-7), which suggests that when given more time to complete each design the depressed patient increases his or her score, and which could be interpreted to mean that low cognitive functioning is a result of slowness. This conclusion would probably be correct if all 32 subjects had used the additional time and increased their scores. Only 17 subjects, however, comprising approximately 50 percent of the sample, actually used the additional time. Of the remaining group, eight subjects had low scores (less than the mean) at admission and still did not profit from additional time, while the other seven had higher scores and had no need for more time. It seems, therefore, that these eight subjects probably functioned according to their actual capabilities and the reason for the low score was not merely slowness. The fact that 14 subjects used the additional time at admission and at discharge indicates that their slowness is probably a result of either basic cognitive capabilities, or that the decrease in depression symptoms occurs before a change in slowed performance. It seems that *not using* more time may indicate cognitive impairment caused by depression without the interference of psychomotor retardation (a slowness occurring sometimes in depression). In conclusion, it is suggested that for those subjects who used the additional time, the factor of

psychomotor retardation has *some* influence on cognitive ability, while for the other group this factor is probably not significant.

The mean BDT score increased significantly between admission and discharge (see Table 13-6), indicating that the BD test is an appropriate test for measuring cognitive impairment in depression. This result is in accordance with the findings of Rapaport and colleagues (1968), which suggested that the BD is especially sensitive to depression. The mean difference on the BDT was 1.3 (from 9.2 at admission to 10.5 at discharge). This number is greater than 1 scaled score, which could be attributed to testing effect (Mandleberg and Brooks, 1975; Quereski, 1968). The mean BD score at discharge was in the range of the normal population score, which suggests that by discharge the depressed patients had returned to normal functioning. This interpretation supports the current description of the normal course of the disease (*DSM III, 1980*).

Depression Scales

According to the data provided by the two depression scales at admission, almost all the subjects were moderately to severely depressed. At discharge their scores decreased, ranging from mild to moderate depression. A significant improvement was found on both scales (see Table 13-6). These results indicate that both scales, whether self-rating or observer rating, are able to measure change in the level of depression.

Two main problems arise when looking at the correlational data for the two scales (see Tables 13-8 and 13-9). First, the two scales were not significantly correlated at admission, while at discharge there was a statistically significant, but low, correlation. According to this result it seems that at admission there was a greater discrepancy between the patient rating and the physician rating. On inspection of the raw data it looked as if the physician rated the patients higher (more depressed) at admission and lower (less depressed) at discharge than did the patients themselves. It is difficult to say who was more accurate, especially as correlational data with the cognitive scales was nonsignificant for both the SDS and the PGR. This result brings us to the second problem, the lack of significant negative correlation, as was hypothesized, between the depression scales and the cognitive test results. This finding was consistent except for one correlation, between SDS and ROCST at discharge (see Table 13-9). Correlations were negative, as expected, but the relationships were not statistically significant. The same result is presented by Braff et al. (1983), who found no significant relationship between degree of depressive symptoms and thought disorder, even though they found significant decrease in abstraction ability in their depressive sample. It seems that there was no strong direct relationship between the level of depression as measured by these depression scales and the cognitive ability measured by most of the tests used in this study. Nevertheless the direction of correlation supported the hypothesis.

CONCLUSION

The general findings of this study support previous studies by Braff and Beck (1974) and Harrow and Quinlan (1977), who found that some kind of cognitive impairment is evident in depression, especially in the more severe phase. This finding agrees in general with Beck's theory (1979) even though it cannot confirm his causal postulate that a cognitive disorder underlies the affective disturbance. It supports also the general postulate of this book, that a temporary cognitive impairment is evident in depressed patients.

On closer inspection it seems that the cognitive impairment was found specifically in abstraction, visual-motor coordination, spatial and visual perception, flexibility to shift set, problem solving us-

ing overt versus covert trial and error, and slowness in test performance. These findings support the results of Friedman (1964), Weckowicz and colleagues (1978), and Braff and colleagues (1983).

In general the areas in which cognitive impairment was visible did not correlate with the level of depression. This result may reflect a loss of energy to sustain performance in depression; or it may be attributed to the level of general psychopathology, as the findings of Braff et al. (1983) suggest, rather than a degree of depression. It may also be explained according to Beck's theory (1979) of an intervening variable, such as negative self-concept, that may influence cognitive performance. Such explanations allude to an indirect relationship between the level of depression and the cognitive ability as measured by test performance. Further research is needed to test these explanations more precisely.

ACKNOWLEDGMENT

Thanks are extended to Robert E. Allen, M.D., and Elizabeth A. Yerxa, Ed.D., O.T.R., who served as members of the theses committee.

REFERENCES

Andreasen, N. C. Do depressed patients show thought disorder? *J. Nerv. Ment. Dis.* 163:186–191, 1976.
Arieti, S. *The Intrapsychic Self.* New York: Basic Books, 1967.
Arieti, S., and Bemporad, J. *Severe and Mild Depression.* New York: Basic Books, 1978.
Bech, P., et al. Quantitative rating of depressive states. *Acta Psychiatr. Scand.* 51:161–170, 1975.
Beck, A. T. *Depression: Causes and Treatment.* Philadelphia: University of Pennsylvania Press, 1967.
Beck, A. T. *Cognitive Therapy and the Emotional Disorders.* New York: International Universities Press, 1976.
Beck, A. T., et al. *Cognitive Therapy of Depression.* New York: Guilford, 1979.

Beck, A. T., et al. An inventory for measuring depression. *Arch. Gen. Psychiatry* 4:561–571, 1961.

Biggs, J. T., Wylie, L. T., and Ziegler, V. E. Validity of the Zung Self-rating Depression Scale. *Br. J. Psychiatry* 132:381–385, 1978.

Braff, D. L., and Beck, A. T. Thinking disorder in depression. *Arch. Gen. Psychiatry* 31:456–459, 1974.

Braff, D. L., Glich, I. D., and Griffin, P. Thought disorder and depression in psychiatric patients. *Comprehensive Psychiatry* 24:57–64, 1983.

Cohen, J. A factor-analytically based rationale for the Wechsler Adult Intelligence Scale. *J. Consult. Psychol.* 21:451–457, 1957 (a).

Cohen, J. A factorial structure of the WAIS between early adulthood and old age. *J. Consult. Psychol.* 21:283–290, 1957 (b).

Colbert, J., and Harrow, W. Psychomotor retardation in depressive syndromes. *J. Nerv. Ment. Dis.* 145:405–419, 1968.

Cole, J. O., Schatzberg, A. F., and Frazier, S. H. (eds.). *Depression.* New York: Plenum, 1978.

Coleman, R. E. Manipulation of self-esteem as a determinant of mood of elated and depressed women. *J. Abnorm. Psychol.* 84:693–700, 1975.

DSM III: Diagnostic and Statistical Manual of Mental Disorders (3rd ed.). Washington, D.C.: American Psychiatric Association, 1980.

Ellis, A., and Grieger, R. *Handbook of Rational-Emotive Therapy.* New York: Springer, 1977.

Feighner, J. P., et al. Diagnostic criteria for use in psychiatric research. *Arch. Gen. Psychiatry* 26:56–63, 1972.

Freedman, A. M., Kaplan, H. I., and Sadock, B. J. *Modern Synopsis of Comprehensive Textbook of Psychiatry II.* Baltimore: Williams and Wilkins, 1976.

Friedman, A. S. Minimal effects of severe depression on cognitive functioning. *J. Abnorm. Soc. Psychol.* 69:237–243, 1964.

Goodwin, D. W., and Guze, S. B. *Psychiatric Diagnosis* (2nd ed.). New York; London: Oxford University Press, 1979.

Hamilton, M. A rating scale for depression *J. Neurol. Neurosurg. Psychiatry* 23:56–62, 1960.

Hammon, C. L. and Krautz, S. Effects of success and failure on depressive cognitions. *J. Abnormal Psychology* 85:557–586, 1976.

Harrow, M., and Quinlan, D. Is disordered thinking unique to schizophrenia? *Arch. Gen. Psychiatry* 34:15–21, 1977.

Herzig, S. I. Occupational therapy assessment of cognitive levels as predictors of the community adjustment of chronic schizophrenic patients. University of Southern California Master's Thesis, 1978.

Hollingshead, A. B., and Redlich, F. C. *Social Class and Mental Illness.* New York: Wiley, 1958.

Katz, N. An occupational therapy study of cognition in adult inpatients with depression. University of Southern California Master's Thesis, 1979.

Kendell, R. E. The classification of depression: A review of contemporary confusion. *Br. J. Psychiatry* 129:15–28, 1976.

Lanzito, B. M., Caldoret, R. J., and Pugh, D. D. Thought disorder in depression. *Am. J. Psychiatry* 131:703–707, 1974.

Mandleberg, I. A., and Brooks, D. N. Cognitive recovery after severe head injury. *J. Neurol. Psychiatry* 38:1121–1126, 1127–1132, 1975.

Matarazo, J. D. *Wechsler's Measurement and Appraisal of Adult Intelligence.* Baltimore: Williams and Wilkins, 1972.

Moore, D. S. An occupational therapy evaluation of sensorimotor cognition: Initial reliability, validity, and descriptive data for hospitalized schizophrenic adults. University of Southern California Master's Thesis, 1978.

Murphy, G. E., et al. Cognitive therapy and pharmacotherapy: Singly and together in the treatment of depression. *Arch. Gen. Psychiatry* 4:33–41, 1984.

Nelson, J. C., Jatlow, P. I., and Quinlan, D. M. Subjective complaints during desipramine treatment. *Arch. Gen. Psychiatry* 41:5–59, 1984.

O'Leary, M. R., et al. Distortion in the perception of depression as a function of level of depression and denial. *J. Clin. Psychol.* 32:527–531, 1976.

Piaget, J. *Biology and Knowledge: An Essay on the Relations Between Organic Regulation and Cognitive Processes*, transl. by B. Walsh. Chicago: University of Chicago Press, 1971.

Piaget, J. *Behavior and Evolution*, transl. by D. Nicholson-Smith. New York: Pantheon, 1978.

Pincus, J. H., and Tucker, G. J. *Behavioral Neurology* (2nd ed.). New York: Oxford University Press, 1978.

Quereshi, M. Y. The comparability of WAIS and WISC subtest scores and IQ estimate. *J. Psychology* 68:73–82, 1968.

Rapaport, D., Gill, M. M., and Shafer, R. The Wechsler-Bellevue Scale. In R. Holt (ed.), *Diagnostic Psychological Testing* (rev. ed.). New York: International University Press, 1968.

Silverman, J. S., Silverman, J. A., and Eardley, D. A. Do maladaptive attitudes cause depression? *Arch. Gen. Psychiatry* 41:28–30, 1984.

Simmons, A. D., Garfield, S. L., and Murphy, G. E. The process of change in cognitive therapy and pharmacotherapy for depression. *Arch. Gen. Psychiatry* 41:45–51, 1984.

Sternberg, D. E., and Jarvik, M. E. Memory functions

in depression. *Arch. Gen. Psychiatry* 33:219–224, 1976.

Wechsler, D. *Manual for the Wechsler Adult Intelligence Scale (WAIS).* New York: Psychological Corp., 1955.

Weckowicz, T. E., et al. Speed in test performance in relation to depressive illness and age. *Can. Psychiatr. Assoc. J.* 23:107–109, 1978.

Williams, L. R. Development and initial testing of an object classification test. University of Southern California Master's Thesis, 1981.

Zung, W. W. K., and Durham, N. C. A self-rating depression scale. *Arch. Gen. Psychiatry* 12:63–70, 1965.

Zung, W. W. K., and Durham, N. C. From art to science. *Arch. Gen. Psychiatry* 29:328–337, 1973.

CHAPTER 14

RESEARCH WITH A NONDISABLED POPULATION

Linda Riska Williams
Claudia Kay Allen

A nondisabled population was selected (Williams, 1981) to explore the similarities and differences between normal and disabled adults. In addition an instrument that could explore further application of the Piagetian hierarchy to adults was developed.

PURPOSE OF THE STUDY

The problem addressed in this study (Williams, 1981) was a description of cognitive abilities as observed in a nondisabled adult population. The study was divided into three parts:

1. An exploration of the usefulness of Piaget's hierarchy for assessing cognitive disabilities beyond the sensorimotor period. The Riska Object Classification Test (ROC) was developed to assess preoperational and concrete operational thinking. Steps were taken to examine the reliability and validity of this test in a nondisabled population.
2. An examination of the relationships between the Allen Cognitive Level Test (ACL) and the ROC in a nondisabled population.
3. An examination of the similarities and differences in ACL scores in this nondisabled population, schizophrenic patients (Moore, 1978; see Chap. 12), and depressed patients (Katz, 1979; see Chap. 13).

INSTRUMENTS

Three instruments were used in this study: the ACL, the Hollingshead Two-Factor Index of Social Position (HISP), and the ROC. The method of administering the ACL is described in Chapter 4; the validity and reliability data available at the time this study was conducted are presented in Chapters 12 and 13.

The HISP (Appendix 14-1) grew out of an investigation of the relationship between mental illness and social class (Hollingshead and Redlich, 1958). It has been acclaimed as one of the most widely used measures of social status (Miller, 1977). The index consists of two seven-point scales with scale scores for two factors: occupation and education. Each factor is weighted, and then the two scores are summed to produce a single index of social position score. These scores fall into five classes, I to V; I is highest, while V is lowest. The two-factor version of the index is used in this study; there is a three-factor version that adds place of residence (Hollingshead and Redlich, 1958). The correlation between judged class and education and occupation was reported to be high ($r = 0.906$); that between judged class and residence, education, and occupation was slightly higher ($r = 0.942$) (Hollingshead and Redlich, 1958). Education and occupation were selected because these two factors may provide a means of controlling for past experiences that may influence present performance. The HISP was used as a subject selection criterion. The aim was to study 10 nondisabled adults in each of the five classes.

Rationale for the Riska Object Classification Test

Herzig's (1978) finding that the cognitive level was a poor predictor of community adjustment led to the idea of developing an instrument that would measure cognition at periods above the sensorimotor period. A further stimulus was the frequent clinical comment by staff members that the level 5, and sometimes level 6, patient has "poor judgment." It was thought that a test of the higher stages of development might provide a clearer description of what is meant by *poor judgment*.

Inhelder and Piaget's (1964) investigations into the development of intelligence during the preoperational, concrete operational, and formal operational stages have included various tasks assessing abilities in seriation, conservation, and classification. The performance of daily life activities seems to be more logically related to classification, with the inclusion of part–whole relations, than to the other Piagetian areas of study. The other tasks may

be skills acquired during educational experiences; indeed, Inhelder and Piaget (1964) suggested this possibility.

The task demands of many activities include flexibility in organizing and classifying information. Some examples will illustrate this point. The homemaker typically needs to organize such household duties as cleaning, laundering, shopping, meal planning, and food preparation. In many cases these duties must be scheduled around meeting the frequent needs of a young child or adjusted by school schedules. Many formal jobs also demand flexibility in organizing various duties to be accomplished within a work period. Unexpected problems that may occur include temperamental machinery, supply irregularities, or indignant customers. Although it has never been demonstrated systematically, probably all of these situations require the person to separate and organize various parts of a task to accomplish the desired end product, whether it is dinner ready at seven o'clock, a daily quota of assembled goods, or satisfied customers. The degree to which the individual is able to arrange and organize the parts of a task mentally in relation to the desired goal may influence his or her effectiveness and efficiency in accomplishing a given task. The ability to consider individual parts of a task while keeping in mind the whole, and simultaneously considering the whole while keeping in mind the individual parts, is referred to by Inhelder and Piaget (1964) as part–whole relations in classification behavior. The potential for generalizing from a test of classification abilities to other routine tasks led to the selection of classification as a focus of study.

Support for the idea that classification abilities are impaired by mental disorders is available. Psychiatric patients have shown significant deficits on classification tests (Kay and Singh, 1975; Kay et al., 1975; Pishkin et al., 1977; Stewin and Martin, 1975; Trunnell, 1964, 1965; Vygotsky, 1962). Classification deficits have also been reported in neurologic disorders such as cerebral palsy, stroke, organic brain syndromes, and possibly learning disorders

(Elliott, 1971; Finnie, 1975). The range of diagnostic groups suggests that classification is an appropriate consideration in relation to cognitive disabilities.

The literature of psychiatry and psychology was reviewed to locate a classification instrument thought to be suitable for occupational therapy use. The results were disappointing. All of the tests reviewed, except one, measure a quantity or end product rather than the quality of a process (Hathaway, 1975). These tests provide a measure of what the patient cannot do, usually in comparison to a healthier population. Tests that measure the correctness of a response, with the expected errors, fail to provide much information about what the patient can do. In addition the relative order, or hierarchy, of the responses is neglected. One can get a score, but what scores mean in relation to the severity of the individual's medical condition or functional abilities is unclear. One test that measures the process of classification, Vygotsky's Block Test (1962), was located. The original design and a revised model by Kasanin-Hanfmann* were both rejected, however, because administration took one hour or longer, which is too much time in clinical practice. A decision was made to develop a new classification test (ROC) and to begin to examine its reliability and validity.

Instrument Development

Inhelder and Piaget's 1964 description of preoperational and concrete operational thinking was used to suggest items that might be included in assessing classification abilities. Inhelder and Piaget used a number of different materials, including toys, flowers, beads, and blocks, to study classification in children. Many of these materials were thought to be inappropriate for an adult population. In an attempt to make the media less childish and to simplify the assessment method, colored forms (Fig. 14-1) were

*Kasanin-Hanfmann Concept Formation Test, Examiner Manual 36118M, Stoeuting Co., 1350 S. Kostner Ave., Chicago, IL 60623.

chosen for the classification task. Such forms have typically been used to assess classification behavior (Kay and Singh 1975; Pishkin et al., 1977; Trunnell, 1964, 1965).

There are two basic philosophies that influence instrument development: psychometric and impressionistic testing. Psychometric testing is rigorous and experimental, while impressionistic testing is not as strict and allows for more flexibility during the testing process. A combination of the two philosophies is considered optimal, although most tests emphasize one over the other (Cronbach, 1960).

The Piagetian method is impressionistic, and the development of the ROC started with this point of view (Hathaway, 1975; Kolberg and Devries, 1969). The first drafts of the ROC were pilot-tested with patients, friends, family members, virtually anyone who would give it a try; trends were identified. The impressionistic method is very time-consuming, and after five or six groupings the volunteers usually reverted to variations within the same, or a simpler, level of classification. This raised questions about how psychometric methods would compare to impressionistic testing. With the same testing materials, a sample of a classification group was given to a subject, who was asked to place the remaining objects in groups like the sample.

Elements of psychometric and impressionistic testing were included in the selected method of administering the ROC. The first part is unstructured (ROCUN) in that patients are given the cardboard shapes and asked to place them in groups, that is, to select their own classification criterion for forming a group. Any classification criterion is accepted, and there are no right or wrong answers. The unstructured part of the test is impressionistic and resembles the open-ended questions used in psychiatric interviews (Maloney and Ward, 1976) in that the patient must spontaneously decide where to start and how to proceed. The therapist observes spontaneous motor actions and records the patient's response to an open-ended demand. Then the patient is asked to identify verbally the classification criterion that guided these motor actions.

Fig. 14-1. Materials for the Riska Object Classification Test, shown actual size. Eighteen forms are used, two of each shape in each of three colors (dark brown, medium brown, and cream). Forms are hand cut so that small irregularities on the edges may be noticeable on close inspection.

The second part of the test is structured (ROCST)—the patient is asked to form classes that are like the therapist's. There is a right and a wrong answer, and the therapist encourages the patient to arrive at the right answer. The classification criteria are selected by the therapist, and in that sense the structure is provided by the therapist.

The impressionistic nature of the ROCUN allows the patient to manipulate the objects in a variety of ways. Therapists must have an in-depth knowledge of the rating criteria (Fig. 14-2) to record scores reliably. To simplify matters the therapist should note that the odd-numbered items are observations of behavior and the even-numbered items call for a verbal comment about the preceding behavior. This order is based on Piaget's (1951, 1971) contention that motor behavior precedes verbal explanation.

Rating Criteria

Our experience in teaching the rating criteria (Fig. 14-2) to therapists suggests that comprehension, and therefore, reliability, is enhanced by a physical manipulation of the materials. Readers may find that the criteria are clearer if they make a replication of the materials (see Fig. 14-1) so that they can see what the classes look like.

1. *Perceptual exploration* refers to extensive random sensory investigation of the objects by physically manipulating, looking at, touching, smelling, or tasting them or purposefully dropping them to produce a slapping sound.
2. *Perceptual comment* refers to a statement regarding the sensory investigations referred to as perceptual exploration.
3. *Exact match* is observed when objects are combined in groups of two with both color and shape matched. The individual groups of two appear randomly arranged with no further organization than that of two objects exactly matched. It is not necessary for all of the objects to be used.
4. *Comment on exact match* means that the subject

Case No. _____   Date _____

	Unstructured classification					Structured classification				
No. of trials	1	2	3	4	5	1	2	3	4	5
1. Perceptual exploration.										
2. Perceptual comment.										
3. Exact match: same color, same shape, group of two.										
4. Comment on exact match.										
5. Sequence dictates criterion. Space dictates criterion. Graphic, picture, story, or geometric pattern.										
6. Comment on sequence, space, or graphic.										
7. One criterion not followed: color, shape, or number started; subject changes or stops before all pieces used.										
8. Identifies criterion changed or stopped. Not all pieces accounted for.										
9. Relies on perceptual organization to reinforce one criterion, all pieces used: groups based on exact match, groups formed by tactile verification.										
10. Identifies criterion that includes all pieces and uses perceptual gestures to validate for self.										
11. One criterion extended to all pieces with random grouping: Like color or shapes placed together.										
12. Identifies one criterion (color, shape, or number); all pieces accounted for, no perceptual gestures.										
13. Uses two criteria simultaneously (color, shape, or number); all pieces used.										
14. Identifies two criteria.										

Final score _____   Final score _____

Scoring instructions: The highest score reached on each part of the test, regardless of the number of trials, is the final score for that part.

Comments:

Fig. 14-2. Score sheet for Riska Object Classification Test.

comments that the group (of two) are the same. The subject may note small flaws in the cut edges of the forms. This shows a strong dependence on tangible features to organize the objects into small groups and is allowable as long as it accompanies a reference to a pair or group of two.

5. *Sequence dictates criterion* refers to organization of the objects according to the order that they are placed on the table by the subject. For example, an oval form is placed first followed by a series of ovals, the last of which is dark brown. A series of dark brown objects are then placed, the last of which is an arrow-shaped form; this is followed by a series of arrows. The classification criterion has changed from shape to color and back to shape. Individual groups are not formed, but an alignment of objects matched according to one criterion, as in the game of dominoes, occurs. Sequence criteria may be difficult to score but can be recognized by the subject's tendency to change the apparent criterion rapidly, which appears to be perceptually aided by the last object placed on the table. It is not necessary for all of the objects to be used.

Space dictates criterion is scored if spatial arrangement on the table is the only criterion used. The angle of an object or the distance between one object and another is used to form groups. Neither shape nor color is used as a criterion. Investigators accustomed to thinking of shape and color will want to take special note that this alternative criterion is possible. It is not necessary for all of the objects to be used.

Graphic, picture, story, or geometric pattern is probably the most easily observed criterion for classification. The test objects are graphically arranged to produce geometric patterns or pictures. Groups may or may not be symmetrical. It is not necessary for all of the objects to be used. Frequently made pictures include stars, clowns, and kites.

6. *Comment on sequence, space, or graphics* is scored if the subject simply states that the groups are the same or points to the forms indicating similar alignment, tells a story, or describes the graphic arrangement.

7. *One criterion not followed* means the subject begins to form groups on the basis of color or shape but stops before using all the pieces. Some mental formation of groups is apparent, but the subject does not recognize that there are other forms on the table that would fit into the group, for example, one arrow is missing. All of the objects are not used consistently.

8. *Comment on one criterion not followed* means the subject is able to identify the one criterion but is unable to account for or is unconcerned about the unused pieces.

9. *Relies on perceptual organization* means the subject is able to retain one mental criterion to include all of the objects but still relies strongly on apparent visual or tactile organization to form groups. Reliance on perceptual organization is indicated by such behavior as (1) frequently looking at both sides of the objects before placing them in groups, (2) carefully placing the objects so that they are partially aligned or stacked, or (3) frequently touching and adjusting the objects.

Groups based on exact match are groups consisting of six objects that are subdivided into three pairs of exact matches. For example, six arrows are placed together with an indication of pairs based on color. All the objects must be included. *Groups formed by tactile verification* refers to groups that consist of six similarly shaped or colored objects that are carefully aligned and frequently stacked. All the objects must be included.

10. *Identifies criterion; tactile* means the subject identifies a single criterion including all of the pieces and may (1) physically manipulate the objects while stating the criterion in an apparent effort to verify that the groups are correctly organized or (2) mention irregularities in the objects while stating the criterion, and may say that they are not "exactly" alike.

11. *One criterion extended; random grouping* means groups of six are formed with color or shape as the criterion. No great care in placement of the objects is observed. The objects are tossed or piled together in a casual manner without regard for mi-

nor irregularities in the objects. All of the pieces must be included.

12. *Identifies one criterion; no gestures* means the subject identifies the criterion without inspecting or rechecking the groups. The subject may use the word *shape* or some other word to describe the classifying criterion. Examples of frequently used terms are *arrows, points, ovals, egg shapes, half circles,* and *half collars*. These terms and others are given credit as proper identification provided excessive gesturing is not used.

13. *Uses two criteria simultaneously* means groups are constructed on the basis of two or more criteria, usually color and shape. Examples of criteria are three different shapes and three different colors (groups of three); three different shapes and two different colors (groups of three). All of the pieces must be used.

14. *Identifies two criteria* means the subject must identify the two, or more, criteria used.

15. *Abstraction cued by physical properties* refers to abstract criteria cued by the physical properties of the objects that may be used to form groups. Examples are all forms with curves, all forms with straight edges, all forms made of cardboard.

16. *Identifies abstraction* means the subject must identify the criterion used.

Test Instructions

The subject is seated at a table in a sufficiently lighted room. The test setting should be as distraction free as possible. Unnecessary clutter and noise should be avoided. The examiner sits adjacent to the subject at approximately a 90-degree angle. The subject is told that the number of responses and time will be noted but there are *no set*, or *right*, responses.

Unstructured Classification

The classification objects are placed in a random fashion in front of the subject. The investigator says, *"Put these objects into groups that are alike."*

An alternative instruction is, *"Make groups that are the same or alike in some way."*

Only if necessary should the investigator repeat the above directions.

After the subject finishes arranging the groups the investigator asks, *"How are your groups alike?"*

The investigator checks the appropriate box on the scoring sheet.

The investigator then says, *"Now make different groups that are alike."*

If after the subject has finished making groups he or she has not stated how they are alike the investigator again asks, *"How are these groups alike?"*

The scoring form is marked appropriately, and the test continues.

The unstructured part of the test is discontinued when the subject states that no additional groups can be made or when 8 to 10 minutes have elapsed. The highest score assigned any grouping is the final score for this section.

The boundaries between groups may be ambiguous; if during the test the investigator is in doubt as to where the subject's groups are, he or she should ask the subject to point to the individual groups before asking how they are alike.

Structured Classification

The second part of the ROC is started immediately after the first. The objects are gathered into a pile by the investigator.

The investigator says, *"Now I am going to make a group. You make as many groups like mine as you can."*

The group presented by the investigator is selected from the piled objects and arranged in front of the subject with seeming randomness such that edges of the objects slightly overlap. The group consists of 1 dark brown arrow, 1 cream quarter circle, and 1 medium brown oval. Sufficient room is left to allow placement of all the subject's "alike" groups below the sample. Instructions are repeated only as needed.

If the subject arranges the groups so that each group includes 3 different shapes and 3 different colors, regardless of sequence, the investigator asks, *"How are your groups like mine?"*

If the subject gives an answer that includes the criteria of 3 colors and 3 shapes, the test is ended. If the subject does not indicate both color and shape the investigator asks, *"Is there any other way your groups are like mine?"*

After the subject responds the scoring form is marked according to his or her second response.

If each of the subject's groups do not consist of 3 different shapes and 3 different colors the investigator says, *"Your groups are like mine in some ways but not in others. Try to make them more like mine."*

The test is continued in this manner until the subject makes the desired response and verbally identifies it, or the subject declines further participation, or 10 minutes have elapsed. The scoring form is marked appropriately, and the test is ended.

The subject is thanked for his or her cooperation, and the investigator completes the scoring form. The highest score assigned to any grouping is noted as the final score for each test section. Any unusual circumstances, behaviors, or responses are noted on the scoring form.

Scoring Difficulties

Scoring an impressionistic test is usually difficult, which is one of the reasons for the disfavor of open-ended tests. During the development of the ROC, rating criteria 9 through 12 consistently proved to be confusing, producing difficulties in attaining rater agreement. Careful observation reveals subtle differences in the motor actions performed during the process of forming groups according to these criteria. The final groups that are formed look similar, but the process differs. A score of 9 or 10 is given when the placement of objects is extremely deliberate, accompanied by frequent touching or adjusting of the objects. The objects may be carefully stacked in neat piles. These motor actions may be interpreted as reliance on tactile or visual cues to verify a classification criterion; a distinction between tactile and visual cues was not included in the scoring of the ROC. A score of 11 or 12 is given when the motor action is casual and sorting is accomplished at a comfortable rate without a reexamination of the colors or shapes. The objects may be gently tossed into a random pile. This may be interpreted as a reliance on an internal thought to guide motor actions.

SUBJECTS

The first subject population consisted of 10 psychiatric inpatients and 10 hospital employees. These volunteers were tested to determine the reliability of the ROC; no further investigations were done with them. The second population, the nondisabled sample, consisted of 58 hospital employees selected by a partially stratified sampling method according to HISP, resulting in five groups. Social selection rather than random selection was employed owing to time constraints. Additional selection criteria included an age of 18 to 65 years, no severe auditory or visual impairments, an adequate understanding of the English language, and no known neurologic or psychiatric disorder. Occupational therapy staff members were excluded. Eight of the fifty-eight subjects were eliminated from the study because they failed to meet the selection criteria.

The final analysis of the data, after data collection was completed, disclosed that one subject who had been placed in Social class V actually belonged in class IV. Stratification was as follows: class I, 10; II, 10; III, 10; IV, 11; V, 9 ($N = 50$). Subjects signed a consent form, and the study was reviewed for the protection of human subjects.

The order of testing was (1) HISP, (2) ACL, and (3) ROC.

RESULTS

Demographic Variables

The nondisabled sample had a mean age of 34.9 years (standard deviation, ± 10.3; range, 18 to 64 years). Twenty-five men and twenty-five women participated in the study. The ethnic makeup of the sample showed an unexpected similarity to that of the total employee population of the hospital where the study was done.

ETHNIC GROUP	RESEARCH SAMPLE (%)	TOTAL POPULATION (%)
White	32	40.71
Black	44	37.00
Mexican American	14	15.22
Asian	6	6.12
Other	2	1.06

Fifteen subjects (30%) had previous leather lacing experience.

No significant correlations were found between the selected demographic variables and the three cognitive scores: ACL, ROCUN, and ROCST (Table 14-1). The lack of the influence of sex is especially noteworthy in relation to the concern that women would score higher than men on the ACL because of their familiarity with sewing. Sex did not seem to influence the ACL score.

Riska Object Classification Test

Interrater Reliability

Interrater reliability on the ROCUN and the ROCST was examined. One of us (L. R. W.) and Katz (see Chap. 13) did simultaneous and independent ratings with the first subject population (described above under Subjects). Pearson product-moment correlations were done; the acceptable level of correlation was set at greater than or equal to $r = 0.80$. The results, using 18 degrees of freedom, were as follows:

Table 14-1. Pearson r correlations between cognitive test scores and selected demographic variables in 50 nondisabled subjects

Variable	ACL	ROCUN	ROCST
Age	−0.109	−0.113	0.045
Sex	0.043	−0.513	0.200
Previous leather lacing experience	−0.123	−0.087	−0.099

ACL = Allen Cognitive Level Test; ROCUN = Riska Object Classification Test, unstructured part; ROCST = Riska Object Classification Test, structured part.
Note: Correlations are nonsignificant in all cases.

TEST	r	p	RANGE
ROCUN	0.835	< .01	4–16
ROCST	0.826	< .01	8–14

These results met the level of acceptance. Six disagreements on the ROCUN and four disagreements on the ROCST were recorded. Eight of these disagreements were on items 10, 12, and 14, which were then refined. These refined scoring criteria are presented in this chapter.

Concurrent Validity

Negative correlations between the ROC and the HISP were expected (1 is the lowest score on the ROC; I is the highest on the HISP). The correlations showed mixed results (Table 14-2). The unstructured part of the test (ROCUN) showed a significant correlation with education, occupation, and the composite social position score, explaining about 33 percent of the variance. The correlations with the structured portion of the test (ROCST) were low, explaining about 4 percent of the variance, and they were not significant.

Discrepancies between the structured and unstructured portion of the ROC, in relation to the HISP, were found in Katz's data (1979; see Tables 13-8 and 13-9) as well. In Katz's study, a significant correlation between education and ROCUN both at

Table 14-2. *Pearson* r *correlations between cognitive test scores and education, occupation, and social position in 50 nondisabled subjects*

Test	Education	Occupation	Social position
ACL	−0.507[a]	−0.526[b]	−0.506[a]
ROCUN	−0.549[b]	−0.589[b]	−0.588[b]
ROCST	−0.217	−0.203	−0.215

ACL = Allen Cognitive Level Test; ROCUN = Riska Objective Classification Test, unstructured part; ROCST = Riska Object Classification Test, structured part.
[a] $p < .0002$.
[b] $p < .0001$.

Table 14-3. *Scores on the Allen Cognitive Level Test (ACL) and Riska Object Classification Test (ROCST and ROCUN) in 50 nondisabled subjects*

Test	Mean	Standard deviation	Range
ACL	5.8	±0.5	4–6
ROCUN	12.9	±2.5	6–16
ROCST	13.5	±1.1	10–14

admission ($r = 0.316$; $p < .01$) and at discharge ($r = 0.309$; $p < .01$) was found. Social position correlated with ROCUN at discharge ($r = 0.404$; $p < .01$) but not at admission. No significant correlations between the ROCST and the HISP were found. The differences (*t*-test values) between admission and discharge scores on both parts of the ROC were not significant; the ROC did not seem to measure improvement in the depressed population (see Chap. 13). The score on the unstructured part of the ROC thus seems to be associated with education in both disabled and nondisabled populations. Occupation and social position seem to be relevant factors in control populations, but not among those with a lower cognitive level.

Further analysis of the data from nondisabled subjects revealed that no subject in Social class I or II scored lower than 12 on the ROCUN, and 13 of the 20 subjects in these two categories scored 16. Subjects in these social positions have a bachelor's or graduate degree (e.g., doctors, nurses, social workers). These subjects classified by at least one criterion, and over half of them classified by multiple criteria. The implication may be that persons in higher social positions may be able to impose their own organization spontaneously in response to an open-ended direction.

The ROCST has a maximum score of 14. Approximately half of Katz's (1979) depressed population

achieved the highest score at admission; there was no room for improvement at discharge. Seventy percent of the nondisabled subjects also obtained the highest ROCST score. The structured score was usually higher than the unstructured score (Table 14-3).

These findings were surprising, and numerous plausible explanations have been considered. At present it may be prudent to make a clear distinction between structured and spontaneous performance. A structured situation, as operationally defined in the ROC, provides a standard of performance. The patient's performance is either right or wrong, that is, it either complies or does not comply with the standard. Therapists administering the test noticed that people who raised their score on the ROCST did so with distress, that is, fidgeting, sighing, and complaining. People were asked, "Make your groups more like mine." Directions that encourage a person to strive for a higher level of performance may produce a false positive by eliciting a level of ability that would not be spontaneously employed during routine task performance. The ROCST may not be a valid indicator of the functional abilities used outside a testing or treatment situation. These findings have important clinical implications; treatment methods that encourage a person to strive for a higher level of performance may be associated with expectations that supercede actual community performance.

The meaning and usefulness of the ROC is still in question. ROCUN scores correlated with the HISP and results of the Block Design of the Wechsler

Adult Intelligence Scale (see Chap. 13). ROCST scores correlated with the Block Design scores and with the patient's self-report of depression at discharge (see Chap. 13). The ROC certainly raises some interesting questions about the kind of instructions given during an observation of task performance and the validity of the therapist's predictions of spontaneous task performance.

Allen Cognitive Level Test

Validity

Pearson correlations computed between the ACL score and the HISP were significant (see Table 14-2). Most of the subjects in this study scored a level 5 or 6 (see Table 14-3), and thus it seems that level 6 is associated with a higher education, occupation, and social position. Forty people (80%) scored at level 6; nine (18%), at level 5; and one (2%), at level 4. The range of performance in a nondisabled population merits further investigation.

The patient population studies (Katz, 1979; Moore, 1978) did not show a significant correlation between education and social position. The patient studies were done in a public institution and were biased in the direction of the lower social positions. This study's stratification across the five social positions may provide a clearer indication of how social position is associated with the ACL. Patient studies conducted with people from the higher social positions will be of interest in refining our performance expectations.

ACL scores below level 6 in nondisabled persons are of interest. The one score of level 4 may be a research artifact; whether this is true or not can only be determined with a larger sample. An inspection of the data indicates that the nine people who scored 5 on the ACL were in Social class IV or V. The data suggest that level 5 may be the usual level of function for some people; a possible implication is that level 5 may also be the premorbid level for some patients. The determination in individual cases still leaves a lot of ambiguity. If, for example,

a class of IV or V had been used to predict an ACL score of 5, the prediction with these data would have been correct 9 times and incorrect 11 times. What can be gleaned from this study is that it is possible to function successfully in classes IV and V with an ACL score of 5, but this expectation should be used with caution.

Relation with Riska Object Classification Test

The second objective of this study was to examine the relationship between sensorimotor and concrete operational abilities, operationally defined by the ACL and the ROC, respectively. Clinical observations of patients assessed at levels 5 and 6 continued to reveal limitations that were difficult to describe objectively. The relationship between these two instruments was examined in the hope of finding a clearer description of these limitations.

Examination of the distribution of ACL and ROCUN scores revealed a strong break between ACL scores and classification ability at item 12 (one criterion; no gestures) on the ROCUN. Cross-tabulations for the chi-square were, therefore, set up for ≤ 12 and > 12 for comparison with ACL scores 5 and 6 (Table 14-4). The one subject who scored a 4 on the ACL was excluded from this analysis. The association ($\chi^2 = 8.98$; degrees of freedom, or df, $= 1$; $p < .003$) may indicate that spontaneous exploratory actions at level 5 may rely on one classification criteria suggested by the material objects. Symbols such as words or images may be required to use two classification criteria at level 6.

No association between the ACL and the ROCST was found. The association between the ACL and the unstructured, but not the structured, part of the ROC is interesting. The instructions given during the ACL can be repeated twice, if the patient wishes a second demonstration. The patient is not compelled to persevere until he or she gets it right. In addition the patient can discontinue the ACL at any time. The philosophies behind the ACL and the ROCUN may explain the associations found between them. The ACL seems to have a greater re-

Table 14-4. Relation between ACL, ROCUN,
and ROCST scores in a nondisabled population

ROC score	No. (%) of subjects	
	Level 5	Level 6
ROCUN[a]		
>12	0 (0)	22 (45)
≤12	9 (18)	18 (37)
ROCST[b]		
>12	7 (14)	33 (67)
≤12	2 (4)	7 (14)

ACL = Allen Cognitive Level Test; ROCUN = Riska Object
Classification Test, unstructured part; ROCST = Riska
Object Classification Test, structured part; df = degrees of
freedom.
[a]Association with ACL score: χ^2 = 8.98; df = 1; p = .003.
[b]Association with ACL scores: χ^2 = 0.11; df = 1; p is not
significant.

lationship to an impressionistic than to a psychometric testing procedure.

Nondisabled Versus Depressed or Schizophrenic Subjects

The third part of the study aimed at comparing the ACL scores of nonpatients with existing data on schizophrenic and depressed patients. The nonpatient sample of 50 subjects achieved a mean ACL score of 5.8; standard deviation was ± 0.5, with a range of scores from 4 to 6. Forty subjects (80%) scored 6 (Table 14-5, Fig. 14-3).

In comparing Moore's (1978) admission data on hospitalized schizophrenics, two subjects were omitted from the patient sample because the data file was lost. In the remaining sample of 30 subjects, the mean ACL score was 4.0, slightly higher than Moore's reported mean of 3.9 for the 32 subjects. Standard deviation for the sample of 30 subjects was ± 1.0, with a range in scores of 2 to 6. Sixty percent or 18 subjects scored 4. The remaining ten subjects were distributed nearly equally among scores of 2, 3, 5, and 6.

The sample of depressed patients (Katz, 1979) at admission fell between the nonpatient and schizophrenic patient samples. The mean ACL score for the 32 subjects was 5.0; standard deviation was ± 0.7, with a range in scores of 4 to 6. Fifteen subjects (47%) scored 5. The remaining subjects were almost equally distributed, scoring either 4 or 6.

An analysis of variance (Table 14-5) showed a significant statistical difference in mean ACL scores between all three samples: F = 59.56; p ≤ .0001; df = 2. These data indicate that the ACL is able to discriminate between the three samples, with schizophrenic patients scoring the lowest, followed by the depressed patients, and with the nonpatients scoring the highest.

DISCUSSION

One of the reasons for developing the ROC was to examine the Piagetian hierarchy as applied to adults with mental disorders. When applied to this group

Table 14-5. Analysis of variance for Allen Cognitive Level Test scores in normal, schizophrenic, and depressed subjects

Subjects	Mean	N	Sum of squares	Mean square	F	Standard deviation
Normal	5.8	50				
Schizophrenic	4.0	30	61.761	30.881	59.56	0.720
Depressed	5.0	32				

Note: p = .0001; degrees of freedom = 2.

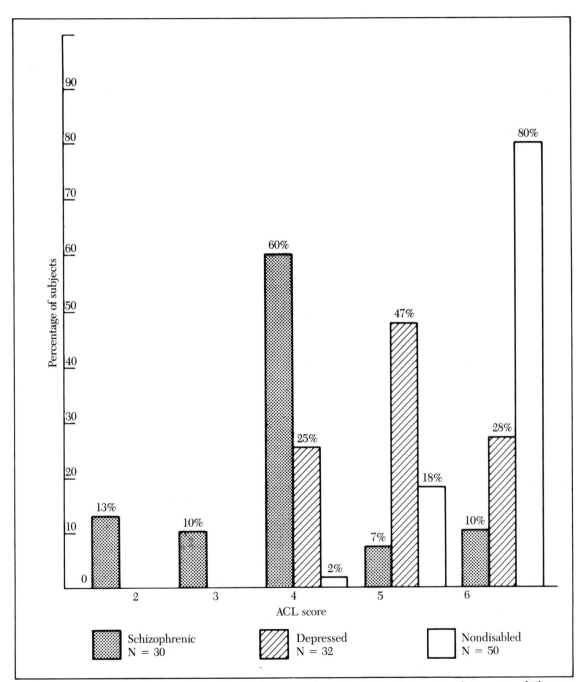

Fig. 14-3. Frequency distribution of Allen Cognitive Level Test scores for nondisabled, depressed, and schizophrenic subjects. (From C. K. Allen, Independence through activity: The practice of Occupational Therapy [Psychiatry]. Am. J. Occup. Ther. 36:731–739, 1982.

the normal growth and development hierarchy collapsed like a folded telescope. Both studies (Katz 1979; Williams, 1981) found an overlap between the operational definitions of sensorimotor period cognition (ACL) and preoperational and concrete operational cognition (ROC). The findings tended to support clinical suspicions. If one assumes that the Piagetian hierarchy is only partially correct in describing the functional behavior of adults with mental disorders, then one must be prepared to look beyond the realm of the Piagetian hierarchy. The studies suggested that a rigorous adherence to Piagetian theory would be counterproductive. There are numerous alternative descriptions of the mental processes that guide behavior. The ROC provides some guidelines for selecting and discarding descriptions of mental processes that could be synthesized with the best attributes of Piagetian theory.

The two parts of the ROC contain methodologic differences that extend beyond testing philosophies and have implications for clinical practice. The statistical analysis showed surprising discrepancies between the structured and unstructured portions of the ROC. The term *unstructured* may be misleading; *spontaneous* may be more accurate. Spontaneous performance occurs in a naturalistic setting; the quality of performance is self-regulated, complying with the patient's self-selected standards of performance. A structure, as operationally defined in psychometric tests, is authoritative. Structured performance occurs in an artificial setting; the quality of performance is judged by another person against an authoritative, and socially sanctioned, standard of performance. Therapists require both methods in clinical practice, but observations of spontaneous performance may provide better information about what the patient will, and will not, do outside the testing and treating situation. The rehabilitation ethic supports the notion that therapists should "push" patients to try to do as much as they possibly can for themselves. Therapists may be disappointed if patients fail to continue to do all of these tasks when they go home. Observations of

spontaneous performance may produce better predictions of what a patient will do after he or she leaves the testing or clinical situation.

Observations of structured performance provide information about how well the patient can comply with social standards of performance. The social standard cannot be set in any old way the therapist chooses; it must be deemed relevant by the patient, family, and community. The problem with many psychometric tests is that they fail to select tasks that are relevant to the social community. The therapist must observe structured performance when there is some question about the patient's ability to comply with socially determined standards of performance.

The use of odd and even numbers on the ROC to score motor and verbal performance was of little value in the studies of depressed patients (Katz, 1979) and nondisabled subjects (Williams, 1981). Most of the subjects were able to provide a verbal explanation for their motor behavior. Clinical experience suggests that the motor performance should be retained: Phencyclidine hydrochloride (PCP) abusers often display motor performance that they cannot describe verbally. Rater agreement on motor performance is difficult to obtain, however. We would suggest that raters draw quick sketches, with notes about the process, and use these to score the ROC after the testing situation is completed.

The comparison of the ACL scores of three different populations (schizophrenic, depressed, and nondisabled subjects) suggests that the test can cut across diagnostic groups and describe a disability. The distribution of these small samples is encouraging but must be viewed with caution. Skewed distributions are a common occurrence with disabled populations. We hope that we can avoid some of the associated statistical problems. The mean scores seem to be following the expected sequence, which lends face validity to the hierarchy of the cognitive levels. Additional patient populations and larger sample sizes are needed to add clarity to this preliminary investigation.

CONCLUSION

The testing of a nondisabled population has provided important information on the proper "fit" of propositions 1 and 2 in the puzzle of describing cognitive disabilities. This research has also provided information regarding the range of cognitive ability within the nondisabled population. The HISP has been identified as an important connecting piece in the puzzle that may help therapists move toward predicting future function for the cognitively disabled. The following additional research is indicated:

1. Replication of the ACL and ROC with patients with other diagnoses and with the various social classes equally represented, to assess better the interaction between the degree of cognitive disability, the diagnosis, and social position.
2. Replication of the study with a larger sample of patients and nondisabled populations to determine further the reliability and validity of the ACL and ROC.
3. Further investigation of the differences between the unstructured and structured parts of the ROC.

ACKNOWLEDGMENTS

We would like to express our thanks to Robert Wolfe, Ph.D. and Jytte Busk, Ph.D. who served on the thesis committee.

APPENDIX 14-1. HOLLINGSHEAD'S TWO-FACTOR INDEX OF SOCIAL POSITION

The Occupational Scale

I. Higher Executives of Large Concerns, Proprietors, and Major Professionals

    A. Higher Executives (Value of corporation $500,000 and above as rated by Dun and Bradstreet)

        Bank
          Presidents
          Vice-Presidents
          Assistant vice-
            presidents
        Business
          Directors
          Presidents
          Vice-Presidents
          Assistant vice-
            presidents
          Executive
            secretaries
          Research
            directors
          Treasurers

    B. Proprietors (Value over $100,000 by Dun and Bradstreet)

        Brokers
        Contractors
        Dairy owners
        Farmers
        Lumber dealers

    C. Major Professionals

        Accountants (CPA)
        Actuaries
        Agronomists
        Architects
        Artists, portrait
        Astronomers
        Auditors
        Bacteriologists
        Chemical
          engineers
        Chemists
        Clergymen
          (professional
          trained)
        Dentists
        Economists
        Engineers (college
          graduates)

Foresters
Geologists
Judges (superior
    courts)
Lawyers
Metallurgists
Military:
    commissioned
    officers, major
    and above
Officials of the
    executive
    branch of
    government,
    federal, state,
    local: e.g.,
    mayor, city
    manager, city
    plan director,
    Internal
    Revenue
    director
Physicians
Physicists, research
Psychologists,
    practicing
Symphony
    conductor
Teachers,
    university,
    college
Veterinarians
    (veterinary
    surgeons)

Brokerage
    salesmen
Directors of
    purchasing
District managers
Executive
    assistants
Export managers,
    international
    concerns
Farm managers
Government
    officials,
    minor, e.g.,
    Internal
    Revenue
    agents
Manufacturer's
    representa-
    tives
Office managers
Personnel
    managers
Police chief; sheriff
Postmaster
Production
    managers
Sales engineers
Sales managers,
    national
    concerns
Store managers

II. Business Managers, Proprietors of Medium-Sized Businesses, and Lesser Professionals

A. Business Managers in Large Concerns (Value $500,000)

Advertising
    directors
Branch managers

B. Proprietors of Medium Businesses (Value $35,000–$100,000)

Advertising
Clothing store
Contractors
Express company
Farm owners
Fruits, wholesale
Furniture business

Jewelers
Poultry business
Real estate brokers
Rug business
Store
Theater

C. Lesser Professionals

Accountants (not
CPA)
Chiropodists
Chiropractors
Correction officers
Director of
Community
House
Engineers (not
college
graduate)
Finance writers
Health educators
Labor relations
consultants
Librarians
Military:
commissioned
officers,
lieutenant,
captain
Musicians
(symphony
orchestra)
Nurses
Opticians
Optometrists,
D.O.
Pharmacists
Public health
officers (MPH)
Research
assistants,
university

(full-time)
Social workers

III. Administrative Personnel, Owners of Small
Businesses, and Minor Professionals
A. Administrative Personnel

Advertising agents
Chief clerks
Credit managers
Insurance agents
Managers,
departments
Passenger agents,
railroad
Private secretaries
Purchasing agents
Sales representa-
tives
Section heads,
federal, state
and local
governmental
offices
Section heads,
large
businesses
and industries
Service managers
Shop managers
Store managers
(chain)
Traffic managers

B. Small Business Owners ($6,000–$35,000)

Art gallery
Auto accessories
Awnings
Bakery
Beauty shop
Boatyard

Brokerage,
    insurance
Car dealers
Cattle dealers
Cigarette machines
Cleaning shops
Clothing
Coal businesses
Contracting
    businesses
Convalescent
    homes
Decorating
Dog supplies
Dry goods
Engraving business
Feed
Finance
    companies,
    local
Fire extinguishers
Five and dime
Florist
Food equipment
Food products
Foundry
Funeral directors
Furniture
Garage
Gas station
Glassware
Grocery, general
Hotel proprietors
Jewelry
Machinery brokers
Manufacturing
Monuments
Music
Package stores
    (liquor)
Paint contracting
Poultry
Real estate
Records and radios

Restaurant
Roofing contractor
Shoe
Signs
Tavern
Taxi company
Tire shop
Trucking
Trucks and tractors
Upholstery
Wholesale outlets
Window shades

C. Semiprofessionals

Actors and
    showmen
Army, master
    sergeant
Artists, commercial
Appraisers
    (estimators)
Clergymen (not
    professionally
    trained)
Concern managers
Deputy sheriffs
Dispatchers,
    railroad
Interior decorators
Interpreters,
    courts
Laboratory
    assistants
Landscape
    planners
Morticians
Navy, chief petty
    officer
Oral hygienists
Physiotherapists
Piano teachers
Publicity and
    public
    relations

Radio, TV
    announcers
Reporters, court
Reporters,
    newspapers
Surveyors
Title searchers
Tool designers
Travel agents
Yard masters,
    railroad

D. Farmers

Farm owners ($20,000–$35,000)

IV. Clerical and Sales Workers, Technicians, and Owners of Little Businesses (Value under $6,000)
  A. Clerical and Sales Workers

Bank clerks and
    tellers
Bill collectors
Bookkeepers
Business machine
    operators,
    offices
Claims examiners
Clerical or
    stenographic
Conductors,
    railroad
Factory
    storekeepers
Factory
    supervisors
Post Office clerks
Route managers
Sales clerks
Sergeants and
    petty officers,
    military
    services

Shipping clerks
Supervisors,
    utilities,
    factories
Supervisors, toll
    stations

B. Technicians

Dental technicians
Draftsmen
Driving teachers
Expeditor, factory
Experimental
    tester
Instructors,
    telephone
    company,
    factory
Inspectors,
    weights,
    sanitary,
    railroad,
    factory
Investigators
Laboratory
    technicians
Locomotive
    engineers
Operators, PBX
Proofreaders
Safety supervisors
Supervisors of
    maintenance
Technical assistants
Telephone
    company
    supervisors
Timekeepers
Tower operators,
    railroad
Truck dispatchers
Window trimmers
    (stores)

C. Owners of Little Businesses ($3,000–$6,000)

Flower shop
Grocery
Newsstand
Tailor shop

D. Farmers

Owners (Value $10,000–$20,000)

V. Skilled Manual Employees

Auto body repairers
Bakers
Barbers
Blacksmiths
Bookbinders
Boilermakers
Brakemen, railroad
Brewers
Bulldozer operators
Butchers
Cabinet makers
Cable splicers
Carpenters
Casters (founders)
Cement finishers
Cheese makers
Chefs
Compositors
Diemakers
Diesel engine repair
    and maintenance
    (trained)
Diesel shovel
    operators
Electricians
Engravers
Exterminators
Firemen, city

Firemen, railroad
Fitters, gas, steam
Foremen,
    construction,
    dairy
Gardeners, landscape
    (trained)
Glass blowers
Glaziers
Gunsmiths
Gauge makers
Hair stylists
Heat treaters
Horticulturists
Linemen, utility
Linotype operators
Lithographers
Locksmiths
Loom fixers
Machinists (trained)
Maintenance foremen
Linoleum layers
    (trained)
Masons
Masseurs
Mechanics (trained)
Millwrights
Moulders (trained)
Painters
Paperhangers
Patrolmen, railroad
Pattern and model
    makers
Piano builders
Piano tuners
Plumbers
Policemen, city
Postmen
Printers
Radio, television
    maintenance
Repairmen, home
    appliances
Rope splicers

Sheetmetal workers
   (trained)
Shipsmiths
Shoe repairmen
   (trained)
Stationary engineers
   (licensed)
Stewards, club
Switchmen, railroad
Tailors (trained)
Teletype operators
Tool makers
Track supervisors,
   railroad
Tractor-trailer trans.
Typographers
Upholsters (trained)
Watchmakers
Weavers
Welders
Yard supervisors,
   railroad
Small Farmers
Owners (Value under
   $10,000)
Tenants who own farm
   equipment

VI. Machine Operators and Semiskilled Employees

Aides, hospital
Apprentices,
   electricians,
   printers, steam
   fitters, toolmakers
Assembly line workers
Bartenders
Bingo tenders
Bridge tenders
Building
   superintendents
   construction

Bus drivers
Checkers
Coin machine fillers
Cooks, short order
Deliverymen
Dressmakers, machine
Elevator operators
Enlisted men, military
   services
Filers, sanders, buffers
Foundry workers
Garage and gas station
   attendants
Greenhouse workers
Guards, doorkeepers,
   watchmen
Hairdressers
Housekeepers
Meat cutters, and
   packers
Meter readers
Operation, factory
   machines
Oilers, railroad
Practical nurses
Pressers, clothing
Pump operators
Receivers and
   checkers
Roofers
Setup men, factories
Shapers
Signalmen, railroad
Solderers, factory
Sprayers, paint
Steelworkers (not
   skilled)
Standers, wire
   machines
Strippers, rubber
   factory
Taxi drivers
Testers
Timers

Tire moulders
Trainmen, railroad
Truck drivers, general
Waiters-waitresses
      ("better places")
Weighers
Welders, spot
Winders, machine
Wiredrawers, machine
Wine bottlers
Wood workers,
      machine
Wrappers, stores and
      factories
Farmers
Smaller tenants who own little equipment

VII. Unskilled Employees

Amusement park
      workers (bowling
      alleys, pool
      rooms)
Ash removers
Attendants, parking
      lots
Cafeteria workers
Car cleaners, railroad
Carriers, coal
Countermen
Dairy workers
Deck hands
Domestics
Farm helpers
Fishermen (clam
      diggers)
Freight handlers
Garbage collectors
Gravediggers
Hod carriers
Hog killers
Hospital workers,
      unspecified

Hostlers, railroad
Janitors (sweepers)
Laborers, construction
Laborers, unspecified
Laundry workers
Messengers
Platform men, railroad
Peddlers
Porters
Relief, public, private
Roofer's helpers
Shirt folders
Shoe shiners
Sorters, rag and
      salvage
Stage hands
Stevedores
Stock handlers
Street cleaners
Struckmen, railroad
Unemployed (no
      occupation)
Unskilled factory
      workers
Waitresses ("hash
      houses")
Washers, cars
Window cleaners
Woodchoppers
Farmers
Sharecroppers

The Educational Scale

The educational scale is premised upon the assumption that men and women who possess similar educations will tend to have similar tastes and similar attitudes, and they will also tend to exhibit similar behavior patterns.

The educational scale is divided into seven positions:

1. Graduate professional training: Persons who completed a recognized professional course that

led to the receipt of a graduate degree were given scores of 1.

2. Standard college or university graduation: All individuals who had completed a four-year college or university course leading to a recognized college degree were assigned the same scores. No differentiation was made between state universities or private colleges.
3. Partial college training: Individuals who had completed at least one year but not a full college course were assigned this position.
4. High school graduation: All secondary school graduates whether from a private preparatory school, public high school, trade school, or parochial school were given this score.
5. Partial high school: Individuals who had completed the tenth or eleventh grades, but had not completed high school were given this score.
6. Junior high school: Individuals who had completed the seventh grade through the ninth grade were given this position.
7. Less than seven years of school: Individuals who had not completed the seventh grade were given the same scores irrespective of the amount of education they had received.

Example of Scoring

SCALE	SCALE SCORE	× FACTOR WEIGHT	= PARTIAL SCORE
Occupation	3	7	21
Education	3	4	12
Index of social position score		=	33

The range of scores in each of five social classes are as follows: Class I (highest), 11 to 17; class II, 18 to 31; class III, 32 to 47; class IV, 48 to 63; class V (lowest), 64 to 77.

Source: The occupational scale and the educational scale are reprinted with permission from A. B. Hollingshead, *Two factor index of social position.* New Haven: Privately printed, 1957.

REFERENCES

Cronbach, L. J. *Essentials of Psychological Testing* (2nd ed.). New York: Harper & Row, 1960.

Elliott, F. A. *Clinical Neurology* (2nd ed.). Philadelphia: Saunders, 1971.

Finnie, N. R. *Handling the Young Cerebral Palsied Child at Home.* New York: Dutton, 1975.

Hathaway, W. E. The Unique Contributions of Piagetian Measurement to Diagnosis, Prognosis, and Research of Children's Mental Development. In G. I. Lubin, J. F. Magary, and M. K. Poulsen (eds.), *Piagetian Theory and its Implications for the Helping Professions* (Proceedings of 4th Interdisciplinary Seminar, February 15, 1974). Los Angeles: University of Southern California Publications Department, 1975.

Herzig, S. I. Occupational therapy assessment of cognitive levels as predictors of the community adjustment of chronic schizophrenic patients. University of Southern California Master's Thesis, 1978.

Hollingshead, A. B., and Redlich, F. C. *Social Class and Mental Illness.* New York: Wiley, 1958.

Inhelder, B., and Piaget, J. *The Early Growth of Logic in the Child,* transl. by E. A. Lunzar and D. Papert. New York: Norton, 1964.

Katz, N. An occupational therapy study of cognition in adult inpatients with depression. University of Southern California Master's Thesis, 1979.

Kay, S. R., and Singh, M. M. A developmental approach to delineate components of cognitive dysfunction in schizophrenia. *Br. J. Soc. Clin. Psychol.* 14:387–399, 1975.

Kay, S. R., Singh, M. M., and Smith, J. M. Colour form representation test: A developmental method for the study of cognition in schizophrenia. *Br. J. Soc. Clin. Psychol.* 14:401–411, 1975.

Kolberg, L., and Devries, R. Relations between Piaget and psychometric assessments of intelligence. Paper presented at the Conference on the Natural Curriculum of the Child, Urbana, Ill., 1969.

Maloney, M. P., and Ward, M. P. *Psychological Assessment: A Conceptual Approach.* New York: Oxford University Press, 1976.

Miller, D. C. *Handbook of Research Design and Social Measurement* (3rd ed.). New York: McKay, 1977.

Moore, D. S. An occupational therapy evaluation of sensorimotor cognition: Initial reliability, validity, and descriptive data for hospitalized schizophrenic adults. University of Southern California Master's Thesis, 1978.

Piaget, J. *Organization and Pathology of Thought,* transl. by D. Rapaport. New York: Columbia University Press, 1951. Pp. 176–192.

Piaget, J. *Biology and Knowledge: An Essay on the Relations Between Organic Regulations and Cognitive Processes*, transl. by B. Walsh. Chicago: University of Chicago Press, 1971.

Pishkin, V., et al. Schizophrenics cognitive dysfunction: a deficit in rule transfer. *J. Clin. Psychol.* 33:335–342, 1977.

Stewin, L. L., and Martin, J. A Comparison of the Developmental Stages Proposed by L. S. Vygotsky and J. Piaget. In G. I. Lubin, J. F. Magery, and M. K. Poulsen (eds.), *Piagetian Theory and its Implications for the Helping Professions* (Proceedings of 4th Interdisciplinary Seminar, February 15 1941). Los Angeles: University of Southern California Publications Department, 1975.

Trunnell, T. L. Thought disturbance in schizophrenia: Pilot study utilizing Piaget's theories. *Arch. Gen. Psychiatry* 11:126–136, 1964.

Trunnell, T. L. Thought disturbance in schizophrenia: Replication study utilizing Piaget's theories. *Arch. Gen. Psychiatry* 13:9–18, 1965.

Vygotsky, L. S. *Thought and Language*. Cambridge, Mass.: M.I.T. Press, 1962.

Williams, L. R. Development and initial testing of an occupational therapy object-classification test. University of Southern California Master's Thesis, 1981.

CHAPTER 15

RESEARCH WITH SUBJECTS HAVING SENILE DEMENTIA

Lois M. Heying

Responding to the recommendations of the studies reported in Chapters 12, 13, and 14, the present study examined the routine task behavior of older persons with senile dementia. There was general agreement that other diagnostic groups that might have a cognitive disability should be explored. There was also agreement that the social consequences of restrictions in routine task performance required further clarification. Dementia was examined with an emphasis on routine task performance, often cited as activities of daily living.

RATIONALE

The cognitive levels, as measured by the Allen Cognitive Level Test (ACL), are a hierarchical system for describing qualitative differences in routine task performance. In fact, this system had limited validation; Moore's study (1978; see Chap. 12) selected routine tasks as presented to patients in a clinical setting. The cognitive levels had not been validated using those activities of daily living needed to maintain oneself in the community (Herzig, 1978; see Chap. 12). Thus a major deficiency was an absence of descriptive data on the strength of any associations between the ACL and independent measures of functional abilities, as observed during the performance of activities of daily living. This study is regarded as a preliminary step in describing qualitative differences in routine task behavior.

Senile dementia was selected because it falls within the realms of both psychiatry and neurology. It seemed logical to study this population next to examine the applicability of the description of the cognitive levels to neurologic disorders. Furthermore, dementia is characterized by a slow progression of greater restrictions in routine task performance (Albert, 1981; *DSM III*, 1980; Zarit, 1980).

Senile dementia is a diagnosis made without reference to specific brain etiology that applies to older persons with multifaceted impairments in cognition, personality, and behavior that interfere with social or occupational functioning (*DSM III*, 1980). The most prominent symptoms are disorientation and progressive memory loss demonstrated by difficulty in learning new information. The major types of dementia have been identified: primary degenerative dementia of the Alzheimer's type, and multi-infarct dementia (*DSM III*, 1980). Since effective medical treatment is unknown and the gradual degeneration may be of chronic duration (2 to 10 years), the focus of management should be on preserving the functional capacity of the impaired person through environmental compensations (Eisdorfer et al., 1980; Mace and Rabins, 1981).

A review of the geriatric literature revealed the need for brief objective measures to assess, monitor, and predict the older person's cognitive and functional status (Abramson, 1977; Cohen and Eisdorfer, 1979; Kane and Kane, 1981). An association between a greater number of errors on a brief mental status examination and restrictions in functional activities, an increased mortality rate, and brain pathology has been demonstrated (Blessed et al., 1968; Goldfarb et al., 1966; Wilson et al., 1973). The effectiveness of a mental status examination that typically taps only orientation and memory is still questioned by some gerontologists (Albert, 1981; Eisdorfer et al., 1980). In addition the gerontology literature indicates a lack of correspondence between results of frequently used psychological tests and actual performance of daily living activities; the lack of correspondence is usually attributed to the intervening influences of social and psychological factors (Albert, 1981; Gurland, 1981; Howell, 1970; Lawton, 1970; Miller, 1981a; Plutchik, 1979; Zarit 1980). To clarify these intervening variables, Miller (1981b) suggests an investigation of the progression of cognitive impairments, spanning the different levels of severity of senile dementia. Therefore a second problem addressed in this study was the association between the severity of the disability in senile dementia and the cognitive levels proposed in this text.

Purpose

The purpose of the study was thus to describe the relationship between cognitive disability and the performance of activities of daily living in persons with senile dementia. Two specific relationships were investigated:

1. The correlation of ACL scores with combined total scores on the Physical Self-Maintenance Scale (PSMS) and Instrumental Activities of Daily Living (IADL) scale.
2. The correlation of ACL scores with individual item scores on the PSMS and IADL scale. In addition, the relationship between the ACL and the PSMS-IADL was examined for the influence of intervening variables.

METHOD

Research Design

The research design of this study was descriptive correlational, examining one nonrandom sample on two main variables, cognition and performance of daily living activities, while controlling for the influence of demographic variables. The independent variable was the ACL score; the dependent variable was a caregiver's report on the PSM and IADL scales.

Instruments

Six instruments were employed in this study:

1. The Mini–Mental State (MMS)
2. The Lower Cognitive Level Test (LCL)
3. The Allen Cognitive Level Test
4. The Physical Self-Maintenance Scale
5. The Instrumental Activities of Daily Living Scale
6. Hollingshead's Index of Social Position (HISP)

The ACL and HISP were used in previous studies and already have been discussed in this book; thus, only their pertinence to this study will be stated here. A brief description of the remaining four instruments will also be provided.

Allen Cognitive Level Test

The ACL, which operationally defines the variable of interest in this study, cognitive disability, was discussed in Chapter 4. Research supporting validity and reliability was reported in Chapters 12, 13, and 14.

Hollingshead's Index of Social Position

The HISP (Hollingshead and Redlich, 1958), an instrument that combines the factors of occupation and education to designate a social position score (which is translated into a social class), was used to control for social influence on performance. The scoring of this measure was described in Chapter 14. The correlation between judged class and education and occupation was reported to be high ($r = 0.906$) (Hollingshead and Redlich, 1958). Women who are, or have been, married, are scored using the occupational and educational levels of the principal wage earner of the household. Although this measure may appear to be male-oriented and outdated, it may adequately reflect the social status of the population of this study (persons over 60 years of age).

Lower Cognitive Level Test

The LCL was devised as part of this study to augment the ACL operational definition of cognitive disability. Criteria were established to differentiate between levels 1 and 2 in the expectation that some subjects would be at the lowest cognitive levels. This simple motor performance test consists of clapping in imitation of a demonstration by the therapist (see Chap. 4). I set the criteria for the LCL during a pilot study of seven inpatients of Los Angeles County–University of Southern California (LAC–USC) Medical Center's psychiatric hospital. Interrater reliability between this researcher and four

staff therapists was 100 percent for 22 subjects with various psychiatric diagnoses.

Mini-Mental State

The MMS is a brief mental status examination developed by Folstein and colleagues (1975) to assist in differential diagnosis of dementia. It consists of 11 items testing the cognitive aspects of mental functions, including orientation, registration, recall, calculation, language, and design copying (Appendix 15-1). Part of the language component requires the subject to follow a three-stage command which, as a motor performance task, bears some resemblance to the ACL.

When the MMS was administered to 69 patients with dementia, depression with cognitive impairments, and uncomplicated depression, the test was demonstrated to be valid and reliable (Folstein et al., 1975). It separated the three diagnostic groups according to the severity of the cognitive difficulty; it also reflected clinical cognitive improvements in acute conditions, such as depression, and a lack of change when the condition was stable for a long period of time, as in dementia. Concurrent validity was shown by a Pearson correlation of the MMS with the Wechsler Adult Intelligence Scale (WAIS) as follows: verbal IQ, $r = 0.776$ ($p < 0.001$); performance IQ, $r = 0.660$ ($p < .011$). Reliability for 24-hour retests was established by a Pearson coefficient for the same tester, $r = 0.887$ ($p < .001$), and for two examiners, $r = 0.827$ ($p < .001$). Additional reliability was verified by using a Wilcoxon T; no significant differences were found. Reliability over time was investigated when the MMS was administered to a clinically stable group 28 days apart; the Wilcoxon T showed no significant difference in the scores and the Pearson correlation coefficient was high ($r = 0.98$, $p < .001$).

The MMS was selected for this study as a criterion measure for subject inclusion since it was being used by the two evaluation centers through which I identified potential subjects. To compensate for possible impaired vision in the elderly, the written command was presented in large print and the complex polygon as a large figure (Appendix 15:1). The test is not timed and usually required only 5 to 10 minutes to administer. The maximum total score is 30. In the Folstein and colleagues' (1975) study, the mean score of persons with dementia was 9.6 with a standard deviation of 5.8 and a range of 0 to 22. The normal range was 24 to 30 with a mean score of 27.6 and a standard deviation of 1.7. I suggest the following levels of severity from a computation using the standard deviation: severe impairment, 0 to 15 points; moderate impairment, 16 to 21 points; mild impairment, 22 to 25 points. Thus, it was proposed that persons with dementia could score from 0 to 25 points. Consequently, a score of 23 or below was set as the criterion for inclusion in this study.

Physical Self-Maintenance Scale and Instrumental Activities of Daily Living Scale

The PSMS and IADL are two instruments that operationalize the domain of activities of daily living. The instruments were developed by Lawton and Brody (1969), and the validity of the instruments was investigated by correlating the scales with the following measures: Physical classification as rated by a physician, based on medical history, physical examination, and laboratory studies; mental status questionnaire, a measure of orientation and memory; behavior and adjustment, a measure of intellectual, personal, behavioral, and social adjustment.

Lawton and Brody (1969) modified the Langley-Porter Physical Self-Maintenance Scale to measure a range of competence in personal care skills (Table 15-1). The PSMS was scored from 0 to 6, one point being given for each task in which the subject is completely independent; thus, the score communicates a general level of self-maintenance. Lawton and Brody (1969) reported high interrater reliability (between pairs of licensed practical nurses, $r = 0.87$; between research assistants, $r = 0.91$) and moderate congruent validity with other functional measures: physical classification ($r = 0.62$), mental

status questionnaire ($r = 0.38$), behavior and adjustment ($r = 0.38$).

The IADL scale was developed by Lawton and Brody to represent those daily tasks that are most relevant to a minimally adequate life in the community after retirement (Lawton, 1971) (Table 15-2). Independence in the community depends on the extent to which the subject can satisfactorily perform these routine tasks. The original scale was scored similarly to the PSMS, except that a person received an additional point for each step of the task that brought the person closer to an accepted level of competence judged necessary for independent living. Lawton and Brody's (1969) study showed that food preparation, housekeeping, and laundry did not scale for men. Interrater reliability ($r = 0.85$) and moderate congruent validity were demonstrated with other functional measures: physical classification ($r = 0.40$), mental status questionnaire ($r = 0.48$), behavior and adjustment ($r = 0.36$), and PSMS ($r = 0.61$).

In the Lawton and Brody (1969) study, the scores for both scales were determined by information obtained from the best and most reliable source available: the subject, family, institutional staff, friends, or combinations of informants. In this study an informant report was used to collect data with these instruments. Although the combined total score of these scales was correlated with the ACL score, it was also the purpose of this study to examine how scores on individual tasks related to cognitive levels. Therefore, the scoring systems used by Lawton and Brody (1969) were altered so that each step of a task received an additional point except for the lowest step which indicates inability to perform the task at all (Table 15-2; see also Table 15-1). A report was given for each item on the scales for both genders. Since the elimination of food preparation, housekeeping, and laundry did not affect the correlation between the ACL and the PSMS-IADL, all items were considered in the scoring for both men and women in this study. Thus, the score of 24 for the PSMS and of 23 for the IADL combined for a possible total score of 47.

Table 15-1. Physical self-maintenance scale as scored by Lawton and Brody and revised for this study

Original score	Revised score	Item
		A. Toilet
1	4	Cares for self at toilet completely; no incontinence
0	3	Needs to be reminded, or needs help in cleaning self, or has rare (weekly at most) accidents
0	2	Soiling or wetting while asleep, more than once a week
0	1	Soiling or wetting while awake, more than once a week
0	0	No control of bowels or bladder
		B. Feeding
1	4	Eats without assistance
0	3	Eats with minor assistance at meal times, with help in preparing food or with help in cleaning up after meals
0	2	Feeds self with moderate assistance and is untidy
0	1	Requires extensive assistance for all meals
0	0	Does not feed self at all and resists efforts of others to feed him
		C. Dressing
1	4	Dresses, undresses and selects clothes from own wardrobe
0	3	Dresses and undresses self, with minor assistance
0	2	Needs moderate assistance in dressing or selection of clothes
0	1	Needs major assistance in dressing but cooperates with efforts of others to help
0	0	Completely unable to dress self and resists efforts of others to help
		D. Grooming (neatness, hair, nails, hands, face, clothing)
1	4	Always neatly dressed and well-groomed, without assistance
0	3	Grooms self adequately, with occasional minor assistance, e.g., in shaving
0	2	Needs moderate and regular assistance or supervision in grooming
0	1	Needs total grooming care, but can remain well groomed after help from others
0	0	Actively negates all efforts of others to maintain grooming
		E. Physical ambulation
1	4	Goes about grounds or city
0	3	Ambulates within residence or about one block distant
0	2	Ambulates with assistance of (check one): a ( ) another person, b ( ) railing, c ( ) cane, d ( ) walker, or e ( ) wheelchair: 1 Gets in and out without help 2 Needs help in getting in and out
0	1	Sits unsupported in chair or wheelchair, but cannot propel self without help
0	0	Bedridden more than half the time
		F. Bathing
1	4	Bathes self (tub, shower, sponge bath) without help
0	3	Bathes self, with help in getting in and out of tub
0	2	Washes face and hands only, but cannot bathe rest of body
0	1	Does not wash self but is cooperative with those who bathe him
0	0	Does not try to wash self, and resists efforts to keep him clean

Source: M. P. Lawton and E. M. Brody, Assessment of older people: Self-maintaining and instrumental activities of daily living. *Gerontologist* 9:180, 1969.

Table 15-2. Scale for instrumental activities of daily living as scored by Lawton and Brody and revised for this study

Original score	Revised score	Item
		A. Ability to use telephone
1	3	Operates telephone on own initiative; looks up and dials numbers, etc.
1	2	Dials a few well-known numbers
1	1	Answers telephone but does not dial
0	0	Does not use telephone at all
		B. Shopping
1	3	Takes care of all shopping needs independently
0	2	Shops independently for small purchases
0	1	Needs to be accompanied on any shopping trip
0	0	Completely unable to shop
		C. Food preparation
1	3	Plans, prepares and serves adequate meals independently
0	2	Prepares adequate meals if supplied with ingredients
0	1	Heats and serves prepared meals or prepares meals but does not maintain adequate diet
0	0	Needs to have meals prepared and served
		D. Housekeeping
1	4	Maintains house alone or with occasional assistance (e.g., heavy-work domestic help)
1	3	Performs light daily tasks such as dish-washing and bed-making
1	2	Performs light daily tasks but cannot maintain acceptable level of cleanliness
1	1	Needs help with all home maintenance tasks
0	0	Does not participate in any housekeeping tasks
		E. Laundry
1	2	Does personal laundry completely
1	1	Launders small items; rinses socks, stockings, etc.
0	0	All laundry must be done by others
		F. Mode of transportation
1	4	Travels independently on public transportation or drives own car
1	3	Arranges own travel via taxi, but does not otherwise use public transportation
1	2	Travels on public transportation when assisted or accompanied by another
0	1	Travel limited to taxi or automobile, with assistance of another
0	0	Does not travel at all
		G. Responsibility for own medication
1	2	Is responsible for taking medication in correct dosages at correct time
0	1	Takes responsibility if medication is prepared in advance in separate dosages
0	0	Is not capable of dispensing own medication
		H. Ability to handle finances
1	2	Manages financial matters independently (budgets, writes checks, pays rent and bills, goes to bank); collects and keeps track of income
1	1	Manages day-to-day purchases, but needs help with banking, major purchases, etc.
0	0	Incapable of handling money

Source: M. P. Lawton and E. M. Brody, Assessment of older people: Self-maintaining and instrumental activities of daily living. *Gerontologist* 9:181, 1969.

The score for each item, which represents the level of specific task competence attained, was also computed. All items are not analyzed evenly for task complexity on the IADL scale; thus, competence for independence could be rated from 2 to 4 (Table 15-2). The highest score for each item on the PSMS was 4 (see Table 15-1).

SUBJECTS

The subjects for this study were 33 persons over the age of 60 with a clinical diagnosis of dementia according to *DSM III* (1980) criteria. All were living in the community with various degrees of caregiver support. Subjects, or caregivers, volunteered by signing an informed consent.

The subjects were referred from five sources to obtain a sample from a wide socioeconomic background. Thirteen subjects were contacted through two medical evaluation centers: the Geriatric Outpatient Clinic of the LAC–USC Medical Center and the Older Adult Health Center of Rancho Los Amigos Hospital. Five subjects were referred from support groups at Andrus Older Adult Center, and the remaining fifteen subjects volunteered through two Alzheimer support group chapters. Most of the 80 potential subjects were excluded because of institutional living or refusal to give consent; two were excluded for visual or hand impairment. Those who exhibited apraxia, a loss in planning skilled motor actions, and aphasia, an impairment in receptive or expressive speech, were not excluded from the study since these impairments were judged to be related to cognitive aspects of mental function as assessed on the MMS.

The age and social class of the subjects were as follows:

	RANGE	MEDIAN	MEAN	SD
Age	61–91	74.8	73.8	7.9
Social class (HISP)	11–77	43.7 (class III)	45.0 (class III)	15.9

Table 15-3. Demographic characteristics of 33 persons with dementia

Variable	No.	Percent
Sex		
Male	11	33
Female	22	67
Race		
Black	3	9
Caucasian	29	88
Hispanic	1	3
Marital status		
Single	1	3
Widowed	7	21
Divorced	4	12
Married	21	64
Previous leather lacing experience		
Yes	0	0
No	33	100
Living situation		
Alone	4	12
With other	3	9
With child	6	18
With spouse	20	61
Residence		
House	25	76
Apartment	7	21
Other (guest home)	1	3
Legal status		
Conservatorship	2	6
Some legal action	6	18
No legal action	25	76
Test location		
Home	22	67
Clinic	11	33
Hospital	0	0

Other demographic characteristics are presented in Table 15-3. Most of the subjects, 63.6 percent, were married, and most were living with a spouse, child, or other relative caregiver, 87.9 percent. All except one who resided in a small guest home were living in family residences.

Diagnostic Credibility of the Sample

In 41 of the 80 persons I contacted for this study, the diagnosis of dementia was assumed to be correct on the basis of a medical chart review either by me or by a reliable staff member at one of the medical referral centers. An examination of persons excluded from the study may lend credibility to the diagnosis of dementia in subjects referred from support groups, for whom the researcher did not have access to medical records. From a list compiled one year previously by one of the Alzheimer support group chapters, 36 persons were contacted by phone. Of this group, two persons were deceased, six were receiving care in nursing facilities, and four were reported as no longer presenting the symptoms of dementia. A total of 15 of the remaining subjects were interviewed and tested; of these, one was excluded for a high score on the MMS, despite a reported medical diagnosis of Alzheimer's disease. This information shows that a third of the persons excluded from participation reported either a worsening of the impairment or a relief of the symptoms over a year's period. The passage of time appears to be a useful index either to confirm or refute the presence of progressive dementia.

The mean scores of the ACL and MMS also lend diagnostic credibility to the sample. The mean score on the ACL of this sample of persons with dementia was 2.6 (original scoring criteria) or 2.8 (revised scoring criteria). (The revision of scoring criteria for the ACL will be discussed in the following section.) This is a lower mean score than for either the depressed sample (mean, 5.0) in Katz's study (1979; see Chap. 13) or the schizophrenic sample (mean, 4.0) in Moore's study (1978; see Chap. 12). Of these mental disorders, one would expect dementia to fall lowest in the hierarchy.

In this study's sample, the mean score on the MMS was 8.7. This score compares favorably to the Folstein and associates (1975) study in which the mean score for persons with dementia syndromes was 9.6. Thus, the present study's sample appears to be a credible representation of those with the medical diagnosis of dementia, a disease that can be confirmed only posthumously.

DATA COLLECTION AND ANALYSIS

Appointments were scheduled with each subject and a caregiver in the home, clinic, or day treatment center. The MMS, the LCL, and the ACL were administered to the subject at the beginning of the interview, followed by the caregiver report on the PSMS-IADL and the HISP. Demographic data (that is, age, sex, race, marital status, living situation, conservatorship status) and previous leather lacing experience were recorded on a data summary form. A more detailed explanation of procedures can be found in my thesis (Heying, 1983).

Data were analyzed using the following statistical procedures: the Spearman correlation coefficient (r^s), paired *t*-test, two-by-two contingency tables and cross-tabulation tables with chi-square statistics or the Fisher's exact test, as well as descriptive statistics including medians, means, standard deviations, and frequencies. The established level of significance accepted for all statistical analysis in this study was $p < .05$.

A nonparametric test, the Spearman correlation coefficient, was used because the variables of interest (the ACL and the PSMS-IADL) did not meet the two underlying assumptions for the use of the Pearson correlation coefficient. Those assumptions are (1) that both variables can be measured on an interval scale, and (2) that both variables are normally distributed (Hinkle et al., 1979). Both the ACL and the PSMS-IADL, as well as most of the demographic variables, yield ordinal, not interval, data. In addition the small sample size did not plot as a normal distribution. Guilford and Fruchter (1973) state that confidence in the Spearman r^s can be almost as great as in the Pearson *r*, given high correlations and an equal sample size. Since the data are converted to ranks, the Spearman test is sensitive to the median as a population statistic.

Revised Scoring Criteria

The r^s was used to describe the associations between the ACL score and the PSMS-IADL combined total score as well as the individual item scores. These correlations were computed twice, first using the original ACL scoring criteria and then using a revision suggested by this study. The revised ACL scoring criteria were derived from the following observations:

1. The task behavior revealed a small group of 5 subjects who were able to perform the whip stitch but unable to untwist the leather lacing even though they recognized an error.
2. The PSMS-IADL total scores of those subjects who were unable to untwist the whip stitch were examined on a scattergram (Heying, 1983). The pattern of their scores resembled that of level 4 performance, so a level 3 score was changed to level 4, in these 5 subjects. The correlations increased between the ACL and PSMS-IADL for the following items: ambulation, bathing, shopping, food preparation, use of the telephone, and managing finances.

The remainder of the data analyses involving the ACL have been computed using these revised scores. The revision resulted in a slight improvement in the r^s between the ACL score and the total combined PSMS-IADL score:

SCORING CRITERIA	r^s	r_s^2
Original	0.813	0.661
Revised	0.822	0.675

There was no change in the level of significance (it was $p < .001$ in both instances).

RESULTS

Primary Findings

The results of the assessment measures are shown in Table 15-4. The median score for each measure is

Table 15-4. Results of assessment measures in 33 persons with dementia

Variable	Range	Median	Mean	Standard deviation
Mini–Mental State	0–23	7.7	8.7	7.4
ACL (original scoring criteria)	1–4	2.7	2.6	0.8
ACL (revised scoring criteria)	1–4	2.8	2.8	1.0
PSMS-IADL total score	2–38	18.0	19.7	10.4

ACL = Allen Cognitive Level Test; PSMS–IADL = Physical Self-Maintenance–Instrumental Activities of Daily Living Scale.

reported because of the ordinal nature of the scales; the mean score is reported for comparative purposes.

A significant, high, positive association was found between the ACL score and the combined total score of the PSMS-IADL, $r^s = 0.822$, $p < .001$. In addition, the results of a series of r^s correlations revealed significant positive associations between the ACL score and all of the individual item scores on the PSMS-IADL (Table 15-5). Four of these fourteen items—feeding, toileting, grooming, and dressing—were substantially correlated with the ACL ($r^s > 0.70$, $p < .001$). Eight of the remaining ten items showed a moderate association with the ACL ($0.50 < r^s < 0.70$, $p < .001$): ambulation, bathing, housekeeping, food preparation, shopping, laundry, use of telephone, and managing finances. Two items, mode of transportation and responsibility for medication, demonstrated a low association with the ACL ($r^s < 0.50$).

Influence of Demographic Variables

Table 15-6 shows the relationship of the ACL with the PSMS-IADL while controlling for demographic variables. The data analyses of these variables represent two procedures. First, variables that could influence the results of the study were correlated

*Table 15-5. Spearman correlations (r_s)
of the ACL score with individual item scores
on the PSMS-IADL in 33 persons with dementia*

Item	r_s	r_s^2	p
PSMS			
Feeding	0.827	0.684	.001
Toileting	0.748	0.553	.001
Grooming	0.739	0.546	.001
Dressing	0.736	0.541	.001
Ambulation	0.673	0.452	.001
Bathing	0.649	0.421	.001
IADL			
Housekeeping	0.680	0.463	.001
Food preparation	0.646	0.417	.001
Shopping	0.641	0.411	.001
Laundry	0.591	0.349	.001
Use of telephone	0.583	0.340	.001
Managing finances	0.524	0.275	.001
Mode of transportation	0.483	0.234	.002
Responsibility for medication	0.318	0.101	.038

ACL = Allen Cognitive Level Test; PSMS-IADL = Physical Self-Maintenance–Instrumental Activities of Daily Living Scale.

singly with the ordinal scales of the ACL and PSMS-IADL. The variables of concern were age, sex, social position, marital status, and living situation. Second, the data on each of these variables were dichotomized as shown on the far right side of the table. These pairs were used as the control variables for computing the chi-square statistic using the dichotomized variables of the ACL and PSMS-IADL or the Fisher's exact text (used when cell frequencies were less than 5). This subsequent analysis indicated whether the relationship of the ACL with the PSMS-IADL was supported while controlling for each of the intervening variable pairs. If the p value from the chi-square analysis or Fisher's exact test on both pairs was significant, the relationship of the primary variables was upheld. A nonsignificant result suggested that an intervening variable confounded the relationship.

The Spearman correlations reported in Table 15-

6 indicate the extent and direction of relationships for each of the combinations of variables. The ACL showed a low positive correlation with age. In this study older subjects scored higher on the ACL than did younger subjects. The ACL demonstrated more moderate significant correlations with marital status and living situations. Reflecting the way the data were scaled, both analyses revealed a negative correlation. The ACL score was higher for single persons and those living alone.

The PSMS-IADL was found to be significantly negatively correlated with marital status and living situation. Those subjects who were single and lived alone performed activities of daily living better than did those living with a spouse.

The findings also revealed a significant positive association between the PSMS-IADL and two other variables, social position and sex. The analysis of social position indicated that subjects with higher social position (i.e., lower scores on the HISP) were generally more impaired in ADL. Two correlations were computed for sex: The analysis of sex with the total score on the PSMS-IADL showed a tendency for women to perform daily living activities better than men; even when food preparation, housekeeping, and laundry were eliminated for men, as recommended by Lawton and Brody (1969), the r^s was nearly the same.

The right side of Table 15-6 depicts the chi-square value, or the p value for Fisher's exact test, for the relationship of the ACL with the PSMS-IADL. (The computer program used for analysis of the data provided only the p value, not the value of the test statistic, for the Fisher's exact test.) When controlling for male sex and living with a spouse, the relationship proved to be nonsignificant, as computed by Fisher's exact test. The findings for all the other variable pairs—female sex, living alone or with a person other than a spouse, low and high age, low and high social position, and being single, widowed, or divorced—agreed with the relationship between the ACL and the PSMS-IADL. The data for the status of being married violated statistical rules and could not be computed.

Table 15-6. Relationship of ACL score with the PSMS-IADL controlling for demographic variables

Demographic variable	r_s with ACL	r_s with PSMS-IADL	χ^{2a}	Fisher's exact test[b]	Pairs
Age	0.294[c]	0.283	—	0.005[c]	Low
				0.006	High
Sex (total score)	0.240	0.439[d]		0.182	Male
			14.160[e]		Female
"Female" items eliminated for men	—	0.453[d]	—	—	—
Social position	0.188	0.414[d]	—	0.004[c]	Low
				0.003[c]	High
Marital status	−0.435[d]	−0.571[e]	13.684[c]		Not married
			Does not compute		Married
Living situation	−0.438[d]	−0.572[e]	14.515[c]		Alone, with other, with child
				0.333	With spouse

ACL = Allen Cognitive Level Test; PSMS-IADL = Physical Self-Maintenance–Instrumental Activities of Daily Living Scale.
[a]Chi-square test with 1 degree of freedom.
[b]p value for result of Fisher's exact test (one-tailed).
[c]$p < .05$.
[d]$p < .01$.
[e]$p < .001$.

Thus in this study the intervening variables of male sex and living with a spouse confounded the relationship of ACL with PSMS-IADL. Regardless of age or social position, the association between the ACL and performance of activities of daily living was supported.

Secondary Findings

A number of secondary findings related to the variables of interest were examined. The major results are summarized below:

1. Cross-tabulation between the ACL and the LCL (Table 15-7) suggested that the LCL discriminated only levels 1 and 2, and not level 3 as anticipated. The LCL may produce a false positive result of level 3.
2. The Spearman correlations of the LCL scores

(range, 1 to 3) with the PSMS-IADL and with the ACL were as follows:

VARIABLE	r^s	r_s^2
PSMS-IADL	0.524	0.275
ACL	0.580	0.341

The correlations with both variables were significant ($p < .001$).
3. The MMS (range, 0 to 23) showed a significant substantial positive correlation with the PSMS-IADL and showed a moderate association with the ACL ($p < .001$ for both):

VARIABLE	r^s	r_s^2
PSMS-IADL	0.749	0.561
ACL	0.656	0.431

The three-stage command portion of the MMS showed a moderate association with the ACL (range, 0 to 3; $r^s = 0.649$; $r_s^2 = 0.421$; $p < .001$).

Table 15-7. Cross-tabulation*
between ACL score and LCL score

LCL	ACL				Row total
	Level 1	Level 2	Level 3	Level 4	
Level 1	3	0	0	0	3
	100	0	0	0	—
	100	0	0	0	9
	9	0	0	0	—
Level 2	0	3	1	0	4
	0	75	25	0	—
	0	30	9	0	12
	0	9	3	0	—
Level 3	0	7	10	9	26
	0	27	38	35	—
	0	70	91	100	79
	0	21	30	27	—
Column	3	10	11	9	33
Total	9	30	33	27	100

ACL = Allen Cognitive Level Test; LCL = Lower Cognitive Level Test.
*Values in each cell, in descending order, are as follows: Count, row percent, column percent, total percent.

Table 15-8. Relationship between ACL score and PSMS-IADL in patients whose caregivers did or did not attend a support group

Variable	N	Range of scores		r_s	r_s^2	p
		ACL	PSMS-IADL			
Support group	20	1–4	2–33	0.867	0.752	.001
No support group	13	1–4	12–38	0.708	0.610	.003

ACL = Allen Cognitive Level Test; PSMS-IADL = Physical Self-Maintenance–Instrumental Activities of Daily Living Scale; r_s = Spearman correlation coefficient.

4. Subjects whose caregivers attended support groups demonstrated a higher correlation between the ACL and the PSMS-IADL than did subjects whose caregivers were not in support groups (Table 15-8).
5. The differences in mean PSMS-IADL score between the cognitive levels were significant except for between levels 3 and 4 (Table 15-9).
6. Cross-tabulations between the ACL and each item of the PSMS-IADL provided examples of behaviors that may correspond to the cognitive levels (see Fig. 2-22).

DISCUSSION

Cognitive Level and Performance of Daily Living Activities

Primary Findings

In this study a highly significant positive relationship was demonstrated between the ACL score and a caregiver's rating of performance of activities of daily living (that is, the combined total score on the PSMS-IADL). This finding is of interest from two viewpoints—Allen's theoretical position and the position prevailing in the gerontology literature.

Allen, in this text, assumes a brain-behavior correspondence as a basis for task performance. The ACL measures qualitative changes in task performance that reflect some brain abnormality. Thus Allen asserts that brain impairment affects the associations made between voluntary motor actions and sensory cues.

The gerontology literature suggests that there is a lack of congruence between cognitive test scores of older persons and their actual performance of daily tasks. In other words, cognitive measures such as mental status examinations do not reliably predict the way a person functions in his or her normal environment. Zarit (1980), for example, states that there is a potential for a brain-behavior association in persons with senile dementia, but he contends that many complex social and psychological factors influence the performance of daily activities.

Table 15-9. Differences in mean PSMS–IADL score between cognitive levels using paired t-tests

Variable	No. of cases	Mean PSMS-IADL mean	SD	F	2-tailed prob	Pooled variance estimate			Separate variance estimate		
						t	df	2-tailed prob	t	df	2-tailed prob
Level 1	3	5.3	3.1	2.58	.259	−4.34	11	.001	—	—	—
Level 2	10	11.5	1.9								
Level 1	3	5.3	3.1	6.92	.266	−3.68	12	.003	—	—	—
Level 3	11	23.2	8.0								
Level 1	3	5.3	3.1	6.24	.291	−5.19	10	.000	—	—	—
Level 4	9	29.4	7.6								
Level 2	10	11.5	1.9	17.88	.000	—		—	−4.68	11.22	.001
Level 3	11	23.2	8.0								
Level 2	10	11.5	1.9	16.14	.000	—		—	−6.86	8.89	.0001
Level 4	9	29.4	7.6								
Level 3	11	23.2	8.0	1.11	.902	−1.77	18	.093	—	—	—
Level 4	9	19.4	7.6								

PSMS-IADL = Physical Self-Maintenance–Instrumental Activities of Daily Living Scale; F = Variance ratio; df = degrees of freedom.

Allen (1982) agrees with the gerontology literature to the extent that, in addition to cognition, a variety of factors including desirability, past experience, medical condition, stress, and environment must be accounted for in interpreting the meaning of poor performance. While acknowledging the influence of those variables, Allen maintains that when conscious awareness is impaired, this impairment is the primary disability of concern. The results of this study support the proposal that the ACL does indeed have the potential to predict routine task behavior.

Secondary Findings

The data were analyzed from several additional perspectives to elucidate further the relationships between the ACL and activities of daily living. Variables considered in this additional analysis included (1) the MMS correlations, (2) support group versus no support group, and (3) the difference in mean PSMS-IADL score between the cognitive levels.

MMS CORRELATIONS. Folstein and coworkers (1975) suggested that the cognitive domains such as orientation, attention, memory, and visual perception assessed by the MMS should have predictive implications for capacity for self-care and managing daily affairs. The results of the present study showed a high correlation of the MMS with the PSMS-IADL, which suggests that the MMS may be useful in predicting current abilities for daily living. The cognitive failures documented by the MMS do indicate potential problems of the impaired person, but a given total score does not present an index of functioning in daily activities.

As reported, the ACL had an even higher degree of association with the PSMS-IADL than with the MMS. Since the cognitive levels of the ACL have been analyzed in terms of a person's abilities and limitations within the environment, the ACL score provides a more precise gauge of task behavior than the MMS does. It could be argued that the MMS

indicates the parameters of cognitive loss in the disease, whereas the ACL designates the degree of functional disability resulting from the disease.

As previously stated, when the MMS results were correlated with ACL scores, there was a moderate association, $r^s = 0.656$ ($p < .001$). This finding suggests that similar domains of cognition, possibly those of attention, registration, memory, sequencing, and visual perception, are assessed by both the ACL and the MMS. Katz's (1979) study demonstrated a much lower significant association between the ACL and the Block Design of the WAIS, $r = 0.457$ ($p < .001$) at admission and $r = 0.396$ ($p < .01$) at discharge. The Block Design subtest was chosen in Katz's study to establish congruent validity for the ACL because its content areas were thought to be most similar to the ACL. The results of the present study suggest that the MMS bears a closer resemblance than the Block Design to the ACL, with the qualification that higher scores for both tests were not assessed in this study because of the lower cognitive status of the population studied.

It is interesting to note that the correlation between the ACL score and the score on the three-stage direction item on the MMS was as great as the correlation of the ACL with the total MMS score. This finding suggests that most of the congruence of the two tests may be accounted for in the three-stage direction item, and most of the variance is due to other factors.

SUPPORT GROUP VERSUS NO SUPPORT GROUP. Another area of the relationship between the ACL and the PSMS-IADL that was explored concerned support groups. Patients whose caregivers belonged to a support group showed a greater association between the variables of interest (activities of daily living and ACL score). This finding is interpreted as reflecting greater reliability of report of daily living activities by caregivers who attended support groups or who had been informed of the diagnosis for at least a year. (Subjects contacted through the support groups were drawn from a list compiled a year before this study was conducted.)

One explanation is that a longer period of time had elapsed since diagnosis for each subject in the support group, providing the caregiver time to adjust to the disability. It is possible that the caregivers of persons newly diagnosed and not in support groups may have been less aware of, or denying, the functional limitations imposed by the disease.

Another explanation is that support groups foster an awareness and acceptance of the disability, promoting an honest assessment of strengths and weaknesses of the impaired person. It was my impression that the caregivers seen in the home (those contacted through support groups) were well-informed about the course of dementia and implications for functional behavior. Many of the support group caregivers had read *The 36-Hour Day* (Mace and Rabins, 1981), a guide for family members caring for persons with dementing illnesses. For the most part, an attitude of promoting the available functional abilities of the impaired person seemed to prevail among this sample of caregivers. Thus, the report of caregivers belonging to a support group may reflect less denial and more realistic expectations of the disabled person's activities of daily living.

DIFFERENCES IN THE MEAN PSMS-IADL SCORE OF EACH COGNITIVE LEVEL. A statistically significant difference between levels 3 and 4 of the ACL in performing activities of daily living failed to be demonstrated. The mean differences between all the other cognitive levels were significant. The wide range of scores (11 to 38) on the PSMS-IADL at level 3 of the ACL appears to be the most probable cause. Even after the five subjects who could not correct the twist of the leather lacing were rescored at level 4, two subjects with a ACL score of level 3 remained in the upper range of PSMS-IADL scoring (34 and 38). A possible explanation for the excessive deviation of these scores is that the reliability of the caregiver report may have been compromised because at the time of the study these two subjects had only recently been diagnosed as having

dementia. In addition the PSMS-IADL scores of two subjects at level 3 fell low (11 and 15), within the range where subjects at level 2 clustered. Although the scores of two subjects at level 4 also fell low (13 and 20), the scores of the remaining seven subjects at level 4 ranged between 31 and 35.

These findings suggest a lack of discriminatory power to distinguish between levels 3 and 4 in either the ACL or the PSMS-IADL scale. The proposed revision of scoring criteria for the ACL resulted in a definite clustering of scores at level 4. The revised scoring criteria also promise to remove some of the variance in scores at level 3.

The numerical ordering of the levels on the ACL makes it appear that there is an equivalent difference in ability between each of the levels. It must be noted that even with the revised scoring criteria used to distinguish level 3 from level 4 subjects, the ACL may measure a small difference in behavior that cannot likewise be discriminated in the behavior in activities of daily living of the two groups. Chapter 3 notes that the levels represent varying degrees of clinical significance with respect to restrictions in task behavior.

Difficulties with the PSMS-IADL were also apparent. During the course of this study, I became aware that the items on the PSMS-IADL were not sensitive enough to delineate the many graduations in task behavior accounted for by caregivers in this sample of persons with senile dementia. This lack of discriminatory power of the PSMS-IADL is discussed further in the following section.

Cognitive Level and Specific Activities of Daily Living

Primary Findings

FINDINGS ASSOCIATED WITH INDIVIDUAL ITEMS ON THE PSMS-IADL. The analyses revealed significant positive associations between the ACL score and results of each of the 14 items on the PSMS-

IADL. The four items that showed the most substantial association were feeding, toileting, grooming, and dressing. Competence in these routine tasks has been developed since early childhood. It is likely that these tasks are retained the longest in a cognitive disability, both because of their familiarity and because the caregiver would tend to encourage the impaired person's participation in these basic functions that preserve life and social dignity. Thus the caregiver would also be more knowledgeable and accurate in reporting the current status of ability. The physical ambulation item, which showed a lesser correlation with the ACL, is an example of an area about which caregivers were often less certain about current status. Because of safety concerns, many caregivers did not allow the impaired person to walk unaccompanied and therefore were not certain if the subject could walk a block away from home and return independently.

The two items that correlated least with the ACL were mode of transportation and responsibility for medication. Both items probably reflect dependence on the caregiver, regardless of the subject's ability, because of the caregiver's precautions concerning safety and compliance with medication. Also, since public transportation or taxis are not commonly used in the area where the study took place, the mode of transportation item probably failed to describe real ability.

LIMITATIONS OF THE PSMS-IADL. Some weaknesses of the PSMS-IADL items may explain the discrepancy in association between the various items and the ACL. First, the extent of assistance required by the impaired person is often not objectively stated in the scales. For example, words such as *minor, moderate,* and *extensive assistance* do not operationally define behavior that is indicative of a specific score.

Second, the scale items were not constructed from the viewpoint of a cognitive orientation toward task behavior. Rating on the ambulation item especially reflected physical components of the task (for example, endurance, use of assistive devices), even though the item was explained to the caregiver in light of prerequisite cognitive ability. Viewed from a cognitive perspective, ambulating within the residence and walking a block distant represent a distinct discrimination in behavioral requirements, yet they are scored the same on the scale. Bathing is another example of an item that is less clear because of intervening physical problems. The process of bathing requires body positioning and interacting with environmental barriers (that is, getting into the tub or shower stall, adjusting the water temperature) that may prove difficult to an older person with decreased range of motion or sensory deficits.

A third weakness of the PSMS-IADL in relation to the ACL concerns the superficial analysis of each task on the PSMS-IADL. Since the scales were intended as an overall competence measure of the older person's capability for independent living, it was not of prime importance to its creator to examine each task in great detail. Most of the items are approached from the viewpoint of how much assistance must be given to the older person for maintenance in the community. The scales do not account for the retained ability of the impaired person to work with the caregiver. For instance, whether or not the impaired person provides assistance to a caregiver in meal preparation by performing a familiar action (for example, scrubbing or peeling potatoes) is not taken into account in the scaling.

Another weakness of the scales is their failure to discriminate consistently and clearly between (1) the performance of a self-initiated task, (2) the carrying through of a task initiated by the caregiver, and (3) incompletion in performing a task. The scales also do not differentiate types of initiation by the caregiver or assistance required, such as verbal reminders, series of directions, one-step directions, demonstrations, tactile cues, and positioning. In addition the scales do not reflect whether the subject is consistent or sporadic in performing a task. Finally, the subject's past experience in performing a task, especially the IADL items, was not accounted for.

In summary, the main shortcomings of the

PSMS-IADL for use in this study, which was concerned with the mental processes guiding function, are the following:

1. Lack of objectivity in wording and precision in scoring.
2. Lack of cognitive orientation toward task behavior.
3. Superficiality of task analysis.
4. Failure to account for initiation, task carry-through, and past experiences.

These shortcomings may account for the inconsistent and moderate to low correlations between some individual items and the ACL score.

Secondary Findings

A revised classification of routine task behaviors was formulated and reported as a secondary finding in the study (the Routine Task Inventory: see Fig. 2-22). As discussed previously, the items on the PSMS-IADL did not discriminate enough to be sensitive to the nuances in ADL behavior reported by caregivers. The associations between the ACL and individual items were varied, perhaps because of the shortcomings suggested above. Furthermore, it was noted that the proportion of variance (r_s^2) described by the linear relationship of the ACL to the findings on the PSMS-IADL was not adequate to make clinical predictions about specific task behaviors. These results suggested the need for a more clearly defined analysis of daily living tasks.

The process of revising the classification of daily living behaviors has facilitated the organization of data, both subjective and objective, into a useful framework for future instrument development. Although several activities of daily living inventories, based on clinical observations, have been attempted by occupational therapists at LAC–USC Medical Center, the proposed classification has the advantage of details garnered from observations and caregiver reports of cognitively impaired persons in their home environment. It was also felt that recent refinements of the theory and analysis of the cognitive levels enabled the current attempt to categorize daily living task behavior according to the taxonomy of the ACL. The next step will be to examine the internal consistency of the Routine Task Inventory and the ACL.

Influence of Demographic Variables

Age

Age showed a low positive significant association with the ACL, and no significant association with the measure of activities of daily living. Interestingly, older subjects scored higher on the ACL than did younger subjects. This finding suggests that the data were skewed toward a higher preponderance of more cognitively impaired younger subjects. This finding may also suggest that increased age does not affect test performance on the ACL from level 1 to level 4, the range of ACL scores in this study. The performance of older persons on the ACL at levels 5 and 6 remains to be examined. The results also showed that, regardless of age, the relationship between the ACL and the PSMS-IADL was supported. This finding is consistent with the belief that chronological age does not correspond with the considerable individual variation in functional abilities of older persons (Zarit, 1980).

Sex

Sex was not significantly correlated with ACL score; however, it was moderately associated with performance of activities of daily living. The findings showed that women scored higher than men on the PSMS-IADL, possibly a reflection of the nature of the IADL tasks, but when the items of food preparation, housekeeping, and laundry were eliminated from the male scoring, the correlation remained essentially the same. This differed from the Lawton and Brody (1969) findings that these items did not scale for men. Possibly those tasks considered to be female occupations are presently being performed equally by men, especially in the retirement population in which there would be role blending. This finding leads to the conclusion that rather than eliminating tasks presumed to be gender related such as cooking, one should eliminate tasks on the basis of inexperience or inaccessibility.

Sex, Living Situation, and Marital Status

An examination of the raw data concerning sex, living situation, and marital status leads one to conclude that these variables are in some way interrelated. The raw data showed that all the men were married and all but one lived with a spouse, but only 46 percent of the women were married (all the married women lived with a spouse). The findings revealed that male sex confounded the relationship between the ACL and the PSMS-IADL, whereas female sex did not. Living with a spouse also confounded the relationship of the ACL and the PSMS-IADL. Therefore, it can be shown that the relationship was confounded in men living with a spouse, but this cannot be known for women since the data regarding living situation were not subsequently analyzed controlling for gender.

It is possible that married men with the condition of dementia become more dependent on their spouse caregivers than their cognitive disability warrants. This behavior may be explained by social and role expectations for the man, the sick person, the husband, or a combination of these roles, expectations reflected in the style of caregiving. Possibly the intimacy of the caregiver spouse role permits more dependent behaviors than a child or other caregiver would allow. This style and its effects were not controlled for in this study.

Both the ACL and the PSMS-IADL were found to be significantly negatively correlated with the variables of marital status and living situation. Those persons who were single and living alone showed a higher level of functioning on both measures. Subjects living alone would be expected to demonstrate higher functioning. The juxtaposition of marital status and lower functioning may be explained by a skew in this sample toward a higher preponderance of cognitively impaired married subjects who were being cared for in the home. It is possible that a spouse would continue to care for the impaired person longer in the home environment than would any other type of caregiver, even when nursing care was justified.

Social Position

Social position showed a moderate significant association with the PSMS-IADL and a nonsignificant relationship with the ACL. Nevertheless, regardless of social position, the relationship between the ACL and PSMS-IADL was affirmed. Those subjects who were designated as holding higher social positions by the HISP (i.e., who received lower HISP scores) were measured as more impaired in activities of daily living (received lower PSM-IADL scores). It is possible that one subject in Class I confounded the data by achieving a score of level 4 on the ACL and a report of daily living behavior more characteristic of level 2. Nevertheless, this finding fails to lend support to Gurland's (1981) proposal that social class and education may account for skills that allow maintenance in the community for a longer period of time. Since the average subject in this study was designated to be of the middle class and since all except one of the subjects were still in family homes, it appears that living in the community may be primarily due to the support systems available to the subject rather than to elements of social position. Unfortunate omissions in data collection—the educational level for the female subjects and the time since onset of disease—make this inference inconclusive.

The nonsignificant association between social position and the ACL in this study does not completely resolve the discrepancy between the results of previous cognitive disability research studies (Katz, Chap. 13; Williams, Chap. 14) concerning the influences of social position on ACL scores. It does suggest an interpretation regarding the issue of social position and the ACL. Using subjects identified by the HISP to be in the lower three social positions, Moore (1978) and Katz (1979) showed that education and social position did not affect performance of the ACL at levels 3 through 5. On the other hand, Williams's (1981) study demonstrated a positive correlation between ACL score and social position in a sample composed of nonpatients distributed more evenly throughout the five social classes. Those subjects who scored at level 4 or 5 were in the lower social class positions. In the present study, the majority of subjects were from the lowest social positions (III, IV, and V). The one subject from Class I whose performance on the ACL was discrepant with performance of daily living activities may have scored at level 4 (high in this study) because of past educational status but was unable to score at level 5 or 6, which require new learning. This relationship was not shown statistically, probably because there were only four subjects in Classes I and II. The foregoing results suggest that social position may make a difference between levels 5 and 6, but when the cognitive disability is as great as that designated by levels 1 through 4, compensation to acquire new learning probably does not occur.

Refinements in Assessing Allen's Cognitive Levels

Revised Scoring Criteria

The primary findings suggested a revision in the ACL scoring criteria, as has been explained. Part of the rationale for revision came from the dependent variable, performance of activities of daily living, but observation of task behavior during the ACL provided the primary insights that suggested a reappraisal of the criteria distinguishing level 3 from level 4.

Five subjects were not able to untwist the leather lacing, although they did recognize the error themselves or when it was pointed out, and each attempted to correct it. A number of explanations for this behavior can be considered in light of the de-

scription of the cognitive levels. It is possible that the subjects lacked motivation to do the task. These subjects appeared to me, however, to be quite goal directed, a level 4 characteristic, and disappointed at their failure to correct the error.

According to the descriptions of the cognitive levels, the subject's attention at level 4 is captured by clearly visible cues. The direction of the lacing tips, inserted through the front of the leather and pulled out from the back, is clearly visible. A twist in the leather lacing is less apparent. The lacing has a right and wrong side that is turned over when twisted. The relationship between the portion of the lacing that is turned over and the portion of the lacing that is correct must be formulated to untwist the lacing. Perception of the relationship required to untwist the lacing may be expected at level 5. At level 4 the researcher had to ask, "Does your stitch look like mine?" The error could be identified but not corrected.

Furthermore, I noted a discrepancy between the ACL instructions and the task analysis for level 4. The ACL instructions direct the therapist to present two consecutive directions to the subject—one to keep the lace untwisted and another concerning the action of the whip stitch. On the other hand, the task analysis suggests that only one direction be given for each step. Perhaps, then, some level 4 subjects may not be able to handle the level 4 instructions on the ACL unless they are given a demonstration with a one-step direction when they encounter the twist problem.

It was apparent to me that subjects who could not untwist the lacing should not be scored at either a level 3 or a level 5. Subjects who performed the ACL at level 3 were unable to bring the lace around consistently to the front and over the edge of the leather to begin the whip stitch. They did not detect even gross errors, which could be interpreted as ignoring a visual cue.

One subject performed the level 5 stitch correctly except for the twisted lace. The description of level 5 suggests, however, that a person scoring at this level should be able to recognize related cues (such as a twisted lace) and solve the problem by overt trial and error. Therefore I scored this subject at level 4. I later noted that this subject's score on the PSMS-IADL clustered with the level 4 scores.

Lower Cognitive Level Test

The LCL was quick and simple to administer. During the reliability study, only 2 of 22 subjects refused, and one of the demented sample refused. Although I did facilitate initiation of the clapping in the sample of persons with senile dementia, I recommend that such action be taken with caution. Persons from other diagnostic groups (especially those with paranoid ideation) may feel threatened and respond in unexpected ways.

In the present format the LCL appears to discriminate only the two lowest levels, level 1 from level 2, thus fulfilling its purpose for this study, in which a number of subjects were expected to be at the lower levels. It was hoped that the test would also distinguish level 2 from level 3 so that an alternative test could be used when a patient refused the ACL. Unfortunately, the data demonstrated a high number of false positive errors, indicating that the test is too simple to distinguish level 2 from level 3. In this study, 7 of 10 subjects who performed the ACL at level 2 were scored 3 on the LCL. There was only one false negative error; 1 subject, of 11 rated at level 3 on the ACL, performed the LCL test at level 2. The moderate Spearman correlations between the LCL and both the ACL and the PSMS-IADL lend validity to the ACL as the more discerning instrument, in association with performance of activities of daily living. Thus it seems to be appropriate to use the ACL as the independent variable in identifying the false positive and false negative errors of the LCL.

CONCLUSIONS

The findings of this study supported the definition of a cognitive disability given in Chapter 2, that a cognitive impairment produces observable limita-

tions in routine task behavior. The sample population, persons with senile dementia, proved to be especially relevant for this study in that their organically based brain disorder manifested itself in dysfunction of the mental processes that guide voluntary motor actions. The impaired person's physical ability to perform an action is left intact, thus allowing observation of a correspondence between brain and behavior that can be attributed to faulty mental processing.

In this study the highly significant association between the ACL score and the PSMS-IADL total score lends support to a brain-behavior correspondence and suggests that the severity of the disability in senile dementia may be described by the cognitive levels. A similar brain-behavior correspondence is suggested by the substantial association between the MMS and PSMS-IADL. The moderate relationship between the ACL and the MMS gives congruent validity to the ACL as measuring similar domains of cognition.

When the ACL was correlated with the individual items on the PSMS-IADL, the associations were less high and varied considerably, which suggests that difficulties with the measurement tools may intervene in the proposed brain-behavior correspondence. A secondary investigation revealed that there was not a significant difference between cognitive levels 3 and 4 in performance of activities of daily living. This finding suggests a lack of discriminatory power in both instruments, the ACL and the PSMS-IADL. The proposed revision in ACL scoring criteria has demonstrated an improvement in item association with the ACL. On the other hand, the PSMS-IADL, which indicated the social consequences of the brain impairment, was not adequate to specify task behaviors for this study. In anticipation of establishing a better correspondence between the ACL and routine tasks, a classification of daily living behaviors (see Fig. 2-22) has been presented as a secondary result in this study.

In addition to the instruments' limitations, some of the variance in individual item association with the ACL may be explained by the caregiver's report. The PSMS-IADL measurement does not explain why subjects were more or less independent; the disease process was assumed to be responsible. The caregiver's report on the PSMS-IADL reflected his or her perception of the subject's performance on those tasks. In this study the association of the ACL with the PSMS-IADL was shown to be higher for subjects whose caregivers were members of a support group than for those whose caregivers were not in support groups. This finding implies that reliability of report can be confounded by any one or a combination of the following: a recent diagnosis of the dementing illness, denial by the caregiver, and lack of support for the caregiver.

The discussion of the demographic variables alluded to the possible variance caused by the caregiver's style, which was not directly controlled for in this study. The findings revealed that male gender and living with a spouse confounded the relationship of the ACL with the PSMS-IADL. The elimination of traditionally female-related tasks from the scoring for men did not strengthen the correlation between sex and the PSMS-IADL, contrary to what would be expected if tasks were removed in which men were inexperienced. Thus, it is suggested that rather than inexperience with task content, men in this study showed unjustified dependency in performing daily living tasks, possibly because of the caregiver style of their wives. These findings emphasize the important relationship between style of caregiving and task behavior and warrant further investigation.

Regardless of age and social position, the relationship of the ACL with the PSMS-IADL was upheld. Since this sample performed the ACL only at levels 1 to 4, it is not known if levels 5 and 6 can be adequately performed by persons aged 60 or older. In this limited sample of persons with dementia, maintenance in family homes appeared to be a matter of support systems rather than of social position, although the data were inconclusive. In addition the results of this and previous studies using the ACL suggest that social position probably cannot compensate for a cognitive disability at levels 1

through 4 in helping a subject acquire new learning.

Finally, the LCL task is recommended to distinguish between levels 1 and 2 in persons with senile dementia. The criteria used in this study need further refinements and empirical study to establish the validity of the LCL as a clinical procedure.

In sum, the findings of this investigation supported the cognitive disability theory proposed in this book and its methodology in occupational therapy practice.

Intervention with Persons Having Senile Dementia

The study's findings lend support to the use of the ACL with persons 60 years and older, although further standardization of the ACL with this population is highly recommended. Few older persons with dementia were physically impeded from performing the task, and none objected to the task content of leather lacing. The task did not appear to create test anxiety, as was exhibited occasionally during the MMS. In addition age did not seem to interfere with the association of the ACL and performance of activities of daily living.

Functional behavior of the cognitively impaired person appears to be influenced by the caregiver. The style of caregiving can be viewed as a continuum with promoting unavailable independence at one end and fostering unwarranted dependence at the other. Using the ACL as a measure of cognitive ability and the task analysis (see Chap. 3), I was able to offer suggestions to the caregiver: to modify the tasks, the environment, or both to facilitate optimal task behavior in the impaired person. The therapist can thus provide support to the family, day treatment center, or nursing facility caregiver in maintaining functional behavior, while monitoring the course of the dementing illness.

Allen Cognitive Level Test as a Potential Predictor of Performance

An ability to predict the performance of activities of daily living from the ACL score has been suggested by these results. Further refinements in the description of daily living activities are, however, essential for prediction in individual cases, and some of the behaviors described by the caregivers interviewed in this study are included on the Routine Task Inventory (see Fig. 2-22). Use of the Routine Task Inventory for health care planning is not justified at this time owing to a lack of empirical study. The ACL, used with any instrument that classifies daily living behaviors, may be found to be more predictive of certain tasks than others. The results of this study suggest that the ACL merits closer scrutiny concerning the internal consistency of the cognitive levels as descriptions of what an impaired person can, and cannot, do.

The fear that the ACL may be used prematurely and inappropriately to predict task ability is not unwarranted. Any brief screening measure, used in isolation from a thorough assessment of the many variables that influence task behavior, would not be an appropriate assessment of competence or readiness for community placement. The study does support the proposition that the therapist's focus on a cognitive disability can provide the family and medical team with valuable information concerning the quality of task behaviors needed for maintenance in the community. The refinement of the description of the cognitive levels may offer increasing assistance in the selection of realistic program objectives, thus enhancing occupational therapy as a profession with interdisciplinary credibility.

Limitations of the Study

The results of the study must be generalized with caution because of a number of limitations that became apparent during the course of the study. Limitations were recognized concerning the following: (1) the PSMS-IADL, (2) the caregiver's report, (3) the caregiver's style, (4) the HISP and education level, and (5) the limited sample characteristics and size.

Physical Self-Maintenance Scale–Instrumental Activities of Daily Living Scale

As discussed previously, the limitations of the PSMS–IADL possibly resulted in subjective scoring of various items. I attempted to interpret the scale items uniformly to each caregiver. As different observations of task behavior were described by caregivers and categorized in terms of the scales, some consistency in interpretation was probably lost.

Caregiver Report

The reliability of the caregiver report was acknowledged as a limitation at the outset of this investigation. In addition to the shortcomings related to the scoring of the PSMS-IADL, a number of other factors may have contributed to inaccurate reporting by the caregiver. First, because the impaired person was present in the room, I could not discuss openly with the informant the extent of daily living impairment. This was especially true with subjects whose suspiciousness and denial were evident. If this lack of privacy appeared to be detracting greatly from a reliable measure, I followed up the interview with a phone conversation.

As discussed previously in the section on support groups, another consideration related to inaccurate caregiver reporting may be denial or inadequate knowledge of the extent of the impairment, owing to the subject's being newly diagnosed. Finally, the caregiver may not have been able to assess realistically the functional impairment of the demented person because of an overwhelming sense of burden and lack of support.

Caregiver's Style

During the data collection, it became evident to me

that the caregiver's expectations and allowances for task behavior were possibly influencing rating on the scales. As discussed in the sections on sex, marital status, and living situation, the style of caregiving appeared to intervene in performance of activities of daily living. Even if the informant's report reflected the actual performance of the subject, it may also have reflected the style of caregiving (that is, promoting or limiting functional independence).

Thus the caregiver issue impinges on this study in two interrelated ways: which task behaviors the caregiver style allows functionally and how the caregiver perceives and reports that function. The goal of the study was to measure task behavior representative of real functional ability so as to obtain a true measure of the association between cognitive ability and functional ability. Although the extent of variance cannot be known, it appears that the intervening variables of caregiver style and report may have compromised this study's measure of functioning on activities of daily living.

Social Position and Level of Education

According to the scaling procedure of the HISP (Hollingshead and Redlich, 1958), the occupation and highest level of education of the main wage earner in the family of the impaired person determined that subject's social position. Consequently, in this sample in which the main wage earner was most often the husband, data concerning educational level of most of the female subjects were missing. This omission limited the study's analysis of the effects of education on the performance of the ACL and activities of daily living.

Limited Sample Characteristics and Size

Since most of the subjects were white, the sample did not reflect the racial characteristics of other populations that therapists see in practice, and these results should be generalized only with caution to other ethnic groups. In addition, since all of the men were married, it is not known how single men aged 60 and older would perform on the ACL and the PSMS-IADL. Finally, because of the limited sample size, the findings of this study must be viewed as suggestive rather than definitive.

RECOMMENDATIONS FOR FUTURE RESEARCH

The following recommendations for future research emerged from this study:

1. Instrument development utilizing the classification of daily living behaviors presented as a secondary result of this study and included in Fig. 2-22. The scaling of task behaviors should correspond to task analysis (see Chap. 3) and account for physical restrictions, types of initiation required, task carry-through, and past experience. Presently, scales for activities of daily living are not specifically oriented toward the cognitive components of task performance.

2. Further investigation of the ACL concerning the revised scoring criterion for the twist problem, and revision of the LCL to discriminate behavior at levels 1, 2, and 3. This research could refine the operational definitions of the cognitive levels.

3. Correlation of the Routine Task Inventory with the ACL in a sample of persons with senile dementia living in family homes. Such a study should include the following: (1) subjects from a wider socioeconomic background, especially from the upper classes; (2) representation of various racial backgrounds; (3) recording of education level for both genders; (4) recording of the time since onset of the disease; and (5) participation of subjects whose caregivers belong to support groups. Such a study could account for the influence of demographic variables and control better for the reliability of the caregiver report while further examining the internal consistency of the descriptions of the cognitive levels.

4. Replication of the study as suggested above with different diagnostic groups in other regions of the United States. This could add to the reliability and

validity of the ACL and suggest further refinements in the listing of daily living behaviors.

5. Analysis of the caregiver's style by examining how various characteristics of the caregiver (such as denial, overprotectiveness, or being overburdened) influences the functioning of persons with dementia at different cognitive levels. Such a study could isolate the effect of caregiver style on performance of activities of daily living.

6. Analysis of the influence of a spouse caregiver versus other types of caregivers on the association between ACL performance and daily living behaviors. The data should be analyzed controlling for gender, marital status, and living situation to determine the effect of various combinations of these variables on the impaired person's behavior.

7. Correlation of the ACL with specific daily living behaviors that are performed at day treatment centers for persons with dementia or other mental disorders. Employing an impartial observer to rate behaviors could ensure reliability of report while further examining internal consistency.

8. A study of the ACL with a random sampling of older persons. The normal elderly population has not been tested with the ACL. (Meal sites where older people are provided with cooked food might be an ideal place to gather data.)

ACKNOWLEDGMENTS

Grateful thanks are extended to Linda J. Davis, Ph.D., O.T.R., who served as the thesis committee Chairperson and Gerald Sharrott, M.A., O.T.R., who served as a member of the thesis committee.

APPENDIX 15-1. MINI-MENTAL STATE

Instructions for Administration of Mini-Mental State Examination (Fig. 15-1)

Orientation

1. Ask for the date. Then ask specifically for parts omitted, e.g., "Can you also tell me what season it is?" One point for each correct.

2. Ask in turn "Can you tell me the name of this hospital?" (town, county, etc.). One point for each correct.

Registration

Ask the patient if you may test his memory. Then say the names of 3 unrelated objects, clearly and slowly, about one second for each. After you have said all 3, ask him to repeat them. This first repetition determines his score (0–3) but keep saying them until he can repeat all 3, up to 6 trials. If he does not eventually learn all 3, recall cannot be meaningfully tested.

Attention and Calculation

Ask the patient to begin with 100 and count backwards by 7. Stop after 5 subtractions (93, 86, 79, 72, 65). Score the total number of correct answers.

   If the patient cannot or will not perform this task, ask him to spell the word "world" backwards. The score is the number of letters in correct order. E.g. dlrow = 5, dlorw = 3.

Recall

Ask the patient if he can recall the 3 words you previously asked him to remember. Score 0–3.

Language

   NAMING. Show the patient a wrist watch and ask him what it is. Repeat for pencil. Score 0–2.

   REPETITION. Ask the patient to repeat the sentence after you. Allow only one trial. Score 0 or 1.

   3-STAGE COMMAND. Give the patient a piece of plain blank paper and repeat the command. Score 1 point for each part correctly executed.

"Mini-Mental State"

Maximum Score	Score	

Orientation

5   ( )   What is the (year) (season) (date) (day) (month)?
5   ( )   Where are we: (state) (county) (town) (hospital) (floor).

Registration

3   ( )   Name 3 objects: 1 second to say each. Then ask the patient all 3 after you have said them. Give 1 point for each correct answer. Then repeat them until he learns all 3. Count trials and record.
Trials _____

Attention and Calculation

5   ( )   Serial 7's. 1 point for each correct. Stop after 5 answers. Alternatively spell "world" backwards.

Recall

3   ( )   Ask for the 3 objects repeated above. Give 1 point for each correct.

Language

9   ( )   Name a pencil, and watch (2 points)
Repeat the following "No ifs, ands or buts." (1 point)
Follow a 3-stage command:
"Take a paper in your right hand, fold it in half, and put it on the floor" (3 points)
Read and obey the following:

Close Your Eyes (1 point)
Write a sentence (1 point)
Copy design (1 point)   ⟶
_____ Total score
Assess level of consciousness along a continuum _____
Alert   Drowsy   Stupor   Coma

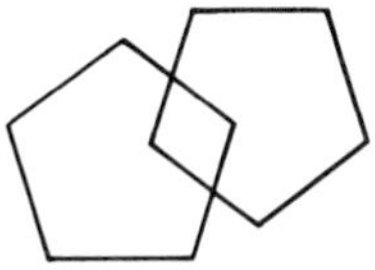

Patient _____
Examiner _____
Date _____

Fig. 15-1. Scoring sheet for the Mini-Mental State. (Designs shown were added to the scoring sheet by the author.) (From M. F. Folstein, S. E. Folstein, and P. R. McHugh, "Mini-Mental State": A practical method for grading the cognitive state of patients for the clinician. J. Psychiatr. Res. 12:189–198, 1975. Reprinted with the permission of Pergamon Press, Ltd.)

READING. On a blank piece of paper print the sentence "Close your eyes" in letters large enough for the patient to see clearly. Ask him to read it and do what it says. Score 1 point only if he actually closes his eyes.

WRITING. Give the patient a blank piece of paper and ask him to write a sentence for you. Do not dictate a sentence; it is to be written spontaneously. It must contain a subject and verb and be sensible. Correct grammar and punctuation are not necessary.

COPYING. On a clean piece of paper, draw intersecting pentagons, each side about 1 in., and ask him to copy it exactly as it is. All 10 angles must be present and 2 must intersect to score 1 point. Tremor and rotation are ignored.

Estimate the patient's level of sensorium along a continuum, from alert on the left to coma on the right.

Source: M. F. Folstein, S. E. Folstein, and P. R. McHugh, "Mini-Mental State": A practical method for grading the cognitive state of patients for the clinician. *J. Psychiatr. Res.* 12:189–198, 1975. Reprinted with the permission of Pergamon Press, Ltd.

REFERENCES

Abramson, J. H. Discussion I. In C. Eisdorfer and R. O. Friedel (eds.), *Cognitive and Emotional Disturbance in the Elderly.* Chicago: Year Book, 1977.

Albert, M. S. Geriatric neuropsychology. *J. Consult. Clin. Psychol.* 49:835–850, 1981.

Allen, C. K. Independence through activity: The practice of occupational therapy (psychiatry). *Am. J. Occup. Ther.* 36:731–739, 1982.

Blessed, G., Tomlinson, B. E., and Roth, M. The association between quantitative measures of dementia and of senile change in the cerebral grey matter of elderly subjects. *Br. J. Psychiatry* 119:797–811, 1968.

Cohen, D., and Eisdorfer, C. Cognitive Theory and the Assessment of Change in the Elderly. In A. Raskin and L. F. Jarvik (eds.), *Psychiatric Symptoms and Cognitive Loss in the Elderly: Evaluation and Assessment Techniques.* New York: Hemisphere, 1979.

DSM III: *Diagnostic and Statistical Manual of Mental Disorders* (3rd ed.). Washington, D.C.: American Psychiatric Association, 1980.

Eisdorfer, C., Cohen, D., and Veith, R. *The Psychopathology of Aging.* Upjohn, 1980.

Folstein, M. F., Folstein, S. E., and McHugh, P. R. "Mini-Mental State": A practical method for grading the cognitive state of patients for the clinician. *J. Psychiatr. Res.* 12:189–198, 1975.

Goldfarb, A. I., Fisch, M., and Gerber, I. Predictors of mortality in the institutionalized aged. *Dis. Nerv. System* 27:21–29, 1966.

Guilford, J. P., and Fruchter, B. *Fundamental Statistics in Psychology and Education.* New York: McGraw-Hill, 1973.

Gurland, B. J. The Borderland of Dementia: The Influence of Sociocultural Characteristics on Rates of Dementia Occurring in the Senium. In N. E. Miller and G. D. Cohen (eds.), *Clinical Aspects of Alzheimer's Disease and Senile Dementia,* (Aging, Vol. 15). New York: Raven, 1981.

Herzig, S. I. Occupational therapy assessment of cognitive levels as predictors of the community adjustment of chronic schizophrenic patients. University of Southern California Master's Thesis, 1978.

Heying, L. M. Cognitive disability and activities of daily living in persons with senile dementia. University of Southern California Master's Thesis, 1983.

Hinkle, D. E., Wiersma, W., and Jurs, S. G. *Applied Statistics for the Behavioral Sciences.* Chicago: Rand McNally, 1979.

Hollingshead, A. B., and Redlich, F. C. *Social Class and Mental Illness.* New York: Wiley, 1958.

Howell, S. C. A symposium on the assessments of functions of the aging adult. *Gerontologist* 10:18–19, 1970.

Kane, R. A., and Kane, R. L. *Assessing the Elderly: A Practical Guide to Measurement.* Lexington, Mass.: Heath, 1981.

Katz, N. An occupational therapy study of cognition in adult inpatients with depression. University of Southern California Master's Thesis, 1979.

Lawton, M. P. Assessment, integration, and environments for older people. *Gerontologist* 10:38–46, 1970.

Lawton, M. P. The functional assessment of elderly people. *J. Am. Geriatr. Soc.* 19:465–481, 1971.

Lawton, M. P., and Brody, E. M. Assessment of older people: Self-maintaining and instrumental activities of daily living. *Gerontologist* 9:179–186, 1969.

Mace, N. L., and Rabins, P. V. *The 36-Hour Day: A Family Guide to Caring for Persons with Alzheimer's Disease, Related Dementing Illnesses, and Memory Loss in Later Life.* Baltimore: Johns Hopkins University Press, 1981.

Miller, E. The Differential Psychological Evaluation. In N. E. Miller and G. D. Cohen (eds.), *Clinical Aspects of Alzheimer's Disease and Senile Dementia* (Aging, Vol. 15). New York: Raven, 1981a.

Miller, E. The nature of the cognitive deficit in senile dementia. In N. E. Miller and G. D. Cohen (eds.). *Aging* (Vol. 15, *Clinical Aspects of Alzheimer's Disease and Senile Dementia*). New York: Raven, 1981b.

Moore, D. S. An occupational therapy evaluation of sensorimotor cognition: Initial reliability, validity, and descriptive data for hospitalized schizophrenic adults. University of Southern California Master's Thesis, 1978.

Plutchik, R. Conceptual and Practical Issues in the Assessment of the Elderly. In A. Raskin and L. F. Jarvik (eds.), *Psychiatric Symptoms and Cognitive Loss in the Elderly: Evaluation and Assessment Techniques.* Washington: Hemisphere, 1979.

Williams, L. R. Development and initial testing of an occupational therapy object-classification test. University of Southern California Master's Thesis, 1981.

Wilson, L. A., Grant, K., Witney, P. M., and Kerridge, D. F. Mental status of elderly hospital patients related to occupational therapist's assessment of activities of daily living. *Gerontol. Clin.* 15:197–202, 1973.

Zarit, S. H. *Aging and Mental Disorders.* New York: Free Press, 1980.

Zarit, S., Reever, K., and Bach-Petersen, J. Relatives of the impaired elderly: Correlates of feelings of burden. *Gerontologist* 20:649–655, 1980.

CHAPTER 16

IMPLICATIONS FOR THEORY DEVELOPMENT

A person's ability to perform a routine task can be influenced by a large number of biologic, psychological, and social factors. Within the confusing array of relevant factors the therapist must decide what he or she can do about a patient's disability. The propositions that have been suggested throughout this text (Table 16-1) can be used as guidelines in identifying relevant evaluations and selecting treatment methods. Therapists can probably identify questions that would benefit from more empirical investigation. This chapter will summarize our current knowledge and attempt to forecast areas requiring further investigation.

PROPOSITIONS

The propositions that have the best empirical support are 1 and 2 (Table 16-1). The social consequences of proposition 9 have placed considerable urgency on the need to describe the routine tasks associated with each cognitive level. The operational definition of the cognitive levels that has been investigated most is the Allen Cognitive Level Test (ACL; see Chap. 4). The ACL has been used to study patients with schizophrenia (Moore, 1978; see Chap. 12), depression (Katz, 1979; see Chap. 13), and dementia (Heying, 1983; see Chap. 15), as well as a nondisabled population (Williams, 1981; see Chap. 14). The significant correlations between the ACL and other measures of cognition, the severity of the disease, selected demographic variables, and routine tasks will be discussed. These studies have suggested some potential instrument refinements and population selection criteria that will be presented. In addition, some theoretical considerations implied by these studies will be discussed.

The propositions sprinkled throughout the text are suggested as statements that can be subjected to empirical investigation. Therapists working in different settings or having different backgrounds are welcome to pursue any of them. The suggested propositions are not meant to be exhaustive; additional propositions, of course, may be investigated.

Table 16-1. Summary of propositions

Proposition	Chapter	Page
1. The observed routine task behavior of disabled patients will differ from the observed behavior of nondisabled populations	2	73
2. Limitations in task behavior can be hierarchically described by the cognitive levels	2	74
3. The choice of task content is influenced by the diagnosis and the disability	3	92
4. The task environment can have a positive or a negative effect on a patient's ability to regulate his or her own behavior	3	93
5. Patients with cognitive disabilities attend to those elements of the task environment that are within their range of ability	3	98
6. Therapists can select and modify a task so that it is within the patient's range of ability through the application of task analysis	3	100
7. An effective outcome of occupational therapy services occurs when successful task performance is accompanied by a pleasant task experience	7	187
8. Steps in task procedures that require abilities above a person's level of ability will be refused or ignored	7	190
9. The assessment of the cognitive level can contribute to the legal determination of competency	11	271

The best available evidence supporting a difference between a disabled and a nondisabled population (proposition 1) is found in the analysis of variance in Williams's study (see Table 14-5 and Fig. 14-3). A significant difference in ACL score between schizophrenic subjects and depressed subjects (see Table 13-7) was also found ($F = 59.56$; $p = .0001$; degrees of freedom, or df, $= 2$).

A difference between the nondisabled population and the depressed population was found at admission and discharge. A two-sample t-test, recently calculated by Katz (1983), showed the following:

ACL SCORE	t	p
Admission	5.631	< .0005
Discharge	1.992	< .05

The difference between depressed and nondisabled subjects is greater at admission, but a significant difference was still present at discharge; the reason for the persistence of these differences several weeks after discharge is unknown and could be an interesting area for further study. Proposition 1 raises some puzzling questions about the natural course of epi-

sodic diseases in which the patient is expected to return to a premorbid level of function. I have assumed that it would be easier, and more important, to substantiate the presence of a grave disability, but this should not be pursued at the expense of ignoring a potential mild disability. There are some clinical suspicions that a mild disability may be present at levels 5 and 6, and ways of describing this disability are still being sought. The study of classification is one approach.

Confirmation of the validity of the hierarchy of the cognitive levels (proposition 2) is tenuous at best. One of the reasons for the creation of the hierarchy was the lack of a valid description of the relative severity of mental disorders. Fig. 16-1 shows the initial ACL scores in three disabled populations and a nondisabled population. The pattern seems to follow clinical experiences and may be evidence of the clinical validity of the hierarchy.

The urgency behind the need to describe how a level of competence predicts social behavior in the community (proposition 9) is implied in Heying's (1983) study. The internal consistency between an ACL score and the descriptions on the Routine Task

369

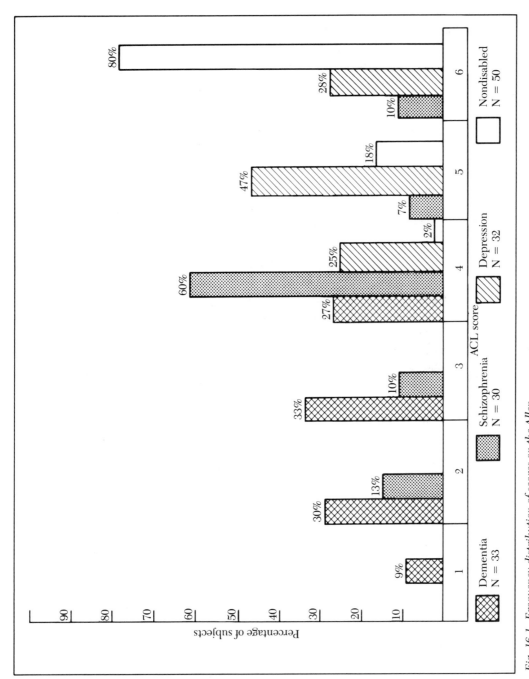

Fig. 16-1. Frequency distribution of scores on the Allen
Cognitive Level Test (ACL).

Inventory (see Fig. 2-22) is not known; studies to investigate this are in process (Heinman and Wilson). One can safely say that more studies, with additional refinements, will be required to provide clinical confidence in our ability to generalize from one task to another.

OPERATIONAL DEFINITION OF THE COGNITIVE LEVELS

The ACL has provided the operational definition of the cognitive level in four studies. A comparison of the significant correlations will be used to gain some perspective on what the cognitive levels are measuring. Two different kinds of correlation statistics have been used: Pearson's, which are parametric, and Spearman's, which are nonparametric. There are different criteria for selecting each statistical tool (Hinkle et al., 1979; Miller, 1977). An inexact examination of Pearson and Spearman correlations done with Heying's (Chap. 15) data showed small differences ($r = \pm .05$), so the following comparisons will not report the statistical tool. (It is reported in Chaps. 12 through 15.)

Allen Cognitive Level Test with Other Cognitive Tests

Statistically significant correlations between the ACL and other measures of cognitive abilities were found (see Table 12-2). The Block Design showed an expected positive correlation with the ACL at admission and discharge in a depressed sample. An expected positive correlation of the ACL with the Riska Object Classification (ROC) test was found in the unstructured (ROCUN) and structured (ROCST) parts of the test at admission, but not at discharge, in the depressed sample. (Correlations between the ACL and ROC were not done with the nondisabled sample.) An expected positive correlation was found between the ACL and the Lower Cognitive Level Test with a demented sample. The correlations are significant enough to provide some validity for the ACL as a measure of cognition. The

Table 16-2. Errors and corrections on the Allen Cognitive Level Test

Running stitch
  Pushes needle down, does not bring it back up
  Skips holes
  Alternates running and whip stitch
  Does whip stitch
Whip stitch
  Goes from back to front
  Fails to recognize twist as error
    Possible visual impairment
    No visual impairment
  Recognizes twist after it is pointed out
  Refuses to attempt to correct twist
  Tries to correct twist, fails
Single cordovan stitch
  Goes from back to front
    Corrects after second demonstration, fails to keep
      needle to left
    Corrects after second demonstration
  Fails to tighten in sequence
    Corrects after second demonstration

correlations, however, are not high enough to suggest that the ACL is a duplication of any of these measures.

Allen Cognitive Level Test with Severity of Disease

Statistically significant correlations between the ACL and other measures of the severity of disease were found (Fig. 16-2). The Brief Psychiatric Rating Scale showed an expected negative correlation at admission and discharge in a schizophrenic population. In addition, the length of hospital stay for the schizophrenic sample showed a negative correlation with the ACL score at admission and discharge (people with a lower score had a longer stay). An expected positive correlation was found with the Mini-Mental State exam as a whole and with the three-stage direction item on the exam in the demented population. An expected correlation between the physician's report (Physician Global Ratr value

1.0 0.9 0.8 0.7 0.6 0.5 0.4 0.3 0.2

Cognitive tests

Block
Design
ROC
ROCUN
ROCST

LCL   0.58 Dementia

−0.46 Depression (admission)
−0.40 Depression (discharge)
0.42 Depression (admission)
0.38 Depression (discharge)

Tests of the severity of the disease

BPRS₁   −0.53 Schizophrenia (admission)
BPRS₂   −0.43 Schizophrenia (discharge)
MMS   0.66 Dementia
MMS₃   0.65 Dementia

Length of hospitalization   0.38 Schizophrenia (admission)
                                        −0.43 Schizophrenia (discharge)

Fig. 16-2. Significant correlations (r) between Allen Cognitive Level Test score and scores on selected cognitive tests and measures of the severity of illness. (ROC = Riska Object Classification Test; ROCUN = ROC, unstructured part; ROCST = ROC, structured part; LCL = Lower Cognitive Level Test; BPRS₁ and BPRS₂ = Brief Psychiatric Rating Scale, at admission and discharge, respectively; MMS = Mini-Mental State; MMS₃ = 3-stage command item on the MMS.)

ing) and the patient's report (Self-rating Depression Scale) of the severity of depression was not found at admission or discharge. In addition the number of hospitalizations in the depressed sample did not correlate with the ACL score.

The ACL seems to be a measure of the cognitive impairment of schizophrenia and dementia, but not of depression. The cognitive impairment of depression may be secondary to the mood disorder, loss of energy, or psychomotor retardation.

Allen Cognitive Level Test with Demographic Variables

Fig. 16-3 shows the statistically significant correlations between ACL score and selected demographic variables. I think that the absence of findings is the most striking feature of the demographic variables: eight significant correlations were found. The most amusing positive correlation is between the ACL score and age with the demented population; older subjects had a higher ACL score. We had excluded people over the age of 65 from the previous studies to avoid a possible confounding factor of intellectual impairment associated with old age. With an older population a negative correlation might be expected. With an older, demented population a positive correlation was found; while the correlation is statistically significant, it is low ($r = + 0.29$). None of the other studies found a significant correlation between ACL score and age. The dementia findings on age may be restricted to a few people in that study. At this point one can be fairly safe in assuming that the ACL assessment of adults is free from the confounding factor of age; developmental disorders, of course, would challenge this assumption.

A significant correlation with sex was never found. This is a bit surprising. I wondered if leather lacing would build on sewing experiences and bias the ACL in favor of women. If it does, the studies have not been able to detect the bias.

Previous leather lacing experience showed a positive correlation with the ACL score in a single in-

stance: the schizophrenic sample at admission. The mean ACL score (3.91) is one of the lowest average ACL scores on a tested sample. The dementia sample had a lower average score, but none of those subjects had ever had any leather lacing experience. The schizophrenic sample contained individuals who have gone in and out of occupational therapy clinics for years, and therapists have taught them how to do leather lacing. Previous experience may be a factor in ACL scores among lower-level samples when therapists have taught the subjects to do leather lacing during previous hospitalizations. The studies suggest that clinicians should inquire about previous leather lacing experience when administering the ACL to check for a false positive score.

Education, occupation, and social position were significant with the nondisabled population. No significant correlation was found in the depressed population, but education was related to the change in ACL score in the schizophrenic population. The disabled populations were principally composed of subjects from the lower educational, occupational, and social positions, while the nondisabled population was spread over the five social positions. Thus it is difficult to make a distinction between the influence of social position and that of disability. The dementia sample contained four subjects in social positions I and II (the highest classes) who scored 4 or below on the ACL. These subjects support the clinical observation that social position is a confounding factor at levels 5 and 6, but that the influence of past education and occupation is less and less apparent as one progresses down the disability hierarchy.

Marital status and living situation demonstrated a positive correlation with the ACL score in the demented population; unmarried persons (single, widowed, or divorced) who were living alone had a higher ACL score. The living situation for the demented population can be compared to residence after discharge for the schizophrenic population; a larger percentage of people with dementia than with schizophrenia are living at home. The differences in available social support systems may ex-

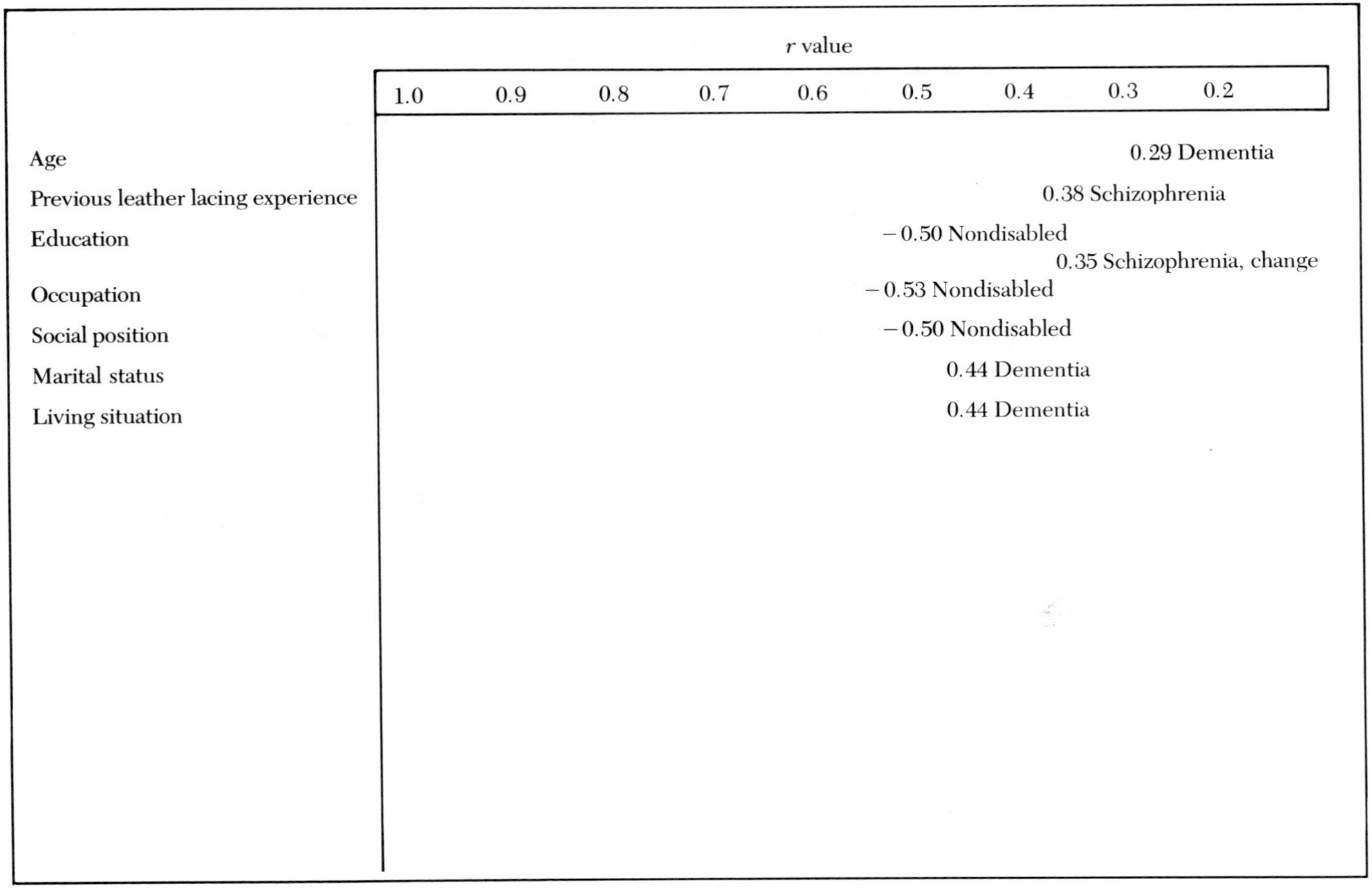

		r value							
	1.0	0.9	0.8	0.7	0.6	0.5	0.4	0.3	0.2
Age									0.29 Dementia
Previous leather lacing experience								0.38 Schizophrenia	
Education						−0.50 Nondisabled		0.35 Schizophrenia, change	
Occupation						−0.53 Nondisabled			
Social position						−0.50 Nondisabled			
Marital status							0.44 Dementia		
Living situation							0.44 Dementia		

Fig. 16-3. *Significant correlations* (r) *between Allen Cognitive Level Test score and selected demographic variables.*

plain these differences. At the time that these studies were done, public funds supported open and closed group homes for people with schizophrenic disorders but not for those with dementing disorders.

All of these studies were conducted in the Los Angeles area and were reviewed for the protection of human subjects by the Los Angeles County–University of Southern California (LAC–USC) Medical Center's research committees. The dementia study included community-based subjects, but the remaining populations were influenced by the LAC-USC Medical Center's admission policies and staffing patterns. I do not know if these findings can be replicated in other institutions or geographical locations; clearly, additional studies conducted in other places are required. A continuous control for demographic variables may help us identify factors that are location specific.

Allen Cognitive Level Test with Routine Tasks

The correlations between the ACL score and selected routine tasks in demented subjects are presented again to allow for comparison of all of the correlations done to date (Fig. 16-4). The correlations between the ACL and routine tasks are stronger than the correlations with other cognitive tests, measures of the severity of the illness, or the demographic variables. If we define a cognitive disability as a restriction in routine task behavior we should expect to find higher correlations in this area of study, and the correlations are high enough to support predictive validity. We cannot, however, be satisfied with these correlations. If we are to move beyond the realm of general populations into predictions in individual cases, we will need to know more about the internal consistency between the ACL and Routine Task Inventory.

Revised Scoring Criteria

Heying's (1983) observations of ACL performance raised numerous questions about the scoring crite-

ria. These questions will be discussed with the understanding that I do not have any answers at present.

There has been a persistent question about what to do about the twist in the leather lacing. The lacing does not always twist and whether it does or not has always been left to chance. Heying noted that the routine task performance of those people who were scored a 3 because of a failure to untwist the lacing more closely resembled the task performance expected at level 4. Revising the score from 3 to 4 made a slight but consistent increase in the correlation between the ACL and the routine tasks scores (Fig. 16-5). This revision raised many questions.

One therapist (Barna, 1983) reported a method for dealing with a chance twist of the lacing: She uses old lacing because it twists more often, and after she demonstrates the whip stitch she quickly twists the lacing within the hole of the leather before handing it to the patient. Other therapists speculated that there seems to be a difference in the errors made in doing the whip stitch: People who fail to go from front to back may be more disabled than people who see the twist as an error but cannot untwist the lacing. In addition people who can untwist the lacing in the whip stitch may fail to untwist it in the single cordovan stitch. The single cordovan is harder to untwist.

The single cordovan introduces another variable, in addition to the twist. The single cordovan must be tightened in sequence. After the first step, putting the leather through the hole, the leather must be tightened before the second step, putting the leather under the lacing. If this sequence is not followed the completed stitch does not look right. A person who sees this problem and spontaneously corrects it is scored a level 6. A person who recognizes a problem but cannot correct it without another demonstration is scored a level 5. In addition the therapist may demonstrate the correction of the error two different ways: (1) by taking the patient's incorrect stitch out and starting over or (2) by demonstrating a correction of the patient's stitch by tightening the stitch in sequence. The second option would seem to be easier; the studies have taken

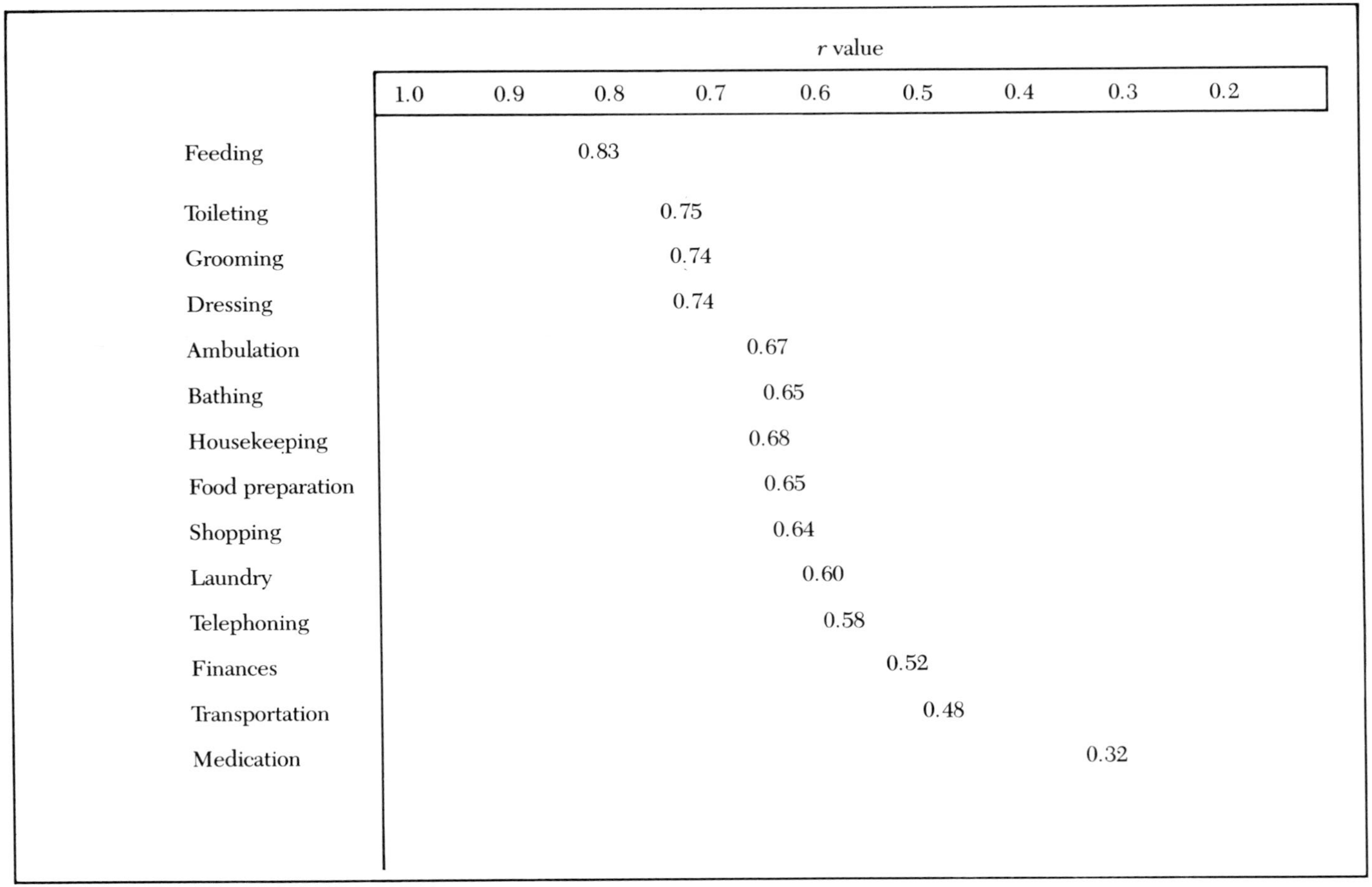

375

Fig. 16-4. Significant correlations (r) between Allen Cognitive Level Test score and score on selected routine tasks in patients with dementia. Routine task scores were obtained by interviewing patient's caregiver.

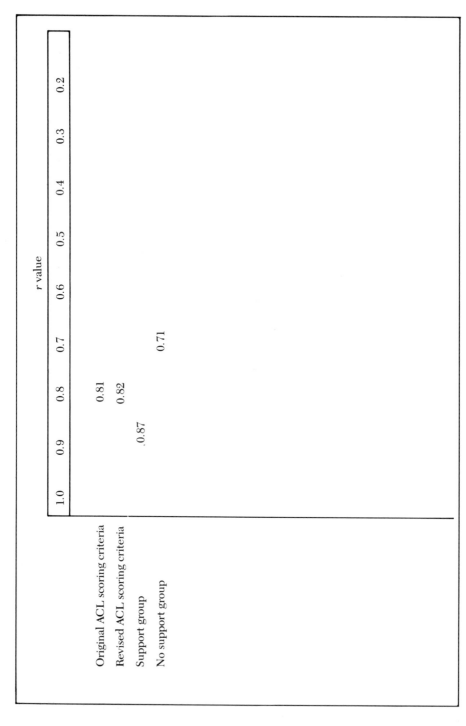

Fig. 16-5. Significant correlations (r) between Allen Cognitive Level Test ACL score and total score on routine tasks in patients with dementia. Routine task scores were obtained by interviewing patient's caregiver.

the stitch out. The differences, if any, between these two forms of demonstration are unknown.

Other errors with the single cordovan include a failure to continue to go from front to back for both steps; this behavior is scored a level 4. Or the patient may fail to keep the needle to the left during the second step; this error seems to fall between the front-to-back error and the tightening error. Therapists have been scoring a spontaneous correction at level 6, correction after a second demonstration at 5, and a failure to correct at level 4. The validity of these scoring criteria should be examined because such a study could lead to refinements in our understanding of the cognitive levels.

Sympathy is extended to those readers who have experienced a twinge of dismay in discovering the ambiguities in the scoring of the ACL. Dismay over ambiguities seems to be a common experience when studying cognitive phenomena. I call it the ice cube experience: Just when I think that I have things neatly packaged into a tangible definition of observable behavior (an ice cube), somebody comes along with a hammer and a nail. The neat package shatters all over the place and begins to melt. Inferences about cognitive phenomena have a way of looking like a shattered ice cube, losing their meaning when one is confronted with unexpected observations of behavior. One approach to the problem is to supply more detail about the common errors in task performance. The discussion of the ACL illustrates this approach.

When Moore and I first began to use the ACL as a research instrument we thought we were being extraordinarily picayune in detailing the materials, directions, and scoring criteria. Now it seems that more detail is required about the common errors observed during test performance (Table 16-2). Because we have not kept records of these errors we do not know what they mean. They may not mean anything, and that would be important, too.

Methodologic Considerations

Further investigations are apt to encounter some obstacles that the researchers, clinicians, and I have thought about but have not directly addressed in these studies. The exclusion criteria have included impairments that may provide alternative explanations for limitations in task performance. Visual impairments are the most troublesome; if a person cannot see the hole in the leather or the twist in the lacing, then vision, not cognitive disability, could explain the error. Hearing impairments or inability to speak English do not seem to pose many problems; if the person watches the demonstration he or she can usually imitate it. Hand impairments have posed fewer problems than anticipated: The therapist can hold the leather for a person who has functional use of one hand. A person who must use a nondominant hand or has tremors may require extra time, but time is not a scoring criterion on the ACL. Obviously, these impairments still need to be taken into consideration; they simply seem to be less confusing than originally anticipated.

A major obstacle has been encountered in studying cognitive disabilities in an acute psychiatric hospital. A person with a functional history that suggests a chronic disability may deny the presence of any deficit. The denial is especially troublesome with patients who do not have a family member or any other person who can serve as a reliable informant. One wonders how disabled the person really is. Heying's selection of a demented population led to an approach to describing the functional disability. She noticed that people contacted through Alzheimer support groups were a rich resource for obtaining detailed descriptions of the functional disability (Fig. 16-5). People with Alzheimer's disease have a relatively stable disability, plus they have caregivers who have in-depth knowledge of what the patients can and cannot do. These caregivers also know how present abilities relate to past experiences; the caregivers are often spouses. A stable disability, coupled with a report from a reliable informant, seems to be an effective approach to describing limitations in routine task behavior. The description of stable conditions can then be used to sharpen our observations of acute and denied disabilities.

378

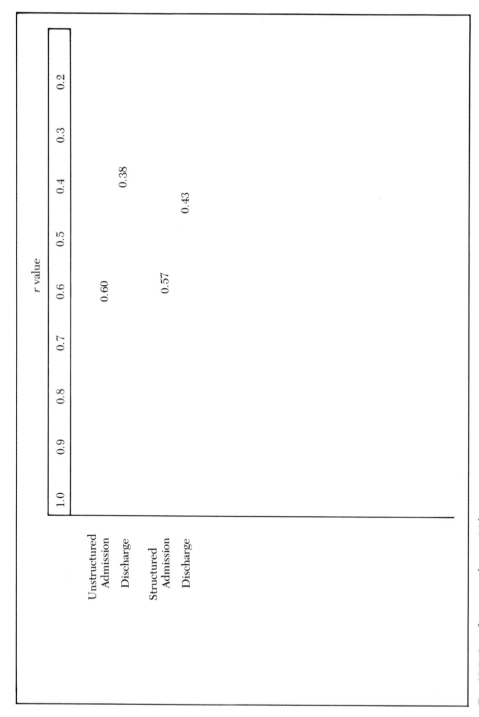

Fig. 16-6. Significant correlations (r) between scores on the Block Design and the structured and unstructured parts of the Riska Object Classification Test in depressed subjects.

CLASSIFICATION

Less is known about the classification instrument (ROC). It has been included because Williams, Katz, and I think it merits further investigation. Significant correlations between the ROC and the Block Design were found in the depressed sample (Katz, 1979). The correlations of both parts of the ROC with the Block Design are stronger at admission than at discharge, which suggests that the symptoms of depression have a similar impact on both measures of cognitive performance (Fig. 16-6). In addition Katz (1983) did more calculations examining her depressed population and comparing the nondisabled population to the depressed sample at admission and discharge using Williams' nondisabled sample. Two-sample *t*-tests had the following results:

$ROCUN_1$, $t = 1.77$ $p < .05$; $ROCUN_2$ $t = 0.60$ (NS)

$ROCST_1$, $t = 2.84$ $p < .005$; $ROCST_2$ $t = 1.35$ (NS)

A significant difference in ROC scores is seen between the first testing of the depressed sample, at admission, and the nondisabled sample. The difference between the depressed sample at discharge and the nondisabled sample is not significant. The two-sample *t*-test results suggest that the depressed patients function within a normal range of classification abilities after the depressive episode is finished. Even though the *t*-test value between admission and discharge scores of depressed patients was not significant (see Chap. 13), the differences between the two populations (depressed and nondisabled) suggests that the ROC may detect a cognitive disability during an acute phase of a disease. The absence of a significant difference at discharge suggests that if a mild disability is present, it is not detected by the ROC.

Scores on the unstructured parts of the ROC are associated with education, occupation, social position, and the number of previous depressed episodes (Fig. 16-7). Scoring on the structured part of the ROC was not associated with any of those demographic variables. These findings suggested the current distinctions made between spontaneous and imitated voluntary motor actions (see Table 2-1).

Assuming that we are trying to detect a mild disability at levels 5 and 6, these limited data suggest that spontaneous actions (unstructured) may be confounded by past experiences. The structured part of the ROC showed a larger (though nonsignificant) difference between depressed subjects at discharge and the nondisabled subjects. The structured part of the ROC may be associated with compliance with an external requirement—placing objects in groups according to two classification criteria. Compliance may be achieved by using mental symbols (shape and color) or by overt trial and error; the researchers have seen it done both ways. More success in detecting a mild disability may come from future investigations into compliance with external standards of performance. The standards will probably need to be refined to differentiate between levels 5 and 6, a distinction that has not been made with the present scoring of the ROC. Refined compliance with standards of performance makes clinical sense. Our biggest clinical problem with patients at levels 5 and 6 has been in advanced crafts in which the standards of performance are often ambiguous. Socially, the implications for successful job performance are apparent, making this an important area of study.

The differences in performance between the structured and unstructured part of the ROC have another intriguing aspect: The mean score on the unstructured part is often lower than that on the structured part. This trend is continuing in some preliminary data with adolescents and a schizophrenic sample (Katz, 1983) (Table 16-3). Perhaps structure improves performance. This is especially interesting when one realizes that the highest possible score on the unstructured part (16) is higher than that on the structured part (14). If structure can improve performance it would raise a number

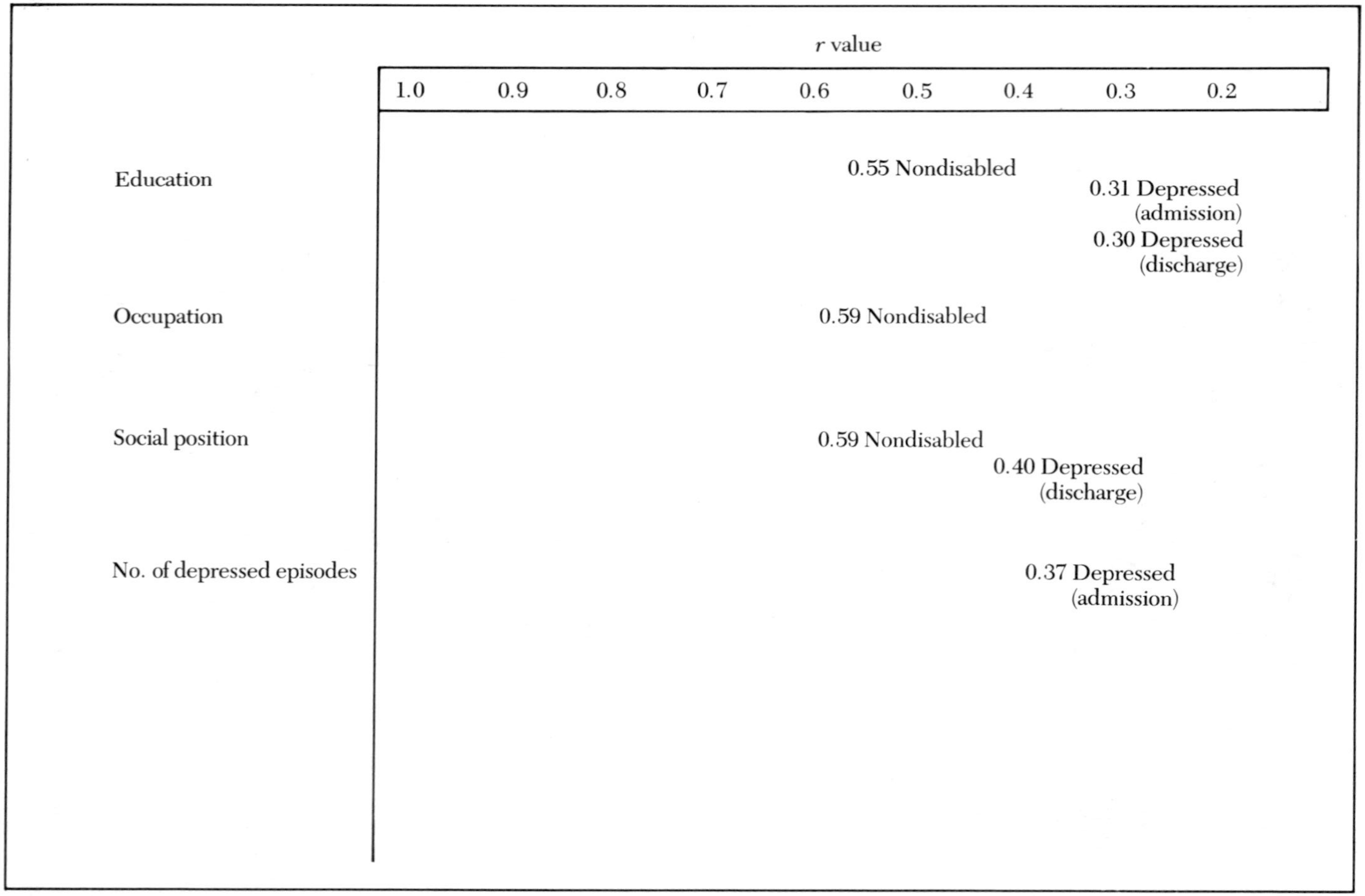

Fig. 16-7. *Significant correlations* (r) *between score on the Riska Object Classification Test, unstructured part, and selected demographic variables.*

Table 16-3. Results of ACL, ROCUN, and ROCST in various patient and control groups

| Group | N | Mean (SD) | | | Difference between ROCUN and ROCST |
		ACL	ROCUN	ROCST	
Adolescents, MBD or MR[a]	22	3.3 (1.8)	7.9 (3.9)	9.5 (3.1)	1.6
Schizophrenics[a]	24	4.9 (0.9)	9.7 (3.4)	10.4 (2.4)	0.7
Depressed patients, admission[b]	32	5.0 (0.7)	11.9 (2.9)	12.5 (2.0)	0.6
Adolescents, controls[a]	22	5.2 (0.9)	10.2 (1.9)	11.7 (1.9)	1.5
Depressed patients, discharge[b]	32	5.5 (0.7)	12.6 (2.0)	13.1 (1.4)	0.5
Nondisabled subjects[c]	50	5.8 (0.5)	12.9 (2.5)	13.5 (1.1)	0.6

ACL = Allen Cognitive Level Test; ROCUN = Riska Object Classification Test, unstructured part; ROCST = Riska Object Classification Test, structured part; MBD = minimal brain dysfunction; MR = mentally retarded.
[a]Data from N. Katz, 1983.
[b]Data from N. Katz, 1979.
[c]Data from L. R. Williams, 1981.

of clinical questions: Is the improvement observed in the OT clinic an artifact of the structured task environment? Will prolonged exposure to structured tasks generalize to spontaneous improvements in performance outside of OT clinic? Is the small difference in mean score (ranging from 0.5 to 1.6) strong enough to be of any clinical significance? The ROC may be able to tap answers to these questions. And, of course, the questions are related to the claims made about the value of occupational therapy services.

DEVELOPMENTAL PERSPECTIVE

The studies done thus far are descriptive; no attempt has been made to investigate the propositions related to treatment methods. The propositions that do relate to treatment stem from the struggle to reexamine the developmental perspective within the context of the advances in the neurosciences. In general the problem has centered around trying to define the relationships between biologic pathology, psychological development, and a social handicap. Some elements of psychological development can be applied to a description of cognitive disability, while other elements seem to be

misleading. The following discussion analyzes the application of developmental concepts.

The occupational therapy literature contains numerous references to studies of normal growth and development. The studies presented in this portion of the text have examined the application of Piaget's view of development to mental disorders. A fundamental question has been implicit in each of these studies: How far can one extend the analogy between development and disability? Stated another way, Does ontogenesis always parallel regression? What differences are there and at what point does the analogy become contrived? Theoreticians and academicians in occupational therapy have not paid much attention to these questions, and the need to describe decline has been difficult to explain. A research study that addressed development and disability might help clarify the differences between these processes.

A study that compared normal children (N = 118) aged 2 to 6 years to cognitively disabled adults with progressive dementia (N = 132) and focal lesions (N = 200) will illustrate the limitations on the developmental analogy. Gianotti (1972) took the ambiguous mental symptom of "closing in" and operationally defined it by a set of graphic tasks. Closing in measured the distance between a graphic model and the subject's copy of the model. Six models were drawn at the top of separate sheets of paper and the subjects were asked to copy the model. Observations of normal children provided the following types of closing in (Gianotti, 1972, p. 431):

(a) scrawling within the models,
(b) tendency to overlap or to bound the lines of the model with the copy,
(c) tendency to trace lines from the model to the surrounding space,
(d) tendency to make copies very near or adherent to the models

Increasing age of the children was associated with a reduction in closing in, roughly following the above sequence. All of the behaviors observed in children were present in adults. In addition the stages of dementia roughly followed a reverse sequence to the stages of development. Similarities between development and decline do exist. The similarities provide a partial description of the behavior observed in children and adults.

Dissimilarities also exist. The children paid attention to the reproduction of angles and simple round figures that are the prerequisites for learning how to write. The adults produced "simple, automatic activities" such as writing their names and had a "tendency to trace unsettled lines" (Gianotti, 1972). The children were *learning* to differentiate forms, while the adults were *reproducing* familiar knowledge. To Gianotti the "analogies are in contrast to the striking differences. . . ."

Clinicians and I have shared Gianotti's observation. The cognitively disabled are not learning, they are reproducing. The developmental perspective is useful in telling us whether a condition is getting better or worse, but that is as far as it goes. When we try to extend the developmental perspective into a statement about treatment objectives, we encounter problems. The therapist can try to direct the patients' attention to higher forms of differentiation, but patients with a stable cognitive disability

often refuse to follow this redirection of attention. They ignore the direction or refuse to have anything more to do with the project.

Patients with an acute cognitive disability display a spontaneous direction of attention to higher sensory cues and motor actions. Spontaneous attention to higher forms seems to be related to medication response and does not seem to be related to attendance in the occupational therapy clinic. The assessment of spontaneous attention seems to provide a relatively accurate measure of a person's most comfortable level of function. Spontaneous attention probably indicates what the patient will do independently, left to his or her own devices.

The therapist can encourage a patient to function at a higher level. Unfortunately, the differences between *encourage, cajole,* and *force* are ambiguous. The first question with acute conditions is, why bother? If the patient is going to function at a higher level spontaneously, do we really need to put ourselves through these projects that are, all too often, torturous for us and the patients? The propositions suggest that unpleasant task experiences be avoided whenever possible. When one is observing for a spontaneous return to a premorbid level of function, therapists should avoid objectives that begin with these habitual phrases: *to increase, to improve, to teach.* The phrases are essentially inaccurate and misleading.

The development perspective can be helpful in evaluating the severity of a condition. When the condition is acute, change is expected. Objective information about the degree and direction of change is important to all members of the treatment team, and the developmental perspective is helpful in providing the information. Extending the developmental perspective into treatment objectives is problematic because the perspective tends to neglect explanations for change other than occupational therapy. With acute conditions, the therapist and the patient are often in the position of waiting for the change to occur. It seems reasonable to suggest that the patient is more apt to endure the waiting if the time is passed as pleasantly as possible. In addition objective and realistic feedback about how the change is progressing can be very reassuring to the patient.

The next question is, should we give up all claims to developmental objectives? The answer is unclear. A United States National Health Interview Survey gathered information on limited activity and physical mobility that may help in answering this question. Between 1966 and 1976 there was a 37 percent increase in the number of people who report disabilities, with more people saying that they are unable to perform their main activity (Colvez and Blanchet, 1981). Therapists, along with many other people in the health care delivery system, have been frustrated by a system that measures the quality of health care by mortality rates. Mortality rates fail to account for the time, energy, and money spent on incapacitating chronic illness. Developmental objectives can be equally harmful by supporting the illusion that our treatment methods can overcome the incapacitating effects of chronic illness. Accurate health care planning requires a realistic appraisal of the outcome of our services, including residual disabilities. Descriptive surveys of routine task behaviors are needed to establish a baseline for health care planning and for measuring the effects of various treatment methods. Viewed from this perspective, developmental objectives can be misleading, with broad social consequences.

The similarities observed between the early development of children and the progressive decline of disabled adults may contain some clues about change in stable mental disorders. The similarities between children and disabled adults may have a biologic explanation. The myelinization of the nervous system of children may explain the emergence of new abilities, while pathologic changes in the nervous system may explain the disappearance of these abilities. Various pathologic changes in the nervous system are being linked to specific diagnoses, and the diagnostic discoveries may help therapists select treatment methods and objectives. Treatment methods that aim at overcoming brain pathology by stimulating dendrite growth, for ex-

ample, may be more effective with one type of pathology than another. Clearer guidelines are needed for selecting different treatment methods and objectives for stable disabilities. More progress may be made by making the selections diagnosis specific. Logigian (1982) has suggested a diagnostic approach, and further investigation into whether developmental objectives are diagnosis specific may be helpful.

Developmental concepts have been used to supply preliminary guidelines for evaluating the severity of a disability. The need for a comprehensive evaluation of the social handicap associated with disabilities has led to a search for limitations in routine task performance that are specific to the expected course of the disease. In this instance development suggested the first step, but further refinements, specific to disability, were required. The extension of developmental concepts into statements about treatment objectives has been problematic and still leaves many questions about the feasibility of achieving those objectives.

SOCIAL SCIENCE APPROACHES TO DISABILITY

The impetus to write this text was derived from the advances in the neurosciences, and as a consequence a great deal has been said about the biomedical views of cognitive disabilities. In addition it has been recognized that a cognitive disability has many social implications. The delineation of the social implications is also dependent on advances in the social sciences, and there are some indications that the practical application of this information is improving.

The application of social science knowledge has been difficult for a number of reasons: Social scientists have had a tendency to draw highly abstract conclusions from severely limited data; the presence of an antagonism toward health care practitioners, especially physicians, may be detected; the utility of the information may be obscured by jargon; and the studies may be interesting but too esoteric to have much meaning in practice. There has been an increasing recognition of these problems, with expressed efforts to correct them (Eisenberg and Kleinman, 1981).

The reorientation of the social sciences toward health and illness seems to be responding to the increase in the number of people who have interminable illnesses. This represents a shift away from the cause and cure of a disease. A chronic illness has already been caused, and it is not cured, it is cared for, for a long time. The reorientation seems to involve shedding some of the sentimental, idealistic, or antagonistic qualities that have jeopardized the credibility of the social sciences

The increase in the number of people with chronic illnesses is a recognized problem in the biomedical and social sciences. The problem is compounded by the realization that approximately one-half of the people who seek medical help for acute or chronic conditions fail to comply with the prescribed medical regimen (Zola, 1981). It is becoming increasingly apparent that care is a shared responsibility—shared among the patient, family, health care practitioners, and society—and that health care costs are a particular concern (Alexander, 1981).

Considerable confusion about the division of responsibilities exists. As one might expect, power struggles and self-serving postures are apparent. The division of responsibilities seems to be especially troublesome when we all lack objective data about the kind of care required by the patient.

Care for a chronic illness is indicated by a functional deficit. Functional deficits are most apparent in the community and are described by qualitative differences in performance. Descriptions of functional deficits can be divided into two categories: behavioral descriptions of what the patient does, and does not, do; and descriptions of the meaning of a functional deficit to the patient and other members of the community. It seems to be logical to assume that descriptions of meaning cannot occur until we have clear descriptions of the behavioral deficits.

There are a number of investigators examining the best approach to describing behavioral deficits. One approach has been suggested by the Routine Task Inventory (see Fig. 2-22). Some other promising approaches are being taken. Berger and Gilson (1981) are working on a Sickness Impact Profile (SIP). The SIP is a performance measure, rating behavior on a given day as it is influenced by the patient's health status. There are 136 items, divided into 12 categories: sleep and rest, eating, work, home management, recreation and pastimes, ambulation, mobility, body care and movement, social interaction, alertness behavior, emotional behavior, and communication. Cluster and factor analytic techniques have been used to identify two groups of disabilities: Physical disabilities seem to influence ambulation, body care and movement, and mobility; cognitive disabilities seem to influence social interaction, communication, alertness behavior, and emotional behavior. The other categories do not cluster and may or may not be influenced by the kind of disability present. One of the advantages of the SIP is that it contains a continuum of dysfunction, from mild illness to severe disability (Berger and Gilson, 1981). The focus on sickness, as opposed to health-related or optimal behaviors, seems to be helpful in selecting behaviors of concern to health care providers.

Weintraub and colleagues (1982) are developing a Record of Independent Living for dementia. Each activity is rated for a change in behavior that may reflect the symptoms of dementia (e.g., memory, sequencing). By using a percentage score, rather than a raw score, they are able to exclude items that are not applicable to a particular patient without falsifying the total score of their instrument (Weintraub, 1983; Weintraub et al., 1982). In general, one can expect disease-specific instruments to contain the signs and symptoms that affect functional performance. Greater specificity seems to be helpful in detecting change in chronic conditions because small, discrete changes in behavior are often occurring. The problem with diagnosis-specific instruments may be that deficits which cross diagnostic categories may be neglected.

The meaning of a functional deficit, to an individual or a cultural group, is still an ambiguous area of study. Some efforts have been made to reduce meaning to people's preferences for one illness over another, but this approach does not seem to be very helpful (Jette, 1980). A recognition of individual and cultural differences may be more productive to an understanding of how the responsibilities for the care of a chronic condition are to be shared (Good and Good, 1981; Stoeckle and Barsky, 1981; Trujillo, 1980).

The growing number of people with chronic disabilities is leading to advances in the social sciences that may be helpful to therapists. The most important contribution may be realistic measures of program effectiveness; the lack of such measures has made it very difficult for us to evaluate the relative merits of our services. Therapists should be able to benefit from, and contribute to, these developments.

THE UNIQUENESS OF OCCUPATIONAL THERAPY

Difficulties with defining the unique knowledge and skill of the occupational therapist is a problem that is far too familiar to many of us. It is not surprising, then, that the recognition of problems with the developmental perspective and the generalist approach should raise questions about occupational therapy's specialized focus of study. The problem has been addressed numerous times throughout the writing of this text; some further thoughts will be presented.

Heritage of the Era of Progressive Reform

Part of the difficulty in suggesting how occupational therapy might be unique can be traced to our origins during the era of progressive reform (1900 to 1940). The progressives based their reform movements on several assumptions that are still evident in occupational therapy:

1. A trust in the benevolent goals of caregivers, assuming that benevolence will mitigate against doing harm
2. A belief that individualized treatment methods are effective, assuming that lengthy evaluations of individuals will produce the information required for effective treatment
3. An assumption that beliefs and trusts need not be subjected to critical analysis and empirical study

These assumptions have been identified as contributing to the failure of progressive reforms (Rothman, 1980).

Progressive assumptions cause problems in occupational therapy practice today. First, many of our professional colleagues think that attendance in OT is probably benign, but unimportant. We have a tendency to present our services as providing an ambiguous "therapeutic atmosphere," which I have heard described as a "nurturing soup." The problem is that the value of our services is not apparent; we keep the patients busy, get them off the ward, or help them wait out the healing process. It has been difficult to communicate the meaning of our clinical observations to other caregivers. In addition, when we are unclear about how to interpret our clinical observations, we are more apt to draw inferences that are incorrect and potentially harmful to the patients.

The second assumption is that lengthy individualized evaluations are the prerequisites for effective treatment. This progressive ideal has been assumed by many theorists; perhaps the most notable instance comes from therapists whose writing use the occupational behavior or human occupation model. Implicit in this assumption is another one: that activities can alter a disease process. A recent text title connotes the continued adherence to the illusion of cure: *Health Through Occupation* (Kielhofner, 1983). These progressive assumptions are questionable. Many conditions, like primary affective disorders, can be treated effectively without a lengthy evaluation. Lengthy evaluations are expensive and the cost is seldom justifiable in acute conditions. The notion that activities can be used to alter the natural course of stable conditions is also questionable. The lack of evidence, coupled with the increasing recognition of the number of people who have chronic mental disorders, place the assumption in jeopardy.

Implicit in the notion that activities can influence a person's health status is the idea that therapists can prevent a known medical problem or alter the natural course of the disease. Practitioners confront a number of difficulties with this assumption because patients have a diagnosis for their disease with a known natural course and expected complications. Within this framework some of the questions posed by practitioners are as follows: Should we be able to prevent the progressive decline of dementia? Should we be able to move a chronic schizophrenic patient from level 4 to level 5? Should people who have had a cerebral vascular accident or a head injury achieve a higher cognitive level with therapy than without? How do we explain the natural healing process following brain trauma? Should therapists be able to prevent the recurrent episodes of primary affection disorders? Can occupational therapy services compete successfully with the documented effectiveness of psychotropic drugs? The concern is that the progressive ideals lead to the wrong set of questions, wrong because it is doubtful that research studies addressed to these questions will be able to demonstrate the effectiveness of our services. Throughout the text I have suggested alternatives that seem to have a better chance of demonstrating effectiveness.

The need to demonstrate effectiveness is related to our economic survival. The progressive era was a period of social history that provided support for the involuntary incarceration of the cognitively disabled, for indeterminate periods of time, so that benign caregivers could effect a cure. The effectiveness of the caregiver's methods was not questioned. The change from the 1920s to the 1980s is important; justifications for economic support must follow a new set of rules. Patients' rights advocates are challenging involuntary incarceration. The length of hospitalization is being established by legal advocates and third party payers. Benign caregivers have been exposed as being negligent, coercive, and even harmful. And finally, promises of program effectiveness are regarded with frank skepticism unless backed by controlled and replicated empirical studies. When progressive ideals are being used to justify the social importance of occupational therapy services, they distract our attention to obfuscating abstractions and mislead us into thinking that we are shielded from the urgency of demonstrating credibility. The justifications are inadequate. The problem with an inadequate justification in the 1980s is that it places jobs in jeopardy. Buttressed-progressive ideals will not protect jobs within the social climate of the 1980s.

Another problem with the recent use of progressive ideals must be addressed. The ideals are widening the division between the roles of our educators and practitioners. The division has always existed; we work for different institutions and answer to different standards of accountability. We are able to bridge the role divisions by a commitment to a common purpose. The sense of common purpose is jeopardized by theoretical ideals that cannot be realistically achieved in practice. We are a small profession and need to be united in collaborative efforts if we are to successfully meet the challenges before us. The progressive ideals are global, suggesting that we can do all things for all people. As we attempt to be more realistic, we will also have to be less global. The unique knowledge of the occupational therapist must identify a realistic focus of study. In addition, a clearer distinction needs to be made between the topics shared with other disciplines and topics that are a unique focus of occupational therapy study.

Shared Focus of Study

The contents that have been selected as a focus of study in this text include the following topics: disabilities—physical, cognitive, or both; voluntary motor actions; attention; conscious awareness; and routine tasks. A review of the literature of other health professions will certainly provide numerous examples of how other professionals describe these topics. The topics are not mutually exclusive; in and of themselves, they will probably not work as criteria for defining the unique nature of occupational therapy practice. Even so, reading the interdisciplinary literature leaves one with the impression that the occupational therapy view of these topics is unique.

A detailed description of the quality of the process observed during task performance seems to be a unique requirement of occupational therapy practice. Once again, the Routine Task Inventory (see Fig. 2-22) can be used as an example. People in other professions tend to use the ends of the descriptions, for example, a person can or cannot dress independently. Efforts to describe the degrees of disability between the extremes are often unspecific from a therapist's perspective, for example, the patient requires major or minor assistance. Therapists, on the other hand, spend a great deal of time defining the type of assistance required. A recognition of the disability is shared; specification of degree of disability is unique.

Therapists are uniquely concerned with the combinations of assets and limitations. Limitations in disabled populations are relatively easy to describe; we must recognize limitations but we do not stop with a description of limitations. In the face of profound disabilities therapists search for remaining abilities. A complete description of task performance contains steps that the patient can and cannot do. Therapists specialize in overcoming problems in performance by identifying remaining abilities and selecting the means of assistance required to complete the steps in a desirable task, for instance, an adapted eating device, a threaded needle, or an arm around the waist.

Observations of task performance seem to introduce a unique set of problems to the occupational therapist. These problems are often shared with the family, other community-based caregivers, and our colleagues in other health professions. Some overlap occurs, but our focus of study differs. A brief description of other investigations of deficits in task performance may help clarify the differences.

Many neuropsychological tests have been developed to establish impairments in voluntary motor actions, commonly referred to as apraxia, agnosia, and aphasia. The tests are used for diagnostic purposes, identifying the site of a focal lesion or differentiating between dementia and depression. Neuropsychological tests also have a tendency to view the various problems with sensory cues and motor actions as separate disabilities: visual agnosia, constructional apraxia, ideomotor apraxia. The separation is pursued to establish distinct sites of focal lesions. Similarities in functional impairments are seldom investigated.

An example of an instrument that may be of interest to therapists will further illustrate the examination of voluntary actions for diagnostic purposes. A Mini–Object Test (MOT) was developed to be "a valid, reliable, cost-effective, portable screening procedure for confirming the diagnosis of aphasia-apraxia-agnosia associated with senile dementia of the Alzheimer type" (Still et al., 1983, p. 52). The test uses 15 miniature models of familiar objects (hammer, saw, ax, ladder) taken from a Jack Straws* game. Subjects are asked what the object is called, using either visual or tactile cues. Then they are asked to show how the object is used. The actions are manual and repetitive so that some correlation between an ACL score of level 3 and the MOT score might be expected. The test was developed to differentiate between dementia, depression, and schizophrenia. A reinterpretation of the test, according to the cognitive level, suggests that the test may be measuring the relative severity of these disorders, rather than symptoms that are diagnosis specific. This test illustrates how various interpretations of limitations in voluntary motor actions can be confusing. It also illustrates the therapist's desire for greater detail in specifying observations of patients' behavior so as to clarify seemingly disparate interpretations.

*Parker Bros., Beverly, Massachusetts.

Tests for visual agnosia can further illustrate investigations that aim at pinpointing the exact nature of an impairment. Studies with neurologic patients have been hampered by visual impairments, which make distinguishing between perceptual distortions and difficulties in the association cortex difficult (Bender and Feldman, 1972). There is some support for the notion that visual agnosia is associated with the cognitive deficits of Alzheimer's disease (Flekkøy, 1976). There is also a study that suggests that visual hallucinations are produced by a distinct information-processing disorder that differs from focal lesions in the occipital cortex (Bazhin et al., 1973). These studies aim at refining the descriptions of differences between diagnostic groups.

Occupational therapists are interested in the results of investigations into differential diagnosis with refined descriptions of the functional disability. The diagnosis is especially helpful in identifying the available medical interventions and the expected course of the disease. To occupational therapists, however, diagnosis is a relevant, secondary concern, not a primary focus of study. Occupational therapists are primarily concerned with overcoming a functional disability that may be associated with a number of diagnoses.

The unique interest of the therapist can be disorienting; the investigations conducted by other health professions often seem to be headed in totally different directions. An impairment that fails to be diagnostic is a disappointing result for our colleagues, but it may be a promising area of study for therapists. Studying an impairment that is not diagnosis specific may help to describe the disability in many different diagnostic groups. In this fashion occupational therapists investigate the same topics as other professionals do, but the purpose of the investigation differs.

Unique Focus of Study

The unique knowledge of occupational therapy can be summarized as follows: Therapists evaluate a disability by describing the assets and limitations that span a number of diagnostic categories; therapists treat by identifying the remaining abilities and selecting the means of assistance required to overcome limitations. The desired activity is selected by patient and caregiver; the information about how to do the activity successfully is supplied by the therapist through the application of a task analysis.

A graphic representation of the therapist's focus is presented at the beginning of this text (see Fig. 1-1). That figure presents the therapist's focus during the intervention process, working toward actualizing the patient's remaining abilities. During the process of developing the description of the cognitive levels, I have found that a shift away from Figure 1-1 is helpful. Theory development aims at establishing criteria for task analysis (Fig. 16-8). Task analysis is a synthesis of the process of doing an activity and the content of the activity.

Recognition of the patient's right to select the desirable task presents a theoretical challenge that occupational therapy theorists have been struggling with for a long time. The difficulty is that any activity in the universe of human activity might be deemed desirable. Age and cultural norms can be used to limit the possibilities in practice, but not in theory because of the diversity of practice. One means of narrowing the possibilities has been found: Chapter 2 describes the disability and Chapter 3 describes the restricted activities. By describing a disability first, the need to describe the universe of human occupations was avoided.

Emphases on the process of doing an activity makes it relatively easy to describe biological implications: the disease norms, medical interventions, acute and chronic disabilities, as well as assets and limitations. The social consequences of a disability require a description of the content of the activity. Problem solving seems to be facilitated by considering process and content in tandems, as follows: Human biological norms are considered within the universe of human occupations; disease norms are related to age and cultural norms; disability is related to restricted activities; assets and limitations are related to desirable tasks; and the information is

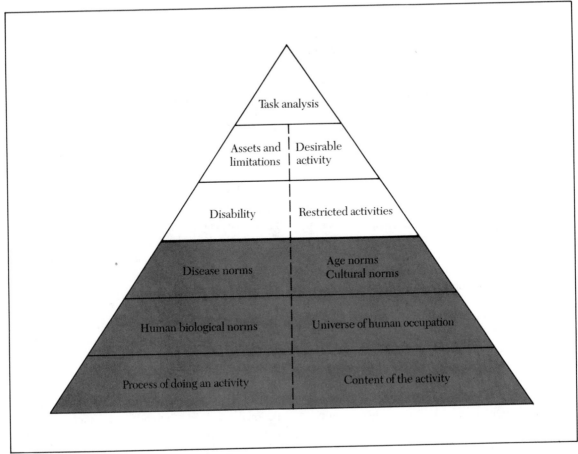

Fig. 16-8. Occupational Therapy's shared and unique focus of study. The base contains shared knowledge; the top shows what is unique.

synthesized into a task analysis (Fig. 16-8).

Task analysis is the therapist's key to application. The criteria for analyzing tasks identify the relative abilities demanded by tasks that patients and their caregivers find desirable, given the present restrictions in possible activities. The criteria for task analysis that are most apt to be relevant to practice can be derived from the assets and limitations associated with disabilities. In my opinion, knowledge development in occupational therapy should focus on these attributes of human activity. The other attributes in Figure 16-8 should be considered, but

we should remember that they are a primary focus of study in other disciplines. The unique and primary focus of study in occupational therapy contains disability, restricted activities, assets and limitations, desirable tasks, and task analysis.

Describing restricted activities is a major theoretical problem. There seems to be a natural tendency to deny the presence of restrictions. The denial is illustrated by the frequency of the following patients' goals: People with a spinal cord injury want to walk again; people with a chronic schizophrenic disorder want to work, and people with dementia want to live independently. Patients and their caregivers cling to the hope that the disability, with the associated restriction in activity, can be removed.

The problem occurs when therapists lack knowledge about how to fulfill these hopes. If therapists promise to fulfill the hopes, they are dangerously close to quackery. If therapists document the restrictions, they provide an unwanted confrontation with reality, and in some instances questions about the need for their services. In stabile conditions, the value of occupational therapy services may not be acceptable until patients and their caregivers have had time to adjust their expectations to the realities of permanent disabilities. The current shift from an industrial society to an information society (Naisbitt, 1984) may make it easier to deal with restricted activities. The change involves a reconceptualization of occupational therapy services. One of the megatrends that Naisbitt identifies is a movement away from institutional help and toward self-help; this trend is supported by Stone's (1976) report of less institutional care for people with cognitive disabilities. Families are being asked to assume more responsibility for the care of their disabled members. What they need is objective information about what the disabled person can, and cannot do. Therapists may be less involved in providing direct services, usually aimed at trying to change the patient, and more involved in providing caregivers with information, usually aimed at describing what to do about the severity of the disability. If this trend is real, it will influence the way we evaluate the quality of our services.

THE QUALITY OF PRACTICE

The quality of a direct service is assessed by measuring treatment effectiveness; in this frame of reference the quality of task performance is changed by the therapist's treatment methods. The quality of an information service is assessed by measuring evaluation effectiveness; in this frame of reference the quality of task performance is changed by the credibility, relevance, and utility of the therapist's report. The therapist's report is used by other caregivers to modify their methods of providing care so

that an improvement in task performance occurs; the therapist's report must merit their attention. A shift from direct services to information services would certainly influence the way we state treatment objectives, a problem that has been addressed throughout this text. The criteria for assessing the quality of occupational therapy services can, at least in part, be derived from the criteria for evaluating the credibility of a research instrument.

Reliability

The first requirement of an evaluation instrument is reliability. The advances in the social sciences and the neurosciences have borne witness to numerous evaluation instruments, and therapists have used a wide range of evaluation tools (Hemphill, 1980). The diversity is a problem; it makes defining occupational therapy very difficult. Writing standards of practice or describing the roles and functions of the therapist is arduous because the current generalist approach seems to include everything that any therapist does. The all-inclusive approach does not seem to work very well; the reliability of the profession lacks credibility. If an institution hires an occupational therapist, there is, at present, no way of knowing what informational or direct services that therapist will provide.

The problem seems to reside in the identification of our domain of concern (Shapere, 1977). The recent definitions of the domain have been so broad that therapists have been able to borrow numerous evaluation instruments developed by people in other disciplines. Instruments developed by therapists that are reliable, valid, cost-effective, and practical are notably lacking. Instrument development must be regarded as a top priority that must be fulfilled to establish the reliability of the profession. Therapists in southern California, Minnesota, Florida, and Maine need instruments that inspire confidence in the notion that we are all talking about the same thing. And, I suspect, we must have confidence in our ability to communicate with each other before we can hope to achieve clarity with

*Table 16-4. Questions related to the validity
of evaluation topics and treatment objectives*

1. How does the topic or objective relate to routine task performance?

2. Does the topic or objective specify a limitation that is secondary to a disease?

3. Is the topic or objective within the unique focus of occupational therapy? If so, what might therapists or other caregivers expect to do about the problem?

4. Is the evaluation and treatment process apt to be cost-effective? Would you pay for it?

5. Is it useful? (a) Will therapists really do it? (b) Will patients and families find it desirable? (c) Will other health professionals see the relevance to their work?

other professionals and the general public. The reliability of the profession must be established before one can hope to make statements about associations, differences, predictions, and effectiveness.

Validity

The current methods of establishing validity follow the rules established by psychologists and other social scientists. Some of the current methods are concurrent, congruent, construct, content, face, and predictive validity (Fox, 1969). In my opinion these methods leave a great deal to be desired because it is quite possible to follow the rules and end up with information that is essentially frivolous.

Some questions that seem to be related to the validity of the evaluation topics and treatment objectives used by a practice profession are listed in Table 16-4. They are questions that can be addressed during the process of selecting a focus of study. One of the things that happens to therapists when they begin to set up a research design is the discovery that one cannot investigate everything. Researchers, like therapists in practice, have a long list of possible questions and set priorities based on some sort of rationale. The questions in Table 16-4 have been used as rationales to guide such selections.

The first question asks for the relationship between a topic or objective and functional performance. Common tasks from normal, everyday life should be identified. The second question concerns the way a disease limits the disabled person's ability to do the everyday activities. The third question is tough: It is relatively easy to identify problems in disabled populations, and many of the problems will be there forever. Identifying problems that are unique to occupational therapy and respond to OT intervention is difficult.

Self-esteem is a good example of a problem that is easy to identify and difficult to define from an occupational therapy perspective. Poor self-esteem is frequently associated with all kinds of disabilities. Many treatment programs aim at improving the patients' or clients' self-esteem. With mental disorders one must decide whether self-esteem is a cause or a complication of the disease. If one assumes that it is a complication, then one must decide what should be done, that is, should evaluations aim directly at self-esteem, or should the evaluation aim indirectly at self-esteem but more directly at disabilities that are amenable to some form of environmental compensation. The effectiveness of both approaches is largely unknown. Self-esteem illustrates the confusion one encounters when trying to select the most important information required by disabled people and their caregivers. The studies reported in Part Three have avoided ambiguous topics and are aimed toward the practical aspects of living with a cognitive disability.

The demands to make assessment procedures and treatment processes as cost-effective as possible have been constant during the last decade. Therapists usually avoid expensive machinery and costly materials, but we have inherited some expensive progressive ideals: lengthy interviews, prolonged observations of performance, and unquestioned belief in our ability to improve the patient's medical condition. The need for cost-effective measures is forcing us to identify priority evaluations that can be used to generalize to other activities. Therapists have complained about cost-effective measures when they produce shorter hospital stays, tending to assume that shorter stays represent poorer care; the validity of this assumption is open to question. The overall effect has been a reexamination of the value of our services, with the specific objectives suggested in this text. The validity of our evaluations and reports will probably be subjected to ongoing evaluation from a cost-effectiveness perspective. Investigations into cost-effectiveness require reliable and valid evaluation tools and accurate descriptions of the natural course of a disease. In addition we have assumed that evaluation instruments must be linked to direct services (our treatment methods). Information services do not require treatment methods, and in instances in which the effective treatment methods are unknown, people may elect to pay for the evaluation but not the treatment.

The practical validity of an evaluation tool can be examined from the point of view of the therapist and the patient. The development of the ACL was concerned with the therapist's requirements: quick to administer, portable, easy to prepare, and inexpensive. The test does not have face validity, that is, its validity is not readily apparent to patients and their families; some patients think that a generalization from leather lacing to routine task performance is silly. An observation of behavior on one of the tasks on the Routine Task Inventory (see Fig. 2-22) may have more meaning to the patient and the family, provided, of course, that the task is relevant to the patient. The ACL may be administered for the therapist's benefit, to assist in efficiently selecting important observations of performance.

The distance between practical validity and theoretical validity must be shortened. The questions suggested in Table 16-4 aim at showing the relationships between theory and practice. Research, in my opinion, is responsible for building the bridge between our wishes (return to normal health) and our realities (forgetting to zip up one's pants). The advances in the social sciences and the neurosciences provide an opportunity to be more realistic about incapacitating disabilities and less embarrassed about the frailties of the human condition.

PROFESSIONAL COHESION

The research process is characterized by questioning, doubting, and criticizing current knowledge, processes that often make people feel uneasy. An emphasis on the weaknesses in our knowledge can have a splintering effect on professional unity. Obviously splintering should be avoided, but the creation of knowledge is derived from critical analysis. What is required is a professional culture that supports the creation of knowledge while protecting itself from divisive nonsense.

The introduction to Part Three briefly described the difficulties encountered in using empirical science to develop a theory of practice. The synergies included (1) abstract ideals + concrete realities = realistic ideals; (2) reduced parts + whole systems = practical theory; (3) doubts + convictions = questioned commitments; (4) known facts + intuitions = inspirations; and (5) individual analysis + group synthesis = professional cohesion (Hampden-Turner, 1981). The synergies are idealistic, and knowledge development seems to be characterized by tipping the continua toward one end or the other. Some of my experiences in dealing with these continua can be shared.

Recently, there has been a tendency to tip the continuum of the first synergy toward abstract ideals, with few clues about how the abstract ideals can be attained in daily practice. Theoreticians who offer ideals that cannot be realized wreak havoc with the confidence of practicing therapists. Therapists, and our consumers, require realistic considerations. As we tip the balance toward concrete realities we must be careful not to tip too far and ignore potential ideals. We will probably teeter-totter around a while before we set the balance straight. Difficulties in achieving the desired balance have certainly been a part of the experience of developing this text; to go, in the space of a few minutes, from reading a philosophical description of a domain of concern to encouraging a depressed woman to wash her hair can be disorienting. One wonders how the bridges between the extremes can ever be explained. To the extent that it has been possible to suggest ideals that may be realized, the struggle seems worthy of continued pursuit.

Achieving a balance between reduced parts and whole systems has been encumbered by an unfortunate misinterpretation of reductionism. There has been a tendency to think that reduced parts are "no-nos," which effectively makes it impossible to develop an operational definition of a theoretical construct. The cognitive levels have been operationally defined by leather lacing, and leather lacing lacks face validity. It should be noted that face validity is the weakest form of validity, and some empirical scientists refuse to recognize it as a measure of credibility. Face validity is in marked contrast to the more desirable forms of reliability and validity gained from a detailed analysis of leather lacing. A detailed analysis of reduced parts seems to work, and we seem to be headed in the direction of requiring more detailed analysis of the ACL and the Routine Task Inventory. These research experiences have been characterized by continual surprises about the amount of reduction required to explain the observations of patients' behavior. The tip toward whole systems may be much more pronounced than originally thought. If this interpretation is correct the implication is that our practical theories require a greater emphasis on reduced parts.

The tone of this text is a deliberate departure from much of the occupational therapy literature of the last three decades. Numerous problems, difficulties, and doubts about our knowledge have been expressed. The intent was to identify issues that might profit from further investigation. We may not have all of the answers now, but that does not mean that we cannot find them. It is hoped that my commitment to resolving difficulties is equally apparent.

The balance between known facts and intuitions is achieved in clinical practice. The facts, as we currently understand them, are taught in school. Intuitions are derived from clinical experiences. Unhappily, the prestige and the pay associated with direct patient care are low. The intuitions required for inspired knowledge development are unavailable to most therapists with graduate degrees. The problem is well recognized; I repeat it here from a different perspective. The research studies and the development of the description of cognitive disabilities enjoyed an immeasurable benefit from the contributions of therapists who have been delivering services for an exceptionally long time. There is no doubt in my mind that I would still be stuck in the mud of theoretical confusion if I had been unable to benefit from their experience. In my opinion a regular dialogue with experienced therapists is an essential part of innovative thought.

Professional cohesion can occur any time a group of therapists gets together. One element of professional cohesion that is frequently underestimated is a debate. During the process of writing this text I have managed to come up with many silly ideas. I was fortunate to present them to therapists who were willing to tell me that the ideas were ridiculous. Many an idea that might sound good on paper was appreciably altered until it made sense in practice. An outsider listening to the debate might have thought that we were ready to kill each other; that is not the case. Frustration is often apparent, but it is shared in mutual attempts to come up with an idea that will work. Many lousy ideas are suggested and discarded; as long as no one takes this discarding personally, the process is effective. Many of the suggestions offered in this text emerged during a debate, and I regard debate as a vital part of the evolution of theory.

A coherent profession is the dream that provided the impetus for writing this text. It seemed that there had to be a better way of pulling together the many different ideas about what occupational therapy is or what therapists ought to be doing. This analysis is offered in the hope that a more cooperative synthesis will be forthcoming. I view coherent profession of occupational therapy as an essential ingredient for improving the quality of life of those who have a cognitive disability.

REFERENCES

Alexander, L. The Double-Bind Between Dialysis Patients and Their Health Practitioners. In L. Eisenberg and A. Kleinman (eds.), *The Relevance of Social Science for Medicine*. Boston: Reidel, 1981.

Barna, F. Personal communication, July 1983.

Bazhin, E. F., Meerson, Y.A., and Tonkonogii, I. M. On distinguishing a visual signal from noise by patients with visual agnosia and visual hallucinations. *Neuropsychologia* 11:319–324, 1973.

Bender, M. B., and Feldman, M. The so-called "visual agnosias." Brain 95:173–186, 1972.

Berger, M., and Gilson, B. S. The Sickness Impact Profile: The Relevance of Social Science to Medicine. In L. Eisenberg and A. Kleinman (eds.), *The Relevance of Social Science for Medicine*. Boston: Reidel, 1981.

Colvez, A., and Blanchet, M. Disability trends in the United States population 1966–76: Analysis of reported causes. *Am. J. Public Health* 71:464–471, 1981.

Eisenberg, L., and Kleinman, A. (eds.). *The Relevance of Social Science for Medicine*. Boston: Reidel, 1981.

Flekkøy, K. Visual agnosia and cognitive defects in a case of Alzheimer's disease. *Biol. Psychiatry* 11:333–344, 1976.

Fox, D. J. *The Research Process in Education*. New York: Holt, Reinhart & Winston, 1969.

Gianotti, G. A quantitative study of the "closing-in" symptom in normal children and brain-damaged patients. *Neuropsychologia* 10:429–436, 1972.

Good, B. J., and Good, M. D. The Meaning of Symptoms: A Cultural Hermeneutic Model for Clinical Practice. In L. Eisenberg and A. Kleinman (eds.), *The Relevance of Social Science for Medicine*. Boston: Reidel, 1981.

Hampden-Turner, C. *Maps of the Mind: Charts and Concepts of the Mind and Its Labyrinths*. New York: Collier, 1981.

Heimann, N. Investigation of the reliability and validity of the *Routine Task Inventory* with a sample of adults with chronic mental disorders. University of Southern California Master's Thesis, in preparation.

Hemphill, B. J. Mental health evaluations used in occupational therapy. *Am. J. Occup. Ther.* 34:721–726, 1980.

Heying, L. M. Cognitive disability and activities of daily living in persons with senile dementia. University of Southern California Master's Thesis, 1983.

Hinkle, D. E., Wiersma, W., and Jurs, S. G. *Applied Statistics for the Behavioral Sciences*. Chicago: Rand McNally, 1979.

Jette, A. M. Health status indicators: Their utility in chronic disease evaluation research. *J. Chronic Dis.* 33:567–579, 1980.

Katz, N. An occupational therapy study of cognition in adult inpatients with depression. University of Southern California Master's Thesis, 1979.

Katz, N. Personal communication, December, 1983.

Kielhofner, G. *Health Through Occupation: Theory and Practice in Occupational Therapy*. Philadelphia: Davis, 1983.

Logigian, M. D. (ed.). *Adult Rehabilitation: A Team Approach for Therapists*. Boston: Little, Brown, 1982.

Miller, D. C. *Handbook of Research Design and Social Measurement* (3rd ed.). New York: McKay, 1977.

Moore, D. S. An occupational therapy evaluation of sensorimotor cognition: Initial reliability, validity, and descriptive data for hospitalized schizophrenic adults. University of Southern California Master's Thesis, 1978.

Naisbitt, J. *Megatrends: Ten New Directions Transforming Our Lives*. New York: Warner, 1984.

Rothman, D. J. *Conscience and Convenience: The Asylum and Its Alternatives in Progressive America*. Boston: Little, Brown, 1983.

Shapere, D. Scientific Theories and Their Domains. In F. Suppe (ed.), *The Structure of Scientific Theories* (rev. ed.). Chicago: University of Illinois Press, 1977.

Still, C. N., Goldschmidt, T. J., and Mallin, R. Mini–Object Test: A new brief clinical assessment for aphasia-apraxia-agnosia. *South. Med. J.* 76:52–54, 1983.

Stoeckle, J. D., and Barsky, A. J. Attributions: Uses of Social Science Knowledge in the "Doctoring" of Primary Care. In L. Eisenberg and A. Kleinman (eds.), *The Relevance of Social Science for Medicine*. Boston: Reidel, 1981.

Stone, A. A. *Mental Health and Law: A System in Transition*. New York: Jason Aronson, 1976.

Trujillo, A. A study of the meaning of activity as conveyed to occupational therapists. University of Southern California Master's Thesis, 1980.

Weintraub, S. Personal communication, February, 1983.

Weintraub, S., Baratz, R., and Mesulam, M. Daily Living Activities in the Assessment of Dementia. In S. Corkin, K. L. Davis, J. J. Growdon, E. Usdin, and R. J. Wurtman (eds.), *Alzheimer's Disease: A Report of Progress* (Aging, Vol. 19). New York: Raven, 1982.

Williams, L. R. Development and initial testing of an occupational therapy object-classification test. University of Southern California Master's Thesis, 1981.

Wilson, D. S. Cognitive disability and routine task behavior in a community based population with senile dementia. San Jose State University Master's Thesis, in preparation.

Zola, I. K. Structural Constraints in the Doctor-Patient Relationship: The Case of Noncompliance. In L. Eisenberg and A. Kleinman (eds.), *The Relevance of Social Science for Medicine*. Boston: Reidel, 1981.

INDEX

INDEX